Teaching Developmental Writing

Background Readings

Teaching Developmental Writing

Background Readings

Third Edition

Susan Naomi Bernstein

University of Cincinnati

Bedford/St. Martin's Boston ◆ New York

For Bedford/St. Martin's

Developmental Editor: Christina Gerogiannis
Production Editor: Amy Derjue
Production Supervisor: Andrew Ensor
Senior Marketing Manager: Rachel Falk
Production Assistant: Lidia MacDonald
Copyeditor: Helen G. van Loon
Text Design: Claire Seng-Niemoeller
Cover Design: Liz Tardiff
Composition: Karla Goethe, Orchard Wind Graphics
Printing and Binding: Haddon Craftsmen, Inc., an R.R. Donnelley & Sons Company

President: Joan E. Feinberg
Editorial Director: Denise B. Wydra
Editor in Chief: Karen S. Henry
Director of Marketing: Karen Melton Soeltz
Director of Editing, Design, and Production: Marcia Cohen
Managing Editor: Elizabeth M. Schaaf

Manufactured in the United States of America.

1 0 9 8 7
f e d c b

For information, write: Bedford/St. Martin's, 75 Arlington Street, Boston, MA 02116 (617-399-4000)

ISBN-10: 0–312–43283–6
ISBN-13: 978–0–312–43283–6

Acknowledgments

Gloria Anzaldúa, From *Borderlands / La Frontera: The New Mestiza.* Copyright © 1987, 1999 by Gloria Anzaldúa. Reprinted by permission of Aunt Lute Books.

Susan Naomi Bernstein, "Teaching and Learning in Texas: Accountability Testing, Language, Race and Place." Copyright © 2004 by the *Journal of Basic Writing.* Reprinted from Volume 23, Number 1, Spring 2004, The City University of New York, by permission.

Patrick L. Bruch, "Interpreting and Implementing Universal Instructional Design in Basic Writing." *Universal Design: Inclusive Postsecondary Education for Students with Disabilities* (Chapter 7, pp. 93–103). Minneapolis, MN: Center for Research on Developmental Education and Urban Literacy, General College, University of Minnesota.

Acknowledgments and copyrights are continued at the back of the book on pages 466–67, which constitute an extension of the copyright page. It is a violation of the law to reproduce these selections by any means whatsoever without the written permission of the copyright holder.

Preface

Welcome to the third edition of *Teaching Developmental Writing: Background Readings,* a book that considers practical questions we ask in our everyday teaching lives. How can we design courses that truly meet our students' needs? How can we accommodate students with different learning styles? How should we approach assessment at both the classroom and the institutional levels, and, perhaps most significant, how do these issues affect our day-to-day teaching? The selected readings in this book can help us address these questions, both as individual teachers/scholars[1] and as a community of professionals in basic writing, developmental education, rhetoric, composition, and related fields.

While the focus here is generally on basic writing, the questions just raised often remain relevant for first-year writing courses and for advanced composition — and for ourselves as teachers/scholars as we practice and theorize about our profession throughout our careers. If we conceive of basic writing as Mina Shaughnessy did, as an opportunity for "inexperienced writers" to gain more experience and practice with learning to write, then we can extend Shaughnessy's description to encompass writers across the spectrum of college writing courses and across the curriculum.[2] Students need to gain experience as they encounter each new writing challenge and rhetorical hurdle. As teachers/scholars, we also have the potential to learn and grow when we face new pedagogical questions. The purpose of *Teaching Developmental Writing: Background Readings* is to help foster that growth for our students and for ourselves.

The editorial apparatus is divided into several sections. Chapter introductions present a context for the selections and offer perspectives on the issues to be discussed. The reading headnotes identify the most important features of the selection. The "Classroom Activities" sections provide suggestions for creating classroom projects based on ideas or concepts from each reading. The "Thinking about Teaching" sections allow room for professional reflection and action, offering ideas for contributing to the discussions taking place in our hallways, offices, staff meetings, and elsewhere in our institutions — and in the forums of our journals, conventions, and Internet listservs.

This edition includes completely new readings on adapting the writing process (Chapter 3) and technology (Chapter 10). There are also new selections on English language learners, particularly Generation 1.5 students (see Chapters 2, 3, 4, 6, 7, and 13). As a result, an Alternative Table of Contents has been added to this edition. The Alternative Table of Contents lists the selections according to more general subject headings, including program design, the creation of syllabi and assignments, English language learners, diverse classrooms, and teacher-based research. Each of these subject headings is explained in a new introduction on page xix as an alternative roadmap to guide you as you chart your journey through this book.

As developmental writing teachers, we often find that our status seems marginal, outside the larger conversations taking place in the rhetoric and composition community. Moreover, the needs of our students as well as the complicated nature of our working conditions often prove more urgent and immediate than abstract theoretical arguments. How can we create a supportive working environment for students who may be under extreme economic and personal pressures that we can only begin to imagine? How can we be effective teachers if we spend our professional lives as "freeway fliers," rushing across town and across communities to our various classrooms?

Although *Teaching Developmental Writing: Background Readings* does not provide easy solutions to these dilemmas, it does present a range of perspectives offered by experienced teachers, and it emphasizes practical approaches to the everyday problems of our classrooms and our institutions. Each article invites us to examine classroom practice and to take part in professional discussions about our students and our teaching.

Acknowledgments

To Bedford/St. Martin's — I would like to thank Joan Feinberg, president; Charles Christensen, former president; and Karen Henry, editor in chief, for their commitment to providing teachers with the best possible tools for meeting the needs of their students. I am also grateful to Denise Wydra, editorial director, who first suggested this project in the spring of 1996; Michelle Clark, who carefully nurtured and served as editor of the first version of *Background Readings;* Talvi Laev, who guided me through the second version of *Background Readings;* Amanda Bristow, editor of the 2001 edition of *Teaching Developmental Writing: Background Readings;* Karin Halbert, editor of the second edition who also offered invaluable assistance on the third edition; Beth Castrodale, for her confidence in offering me the challenge of refashioning this book for its third edition; and, finally, Christina Gerogiannis, my current editor, for thoughtful discussions and critical feedback as this new edition was shaped and reshaped.

To my colleagues at the Center for Access and Transition at the University of Cincinnati who value and support my work and who cheered me on as I was writing this book, I offer my thanks.

I am also grateful to my colleagues across the country who provided invaluable support all along this journey, including (but not inclusive): Jonathan Alexander, Kathleen Baca, Stuart Blersch, Charles Brady, Shannon Carter, Cassie Cleverly, Linda Fellag, Doe Gavin, Michelle Gibson, Gregory Glau, Barbara Gleason, Ann E. Green, Valerie Felita Kinloch, Missy Laine, William Lalicker, David Leonard, Jen Lile, Christine Lottman, Eric Mast, Deb Meem, Alan Meyers, Tom Ott, Eric Paulson, Terry Peters, Mary Pat Raupach, Robin Reagler, Janet Reed, Jon Reid, Deborah Sanchez, Johanna Schmertz, Gregory Stewart, Karen Uehling, Amy E. Winans, Francie Blake Woodford, and James Wrable.

I would like to thank those instructors who reviewed the first edition for their valuable insights and advice as well as my reviewers of the second edition who provided helpful suggestions for revision: Mary Ann Gauthier, St. Joseph College; Guy Kellogg, Kapiolani Community College; Matthew Parfitt, Boston University; Alice Savage, North Harris Community College; and Karen Uehling, Boise State University.

To my current and former students in Ohio, Texas, and Pennsylvania: Your writing and your lives move me beyond words.

To my niece Missy Starcher and the rest of the crew of nieces, nephews, grandnieces, and grandnephews; to my brother David Bernstein; to my cousin Debbie Sternecky and to her daughters, Kate and Jane; and to the memory of my mother-in-law, Eleanor Cormany. All of you remind me why writing — and writing this book — is important.

To my brother Aaron Bernstein, who, in 1996, offered me a ride from Chicago to Milwaukee after I missed the train so that I would arrive on time for the meeting that began the work of this book.

To my 12th grade English teacher, Dr. Angela W. Graham, who had the opportunity to meet Mina Shaughnessy in the mid-1970s and who infused her own teaching with the excitement of that time in history. It is Angela who inspires my desire to teach and to write — and who emphasizes the ethical responsibilities of both.

To my life partner, Stephen Cormany, who shares my dream of bringing writing into the world by any means necessary. He would want me to acknowledge our tabby cat, Patty Paws, and so I do. Any remaining exclusions or infelicities I claim as my own.

SUSAN NAOMI BERNSTEIN

Notes

1. I use the term *teachers/scholars* to suggest that as instructors of basic writing we simultaneously teach and study our own teaching. Such self-study provides opportunities to add to the scholarship of teaching and learning by creating innovations in our own pedagogies — and by implementing these innovations in our classrooms and sharing what we have learned with our colleagues and other professional communities. See the "Reflective Practices for Teachers/Scholars" (p. xxix) for more on the term *teachers/scholars,* including a discussion of Marilyn Cochran-Smith and Susan Lytle's work on teacher-based research.
2. I am grateful to Barbara Gleason for this insight. See also Irene Ward's introduction to her book *Literacy, Ideology, and Dialogue: Towards a Dialogic Pedagogy* (Albany, NY: State University of New York Press, 1994) and the collection edited by Gerri McNenny, *Mainstreaming Basic Writers: Politics and Pedagogies of Access* (Mahwah, NJ: Erlbaum, 2001).

Contents

1. Basic Writing: Teachers' Perspectives   1

Mina Shaughnessy
Some New Approaches toward Teaching   2

Shaughnessy views students in basic writing courses as inexperienced
rather than "unskilled" writers. She discusses where and how to begin
a course in basic writing.

Lalicker describes a baseline or prerequisite model of a basic writing program, as well as five "alternative" models: the stretch model, the studio model, the directed self-placement model, the intensive model, and the mainstreaming model.

Uehling presents the guidelines and goals for developing the basic writing course at Boise State University, "a commuter institution of 17,000 part- and full-time students with an average age of about twenty-seven"; included in these guidelines are competencies for portfolio assessment and teaching suggestions for instructors.

2.   Basic Writing: Students' Perspectives   39

Kinloch offers pedagogical strategies for supporting linguistic diversity in the writing classroom and includes a thorough discussion of the 1974 position statement *Students' Right to Their Own Language*. Students' voices permeate and inform Kinloch's argument in these excerpts from her longer article.

Maher describes the roles of writing and education in the lives of her pre-college students, inmates of a women's maximum-security prison outside New York City. Maher includes notes that students have written to her, as well as a complete student essay, composed for readers "who knew nothing about her but who sincerely wanted to understand what she wanted and needed to say."

Ann E. Green
My Uncle's Guns 73

Green's narrator in this short story is a young woman who lives in a rural, white, working-class, poor community who is enrolled in a beginning college writing course taught by an instructor who is an outsider to the community.

3. Adapting the Writing Process 83

Dana R. Ferris
One Size Does Not Fit All: Response and Revision Issues for Immigrant Students 83

Ferris examines the role of teacher feedback in the revision process and offers specific suggestions for commenting on writing by Generation 1.5 (immigrant) students.

Michelle Gibson
From The Peculiar Case of Contessa: Postmodernism and Basic Writing Pedagogy 100

In these excerpts from a case study of her student "Contessa," Gibson explores the intersections and contradictions of process pedagogy, postmodernist identities, and her own position as a lesbian professor of composition.

4. Writing and Reading 113

Jeanne Henry
From If Not Now: Developmental Readers in the College Classroom: Literary Letters 113

In these excerpts from *If Not Now,* Henry uses teacher research to explore writing "literary letters" and summaries of books and short stories to help students to become more intellectually engaged as readers and writers. Henry includes sample student summaries to illustrate her ideas.

Leki suggests that reading is not simply focusing on finding the main idea or looking for answers for post-reading questions. Such skills are often presented in isolation and are disconnected from making meaning from the text itself. Leki's findings are relevant for English language learners and for native speakers of English.

Neuleib and Brosnahan observe the ineffectiveness of having students simply memorize grammar concepts and believe instead that it is important to teach students how to recognize patterns of error.

Weaver presents creative strategies to help students add variety to their sentences and to develop a more sophisticated writing style. Using their own writing, students learn general grammar concepts and gain experience playing with language and ideas.

Bruch demonstrates the link between social justice work and universal instructional design for basic writing pedagogy; he discusses how this theory works in practice and offers a writing assignment that features inclusive participation for students with (and without) apparent learning disabilities.

White analyzes the social construction of learning disabilities research and teaching methods; she also examines the implications of social class and race in the diagnosis of learning disabilities. As a result, she argues for a constructivist pedagogy that will address the needs of all students.

Feminist poet and essayist Adrienne Rich reflects on the joys and challenges of teaching basic writing in the early years of open admissions at City College of New York, where she taught under the direction of Mina Shaughnessy.

Nixon-Ponder considers the needs of adult learners as she presents the concept of problem-posing dialogue. This student-centered classroom structure provides opportunities for even the most reticent students to begin to speak.

Gleason describes her writing course for working adults at City College's Center for Worker Education and presents the case studies of two very different students. By studying the progress of these students throughout the course, Gleason illustrates the success of a particular assignment sequence that introduces students to ethnographic research.

8. Critical Thinking

Nancy Lawson Remler
**The More Active the Better: Engaging College
English Students with Active Learning Strategies**

Remler urges teachers to consider active learning strategies by providing sample lessons from her own classrooms. Students who are actively involved in a lesson, Remler suggests, will develop stronger critical thinking skills than students who passively absorb information.

Glynda Hull and Mike Rose
**"This Wooden Shack Place":
The Logic of an Unconventional Reading**

Hull and Rose take a close look at the critical thinking processes of Robert, a student in basic writing at UCLA. Hull and Rose examine Robert's "unconventional reading" of a poem by Garrett Kaoru Hongo, allowing the reader to follow along as Robert reveals how social class and cultural background affect his processes of critical thinking and close reading.

9. Collaborative Learning

Peter Elbow
Using the Collage for Collaborative Writing

Elbow provides step-by-step collaborative learning activities that may appeal to students who are not usually comfortable working in groups. His collage activity will be helpful to instructors interested in trying out new approaches to collaborative learning.

Richard Raymond
**Building Learning Communities
on Nonresidential Campuses**

Raymond describes a collaborative learning community he helped to create with teachers of speech communication and anthropology at the University of Arkansas–Little Rock. A class of first-year, primarily nonresidential students took linked courses in these disciplines, as well as Raymond's composition course. Raymond documents the collaboration that took place as teachers and students came together as a community of learners.

10. Technology 286

Pavia offers case studies of two students in basic writing with limited access to computers outside of the classroom. Pavia documents changes that she made to her pedagogy based on the findings of her teacher research; she also describes the "technology narrative" that she assigns.

Cummings writes about her experiences in Japan with computer-mediated instruction and EFL students who are enrolled in a basic writing course taught entirely in English. Cummings discusses how she created an online version of this course and presents an Internet-based assignment that develops students' ability to read, write, and communicate in English.

11. Engaging Difference 328

In this excerpt from her groundbreaking book, *Borderlands/La Frontera: The New Mestiza,* Chicana tejana lesbian feminist Gloria Anzaldúa reflects on coming of age in the borderlands of the Rio Grande Valley in South Texas, and the inseparable intersections of language and culture.

Jordan presents a teaching narrative that argues for the power and persistence of Black English in a society that valorizes the cultural practices of Standard (white) English. Jordan's article includes excerpts from student texts on Black English, ending with a compelling statement of purpose written by her student, Willie Jordan.

Thurston writes about challenges facing students at Navajo Community College. In describing the cultural background of her students, she also challenges white teachers of composition to confront their own Western ethnocentrism and to begin to envision a more inclusive course design that would "mitigate barriers" between Eurocentric ideas of education and a Navajo approach.

12.   Teaching ESL and Generation 1.5 Students   369

Dong asks students to write literacy autobiographies about their experiences with writing and reading in their first language so that students can understand the continuum of the writing process. Throughout this article the voices of Dong's students speak clearly and poignantly about their experiences with literacy in their countries of origin.

In these excerpts from their longer article, Hartman and Tarone examine the intersections of high school and college writing for Generation 1.5 learners whose first language is Vietnamese; they offer a set of best practices and recommendations for facilitating the high school-to-college transition for these English language learners.

13.   Assessment   390

In 1993, the Executive Committee of the Conference on College Composition and Communication charged the CCCC Committee on Assessment with developing an official position statement that would help writing teachers explain assessment in composition courses to administrators and other stakeholders. This document, adopted in 1995, is presented in hypothetical (if not utopian) terms.

Kay Harley and Sally I. Cannon
Failure: The Student's or the Assessment's?   400

Harley and Cannon contend that much assessment deals with what a writer doesn't do, how his or her writing doesn't measure up, rather than with the incipient strengths of the writing, such as the developing personal voice of the writer. To explore the notion of assessment, they present a case study of Mica, a student enrolled in a pilot program that combined basic and first-year writing courses. Mica's voice resonates throughout the article, arguing for a reconsideration of what it means to be identified as a "basic writer."

Susan Naomi Bernstein
***From* Teaching and Learning in Texas:**
Accountability Testing, Language, Race, and Place   417

In these excerpts from an article first published in the *Journal of Basic Writing* in 2004, Bernstein examines the impact of state-mandated accountability testing on students transitioning from high school standards-based writing to college basic writing, including a case study of Noah, a student identified as an English language learner. Noah's testimony documents the challenges of learning English in urban public schools that focus on preparation for state-mandated accountability tests. This testing system would eventually serve as a model for the No Child Left Behind Act of 2001.

14.   Basic Writing and the Writing Center   429

Gregory Shafer
Negotiating Audience and Voice in the Writing Center   429

As a writing center tutor, Shafer attempts to negotiate basic writing students' struggles with voice and instructors' emphasis on teaching five-paragraph themes and other "basic skills." Shafer articulates the purpose of the writing center as a site of democratic education and critical pedagogy and cites the work of the late Brazilian educator Paulo Freire and the African American educator bell hooks to support such pedagogy.

Introduction

The questions that our students and our classrooms present to us do not fall into neat or easy categories. For instance, a question that at first appears to involve only technology may also engage issues of learning styles, language acquisition, and reading and writing (for example, see Pavia and Cummings in this edition). Such pedagogical inquiries may be most usefully approached from multiple perspectives. The following Alternative Table of Contents was created with these concerns in mind. You will find six subheadings that group the readings into separate, yet overlapping categories. The readings are listed in the order in which they are found in this edition.

The introduction is also divided into separate subheadings that correspond to the categories of readings and that serve as a guide to the Alternative Table of Contents. The selections cited throughout the introduction are all included in this edition. Page numbers for these selections can be found in the initial Table of Contents that begins on page ix.

Alternative TOC

1. Brief Histories of Writing Programs and Program Designs

4. English Language Learners: ESL, Generation 1.5, and Foreign Language Students

6. Reflective Practices for Teachers / Scholars: From Teaching Journals and Teacher-Based Research to Conference Presentations and Publications

Brief Histories of Writing Programs and Program Designs

In 1967, Mina Shaughnessy was appointed to direct the pre-baccalaureate writing program at the City College of New York (CCNY), part of the City University of New York (CUNY) system.[1] While open-access programs no longer exist at CUNY's four-year campuses, Shaughnessy remains one of our field's germinal teachers/scholars nearly thirty years after her death from cancer at age fifty-four. Shaughnessy invited us to envision students in basic writing,[2] as "inexperienced" writers, who, through their enrollment in college, can gain access to and experience with academic writing. She rallied against the perception, common in her time and ours, that students in basic writing are intellectually deficient and otherwise incapable, or even unworthy, of the challenges and privileges of higher education.

Adrienne Rich, who taught with Shaughnessy in the late 1960s and early 1970s, weighs in with a teaching narrative about her experiences at CCNY. Rich's narrative reflects both the turbulence and the exuberance of living and teaching in New York City in the Vietnam War era. Her consideration of race, social class, and gender in the context of open-access education, first published in 1972, provides a provocative history of "teaching language in open admissions" that is still relevant today.

Nearly four decades after Shaughnessy and Rich's work at CUNY, models of basic writing program design continue to evolve (Lalicker), from first-year learning communities (Raymond), to online classrooms (Cummings) to worker education (Gleason). Uehling presents a model of basic writing program design based on intensive teacher-based research, while Harley and Cannon describe a portfolio-driven basic writing course. The CCCC position statement on assessment discusses elements of program design of significance for students, faculty, administrators and higher education governing boards, and legislators that provide our profession's standpoint on the high-stakes testing issues that continue to have a serious impact on students and the basic writing courses in which they are enrolled. Our history as a field is rich and varied and not without controversy as programmatic concerns have a direct effect on the work of teaching and learning.[3]

Designing Syllabi and Course Assignments: Fostering College Success in Basic Writing Classrooms and Beyond

In "Some New Approaches toward Teaching," Mina Shaughnessy addresses the difficulties of where to begin a course in basic writing; she observes, "Meanwhile, students confuse the issue by learning to write and not learning to write under almost all approaches." With that in mind, in the second section of the Alternative Table of Contents, readers will find a wide variety of approaches to the work of the classroom, as well as ideas to assist in designing course syllabi and assignments. Examples of student writing also can be found in many of these selections.

There are several common threads that link the articles in this second section together. The higher the bar is set for students — the more that students are challenged to reach beyond their comfort zone — the greater the likelihood that students will achieve writing proficiency at higher and more sustainable levels. In other words, students can engage with writing in the context of real-world literacy and life experiences, as the articles in this section demonstrate. Teachers/ scholars in many of these selections (Kinloch, Maher, Bruch, Nixon-Ponder, Gleason, Hull and Rose, Pavia, Cummings, Jordan, Dong, Harley and Cannon, Bernstein) have created curricula based on the local needs of their students, while at the same time addressing more global concerns.

For instance, Uehling suggests that basic writing courses can "preview" first-year college composition courses. Henry presents the strong interconnections of reading and writing. Neulieb and Brosnahan and Weaver insist on teaching grammar within the contexts of the students' own writing. Elbow, Raymond, and Remler argue for active — and interactive — learning strategies that invite opportunities for building classroom communities of learners.

While courses in basic writing may be organized in a variety of ways, many of the above selections, in general, seem to present the following approach:

- Select a general theme for the course, such as "Education," "Work," "Community."

- Choose readings that address this theme (nonfiction or fiction books, Internet sources, newspaper articles, anthologies, readings that students select or write themselves — or a combination of genres and electronic and nonelectronic texts).

- Create writing assignments that call for increasing degrees of difficulty or scaffolding.[4] Some teachers/scholars move from more personal narrative to persuasive analysis. Others require that students incorporate course readings and/or other outside sources as part of all of their assignments. Still others advocate for a course that ends with a researched essay.

- Present grammar and mechanics through the use of the students' own writing and reading.[5] Many teachers/scholars offer students the opportunity to work on grammar via extensive revision, culminating in a final portfolio that includes students' best writing from the course. Still others introduce and invite students to use a handbook and/or online sources as part of the revision process.

As the reader can see from the variety of course arrangements and writing assignments offered in this book, there are myriad ways of creating opportunities for students to write.

Technologies: Reading, Writing, and Learning Styles

In the early twenty-first century, the word "technologies" conjures visions of electronic communication, whether via the Internet and other new media, computer lab classrooms, course management systems such as Blackboard or Web CT, distance-learning courses, instant messaging, cell-phone text messaging, e-mail, and so on. For those who came of age before electronic communication was in wide use — and for those without reliable and sustainable access to computers — the results can be quite daunting (Pavia). Yet electronic communication also provides new and challenging opportunities for students and teachers/scholars of basic writing, as they engage with innovative new literacies[6] and confront issues such as electronic plagiarism (Cummings).

The selections under the "Technologies" heading invite readers to consider electronic communication, as well as the technologies of reading and writing — and the relationship of all of the above to students' learning styles. Henry, Leki, and Hull and Rose emphasize the significance of reading for developing the critical thinking so necessary for writing. Their selections draw particular attention to the ways in which reading, writing, and critical thinking are overlapping processes and technologies for successful communication in academic environments.

Several authors in this section encourage the use of innovative pedagogical methods that account for the variety of students' learning styles (Shaughnessy, Bruch, White, Remler, Elbow, Raymond). Still others emphasize that cultural and language backgrounds remain inseparable from students' individual and collective approaches to learning (Kinloch, Green, Ferris, Gibson, Nixon-Ponder, Gleason, Anzaldúa, Jordan, Thurston, Dong, Hartman and Tarone, Harley and Cannon, Bernstein, Shafer, and DiPardo).

In other words, what instructors might interpret as "problems" with classroom behavior or student motivation may in reality be the diversity of approaches that constitute students' learning styles. By employing a variety of technologies, whether new media or old, teachers/scholars and students working together can co-create an accessible — and intellectually engaging — space for learning.

English Language Learners: ESL, Generation 1.5, and Foreign Language Students

The students and teachers/scholars in this section write from a variety of locations, such as Arizona, California, Massachusetts, Minnesota, New York, and Texas in the United States, as well as from Japan. The student writing featured in this section offers a diversity of perceptions and perspectives about what it means to be identified as an English language learner in a global world. In this regard, language, culture, and learning styles remain intimately intertwined as several of the authors in this section remind us (Anzaldúa, Thurston, DiPardo). Second-language writing[7] offers a teachable moment of self-reflection for our students who arrive in our United States ESL classes from all over the world (Dong).

The selections under this heading demonstrate the diversity of students who are categorized as English language learners. Often students are tracked into separate classes that may be designed to address their specific needs. Increasingly, however, many English language learners find themselves in basic writing classrooms with native speakers of English (Pavia) — and instructors who remain uncertain of how to accommodate the diverse language backgrounds of all of their students. In this regard, readers will find much overlap between the selections in this section and the previous section on "Technologies: Reading, Writing, and Learning Styles" and the following section on "Diverse Classrooms: Perspectives on Basic Writing and Race, Social Class, and Gender."

Generation 1.5 students, for example, may be heritage speakers of a language other than English; they and/or their families of origin may have immigrated to the United States. These students may have lived their entire lives as citizens, or the majority of their lives as residents of the United States; some students, who are relatively recent émigrés, may have graduated from high school in the United States. Whatever their cultural background, Generation 1.5 students may well have experienced the prejudice that often comes with being labeled "language minority" and may not be fluent in writing or reading their "home" or heritage language(s) — or they may well have read and written widely in their native language. In other words, Generation 1.5 students are not easily categorized in terms of either language use or immigration status (Kinloch, Bernstein).[8]

Moreover, because of globalization and the use of English as an international language of commerce, it is also critical to consider the varieties of World English[9] in this discussion of English-language learners. As Cummings suggests, students learning English as a foreign language (EFL) in their countries of origin where English is not the primary language may see little practical value in learning basic writing, beyond fulfilling course requirements for graduation.

Cummings ultimately views this development as an opportunity to create new pedagogies, rather than as an obstacle to teaching EFL.

In addition, several authors in this section suggest that pedagogical practices that facilitate learning for English language learners also enhance writing and reading instruction for native speakers of English (Leki, Ferris). As Hartman and Tarone suggest, English language learners benefit from intensive instruction in intellectually challenging modes of writing, such as analysis and persuasion, rather than lessons in rote memorization of grammar rules or in writing personal narratives. As many teachers/scholars confirm elsewhere in *Teaching Developmental Writing: Background Readings,* an emphasis on rigorous intellectual engagement with writing and reading provides rich opportunities for increased college literacy — as well as for studying English in all of its varieties and forms.

Diverse Classrooms: Perspectives on Basic Writing and Race, Social Class, and Gender

In the second edition of *Teaching Developmental Writing: Background Readings,* Chapter 11 was entitled "Writing and Race, Class, and Gender." During the revision process, however, it became clear that many selections would fit under that broad chapter title. It also was apparent that the categories of race, social class, and gender often overlap and are not easily separated from each other.

With this in mind, the readings in Chapter 11 remain the same, but the chapter title has been changed to "Engaging Difference." While Anzaldúa, Jordan, and Thurston do in fact address writing and race, class, and gender, in addition each of these authors also engages *difference.* From an academic perspective, the idea of difference would seem to imply that which falls outside the mainstream of standard written English. This perception would, in part, account for the presence of basic writing courses in institutions of higher education — and for Shaughnessy and Rich's proactive work on behalf of students enrolled in basic writing at CCNY.[10]

Yet it also seems as if "difference," like its synonyms "diverse" and "multicultural," cannot begin to describe the material realities of our basic writing classrooms. For many students and teachers/scholars, our basic writing classrooms are reflections of — and are directly affected by — the local and global upheavals and social changes of the late twentieth and early twenty-first centuries. Whether "difference" describes the plethora of racial, ethnic, language, social class, and gendered backgrounds of our students and ourselves, or differences between teachers/scholars and students, we are fortunate to have a variety of perspectives on the categories of identity that constitute the cultures of our classrooms.

Language diversity, as presented in the previous section, is one of many overlapping categories of identity (Kinloch, Ferris, Leki, Cummings, Anzaldúa, Thurston, Dong, Hartman and Tarone, Bernstein, DiPardo). Furthermore, as Jordan states, "as children, most of the thirty-five million Afro-Americans living here depend on [Black English] for our discovery of the world." In addition to Jordan, Kinloch, Gibson, Bruch, Harley and Cannon, and Shafer discuss working with African American students in urban and other settings.

Other categories of difference in this section are students studying at commuter institutions (Uehling, Henry, Raymond), working class, working poor, and destitute students (Shaughnessy, Uehling, Kinloch, Maher, Green, Gibson, Henry, Bruch, White, Rich, Nixon-Ponder, Hull and Rose, Pavia, Anzaldúa, Jordan, Thurston, Harley and Cannon, Bernstein, Shafer, DiPardo). Bruch and White examine learning differences and universal design; and Anzaldúa and Gibson address queer theory. Differences between teachers/scholars and students as well as the tensions and rewards of those differences are engaged by Kinloch, Maher, Green, Gibson, Rich, Nixon-Ponder, Hull and Rose, Thurston, Harley and Cannon, Bernstein, Shafer, and DiPardo.

Clearly, "diverse classrooms" take on a variety of forms, whether teaching and learning take place in a women's maximum security prison (Maher) or online (Cummings). This section offers views of intersecting, overlapping, and conflicting categories of identity. The reader is invited to continue exploring the meaning(s) of "difference" — both locally and globally — in his or her own terms.

Reflective Practices for Teachers/Scholars: From Teaching Journals and Teacher-Based Research to Conference Presentations and Publications

Throughout the apparatus of *Teaching Developmental Writing: Background Readings,* readers will find numerous suggestions for engaging in teacher-based research. The term *teacher/scholar* is inspired, in part, by the work of Cochran-Smith and Lytle, who define teacher-based research as "systematic and intentional inquiry about teaching, learning, and schooling carried out by teachers in their own school and classroom settings" (27).[11] In other words, teachers are also scholars who research and inquire into their own students, classrooms, and pedagogical practices.

Many of us already do this work, often without realizing it. For example, one form of teacher-based research that instructors may encounter on a regular basis is a question of consistency: A lesson that was particularly successful in the evening basic writing class falls flat in a different section of basic writing the next morning. What accounts for the differences? What changes need to be made in order for the lesson to succeed in the morning class? As soon as a teacher/scholar asks a question about his or her pedagogical practices and begins envisioning plausible responses, he or she has begun teacher-based research.[12]

Cochran-Smith and Lytle also state that, "through inquiry, teachers generate knowledge." They divide the audience for this knowledge into three categories: "for their own practice; for the immediate community of teachers; [and] for the larger community of educators" (44). In the apparatus of *Teaching Developmental Writing: Background Readings,* readers will find suggestions that address each of these audiences, from individual reflection, to teacher/scholar-based discussions (both face-to-face and online), to conferences, presentations, and publications.[13]

Keeping a journal can be a helpful means of documenting inquiry and reflection on teaching/research, whether that journal is written on a laptop, in the margins of a grade book or daily planner, or in the lined pages of a leather-bound diary. Cochran-Smith and Lytle describe journals as "teachers' accounts of classroom life over time" which can include:

- Records of observations

- Analyses of experiences

- Reflections and interpretations of practices (27)

As part of her article, Cummings quotes from her journal to analyze her experiences of teaching in Japan. My own study of standardized testing and Generation 1.5 students began with records of my observations of student writing on education, especially students' responses to the standardized tests mandated by the state of Texas for public school students. Uehling and her colleagues kept track of their reflections and interpretations of practices of teaching basic writing in order to plan a new curriculum at Boise State University. Initially this research was conducted for their immediate community of teachers, but eventually the project was expanded for a larger community of educators as a conference presentation and an article.

Other examples of systematic inquiry that address multiple audiences include reflections on teaching practices and student learning (Shaughnessy, Maher, Gibson, Henry, Bruch, Nixon-Ponder, Gleason, Raymond, Pavia, Jordan, Dong, Harley and Cannon, Shafer, and DiPardo); several of these selections also include case studies of individual students or of specific classrooms. Still other teacher-based inquiry examines systemic practices in education (Ferris, Hull and Rose, Thurston, and Hartman and Tarone).

An additional example of what Cochran-Smith and Lytle identify as conceptual research (theoretical/philosophical work or the analysis of ideas) takes the form of classroom narratives. Cochran-Smith and

Lytle categorize these narratives under the category of "Essays: Teachers' interpretations of the assumptions and characteristics of classroom and school life and/or research itself" (27). Many of the reflections in this section use some form of narrative to exemplify conceptual frameworks. Maher, Rich, and Jordan employ narrative as the main focus of their work, using storytelling to indicate significant instances of their theoretical/philosophical work. Green creates a fictional narrative in order to analyze her ideas about schooling and working-class rural life.

Class preparation, large student loads, grading, committee work, commuting, and other realities faced by instructors of basic writing may seem to limit our time for teacher-based research. Yet as we engage with the struggles and pleasures of writing, we create the potential to grow and learn as teachers/scholars and as writers. In this regard, we have the potential to inspire the practices of colleagues, both globally and locally, for the benefit of our profession — and for the benefit of our students and ourselves.

Notes

1. See Jane Maher's extraordinary biography, *Mina Shaughnessy: Her Life and Work* (Urbana, IL: National Council of Teachers of English, 1997) for a more comprehensive history of this period.

2. In using the term "students enrolled in basic writing," instead of "basic writers," I reference the important work of Laura Gray-Rosendale in *Rethinking Basic Writing: Exploring Identity, Politics, and Community in Interaction* (Mahwah, NJ: Erlbaum, 2000) and Linda Adler-Kassner and Susan Marie Harrington in *Basic Writing as a Political Act: Public Conversations about Writing and Literacy* (Creskill, NJ: Hampton, 2002). Also see Linda Adler-Kassner's "Review: Structure and Possibility: New Scholarship about Students-Called-Basic-Writers" in *College English* 63.2 (2000): 229–43. Gray-Rosendale, Adler-Kassner, and Harrington resist stereotyping a typical basic writer, but instead invite the reader to examine more closely what students enrolled in basic writing courses are capable of accomplishing.

3. For an introduction to the field of basic writing, see Linda Adler-Kassner and Gregory R. Glau's Introduction to *The Bedford Bibliography for Teachers of Basic Writing*, 2nd edition (edited by Adler-Kassner and Glau, Boston/New York: Bedford/St. Martin's, 2005), and Karen Uehling's "The Conference on Basic Writing, 1980–2005" in the same volume. This annotated bibliography provides a comprehensive list of articles in the field of basic writing, and includes chapters on "History and Theory: Basic Writing and Basic Writers," "Pedagogical Issues," "Curriculum Development," "An Administrative Focus," and "Developmental Books from Bedford/St. Martin's."

4. Bloom's taxonomy is one example of the concept of scaffolding assignments in order of increasing degrees of difficulty. See "Illinois Online Network: Educational Resources" at <http://www.ion.uillinois.edu

/resources/tutorials/assessment/bloomtaxonomy.asp> for a useful explanation of Bloom's taxonomy.

5. For suggestions for incorporating the study of grammar in the context of
students' own writing and reading, see Laura Micciche's "Making a Case
for Rhetorical Grammar." *College Composition and Communication* 55.4
(2004): 716–37.

6. For more about New Literacy Studies, see James Paul Gee's *What Video
Games Have to Teach Us about Learning and Literacy* (New York:
MacMillan Palgrave, 2001) and *Social Linguistics and Literacies:
Ideology in Discourses,* 2nd ed. (Bristol, PA: Taylor and Francis, 1996).

7. See the introduction to Paul Kei Matsuda, Michelle Cox, Jay Jordan and
Christina Ortmeier-Hooper's collection *Second-Language Writing in the
Composition Classroom: A Critical Sourcebook* (Boston/New York:
Bedford/St. Martin's, 2006) for a critical perspective on the term "second-
language writing," which they regard as more specific to composition
studies than "English language learner." I use the term "English language learner" throughout this section to emphasize the interconnections in learning the English language arts of reading, writing, critical
thinking, speaking and other forms of communication. I would argue
that native speakers of English also may be conceptualized as English-
language learners. As native and non-native teachers/scholars of basic
writing, we may often find ourselves learning more about how English-
language works, no matter what our heritage languages or vernaculars.

8. For more about issues faced by Generation 1.5 students, especially in the
transition from high school to college, see Linda Harklau's important
study "From the 'Good Kids' to the 'Worst': Representations of English
Language Learners Across Educational Settings" in Paul Kei Matsuda,
Michelle Cox, Jay Jordan and Christina Ortmeier-Hooper's collection
*Second-Language Writing in the Composition Classroom: A Critical
Sourcebook* (Boston/New York: Bedford/St. Martin's, 2006). Also see
Linda Harklau, Kay M. Losey, and Meryl Siegal's *Generation 1.5 Meets
College Composition: Issues in the Teaching of Writing to U.S. Educated
Learners of ESL* (Mahwah, NJ: Erlbaum, 1999).

9. For a critical perspective on World English, see Min-Zhan Lu's "An Essay
on the Work of Composition: Composing English against the Order of
Fast Capitalism." *College Composition and Communication* 56.1 (2004):
16–50 and Bruce Horner and John Trimbur's "English Only and U.S.
College Composition." *College Composition and Communication* 53.4
(2002): 594–630.

10. I am grateful to Amy E. Winans for this suggestion. See Winans's "Local
Pedagogies and Race: Interrogating White Safety in the Rural College
Classroom." *College English* 67.3 (Jan. 2005): 253–73 for an excellent
discussion of engaging difference in a first-year writing classroom at a
small university in rural Pennsylvania. Also see Deborah Mutnick's
*Writing in an Alien World: Basic Writing and the Struggle for Equality
in Higher Education* (Portsmouth, NH: Boynton, 1995).

11. For another perspective on this subject, see Bruce Horner and Min-Zhan
Lu's *Representing the "Other": Basic Writers and the Teaching of Writing.*
Urbana, IL: National Council of Teachers of English, 1999.

12. See Marilyn Cochran-Smith and Susan Lytle's *Inside / Outside: Teacher Research and Knowledge.* (New York: Teachers College Press, 1993). I am also grateful to Susan Lytle and Elizabeth Cantafio for facilitating a practitioner-inquiry project on the Community College of Philadelphia in 1995–96, where, as a faculty member just out of graduate school, I participated with colleagues in teacher-based research. My work there in the mid-1990s, especially with Francie Blake Woodford, remains germinal to my teaching and scholarship more than a decade later. See Blake Woodford's article "Identity, Community, and the Curriculum: A Call for Multiculturalism in the Classroom" in the online *Community College of Philadelphia Journal of Developmental Education* at <http://www.ccp.edu/vpacaff/divess/jde/blake.htm>.

13. For information about ethical research and institutional review boards, see the Conference on College Composition and Communications' "Guidelines for the Ethical Conduct of Research in Composition Studies" at <http://www.ncte.org/cccc/resources/positions/123781.htm>.

   Online discussion groups for basic writing can be found at <http://www.asu.edu/clas/english/composition/cbw/listserv.html#subscribe> (sponsored by the Conference on Basic Writing, a special interest group of the Conference on College Composition and Communication) and http://www.mhhe.com/socscience/english/tbw/ (moderated by Laura Gray-Rosendale and sponsored by McGraw-Hill). For publications and organizations that address basic writing and composition studies and related topics, see:

- *Journal of Basic Writing*
  <http://www.asu.edu/clas/english/composition/cbw/jbw.html>

- National Council of Teachers of English   <www.ncte.org>

- *College Composition and Communication*
  <http://www.ncte.org/pubs/journals/ccc>

- *College English*   <http://www.ncte.org/pubs/journals/ce>

- *Teaching English in the Two-Year College*
  <http://www.ncte.org/pubs/journals/tetyc>

- *Journal of Research and Teaching in Developmental Education*
  <http://www.nyclsa.org/>

- *National Association of Developmental Education*
  <http://www.nade.net/>

- *Teaching English to Speakers of Other Languages*
  <http://www.tesol.org/s_tesol/index.asp>

- *International Reading Association*   <http://www.reading.org/>

Basic Writing: Teachers' Perspectives

What is "basic writing"? This chapter introduces you to ways in which this question has been framed by professionals in the past quarter century. We begin with Mina Shaughnessy, who defines basic writing from a teacher's perspective. Shaughnessy arrives at her definition based on her classroom observations of urban open-admissions students in the 1970s. She is a firm believer in "buil[ding] upon the skills the student already possesses."

William B. Lalicker, writing almost twenty-five years after Shaughnessy, looks at basic writing from the point of view of a writing program administrator. His article describes the advantages and disadvantages of several program models. He urges readers to create a program that is "most achievable with your institution's mission and resources." Karen Uehling's article demonstrates the possibilities of creating such a program. She presents the guidelines and goals for developing the basic writing course at Boise State University, a "commuter institution of 17,000 part- and full-time students with an average age of about twenty-seven." Included in these guidelines are competencies for portfolio assessment and teaching suggestions for instructors. Seen together, these three articles give readers a sense of the beginnings of basic writing as its own academic discipline — and of our discipline's future in the twenty-first century.

Some New Approaches toward Teaching

Mina Shaughnessy

First published in 1970 in A Guide for Teachers of College English *(and later reprinted in a 1994 edition of the* Journal of Basic Writing*), the following essay grew out of Mina Shaughnessy's experiences working with basic writing students at the City College of New York. The essay, which includes helpful examples, useful insights, and practical strategies for teaching developing writers, presents Shaughnessy's early theories on basic writing, theories on which she later expanded in her pioneering book* Errors and Expectations *(1977). Here she lays out her ideas about where to begin a course in developmental writing, and as in all her work, she bases her ideas on the belief that her students are not unskilled but rather inexperienced.*

Teaching Basic Writing

I

The term "basic writing" implies that there is a place to begin learning to write, a foundation from which the many special forms and styles of writing rise, and that a college student must control certain skills that are common to all writing before he takes on the special demands of a biology or literature or engineering class.* I am not certain this is so. Some students learn how to write in strange ways. I recall one student who knew something about hospitals because she had worked as a nurse's aide. She decided, long before her sentences were under control, to do a paper on female diseases. In some way this led her to the history of medicine and then to Egypt, where she ended up reading about embalming — which became the subject of a long paper she entitled "Postmortem Care in Ancient Egypt." The paper may not have satisfied a professor of medical history, but it produced more improvement in the student's writing than any assignments I could have devised.

Perhaps if students with strong enthusiasms in special fields were allowed to exercise themselves in those fields under the guidance of professors who felt responsible for the writing as well as the reading of students, we could shorten the period of apprenticeship. But clearly this is not the way things are, and students who need extra work in

*Note that although Shaughnessy uses the referent pronoun *he* throughout the article, she herself notes that she was writing in less enlightened times. In a footnote to *Errors and Expectations,* Shaughnessy offers: "After having tried various ways of circumventing the use of the masculine pronoun in situations where women teachers and students might easily outnumber men, I have settled for the convention, but I regret that the language resists my meaning in this important respect. When the reader sees *he,* I can only hope *she* will also be there" (4). [Editor's note] writing are therefore placed in courses called Basic Writing, which are usually taught by English teachers who, as specialists themselves, are inclined to assume that the best way to teach writing is to talk about literature. If such talk will stimulate the student to write, however, then it will serve most students at least as well as mummies, for the answer to improved writing is writing. Everything else — imaginative writing texts, thoughtfully designed assignments, elaborate rationales for teaching writing this way or that — is merely part of the effort to get writing started and to keep it going.

There are many views on the best way to do this and there is some damning evidence piled up against some of the ways that once seemed right. Since English teachers are often considered both the victims and the perpetuators of these apparently mistaken approaches, it becomes important for them to try once in a while to think away everything except the facts and insights that their experiences with students as writers have given them.

The following pages are my effort to do this.

II

Writing is the act of creative reading. That is, it is the encoding of speech into lines of print or script that are in turn decoded into speech by a reader. To understand the nature of writing, and therefore the way writing can be learned, it is necessary to understand the connections and distinctions between speech, writing, and reading and to identify the skills that are implied in the ability to write.

For most people, speech is easy and writing is difficult; the one is inevitable, the other acquired, generally under conditions that seem to violate rather than use the natural learning abilities of people. Because of this violation, learning to write requires almost as much undoing as doing, whether one is involved with those skills implied in the encoding process itself (handwriting, spelling, and punctuation) or those skills that are carried over from speech to the page (making and ordering statements).

Beyond these two types of skills, there is an additional opportunity in writing that distinguishes it both as a skill and as a product: the opportunity to objectify a statement, to look at it, change it by additions, subtractions, substitutions, or inversions, the opportunity to take time for as close and economical a "fit" as possible between the writer's meaning and the record of that meaning on the page. The typescript of a taped discussion is not, therefore, writing in this sense; it is, rather, a repetition on the page of what was spoken. And the goal in writing is not simply to repeat speech but to overcome certain disadvantages that the medium of sound imposes upon speech. (In speech, time says when you are finished; in writing, you say when you are finished.)

Writing thus produces a distinctive circuitry in which the writer continually feeds back to himself (as writer and reader) and acts upon that feedback at any point and for as long a time as he wishes before his statement is finally put into circulation. This opportunity for objectifying a statement so as to "work" on it is the distinctive opportunity of writing, and the central goal of any writing class is therefore to lead the student to an awareness of his power to make choices (semantic, syntactic, organizational) that bring him closer and closer to his intended meaning. Ideally, this opportunity should free the writer because it increases his options; it should give him pleasure because it sharpens his sense of what to say and thereby his pleasure in saying it; and it should make him feel comfortable with so-called mistakes, which are simply stages in the writing process. Unfortunately, the fact that writing can by its very nature produce a more precise and lasting statement than speech has led teachers to expect (and demand) a narrow kind of perfection which they confuse with the true goal in writing, namely, the "perfect" fit of the writer's words to his meaning. Teachers, in other words, have not only ignored the distinctive circuitry of writing — which is the only source of fullness and precision — but have often shortcircuited the writing activity by imposing themselves as a feedback. Students, on the other hand, have tended to impose upon themselves (even when bluebook essays do not) the conditions of speech, making writing a kind of one-shot affair aimed at the teacher's expectations. Students are usually surprised, for example, to see the messy manuscript of pages of famous writers. "You should see how bad a writer Richard Wright was," one of my students said after seeing a manuscript page from *Native Son*. "He made more mistakes than I do!" Somehow students have to discover that the mess is writing; the published book is *written*.

A writing course should help the student learn how to make his own mess, for the mess is the record of a remarkable kind of interplay between the writer as creator and the writer as reader, which serves the writer in much the same way as the ear serves the infant who is teaching himself to speak. No sooner has the writer written down what he thinks he means than he is asking himself whether he understands what he said. A writing course should reinforce and broaden this interplay, not interrupt it, so that the student can use it to generate his own criteria and not depend upon a grade to know whether he has written well. The teacher can help by designing writing situations that externalize the circuitry principle. The teacher and the class together can help by telling the writer what they think he said, thereby developing an awareness of the possibilities for meaning or confusion when someone else is the reader.

But if the student is so well equipped to teach himself to write and the teacher is simply an extension of his audience, why does he need a teacher at all? The answer is, of course, that he doesn't absolutely

need a teacher to learn to write, that, in fact, remarkably few people
have learned to write through teachers, that many, alas, have learned
to write in spite of teachers. The writing teacher has but one simple
advantage to offer: he can save the student time, and time is important to students who are trying to make up for what got lost in high
school and grade school.

To help in even this limited way, a teacher must know what skills
are implied in the ability to write what is called basic English and he
must understand the nature of the difficulties students seem to have
with each of them. The following list is a move in that direction.

HANDWRITING   The student has to have enough skill at writing to
take down his own dictations without getting distracted by the muscular coordination writing requires. If a student has done very little
writing in high school, which is often the case, he may need to exercise
his writing muscles. This is a quantitative matter — the more of anything he copies, the better the coordination. Malcolm X's exercise of
copying the dictionary may not be inspiring enough for many students, but if a student keeps copying something, his handwriting will
begin to belong to him. Until then, he is likely to have his problems
with handwriting mistaken for problems with writing.

SPELLING AND PUNCTUATION   To write fluently, a student must feel
reasonably comfortable about getting the words and punctuation
down right, or he must learn to suspend his concern over correctness
until he is ready to proofread. If he is a bad speller, chances are he
knows it and will become so preoccupied with correctness that he will
constantly lose his thought in order to find the right letters, or he will
circumlocute in order to avoid words he can't spell. A number of students enter our classes every semester so handicapped by misspelling
and generally so ineffectively taught by us that they are almost certain not to get out of basic writing. It is a problem neither we nor the
reading teachers have willingly claimed, but it presses for a solution.
The computer, which seems to hold great promise for misspellers, is
still a laboratory. The Fidel chart, so successfully used by Dr. Gattegno
in teaching children and illiterate adults to read, has not yet been
extensively tried in college programs such as ours.[1]

Students are generally taught to think of punctuation as the scribal
translation of oral phrasing and intonation. Some students have, in fact,
been taught to put commas where they breathe. As a translation of voice
pauses and intonations, however, punctuation is quite crude and almost
impossible to learn. Commas can produce as long a pause as a period,
and how much time does a semicolon occupy? Most students solve the
problem by working out a private punctuation system or by memorizing
a few "rules" that often get them into more trouble than they are worth
(like always putting a comma before "and").

In the end, it is more economical for the student to learn to translate punctuation marks into their conventional meaning and to recognize that while there are stylistic choices in punctuating, even these choices are related to a system of signs that signal grammatical (or structural) information more accurately than vocal spacing and intonation. The marks of punctuation can in fact be studied in isolation from words, as signals that prepare a reader for certain types of constructions. Whether these constructions are given their grammatical names is not important, but it is important that a student be able to reconstruct from a passage such as the following the types of constructions he — and other readers — would expect:

_____ . _____ :
_____ . _____ , and
_____ . _____ , ____ ,
_____ . _____ : ____ , ____ , ____ .

Sentence fragments, run-ons, and comma splices are mistranslations of punctuation marks. They can occur only in writing and can be understood once the student understands the structures they signal. This suggests that punctuation marks should not be studied in isolation from the structural units they signal. For example, when the student is experimenting with the ways in which information can be added to a subject without creating a new sentence (adjectival functions), it is a good time to look at the serial comma, the appositional commas, and the comma in the nonrestrictive clause.

MAKING SENTENCES   An English-speaking student is already a maker of statements that not only sound like English but sound like him. Because he has spoken so many more years of sentences than he has written, however, there is a gap between what he can say and what he can write. Sometimes the writing down of sentences is in fact such a labor that he loses his connection with English and produces a tangle of phrases he would never speak. Such a student does not need to learn how to make statements but how to write them at least as well as he speaks them. Other students with foreign-language interferences may have to work on English sentence structure itself, but even here their speech is doubtless ahead of their pens. Learning to write statements, therefore, is at first a matter of getting the ear to "hear" script. Later, when the writer wants to exploit the advantages that writing has over speech, the advantage of polishing and perfecting, he may write things he would not be likely to say, but this happens after his pen has caught up with his voice. Students who have little confidence in their voice, or at least in the teacher's response to that voice, have often gone to a great deal of trouble to superimpose another voice upon their writing — sometimes it represents the student's version of a textbook voice; sometimes it is Biblical; sometimes it is a business letter voice — but almost always it seems to keep the writer from understanding clearly what he wants to say. The following sentence, which seems to be a version of the textbook voice, illustrates the kind of entanglement that can result:

> In a broad sense admittance to the SEEK program will serve as a basis of education for me in terms of enlightenment on the tedious time and effort which one must put into all of his endeavors.

A student will usually not abandon this acquired voice until he begins to recognize his own voice and sees that it is safe to prefer it.

There is another skill with sentences which affects the quality of a student's theme as well as his sentences. It involves his ability to "mess" with sentences, to become sensitive to the questions that are embedded in sentences which, when answered, can produce modifications within the sentence or can expand into paragraphs or entire essays. It involves his awareness of the choices he has in casting sentences, of styles in sentences. As Francis Christensen has illustrated in *Notes toward a New Rhetoric,*[2] the sentence is the microcosm. Whatever the writer does in the sentence when he modifies is in principle what he does in paragraphs and essays. The principle of coordination and subordination can be learned there. The foundation of a paragraph, a chapter, a book is there. It is tempting to say that a student who knows his way around the sentence can get anyplace in writing. And knowing his way means working on his own sentences, not so much to polish them as to see how much of his meaning they can hold.

But for many students, putting sentences on a page seems a little like carving something on stone: an error cannot be ignored or skimmed over as it can be in speech. It is there forever. "Everything has to be exactly right," explained one of my students, "and that makes me nervous." The page disconnects the student from his product, which will appear alone, before strange eyes, or worse, before the eyes of an English teacher who is a specialist at finding mistakes. To make matters worse, most students feel highly mistake-prone about sentences. They half remember prohibitions about beginning with certain words, but they aren't certain of which words or why (probably the result of lessons on sentence fragments). In short, they feel they are about to commit a verbal sin but they aren't certain what sin it is. In such a situation, it seems safer to keep still. It is not unusual to have students at the beginning of the semester who sit through several class periods without writing a word, and when they explain that they don't know how to begin, they are not saying they don't have an idea. They are saying they are not certain which are the "safe" words to begin with.

Students who become observers of sentences and experimenters with sentences lose their fear of them. This experimentation can take many forms. Sentences can be examined as if they were separate compositions. A sentence such as the following by Richard Wright can be written on the board without reference to its context:

> Those brave ones who struggle against death are the ones who bring new life into the world, even though they die to do so, even though our hearts are broken when they die.

Students can talk about the way the sentence is built; they can try to imitate it or change it; or they can try to build a paragraph by expanding some part of it.

There is a kind of carpentry in sentence making, various ways of joining or hooking up modifying units to the base sentence. Suffixes added to make adjectives or adverbs, prepositions, "wh" words like where, when, who, which, etc., the double commas used in appositional constructions — all of these can be seen as hooking devices that preserve us from the tedium of Dick-and-Jane sentences. As a form of sentence-play, students can try to write fifty- or one-hundred-word sentences that contain only one independent clause. Once discovering they can do it, they usually lose their inhibitions about "real" sentences. Some even move from carpentry to architecture. This sentence was written by a student who was asked in an exam to add information to the predicate of the sentence: "The problem will be solved."

> The problem will be solved with the help of the Almighty, who, except for an occasional thunderstorm, reigns unmolested, high in the heavens above, when all of us, regardless of race or religious differences, can come together and study this severe problem inside out, all day and all night if necessary, and are able to come to you on that great gettin' up morning and say, "Mrs. Shaughnessy, we do know our verbs and adverbs."

ORDERING SENTENCES   Order is an arrangement of units that enables us to see them as parts of something larger. The sense of orientation that results from this arrangement creates a pleasure we call understanding. Perhaps because writing isolates a reader from everything except the page, whereas speech is supported by other gestures and by the right of the audience to query and disagree, we seem to be more tolerant of "disorder" (no clear pattern) in speech than in writing. The talker is not, therefore, committed to knowing where he is going in quite the way that a writer is although he often gets someplace in a way that turns out to have order to it. The writer, however, puts himself on the line, announcing where he is going to go before he sees how he is going to get there. He has to move in two directions at the same time — ahead, point by point toward a destination he has announced but never been to, and down, below the surface of his points to see what they are about. Sometimes, having decided on or having been given an overall arrangement (or plan) that seems a sensible route to where he is going, the writer hesitates to leave the security of this plan to explore the parts of his paper. Result: a tight, well-ordered but empty paper. At other times, the writer stops to explore one point and never gets back because he cannot get control over the generating force of sentences, which will create branches off branches off branches unless the writer cuts them off. Result: a wilderness.

The skill of organizing seems to require a kind of balance between the demand that a piece of writing get someplace along a route that is sufficiently marked for a reader to follow and the demand that there be freedom for the writer to explore his subject and follow where his questions and inventions take him. The achievement of this balance produces much of the "mess" in writing. Often, however, teachers stress the "administrative" aspects of writing (direction and proce-dure) over the generative or even assume that the generative is not a part of the organizing skill. This assumption in turn seems to lead to the formulation of organizational patterns in isolation from content (pyramids, upside-down pyramids, etc.) and the efforts to get students to squeeze their theme materials into these patterns. I do not mean to say that restrictions or limits in writing are necessarily inhibiting. They can be both stimulating and liberating, as the sonnet illustrates. But the restrictions I speak of here merely hint at forms they are unable to generate, leaving the reader with the feeling that there is a blank to be filled in but with no sense of how to do it.

Because of this isolation of form from content, students have come to think of organization as something special that happens in themes but not in themselves, daily, as they think or talk. They do not notice that they usually "talk" a better-organized paper than they write, that they use illustrations, anticipate questions, repeat thematic points more effectively in conversation than in writing, whereas the con-scious effort to organize a theme often cuts them off from the real con-tent of the theme, giving them all the organizational signposts but no place to go. In talking, they are evolving order; in writing, they often feel they must impose it.

This is not to say that developing a paper is as easy as talking but simply that the difficulty lies not in fitting an amount of raw content into a prefabricated frame but in evoking and controlling the generat-ing power of statement. Every sentence bears within it a new set of possibilities. Sometimes the writer chooses to develop these possibili-ties; sometimes he prefers to let them lie. Sometimes he decides to develop them fully; at other times, only slightly. Thus each step in the development of a base or thesis statement must inevitably send the writer into a wilderness of possibilities, into a fecundity as dense and multiform as thought itself. One cannot be said to have had an idea until he has made his way through this maze. Order is the pattern of his choices, the path he makes going through.

The initial blocking out of a paper, the plan for it, is a kind of hypothesis which allows the writer to proceed with his investigation. Any technique of organization, however, that ignores the wilderness, that limits the freedom of the writer to see and make choices at every step, to move ahead at times without knowing for certain which is north and south, then to drop back again and pick up the old path, and finally to get where he is going, partly by conscious effort but also by some faculty of intellection that is too complex to understand — any technique that sacrifices this fullest possible play of the mind for the security of an outline or some other prefabricated frame cuts the student off from his most productive thinking. He must be allowed something of a frontier mentality, an overall commitment, perhaps, to get to California, but a readiness, all along the way, to choose alternative routes and even to sojourn at unexpected places when that seems wise or important, sometimes, even, to decide that California isn't what the writer really had in mind.

The main reason for failure in the writing proficiency test at City College, a test given to all upperclassmen, has not been grammar or mechanics but the inability to get below the surface of a topic, to treat a topic in depth. The same problem arises in bluebook essays. It is the familiar complaint of students: "I can't think of anything more to say." They are telling us that they do not have access to their thoughts when they write. A part of this difficulty may be related to the way they have learned to write. And a part of the answer may lie in our designing assignments that make the student conscious of what the exploration of an idea is and how this exploration relates to organization.

GRAMMATICAL CORRECTNESS   Correctness involves those areas of a dialect where there are no choices. (The "s" on the present tense third-person singular is correct in standard English; the use of a plural verb with the subject "none" is a choice; the comparison "more handsome" is a choice but "more intelligenter" is incorrect.) Native speakers of a dialect are not concerned with correctness; they unconsciously say things the correct way. Non-native speakers of a dialect must consciously acquire the "givens" if they want to communicate without static in that dialect. This is a linguistic fact that seems at the outset to put speakers of a nonstandard dialect at a disadvantage. But it is a strange logic that says having access to one dialect is better than having access to two, particularly when we know that every dialect or language system sets limits on the ways we can perceive and talk about the world.

Unfortunately, this is not the way speakers of other dialects have been encouraged to think about their dialects, with the result that writing classes and writing teachers seem to put them at a disadvantage, creating either an obsessive concern with correctness or a fatalistic indifference to it. The only thing that can help the student over-come such feelings is to help him gain control over the dialect. It is irresponsible to tell him that correctness is not important; it is difficult to persuade him after years of indoctrination to the contrary that "correctness" plays a subordinate role in good writing; but it is not impossible to give him the information and practice he needs to manage his own proofreading.

The information will inevitably be grammatical, whether the terminology of grammar is used or not. But it is more important to remember that the student who is not at home with standard English has most likely had several doses of grammar already and it hasn't worked. For reasons that he himself doesn't quite understand, the explanations about things like the third-person "s" or the agreement of subject and verb haven't taken. He is not deliberately trying to make mistakes but for some reason they keep happening. What he often does not realize, and what the teacher has to realize is that his difficulties arise from his mastery of one language or dialect, and that changing to another often involves at certain points a loss or conflict of meaning and therefore difficulty in learning, not because he is stubborn or dumb or verbally impoverished but because he expects language to make sense. (The student, for example, who finally told me he *couldn't* use "are" to mean something in the present because it was too stiff and formal and therefore faraway, and the Chinese student who could not make a plural out of sunrise because there is only one sun, were both trying to hold on to meaning, as Will James, the cowboy author, was when he continued to use "seen" for the past tense because it meant seeing farther than "saw.")

These are obviously grammatical matters, but this does not mean they require the traditional study of grammar. The question of what they do require is widely debated. Certainly it should be apparent that teachers working with students who have black dialect or Spanish or Chinese or some other language background should be familiar with the features of those languages that are influencing their students' work in Standard English. This should be part of the general equipment of us all as teachers. And the new insights that come from the linguists should also be ours. But none of this information will be of much use if we simply make pronouncements about it in class. Students cannot be expected to get more help from memorizing two grammatical systems instead of one, and the diagrams in transformational grammar are still diagrams. The acquisition of new information will not automatically make us better teachers. To make this happen, we need to develop a sharp sense of the difference between talking and teaching. We need to design lessons that highlight the grammatical characteristics of a dialect so that the student can discover them for himself. (It is one thing to tell a student about the "s" in the third-person present singular; it is another for him to discover the power of that schizophrenic letter which clings so irrationally to its last verb to mark its singularity while it attaches itself to nouns to mark their plurality, and then, confusing things further, acquires an apostrophe and marks the singular possessive.) We need to devise ways of practicing that the student enjoys because he is able to invent rather than memorize answers. We need, finally, to teach proofreading as a separate skill that uses the eye in a different way from reading and places the burden of correctness where it belongs — at the end of (rather than during) the writing process. To do things for the student that he can do himself is not generosity but impatience. It is hard work for a teacher not to talk, but we must now be very industrious if we want our students to learn what we have to teach.

III

I have been speaking about the skills that seem basic to writing, but basic writing courses that prepare students for college writing are actually concerned with a rather special kind of prose called exposition, a semiformal analytical prose in which the connections between sentences and paragraphs surface in the form of conjunctive adverbs and transitional sentences. More simply, it means the kind of writing teachers got B's and A's for in college, a style whose characteristics they have now internalized and called a standard.

Teachers of basic writing are thus responsible for helping their students learn to write in an expository style. They must also give them practice in writing to specification (i.e., on a special topic or question and in a certain form) since many assignments require it. The question of how to reach such objectives and at the same time give each student a chance to discover other things about writing and about his individual powers as a writer troubles many teachers and creates many different "positions." Where, for example, on the following list, ranging from highly controlled to free assignments, it is best to begin a course in basic writing:

1. paraphrase

2. summary

3. exegesis of a passage

4. theme in which topic sentence and organizational pattern are given

5. theme in which topic sentence is given (includes the examination question which is usually an inverted topic sentence)

6. theme in which subject is given

7. theme in which form is given — description, dialogue, argument, etc.

8. theme in which only the physical conditions for writing are given — journal, free writing, etc.

Teachers take sides on such a question, some insisting that freedom in anything, including writing, cannot exist until there is control and that this comes through the step-by-step mastery of highly structured assignments; others insist that students must begin not with controls but with materials — the things they have already seen or felt or imagined — and evolve their own controls as they try to translate experience into writing. Meanwhile students confuse the issue by learning to write and not learning to write under almost all approaches. I prefer to start around #7, with description. But then, I have to remember the student who started a research paper on mummies before she could manage her sentences. "Positions" on curriculae and methods are somehow always too neat to say much about learning, which seems to be sloppy. They tend to be generalizations about students, not about the nature of the skills that have to be mastered, and the only generalization that seems safe to make about students is the one they persistently make about themselves — that they are individuals, not types, and that the way to each student's development is a way the teacher has never taken before. Everything about the teacher-student encounter should encourage a respect for this fact of individuality even though the conditions under which we must teach in large institutions often obscure it. Books do have to be ordered and teachers do have to make plans. But perhaps the plans need not be so well laid that they cannot go awry when the signals point that way. A teacher must know deeply what it is he is teaching — what is arbitrary or given and what is built upon skills the student already possesses. This is his preparation. But he cannot know about his student until both meet in the classroom. Then teaching becomes what one student described as "simply two people learning from each other."

In the confusion of information on methods and curriculae that comes to us from publishers — and from each other — it is probably important to emphasize this single truth.

Notes

1. Caleb Gattegno, *Teaching Reading with Words in Color* (New York, Educational Solutions, 1968).
2. Francis Christensen, *Notes toward a New Rhetoric* (New York, Harper & Row, 1967).

Classroom Activities

Have students generate lists of three to five rules that they have learned about writing (this may be done individually or in small groups). Then compile the separate lists into one long list that will be distributed to the entire class. You may wish to use the following questions as a starting point for class discussion:

- Is there more than one way of stating the same rule?
- Are some rules more difficult to understand than others?
- Which of the rules seem contradictory?
- Which rules seem helpful?
- Are there writing situations in which these rules may be broken?
- What are the consequences of breaking the rules?
- What are the choices that writers can make about how to compose their writing?

Thinking about Teaching

As you read the essays in *Teaching Developmental Writing: Background Readings,* you are encouraged to keep a journal to record your reactions to the readings and to write down student responses to class activities. Think about sharing your journal entries with other teachers — and especially with your students. The pedagogy that Shaughnessy advocates implies engaged involvement between students and teacher. Journaling with your students can be an important means of creating an engaged classroom.

Record your impressions of your students' responses to the above activity. Were you surprised by their lists or by the discussion of rules? What ideas from the lists or from the discussion can you use in class?

Shaughnessy, writing in the mid-1970s, lists the following skills as critical for "the ability to write what is called basic English": spelling and punctuation, making sentences, ordering sentences, and grammatical correctness. Can you think of any others (some examples might be keyboarding and awareness of audience and purpose)? Are there any skills that you would eliminate or revise from Shaughnessy's list? What has changed since Shaughnessy first wrote this article?

Shaughnessy suggests that one way of answering the question of where it "is best to begin a course in basic writing" may be for teachers to evolve a working metaphor of their own practice. "There is a kind of carpentry in sentence making," Shaughnessy writes, "various ways of joining or hooking up modifying units to the base sentence." What metaphors would you use for your own practice of writing and of teaching writing? Why do you find those metaphors particularly helpful or descriptive?

A Basic Introduction to Basic Writing Program Structures: A Baseline and Five Alternatives

William B. Lalicker

In 1999, William B. Lalicker conducted a survey on the Writing Program Administrators' listserv in order to determine the different kinds of basic writing program models at a variety of institutions. From these results, he was able to describe a "baseline" model of a basic writing program and five "alternative" models. In the following article, first published in 2000 in Conference on Basic Writing: Basic Writing e-Journal, *he lists the advantages and disadvantages of each model, as well as such important features as credit status, placement, and grading. These descriptions give us a sense of the variety and scope of the programs in place and the program options available at various institutions.*

In January 1999, I conducted a brief survey of writing program administrators to determine the alternative structures for basic writing programs. My query on the Writing Program Administrators listserv asked respondents to identify their basic writing program structures according to five models I'd identified from a general search of scholarship on the subject. Respondents not only described their basic writing programs as variants of the five models; they provided useful insights concerning the advantages and disadvantages of each model in their specific institutional contexts. (Examples of basic writing programs herein, when not otherwise cited, are taken from that listserv survey.) The following is a summary, a kind of primer, about those models and their features.

Although the appropriateness of each model relies strongly on a combination of site-specific conditions such as the institution's mission, its demographics, and its resources, no pattern emerged linked to the generic type of college or university in question. Institutions of every type have developmental writing programs. One might expect research universities, comprehensive state universities, liberal arts colleges, and community colleges to favor particular models according to institutional type, but such seemed not to be the case. Individual institutional needs — and, possibly, the theoretical or epistemological assumptions driving the writing program — seemed to be a stronger determinant.

Basic writing program directors, then, should be able to borrow from a range of structural alternatives in designing the best possible program for their students. The introduction below will begin by describing a baseline approach — the "prerequisite" model. (Since critiques of this model, especially of its placement and grading systems, are prolific in basic writing journals, I will refrain from extensive analysis and will simply describe this system in order to provide a starting point for comparing the alternatives.) I will use a parallel descriptive structure to sketch the key features of alternative approaches.

Baseline: The Prerequisite Model

- *Description:* This is the "current-traditional" approach to basic writing. This model assumes that basic writers are provisionally allowed to enter college despite literacy abilities that are sub-college-level. Writers may earn their way into the college-worthy elite (signified by admission to standard composition) by successfully completing the basic writing course; the course frequently focuses more on grammatical conformity than on rhetorical sophistication. Many institutions have used this model for decades. Some examples of this model still rely on grammar-drill workbooks and limit the scope of student writing to the paragraph level; others attempt to apply more progressive rhetorical theory within a structure unchangeable due to local political or budgetary limitations.

- *Credit status:* The prerequisite model carries with it the assumption that basic writing isn't really "college-level" writing. Although this assumption seldom if ever prevents the college or university from collecting tuition for the course, it usually prevents the institution from awarding college credit. Typically, the three credit hours of the basic writing course are allowed to count toward full-time enrollment status for a student's financial aid qualification, but do not count toward the number of credit hours required for a degree, and do not count as part of the general education core.

- *Placement:* Initial placement is usually determined by locally decided threshold scores on a standardized national examination (ACT-English, SAT Verbal, or infrequently the Nelson-Denny test). A locally developed writing examination — usually a short, timed, impromptu, no-revision-allowed essay — administered near the start of classes may influence placement. Although the timed impromptu essay has its champions (see White), most in the field find alternatives preferable (see Harrington). More rarely, a portfolio of writing solicited as part of the admissions application, or high school grades, may also be used. (For two useful surveys of the most common approaches to placement, see Huot, and Murphy et al.)

- *Grading:* Students may earn a grade on the regular A-through-F four-point scale, or may take the course pass-fail. Grading may be affected by a heavily weighted exit examination, sometimes a test of isolated grammatical questions. Additionally, a number of institutions dictate a higher minimum passing grade: if D is the minimum passing grade in most (that is, "college-level") courses, a C may be the minimum grade for a student to complete the basic writing prerequisite and continue to standard general-education composition.

- *Advantages:* This system can be simple to administer and staff, due to its compatibility with standardized placement, mechanical grammar drill, and Scantron-ready exit exams. Depending on the degree of mechanical standardization in the placement and exit exam practices, this system may be inexpensive to provide. Moreover, it powerfully refutes accusations of grade inflation and general mollycoddling of underprepared students. (Some educators and politicians apparently see this as a "tough love" system: applying this basic writing hazing, we'll have done our students the good service of preparing them for the rigors of academic discourse.)

- *Disadvantages:* Stigmatizing elements of the system, and arbitrary-appearing placement and exit exams, can raise resentment in students and parents. Lack of graduation and general education credit raises similar resentments. Outcomes of this approach to basic writing may not be theoretically or epistemologically compatible with outcomes being assessed for the composition program as a whole, especially if the composition program is driven by progressive rhetorical theory.

Alternative 1: The Stretch Model

- *Description:* "Stretch" programs serve basic writers by allowing them to complete a typical introductory standard composition course over two semesters instead of one. After taking this two-semester version of English 101, students take other general-education writing courses as required by the institution's standard curriculum. The stretch program might be numbered as, for instance, ENG 100 and ENG 101, retaining the standard composition course number but adding a prerequisite for some students (the system at Arizona State University, a prominent stretch model). Alternatively, it might be numbered, for example, ENG 099 and ENG 100, with the two courses together carrying general education credit equal to (and substituting for) ENG 101. Some stretch models structure the course as a truly integrated one-year version of introductory composition; others make the basic writing course a discrete prerequisite for standard composition, but allow that prerequisite to carry general-education, elective, or graduation credit.

- *Credit status:* A stretch sequence typically carries general-education credit — but requires students to have three additional composition credit hours compared to students not in the developmental sequence.

- *Placement:* Standard placement methods (SAT Verbal score, writing exam, entrance portfolio, or sometimes pre-enrollment writing sample or high school grade).

- *Grading:* Standard options — may be regular grade; may be pass-fail; or first course in sequence may be pass-fail, with second course being regular grade (to keep number of regular-grade general education credit hours equal for basic writers and non-basic writers).

- *Advantages:* Number of credit hours and resources devoted to composition remains essentially unchanged from system in which some students are required to take a basic writing prerequisite to standard composition. Faculty roles, number of faculty credit hours taught, and general logistics remain the same as in the baseline programs. Moreover, more faculty may be willing to teach the basic writing course once it's declared 100-level and credit-bearing, since some faculty (like some students) bring a sense of stigma or fear to any course called 0-level. Placement methods are flexible; options are essentially the same as for any other model. Not only students and faculty, but also parents, may find less stigma when starting with general-education credit-bearing, 100-level courses. In the stretch model, all students begin English Comp as university students — members of the academic community — rather than as nonqualifying, 0-level, pre-college-level outsiders. Yet basic writing students get the extra practice they need. Basic writing students begin work on the same general-education objectives as standard comp students, but have more time to reach those outcomes.

- *Disadvantages:* Simply renaming ENG 099 as ENG 100, and then requiring basic writing students to take ENG 101, doesn't necessarily change the substance and perception of a course that is often ghettoized and stigmatized. Also, students are required to earn three additional credit hours to graduate, compared with students not in the basic writing sequence. Although additional required credit hours are a feature of almost any basic writing model, the promotion of basic writing to credit-bearing status in the stretch (or any) model doesn't prevent basic writers (or their parents) from resenting that requirement, especially if it means extra tuition to pay. And a credit-bearing basic writing course may be illegal in states where legislators (or in institutions where administrators) mandate an absolute requirement that students with low SAT, ACT, or Nelson-Denny scores take 0-level courses.

Alternative 2: The Studio Model

- *Description:* A "studio" program typically allows all students to begin their general-education English Composition in the standard comp course, but places certain students in small required group sessions to supplement the work in that standard course. The studio course runs concurrently with the standard comp course and may have the same instructor, a different instructor, or may use teaching assistants or Writing Center tutors. Studio sessions, consisting of six or eight students, discuss grammatical and rhetorical issues from the composition course and do writing workshops to improve the essay drafts assigned in the standard course.

- *Credit status:* Regular general-education credit, although typically the course earns only one credit hour. May be analogous to a science "lab section" — a fourth credit hour added to a three-hour course.

- *Placement:* At the institution that initiated the studio model (the University of South Carolina), students are placed by recommendation of their composition instructors during the second week of the standard comp course. Instructors use two student writing assignments, plus portfolios of writing submitted upon university admission, to decide whether students are assigned to a studio. Some students self-select the studio to improve their skills. However, students might be placed in the studio course by any of the standard methods (SAT Verbal score, or locally designed writing examination, for instance).

- *Grading:* Studio sections are usually (but not necessarily) pass-fail; work in the studio section is assumed to influence the comp course grade indirectly (work in studio section leads to better work and a higher grade in the comp course).

- *Advantages:* Studio sections can mitigate stigma by allowing students to get general-education credit and take standard composition concurrently with raising ability levels for basic writers; many parents and students currently complain that taking basic writing before standard comp (the prerequisite approach) puts them "behind schedule" toward graduation. The studio model unites the curriculum of basic and standard comp: the writing outcomes of basic writers and standard comp are the same, with assessment in the comp section only. This enforces the notion that basic and standard composition students are all working equally and collaboratively toward fluency in academic discourse and critical discourse consciousness (rather than segregating basic writers in a simplistic linguistic world where grammatical conformity dominates). According to Grego and Thompson of the University of South Carolina, "the Studio program gives body and voice to a part of the academic institution which is working to see the personal and interpersonal aspects of learning as part of the 'thinking' that constitutes academic discourse" (81).

- *Disadvantages:* At some institutions, it could be logistically tricky for the registrar to allow students to enroll in a class two weeks into a semester. (Presemester placement, as in the intensive model described below, would solve this problem, albeit with the reintroduction of some stigma and stress for parents and students.) If the studio course is one credit hour, this will significantly reduce (by two-thirds) the number of credit hours generated now by basic writing (reducing course-generated income that supports faculty and programs — an issue in some departments). Studio sections might cost more than the three-hour-requirement system on a per-student basis if the three-hour basic writing course section is larger than eighteen. (An instructor in the studio model teaches only eighteen students if there are six students per studio; but if an instructor teaches three eight-student studio sections, the total of twenty-four students is larger than most basic writing three-credit sections.) The studio system places heavy responsibility for placement on instructors, if the South Carolina placement system is adopted. (This isn't necessarily bad; as Susanmarie Harrington notes concerning placement, "The newer models rely on teacher expertise to sort students into appropriate courses" [53]; William Smith defends this approach based on his experience at the University of Pittsburgh [142–205]. But I tend to share the view of Richard Haswell and Susan Wyche-Smith, whose work with the system at Washington State University leads them to emphasize the care and training such instructor-reliant placement requires [204–07].) Finally, the studio model may not be an option where non-credit-bearing "remedial" writing is required based on entrance test score or other placement measures.

Alternative 3: The Directed Self-Placement Model

- *Description:* "Directed Self-Placement" might be called "Basic Optional": advisors and the writing program administrator (or basic writing director) suggest or persuade, rather than require, designated students to start with basic writing rather than standard English Comp. In fact, directed self-placement isn't really a model in the structural sense: it can be used with a wide variety of course and credit arrangements. But the attitudinal change it seeks to foster in students — that basic writing is something students choose because they know they need it, rather than something forced upon them — may make a number of creative and effective course structure alternatives politically possible, even palatable, in the eyes of some constituencies (students, parents, faculty, administrators). (See Royer and Gilles for a complete description of the model and its effects at Grand Valley State University.)

- *Credit status:* At Grand Valley State University (Michigan), which has pioneered this model, students may choose to take ENG 098, a three-credit-hour, non-general-education-credit course. Programs have the option of using this model with 100-level elective basic writing courses offering general-education credit.

- *Placement:* The writing program administrator at Grand Valley State addresses an assembly of all incoming students during orientation, directing them to respond for themselves on key statements defining their literacy levels. Students consider statements such as "I read newspapers and magazines regularly." "In high school, I wrote several essays per year," and "My ACT-English score was above 20" (analogous to "My SAT Verbal score was above 490"). Then, for students who answer "No" to the questions, he makes the case for ENG 098 instead of standard comp, and students sign up for the course in which they believe they belong.

- *Grading:* The basic writing course may be traditionally graded or pass-fail.

- *Advantages:* Students take responsibility for their own literacy — and for their own placement in English Composition. This may lead students to resent their placement less, and to motivate themselves more energetically in whatever writing course they choose. Placement is less expensive and time-consuming: no local testing systems or portfolio assessment necessary. As the subtitle of the Royer and Gilles article concludes, "Directed Self-Placement Pleases Everyone Involved" (65).

• *Disadvantages:* Although Grand Valley State's conclusion is that the students who should have been taking developmental comp all along tended to place themselves in it, there is the possibility that some students who would benefit from the developmental course would avoid basic writing. Some students may self-place inaccurately, be overwhelmed by early academic expectations, and perform more poorly in standard comp and other university writing tasks. If self-directed placement leads to significantly fewer basic writing sections, a loss of income-generating credit hours or critical program mass may lead to a marginalized program without resources to serve its constituency. Directed self-placement may depend upon an enhanced Writing Center (and a commitment to an enhanced Writing Center budget) to provide support to students who might receive extra instruction through basic writing but are placed in standard comp. Finally, the "optional" quality of self-directed placement may not be legal in states where legislators (or campus administrators) mandate placement in "pre-college-level" writing based on test scores or other standardized measures.

Alternative 4: The Intensive Model

• *Description:* The "intensive" model offers two kinds of standard composition sections: the regular sections, plus "intensive" sections that include additional instruction time or writing activities tailored for basic writers. To some degree, the intensive model is a variation on the studio model, usually differing from the standard studio model in two ways. First, in intensive-model basic writing, students start in special intensive composition sections from the first day of classes, based on common placement methods such as test scores or portfolio ratings. Second, in the intensive model, students usually are part of one five-credit class group, while in the studio model, students from several different sections of standard composition come together at random in the studio lab sections; each structure leads to different pedagogical possibilities.

• *Credit hours:* Intensive sections of comp generally offer five credit hours for the course, rather than the standard three-credit-hour sections. All sections — intensive and standard — carry general-education credit.

• *Placement:* Any placement system may be used; institutions presently using the intensive system tend to use SAT Verbal scores for placement.

- *Grading:* Students in intensive sections get regular grades, counting for five credit hours for the initial general-education composition course, rather than the standard three credit hours.

- *Advantages:* Writing program administrators at two of the noted programs using this system (Illinois State University and Quinnipiac College) endorse the intensive model; Mary T. Segall says that the intensive model has removed the basic-writing stigma and increased motivation (38–47). The system also may remove the complaint about prerequisite basic writing delaying the start of general-education comp, may integrate students into mainstream academic writing situations more quickly, and may help unify basic writing and English Comp writing standards and assessment outcomes. Students who are part of a unified classroom group for all of the work that five credit hours implies may find it easier to collaborate with the stable community of student-colleagues. The two-credit-hours' worth of added work in each intensive section is focused on the tasks of one course section (unlike in the studio system, where studio work may include students comparing perspectives from slightly differing course sections).

- *Disadvantages:* In a five-credit-hour system, one-third fewer credit hours would be generated by basic writing than are generated in a prerequisite basic writing system (with possible budgetary consequences). Five-credit courses might be logistically tricky to work into instructors' nine- or twelve-credit-hour loads (and adjunct faculty at many institutions are paid by three-credit-hour course), necessitating some special prorated pay arrangements or overtime salary. If credit is awarded for intensive courses, this policy may violate state or institutional mandates that low-performing entrants take non-credit-bearing "remedial" writing.

Alternative 5: The Mainstreaming Model

- *Description:* "Mainstreaming" essentially eliminates basic writing classes and puts all students, no matter what their apparent writing ability, into standard comp classes. Students address deficiencies in their writing through their own initiative in the Writing Center or use other tutoring options (including increased one-on-one help from professors in conferences).

- *Credit:* Regular general-education credit — basic writers take standard composition.

- *Placement:* No placement into basic writing necessary.

- *Grading:* Same as in standard composition.

- *Advantages:* "Mainstreaming" — teaching special needs students (in this case, basic writers) in standard classes — has been championed in many levels of education for social reasons, mainly the elimination of the "outsider" status of a segment of the student population. Some mainstreaming schools (such as the City College of New York) adopted mainstreaming for the philosophical view that all students should be part of a united community without stigmatized segments (before the CCNY trustees eliminated basic writing in an anti-remedial-education move). In practical terms, there is some evidence that mainstreamed students improve their writing faster when immersed in the higher-level academic discourse of the standard comp class. Some institutions (such as Essex Community College in Maryland) claim that basic writers placed in basic writing classes are ultimately less successful in college writing tasks than basic writers who skip basic writing and go into standard comp (Adams 22–36) (although this may be an argument for "directed self-placement" rather than mainstreaming). Mainstreaming eliminates costs of basic writing placement.
- *Disadvantages:* Some basic writing students might find themselves overtaxed in standard comp classes, with possible consequences ranging from poorer overall student writing performance to decreased retention and graduation. Instructors in standard comp classes would need to be prepared to do more diagnostic work and one-on-one tutoring. Mary Soliday and Barbara Gleason at CCNY warn that mainstreaming requires increased tutoring support and faculty development to meet the needs of basic writers (22–36). Inadequately supported Writing Centers would likely be overwhelmed by demand for service, and might need increased and sustained resources. Alternatively, the regular general-education comp courses might have to lower established standards and expected outcomes, or be revised with an eye toward what has been basic writing instruction (possibly serving basic writers adequately, but more prepared writers less appropriately than under the status quo). Mainstreaming would mean the elimination of basic writing; in some cases, this may mean the elimination of basic writers, especially in jurisdictions where basic writing is mandated for low-scoring students — a violation of many institutions' missions to serve disadvantaged populations or broad regional needs. In some systems, mainstreaming means the loss of budgetary dollars generated by basic writing credit hours (erstwhile basic writing students would be taking three fewer credit hours).

Which model should you adopt? Should you copy the key features of a typical system as described here, or design a variant by playing mix-and-match? A greater understanding of the alternatives will help you determine the answer most suited to your program's theories and goals, most achievable with your institution's mission and resources, and most successful for meeting the literacy challenges of your basic writing students.

Works Cited

Adams, Peter Dow. "Basic Writing Reconsidered." *Journal of Basic Writing* 12.1 (Spring 1993): 22–36.

Grego, Rhonda, and Nancy Thompson. "Repositioning Remediation: Renegotiating Composition's Work in the Academy." *CCC* 47.1 (Feb. 1996): 62–84.

Harrington, Susanmarie. "New Visions of Authority in Placement Test Rating." *WPA: Writing Program Administration* 22.1/2 (Fall/Winter 1998): 53–84.

Haswell, Richard, and Susan Wyche-Smith. "A Two-Tiered Rating Procedure for Placement Essays." *Assessment in Practice: Putting Principles to Work on College Campuses.* Ed. Trudy Banta. San Francisco: Jossey-Bass, 1995. 204–07.

Huot, Brian. "A Survey of College and University Writing Placement Practices." *WPA: Writing Program Administration* 17.3 (Spring 1994): 49–65.

Murphy, Sandra, et al. Report to the CCCC Executive Committee: Survey of Postsecondary Writing Assessment Practices. 1993.

Royer, Daniel J., and Roger Gilles. "Directed Self-Placement: An Attitude of Orientation." *CCC* 50.1 (Sept. 1998): 58–70.

Segall, Mary T. "Embracing a Porcupine: Redesigning a Writing Program." *Journal of Basic Writing* 14.2 (Fall 1995): 38–47.

Smith, William. "Assessing the Reliability and Adequacy of Using Holistic Scoring of Essays as a College Composition Placement Technique." *Validating Holistic Scoring for Writing Assessment: Theoretical and Empirical Foundations.* Ed. Michael M. Williamson and Brian Huot. Cresskill, NJ: Hampton, 1993. 142–205.

Soliday, Mary, and Barbara Gleason. "From Remediation to Enrichment: Evaluating a Mainstreaming Project." *Journal of Basic Writing* 16.1 (Spring 1997): 64–78.

White, Edward M. "An Apologia for the Timed Impromptu Essay." *CCC* 46.1 (Feb. 1995): 30–45.

Classroom Activities

Encourage students to reflect on their own education by thinking about the six models for basic writing that Lalicker presents. In order to offer a more relevant approach to the idea of an educational model for students, you might ask them to respond to the following prompts:

- Describe your experiences with studying writing and reading in grade school, high school, or GED or ABE programs. What was the best experience you ever had with writing? What was the worst? What made these experiences memorable?

- Compare your previous experiences with writing to your basic writing course(s) in college. What differences do you see? What similarities? Are the expectations for writing in college similar or different from your previous education? Why or why not?

- How does your education in writing compare or contrast to your education in some other discipline(s) (math, science, social studies, and so forth)? What similarities do you see in how these disciplines are taught? What differences? How are these similarities and differences important to your education as a whole?

Thinking about Teaching

In your teaching journal, reflect on your students' responses to the above questions. What surprised you or otherwise jogged your thinking? How can you use your insights about this discussion to help shape activities in your classroom?

Examine the baseline model and the alternative models represented in Lalicker's article. Which model(s) seem to be used in the institution(s) in which you teach? Does this model seem to be appropriate for the student population and the mission of the institution? Why or why not? Do you have questions about how the model came to be used in your institution?

Can you conceptualize another kind of model, one not described in Lalicker's essay? What would that model look like? How would a new model benefit students? How would it facilitate teaching? Are there any details that Lalicker left out of his descriptions of the models? What are they?

As appropriate, share your reflections and questions on the above issues with students, faculty, and administrators. What kinds of questions does your institution need to ask about basic writing? Why?

Creating a Statement of Guidelines and Goals for Boise State University's Basic Writing Course: Content and Development

Karen S. Uehling

During the 2000–01 academic year, Karen Uehling and five adjunct colleagues at Boise State University collaborated in composing a "Statement of Goals and Guidelines" for their institution's basic writing course. In this selection, Uehling documents the process of creating the statement and includes the final product that evolved from this process. The statement features a description of local conditions for teaching basic writing at BSU as well as minimum course requirements, course competencies, and suggestions for teachers. Uehling's selection responds to the question "What is basic writing?" based on the immediate circumstances of her home institution. At the same time, the "Statement of Guidelines and Goals" demonstrates the strong confluence of pedagogy, theory, and classroom practice in basic writing as a discipline.

My institution, Boise State University, created a statement of guidelines and goals for our basic writing course in 2000–2001.[1] To develop our statement, we wrestled with the relationship between basic writing and our two required first year composition courses. Ultimately, we envisioned a course that prepares students for English 101 in several ways. We hope students will be prepared "because they have begun to develop confidence in their reading and writing abilities, learn the conventions and expectations of university classrooms, [and] develop an awareness of the activities in writing classrooms and the terms used to talk about writing" (Boise State University). Like other documents of this kind, our curricular statement was developed in response to local conditions.

Boise State University (BSU) in Boise, Idaho, is a six-year urban, commuter institution of 17,000 part- and full-time students with an average age of about twenty-seven. BSU also fulfills a community college function through a vocational technical program that offers two-year degrees and certificate programs. The Idaho State Board of Education, in its mission statement for the institution, describes Boise State University as "a comprehensive, urban university serving a diverse population. . . ." Further, the mission statement calls for the university to "maintain basic strengths in the liberal arts and sciences, which provide the core curriculum or general education portion of the curriculum." Our basic writing course is within the English Department and thus within the College of Arts and Sciences; the college mission statement reads, in part: "In teaching, the College of Arts and Sciences offers a core curriculum that prepares undergraduate students for future lives and careers by developing their communication, numerical, and analytical skills, enhancing their creative abilities, fostering in them a greater awareness of human values and needs, and encouraging in them a lifelong appreciation of learning for its own sake." It was within these contexts that we worked to produce our statement of guidelines and goals for basic writing.

Numbered English 90, our basic writing class, is a one-semester, non-credit course, the equivalent of three credits.[2] Passing the course permits students to enroll in English 101. Our institution places students in basic writing based on test scores. Beginning fall term 2000, the Idaho State Board of Education raised the scores necessary for admission to first year composition, and consequently doubled the number of students in basic writing. In addition to those students who are required to take basic writing, some, primarily older, returning students, choose to take the course as a review.

Since the test scores were raised, the quality of writing has improved in the class, and the students now fall in two groups — those typical of students who enrolled previous to the change in test scores who have clear surface level writing problems and those who can write relatively correct prose, but whose texts seem vacant, vague, and disorganized. The current group of students in our basic writing course might be characterized as upper-level basic/lower-level freshman composition students.

Our Statement of Guidelines and Goals for Basic Writing

Our statement of guidelines and goals for basic writing (see Appendix A) contains several headings: an introduction, and sections called "Transforming Attitudes," "Making the Transition to the University" (which includes "Relationship to English 101"), "Demonstrations, Examples, and Models," "Consistent Goals and Methods," "Language Study," "Minimum Requirements," "Specifics," "Competencies," and "Suggestions for Teachers."

The framework for this document derived from curricular documents already developed by Boise State faculty for the two required first year writing courses at our institution, English 101 and 102. New features that the basic writing faculty added were "Relationship to English 101" and "Suggestions for Teachers."

The heart of this document is the seven competencies for basic writing because the competencies are tied to portfolio assessment and thus significantly influence what goes on in class. I will explain our thinking about and approaches to each competency in turn.

The Competencies

1.   They have confidence in themselves as writers and readers within a college environment.

Students need confidence to access the skills they have. Many do not trust their own instincts about language. Students also need confidence to develop new skills, try out new processes and approaches, allow themselves to make mistakes, and learn. Some have had bad experiences with English in high school; for older students, negative feelings may have festered for years, and often students don't give themselves credit for having any language skills. Some students are "generation 1.5" learners who have used two languages or dialects since birth, and they may distrust standard English. Some students dropped out of high school and obtained GEDs and believe there is a vast world of education they missed in high school. Most hold a university in awe — they do not see themselves as peers of other students or capable learners.

2.   They can engage in a multi-faceted process of writing, that includes invention, development, organization, feedback, revision, and editing / proofreading.

In our course we introduce and practice various methods of invention — free writing, brainstorming, clustering, listing, and other processes. We develop papers step-by-step over time. Students may draft five papers and later revise three in the last third of the course. We teach editing/proofreading as a separate step generally at the end of writing. Revised and edited papers become part of a portfolio due at the end of the course. The English 90 portfolio is fifteen pages, in line with twenty pages for English 101 and twenty-five for English 102: thus each course steps up five pages in portfolio length.

3.   They are willing to use multiple strategies to view, revise, and edit their evolving written texts over time, moving from writer- to reader-based prose.

Students observe pieces of writing evolving and changing over time. Often the instructor demonstrates this process with her own drafts, by handing out raw invention materials, then a rough draft; next, after soliciting student feedback, a revised draft. Student assistants also model the invention and response processes with drafts of papers on later projects. And students see their own and their peers' papers shifting and developing as they focus and revise. Eventually students come to view the same text differently as they get reader response and reread a paper later in the term that had earlier seemed "finished." We want them to experiment with changing a text that they thought was completed; this is a key transition to English 101 and critical for English 102.

4.   They can produce writing that has a beginning, middle, and end developed with relevant details and examples.

For this competency, we draw attention to how writers open and close pieces, such as the use of anecdote or dialogue as an opening strategy or returning to the beginning idea as a closing strategy. We point out how titles are not random or merely topic announcements but have some integral connection to the text. We review some essential organizational strategies, like chronology, categorization, and final emphasis. We push students to find these structures in readings and imitate them. Of course, we stress concrete details and specific examples and ask for figures, names, species, colors, ages, dates, and dollars and cents.

5.   They can produce writing in a format appropriate to its purpose.

By "format," we mean these kinds of features: typed, double spaced, 1″ margins; standard, 12-point font; left justified; paragraphs indented .5″; all important words of title capitalized, and title not all capitals, bold, underlined, in quotes, in italics, or in a larger typeface. "Format" in this competence also includes basic academic conventions like referring to the author by his or her last name, not first name; checking that the name is accurate and not in a similar or rough form; capitalizing the name; and spelling it right.

We also work on identifying and labeling work, and the basics of responding to a question: answering the question asked with adequate length and carrying out the number and kinds of tasks for which the question asks. We emphasize the need to answer questions using complete sentences and to make responses self-contained, so that the reader who does not have the question handy can still understand the response. We examine when and how to insert a quotation and the word choice needed to talk about quotations.

6.   They can read actively and critically and engage in a dialogue with a text.

Students read essays that connect directly to the kinds of essays they are writing; they also read the textbook, their own and others' drafts, and in many sections, a complete challenging nonfiction book. The textbook used most recently was *Reading Critically, Writing Well,* edited by Rise B. Axelrod and Charles R. Cooper, which is especially effective at connecting reading and writing assignments. Typical full-length books that we might assign are *Lives on the Boundary,* by Mike

Rose, or *Bootstraps,* by Victor Villanueva, both literacy narratives that focus on the transition to college. Students write reading log responses to such works, answering specific questions. We ask for a variety of responses, beginning with if they liked the reading or not and why and proceeding through such investigative processes as speculation about the title, use of sensory description and specific development, imitation of powerful lines, the meaning of the text, and connection with other texts. Some of us ask students to write midterm and final exam essays based on questions from the nonfiction book.

7.   They can edit their work for mechanical errors to the extent that, while perhaps not "perfect," surface features of the language do not interfere with communication.

English 90 is the primary class we offer that includes some direct language work, as a review. We teach a minimal grammar; I favor Rei Noguchi's "writer's grammar." I show a video of a colleague coaching a student as she edits her paper for fragments and run-ons using this writer's grammar. We talk about proofreading as a different kind of reading from reading for meaning. We ask students to engage in self-study of problem areas and thus make them responsible for their errors; and we offer tips and hints for editing. And, all of this, we hope, is in an atmosphere of language play. Reading a challenging nonfiction book is also critical because a text that forces a reader to stop, look, and think about language helps develop awareness of language and the kind of seeing required for effective editing.

So that is the heart of our document. The final section of our statement is called "Suggestions for Teaching." Each competency connects with and is supported by the teaching suggestions. I will consider one example, our first competency: 1. They have confidence in themselves as writers and readers within a college environment.

The teaching suggestion *Making the Transition to the University* supports confidence in that we introduce students to campus resources for academic services and support through guest speakers from groups like the Writing Center and student success and support programs; and we offer information on where and how to learn to type or learn basic word processing skills. We also build student confidence by reviewing and re-enforcing basic study skills. At one time Boise State University had a learning community program that linked basic writing students through grouped courses, including basic writing, study skills, and core courses, and we still try to support study skills in the basic writing class.

Consistent Goals and Methods is a teaching suggestion that also supports confidence; we offer an overview of the course at the beginning, and we make course goals and methods clear throughout. We repeat reading, writing, discussion, and feedback activities in a predictable format. And we present extended assignments in a step-by-step sequence.

Developing the Statement of Guidelines and Goals

The key to the development of the statement of guidelines and goals was a collaborative process, what Bruce Ballenger, our Director of Writing, characterizes as a "focus group." The group was initially created to increase the number of trained faculty prepared to teach basic writing. The group consisted of six adjunct faculty, chosen for their talent and experience teaching freshman composition, and me; I was asked to mentor these instructors during the first term they taught basic writing, fall 2000. An important feature of this training was administrative support. The adjunct faculty received an honorarium for participating in the training and collaborative work, and I received a course release for undertaking the mentor's role.[3] As part of the training and mentoring, I wanted to engage the group in a substantive contribution to the basic writing endeavor on our campus, and producing the statement of guidelines and goals seemed timely and important;[4] and, for once we had the time to engage in serious reflection on our work as basic writing teachers.

We spent several of our weekly mentoring meetings working on the statement. We began by listing everything we did in basic writing, especially what we thought was critical or unique to the course. Next I categorized this list and gave it back to the group for discussion. At the same time, I had posted a request on the Conference on Basic Writing Listserv (CBW-L) asking for sample guidelines, goals, and mission statements, and I gave these samples to the group as well. Although our group did not directly consider the formal mission statements of the university and college when we initially drafted our statement, clearly it would be preferable to do so; however, the course we describe does support those mission statements. After all, we are directly engaged each day with the students the mission statement describes, an "urban university serving a diverse population," and we work to develop students' core communication skills in reading and writing.

Based on the group's feedback to my list of basic writing activities, I drafted the first full statement for group review and consensus. When we had a draft we could agree on, I sought response from two tenured colleagues who also teach the course. The revised document was then presented to the chair and Writing Committee.

The next term, spring 2001, the adjunct faculty and I met with the Writing Committee a few times and together we revised the document further. In the summer, the Writing Program carried out a preliminary assessment of basic writing portfolios based on the proposed competencies. Our students did well in this pilot assessment, revealing that the statement of guidelines and goals appeared appropriate. Further, there was informal evidence that students who took English 90 often did better in English 101 than those who did not take it. In October of 2001, the Writing Committee brought the statement of guidelines and goals to an English Department meeting where it was ratified and then the document was posted on the Writing Program website.

The collaborative nature of this process produced several benefits. Obviously, the faculty group, using a collective brainstorming method, generated more good ideas than could have been articulated by any one person. The initial focus group process also gave the instructors ownership of the document because they helped create it. The instructors thus "bought" into the process and the resulting course. The follow-up with other tenured instructors and the Writing Committee, which included the Director of Writing, strengthened the document, especially by aligning it more closely with our existing statements. When the statement was brought to the department, this development process gave it legitimacy; there was little discussion before approval because it had already been tested and revised. The creation of the statement of guidelines and goals brought visibility to our basic writing course; I feel the department better understands basic writing now and takes it more seriously as a course.

The development of the English 90 *Statement of Mission and Minimum Requirements* has also affected other first-year writing courses. The Writing Committee and Writing Program administrators liked the features the basic writing faculty added to the template of the document, which were "Relationship to English 101" and "Suggestions for Teachers," and there are plans to add similar sections, developed collaboratively, to the English 101 and 102 documents. Also the writing program plans eventually to develop statements of guidelines and goals for our other first year courses, honors composition and our English as a Second Language (ESL) sequence.

One of the most interesting aspects of creating our statement of guidelines and goals was trying to articulate how basic writing differs from English 101 and how it is the same. Ultimately, we framed our thinking in these terms: previewing, practicing, working on language, explaining writing courses, and developing confidence. We *preview* some of the academic work of English 101 and of the university as a whole. We *practice* reading and writing. We are the primary class that includes *some language instruction*. We *explain* what goes on in a college writing course and why. This information is especially important for students who have been out of school for a while. Adult learning theory suggests that learners need to know why they are being asked to do something and how it fits into the big picture of the course or the field of study (Knowles 174). This means we have to justify our goals and methods of instruction, for instance, why we ask for early free writing or peer response in feedback groups or editing as primarily the last step. We hope that we *develop confidence* through all of these activities.

Our English 101 course is now taught largely by teaching assistants who use a modified expressivist and reading process approach with free writing, conferencing, and group work. We hope our basic writing students will be ready to thrive in an atmosphere of this kind, especially where TAs may not be adept at articulating exactly why these teaching strategies are effective. Our students will be able to trust this process.

Notes

1. Although titled a *Statement of Mission and Minimum Requirements,* our document is not a traditionally conceived mission statement, that is, a concise statement of a group's mission and identity. Rather, our basic writing statement is a document of several pages that details course rationale and describes and explains curriculum; thus I refer to this statement as a statement of "guidelines and goals."
2. I think the course should carry elective credits, and, as a step in that direction, in fall 2002 I piloted a dual enrollment combined basic writing/freshman composition course, which met for six hours per week and offered the noncredit equivalent of three credits for English 90 and three regular credits for English 101; the course was successful enough that it will be offered again in fall 2003.
3. Recently, all tenured faculty in writing, including the Director and Assistant Director of Writing, participated in some of the basic writing training so that they will eventually be prepared to teach basic writing. This clear administrative support for basic writing strengthens the sense of commitment and community of those who teach basic writing and increases the visibility of the course to other faculty and campus administrators.
4. The group of faculty who helped draft the initial statement included Julie Ewing, Jill Heney, Joy Kidwell, Siskanna Naynaha, Kate Pritchard, Marian Thomas, and Karen Uehling.

Works Cited

Axelrod, Rise B., and Charles R. Cooper, eds. *Reading Critically, Writing Well: A Reader and Guide.* 6th ed. NY: Bedford/St. Martin's, 2002.

Boise State University. *English 90: Statement of Mission and Minimum Requirements.* Boise, ID: last revised 12 Nov. 2001. 19 Feb. 2003 <http://english.boisetate.edu/writing/Mission.090.htm>.

Knowles, Malcolm S. *The Adult Learner: A Neglected Species.* 3rd ed. Houston: Gulf, 1984.

Noguchi, Rei. *Grammar and the Teaching of Writing: Limits and Possibilities.* Urbana, IL: NCTE, 1991.

Rose, Mike. *Lives on the Boundary: The Struggles and Achievements of America's Underprepared.* NY: Penguin, 1990.

Uehling, Karen S. "Mission Statement for Boise State University's Basic Writing Course: Content and Development." Paper presented at the Conference on College Composition and Communication. Chicago, March 2002.

Villanueva, Victor, Jr. *Bootstraps: From an American Academic of Color.* Urbana, IL: NCTE, 1993.

APPENDIX A

English 90
Boise State University

Statement of Mission and Minimum Requirements
Fall 2001

Introduction

One of the strengths and challenges of Boise State University is the rich diversity of its students, and ENGL 90 students are often some of the most diverse students on campus. They may be adults, returning to college after many years; they may work full or part-time as they attend school; they may be speakers of more than one language or dialect. ENGL 90, an introduction to college writing, is required if a placement test or writing sample demonstrates need, and it also provides review for those who wish further preparation before taking ENGL 101. ENGL 90 offers students extra time to work on their writing with attention to fluency, development, organization, revision, and editing/proofreading. ENGL 90 counts as the equivalent of 3 credits, though the credits do not count toward graduation.

Transforming Attitudes

Students in ENGL 90 are usually just entering the university and can often be distinguished by their lack of confidence. Yet to thrive in college, students must become confident as readers and writers and as members of the academic community. ENGL 90 is a course that builds both confidence and skill. We believe that students' experiences with language and language use in the course should be positive, and that this will provide the basis for the development of writing skills. As a consequence, ENGL 90 focuses, like ENGL 101, in part on the affective dimension of writing and thinking processes; that is, the course hopes to encourage students to believe that reading and writing are meaning-making activities that are relevant to their lives, within school and without.

Making the Transition to the University

ENGL 90 serves as a bridge between the community and the university. Instructors should assist students with this transition into the world of studenthood. Essential topics include active, critical reading; an introduction to the culture of the academy and to basic terms of academic analysis; review of study skills; and an introduction to campus resources for academic support.

ENGL 90 students will be prepared to enter ENGL 101 because they have begun to

- develop confidence in their reading and writing abilities

- learn the conventions and expectations of university classrooms

- develop an awareness of the activities in writing classrooms and the terms used to talk about writing

Demonstrations, Examples, and Models

Students may have not seen writing develop over time and may be unfamiliar with the processes writers engage in to produce writing. Thus, students will observe how writing is produced.

Consistent Goals and Methods

We believe ENGL 90 students thrive in an atmosphere that is predictable. Clear goals, repeated routines, and "scaffolded" assignments are likely to create an atmosphere that builds student confidence and provides the basis for the development of writing skills.

Language Study

ENGL 90 is one of the few courses in which editing and proofreading skills are taught; however, such skills are only one part of ENGL 90, which is clearly a writing course. Language skills should be taught largely within the context of the student's own writing.

Minimum Requirements

Specifics

Students in writing classes should continuously produce written work. This includes evaluated work, such as formal assignments and subsequent revisions, as well as informal and non-evaluated work, such as journal entries, in-class writing exercises, rough drafts, and peer responses. ENGL 90 students will produce, on average, the equivalent of 3 to 3.5 double-spaced and typed pages — about 1000 words — a week. The equivalent of 15 pages of double-spaced and typed writing will be the basis for assessing students' final grades in the course.

Students will write several informal responses to reading materials using a variety of strategies for active, critical reading.

Students will begin to learn the terms, processes, and conventions of academic writing necessary for success in ENGL 101 and other university classrooms.

Students will meet all the attendance and class participation requirements and submit required assignments on deadline.

Competencies
Students will demonstrate that:

1. they have confidence in themselves as writers and readers within a college environment.

2. they can engage in a multi-faceted process of writing, that includes invention, development, organization, feedback, revision, and editing/proofreading.

3. they are willing to use multiple strategies to view, revise, and edit their evolving written texts over time, moving from writer- to reader-based prose.

4. they can produce writing that has a beginning, middle, and end developed with relevant details and examples.

5. they can produce writing in a format appropriate to its purpose.

6. they can read actively and critically and engage in a dialogue with a text.

7. they can edit their work for mechanical errors to the extent that, while perhaps not "perfect," surface features of the language do not interfere with communication.

Suggestions for Teachers

MAKING THE TRANSITION TO THE UNIVERSITY.   Demonstrate how to view a text not as a "flat landscape" but as a rich, living piece of discourse; have students practice engaging in a dialogue with the author. Preview some of the terms, processes, and conventions of academic writing. Review and re-enforce basic study skills. Introduce students to campus resources for academic services and support.

DEMONSTRATIONS, EXAMPLES, AND MODELS.   Conduct demonstrations of writing in progress, both step-by-step examples of major assignments and examples of informal assignments. Several examples will provide a range for students rather than a single model to follow. Student interns can provide additional supporting demonstrations.

CONSISTENT GOALS AND METHODS.   Present an overview of the course at the beginning of the term, carefully explaining course goals and methods of instruction. Repeat and practice reading, writing, discussion, and feedback procedures in a predictable format. Present extended assignments in a step-by-step, staged, and sequence manner.

LANGUAGE STUDY.   Foster a playful, inquisitive attitude toward language and its richness, encouraging students to take an investigative approach to language phenomena. Practice individual error analysis, and teach editing and proofreading as a special task that requires its own particular ways of seeing and responding to text. Offer students practical tricks and hints for editing their own work rather than an exhaustive review of grammar.

Classroom Activities

Invite students to assess their own progress in the course using the list of seven competencies described by Uehling. Or substitute your own institution's list of course competencies for basic writing. Students can evaluate how and why they have achieved specific course competencies; they also can consider course competencies in which they have not yet gained proficiency.

If your course uses a portfolio-based evaluation system, students can use their self-assessment as a portfolio cover letter, including examples of their writing from the portfolio as supporting evidence. Students also can implement this self-assessment strategy for individual essays throughout the term.

Thinking about Teaching

Uehling and her colleagues initially engaged in a self-study of their basic writing course as part of teacher training. "We began by listing everything that we did in basic writing, especially what we thought was critical or unique to the course," Uehling explains. Consider creating a list of significant activities in your own basic writing course and joining with a group of colleagues to compare notes. From this self-reflection, you can evolve guidelines for new teachers such as the "Suggestions for Teachers" listed in Uehling's appendix. You also may wish to develop a statement that would be useful for describing the course to other department members, institutional administrators, or other stakeholders.

2

Basic Writing: Students' Perspectives

Who are basic writing students? Whether you are a first-year or veteran teacher, this chapter will help you think through your own response to this question. In addition, you will find a collection of students' perspectives on their experiences with education and writing. Some students, for instance, may have graduated from under-funded inner-city or rural high schools; other students may be returning to school after several years away and need extra support as they begin college. Still other students come to college from GED or ABE programs; and a growing number of students would describe themselves as bilingual or multilingual. Students represented in this chapter come from a wide variety of backgrounds, reflecting the diversity of those enrolled in many basic writing courses.

Valerie Kinloch, in "Revisiting the Promise of *Students' Right to Their Own Language:* Pedagogical Strategies," analyzes the work of her writing students as they grapple with home and school languages. As a result of her classroom observations, Kinloch offers pedagogical strategies for supporting linguistic diversity in the writing classroom and includes a thorough discussion of the 1974 position statement *Students' Right to Their Own Language.* Students' voices permeate and inform Kinloch's argument in these excerpts from her longer article.

Jane Maher's "'You Probably Don't Even Know I Exist': Notes from a Prison College Program" describes the roles of writing and education in the lives of her pre-college students, inmates of a women's maximum-security prison outside New York City. Maher includes notes that students have written to her, as well as a complete essay, composed by her student Kecia Pittman, written, as Maher suggests, for readers "who knew nothing about her but who sincerely wanted to understand what she wanted and needed."

Ann E. Green, in "My Uncle's Guns," creates the voice of a fictional basic writing student who lives, works, and writes in a white, working-class farming community in Pennsylvania. The main character writes a "personal narrative" much like one assigned in many basic writing courses. The narrator comments on her own writing process throughout the story. Green presents critical issues of social class and region that influence the interactions of basic writing teachers and students. Her short story urges the reader to consider how social class is constructed and represented in basic writing classrooms — and in the writing process itself.

From Revisiting the Promise of *Students' Right to Their Own Language:* Pedagogical Strategies

Valerie Kinloch

In these excerpts from a longer article first published in College Composition and Communication *in 2005, Valerie Kinloch presents strategies for engaging linguistic diversity in a writing course whose working-class Generation 1.5 and African American students initially describe themselves as on the "margins" of the educational mainstream. Kinloch invites students to question their position within the university through critical reading, writing, and discussion of essays by June Jordan (see Chapter 11 of this volume), bell hooks, and the 1974 CCCC resolution* Students' Right to Their Own Language. *Kinloch also introduces her own subject position as an African American educator who "know[s] how to code switch and [whose] primary form of communication is partly influenced by the Gullah culture of the Sea Islands."*

Significant pedagogical implications emerge from the students' work in this course, and Kinloch offers a list of seven strategies for approaching linguistic diversity in the composition classroom, stating that "Experimentation with new strategies points to an awareness of the changing student demographics within the university. . . ." In addition, Kinloch includes a document composed by her own students, a "resolution on student willingness to be a part of an academic community." As a result, student voices permeate and inform Kinloch's argument throughout this selection.

Classroom vignette 3

Issues of language and class, as with issues of race, are present throughout the supporting document of the *Students' Right* resolution. One section reads:

Students who come from backgrounds where the prestigious variety of English is the normal medium of communication have built-in advantages that enable them to succeed, often in spite of, and not because of, their schoolroom training in "grammar." They sit at the head of the class, are accepted at "exclusive" schools, and are later rewarded with positions in the business and social world. Students whose nurture and experience give them a different dialect are usually denied these rewards. As English teachers, we are responsible for what our teaching does to the self-image and the self-esteem of our students. (2)

After reading this passage with my class, I awaited their individual responses. Many of them expressed feelings of rage, not because of what the passage says, but because of the reality of class privilege in this democracy. "Minh," a student in the class, shared with us how her Chinese language was considered an "interference" with her acquisition and mastery of Standard Written and Spoken English: "My twelfth-grade English teacher once said: 'You know, Minh, if you want to one day live in power, then you'll have to work on *downplaying* your accent . . . and you must stop using Chinese words and phrases when trying to express a complete thought. If you must, then translate privately, but never make it a public act. Your speech will determine your class status.'"

Other students in the class became even more enraged after Minh's comment, and wanted to further investigate the *Students' Right* passage in light of one of the course readings on language and class. For the next reading discussion, they unanimously selected bell hooks's "Confronting Class in the Classroom," and Minh volunteered to lead the discussion.

When Minh's presentation day arrived, she asked me to provide an introduction to the piece. Not knowing where my introduction would fit into Minh's discussion, I decided to begin with the following passage from "Confronting Class in the Classroom": "[A]ny professor who commits to engaged pedagogy recognizes the importance of constructively confronting issues of class. That means welcoming the opportunity to alter our classroom practices creatively so that the democratic ideal of education for everyone can be realized" (189). Minh jumped in by talking about the mantra of class issues in the classroom as representative of controversial fields of contact in which, according to Minh, "students can easily be exposed to others and can feel so uncomfortable if the teacher does not provide the space and time for students to talk about their feelings and hear different reactions from other people in the classroom" (hooks's engaged pedagogy). Minh made a connection between hooks's talk of class and the *Students' Right* resolution's talk of students from privileged versus nonprivileged backgrounds by saying: "I was offended when my twelfth-grade teacher told me to *downplay* my accent because of what she thinks is my unprivileged cultural background. Well, I think it's important to know that regardless of language and accent and dialect, we all have a right to our language and the language of social class mobility. I care about my Chinese language and my English language, and I need to know how to nurture them as I move up the class ladder." At the closing of this class session, another student confessed, "I'm black, I'm male, I'm poor, and yet I speak Standard English. Do I give a damn about differences in language and class? Yeah, I do, because language defines class and class defines social and political status, power, and, in some way, it all defines who we are or who we want to eventually be. But will I give up my right to my own language? Now that I know I have a right, no!"

From this class session and for the remainder of the semester, students productively interrogated the fundamental principles outlined in both the Jordan and the hooks essays, and their doing so is demonstrative of how language and class issues can motivate students to critically reflect on their own experience while cultivating their own expressive powers through methods of inventiveness and analysis. They reread the essays, bringing into subsequent class sessions highlighted paragraphs to share with one another; they questioned Jordan's statement, "I believe that somebody real has blinded America in at least one eye. And, in the same way that so many Americans feel that 'we have lost our jobs,' we suspect that we have lost our country. *We know that we do not speak the language*" ("Problems" 232). Additionally, the students made connections between Jordan's emphasis on language being a common currency and hooks's implication that people need to talk about class distinctions by using language. One student even brought into class a quotation from Toni Morrison's *Lecture and Speech of Acceptance, Upon the Award of the Nobel Prize for Literature,* and as he stood tall to read a passage from the text, everyone fell speechless. He stated, "Since we're talking about the power of language this semester, about how students do have a right to their language, and about how we can use language to talk about issues like class, I brought in something to share." He then said, "Toni Morrison writes, 'We die. That may be the meaning of life. But we *do* language. That may be the measure of our lives'" (22).

Lessons from the vignettes

Clearly, "we do language." In doing language, my students and I confront issues of language abuse inside the writing classroom. When students become silent after reading a text on language and class issues, when they make use of their native languages and dialects (see Elbow) to assert their beliefs the best way they can, when they turn to the course texts in search of a deeper meaning, and when they take classroom work into their homes and communities, bringing back other people's reactions, then we are doing the work required of an engaged pedagogy. We are participating in a rhetoric of rights. We are reading, talking, discussing, sharing, and writing about issues circulating around language rights, but more important we are confronting our own sense of reality, which often gets ignored in classrooms. We are, in the sentiments of Karla Holloway in "Cultural Politics in the Academic Community: Masking the Color Line," confronting the very lived realities comprised in our ever-so-expanding classrooms: "Our classrooms are populated by the 'them' we once studied. Those we theorized about [. . .] not only are in front of the classroom, but are now its students" (611). Holloway goes a step further to assert that educators should

> [e]mbrace to our own ends the identity politics — the perspectives of race, culture, gender, and ethnicity — inherent in language. We can claim the power of our voices, and their complexity, *and their complexions* to assert the dimensions of our concerns, to call attention to our success in vitalizing the community of the university — both its faculty bodies and its student bodies. (617)

This type of engagement, whereby teachers are embracing the politics of language identity and students are sharing their perspectives on language diversity, represents a vital intersection of Nino's interpretive attitude, Jordan's legitimatization of black English and *languages,* and the adoption of the *Students' Right* resolution: the availability of a public discourse to talk about educational and political concerns is often absent shared democratic values when groups of people do not participate in evaluating and reimagining the possibilities of our commitments. In the sentiments of Nino, an interpretive attitude would mean that we are publicly confronting tensions surrounding, for example, the politicization of language rights, linguistic diversity, and democratized systems. I seek not to oversimplify the case for linguistic diversity in classroom practices by encouraging teachers to wear an interpretive attitude and go on about the business of teaching. What I want to do, as evidenced by my involvement with writing students, is to reimagine our educational commitments, our shared values, in ways that mobilize public and professional attitudes circulating around the education of monolingual and multilingual students. This mobilization, I believe, needs to be grounded in linguistic and cultural negotiation and not in a wrong language/right language debate.

An interpretive attitude allowed me to accept responsibility "for what [my] teaching does to the self-image and the self-esteem of our students" (*Students' Right* 2) as students produced classroom work using traditional academic writing, a combination of academic writing with linguistic varieties, and mixed-genre writings.[1] They used their multilingual and bidialectical voices to discuss, debate, and reflect on course readings, to make meanings, and to construct sophisticated written and verbal arguments. By the semester's end, they all embraced *Students' Right,* witnessed how the resolution could indeed be implemented inside a classroom focused on student involvement and student voice, and they all agreed with James Berlin, in "Composition Studies and Cultural Studies" that "[r]hetoric, after all, was invented to resolve disputes peacefully, as an alternative to armed conflict, and it remains the best option in a perilous time" (116).

Our collective endorsement of Berlin's belief in rhetoric, along with our "interpretative attitude," to borrow Nino's phrase, taught us valuable lessons as we established connections between language and struggle, language and cultural and academic selves. Minh articulated her frustration not with language, but with the teachers and academic systems that alienated her cultural and linguistic registers from classroom practices, forcing her to immediately assimilate into "a language of otherness that doesn't acknowledge the history of my people." José, obviously moved by Minh's comment, responded, "If we [students] must master . . . the codes of power . . . Standard English . . . academic writing . . . pass all the tests, for the classes and the state, then shouldn't there be an awareness of our conditions, our languages, our lives and literatures, by teachers?" A different student interrupted, "By the whole system, José, by the whole system!"

José, Minh, and the other students were in agreement. José then asked if we could return to hooks's article, "Confronting Class in the Classroom." He pulled out the article along with hooks's text, *Talking Back: Thinking Feminist, Thinking Black* (as students snickered, "Man, you bought that book? You trying to outdo us?"). He read the selected passages:

> Students who enter the academy unwilling to accept without question the assumptions and values held by privileged classes tend to be silenced, deemed troublemakers. ("Confronting Class" 179)

> To avoid feelings of estrangement, students from working-class backgrounds could assimilate into the mainstream, change speech patterns, points of reference, drop any habit that might reveal them to be from a nonmaterially privileged background. ("Confronting Class" 181)

> Coming to Stanford with my own version of a Kentucky accent [. . .] I learned to speak differently while maintaining the speech of my region, the sound of my family and community [. . .]. In recent years, I have endeavored to use various speaking styles in the classroom as a teacher and find it disconcerts those who feel that the use of a particular patois excludes them as listeners, even if there is translation into the usual, acceptable mode of speech. Learning to talk to different voices [. . .] challenges the notion that we must all assimilate. (*Talking Back* 79)

After his reading, students discussed hooks's journey to enter a world different from her "nonmaterially privileged" world in the South and the struggles that resulted. One student made the connection between hooks's efforts to maintain her home practices and Jordan's argument to embrace the language, culture, family, community, and rights that are ours as we work to erase boundaries of right/wrong, standard/nonstandard. This discussion was met with a peculiar student request: to devise a resolution on student willingness to be a part of an academic community. The following is what resulted:

1. Students, hereafter referred to as "we," are willing to negotiate who we are, the languages we speak, and the codes we use only if this negotiation is embraced in the classroom as "negotiation" and not "abandonment";

2. We are willing to accept and critically engage in academic challenges that promote various theories and conventions as long as we are not prohibited from making our own meaning and producing our own arguments that may, at times, oppose or challenge traditional arguments and positions;

3. We are willing to work, even struggle if need be, to understand the content as long as this struggle includes working with both content and spoken discourse — we don't want to privilege one by devaluing the other. We know this may be hard, so we'll appreciate all attempts;

4. We are willing to embrace the language diversity and variety of the people in this class so we can prepare ourselves to accept the variety of other people we will eventually encounter. We refuse to believe that we are linguistically inferior.

This student-devised resolution allowed other lessons to emerge during the remainder of the academic semester. More specifically, we agreed that to be on or at the margins . . . does not have to mean that students are "linguistically inferior" or "underprepared." My students have helped me to realize that being on or at the margins is to occupy a space of critical inquiry, one that moves beyond labels of inequality, social injustice, and marginalization and into relationships of reciprocity, linguistic virtuosity, and understanding: "And humanity tells us that we should allow every [person] the dignity of his [or her] own way of talking" (*Students' Right* 18).

Additionally, we learned that invention of the university does not mean that students, and teachers alike, should deny who they are and whence they come (our Class Resolution 1). Nor does it mean that the ways students learn of and eventually come into academic discourse communities of critical inquiry depend on the denial of dialect diversity: "Diversity of dialects will not degrade language nor hasten dele-terious changes. Common sense tells us that if people want to under-stand one another, they will do so" (*Students' Right* 18). Students, using various dialects and language forms, can contribute to the mis-sion of pedagogically sophisticated classrooms at the same time that their messages are received and recognized (the student resolution on willingness is a good example of this). My students asked me to honor our resolution, their language rights, as they agreed to honor, with questions, my teaching practices and academic assignments. It was a difficult, yet successful semester.

SRTOL, points of engagement, and pedagogical practices

The success of the semester unveiled itself as we began to trust one another, thus, divulge critical information about our identities. I remember one student sharing her journal entry on the consequences of not doing language (a message from Morrison's *Nobel Lecture* speech). As she scrambled through her entry, trying to make sense of her writing in light of the arrows, marginal notes, and scratched-out sentences, she frustratingly stopped and asked to be skipped over. Without hesitation, her writing partner said, "No! Just read it." What she eventually shared with the class was her social location: she was a resident of a local barrio, a first-generation college student, a fluent Spanish and Spanglish speaker, and the only fluent English speaker in her extended family. She then said that to not do language was not a part of her vocabulary and experience, and she could not understand how people could not do and love and feel language, "the only thing that heals the pain."

She sat, and nothing in the room moved, until Anthony's hand went up. He thanked this student for her honest reflection and then informed us of his social location: he was a resident of the third ward, a historic black inner-city community, son of working-class parents, and a user of "any language form I can get my hands on." Anthony's connection to language comes from his interaction with the people, his "street mentors" in his community, who can smooth-talk one minute and theorize the next. Anthony and the other student speakers and lis-teners reminded me that any classroom teacher who wants to confront language issues circulating around the politics and the teaching of writing must acknowledge, trust, and value students as knowledgeable people from various discourse communities.[2] They also taught me that listening to and critiquing students' realities can lead to self-reflection and critical consciousness of differences as an increased sense of agency for students, teachers, and governing systems is established.

In drawing on the plethora of knowledge students have and can bring into the classroom, I turn to Smitherman and her invitation to educators to reflect "How can I use what the kids *already* know to move them to what they *need* to know? This question presumes that you genuinely accept as viable the language and culture the child has acquired by the time he or she comes to school" (*Talkin and Testifyin* 219). Smitherman's assertion legitimizes the varieties of linguistic and cultural diversity that intersect with dynamics of privilege, identity, and schooling. In this way, the dilemma of *Students' Right* becomes a concern for how composition scholars locate meaningful teaching practices inside of classrooms while asking the questions: What else could the resolution say about language variety? How else could the resolution challenge educators to adopt a rights rhetoric of and for student differences/voices inside classrooms? And how far is too far for educators to go in discussing and advocating the rights and values of students?

The contributions of José, Minh, Anthony, and the other students to class conversations on language prove that, at times, going too far is not going far enough. Their honest responses to class readings, discussions, and journal reflections on topics ranging from "being on the margins," "social class (im)mobility," and "a privileged language" speak directly to the politics of teaching writing in these United States, given our national history with social injustice. So, writes Smitherman,

> One major result of the social movements of the 1960s and 1970s was the creation of educational policies to redress the academic exclusion of and past injustices inflicted upon Blacks, Browns, women, and other historically marginalized groups. Programs and policies such as Upward Bound, open enrollment, Educational Opportunity Programs (EOPs), preferential/affirmative action admissions, and the development of special academic courses ('basic' writing) brought a new and different brand of student into the college composition classroom. ("CCCC's Role" 354)

The politics of teaching writing require educators to recall, as Smitherman does, the social movements and educational policies birthed in the 1960s and 1970s so as to complicate our thinking about writing, reading, language, and literacy practices. In "CCCC's Role in the Struggle for Language Rights," Smitherman presents the reality of the new student with a different, albeit nontraditional, Americanized culture. In *Bootstraps: From an American Academic of Color,* Victor Villanueva, Jr., goes a step further in talking about the new student, whether Latina/Latino, Puerto Rican, or African American, as not so new, and not so foreign, and he used himself and his linguistic fluencies as examples. In this mixed-genre autobiography, Villanueva writes of his multilingual skills — as a speaker of English, Black English (or African American Language), Spanish, and Spanglish — as he reflects on the language of other speakers of color:

He looks at the experiences of the African American speaker of Black
English, the Spanish-speaking Mexican American, Puerto Rican, or
other Latino, and says, "They lack sophisticated speaking skills in the
language of the majority." Then he remembers having spoken Spanish
and Black English and the Standard English required at the school,
seems like always [. . .] (xiv)

He then chronicles the existing distances (located in assumptions)
between teachers and students by recalling an early school experience: "Spanish was taught by Mr. Hauser (trying to teach Spanish to
thirty bilingual kids). We didn't know about dialects, prestige, or the
like, just about right and wrong. He was wrong [. . .]" (3).

In relation to Villanueva's powerful experiences and Smitherman's talk of the new student is Jordan's insistence that "Black
English is not a linguistic buffalo; as children, most of the thirty-five
million Afro-Americans living here depend on this language for our
discovery of the world" ("Nobody" 175). We can also turn to Min-Zhan
Lu's confession that "if I watched myself carefully, I would figure out
from the way I read whether I had really mastered the 'languages.'
But writing became a dreadful chore. When I tried to keep a diary, I
was so afraid that the voice of school might slip in that I could only list
my daily activities" (141–42).

Collectively, Smitherman, Villanueva, Jordan, and Lu encourage
us all to critically discuss the democratic possibilities of educating students not simply by avowing differences in language and culture but
also by problematizing and complicating them as essential components of academic literacy. One way to do this type of work is to
reimagine the promise of *Students' Right* through our history's social
movements. Another way is to use the resolution to engender multilingual, multicultural, multigenerational perspectives, grounded in
critical and creative pedagogies, in the composition class. Either way,
we must, according to Lu, "complicate the external and internal scenes
of our students' writing [. . .]. Don't teach them to 'survive' the
whirlpool of crosscurrents by avoiding it. Use the classroom to moderate the currents. Moderate the currents, but teach them from the
beginning to struggle" (147). How do we complicate and moderate, and
how can we effectively *do* such work in our classrooms?

I offer the following strategies for engaging in such work in the
space of academic classrooms. Some strategies have been tested
numerous times and have yielded successful classroom discussions
and assignments. Others have been partly tested, depending on the
course level, readings, and requirements.

1. Invite students to examine the spatial location and demographic
   trends of their university community juxtaposed with their home
   community affiliation(s). I begin by asking students to consider

such questions as: How would you describe the university in terms of cultural and linguistic practices, male-female attendance, and location within the surrounding community? What does your descriptive observation say about who you are as a member of this academic community? Would you describe the university and the students as multilingual and multicultural, and if so, how are you using such terms? What do the terms signify? (This requires students to consider arguments by Banks, Keith Gilyard, and Baugh, for example.)

2. Ask students to listen to the languages of other people (the faculty and student bodies of their university community) by paying attention to and documenting the structures and patterns, codes and language shifts of speakers. What do such patterns and shifts indicate about communicative practices, about the ways people interact with one another, and about "academic" and "nonacademic" conventions? How do you linguistically engage with the members and the nonmembers of your discourse community, and what do such implications imply?

3. Ask students to write out the lyrics to popular songs and invite volunteers to play a sample of the selected songs with the class before sharing the written lyrics (we compare what we hear with what we read). In this comparison, we are listening to and reading the words (form and pronunciation) before analyzing, synthesizing, citing, and even rewriting the content as exercises in revision.

4. Engage students in a discussion of how socioeconomic status and geographic location, or region, influence language practices by listening to music samples of various East and West Coast artists. We take note of how meaning is read as comprehensible and is popularized across linguistic and spatial differences. Students could then write a response to the rap lyrics by considering their own positions juxtaposed with the position(s) of the rapper as writer.

5. Invite students into a discussion of phonology, semantics, syntax, accent, and dialect. This can lead to an examination of the *Students' Right* resolution and various theories of language acquisition, grammar, and vocabulary. It follows that students often become so interested in the topic of language development and rights that they explore the language histories of friends and family members through interviews, surveys, and informal conversations. This strategy can be enhanced if connections are established between the composition instructor and an instructor whose research area is in sociolinguistics, the teaching of grammar, and/or the teaching of the English language. This instructor

could be invited to lead a class discussion on the history of the language and the connections of the language to speech acts and writing skills.

6. On occasion, I ask students to listen to recordings of selected poetry and prose read by Langston Hughes, noting how he combines the language of the blues with his oration of the language of everyday people. This has proven very successful, especially in encouraging students to explore the nature of mixed genres and the skills involved in code switching. Writing assignments follow.

7. A most important strategy is to create a comfortable, safe environment in which students trust one another enough to share their beliefs about language diversity. This is not always an easy strategy to fulfill, for it means that we must consciously work at getting to know our students in an abbreviated amount of time. To do this, it is helpful to know students by their first names, to support their collective and individual explorations of language, and to ask for volunteers to lead class discussions and be responsible for a major component of the class work. At the beginning of the semester, work into the culture of the classroom time for freewriting/journal writing. If at the beginning of class, ask students to respond to a topic or a set of topics related to the class readings. Then ask student volunteers to share parts of their entries, sharing that can lead into the class lesson for that day. If at the end of class, remind students that they will be asked to share their responses at the beginning of the next class session, and their sharing can lead into that class lesson. I like to have students see how I consciously connect themes from their journal entries to class lessons and assignments. Throughout the semester, students are invited to return to earlier journal entries as they brainstorm topics for academic essays, prepare for in-class presentations, and work in groups to analyze pressing issues circulating around language rights.

I have discovered that such strategies not only establish connections between class readings/theories and student realities, but they also encourage students who are normally silent to participate in class conversations. Over time, students become less reluctant to use their own language form in the classroom as they attempt to master the negotiation of home practices with academic practices. The struggles of my students to negotiate indicate my lifelong struggle to work at dismantling the social and political dimensions of power, politics, and literacy evident in the larger society (this is a lifelong struggle, indeed). My strategies, then, are influenced by my interpretive attitude (see Nino) to make public the very realities and struggles of students as they become comfortable with their academic identities.

To implement new strategies for working with students means that teachers cannot lambaste their homes or communities or first languages. Experimentation with new strategies points to an awareness of the changing student demographics within the university, changes that require critical conversations about language and writing so choices can be made, arguments supported, context and audience defined, and variations studied. This is the type of work I engaged in with my undergraduate composition students; it is the same type of work I am committed to as I now work with preservice and inservice graduate students and public high school students.

Conclusion: Returning to *Students' Right to Their Own Language*

My overall argument, that communicative actions regarding student differences should become a central part of classroom pedagogy, is a difficult one to put into and keep in practice. I am quite aware that this movement is not easy. As an African American educator familiar with home and academic language variations, I realize the power of language, particularly as it constructs identity and positions people in certain classes.[3] I am also aware that the discourses of institutional and public politics are profoundly committed to the markers of white middle- and upper-class socioeconomic values that many of my students attempt to imitate in becoming *insurgent* intellectuals (see hooks and West) of mainstream culture. Nevertheless, as I inform my students, becoming insurgent intellectuals requires a personal investment in the world of and the sharing of ideas, however diverse or not, are the methods by which those ideas are presented. And this claim clearly supports the *Students' Right* resolution regarding the affirmation of language varieties students bring into the classroom.

Or, in the sentiments of two of my students: "So you mean, like, I do have a right to speak the way I be speakin' in class, even while I be learnin' a standard?" and "See, them other teachers don' really wanta hear dat from the get go, so I don' be talkin'. They don' know about affirmin'."

My students represent the lives of people whose language variations should be affirmed and respected. They must learn to believe, as we should, that in their language patterns and varieties can be found sophistication, meaning, and power. I am not afraid to tell my students that I know how to code switch and that my primary form of communication is partly influenced by the Gullah culture of the Sea Islands. I am not afraid to tell them that my family members frequently mix "black" English with "white" English, and that I am able to demonstrate mastery of both language forms. Oftentimes, the next question from my students is an inquiry into how they can achieve such mastery in using both the language forms they already know and the language patterns of mainstream society.

With this inquiry came our acceptance of their language form as powerful and meaningful. This acceptance forced me to invite students to use their "mother tongues" in the classroom, and they invited me to make use of my "mother tongue" when I felt the need to. Asking students to engage in this process reiterates Peter Elbow's argument:

> If we want our students to take on the power of full mainstream literacy, we can never remove the difficulty or even identity anxiety that some of them may experience in having to move past an oral culture (not necessarily to leave it) and take on a culture of literacy. But we can substantially mitigate their anxiety by inviting them to take on *full literacy* in their oral dialect. (372)

I agree with Elbow that our students should be invited "to take on *full literacy* in their oral dialect," which leads me to another valuable lesson: students must be exposed to various forms and expressions of literacy. Lisa Delpit, in *Other People's Children: Cultural Conflict in the Classroom,* asserts, "All we can do is provide students with the exposure to an alternate form, and allow them the opportunity to practice that form *in contexts that are nonthreatening, have a real purpose, and are intrinsically enjoyable*" (54). Encouraging students to use alternate forms of expression in the classroom can demonstrate the richness of languages in communication, engagement, participation, and understanding in literacy learning.

For example, when I first made use of my "mother tongue" in the classroom, I explained to students that there are many ways of saying the same thing; the significance of which expressive form to use depends on defining the audience and the context. Soon thereafter, students who were silent because of perceived language barriers began to share interpretations of class readings — they began to demonstrate proficiency in language and literacy, but, more important, they began to critically understand the power of the "mother tongue" in an academic environment. As declared by Judge Charles C. Joiner in his order that a school district in Ann Arbor, Michigan, could not use children's language as reason to register them into learning disability courses, teachers must "recognize the existence of the language system used by the children in their home community and to use that knowledge as a way of helping the children to learn to read standard English" (*Martin Luther King Elementary School Children v. Ann Arbor School District Board*).

While my composition students can in fact read Standard English, many of them were initially reluctant to engage in discussions for fear that linguistic (in)competence in Standard English would measure their success or failure. In thinking about my students' fear, I recall

Henry Giroux's argument that "the discourse of standards represents part of the truth about ourselves as a nation in that it has often been evoked in order to legitimate elitism, racism, and privileges for the few" (190). One way to confront this truth so as to not maintain it is by using *Students' Right* to enact a democratic platform in which theorizations of student differences, incompetencies, and disadvantages become expressions of the contradictions of the struggle for success, acceptance, and competency as measured through schooling. By bringing the resolution into the space that it is meant to occupy — the classroom — we can work to enact a multilingual policy that respects, upholds, and legitimizes every person's right to his or her own language while affording him or her access to "multiple aspects of the communication process [whereby] we can be sure we are dealing with the totality of language, not merely with the superficial features of 'polite usage'" (*Students' Right* 12).

Contemporary conversations about and practices of language variation stem from the promise set forth in *Students' Right* that says that teachers "must decide what elements of our discipline are really important to us, whether we want to share with our students the richness of all varieties of language, [and] encourage linguistic virtuosity" (2). It is essential that we, as a profession, privilege the language rights of our students by exposing them to the multiplicity and creativity inherent in expressive forms of literacy. This means that educators should rethink the implications of the resolution in ways that parallel the justice of our classroom pedagogy with the legacy of the resolution. We must do more than theorize about student differences and language variation. We must use a rights rhetoric such as *Students' Right* to encourage students to become active learners and critical thinkers inside and outside of classrooms if we are, in the words of Smitherman, "taking care of business" (*Talkin and Testifyin* 216). Clearly, we can engage in complex discussions of language in composition courses in ways that pay attention to the *Students' Right* resolution, Jordan's argument regarding our common currency, hooks's attention to the language of class, Nino's interpretive attitude, and Smitherman's analysis of language rights if we are ever to repudiate the inequities of social class, language abuse, and racism. Let us affirm the rights of students to their own language by affirming the practices they bring into classrooms as they enhance their critical thinking, reading, writing, and performing skills.

Acknowledgments

I am indebted to Professors Jia-Yi Cheng-Levine, Maisha Fisher, Min-Zhan Lu, Andrea Lunsford, and Erica Walker for their critical and insightful responses to earlier drafts of this article. I would like to acknowledge members of the NCTE Commission on Language and the mentors/mentees of the NCTE grant program, "Cultivating New Voices among Scholars of Color" for their stimulating discussions and critical insights on the *Students' Right to Their Own Language* resolution.

Notes

1. Because this preliminary study of the historical and pedagogical significance of the SRTOL resolution examines classroom conversations and engagements with course readings, I do not offer substantive data from student writings as a way to demonstrate the "ultimate" effects of my pedagogical strategies. I will take up the challenge of demonstrating the effects of my strategies on student writings in a future study.
2. My own reflections on this course are ongoing: in part, I seek to enhance my own methods of engaging students in the very complex issues highlighted throughout this article; in another way, I reconsider how my actual pedagogical practices speak to the difficulties of student writers on writing. While I attempt to illustrate methods and pedagogical practices throughout this article, I am aware that this article highlights students' thinking (talking, presenting, and engaging with the texts, with one another, and with the teacher) rather than their doing (the act of writing and the difficulties that may come with this process).
3. I recognize that my own positionality affects my abilities to work with the suggested strategies. The ways in which my students see and react to me — insofar as race, class, age, and academic status are concerned — are oftentimes inviting "of classroom environments supportive of imaginative explorations, freedom of idea expression and generation, and the journeys of the writing process" (Kinloch, "Poetry" 111). It does not, nonetheless, become easy to teach complex thematic issues, to ask students to discuss such issues openly and honestly in the classroom and, subsequently, to have students produce written, academic arguments.

Works Cited

Berlin, James. "Composition Studies and Cultural Studies: Collapsing Boundaries." *Into the Field: Sites of Composition Studies.* Ed. Anne Ruggles Gere. New York: MLA, 1993. 99–116.

Conference on College Composition and Communication. *Students' Right to Their Own Language.* Spec. issue of *CCC* 25.3 (Fall 1974): 1–32.

Delpit, Lisa. *Other People's Children: Cultural Conflict in the Classroom.* New York: New Press, 1995.

Elbow, Peter. "Inviting the Mother Tongue: Beyond 'Mistakes,' 'Bad English,' and 'Wrong Language.'" *JAC* 19.3 (Summer 1999): 359–88.

Giroux, Henry. "Pedagogy and Radical Democracy in the Age of 'Political Correctness.'" *Radical Democracy: Identity, Citizenship, and the State.* Ed. David Trend. New York: Routledge, 1996. 179–93.

Holloway, Karla. "Cultural Politics in the Academic Community: Masking the Color Line." *College English* 55 (1993): 610–17.

hooks, bell. "Confronting Class in the Classroom." *Teaching to Transgress: Education as the Practice of Freedom.* New York: Routledge, 1994. 177–89.

———. *Talking Back: Thinking Feminist, Thinking Black*. Boston: South End, 1989.

hooks, bell, and Cornel West. *Breaking Bread: Insurgent Black Intellectual Life*. Boston: South End, 1991.

Jordan, June. "Nobody Mean More to Me Than You and the Future Life of Willie Jordan." *Moving Towards Home: Political Essays*. London: Virago, 1989. 175–89.

———. "Problems of Language in a Democratic State." *Some of Us Did Not Die: New and Selected Essays of June Jordan*. New York: Basic, 2002. 223–32.

Kinloch, Valerie. "Poetry, Literacy, and Creativity: Fostering Effective Learning Strategies in an Urban Classroom." *English Education* 37 (2005): 96–114.

Lu, Min-Zhan. "From Silence to Words: Writing as Struggle." *Women/Writing/Teaching*. Ed. Jan Zlotnik Schmidt. New York: SUNY P, 1998. 133–48.

Martin Luther King Elementary School Children v. Ann Arbor School District Board. Civil Action No. 7-71861. 473 F. Supp. 1371. 1979.

Morrison, Toni. *The Nobel Lecture in Literature, 1993*. New York: Knopf, 1993.

Nino, Carlos Santiago. *The Constitution of Deliberative Democracy*. New Haven: Yale UP, 1996.

Smitherman, Geneva. "CCCC's Role in the Struggle for Language Rights." *CCC* 50.3 (1999): 349–76.

———. *Talkin and Testifyin: The Language of Black America*. Detroit: Wayne State UP, 1977.

Villanueva, Victor. *Bootstraps: From an American Academic of Color*. Urbana, IL: NCTE, 1993.

Classroom Strategies

Invite students to read and discuss the text composed by Kinloch's students, "a resolution on student willingness to be part of an academic community." As a corollary activity, students also can read CCCC's *Students' Right to Their Own Language* (available at <http://www.ncte.org/about/over/positions/category/lang/107502.htm>).

As a response to these readings, students can engage in the first two strategies from Kinloch's list:

1. Invite students to examine the spatial location and demographic trends of their university community juxtaposed with home community affiliation(s). . . .

2. Ask students to listen to the languages of other people (the faculty and student bodies of their university community) by paying attention to and documenting the structures and patterns, codes and language shifts of speakers. . . .

Taken together, these activities can help students to compose their own "resolution" and to define for themselves the meaning(s) of "academic community."

Thinking about Teaching

In your teaching journal, as Kinloch suggests, consider the public and professional communities with which you engage. Such communities may include your colleagues on campus, your home community, and your professional contacts at local, regional, and national meetings. What attitudes do the members of these communities hold toward "the education of monolingual and multilingual students"? Do these attitudes impact your perspectives and approaches to teaching monolingual and multilingual students? What do you see as the differences between "be[ing] grounded in linguistic and cultural negotiation and not in a wrong language/right language debate"?

As you respond to these questions, reflect as well on Kinloch's call "to reimagine our educational commitments, our shared values, in ways that mobilize [these attitudes]." What contributions and/or changes would you make to your classrooms and to your public and professional communities? How can you begin to advocate and implement these changes?

"You Probably Don't Even Know I Exist": Notes from a Prison College Program

Jane Maher

In this selection, Jane Maher writes about her experiences teaching basic writing at Bedford Hills Correctional Facility, a women's maximum-security prison. Maher's writing clearly evokes the material realities of the prison and emphasizes the necessity of college education in the lives of the inmates. When state and federal support for higher education for prisoners ended in the mid-1990s, the women's morale greatly deteriorated and prospects for containing recidivism declined. Private funds, while remaining precarious, were raised to reinstate the college program and Maher was subsequently invited to teach the basic writing course.

As Mina Shaughnessy's (see Chapter 1) biographer, Maher shares Shaughnessy's belief in the urgency that writing holds for the lives of her students. Maher includes many examples of student writing in her article, including a full-length essay by Kecia Pittman. The focus on student writing is especially compelling here because, as Maher affirms, "writing

*— as hard as it is to teach and learn — is a skill that will not only help
the women succeed in their college courses, it will help them succeed in
negotiating prison life and life after prison in a way that few other skills
will."*

When I was asked in 1997 to teach a basic writing course to the
female inmates at the Bedford Hills Correctional Facility in
Westchester, New York, I knew a lot about teaching writing, but I
knew absolutely nothing about prisons, prisoners, their need for post-
secondary education, or the way their past personal and educational
experiences would impact on their ability to succeed in college.

Now, I sometimes think I know far too much: about the conditions
that contributed to the circumstances that brought many of the
women to prison in the first place; about the pain and angst they suffer upon being separated from their families, particularly their children; about the poor (or nonexistent) educations they received before
arriving at prison; about the inequality of sentencing based on race
and class; about the diseases that ravage these women and their families as a result of poverty; about the way that drugs can destroy two,
even three generations of the same family; about the way many
people in society view these prisoners ("Aren't you afraid of them?" is
the question I am most often asked about my work); about the way
that politicians support harsh sentencing to win public approval, from
the draconian but ineffectual Rockefeller drug laws to the decisions
handed down day after day by parole boards, keeping even non-violent
offenders behind bars until they "max" out; about the fact that Pell
and TAP grants for prisoners were withdrawn in 1995 in order to save
the taxpayers' money, despite the fact that the amount being spent on
post-secondary education for prisoners was only a minuscule portion
of the total budget — about six cents of every ten program dollars
(Kunen 38); about the fact that this country imprisons more people
than any other country in the world — half a million more than
Communist China (Schlosser 52); about the fact that hundreds of
thousands of the almost two million prisoners in the United States
will be released in the next ten years having received little or no training or education to prepare them for reentry (Schlosser 58); and most
disturbing of all, about the fact that these conditions, coupled with
scores of others, often leave the prisoners feeling frustration, rage,
helplessness, or a sense of worthlessness.

But I also know that good things can happen in prison, as contradictory as that sounds. One of them, in fact, is the non-profit Women's
Prison Education Partnership college program, one of several programs that exist at Bedford Hills because of the extraordinary courage
and wisdom of Elaine A. Lord, the recently retired superintendent. In
the midst of the "get tough on crime," "race to incarcerate," "three

strikes and you're out," "send them back to prison for minor parole infractions," "build more prisons than schools" mentality that has overtaken the United States, Lord has steadfastly focused on programs that will help the women prepare for release. "Empowerment is what I aspire to bring to the women," she said in a recent interview. "I struggle with whether this is a valid concept in a prison, but the women report that they felt safe at Bedford, sometimes for the first time in memory, and that they were able to learn and think" (Wilson 25).

For the past twenty years, Bedford Hills has been a model facility for those who believe that prisons can actually be places where inmates are able to benefit from education, training, and counseling. As one of the college students wrote, "Bedford is the place that cured me of the diseases that brought me here."

Evidence of this curing environment is everywhere. The college program's computing and learning center (Bedford is one of the few prisons in New York State where inmates are permitted to have access to computers) is located in the basement of the facility's administration building, right next door to the children's center, where inmates can spend time visiting with their children. In the children's center, women learn to read so they can make tapes to send to their children; take courses in child care and development (overseen by volunteers from Bank Street College); contact their children's social workers, care givers, and teachers; and learn parenting skills. Women who are pregnant when they are arrested (provided they satisfy certain requirements) can keep their babies with them in the prison nursery for 18 months — one of the few prisons in the United States where such a program exists (and the model for prison nurseries in several European countries). Members of the local chapter of NOW (the National Organization for Women) meet regularly to conduct book discussion groups with some of the inmates; lawyers from Columbia Law School hold seminars with the women to help them understand their cases and their rights of appeal; members of church groups provide much-needed services to the women — from preparing food for visiting family members (who often travel for hours with young children via public transportation) to collecting clothes for the women to wear when they are released. The women are able to participate in the Puppies Behind Bars program, in which they train puppies for eventual service as guide dogs for the disabled. Although Bedford Hills looks very much like a prison, with rows of razor wire surrounding its perimeter, the presence of black Labrador puppies learning to walk up and down staircases and children crawling around the playroom can make it seem like a very human place at times. The women receive mandatory counseling for drug and alcohol addiction, participate in family violence prevention programs, sexual abuse workshops, and learn about anger management. During the summer, through the Host Family Program, inmates' children reside with local families so they can spend entire days for a week or two with their mothers at the prison. The inmates are required to participate in literacy programs — ABE (Adult Basic Education) and GED (General Educational Development)—sponsored by the Department of Correctional Services, and the GED passing rate at Bedford Hills is far higher than in most U.S. prisons. This success is the result of an aggressive and determined effort on the part of New York State Department of Corrections Deputy Superintendent of Education, Dr. John Nuttall, to improve the quality of instruction and participation in these classes.

In fact, the policies and practices at the prison are so progressive that in the late 1980s, long before doctors and other medical personnel fully understood the causes and treatment of AIDS, the inmates at Bedford Hills had, with the full approval and cooperation of the superintendent, set up a program whereby they could learn and then teach each other about the disease, care for each other, and educate people both inside and *outside;* in fact, the inmates collaborated in writing a book about the ACE (AIDS Counseling and Education) program, in which they described their experiences as they joined together to overcome the fear and ignorance that existed among the inmates and the corrections officers as more and more inmates were diagnosed with HIV and AIDS.

A volunteer at the prison who had also worked at several other prisons once told me that the women at Bedford Hills actually *look* different than prisoners at other facilities: they walk with their heads held higher, make eye contact, engage in conversation in a way that indicates a sense of pride and self-worth. "Bedford Hills is a prison, of course," she noted, "but it is *less* of a prison because the women are still being encouraged to think, to change, and to hope."

Despite this environment, however, when I arrived at Bedford Hills in the late 1990s, the college program was barely functioning. When TAP (New York State Tuition Assistance Program) and federally financed Pell grants were withdrawn in 1995, the thriving, full-time college program administered by Mercy College ceased to exist, along with 350 other prison college programs across the United States (despite an aggressive lobbying campaign mounted by college administrators and educators who produced reams of evidence showing the benefits to society of post-secondary prison education). At Bedford Hills, the impact of losing the college program was immediate and severe. Several inmates were tantalizingly close to earning their degrees, and they were crushed by the prospect of never completing their college education. Many of the inmates had painstakingly completed all of the non-credit requirements and had finally begun to earn college credits. "My son and I were going to start college at the same time," one of the inmates recalled, "and I knew that it was so hard for him on the outside that when I told him I wasn't going to be able to go to college, it would take away his incentive — it was the one time in his life that I had been a positive role model to him, and now I didn't even have that to offer him." Use of the library dropped, as did interest in the GED program. There was an increase in suicide attempts. Fighting on the living units increased. And the officers noticed that the women who had formerly participated in study groups or tutored other students were now struggling to find a way to replace college. "The card games, boring television, street talk, gettin' it on did not satisfy them anymore," one of the officers noted.

Within two months of the withdrawal of college, several of the inmates asked the superintendent if they could try to find volunteers who would be willing to reinstate the college program without using public funds. As usual, the superintendent not only agreed, she helped to identify and contact potential resources. A community organizer and long-time prison volunteer, Thea Jackson, responded with great enthusiasm — and efficiency. Through her friendship with Dr. Regina Perrugi, who was President of Marymount Manhattan College at the time, she was able to organize a consortium of several metropolitan-area colleges that agreed to provide instructors and other resources, with Marymount Manhattan functioning as the degree-granting institution. It was a grand scheme — but a risky one. There was no precedent, and no money. Would people make donations to a program that had just lost public funding based on the decisions of their own elected officials?

Running a college program in a maximum-security facility is difficult under the best of circumstances: security rules prohibit the use of fax machines, the Internet, e-mail, calculators, palm pilots, cell phones. All visitors must be approved by the Department of Correctional Services in Albany before they are permitted to enter the facility (a process that can take up to two months), and, in addition, all approved visitors must have their name placed on a gate clearance *each and every* time they enter the facility — a time-consuming practice that eliminates any possibility of a professor just "dropping in" to confer with students. All academic supplies must be approved in advance and inspected upon arrival — no workbooks with metal spiral bindings (the mentally ill inmates might use them to self-injure). The student-inmates can only move from place to place within the facility at certain times and under certain conditions. Instructors can only communicate with the inmates during class time or during prearranged appointments in the learning center. Give the way the inmates' days are scheduled and the availability of classrooms, college courses can only be offered in the evenings — from 6:30 until 9:30 — at the end of very long days for both the inmate-students and the professors. The prison is located in one of the most beautiful (and expensive) areas in lower Westchester County, a place where few college professors can afford to live; therefore, professors who volunteer to teach often have to travel relatively long distances to get to and from the prison. Department of Correctional Services' rules prohibit volunteers from sharing personal information with the inmates in order to protect the volunteers' safety, but this practice is often antithetical to the open and questioning climate that exists in college classrooms; professors must refrain from using personal examples to illustrate, to model, to inspire the students.

Negotiating these conditions was difficult enough when Mercy College had a full-time administrator in place. (Mercy's program was a model among prison college programs, and Mercy College continues to support the "new" program with extraordinarily generous donations — each semester, they cover the cost of four or five courses.) When the "private" college program returned, particularly during its first semester of operation, when it had not yet raised any money, when it had no office supplies, when it had no facilitator, it was a logistical nightmare.

Yet we managed, not only because of the enthusiasm of the students, the faculty, and the community organizers, but because of the good will of the facility's staff. Of course, there was the occasional officer who wondered why prisoners should be entitled to a free college education when they could not afford one for themselves or in many cases for their children, but, for the most part, the officers understood what the politicians and the public who voted for these politicians had not. As one officer explained, "I see these women, girls really, no more than 17 or 18 or 19 or 20, coming back again and again because of drugs or the street life, and I know that they came back because they went home the same way they came — with no education, no job prospects. Pimps, drugs, abuse, prison — it's a cycle. Maybe college can break that." The officers even help the women with their homework. "I think this essay is ready for our class publication," one of the students wrote in a note to me. "I moved the second paragraph to the end. At first I didn't agree with you but the officer tonight read it and he said I should move it, he sees your point."

College can break the cycle. As the new college program gained stability, Dr. Michelle Fine, a renowned sociologist from the City University of New York (CUNY) Graduate Center and a former volunteer in the program, conducted (with several student inmates as co-researchers) an intensive qualitative and quantitative study showing that the recidivism rate of female offenders decreases in direct proportion to the amount of college education they receive in prison (*Changing Minds*).

When I first began to teach in the college program at the prison in 1997, however, I was not aware of many of these facts and circumstances. In fact, the reason I was asked to participate was that although those students who had already participated in college were doing okay (in fact, they were working harder than ever, reinvigorated by the fact that college had returned), the new students, those who had no college experience and particularly those who had recently entered the prison system, were struggling mightily: extremely low scores on the admissions examinations, poor attendance, low confidence, inappropriate classroom behavior, high attrition. I recognized and identified these students immediately. My years of experience teaching basic writing first at Kingsborough Community College, CUNY, as an adjunct, and then at Nassau Community College as one of the founders of the Basic Education Program, my graduate work in composition studies at New York University, my research and writing of the biography of Mina Shaughnessy — all had prepared me to identify and help those students who, as Shaughnessy once said, "come to us at the last moment of their formal education, expecting, needing to encounter teachers who will finally make a difference" (qtd. in Maher 309).

But as I came to know these students, I began to realize that although they were similar in some ways to those students on the "outside" (a term the inmates use) who are required to take non-credit courses, they were different in ways that would affect and impact my teaching — and their learning. Shaughnessy had talked about the "last moment"; I began to feel that these students were beyond that already precarious point in their educational careers, perhaps even in their lives.

These differences are difficult to describe and were, at first, difficult to identify. In most cases, the students' reading and writing skills were slightly better than those of the students whom I taught on the outside. I was not quite sure how to account for this because as I began to get to know the "pre-college" students (a term that the inmates themselves began to use to refer to the students in non-credit classes), I realized that their educational experiences had been truly dismal, either because of the poor quality of the schools they had attended or because their lives had been so chaotic that they had not attended school very much, if at all. I later began to think that their stronger literacy skills were a result of the fact that the primary means of communicating with those on the outside was through letter writing; phone calls are prohibitively expensive and many family members are unable or unwilling to visit. The exception to this was the Latina students, most of whom earned their GEDs in Spanish at the prison and thus were unable to pass the admissions examinations in English, despite the implementation of ELL (English Language Learning) workshops.

Despite these better skills, however, many of the pre-college students had little or no confidence in themselves, and little or no sense of the connection between their poor educational experiences and their current status. In contrast to the resistance or even bravado sometimes exhibited by my students on the outside — "I didn't take the admissions test seriously"; "These non-credit classes are a waste of my time"; "Why do I have to pay money when I'm not earning credit?"

— many of the women who placed into the pre-college courses at Bedford Hills seemed to believe that they had relinquished all rights to any kind of attention at all, much less a college education. This sense of worthlessness was reflected in one of the first notes I received from an inmate interested in enrolling in the college program, the note from which I have taken my title. "You probably don't even know I exist," the note began:

> You are a very busy person and may not have time for me. And I don't know if I can come to college at all. I just earned my GED at Rikers and my scores were good, at least that is what my counselor said, but I have never been a good student and I have no money to pay for fees or books. I never thought I was smart at all because I didn't get good grades and everyone said it was okay when I dropped out of high school at a young age and pregnant. If I can't come to college I understand, but do you have college books that I can read and memorize so I can educate myself a little more and keep up with my peers on the unit?

Other notes and conversations confirm this sense of not belonging, of a lack of entitlement. I have saved these notes, first in the hope of using them to write a book about the program (when there is time for such a project), but now because they are very special to me, both as a writing instructor and as a human being. They represent and reflect the challenge I and others in the program face: to help these women overcome a pervading sense of not belonging, of not being worthy of attention, of not having a voice, a place, a future. For those who wonder what became of the children described in Jonathan Kozol's *Savage Inequalities,* I fear I have the answer in this two-inch-thick packet of notes I have accumulated over the past seven years. I remember clearly the early Saturday morning about five years ago when I began to read the responses my students wrote in reaction to Cedric Jennings' struggle to succeed at Brown University after having attended one of the worst high schools in the nation (reported by Ron Suskind in *A Hope in the Unseen*). I had expected the women to relate to Cedric's struggles, to sympathize with the inequities he endured, to realize how difficult it was for him to grow up with his father in prison. Instead, they said he was lucky: "He has a roof over his head, a mother who works. He has never been shot or stabbed. That's more than my kids have."

One student recalled being referred to as "fat house" through the first two years of high school; she dropped out, became a prostitute, and was eventually sentenced to ten years for a drug-related crime. "I was being abused at home sexually, but then going to school I didn't fit in so I went to the streets. And now here I am. I got my GED after two tries. Now let's see if I can do college. I won't tell my family I'm trying for college they'll just tell me I'm stupid and wasting my time."

Another student wrote, "I did not like the movie [*The Sweet Hereafter*]. It brought back memories. Do not show that movie to us anymore. I'm not the only one."

At one of the first sessions of one of the first basic writing courses I taught at Bedford Hills, I asked the women to tell me what kind of writing they did in prison and what kind of writing they needed help with. Their responses were further reminders of the differences between them and the students whom I usually taught: My students on the outside occasionally remind me that as soon as they complete their college writing requirements, they will never have to write again. The women in my course at Bedford Hills, however, told me about writing projects that had profound and permanent effects upon them.

> Writing a formal letter to the family that would take care of my baby when she left me and the [prison] nursery program to go into foster care. I read it to her in the middle of the last night we were together. I leaned over her crib knowing she did not understand the words but the family will know the words have meaning. In the letter I asked the family to love her for me. I did not need help with that letter. It came from my heart. Mistakes were not of concern to me just that the family knew this was a loved and wanted baby.

> Breaking the news to my grandmother that I am HIV positive. She does not understand that there is medication today. I have to tell her so she can have my children tested.

> Writing to my children's teachers. They are going to see the envelope saying the prison and the inmate box number. I don't want to bring more shame on my children but I have a right to know how they are doing. I want to know if they are getting extra help that they need.

> I want to be in college and need writing skills for that. Please help me. My way out of this life is an education. I have to start over when I get out. Be where nobody knows me. I will have to read job ads, find an apartment, find my children.

> I am going to write about my educational failures so others can be warned — no they are not my failures. I was told to take vocational classes because I am a woman. Because I am black. Because I had no one to look out for me.

The women explained in their notes that they must write to judges, court-appointed lawyers, social workers, case workers, doctors, correctional services personnel, even funeral directors. And in almost every note to me, they wished that they could write better, more clearly, "say it right" so that attention would be paid. Perhaps the most painful notes for me to read were those that explained that the woman had not done any writing recently for they had no one to write to.

Approximately 45 percent of the women at Bedford Hills suffer from mental illness, and some of these women place into the pre-college program. "I'm going to write to request that my mental meds be reduced so I don't fall asleep in class or while doing my homework."

Other notes reflect the overwhelming factors working against these students as they begin college, often at the same time they are beginning to serve their prison sentences. The students whose reading and writing skills (and self-confidence) are weakest are the ones who are most overwhelmed by the circumstances that arise as they begin their long periods of incarceration. (Because Bedford Hills is a maximum-security prison, only women with sentences longer than eight years are usually sent there. Ironically, this is an advantage in terms of the college program because it affords the women — who are able to take two courses per semester — enough time to earn a two-year and sometimes a four-year degree.)

> I have been here for two months after almost a year in the county jail. I can't concentrate on school right now and I am going to drop out and return my books. I read the first pages of homework over and over but can't seem to realize what it says. I can only think of the pain I have caused my mother. And can her health hold up under the stress of caring for my children and her own children still at home (my two brothers).

Often, as I make the long drive home from the prison at 9:30 at night, I wonder how even the strongest women function under the circumstances they encounter in prison. While I am frequently amazed at the way my students on the outside manage to juggle the responsibilities of family, work, and school, these issues seem more manageable than the circumstances faced by the inmates. When I first began to volunteer at the prison, I believed that the women would be able to concentrate on college in a way that students on the outside could not. After all, they had "time" on their hands and they had few other responsibilities. I quickly realized what a serious (but common) misconception this was. The women, like all New York State inmates, are required to participate in work, study, and counseling programs that take up most of their day. Those who work in the mess hall, for example, have shifts that begin at 5 a.m. They serve hundreds of inmates, scrub huge pots, stir gallons of oatmeal or soup or some other hot, heavy liquid. "I am coming late for class," one inmate wrote, "not because I don't want to be there, but because I have to shower after my shift in the mess hall. I smell nasty and don't want to come to class like that."

Those who work in the laundry are on their feet all day, working with steaming hot equipment in rooms that sometimes reach 115 degrees in the summertime. The "pay" averages from 15 to 30 cents an hour. Those women who do not get any help from outside in the form of money or packages of food or small pre-approved items must use this money to pay for personal hygiene products that are not provided by the system. (I learned about this when one of the officers expressed sympathy for one of the students whom he described as "wearing state, eating state." In prison, as on the outside, there are the haves and have-nots.) The students in the college program are required to pay tuition of five dollars per semester, and although we make it clear that students who cannot afford to pay this amount do not have to do so, very few students ask for an exemption.

The inmates are separated from their families, particularly their children, and this causes them to greatest pain and worry. (Seventy-five percent of the women in the pre-college program are mothers, more than half with children under the age of six.) These mothers carry pictures of their children, and they keep small personal items that belong to their children with them all the time: hair barrettes, tiny plastic action figures, a stone found on a path during a visit.

In an article that appeared recently in the *New York Times,* Sara Rimer explained the conditions that Elaine Bartlett, a former Bedford Hills prisoner and college student, found on the day she was released and returned home to her four children:

> [Bartlett] had fantasized about the welcome party her family would hold in their apartment in a housing project on the Lower East Side, where they have moved in her absence. . . . What greeted her instead was a disaster scene. "There was no food in the refrigerator, no toilet paper," she said. "The toilet seat was broken — the sink was full of dirty dishes. There were roaches and mice running around. The ceiling was black with dirt. . . ." Ms. Bartlett had returned home to find that her family had created its own prison in a housing project, and that she had been living better behind bars than the rest of the family outside. (Rimer B1)

Research has shown the high correlation between poverty and illness, and nowhere is this more evident than in the lives of these inmates, many of whom are HIV positive or suffer from diabetes, cancer, or high blood pressure. The grandmothers, who often raised them, are now raising their children — and the inmates feel anguish and guilt as they watch the toll such responsibility takes: heart disease, asthma, diabetes are common, and deadly. When a grandmother dies, the inmate must then either identify another relative who can take over the care of her children or look on helplessly as the child enters the foster care system. There is an expression among counselors who work with prisoners: "When a man is released from prison, he returns to a woman who has been caring for his children, holding his house together. When a woman is released from prison, she returns to a woman who has been caring for her children, holding her house together."

Many of the women were sexually or physically abused as children and fear that their children will be abused; in addition to the other permanent and devastating effects of such abuse, research has shown that sexual abuse has a detrimental effect on a student's confidence and ability to learn. Many of the inmates were addicted to drugs and/or alcohol when they were arrested and are struggling to overcome these addictions. Although the prison offers highly effective programs, one of the greatest challenges the security officers face is making sure visitors are not carrying in drugs for the prisoners — they are sometimes hidden in the diapers of visiting infants.

Prison living conditions are difficult, even frightening. Bedford Hills may be a model facility in terms of programs, progressive treatment, a staff that supports and encourages growth and change through programs, but it is still a prison. Inmates live in close proximity to other inmates, many of whom are mentally ill, hostile, or violent. The loss of personal choices and freedoms is difficult to adjust to, particularly the state-issued uniforms; highly restricted use of telephones; loss of privacy (phone calls can be monitored and mail can be read); control over every aspect of day-to-day life, including the type of make-up that can be worn, the time one eats, sleeps, works, and moves from one location to another; pat-frisking by male officers (a practice that is being challenged in court); the potential for harsh punishment such as placement in the solitary housing unit (SHU), or loss of other privileges for infractions that often seem arbitrary or capricious; being set up, robbed, or attacked by other inmates. One of the counselors once told me that it takes up to three years for inmates to fully accept the fact that they are "doing time." They often hold out hope — against serious odds — that their appeals will be successful; they are often so ill or run down by the life they had been leading that they are not at first aware of the severity of their sentences. As one of the college students said in an essay about her life before and after prison:

> I can't believe I am saying this, but I am almost grateful for prison. If I weren't here, I'd be dead. I had no job and had not had one for seven years. I had lost my kids to crack and I mean lost, I did not even know where they were. I was committing more crimes while awaiting trial for previous crimes. I was in an abusive relationship that was worse than the one I had left two years before. I didn't know who I was anymore, and I didn't care. A counselor once tried to tell me that I had to come to terms with the sexual abuse I had suffered in my childhood, that I was self medicating, but I remember thinking he had no idea of the deal — did he think I could just pick myself up and go to therapy? Would that be before or after my pimp came to collect?

The younger student inmates, the ones most likely to place into the pre-college program, face an even more difficult time adapting. As Superintendent Elaine Lord noted in an interview:

The younger women are more unruly, and they haven't learned how to adapt to prison routines yet. They expect the prison to adapt to them, just like kids on the streets think they have the world in their hands. They can be like teenagers in high school — focusing on relationships and how they look to peers. They are not thinking much about the future; they live in the now. If they have a long sentence, they really can't conceive of it. A 40- or 50-year sentence to someone who has only lived 17 or 18 years is meaningless. They are more concerned with meeting other young women coming off the intake bus that they might have met at the county jail. They are concerned about how they look. They engage in relationships and experiment with homosexuality because they are fiercely interested in all things sexual — just as many teens in the community are. Too often they see the world as a place where they have to take what they can or be left without. We forget that at this age all teens are still growing and learning how to be people. (Wilson 23)

One of those teens was dismissed from the college program because she was "out of place"; in other words, she had told her unit officer that she was coming to the school building to work on a college writing assignment, but instead she sneaked off with her girlfriend. During this time, she got involved in a fight and seriously hurt someone. "I'm returning my books," she explained. "I can no longer attend college because of a distraction. It's been nice knowing you. Don't worry about me." Her work habits and performance had been exceedingly poor. Her attitude had been so defensive and at times hostile that she was one of the few inmates with whom I felt uncomfortable, even afraid; the other inmates expressed similar feelings about her. I "lose" students on the outside frequently, but losing students in prison is different. There is truly nowhere else for them to go. That closing line, "Don't worry about me," was, I believe, pure bravado. I am convinced that there has not been anyone in that inmate's life who worried about her, and that is why she was so tough, so defensive, so unable to get along with others. I worried enough to negotiate a one-year suspension rather than a dismissal (again, through the kindness and support of prison officials).

And there is my favorite note of all — actually two notes — from the same inmate. I had just returned a set of essays to my students. After about five minutes Robin (not her real name) approached my desk and placed her essay in front of me. By the time I had finished commenting on her essay, I had written more than she had, and clearly my comments had offended her. I looked down and saw that she had printed, in large letters, the following words: "Are you dissin' me?" The other students were still reviewing their essays, so I had a chance to respond: "No, Robin, I'm not dissin' you, I'm trying to help you become a better writer so you can succeed in this course." When we had a chance to talk (out in the hall, away from the other students, but within earshot of an officer), I discovered that Robin had completed three years of high school, but during those three years, she had not written one essay, "not even one page, not even one paragraph, not even one word," yet she had passed all of her English courses. Robin was furious that I had "messed up" her essay "with all that shit you wrote. If you don't like my writing, just give me a bad grade."

At the end of that semester, after scores of such "discussions" since Robin questioned every one of my comments and corrections, she managed to pass my course and the exit examination and qualify for credit-bearing classes. On the last night of classes, Robin approached my desk in much the same way she had early in the semester; the similarity was clearly intentional. This time, she placed the following note on my desk: "Jane, I really appreciate your suggestions and I also appreciate your position in my life. I am intrigued by learning. I look forward to fighting every Monday. Teach me, Jane, teach me."

It is notes like these that I concentrate on as I go about the task of teaching writing to the women in the pre-college program at Bedford Hills. I am not naïve enough to think that the problems I've listed (and there are scores of others) will either go away of their own accord or be solved entirely by the inmates' participation in college courses, and I am not naïve enough to believe that the students whom I teach are in prison because of conditions entirely beyond their control. And I am constantly consumed with the fear that I and other incredibly hard-working volunteers will not be able to continue to raise the funds we need to keep this extraordinary program going. When the program was in such dire need of funding that we were not sure we would be able to continue for another semester, one of the inmates wrote to me saying "I know how hard it is, but please don't take college away. My only way out of this life is an education."

If I have learned anything as a result of my work in the college program at Bedford Hills, it is that what we do matters, helps, makes things better. And that writing — as hard as it is to teach and learn — is a skill that will not only help the women succeed in their college courses, it will help them succeed in negotiating prison life and life after prison in a way that few other skills will.

I will end not with a note, but with an entire essay written by Kecia Pittman, a 27-year-old former pre-college student (she earned her associate's degree last year and was the salutatorian) who "hit" the streets when she was 13 (her mother could not care for her because of a drug addiction), spent the next six years in a series of foster homes, and is serving her third term at Bedford Hills. This essay was written at my request after she sent me a note saying I could never understand her so she wasn't going to do a particular writing assignment. After scores of conversations and writing conferences, I agreed that perhaps she was right, but she would never know unless she tried. I also asked her not to imagine me as a reader, but to imagine "other" readers who knew nothing about her but who sincerely wanted to understand what she wanted and needed to say.

Writing about my college experience is not easy to do because my psyche is wrapped up in it. My personal experiences, my inadequacies, my ideas about success, my family history, and who I am now as opposed to who I was before, influence and shape how I feel about college. Do not get me wrong: I love my education. However, I think and exist in an agonizing dichotomy of future optimism and past failures. My apprehensions are fed by my anger and my hunger for a better life. I look for a release from a gripping past that will threaten me as soon as I step out of these gates.

Because of college, this is the first time in my life I am trying to discover who I have become. Writing for the purpose of sharing this discovery with people I have never met is so difficult because it is so impersonal. Yet strangely, something inside me wants the reader involved in this process. I want to convey the complexities of revelations and conclusions as they evolve. I shall make every effort to write as if the reader is here with me having an intimate conversation as I churn out ideas about who I am for the very first time.

I do not think the impact college has had on me can be fully understood until I define who I was and still am to some degree. I am the only child of a single-parented African-American home. I went up to the eighth grade. Somehow at age 13, I failed my mother or she failed me because I've been in the street ever since. There are a lot of hurts and disappointments swimming around like sharks in my memory. I survived the group homes and the streets. Decisions were made on pure impulse and they resulted in actions based solely on the inexperience of my 13-year-old mind. I am not feeling sorry for myself, but can you imagine the baggage I carry? There were never trophies or certificates indicating that I was doing the right thing. Instead, my rewards came in good-time sensations and short-lived comforts, no matter how dangerous. Nobody loved me enough to tell me to do different.

Even now I still feel like that 13-year-old child. Surviving. In college, I've learned that since I'm still alive, I've beaten the odds. I survived, yes, but I was never in one home long enough to submerge myself in the healthiness of school, friends, class trips, favorite teachers or prom night. It saddens me to write this because I never was forced to think of my life this way. The loss of my education and everything it represented early in my life contributes to the dichotomy of my fear of failure crowding in on my desire to be optimistic. Although my college experience does not render me automatically healthy, it does make me feel as if someone threw me a lifeline as an alternative to a pre-established pattern of thinking.

Education, no matter how late obtained, has a way of destroying the misconceptions that I lived by. I loved myself but in a submissive and low self-esteem kind of way. I now think that this stunted my ability to avoid many defeatable situations. My psyche was always saying, "I can't, I don't know how." In 1997 I met a college professor here in BHCF who literally turned red in his urgency to teach me otherwise. His main goal was to convince that thing inside me that it was not my fault, something true but so foreign to my understanding of life, of myself.

The one hard truth for me is that although I have made my way to prison three times, this is the first time I will emerge educated. The dichotomy of optimism and fear of failure is a mixture of this time's college experience and last time's unsuccessful releases. The truth is, college has spliced in new ideas to help me consider old perceptions. My understanding of life and my approach to problem solving has been altered in a way that leaves me vulnerable to new heights of optimism for the future but also fears of failing without the excuse of ignorance. The truth is that I now acknowledge myself as an intellectual human being and a symbol of strength by overcoming the odds. Not even the most successful among you may have survived what I have survived.

However, lurking in the depths of my mind is the low self-esteem warning me of who I was and not to trust who I am becoming. I feel like I am sitting between two worlds. You must understand: I have not had a chance to know what this experience will mean when I return to the old boulevards, the ratty tenements, the crackhead avenues. I am mostly concerned that the animalistic drive to survive will take over when I hit the streets again.

I am learning at this moment. I am, for the first time, actively and knowingly dialoging with myself for the purpose of truly figuring out who I am. I like sharing this with you, whoever you are. I am intellectualizing my experience. The fact that I could not have done this before is a revelation popping into my head as I write. I never had a reason to ask myself who I am, never thought my mind could check itself out. Optimism! That is what positive use of my prison time means. I am not involved in the nothingness of doing time. The day-by-day drifting of meaninglessness and depression that can consume a person. As I write I am engaged in an assignment for my professor, Jane Maher, but right now I am discovering college's impact on me. Right now at this writing moment.

College gave me a need and a reason to believe I could do something with my life even though there are so many things going against that belief. I am so afraid and so hopeful at the same time. My mind feeds on the collision of past and future. Without college there was nothing to hope would change. Without my past there would be nothing to look forward to changing. I am angry at my situation, yet in prison I could waste this anger on so many things that will never change. However, instead I use my anger to drive my academic achievements. My memories of failure keep me fearful enough to see optimism as the only possible route out of an indescribable, madness, (meaning anger and insanity).

College has been a bridge over some very troubled waters. The impact it has had on me is most of what you have just read. The things I cannot convey are made of words not yet formed in my head to explain. They will come. However, without college nothing would have been needed to be said, because nothing inside of me would have changed.

Works Cited

Changing Minds: The Impact of College in a Maximum Security Prison. Ed. Michelle Fine et al. 24 May 2004 <http://www.changingminds.ws>.

Kozol, Jonathan. *Savage Inequalities.* New York: HarperCollins, 1992.

Kunen, James S. "Teaching Prisoners a Lesson." *The New Yorker* 10 July 1995: 34–39.

Lamb, Wally, and Carolyn Adams Goodwin, with Women of the York Correctional Institution. *Couldn't Keep It to Myself: Testimonies from Our Imprisoned Sisters.* New York: HarperCollins, 2003.

Maher, Jane. *Mina P. Shaughnessy: Her Life and Work.* NCTE: Urbana, IL, 1997.

Rimer, Sara. "At Last, The Windows Have No Bars." *New York Times* 29 Apr. 1995: B1.

Salzman, Mark. *True Notebooks.* New York: Knopf, 2003.

Schlosser, Eric. "The Prison-Industrial Complex." *The Atlantic Monthly.* Dec. 1998: 51–77.

Suskind, Ron. *A Hope in the Unseen: An American Odyssey from the Inner City to the Ivy League.* New York: Broadway Books, 1999.

Wilson, Tracy Payne. "A Warden's View: Interview with Elaine Lord." *Finding Our Place* Special Issue 4 (2003): 19, 22–25.

Classroom Activities

Ask students to read and respond to the student essay written by Kecia Pittman that Maher includes at the end of the article. In introducing the essay, be sure to include Maher's advice to Pittman, "to imagine 'other' readers [as the audience] who knew nothing about [Pittman] but who sincerely wanted to understand what she wanted and needed to say."

Pittman writes:

> I am learning in this moment. I am, for the first time, actively and knowingly dialoging with myself for the purpose of truly figuring out who I am. I like sharing this with you, whoever you are. I am intellectualizing my experience.

Invite students to consider what Pittman means by this statement and to identify Pittman's audience and purpose for the essay. Students also can consider the strategies that Pittman uses to address audience and purpose. In what ways can students adapt such strategies for their own writing?

Thinking about Teaching

Jane Maher presents a compelling and persuasive argument for the rights of prisoners to a college education. As Maher writes, "College can break the cycle [of recidivism]" and indeed, in the midst of a funding crisis for the Bedford Hills program, one of Maher's students writes, "I know how hard it is, but please don't take college away. My only way out of this life is an education."

Federal funding for higher education programs for prisoners was abolished more than a decade ago. Nonetheless, Maher affirms the necessity for programs like the one at Bedford Hills. Investigate whether or not such programs exist in your region and how you might contribute to them. If no program currently exists, consider the logistics of advocating for such a program or participating in other initiatives for higher education for prisoners. See Michelle Fine's study *Changing Minds* (cited by Maher) at <http://www.changingminds .ws> for more information. This site includes Fine's study of Bedford Hills and suggestions for continued advocacy for higher education for prisoners. The "Community Brochure" link is particularly helpful.

My Uncle's Guns

Ann E. Green

In her short story "My Uncle's Guns," Ann E. Green creates a first-person narrative from the point of view of a basic writing student from a working-class and poor white community in rural Pennsylvania. As the narrator tells this story, she includes metacognitive comments that demonstrate the frequently ignored impact of social class differences on students and teachers. The story was first published in 1997 in Writing on the Edge.

My uncle, who is not really my uncle but my father's best friend since grade school, bought an antique gun from the First World War. We saw it when we went over to my uncle's house to visit. Dad and T.J. were talking, having conversations with long pauses, while I watched out the living room window.

I'm not sure how these essays are supposed to start. You said in class that a narrative should tell a story. How much of the story do I have to tell? Should I put in a reflection now? Should I tell you about smoking? Growing up, I watched men have conversations with each other filled with these long moments of silence where they smoked. One of them would light another cigarette or refill his pipe or, on a special occasion, smoke a cigar. If they didn't smoke, they chewed, either wintergreen Skoal or a pipe stem or a long piece of hay. Dad smoked a pipe with Old Hickory Tobacco until he quit farming. T.J., according to Dad, used to have every vice imaginable and then some, but he had quit smoking both cigarettes and cigars, almost entirely stopped chewing tobacco, and even cut back on his drinking since his heart attack. Every time I watch Dad talk, I remember how he smoked. Should this be part of the story?

While I was looking out the window, two deer appeared from the woods and strolled out into the yard. Although T.J. and Dad hunted together every year, T.J. fed wild animals, birds and rabbits, deer and even stray dogs in his back yard. The two deer went to pick at the food that had fallen from the bird feeders. One was a good-size doe, the other a late-born fawn with spots on its rump yet. When I walked up to the window to get a closer look, the deer spooked and leaped over the stone wall separating the lawn from the woods. Dad said, "Damn it, T.J., where's your camera?"

"Don't own one. If I shoot something, it ain't going to be for a god damn picture, anyway." He paused and slowly stood up from his recliner. "Come here, I'll show you what I'll shoot it with come December."

Dad and I went into T.J.'s spare bedroom to his gun cabinet, and he pulled out the WW I gun, a rifle whose stock had been cut off and refinished, evidently as a deer hunting gun. T.J. said, "It's my gun from the First World War." And then he laughed long and hard at his own joke. His laugh, as usual, drowned out any other sound and ended with a couple of snorts after which he laughed again. T.J. hadn't seen any combat after he enlisted. His ROTC scholarship paid for Penn State, but instead of sending him to Korea where the fighting was, the Army sent him to West Germany as a stretcher carrier in a medical unit. For the Army, it hadn't been bad, T.J. said. They spent most of their time moving the mobile medical unit along the East German border, to practice in case of a communist attack.

My father took the gun from T.J.'s hands. "Nice job cutting it back. Craig .340."

The gun didn't look any different to me than the dozens of other guns I'd seen and handled. I didn't hunt, or at least I didn't shoot, but I occasionally had gone out for turkey with Dad in the spring. We'd never even seen one, but it was beautiful in the woods at dawn.

At twelve, my first date was a picnic on roast woodchuck in a field near home; the gun that shot the chuck was a bolt-action 30.30. Everyone in my class took the Hunter Safety course in sixth grade, before it was legal for us to hunt at twelve. All of my boyfriends and a good many of my girlfriends owned guns for shooting or hunting purposes, and school was canceled for the first day of buck season in December. In the fall, I was late home from dates because any boy I was with would use the drive home as a good opportunity to spotlight deer, to see how many there were before hunting season.

Are these the kinds of details that you mean when we talk in class about significant details? How am I supposed to know which details are important to you?

I feel like I have to tell you all the details about deer hunting so you won't think we're simple or backward or country, getting all excited about looking at somebody's gun. Even though you assign us those Tim O'Brien stories with lists, you really don't think we'll write like that do you? And you would tell us we were too repetitive if we did. You're not from around here, and I can see you don't like us sometimes when we go outside on break from class and smoke and talk too loud about how we hate our jobs.

You look at us and think that we don't know anything. You think that teaching us how to write can't help us cause we're not going to change our lives by reading some essays. But we all want to do well in this class. Can't you just tell us what you want us to write about?

As Dad looked the Craig .340 over, peering down the barrel, checking to see if it was loaded, he said, "Let's try the son-of-a-bitch out in November at the fireman's shoot-in and pig roast." We left then, in our pickup, complete with spotlight and gun rack in the cab. Dad had to get home to go work as a janitor at 7 a.m., while I had to make it in early to run the drive-by window at the bank. We saw twelve deer in a field on the way home, and nothing was unusual.

In fact, the night that it happened I had gone to the fair with Dad and his new woman, Louise. It was about time Dad found somebody else, and I was glad it was Louise, who was younger than Dad but older than me by quite a bit. I'd seen what other kinds of women men found after their first wives.

I'll cut Louise out of this paper later, because I know that you'll think she's extra, just one more person who's not really in the rising action of this story, but right now it's important to me that she stay in here. Most of the time I'm too busy trying to figure out how I'll pay for my next class and my car insurance to sit around and think about how I feel about somebody who's important in my life, but not a pain in my ass in some way. Louise has just been a fixture, a nice addition to Dad's life that makes him leave me alone more.

I rode down to the fair that night with Dad and Louise, knowing that I'd most certainly see somebody I knew and come home with whoever was there. T.J.'s volunteer fire company had beer at its fair, so it was a big event. It was high school reunion week, but nobody had called me to go as a date. I guess after this long, everybody brought their wives. What I didn't expect at the fair was that Mike would show up, looking better than the last I'd seen him, appearing between the clam and the beer tents while Dad brought Louise and me beers. He wasn't wearing anything Army. Evidently he no longer needed to show his pride in the uniform by wearing it to public events. He came over and asked Dad how he was and what he was doing since he wasn't farming. Mike nodded to Louise, but he was looking me up and down, checking to see if I had a wedding band, if weight had settled on my legs or on my ass, trying to see if the rumor about me taking college classes could be true. Dad said, "Mike, are you staying with your folks? Could you run Maria home on your way?"

I was mad that Dad was passing me off on Mike, even if I did plan on staying later. I could find my own way home and always had.

"I'll take her home. No problem," Mike said, grinning at me. "Does she have to be home at any particular time these days?"

We all laughed, because even when there were particular times, I had often missed them. Mike and I had another good long look at each other. No beer belly. No visible scars. Lines around his eyes. Teeth still straight and white. The Army has good dental.

> The good dental is an important detail, and you probably don't know that. If you're on welfare, you get dental, same if you're in the Army, but if you work loading potato chips on tractor trailers you don't get dental, the bank gets some dental (because otherwise who'd deposit their paycheck with a teller-girl minus a front tooth?) but if you're self-employed or working in a stone quarry, you don't get dental. First thing that goes on people round here, makes them look older than they are, are teeth. That's why kids in Head Start are fluoridated almost to death. Mary, from our class, her kid is in Head Start, and she says they make those kids brush their teeth twice in the three hours they're there. It's like that Head Start teacher believes Mary's teeth are bad because she doesn't brush them, not because her Mom raised her on potato chips and soda. If those kids don't look poor, if they have good teeth, a decent set, they might just make it.

"How's the babies doing?"

"Fine. Growing like weeds. They're still in Texas. This is a short trip, just me seeing Mom and Dad and going to the reunion. Karen's pregnant again, and she don't travel too good."

I remembered the one time I'd seen Karen, she was a dishwater blond with circles under her eyes and a crooked, white smile. Mike had met her at basic training in Oklahoma. Mike just came back from that last ten day brutal basic training hike in the desert and proposed. They were married before he was shipped to Germany, and they were in Germany when Mike got shipped to Saudi. She had stayed in Germany, praying that what was at first a conflict wouldn't last too long, and then praying that the war wouldn't kill him before their first child was born.

We decided to go get a drink at our favorite bar, the Tea Kettle, because it had been a good place to skip an afternoon of school when we were growing up. It seemed like a perfect place to fill Mike in on the local gossip.

Mike was driving a familiar car, his Dad's ancient, rust and white colored Ford Fairlane, the passenger seat littered with the usual collection of empty cigarette packages, a partially filled bottle of oil left over from a previous oil change, and an oil filter wrench. Mike threw the junk into the back seat on top of a light-weight fluorescent orange hunting vest with the license pinned in the back and an ancient red hunting cap. I smiled because the clutter in the back seat was so familiar. The extra flannel shirts and jumper cables didn't seem to have moved in the years since I'd ridden with him.

> You said something in class about Tim O'Brien and parataxis. Is that a list or something? Does this description of Mike's back seat count? Should I describe the flannel shirts? Do you even know what an oil filter wrench looks like?

At the Tea Kettle, we started drinking shots and went through our high school classmates, listing births, deaths, marriages, divorces, and affairs. We'd each graduated with about seventy people, most we'd known all our lives, and we had talked about almost everybody when I started asking him about his time in the Gulf.

"It was lots of sand and way too hot," he said. "But in that way it was like Oklahoma and basic all over again. MREs and sweat. No black widow spiders, though. Did I tell you about that?"

"No. Don't we have black widow spiders around here? The males have the red hour glass on their backs?"

"No, the females. They bite their mates after they have sex and kill them."

"But what about the Gulf? Your Mom told Dad that you were in the actual fighting and some of the digging of the bodies out of the bunkers after stuff was over."

"It wasn't that big a deal. The hardest thing was losing the barracks to the Scud. I knew those people to speak to. . . . They were Pennsylvanians, reserve, not career military. Stupid loss, shouldn't have been there.

"But anyway, I was on maneuvers in the Oklahoma desert," Mike continued. "Last ten day stretch of basic. The Army has convinced you, you can't brush your teeth unless somebody else says it's O.K. and shows you how, and we're supposed to be out surviving in combat conditions. I'm in my tent putting on socks . . ."

"Putting on socks?"

"Yeah. We had to march ten miles back and my feet are blistered, so I'm putting on a pair of these stupid army issue socks. I'm pulling the left sock on and I feel this sharp pain, and I look down and there's a god damn black widow spider stuck to my leg. And we'd been told there are no black widow spiders in the Oklahoma desert, no dangerous spiders at all."

"Wait a second. No bad spiders. How in the hell did it end up on you then?"

"Christ, I don't know. But this drill sergeant has been giving me shit since the beginning, saying that it don't matter if my father was in Asia, that I'm such a smart ass that I'm not going to make it through basic. And since I think I'm so god damn intelligent, I should try for an ROTC scholarship in the Air Force, and just look at war on a computer screen, like Space Invaders. He's been busting on me for weeks, and now he's not going to let me finish basic. Or he's not going to believe me, and by the time he does I could be dead."

"Why are they such sons-of-bitches?"

"Right now you can only be career Army if they keep moving you up the chain of command. Career Army means retirement at thirty-eight and a new life. This weekend warrior shit means dying whenever somebody who's been away for a while forgets the rules and has an accident and you're in the line of fire or in the tank that he mistakes for the enemy."

I don't know if this is the kind of dialogue that you say "reveals charac-ter." We said "fuck" a lot more than I'm writing down now, but you prob-ably don't want that in a paper. It's probably one of those things that a professional author can use, but that we can't yet. Like we have to get good at knowing how to use big words first, before we can write like we talk. See, for me the spider symbolizes what Mike's life has been like, something always biting him on the ass at a crucial moment and screw-ing things up, but I don't know if you'll get the spider comparison. It doesn't seem "realistic," but it's what he said really happened, so it must be true.

Is this the language of "the oppressed" that you've been talking about in class? Like that guy who taught those peasants, those peasants prob-ably said "fuck" in Spanish a lot, too, but that probably wasn't included in their essays, right?

"So, anyway, you're still in the Army," I said, motioning the bar-tender to give me another chaser. "So what did you do about the spider?"

"Well, the Army gives you this stuff that freezes on contact. Why not just a bottle of bug spray, I don't know. So I'm hopping up and down and grabbing the can from my kit, dumping stuff all over, and the spider's trying to beat a hasty retreat and I'm hopping after it, knocking the tent down, till I finally freeze the sucker. I'm trying to figure out . . ."

The door to the Tea Kettle slams, and Candy Dimock, now married to a Brown, bursts in, talking before she's in the door.

"There's bodies in the road. Please come help. They're dead. We think they're dead, but we're not sure. Bodies . . ."

"What bodies, Candy?" I ask, but people are already standing up and pushing forward. "What road, where?"

"Up the hill," she says. I had seen her from a distance at the fair grounds earlier with her husband. They must have been driving home and seen something. "Danny went to call the state cops, the ambulance."

"Run over?" I ask. Candy says, "Blood in the road. I don't know . . ."

Mike grabs Candy by the arm. "Come show us where you saw them," he says. "We'll see if we can help. Maria, you know CPR, right?" He pulls Candy toward the Ford and throws open the back seat door for her. Reaches around and pulls a thirty-thirty out from underneath the hunting clothes. "Get in," he says, and pushes Candy inside, handing me the rifle. "There are shells in the glove box." Other people are getting into their cars, some still holding their beers. Some are unpacking knives and deer rifles from beneath their back seats. They are waiting to follow us. I fasten my seat belt and open the glove compartment while Mike gets in the car. When I open the glove box, Mike's grandpa's service issue revolver tumbles out with boxes of shells, pink registration information, and their Family Farm insurance card. Mike backs up fast, while I start slipping long yellow-colored bullets into the chamber of the thirty-thirty, load it and put the safety on. Candy says, "Maria, do you remember two-man CPR in case we need it? I can't remember how many breaths per second . . ."

"How far," Mike asks, voice calm. He doesn't wait for an answer before he says, "Load the Colt, too."

I am already filling the Colt from the other box of bullets. The only gun I have shot on a regular basis. Friday nights shooting bottles filled with water and watching them explode. Saturday nights shooting mailboxes at midnight driving too fast, throwing beer bottles at the mailboxes if it wasn't your turn with the gun.

"Here," Candy says, but at first we see nothing. Then we spot the white in the ditch, the unmoving white in the ditch.

I remember (from first aid class):

— gun shot wounds are to be treated as puncture wounds;

— knife wounds also puncture (don't remove the knife);

— cover and try and prevent bleeding with direct pressure.

Mike gets out of the car with the thirty-thirty, metal glinting, catching the light from a car pulling up behind us. Others pull up behind us, also get out. Slowly. Moments drag on and on. I hold the forty-five. The bodies are end to end in a ditch by the road side. Blood has run from the man's chest onto the road and pools on the asphalt. In the headlights, it's not clear whether the woman's sweatshirt is gray or white. She lies on her side, and I can see that she was shot from the front because the exit wound on her back is big enough for me to put one of my hands in.

"Two," Mike says, his hand gently lifting the man's dark hair from his neck as he feels for the carotid pulse.

My fingers probe the woman's neck for the artery, any sign of life. Their clothes are red and maroon, fresh and bright, partly dried blood.

Her eyes are wide open, but she is dead. It is silent as we gather around the bodies, not moving them. Sticking the guns back in the vehicles, finishing the beers, lighting cigarettes, waiting for the cops. No one recognizes the two dead.

We found out later it was a lover's triangle involving newcomers. The guy who did the killing went to the fair with his ex-girlfriend. She wanted to be friends and invited him to come with her to meet her new boyfriend. The old boyfriend was in the back seat of the car, pulled out a gun, shot through the seat and killed the boyfriend. She stopped the car, turned around, and said, "What the hell is going on?" and was shot in the chest. He panicked, threw the bodies in the ditch and drove off. Threw the revolver and its clip out at different places on his way out of town, but was caught before he hit the interstate because a cop stopped him and noticed the blood and rips on the passenger seat. The cops found the clip the first day, on the five mile strip of two lane that was most likely, but they couldn't find the gun. T.J.'s fire company cleaned up from the fair and then helped hunt for the gun. T.J. found the weapon three days later, ten yards from the road, in the rain. He knocked over some strands of purple and white vetch with a branch when the stick hit the gun. It was his sixtieth birthday, and after he found the gun, all the state cops shook his hand. His picture, holding his walking stick and grinning, was in the local paper.

That night, after we'd talked to the cops, Mike drove me home and finished telling me about the Gulf.

"Since I'm in for twenty years and already served almost half, they stuck me in a tank with more firepower than you'd ever imagine, guarding some West Point son-of-a-bitch commander who'd never even sweated in a desert. He was trained in jungle warfare, a kind of leftover. It was just miles and miles of tunnels, sand, and oil. And we were going to suffocate them in their bunkers anyway."

As I sit here trying to write this story, I try and remember what was said about a good narrative, what a good narrative consists of, but I don't have a conclusion in this story, just more fragments: Dad and T.J. hunted deer and came back empty-handed; Mike's mother sent over a venison roast from one of their deer; we ate the venison roast today at noon, with potatoes. And I don't have any questions for peer reviewers, because now that I'm in these night classes with these eighteen-year-olds, they don't understand my life anyway. At least in the continuing ed classes we had a variety of experiences, like shitty jobs or boyfriends, and shared ideas about good writing, like no comma splices and clear words. These girls can't even tell the difference between a Honda and a Ford, a double barrel shot gun and a pellet gun, or even, a buck and a doe. Some of them aren't even sure what their major is, while I'm trying to get enough algebra in my head to pass chemistry, qualify for the nursing program.

The assignment sheet said that this narrative should contain reflections, reveal something about ourselves and how we were changed by an event. But how should I be changed by finding a couple of bodies on a strip of two lane a couple of miles from home? Should I have a moral about how guns are dangerous and bad and nobody should have them anymore? Should I lie and tell you that I'll never be around guns anymore, that I'll be a good girl now and stay away from violent people and places?

How can I explain to you or to the other people in class that I finally decided that the noise I'm hearing outside the window as I write this isn't firecrackers, but gunfire. And that the phone just rang, and I talked to my neighbor who apologized for shooting his gun off, although it's ten on a Sunday night. I told him no big deal and he said, "I'm sorry for what I done, but I needed to do that, or I'd have to go somewhere and hit somebody." I don't tell him that Dad's not here, and that I'm trying to finish writing an essay.

And that he scared me.

And that while I've been listening to the shooting, I've propped the twelve-gauge at the front door and the thirty-thirty at the back.

Classroom Activities

Ann E. Green's short story resembles a "think-aloud protocol" in that the narrator includes metacognitive comments about her writing process, her teacher and the other students, and her story itself. Invite students to include their own metacognitive comments in a draft of their next essay or short story. What were they thinking about as they were writing? How might that thinking be included as part of a revised version of their text?

"My Uncle's Guns" is a story that foregrounds differences in social class and cultural and regional origin between teachers and students. Have students write an essay or short story that highlights social class, race, gender, region, and/or other cultural differences in the lives of the characters. Students can also try writing their essay or story first from their own perspective, and then from the perspective of a teacher or other authority figure.

Give students "My Uncle's Guns" as a reading assignment and ask them to respond to what seems interesting about the form and content of the story. Do the narrator's comments on her own story seem appropriate? Are cultural differences important to an understanding of the story? What else seems striking about the story?

Thinking about Teaching

Record your students' responses to any of the above classroom activities. What issues seemed to be important for the students in discussing the structure of the narrative? What concerns do students have in discussing cultural differences? What insights did students provide on the relationships between students and teachers in a basic writing classroom? Share your reflections with students. In your journal, or in discussion with other teachers, disclose your own assumptions about your relationships with your students, and about cultural differences. Which issues are easy for you to discuss, and which are difficult? How do you account for this difference? For instance, how do you interpret the following statement by Green's narrator: "You look at us and think that we don't know anything. You think that teaching us how to write can't help us cause we're not going to change our lives by reading some essays. But we all want to do well in this class. Can't you just tell us what you want us to write about?"

Write a short story or personal narrative about a classroom incident from your perspective as a teacher. Then write about the same incident from the point of view of a student. What differences do you notice? How can those differences help inform your classroom practices? As appropriate, share your reflections and questions on the above issues with students, faculty, and administrators.

3

Adapting the Writing Process

S ometimes the most difficult part of learning to write is understanding that good writing is the result of a process. Yet this
process is not a series of rote, predetermined steps. Good writing
comes from continually asking questions such as, Why am I writing?
For whom am I writing? What do I want to say? How can I clarify my
meaning? How can I identify and avoid errors that confuse my meaning? The articles in this section also challenge us to think of writing as
an interactive process, one that requires reflection on the part of
teachers as well as of students. Dana R. Ferris examines the role of
teacher feedback in the revision process and offers specific suggestions
for commenting on writing by Generation 1.5 (immigrant) students.
Michelle Gibson explores the intersections and contradictions of
process pedagogy, postmodernism identities, and her own position as a
lesbian and as a professor of composition.

In their studies of students' writing processes, Ferris and Gibson
demonstrate the need for observation, research, and reflection as part
of an informed pedagogy. As a result of such pedagogical explorations,
students can learn new approaches to composing essays and can come
to see writing as a negotiated and developing process.

One Size Does Not Fit All: Response and Revision Issues for Immigrant Students

Dana R. Ferris

*In the selection that follows, Dana R. Ferris summarizes recent writing
process research that strongly suggests differences in the ways that immi-*

grant (Generation 1.5) students and international students respond to and make revisions based on teachers' commentary and corrections on student writing. Teachers and researchers, Ferris emphasizes, need to avoid conflating these two groups of English-language learners and also need to avoid making broad generalizations about either group. Instead, Ferris argues for the importance of evaluating the cultural contexts in which English language learners study and learn about English language speaking and writing and the writing process.

Although international students may have more instructional, classroom-based knowledge of their second language (L2), immigrant students "can benefit from instruction and practice which takes advantage of their [non-instructional] L2 competence." Ferris concludes instructors need to, "examine and carefully consider contrasts across L2 student populations —especially between immigrant and international students — in designing research and instruction and in constructing responses to student writing."

As process-oriented composition teaching approaches, with their emphases on multiple drafts, feedback, and revision, have permeated U.S. college classes, teacher commentary has become a much more vital and significant aspect of writing instruction. Early first-language (L1) and second-language (L2) process advocates (e.g., Hillocks, 1986; Krashen, 1984; Zamel, 1982, 1985) argued that teacher feedback is much more effective at intermediate steps of the writing process than at the end of it (Leki, 1990). Although the process approach has also led to an increased focus on other forms of response, such as teacher–student conferences (Carnicelli, 1980) and peer feedback (Ferris & Hedgcock, 1998; Mittan, 1989), neither type of feedback is identical to written teacher commentary and neither, for a variety of reasons, can or should replace it. Thus, because written teacher commentary is likely to continue as a crucial part of composition instruction, it is important that we carefully examine the nature and effectiveness of such responses.

Unfortunately, research on teacher response to L2 writing (whether written or oral) has been scarce and, for a number of reasons, inadequate. Such research as there is has been limited by the absence of systematic data collection and/or analysis procedures, of longitudinal research designs, and of adequate consideration of the larger pedagogical context (Ferris, Pezone, Tade, & Tinti, 1997; Leki, 1990; Mathison-Fife & O'Neill, 1997; Reid, 1994). Because of this insufficient database, much of the advice given to ESL writing teachers about response to L2 student writing tends to follow directly from that given to teachers of native English-speaking (NES) writers, a trend that has been increasingly questioned and challenged by L2 writing researchers and theorists (Ferris et al., 1997; Leki, 1990; Silva, 1988, 1993; Zhang, 1995). Furthermore, examinations of teacher response and student revision in L2 contexts have been almost exclusively concerned with either foreign language (FL) students (specifically NES college students studying French, Spanish, or German in the United States) or with international students pursuing their education in United States academic settings. There is little published research available on teacher feedback to immigrant student writers and none at all (as of this writing) that attempts any direct comparisons between this group of students and international or FL novice writers.

This chapter begins by highlighting several key differences between international and immigrant English as a Second Language (ESL) students with respect to issues of teacher response. It then describes several recently completed studies on the immigrant student population, which were intended to address some of the gaps in the previous literature. Based on this discussion, key issues and strategies for future research on this important but relatively neglected aspect of ESL composition instruction are highlighted. The chapter concludes with implications for responding to L2 writers, focusing particularly on strategies for student writers who are long-term United States residents.

Background: Differences Across L2 Student Populations

In large part because there has been so little research of any kind about teacher feedback and its effects on L2 student writers, previous reviews of research considered all studies of L2 writers together, regardless of differences across contexts and student populations (cf. Leki, 1990; Silva, 1993; Truscott, 1996). For instance, Cardelle and Corno (1981) warned teachers against giving students too much praise in their commentary, arguing that it may cause students to become complacent or may actually discourage them from revising ("My teacher liked this part of my paper, so I shouldn't change it."). But their subjects were NES students studying Spanish at the college level; it could certainly be argued that U.S. undergraduate students and ESL writers have different affective responses to positive feedback from their teachers. It has also been argued that FL students and instructors have different attitudes toward composition in the FL class than do ESL instructors and students, with the former group seeing writing primarily as language practice and the latter seeing it as a necessary survival skill for L2 academic settings (e.g., Cohen & Cavalcanti, 1990; Hedgcock & Lefkowitz, 1994, 1996). This difference in perceptions and goals influences teachers' response strategies and students' willingness and ability to consider their teachers' feedback carefully and to revise. It is not appropriate, therefore, to lump all L2 writing research together as if the studies and findings were comparable simply because subjects were writing in a second language.

In addition to considering differences between ESL and FL contexts, it is crucially important in analyzing and considering response to draw distinctions between international ESL students and immigrant students or other long-term United States residents. These distinctions have been examined in some detail in this volume and elsewhere (e.g., Ferris & Hedgcock, 1998; Leki, 1992; Reid, 1997; Spack, 1994); this discussion focuses on the implications of these differences for teacher response. Although some generalizations about these two groups of college students are made in this discussion, it must always be remembered that international and immigrant students are two internally diverse and heterogeneous groups of writers.

International Students

Depending on their specific linguistic, cultural, and educational backgrounds as well as their prior experience with U.S. higher education, international students may resist the notion of multiple drafting and revision and may not, at least initially, see the purpose of teacher commentary on preliminary essay drafts. Like U.S. FL students, writers whose primary English education has occurred in their home countries may not value either composing as a means to discover ideas or writing as a means to accomplish instrumental academic or professional goals, having experienced L2 writing mostly as a way to practice new vocabulary or grammar constructions (Reid, 1997). International students may also lack the pragmatic and cultural awareness that teacher feedback is meant to be taken seriously and considered carefully, regardless of whether it is in statement or question form, or whether hedges (such as "maybe") are used. Indirectness on the part of the teacher may be perceived as a lack of confidence or competence and cause the student to lose respect for the instructor (Leki, 1992; Levine, 1983, cited in Scarcella, 1990, p. 94).

Immigrant Students

Students who have been partially, primarily, or wholly educated in the United States will likely be more familiar and comfortable with teacher–student communication patterns, feedback, and the notion of revising after receiving feedback (Ferris & Hedgcock, 1998; Reid, 1997). They may also be more aware of U.S. pragmatic phenomena and thus able to correctly interpret a comment like "Could you maybe give an example here?" as "I would like you to provide an example at this point."[1] However, they may struggle with two important issues in rela-

---

[1] In an earlier study (Ferris, 1997), I found that the presence or absence of hedges in teacher commentary had no noticeable effects on the number and quality of revisions made by the student writers.

tion to teacher feedback. First, even immigrant students who have resided in the United States for a number of years may still be acquiring academic literacy skills, although they may be highly fluent in everyday English. Like many of their NES counterparts, they may have failed to acquire the critical thinking skills prized by university instructors and assumed by teachers' higher order questions on their papers that challenge their logic (Atkinson & Ramanathan, 1995; Collier, 1989; Ferris & Hedgcock, 1998; Leki, 1992; Reid, 1997). Second, because they learned English in U.S. communication-oriented immersion–submersion settings, such students often lack the knowledge of metalanguage used by teachers to make comments about rhetorical aspects of student writing ("thesis," "topic sentence," etc.) — terms used in academic ESL textbooks that international students may have encountered in their home countries or in intensive English programs in the United States — and especially about grammatical and mechanical problems (Ferris & Hedgcock, 1998; Reid, 1997).

Examples of the possible gaps in immigrant students' formal grammatical knowledge were observed in a recent study by Ferris, Harvey, and Nuttall (1998) on the effects of a grammar training program on immigrant student writers' linguistic knowledge and accuracy. The researchers found that the subjects — junior-level university students taking an advanced "Writing for Proficiency" course — were able at the beginning of the program to label only 8% to 12% of common errors (noun plural/possessive, verb tense/form, run-ons, etc.) in a student essay excerpt. Unfortunately, most discussions of teacher feedback strategies and accompanying teaching materials overlook immigrant ESL students' lack of knowledge of formal grammar terminology. For instance, in preparing materials for the same grammar training project on the topic of subject–verb agreement for advanced university ESL students who were long-term United States residents, I consulted six grammar/editing books. All six assumed students' prior knowledge of the terms *subject, verb,* and *agreement,* and assumed that the students simply needed to know rules for avoiding errors in agreement. But when asked what they knew about subject–verb agreement, students in the program responded, "If the noun has an 's,' then the verb must also have an 's,' so they agree."

The foregoing discussion of immigrant students and teacher feedback leads to several questions that lend themselves to empirical investigation:

1. How do immigrant ESL writers react to teacher feedback?

2. What kinds of revisions do immigrant students make after receiving teacher feedback?

3. What kind of grammar feedback is most helpful for immigrant student writers?

The following sections discuss recently completed research that addresses these questions. In some cases, comparisons between research that has focused on international students and other studies that have focused on immigrant students are discussed. In other instances, no such comparisons are possible because relevant research does not exist. This discussion is followed by a summary of findings and of ways in which future researchers should consider investigating questions that remain.

Research on Feedback to Immigrant Student Writers

How Do Immigrant Student Writers React to Teacher Feedback?

Early studies of ESL students' reactions to or preferences regarding teacher response typically reported that student writers disregarded teacher feedback and/or had limited strategies for utilizing it in subsequent writing tasks. It was also found that L2 student writers had strong preferences for grammar-focused feedback over responses to the content and organization of their essays (Cohen, 1987; Cohen & Cavalcanti, 1990; Leki, 1990, 1991; Radecki & Swales, 1988). However, these studies were conducted in single-draft settings in which students were not expected to revise their work after receiving feedback or in English as a Foreign Language (EFL) contexts or with international students in the United States.

Recently, several researchers examined student reactions to teacher feedback in settings where some or most of the student subjects were long-term U.S. residents (Ferris, 1995b; Hedgcock & Lefkowitz, 1994; McCurdy, 1992). In these studies, students reported that they consider teacher feedback very seriously and find it extremely helpful in revising their work and in later writing projects. In a previous study (Ferris, 1995b), for example, 155 university ESL students at high intermediate to advanced levels of English proficiency, nearly all of whom were long-term U.S. residents, were surveyed about their attitudes toward written teacher commentary on intermediate and final drafts of their essays. The students claimed to attend to teacher commentary on both preliminary and final drafts of their essays and to value feedback on both content and grammar issues. More than 96% of the respondents felt that their teachers' feedback helped their writing to improve. At the same time, the students reported experiencing at least occasional confusion over their teachers' questions in margins or endnotes and over grammatical symbols, corrections, and terminology. These results therefore support the previous generalizations that immigrant students are comfortable with feedback-and-revision cycles, that they perceive the value of improving their writing and of teacher feedback in achieving that goal, and that they may experience some confusion with regard to specific teacher response strategies.[2]

With regard to student reactions to teacher feedback, a helpful comparison may be made between Cohen (1987) and my earlier study (1995b), because my study was a third-generation replication of the former. Cohen reported that his student subjects had a "limited repertoire of strategies for processing teacher feedback" and that teacher feedback "may have a more limited impact on the learners than the teachers would desire" (pp. 65–66). In contrast, my subjects reported utilizing "a variety of resources to deal with teacher commentary" (p. 44). I attributed the differences to the process-oriented, collaborative nature of the writing classes being studied. However, the contrast may also be explained by the fact that the subjects in my study had more extensive experience in U.S. academic settings and that they felt more highly motivated to revise and improve their work because they saw development of their writing skills as important to their future academic and career pursuits.

What Kinds of Revisions Do Immigrant Students Make after Receiving Teacher Feedback?

There have been few studies of ESL students' revision patterns and even fewer that have specifically linked teacher feedback to student revision (see Ferris, 1997, for a review). L1 researchers have reported that inexperienced student writers are primarily focused on microlevel changes in their writing, seeing "revision" as mechanical correction and cleanup (Beason, 1993; Faigley & Witte, 1981). Similarly, research on L2 writers' revisions has generally found that student writers make primarily surface-level changes and relatively few macrolevel, content-focused revisions. However, most of those studies have focused on international students or EFL writers, who may have limited experience with or training in strategies for substantive revision and/or insufficient motivation for making major changes in their papers.

In contrast, in a longitudinal discourse-analytic study, I (Ferris, 1997) examined the effects of teacher feedback on a sample of 220 student papers (first draft/revision pairs), nearly all of which were written by immigrant ESL students, and more than 1,500 teacher comments provided on students' preliminary essay drafts. The results indicated that students utilized a great majority of the teacher's comments to make substantive and effective revisions. However, it was

[2]It may also be the case that international student writers are equally confused by teacher questions and by various types of grammar feedback; however, there is no research on this point which directly compares the two general populations.

also found that some types of feedback were more likely than others to lead to effective student revisions.

A similar study (Patthey-Chavez & Ferris, 1997) utilized a case study approach to examine the effects of teacher–student writing conferences on the subsequent writing of several highly competent university international students. Data examined included students' first drafts, audiotapes and transcripts of teacher–student conferences, student revisions of the same paper, and first drafts of papers from the next essay assignment. Quantitative and qualitative differences were found between the conferences of the stronger and weaker writers, and the stronger writers produced more extensive and effective revisions. It was possible to trace effects of the conference discussions not only in the revisions of the paper that had been discussed, but also in the first drafts of the next assignments. Like the immigrant students whom I studied (Ferris, 1995b, 1997), the international students in this context also appeared highly motivated to improve their writing, as all of them had to pass an in-class essay examination at the end of their respective writing courses. In addition, the ESL and composition programs in which they were enrolled placed great value on multiple drafting and teacher feedback (cf. Atkinson & Ramanathan, 1995). Finally, it was apparent from the conference transcripts and from the revisions that there was mutual respect between teachers and students and that the students valued teacher feedback and appreciated the time their teachers took to meet with them.

In summary, these studies suggest that teacher feedback (whether oral or written) can have significant, positive effects on student revision when the feedback is thoughtful and focuses primarily on student ideas, when students are motivated to revise, and when they respect their teachers' efforts on their behalf. However, as I noted previously (Ferris, 1997), the findings "suggest two conflicting but coexisting truths: that students pay a great deal of attention to teacher feedback, which helps them to make substantial, effective revisions, and that students sometimes ignore or avoid the suggestions given in teacher commentary" (p. 330).

In an attempt to examine the characteristics of teacher commentary that lead to more or less effective student revisions, I (Ferris, forthcoming) examined 24 pairs of student first drafts and revisions completed by eight ESL student writers (seven immigrant students and one international student). It was found that the subjects were able to effectively address questions that asked for specific information from their own experience or from assigned course readings, feedback that suggested microlevel (word or sentence) revisions as opposed to global changes, and verbal summary feedback about specific patterns of grammatical error, combined with underlined in-text examples of these patterns. They were less able to cope with higher order questions or statements (Carlsen, 1991; Dillon, 1982; Kusnick,

1996) that challenged their logic or argumentation, and tended to either ignore or avoid such advice or to make ineffective revisions which failed to improve or even weakened their original texts.

Because there have been no direct comparisons to date between immigrant and international ESL students as to their ability to utilize teacher commentary in revision, it would be inappropriate to suggest that either group is more or less capable of or willing to incorporate teacher feedback in their revisions. What can be said, based on the fairly substantial sets of survey and discourse-analytic data collected from immigrant students in my earlier studies (Ferris, 1995b, 1997), is that teacher feedback can have a very significant influence on students' revisions and that this feedback may at least occasionally be problematic for students. If nothing else, this conclusion suggests that teachers need to construct their feedback to immigrant student writers very carefully, knowing that their students will likely do their utmost to respond to teacher input in their revised texts.

What Kind of Grammar Feedback Is Most Helpful for Immigrant Student Writers?

A recent review essay by Truscott (1996), arguing that ESL writing teachers should dispense with all error correction, has caused researchers and teachers to focus on the issue of whether teachers should give grammar feedback to their students at all, and if so, what form(s) it should take. As with most other ESL writing research, the studies cited by Truscott to support his thesis focus almost exclusively on FL students or international students. As of this writing, no study has examined differences between international and immigrant students in their ability to process and benefit from error feedback and grammatical explanations. However, in her discussion of the differences between "eye" learners (international students) and "ear" learners (immigrant students), Reid (1997) pointed out that, although immigrant students have learned English "principally through oral trial and error" (p. 4), international students "know, understand, and can explain English grammar" (p. 6). These generalizations would imply that immigrant students may need different types of grammatical explanation and error feedback than do international students.

One weakness of Truscott's argument against error feedback in L2 writing classes is his lack of definition of the term *error correction*. One need only to survey different editing textbooks and error correction studies to conclude that the term *error correction* does not mean the same thing to all teachers and researchers. International students, for instance, may benefit from a very precise system of error correction that identifies and labels various error types so that they can access their previously learned knowledge of grammatical rules in editing their writing (see Lane & Lange, 1993, for an example of such a system). On the other hand, immigrant students may cope better with indirect feedback (Ferris, 1995c; Ferris & Hedgcock, 1998; Hendrickson, 1980) that simply locates errors for them without offering labels or corrections. This system allows them to use their acquired oral competence in the L2 to self-correct errors (Brown, 1994) in much the same way as NES self-edit, without reference to a system of grammatical terms and rules to which they may never have been formally exposed.

Although there is little hard evidence as to what types of error feedback work best for immigrant students, several recent studies report results that at least suggest support for indirect error correction methods. In an earlier study (Ferris, 1995a), 30 immigrant ESL students were systematically taught to self-edit their work over the course of a 15-week semester (using a pedagogical approach outlined in Ferris, 1995c). Error feedback consisted of verbal commentary (in an endnote) about one to three major patterns of error observed in a given paper, paired with underlined examples of each error type in the students' texts. At the end of the semester, examination of two in-class essays and three revised out-of-class essays showed that 28 of the 30 subjects showed at least some reduction in error frequencies of targeted patterns of error. Furthermore, as already noted, the discourse-analytic data reported in my earlier work (Ferris, 1997) showed that the teachers' verbal end comments on students' errors (again paired with underlined textual examples) were highly effective in helping students to produce improved revisions.[3]

In Ferris et al. (1998), we addressed immigrant students' lack of prior grammatical training by assessing the effects of a 10-week grammar/editing tutorial program. This program consisted of minilessons (including definitions of key terms, examples, discovery and error correction exercises, and editing strategies) on writing problems common to the immigrant student population in that context (a large suburban 4-year public university in Northern California).[4] Pretest data confirmed that the 40 students who began the program had very limited ability to identify the types of errors addressed in the tutorials, either in isolated sentences or in connected discourse. However, they showed dramatic improvement on these tasks on posttests. This study provides at least limited confirmation both that college-level immigrants

---

[3]In both studies, students had also received input from their teachers about grammatical rules and editing strategies in the form of in-class minilessons and/or out-of-class individualized assignments in an editing handbook. In other words, indirect teacher feedback about errors was not the only form of grammar/editing information given to students.

[4]Topics covered were subject-verb agreement, nouns (types, plurals, possessives, articles/determiners), verbs (present vs. past tense, past vs. present perfect, modal auxiliaries), and sentence structure (types of clauses, punctuation of clauses, avoiding run-ons and fragments).

lack specific types of formal grammatical knowledge and that they can benefit from focused instruction on grammar terms and rules and editing strategy training that addressed the gaps in their knowledge while building on their acquired competence in the L2.

To summarize, previous studies of immigrant student writers on issues related to teacher feedback and student revision have suggested the following conclusions:

- Immigrant student writers take teacher feedback very seriously and value it highly (Ferris, 1995b);

- Immigrant student writers are capable of utilizing teacher feedback to improve their papers during revision (Ferris, 1997; see Patthey-Chavez & Ferris, 1997, for similar findings with international students);

- Immigrant student writers utilize specific types of teacher feedback in revision more successfully than other types (Ferris, 2001);

- Immigrant student writers can utilize indirect error feedback from their teachers to produce more accurate texts (Ferris, 1995a, 1997);

- Immigrant student writers have limited formal knowledge of formal grammar terms and rules, but can benefit from instruction and practice which takes advantage of their acquired L2 competence (Ferris et al., 1998).

However, there still remain a number of unanswered (and largely unexplored) questions with regard to teacher feedback to immigrant student writers. First, it is important to consider feedback and revision by a wide spectrum of teachers and students. Given the discussion in this chapter, it is especially important to study and describe different populations of immigrant student writers, both to contrast them with international students and to identify various factors in immigrant students' backgrounds (linguistic and cultural differences, educational experience, etc.) that may affect not only the response and revision dynamic but the students' development as writers in general. Second, in designing research on teacher feedback, it is crucial that we provide precise descriptions of what teachers do as they comment and how students process those comments, and that we consider more carefully the students, settings, and tasks being studied. Previous response-and-revision research has been justly criticized for not adequately considering contextual variables. Studies of teacher response need to take a variety of factors into account, including, but not limited to, the following classroom variables: the type of assignment/ genre of writing being completed, the point of the term at which the feedback is given, the number of drafts/papers being written and the relative weight given to each in the final evaluation, other types of response (e.g., peer, tutor, self-evaluation) received by students, turn-around time between submission of drafts and teacher feedback, the availability of in-class explanation of teacher response strategies and in-class opportunities for students to process and ask questions about teacher feedback, in-class instruction that could affect the form and content of the teachers' comments and the nature of the overall relationship between the teacher and his or her class. In addition to discourse-analytic, survey, and experimental techniques that have already been used, ethnographic interviews and teacher and student think-aloud data may be helpful at getting at these issues in greater depth.

Implications for Composition Instruction

Though the review of the literature presented in this chapter points out a number of limitations and gaps in the previous research, it also yields some preliminary insights and generalizations potentially useful for L2 writing pedagogy as it relates to response and revision for ESL writers, particularly those who are long-term United States residents. These suggestions fall into two general categories; implications for teachers as they construct responses to their students' papers, and implications for helping students to process teacher feedback and to utilize it effectively in constructing subsequent texts.

Considering Students' Competence

In writing comments to students, teachers need to consider carefully the knowledge and abilities of their students. For instance, as previously discussed, immigrant students may have little formal knowledge of grammatical terminology; marginal or terminal comments or error-labeling corrections may therefore have limited effects on their ability to produce more accurate papers. On the other hand, such students, particularly those at advanced levels of proficiency, may have a great deal of acquired competence in English and may be able to self-correct errors if they are pointed out (Brown, 1994). Similarly, teachers should not assume that their students are familiar with composition jargon such as "thesis statement," "topic sentence," or "transition." Before providing any feedback about content, organization, or grammar/mechanics, teachers should consider administering some form of survey or test to find out what their students already know (or do not know) of this metalanguage (cf. Ferris et al., 1998).

Considering Students' Preferences

In addition to considering students' knowledge, instructors should also explore students' expectations regarding feedback: Do they prefer oral or written? Would they like comments in the margins, at the end, on a separate sheet, or some combination of these? Do they expect comments of praise or constructive criticism? Would they rather have content and form issues addressed together or on separate drafts? Do they want all errors corrected or pointed out, or only a select few? With such information, teachers can either provide students with the types of feedback they prefer or explain to students their rationale for *not* doing what the students want. In either case, the students will likely feel more empowered and listened to than if the teacher merely imposed his or her own feedback style on them.

Assessing the Effectiveness of Commentary

Teachers should assess the effectiveness of their own responses by getting feedback from students as to what they appreciated or were confused by in the teacher's comments and by examining subsequent student papers to see whether or not the teacher response was helpful to students as they revised. Some practical steps toward such self-assessment could include providing in-class time for students to ask questions about and write brief summaries of the teacher comments after returning marked drafts (Ferris, 1995b), and requiring students to turn in all previous drafts with their revisions, perhaps with a cover letter explaining how they addressed the teacher's feedback on the prior draft or why they chose not to (Ferris, 1997).

In examining student revisions to assess the effects of commentary, teachers should pay particular attention to the effects of their own questions, especially higher order questions designed to challenge students' logic or stimulate critical thinking (Carlsen, 1991; Dillon, 1982; Ferris, 1997; Kusnick, 1996). Carlsen's (1991) review of educational studies of classroom questioning found little evidence of a relationship between higher order questions and student achievement. In a recent article on teacher questions, Kusnick (1996) noted that "despite our widespread cultural belief that questioning is an essential part of teaching, educational research has never demonstrated that asking students questions enhances learning" (p. 2). In my own recent research (Ferris, 1995b, 1997, 2001), it was found that ESL students expressed confusion about the intent of teacher questions and that both L1 and L2 students were less likely to make effective revisions in response to higher order questions than to other types of comments (e.g., statements, imperatives, or lower order questions asking students to provide specific information). Although I am not advocating that teachers abandon such questions altogether, it is important to assess whether students are understanding and utilizing this type of feedback, and, if not, to help them to do so during the revision process.

Assisting Students With Revision

An important but overlooked step in the process of teacher response and student revision is actively helping students to utilize feedback, whether from teacher or peers, in shaping their revisions. Teachers all too often simply assume that students will understand the feedback itself and how to incorporate suggested changes skillfully in their revisions. However, recent research findings suggest that immigrant student writers may ignore or avoid comments when they do not feel competent to make the changes necessitated by those comments, even deleting material rather than attempting to improve it (Ferris, 1997, forthcoming), or making the change without the corresponding rhetorical or syntactic adjustments needed to make the revision flow smoothly. Teachers can provide practical help in the following ways:

1. Pairing their higher order questions or statements with concrete suggestions that could help students know how to address those comments.

2. Discussing revision strategies with the whole class, including showing a marked student essay and talking about what types of changes the teacher comments suggest and how those suggestions could be implemented in this paper.

3. Providing individualized assistance to students, via teacher–student conferences, to help them process the feedback and revise successfully.

Conclusion

Several major points have been advanced in this chapter:

1. Teacher response is an important part of the writing class and therefore needs careful examination by researchers.

2. Differences exist between immigrant student writers and other groups of L2 student writers that have implications for teacher response strategies.

3. Research findings suggest that both teachers and students need to consider response and revision much more carefully and systematically and in much more depth.

In closing, it is important to echo the warnings of L2 researchers and theorists that we not apply uncritically the findings and prescriptions of L1 composition research to the endeavor of responding to L2 student writing (Ferris et al., 1997; Leki, 1990; Silva, 1988, 1993,

1997). Not only do L2 writers need "more of everything" (Raimes, 1985, p. 250) in terms of linguistic and rhetorical information, but they are widely diverse in their cultural expectations of and educational experiences with teacher–student relationships, feedback, composing and revision. Because of this diversity, it is important not only that we recognize differences between L1 and L2 writers but that we examine and carefully consider contrasts across L2 student populations — especially between immigrant and international students — in designing research and instruction and in constructing responses to student writing.

References

Atkinson, D., & Ramanathan, V. (1995). Cultures of writing: An ethnographic comparison of L1 and L2 university writing/language programs. *TESOL Quarterly, 3,* 539–66.

Beason, L. (1993). Feedback and revision in writing across the curriculum classes. *Research in the Teaching of English, 27,* 395–421.

Brown, H. D. (1994). *Principles of language learning and teaching* (3rd ed.). Englewood Cliffs, NJ: Prentice-Hall.

Cardelle, M., & Corno, L. (1981). Effects on second language learning of variations in written feedback on homework assignments. *TESOL Quarterly, 15,* 251–61.

Carlsen, W. (1991). Questioning in classrooms: A socio-linguistic perspective. *Journal of Educational Research, 61,* 157–78.

Carnicelli, T. A. (1980). The writing conference: A one-to-one conversation. In T. Donovan & B. McClelland (Eds.), *Eight approaches to teaching writing* (pp. 101–31). Urbana, IL: National Council of Teachers of English.

Cohen, A. (1987). Student processing of feedback on their compositions. In A. L. Wenden & J. Rubin (Eds.), *Learner strategies in language learning* (pp. 57–69). Englewood Cliffs, NJ: Prentice-Hall.

Cohen, A. D., & Cavalcanti, M. C. (1990). Feedback on compositions: Teacher and student verbal reports. In B. Kroll (Ed.), *Second language writing: Research insights for the classroom* (pp. 155–77). New York: Cambridge University Press.

Collier, V. P. (1989). How long? A synthesis of research on academic achievement in a second language. *TESOL Quarterly, 23,* 509–31.

Dillon, J. T. (1982). The effects of questions in education and other enterprises. *Journal of Curriculum Studies, 14,* 127–52.

Faigley, L., & Witte, S. P. (1981). Analyzing revision. *College Composition and Communication, 32,* 400–14.

Ferris, D. R. (1995a). Can advanced ESL students be taught to correct their most serious and frequent errors? *CATESOL Journal, 8*(1), 41–62.

Ferris, D. R. (1995b). Student reactions to teacher response in multiple-draft composition classrooms. *TESOL Quarterly, 29,* 33–53.

Ferris, D. R. (1995c). Teaching ESL composition students to become independent self-editors. *TESOL Journal, 4*(4), 18–22.

Ferris, D. R. (1997). The influence of teacher commentary on student revision. *TESOL Quarterly, 31,* 315–39.

Ferris, D. R. (2001). Teaching Writing for Academic Purposes. In J. Flowerdew & M. Peacock (Eds.), *Research Perspectives on English for Academic Purposes*. Cambridge, England: Cambridge University Press.

Ferris, D., Harvey, H., & Nuttall, G. (1998, March). *Assessing a joint training project: Editing strategies for ESL teachers and students*. Paper presented at the annual meeting of the American Association for Applied Linguistics, Seattle, WA.

Ferris, D., & Hedgcock, J. (1998). *Teaching ESL composition: Purpose, process, and practice*. Mahwah, NJ: Lawrence Erlbaum Associates.

Ferris, D., Pezone, S., Tade, C., & Tinti, S. (1997). Teacher commentary on student writing: Descriptions and implications. *Journal of Second Language Writing, 6,* 155–82.

Hedgcock, J., & Lefkowitz, N. (1994). Feedback on feedback: Assessing learner receptivity to teacher response in L2 composing. *Journal of Second Language Writing, 3,* 141–63.

Hedgcock, J., & Lefkowitz, N. (1996). Some input on input: Two analyses of student response to expert feedback in L2 writing. *Modern Language Journal, 80,* 287–308.

Hendrickson, J. (1980). Error correction in foreign language teaching: Recent theory, research, and practice. In K. Croft (Ed.), *Readings on English as a second language* (pp. 153–73). Boston: Little, Brown, and Co.

Hillocks, G., Jr. (1986). *Research on written composition: New directions for teaching*. Urbana, IL: ERIC Clearinghouse on Reading and Communication Skills and the National Conference on Research in English.

Krashen, S. (1984). *Writing: Research, theory, and application*. Oxford: Pergamon Press.

Kusnick, J. (1996). Classroom questions. *Teaching Newsletter, 8*(2), 1–4.

Lane, J., & Lange, E. (1993). *Writing clearly: An editing guide*. Boston: Heinle & Heinle.

Leki, I. (1990). Coaching from the margins: Issues in written response. In B. Kroll (Ed.), *Second language writing: Research insights for the classroom* (pp. 57–68). New York: Cambridge University Press.

Leki, I. (1991). The preferences of ESL students for error correction in college-level writing classes. *Foreign Language Annals, 24,* 203–18.

Leki, I. (1992). *Understanding ESL writers*. Portsmouth, NH: Heinemann.

Mathison-Fife, J., & O'Neill, P. (1997). Re-seeing research on response. *College Composition and Communication, 48,* 274–77.

McCurdy, P. (1992, March). *What students do with composition feedback*. Paper presented at the 27th annual Teaching of English to Speakers of Other Languages Convention, Vancouver, B.C.

Mittan, R. (1989). The peer review process: Harnessing students' communicative power. In D. M. Johnson & D. H. Roen (Eds.), *Richness in writing: Empowering ESL students* (pp. 207–19). New York: Longman.

Patthey-Chavez, G. G., & Ferris, D. R. (1997). Writing conferences and the weaving of multi-voiced texts in college composition. *Research in the Teaching of English, 34,* 51–90.

Radecki, P., & Swales, J. (1988). ESL student reaction to written comments on their written work. *System, 16,* 355–65.

Raimes, A. (1985). What unskilled ESL students do as they write: A classroom study of composing. *TESOL Quarterly, 19,* 229–58.

Reid, J. (1994). Responding to ESL students' texts: The myths of appropriation. *TESOL Quarterly, 28,* 273–92.

Reid, J. (1997). "Eye" learners and "ear" learners: Identifying the language needs of international student and U.S. resident writers. In J. M. Reid & P. Byrd (Eds.), *Grammar in the composition classroom: Essays on teaching ESL for college-bound students* (pp. 3–17). Boston: Heinle & Heinle.

Scarcella, R. (1990). *Teaching language minority children in the multicultural classroom.* Englewood Cliffs, NJ: Prentice-Hall.

Silva, T. (1988). Comments on Vivian Zamel's "recent research on writing pedagogy": A reader reacts. . . . *TESOL Quarterly, 22,* 517–20.

Silva, T. (1993). Toward an understanding of the distinct nature of L2 writing: The ESL research and its implications. *TESOL Quarterly, 28,* 657–77.

Silva, T. (1997). On the ethical treatment of ESL writers. *TESOL Quarterly, 31,* 359–63.

Spack, R. (1994). *Blair resources for teaching writing: English as a second language.* Englewood Cliffs, NJ: Prentice-Hall.

Truscott, J. (1996). The case against grammar correction in L2 writing classes. *Language Learning, 46,* 327–69.

Zamel, V. (1982). Writing: The process of discovering meaning. *TESOL Quarterly, 16,* 195–209.

Zamel, V. (1985). Responding to student writing. *TESOL Quarterly, 19,* 79–102.

Zhang, S. (1995). Reexamining the affective advantage of peer feedback in the ESL writing class. *Journal of Second Language Writing, 4,* 209–22.

Classroom Activities

Based on reviews of her own research, Ferris "[finds] that both L1 [students whose first language is English] and L2 [students whose second language is English] were less likely to make effective revisions in response to higher-order questions than to other types of comments (e.g., statements, imperatives, or lower-order questions asking students to provide specific information)." She also suggests that "error-labeling corrections may . . . have limited effects on [immigrant students'] ability to produce more accurate student papers." However, immigrant students with "acquired competence in English . . . may be able to self-correct errors if they are pointed out" (Brown 1994).

For Ferris, the implications of these findings strongly suggest that teachers investigate what students already know about "composition jargon" and what students still need to practice or learn. Ferris offers two strategies that may particularly benefit developing writers, including but not limited to

- inviting "students to . . . write [and turn in] brief summaries of the teacher['s] comments after [teachers return] marked drafts" (Ferris 1995b).

- "[d]iscussing revision strategies with the whole class" as well as "via teacher-student conferences."

Teachers can combine these strategies for effective revision. After reviewing students' written feedback on teacher comments, teachers can address students' questions or concerns in class discussion or in individual conferences to further explain their approaches to composition pedagogy and to acknowledge students' feedback. Such strategies can help students review and build on what they already know about the writing process and can allow students to actively learn academic vocabulary often used in college writing courses.

Thinking about Teaching

Ferris points out that there are "a number of unanswered (and largely unexplored) questions with regard to teacher feedback to immigrant student writers." In particular, Ferris recommends examining "different populations of immigrant student writers [in contrast to] international students and to identify various factors in immigrant students' [linguistic, cultural, and educational] backgrounds . . . that may affect not only the response and revision dynamic but the students' development as writers in general."

Several articles in this edition of *Teaching Developmental Writing: Background Readings* address such research as well as the implications for teaching L2 writers. These articles are included in the Alternative Table of Contents under the heading "English Language Learners." Consider the needs of your own classroom as you read these articles and design a study that assesses and addresses how and why students interpret and adapt particular writing process strategies.

From The Peculiar Case of Contessa: Postmodernism and Basic Writing Pedagogy

Michelle Gibson

In these excerpts from a longer article first published in Transformations *in 2004, Michelle Gibson analyzes the ways in which postmodernism functions in the writing classroom. Gibson employs a case study of her student "Contessa" (a pseudonym) to examine this student's "competing identities" as demonstrated in successive drafts of an essay on homophobia. In these drafts and in the final essay, Contessa demonstrates her*

competing identities as she supports a gay friend confronted by homopho-
bic harassment — and as she identifies herself as a church member who
"[asserts] that homosexuality is a sin." Contessa's struggles with the writ-
ing process are represented by excerpts from her drafts, Gibson's com-
ments on Contessa's drafts, Contessa's metawriting on her goals for revi-
sion, and excerpts from interviews with Gibson's colleague Margaret
Lingren.

Gibson further examines how she, as Contessa's professor, "performed
my multiple identities . . . as a teacher who wanted [Contessa's] essay to
have more focus and clarity" and as an out lesbian who is "involv[ed] in
lesbian-feminist communities" (Gibson does not mention her sexual orien-
tation in her comments on Contessa's drafts). In the introduction to this
article (not included here), Gibson states, "The commitment to a social
justice mission has been one of the driving forces behind my work as a
teacher of basic writing" (2). The challenges and rewards of Gibson's com-
mitment are strongly reflected in the following excerpts.

A Basic Writer in First-Year Composition

Contessa enrolled in my English Composition 101 course during
the winter quarter of her first year in college and in the English
Composition 102 course I taught in the spring quarter of the same
year. Though it might seem that when Contessa completed the basic
writing course and began the English Composition sequence, she was
no longer a basic writing student, I have come to believe that such an
assumption ignores the real-life experiences of basic writing students
and teachers. Like many other basic writing students, Contessa had
demonstrated that she was ready to take the initial course in the
English Composition sequence. However, also like many of her peers
Contessa took a number of what I will call "basic writing characteristics" with her into the English Composition 101 course. My experience
of Contessa indicated to me that she was extremely intelligent but
easily frustrated by the conflict she experienced between the complexity of her thinking and her inability to articulate that complexity.
Though I believe that Contessa originally "belonged" in a basic writing class, she was not underprepared. And, though I am convinced
that one of the problems Contessa faced was that her intellect and
insights were more developed than her ability to express herself, I also
do not believe that she could be called a "developmental writing" student. Instead, I believe that Contessa was trying to balance the modernist values of the academy, which I was communicating to her
through my use of process pedagogy and my sometimes dialogic, sometimes directive comments on her writing, and a postmodern awareness of her multiple selves, which she was communicating to me
through essays characterized by a kind of exploratory antiform.

In my department, we teach a large number of what we call
"trailer" courses, so named because they trail behind the regular basic

writing or English Composition sequence by one, two, or even three academic terms. Students who either began in the basic writing sequence or failed at least one of the courses in the English Composition sequence populate these courses. My own experience of these trailer courses is that there is often a conflict between the title of the course (English Composition 101, 102, or 103) and the types of students in the courses. Many of the students in trailer classes who supposedly no longer fit into the category of "underprepared" have a number of characteristics that distinguish them from students placed in English Composition in the first quarter of their first year in college. First, many of these students have intellectual ability that far exceeds their ability to express themselves in writing. Second, they often have conflicting desires — they want to challenge themselves intellectually at the same time that they want to maintain the safety of unchallenged values. Third, their own sense of themselves as intelligent yet unable to write often results in a deep defensiveness when it comes to interpreting what they consider critical teacher commentary (verbal or written) on their writing. Fourth, they often come from families that tend to value education as a means to a "better life" economically, but who also place extreme pressure on their children to be present at family events — even if those events interfere with school work. And finally, while they believe that the way to pass a writing course is to "write what the teacher wants to hear," they are also at once resistant to giving up their ways of thinking and not particularly astute at determining what the teacher believes. Contessa possessed many of these characteristics (all but the fourth).

Knowing that I would be teaching a "trailer," I designed the 101 course that Contessa took so that students would be able to choose their own topics and write about issues that interested them and in which they had some investment. I used Jeff Sommers and Cynthia Lewiecki-Wilson's *From Community to College: Reading and Writing across Diverse Contexts* as a reader and Barbara Fine Clouse's *Working It Out* as a rhetoric. My thinking about and reading in the theory of feminist and social constructionist pedagogy had led me to believe that students needed the opportunity to examine their inherited assumptions and to write their way into complex thinking about social issues. Students were asked to use the readings we were discussing to help them identify and critique their own feelings about issues they felt were important.

The 102 course Contessa took with me, which was designed around R. J. Willey and Jennifer Berne's *Process of Discovery: A Writer's Workshop* and Dorothy Allison's *Bastard out of Carolina,* was also informed by social constructionist and feminist pedagogical theory. My intention was to use the rhetoric as the source for in-class writing activities, but to focus class discussion almost entirely on issues raised in the novel. I hoped to help students examine and critique popular rhetoric about oppression and then apply it both to Allison's work and to their own lived experiences. To that end, students were asked to collect articles and essays about the types of oppression Allison's characters experienced (sexual abuse, sexism, racism, homophobia, and classism, for instance) from print and electronic media. With some help from me, the students used the articles and essays to establish a kind of linguistic "collection" of language to discuss oppression and then tried to determine how that language either elucidated or worked against a clearer understanding of the novel and/or their own experiences.

Over the course of these two ten-week quarters, Contessa wrote and revised six essays. Because I comment on but do not "grade" individual essays (I use a "contract" grading system much like that popularized by Peter Elbow), Contessa generally wrote three versions (an early draft and two revisions) of each essay. What I recognize as I look back on Contessa's writing from those two quarters is that several of her essays in both classes shared a common goal: to challenge popular definitions of oppression in order to show that not everyone who resists activist movements intends to oppress. As she attempted to meet this goal, though, Contessa also seemed to be trying to manage several distinct identities that stood in opposition to one another: (1) a Christian who believes in the moral mandates set forth in the Bible and by her minister; (2) a strong believer in the Christian mandate to "love the sinner, but hate the sin"; (3) an independent thinker who wishes to make her own decisions about who to have as friends; and (4) a diligent and thoughtful novice academic who cares deeply about doing good work and maintaining a relationship with her teacher. One result of the attempt to give voice to all of these identities simultaneously was that Contessa's writing, as well as her interactions with me, became marked by a growing sense of frustration. One of the essays Contessa wrote, about homophobia, revealed that she lacked the ability to express the conflicts among her identity fragments.

The problems she was having expressing those conflicts played itself out in several ways, the most distinct of which was that Contessa became increasingly dependent on me and began to view me as the only reader qualified to respond to her writing. Contessa was exposed to a number of readers in all three of the classes she took with me. In the tradition of process pedagogy, I provided opportunities in class for discussion among peers and with tutors; I also required that students show evidence of discussions about their writing with friends, family, and so on outside of the college. Also in the tradition of process pedagogy, I had made distinct and overt connections among the essay assignments — in terms of both content and skills application. I wanted students to resist oversimplifying individual comments on their writing (particularly mine) and to think about response as socially constructed and provisional. I also wanted them to see writing as a social process in which competing voices struggle to be heard. I believed that by infusing my process pedagogy with social constructionist theory I could help my students move beyond the "skills" approach to writing and toward an expanded definition of "good writing" that they could actually use as they wrote for other classes.

Multiple Identities and Explications of an Essay

Contessa's work on the essay about homophobia revealed some of the problems a student can face when she tries to bring her identity fragments to consensus in order to "write well" in the academy. Because she experienced herself simultaneously as a Christian whose church teaches that homosexuality is a sin, as a friend to at least one lesbian and one gay man, and as a moral person who cared about people, Contessa's writing exhibited much conflict around issues related to homosexuality. Her concern for the material and emotional conditions under which her friends live directly opposed her strong belief in her church's teaching, and this conflict became evident when, instead of avoiding the issue of homosexuality, Contessa chose to write the homophobia essay. When Margaret asked her why she wrote about homophobia, she explained, "because I couldn't find anything good on sexual harassment." She told Margaret that the assignment involved choosing a topic from among those discussed in the class's reader, and that as she saw it, the topics she had to choose from were sexual harassment and homophobia. She went on to explain that the assignment itself felt constraining to her because she had to augment her "opinion" with some kind of library research.

Once she chose the topic, though, Contessa was aware that it would be difficult to write about. She told Margaret that she did not "believe in" homosexuality, but that she also believed that people must act compassionately toward one another. She went to explain her stance on the issue more fully:

> It's like those guys in the beginning [of the essay] saying weird things to my friends; I mean, I don't like it at all. If I was there and they said something probably — you know, 'cause it's not right for anybody to be treated like that about anything. But, I don't think it was because they necessarily hated gay people or were afraid of gay people; I think they're just jerks.

This description of the essay's thesis jibes with what Contessa wrote. She decided to argue that the popular definitions of homophobia are too far-reaching and that the word homophobia does not sufficiently describe the actions of people who, like her, believe that homosexuality is "a sin." She also wanted to distinguish between anti-gay rhetoric and verbal violence against gays and lesbians and what she perceived to be the loving, Christian approach to homosexuality, which involved a complete "acceptance" of the gay/lesbian individual, but an absolute rejection of homosexual activity.

Contessa began the first draft of her essay by describing an incident of harassment experienced by her gay friend, Robert:

> My gay friend, Robert, is a waiter at a restaurant. Last week he waited on a few men whom Robert described as homophobic. They kept making comments to him about his sexuality, such as "faggot" and "freak." Robert told me they were speaking with a lisp, "trying to sound feminine." Their harassment finally got to Robert and he told them to shut up or get out. They laughed at him, as if a gay man could not make them leave. When they did leave, one man rudely commented to Robert, "Now tell me you don't take it in the ass." Robert simply told that guy that he had a problem with his own sexuality. I asked Robert about how this circumstance made him feel. He told me, "It pissed me off more than anything because I wanted to go off on him and show him a 'faggot' could kick his ass." Robert told me that this kind of situation is rare. Most people who find out he's gay think that it's "cool."

I quote the entire introduction here because I am struck by what it implied about the rest of the essay. When I first read it, I believed that this introduction indicated that the essay would be a sensitive treatment of issues related to homophobia, and that the writer, who identified Robert as her "friend," would explore the effects of homophobia on the lives of the people who experience it. After all, according to Contessa, the harassers were rude, and she was careful to point out that she cared how Robert felt about the harassment.

In the next paragraph, though, Contessa immediately changed her tone about the situation. She provided Esther Rothblum and Lynne Bond's definition of homophobia as "an irrational, persistent fear or dread of homosexuals," then addressed her readers with this question: "Were the men who harassed Robert homophobic?" Her answer was that she didn't know "because [she] didn't get to meet them or talk to them." She focused on the notion that homophobia is about fear and then came to the conclusion that "a person can love the homosexual but not his homosexuality." Here was where Contessa's writing began to show the way the fragments of her identities were competing for voice. On the one hand, as Robert's friend, she felt protective of him and irritated with his harassers; however, she also wanted to take the academic's approach and challenge clichéd definitions of homophobia; and she wanted to give voice to the Christian in her who believed that homosexuality is a sin. In the span of only two and a half pages, Contessa performed all of these fragments; she narrated one more event, referred to another piece of theory about homophobia, and returned in her conclusion to the "moral issue of homosexuality."

The second incident Contessa narrated had to do with an experience she had when she took her lesbian friend to church. When the pastor asserted, "a homosexual would be a lot easier to reach than a religious fanatic," the friend, offended, "got up and marched out [of the church]." Contessa's third sentence in that paragraph summed up her interpretation of her church's stance on homosexuality: "My church loves the homosexual, but not the homosexual lifestyle." I think that Contessa believed this to be a humane stance, one that stood in direct opposition to the one taken by the young men who harassed Robert. In a conference with me, Contessa responded to my comment that I would probably have walked out of the church too by laughing and saying she thought that kind of reaction was silly. Among other things, my written remarks on this draft (1) challenged Contessa to explain more fully why she believed that rethinking the definition of the term homophobia was important, and (2) asked her to try to understand why a lesbian might respond negatively to the kinds of comments Contessa's pastor was making.

By the time Contessa wrote the final, portfolio version of this essay, she had decided that, in order to "focus" her argument, she must settle on an identity and perform it consistently throughout the text. The final version of the essay began with exactly the same introduction as it had in earlier versions (one that I had, by the way, characterized as "good"), but then took an immediate and interesting twist. The second paragraph began with these sentences:

> Homosexuality is a moral question one must face before understanding homophobia. Since this is my essay the readers will have to see the issue from my point of view. The homosexual lifestyle is wrong. Treating people in a hateful way is also inappropriate behavior. Where is the balance on how to treat a homosexual person?

I would assert that there were several things going on in this passage. First, Contessa was trying to give voice to two fragments of her identity — the one that believed that homosexuality was wrong and the one that wanted to treat people ethically. Second, she wanted to draw a distinction between two types of behavior; while homosexual behavior is unequivocally "wrong," harassment of homosexuals is merely "inappropriate" in Contessa's mind. Third, Contessa was addressing a reader (me) whom she knew would disagree with much of what she was arguing. She wanted to take ownership of her essay by pointing out that it was, after all, her essay and by insisting that I would have to show her the courtesy of trying to understand her point of view. Finally, she wanted her readers to be aware that she was looking for what she called "a balance" in the treatment of homosexuals. This is an extremely interesting assertion on Contessa's part because I sense that she was also looking to create a balance among her competing identities, to give them all some voice, some space in the text, but to present them as if they had come to consensus.

Throughout the final version of the essay, Contessa said things like, "Even though I disagree I try to empathize because no matter what I believe or what the world believes there is an absolute truth. Even though people know the truth, life is still a struggle. If someone rejects homosexual behavior, that someone isn't necessarily homophobic." These comments were juxtaposed with more clearly stated assertions like, "Homophobic behavior is just as wrong as homosexual behavior," and "I think on this moral issue of homosexuality and homophobia I've got the right idea: tell the truth, while loving people regardless of their actions." In the end, though, nothing was resolved by writing the essay; the final version was neither a coherent modernist text nor a fully realized, exploratory postmodern essay. In the final revision, Contessa was no more able to fully articulate the complex interactions among her multiple ways of seeing this issue than she had been when she began writing.

Postmodernisms, Teacher Commentary, and the Modernist Academy

In "Rend(er)ing Women's Authority in the Writing Classroom" Michelle Payne says, "By sharing my personal experience, and certainly my feelings, I may be inviting someone to come along and determine I am unfit, unstable, too emotional to be in a position of power — that my presentation of efficiency and capability is exactly that, a presentation" (100). As I write this article, I am struck by the same kinds of insecurities. I keep running into the feeling that my discussion of Contessa's writing and my responses to it will reveal that I simply failed to respond to the needs of a student who was struggling to express her beliefs in academic discourse. And, writing this section of the article only heightens that feeling, for here is where I focus on the aspects of my own autobiography which influenced my responses to what Contessa wrote. Here, I acknowledge that as a lesbian, I found myself struggling to balance aspects of at least two distinct fragments of my own identity — lesbian and teacher — when I responded to Contessa's essay. In essence, Contessa wrote an essay that illustrated conflicts among her own competing identities and I responded to those essays out of my own postmodern identity crisis. Because I identified as her writing teacher, I wanted to help Contessa express her beliefs as fully as possible, but because I also identify as a lesbian, I often found myself angry, hurt, and baffled by what I was reading.

My written commentary on Contessa's essay reflected not only my belief in process pedagogy, but also my very personal feelings about Contessa's assertions that homosexuality is a sin. My involvement in lesbian-feminist communities, and my out lesbian identity led me to

moments of near shock that a student I felt was thoughtful and intelligent — and for whom I felt a deep fondness — could take a number
of stances on homosexuality that I found appalling. In my comments
on the essay, I performed my multiple identities in much the same way
as Contessa performed hers in the essay. I responded as a reader who
didn't understand Contessa's purpose in challenging the definition of
homophobia and as a teacher who wanted the essay to have more
focus and more clarity. In her interview with Margaret, Contessa
explained the interaction between her early draft and my comments
this way:

> Like she was saying, "What difference does it make what you call it or
> why it happens? It's awful, cruel, stupid behavior. You seem to be
> defending these guys." I don't think I was defending them, but — okay,
> so maybe the word's wrong, but that's just . . . "How would you like it if
> people started saying, 'I love Contessa, but she's a person who engages
> in horrible, evil behavior?' Would you feel loved?" I think she was just
> kind of maybe — this would be my opinion. I mean, I don't care either
> way. If your teacher agrees or disagrees, it really doesn't matter. It's just
> like they're there to help you focus better. But, we talked about it, and . . .
> I think she might have misunderstood me — that I was saying, like I was
> defending these people and stuff.

What seems clear to me from this characterization of my comments is that Contessa was simply confused by what I wrote, partially
I believe, because my commentary did not acknowledge either
Contessa's or my own competing identity fragments. She wanted to
separate me from the text itself, perhaps because my voices, when
combined with hers, seemed to complicate the issues even more than
they already were in her own mind. I think, though, that another reason for the confusion was that I did not "come out" as a lesbian when
I responded to Contessa's essay. Because I am very "out" on campus,
many of my students already know about my lesbianism or figure it
out immediately when they come to my office for a conference and see
the small collection of lesbian memorabilia I have there, so I suspected
that Contessa was trying not to recognize my lesbianism. And, I knew
that Contessa had out gay and lesbian friends, so I also suspected that
my coming out would only amount to adding one more voice to an
already confusing chorus of voices.

Before she revised her essay, Contessa wrote a piece of metawriting in which she identified the issues she wanted to address in the
revision. She said, "The voice in this essay is too harsh. I was bitchy in
essay 2, but that isn't how I want to be now. I need to sound firm in
my beliefs but loving as well. I don't understand exactly how to sound
loving, but it won't hurt to try . . . I have a bad feeling about this essay
— that it will only get worse." Though neither Contessa nor I was able
to articulate it, I want to suggest that this metawriting indicated that,

on some level, she was aware of the competition for voice in which her identities were engaged. She seemed to know that there was a distinction between her firm beliefs in her church's rejection of homosexuality and its insistence on "loving" homosexuals. She also seemed aware that it would be nearly impossible for a student writing at the level she was writing to express rejection and acceptance simultaneously. And, though it is not clear in her metawriting, Contessa was very much aware of my presence as a reader who would challenge her beliefs and as a teacher who would finally evaluate her writing when she revised the essay. Her handwritten revisions on the first draft are all provided in response to in-text comments made by me, and in her first revision, all of Contessa's changes are like dialogic answers to my remarks.

Conclusion

In the introduction to their volume entitled *Feminism and Postmodernism,* Margaret Ferguson and Jennifer Wicke argue that postmodernism is "a name for the way we live now, and it needs to be taken account of, put into practice, and even contested within feminist discourses as a way of coming to terms with our lived situations" (1). My experiences and observations of Contessa and her writing lead me to believe that their assertion is true. Though it flies in the face of much of what I have been trained to believe about the teaching of writing — particularly process pedagogy — what I feel I have learned from Contessa is that I can no longer ignore the postmodern condition. Contessa's writing reveals that throughout the time she spent in my writing classes she was struggling to give voice to a number of competing identity fragments. My own observations of my interactions with Contessa and my responses to her writing reveal to me that because I was engaged in my own, unarticulated identity negotiation, I failed to recognize an important barrier to Contessa's production of the univocal, modernist writing that is expected in the academy. I believe that Contessa, unlike the "underprepared" or "developmental" basic writing student we have constructed in our theoretical discussions about basic writing, might well have been "up to" the task of writing in the academy if only I had been able to articulate to her in language that she could understand the tensions between her postmodern condition and the academy's modernist requirements. Contessa was making an attempt to be "true" to her experience of the world and to make her writing communicate an intellectual phenomenon that I believe she recognized but could not name.

All of this said, my own observation that Contessa's story is intimately connected to postmodern theory leaves me somewhat cold because I wonder how the material conditions under which I work will allow me to put that recognition into practice. I teach in an institution where basic writing teachers carry a four-course load and where the academic calendar is still organized around ten-week quarters. Faculty at my institution are expected to perform service to the college and university and to their national communities, as well as to publish in professional journals. These circumstances mitigate against my having the kind of time I would need to spend with individual writing students if I wanted them to grasp and be able to apply even modified versions of postmodern theories of multiple identities in their writing. And, even if I could find a way to address these issues with my students, I would have to find a way to allow students to explore their postmodern condition in writing. The kind of writing the students would produce during that exploration, though, would be nothing like the more traditional writing they would be required to produce in other classes. The fact of the students' placement in basic writing classes indicates that the institution believes they need "extra" instruction in writing if they are going to perform effectively in their other classes. If I were to teach a kind of postmodern discourse, I would be doing my students a great disservice.

How, then, does my recognition of the connection between postmodern theories and Contessa's writing change my pedagogy? And, how can that recognition be used to create agency rather than to remove it? Though Contessa does not, many of my students do "fit" the traditional definitions of basic writing students, by which I mean that many of my students are underprepared. The discussion of postmodern theories with those students must occur face-to-face and perhaps without direct reference to theory itself. Without me there to help students articulate the ways they perform their multiple identities, and by way of example to perform my own, many of my students would neither care about nor understand postmodern identity theory's relevance to their work. With basic writing students like Contessa — students whose primary difficulty with writing is an inability to understand and articulate the complexity of their intellectual insights — pointing out and perhaps even consciously performing the identity fragments I see competing for voice in their work might help us work together to come up with controlling ideas that explain that competition. I also believe that with students like Contessa I could change my methods for response to essay drafts. I could, for instance, identify the voices I see in the text, bracketing them off or highlighting them so that the student could see how the competition is performed in the text. And finally, I could provide students like Contessa with simple explanations of basic tenets of identity theory so that they might be able to consider for themselves whether the experiences the theory describes are in sync with their own experiences of the world.

While the scholar in me may be interested in theory for theory's sake, as a teacher who spends the vast majority of her time working with basic writing students, I am more interested in how theory can help teachers and students perform in the basic writing classroom and in their other courses. And, though I suspect that a teacher of basic writing who tried to "teach" postmodernism in her classroom would find herself frustrated, I believe that the simplified version of the postmodern theory of multiple, fragmented identity can be usefully performed in some interactions between students and teachers. Many of our basic writing students recognize a tension between their experiences and the world's expectations of them. If I can offer those students a version of postmodern theory that helps them articulate that tension, then perhaps I can help them be both more thoughtful and more successful as writers and students.

Bibliography

Allison, Dorothy. *Bastard out of Carolina*. New York: Plume, 1993.

Carroll, Lee Ann. "Pomo Blues: Stories from First-Year Composition." *College English* 59 (1997): 917–33.

Clouse, Barbara Fine. *Working it Out: A Troubleshooting Guide for Writers*. New York: McGraw-Hill, 1996.

Ferguson, Margaret, and Jennifer Wicke, eds. *Feminism and Postmodernism*. Durham, NC: Duke UP, 1994.

hooks, bell. "Black Identity: Liberating Subjectivity." *killing rage: Ending Racism*. New York: Holt, 1995. 240–50.

Lunsford, Andrea. "Composing Ourselves: Politics, Commitment, and the Teaching of Writing." *College Composition and Communication* 41 (1990): 71–82.

Orleans, Ellen. *Who Cares If It's a Choice? Snappy Answers to 101 Nosy, Intrusive and Highly Personal Questions About Lesbians and Gay Men*. Bala Cynwyd, PA: Laugh Lines, 1994.

Owens, Derek. "Composition as the Voicing of Multiple Fictions." *Into the Field: Sites of Composition Studies*. Ed. Anne Ruggles Gere. New York: MLA, 1993. 159–75.

Payne, Michelle. "Rend(er)ing Women's Authority in the Writing Classroom." *Taking Stock: The Writing Process Movement in the '90s*. Eds. Lad Tobin and Thomas Newkirk. Portsmouth, NH: Boynton/Cook Heinemann, 1994. 97–111.

Reynolds, Nedra. "Interrupting Our Way to Agency: Feminist Cultural Studies and Composition." *Feminism and Composition Studies: In Other Words*. Eds. Susan C. Jarratt and Lynn Worsham. New York: MLA, 1998. 58–73.

Sommers, Jeff, and Cynthia Lewiecki-Wilson, eds. *From Community to College: Reading and Writing across Diverse Contexts*. New York: St. Martin's, 1996.

Trimbur, John. "Composition Studies: Postmodern or Popular." *Into the Field: Sites of Composition Studies*. Ed. Anne Ruggles Gere. New York: MLA, 1993. 117–32.

Willey, R. J., and Jennifer Berne. *Process of Discovery: A Writer's Workshop*. New York: McGraw-Hill, 1997.

Yagelski, Robert. "Who's Afraid of Subjectivity? The Composing Process and Postmodernism or a Student of Donald Murray Enters the Age of

Postmodernism." *Taking Stock: The Writing Process Movement in the '90s.* Eds. Lad Tobin and Thomas Newkirk. Portsmouth, NH: Boynton/Cook Heinemann, 1994. 203–17.

Classroom Activities

Gibson offers particular strategies for "students whose primary difficulty with writing is an inability to understand and articulate the complexity of their intellectual insights." One strategy is for teachers to "poin[t] out and perhaps even consciously perfor[m] the identity fragments I see competing for voice in their work [which] might help us work together to come up with controlling ideas for explaining that competition." This strategy might be especially useful, as Gibson suggests, in helping students to deal with competing voices on issues such as homophobia.

Students can freewrite monologues for each competing voice or perhaps conversations between voices. As students move through the writing process, they can create controlling ideas as suggested above. This process would provide students with an opportunity to address the complexity of their own ideas, which is an important step for growing as writers and critical thinkers.

Thinking about Teaching

The introduction to Gibson's article (not included here) presents several research questions that guided her case study of Contessa. In particular, Gibson asks, "What can we learn from the inevitable confusion caused by the interactions among basic writing teachers' and students' multiple identities?" (3). To explore this question for yourself, write a series of reflective journal essays in which you consider your own multiple identities, especially in regard to race, social class, gender, and sexual orientation. How do these identities conflict and coalesce? What impact do these identities have on your interactions with students in your basic writing classrooms?

4

Writing and Reading

A significant body of research on basic writing and reading highlights the connections between the two activities, treating reading
and writing as similar composing processes for making meaning.
Drawing on such research, the articles in this section persuasively
make the case that reading should not be taught in isolation from
writing, and that developmental students can usefully and successfully engage the interconnections and similarities between these
processes.

Jeanne Henry uses teacher research to explore writing "literary
letters" and summaries of books and short stories to help students
become more intellectually engaged as readers and writers. Ilona Leki
shows how an understanding of the connections between reading and
writing processes can be beneficial for students whose home language
is not English (as well as for developmental writers and readers from
other backgrounds). In addition to demonstrating the power of writing
and reading as complementary interconnected processes, Henry and
Leki also offer practical classroom applications of their ideas.

From *If Not Now: Developmental Readers in the College Classroom:* Literary Letters

Jeanne Henry

The following excerpts are from Chapter 5 of Jeanne Henry's book If Not
Now: Developmental Readers in the College Classroom. If Not Now *is a
revision of Henry's doctoral dissertation, a teacher-research-based study*

of students enrolled in her Reading Workshop course at Northern Kentucky University. The Reading Workshop course is based on "[Louise] Rosenblatt's [transactional] theory that reading entails both public and private meanings, along with [Nancie] Atwell's reading workshop approach, with its free reading selection, individualized instruction, and literary letters" (Henry xiv).

In these excerpts, Henry explains the audiences and purposes for writing "literary letters" and offers several examples of students' summaries to illustrate the interconnections of reading and writing. Students in Henry's class spent the term reading books of their own choice and writing letters to Henry in response to their reading. In the process of her teacher research, Henry discovered that this integrated approach to language arts proved successful for her developmental students as they grew into more competent and confident readers and writers.

There is very little reason for us to write letters any more. AT&T has wired up the world, so I can forget what time it is and call and wake up my mother just as easily from New Zealand as I can from Northern Kentucky. And all you have to do is "surf the 'Net," as my students say, to know that you can e-mail a friend a thousand miles away faster than you can lick a stamp and walk to the post office. And fax machines! I love these things. Words out of wires. But even though we have little reason to write letters anymore, we still do. I suspect we always will. Letters get things on record, and we seem to like that. People can also say things in letters they are unwilling to say face-to-face, like "I am leaving you" or "I think I love you" or "It has come to our attention." We like that about letters too. There are letters of application, intent, thanks, apology, invitation, regret, condolence, recommendation, and acceptance. And what about chain letters? The part of your brain that evolved over the last ten million years knows these things need to be promptly transported to the trash, but your more primitive, reptilian tissue makes you hesitate, wondering what the vengeful gods will send your way if you break the chain. The mere sight of certain letters in the box can instantly take your blood pressure up a notch, but then there is nothing like getting your hands on a letter you have been longing to see. Letters get to us.

It was inevitable that letter writing would find its way into the classroom. For years we have been asking students to write letters to the editor or to the president or to soldiers stationed overseas. Sometimes these exchanges are merely one-sided exercises in audience, but I once asked my Northern students to write to the college students I was teaching in a maximum security prison for youthful offenders. A lesson in audience awareness was had by all. One of my freshmen asked an incarcerated student if he was looking forward to going home for Christmas, and one of the prison students asked why all college kids drove Corvettes. I wanted the exchange to continue, as did both sets of students, but the prison administrators went ape and I had to abandon the plan. We get to know each other well through letters, sometimes too well.

Asking students to address those letters to us, their teachers, and for us then to write back a reply, does not seem to have occurred to anyone until the mid-sixties, when a sixth-grade teacher named Leslee Reed engaged her students in on-going letter exchanges about their lives and academic work that came to be known as dialogue journals (Staton et al. 1988). And of course, Nancie Atwell (1984, 1987) later developed "literary letters," in which the student-teacher letter exchange focused entirely on reading. But I had some questions about these literary letters. In Nancie Atwell's skilled hands, the letters were collaborative, involved and involving, mutual. But not everyone is the teacher Nancie Atwell is. I had seen response journals, a format intended to give students an opportunity to explore meaning, corrupted by colleagues. One in particular told me she used journals as a means of "letting students get their silly ideas out of their systems before I tell them what the piece is about." So what would the letters be like in my novice hands? I wondered about the extent to which these letters could be collaborative, given the unequal authority and expertise of the correspondents. While *collaboration* can be defined as joint intellectual endeavor, it is also the word used to describe treasonable cooperation. Would I use letters to do what reading teachers traditionally seem to fall back on — telling students the meaning of what they have just read — or would I help sustain, maintain, and extend their reading? Bottom line, I studied literary letters because I was dying to know what students might write in them, as well as whatever I might say in response.

Summary Writing

I was a mess during the first workshop class. I did not have a lot of time to reflect on the letter exchange, since I was up to my elbows in literary letters, research, graduate course work, and the two other classes I taught, but I knew from the very beginning that the students' letters were filled with plot summary. I kept a teaching journal throughout my research, and my comments indicate I had myself in an uproar: "They're writing too much summary." "What am I going to do about all this summary?" "If I suggest they write less summary, will they just write shorter letters?" My assumption was that summary writing, especially in response to literature, was uncritical, unselective, lazy, low-down, and dumb. In learning hierarchies, the rank of summary writing is roughly equivalent to that of where coelenterates fall in the food chain. If literary letters produced so much summary, at least in my instructional hands, I had to wonder how valuable they really could be.

Once again, professor Chet Laine, patron of strung out doctoral students, listened to me talk this through. All he said was, "Now you hadn't read most of the books the students did, right?" Right. So? Oh. These students read ninety-three different books, only fifteen of which I had read previously, and many of those I had read ten or more years ago. When any two people discuss a book one of them has not read, there is an obvious need for a little summation of the plot. I was so used to artificial talk with my students about reading, I did not recognize the real thing when it was under my nose. Of course they had to summarize the plot if I was going to understand their interpretations of or reactions to their books. I never told students to include enough summary so that I could get a solid sense of what their books were about. They intuitively knew that I would not understand what they had to say about the meaning of a book if I did not know the plot in some detail.

This hunch that students were summarizing for the benefit of their reader rather than because of some character flaw was refined when I broke down students' summary passages into two types: summaries written about books I had read and those produced about books with which I was unfamiliar. All combined, students wrote roughly forty-three thousand words of summary. Eighty-four percent of those many, many words were devoted to summarizing the books I had not read. Only sixteen percent (about seven thousand words) covered those books I had read sometime in the last decade. The students knew that it was not necessary to summarize a book that I had already read, unless they needed to let me know where they were in the book or to frame an interpretive remark. They wrote *purposeful* summaries, and this was essential if we were to talk coherently about their books.

But I don't let myself or workshop off the hook so easily. Even though these were purposeful summaries, I still wondered if the fact that students needed to devote so much of their writing simply to filling me in might be robbing them of time and attention better spent analyzing their books in more critical or at least more entertaining ways. Was this a problem with workshop? If the teacher has not read the student's book — and even with my regimen of trying to read everything students drag in, I am still unfamiliar with fifty percent of what they read — did the approach foster more summary writing than we might desire? When I raised that question, I was still operating under the belief that writing summaries required little critical thinking. But when I cruised through my students' summary passages again for the third or fourth time, my English teacher assumptions about summary writing started to fall apart.

First, these summaries were not uncritical or unselective. The students boiled down the plots of two- and three-hundred-page books to three to five pages (when totaled — summaries were always interrupted by interpretive comments and written across the course of two to four letters). I have no idea how students decided what to include in their summaries, but clearly each writer made choices about what I needed to know in order not only to understand the book but also to *experience* its dramatic moments. The students also seemed to want to make their summaries compelling, which they did by including important bits of dialogue and vivid descriptive details. Take a look at Jerry's letter about a book called *Twice Pardoned,* Harold Morris's confessional account of his murder conviction and later conversion to Christianity. The climax of the book comes with Morris' arrest, which he had not been expecting:

> . . . a bunch of police officers kicked open the door about 11 pm at night. Harold was then put under arrest. He was asked a lot of questions in the police car but he did not answer because he knew his rights.
>
> His bail was set at $10,000. We was in his cell when a FBI agent came in and said that "bail has been dropped for you, Harold Morris. You are charged for six armed robberies, and murder one, no bond."
>
> Harold thought this was a nightmare but the bars reminded him that it wasn't.

Lucy's writing was equally vivid. In her summary of an Alice Walker story entitled "Nineteen Fifty-Five," Lucy explained that a character named Traynor, a white singer who became known as the "emperor of rock and roll," had bought all of the songs he sang from a black songwriter who had not been able to break into the music business. Lucy summarized an important moment of the story:

> Traynor came by one day to see how Gracie Mae (oh by the way that was her name) was doing and he invited her out to his house for dinner. He had her picked up in a limo and she was speechless when she visited his house. She said he was starting to gain weight and [that he] complained about life a lot. He asked her about the song she wrote. "What did it mean?" She said "you've been singing this song and making a lot of money off this song and do not know what it means?" He did not know what to say.

A passage from one of Lance's letters (putting me in mind of a young Yukio Mishima) also makes my point:

> The Shawnee Indian tribe had captured a colonel by the name of Crawford. The torture they put him through was tremendous. They tied him up at the stake, built a fire around him, and burned him. They cut his ears off, stabbed him with hot spears, threw hot coals at him, and at one time while he was still alive his face was black and began to actually burn. And when they were done playing with him they threw him in the fire.

Because of these detailed and proficient summaries, I had a very clear sense of what students were reading, which helped me understand and respond to their interpretations, hard spots, and enthusiasms. As I wrote to Jerry, "I feel like I'm reading over your shoulder." The students' summaries were detailed enough, their sense of what a reader would need to know precise enough, that most of the plot synopses I provide here are based solely on the knowledge I acquired through the students' writing. Now, it is not as if I were the only one who considered summary writing as a shallow way for adults to respond to literature. Why is this? In traditional reading and literature classrooms, the teacher has already read the book the student is writing about because, well, he or she assigned it. We do not need to be told what we already know, so summary looks like a substitute for substance.

But summary writing proved more than a necessary evil in these literary letters. Because they were purposeful summaries, written for a real audience with a real need to know, students had to write with a sound sense of audience awareness, and they explained themselves, defined their terms, and made their summaries riveting. It is hard enough for any writer to "dissociate from the text and read it through the eyes of potential readers" (Rosenblatt 1989, 167), and this is particularly true for the inexperienced. These students had to imagine what I could reasonably be expected to know about their books, what I might want or need to know, and eventually even the questions I would be likely to ask. This is not a talent that leaps to mind when I think about the writing ability of underprepared freshmen. Even if all students are doing is retelling plot, they are still reflecting on what they have read. As Paris, Wasik, and Turner inform us, good readers "ask questions . . . and invoke strategies to review the text and their comprehension" (1991, 614). In other words, they continue processing after the reading is completed. Now, the act of writing does not guarantee advanced processing, but to summarize a book does require that students review and reconsider its events. The book is reopened, in a sense, after the student is done reading. Students also had to tell me what was happening in the story to support, frame, or explain their thoughts about a character's motivation or psychological make-up or morality. The National Assessment of Educational Progress found that the majority of seventeen-year-olds were not able to provide adequate evidence to support their interpretations (1981, 16–17). Yet my remedial readers were very able to tell me enough about the books they read to explain why they thought the things they did. Go figure.

You bet, literary letters used in a free-choice reading class require students to write considerable summary. But there may be advantages to this situation in which a teacher has not read the book a student is reporting on, regardless of how much summary writing this kind of correspondence demands. And chief among them is the authenticity of the exchange. Carole Edelsky describes one type of inauthentic writing (or "writing," as she abbreviates) as making use of print for the professed purpose of informing an audience that, in reality, is better informed than the writer (1986, 174). There was no pretense here; I actually was less informed than the students. Yes, I asked them to write these letters — the students may not have had a yearning deep in their souls to talk to me or anyone else about books — but once the exchange was set in motion, it was authentic. The students accepted "the ostensible purpose," telling me about their books, "as their own" (Edelsky 1986, 177). These letters, with their jokes and confidences, their engagement, and their efforts to explain, insist on the authenticity of the exchange.

Bibliography

Atwell, N. 1984. "Writing and Reading Literature from the Inside Out." *Language Arts* 61 (3): 240–52.

———. 1987. *In the Middle: Writing, Reading, and Learning with Adolescents.* Portsmouth, NH: Boynton/Cook.

Carbo, M. 1981. *Reading Style Inventory Manual.* Roslyn Heights, NY: Learning Research Associates.

Dorfman, M. 1985. "A Model for Understanding the Points of Stories: Evidence from Adult and Child Readers." Paper presented at the Seventh Annual Conference of the Cognitive Science Society, Irvine, California. ERIC, ED 335605.

Edelsky, C. 1986. *Writing in a Bilingual Program: Habia Una Vez.* Norwood, NJ: Ablex.

Goodman, K., and Y. Goodman. 1983. "Reading and Writing Relationships: Pragmatic Functions." *Language Arts* 60 (5): 590–99.

Henry, J. 1990. "Enriching Prior Knowledge: Enhancing Mature Literacy in Higher Education." *The Journal of Higher Education* 61 (4): 425–47.

Murray, D. 1986. "Reading While Writing." In *Only Connect: Uniting Reading and Writing,* ed. T. Newkirk, 59–86. Portsmouth, NH: Boynton/Cook.

National Assessment of Educational Progress. 1981. *Reading, Thinking, and Writing: Results from the 1979–1980 National Assessment of Reading and Literature.* Denver, CO: National Assessment of Educational Progress.

Newman, J. M. 1985a. "What About Reading?" In *Whole Language: Theory in Use,* ed. J. M. Newmann, 99–110. Portsmouth, NH: Heinemann.

Paris, S. G., B. A. Wasik, and J. C. Turner. 1991. "The Development of Strategic Readers." In *Handbook of Reading Research,* vol. 2, ed. R. Barr, M. L. Kamil, P. Mosenthal, and P. D. Pearlson, 609–40. New York: Longman.

Rosenblatt, L. M. 1938. *Literature as Exploration.* New York: Noble and Noble. Reprint, 1968.

———. 1978. *The Reader, the Text, the Poem: The Transactional Theory of Literary Work.* Carbondale, IL: Southern Illinois University Press.

———. 1985a. "Language, Literature and Values." In *Language, Schooling and Society,* ed. S. N. Tchudi, 64–80. Portsmouth, NH: Boynton/Cook.

———. 1985b. "The Transactional Theory of the Literary Work: Implications for Research." In *Researching Response to Literature and the Teaching of Literature: Points of Departure,* ed. C. R. Cooper, 33–53. Norwood, NJ: Ablex.

———. 1989. "Writing and Reading: The Transactional Theory." In *Reading and Writing Connections,* ed. J. M. Mason. 153–76. Boston: Allyn and Bacon.

Sadoski, M., and E. Goetz. 1985. "Relationships Between Affect, Imagery, and Importance Ratings for Segments of a Story." In *Issues in Literacy: A Research Perspective,* 34th Yearbook of the National Reading Conference, ed. J. Niles and R. Colik, 180–85. Rochester, NY: National Reading Conference.

Sadoski, M., E. Goetz, and S. Kasinger. 1988. "Imagination in Story Response: Relationships Between Imagery, Affect, and Structural Importance." *Reading Research Quarterly* 23 (3): 320–36.

Smith, F. 1983a. *Essays into Literacy: Selected Papers and Some After-thoughts.* Portsmouth, NH: Heinemann.

———. 1983b. "Reading Like a Writer." *Language Arts* 60 (5): 558–67.

———. 1985. *Reading Without Nonsense.* New York: Teachers College Press.

———. 1986. *Understanding Reading: A Psycholinguistic Analysis of Reading and Learning to Read.* Hillsdale, NJ: Erlbaum.

Stahl, N. A., M. L. Simpson, and W. G. Brozo. 1988. "The Materials of College Reading Instruction: A Critical and Historical Perspective from 50 Years of Content Analysis Research." *Reading Research and Instruction* 27 (3): 16–34.

Station, J., R. W. Shuy, J. K. Peyton, and L. Reed. 1988. *Dialogue Journal Communication: Classroom, Linguistic, Social and Cognitive Views.* Norwood, NJ: Ablex.

Sternglass, M. S. 1986. "Writing Based on Reading." In *Convergences: Transactions in Reading and Writing,* ed. B. T. Petersen, 151–62. Urbana, IL: National Council of Teachers of English.

———. 1988. *The Presence of Thought: Introspective Accounts of Reading and Writing.* Norwood, NJ: Ablex.

Classroom Activities

Take students to the campus or other local library or bookstore to search for a book that they would enjoy reading on their own, or offer students the opportunity to choose their own reading from the required reading list. If appropriate to your term schedule, arrange part of each week for silent, in-class reading. To help draw connections between reading and writing, assign students to write a series of literary letters or e-mails to you, culminating in a three- to five-page extended summary of the book they chose to read. Offer students tips for summary writing based on these suggestions from Henry:

• Boil down the plot of the book to one to two paragraphs.

- Give the reader the opportunity to experience the most dramatic moments of the book.

- Include important bits of dialogue and vivid descriptive details.

Thinking about Teaching

Henry employs a strong narrative voice as she analyzes the findings of her research. Consider creating a teacher research project of your own or with others and presenting the results as a written classroom narrative or as a conference presentation told as a story.

Also, consider studying your own students' reading and writing processes. You can interview and invite students to write about the kinds of reading and writing they have enjoyed in the past and when and where they read and write for your course. Write up the results of your study as a narrative as described above and consider whether your findings hold implications for transforming your own approaches to developmental reading and writing pedagogy.

Reciprocal Themes in ESL Reading and Writing

Ilona Leki

> *Originally published in 1993 in* Reading in the Composition Classroom: Second Language Perspectives,* *Ilona Leki's essay presents a particularly effective analysis of how changes in our understanding of ESL students' writing processes have "reciprocal themes" in studies of reading processes. She suggests, for example, that the notion of writing for specific purposes correlates to the idea of reading for specific purposes. Leki argues that focusing simply on reading for "the main idea" or for answers to post-reading questions in a textbook is unhelpful for students because such skills are often presented in isolation from "making meaning" from the text itself. In the same vein, Leki suggests that "we are preventing the very grappling with meaning that would allow students to develop their own strategies for rapid and accurate text processing," including discovering internal motivation for reading. Although Leki emphasizes the importance of such processes for ESL students, her findings are also relevant for other developmental reading students who are often enrolled in our basic writing classes.*

*Throughout her essay, Leki's references to "this volume" pertain to *Reading in the Composition Classroom: Second Language Perspectives,* ed. Joan Carson and Ilona Leki (Boston: Heinle, 1993).

> Reading, like writing, begins in confusion, anxiety and uncertainty . . . it is driven by chance and intuition as well as by deliberate strategy and conscious intent . . . certainty and authority are postures, features of a performance that is achieved through an act of writing, not qualities of vision that precede such a performance. (Bartholomae & Petrosky, 1986, p. 21)

Over the last ten to twenty years, research in L2 reading and writing has progressed almost entirely independently, yet their findings echo each other. Relying heavily on insights from L1 research and on psycholinguistic studies of reading and composing processes, L2 researchers have made extensive use of miscue, protocol, and think-aloud analyses of the reading and writing of proficient and less skilled L2 readers and writers. As a result of these studies, we have some idea of where L2 readers focus their attention as they try to make sense of a text — to what extent they predict upcoming text and relate it to what they have already read (Carrell, 1983b; Clarke, 1979; Cziko, 1978; Devine, 1988; Hudson, 1982; Rigg, 1977). We also have an idea of what goes on in the minds of experienced and inexperienced L2 writers as they compose — how much they plan, how much they translate from their L1, where they focus their attention, how they handle vocabulary problems (see Krapels, 1990 for an overview of L2 writing research; Arndt, 1987; Cumming, 1989; Hall, 1990; Jones & Tetroe, 1987; Raimes, 1985; Zamel, 1983).

Often (but not always — see Raimes, 1985) these studies reveal that less skilled readers and writers both appear to attend to the same thing, to the text on the page rather than to the meaning potential of that text, to the forms of the letters and words rather than to the overarching connections between them. Inefficient L2 readers read too locally (Cohen et al., 1979), failing to link incoming text with previous text, and because they are unskilled in rapid text processing in L2, depend too heavily on bottom-up strategies to decode or extract the message assumed to exist in the text (Carrell, 1988b; Hosenfeld, 1984; McLaughlin, 1987; Stanovich, 1980).[1] Poor L2 writers focus excessively on word- and sentence-level grammatical and print code concerns (Arndt, 1987; Hatch, Polin, & Part, 1970; Silva, 1990).[2] All of this is to the detriment of meaning. Good readers and writers, on the other hand, are better able to focus on broader concerns related to communication.

Further parallels between cognitive research in reading and in writing indicate that proficient L2 readers and writers use strategies not hierarchically or linearly, but interactively in reading and recursively in writing (Carrell, 1983b; Zamel, 1983). The unifying characteristic of good readers and good writers seems to be flexibility, the ability to use and reuse different strategies as the moment calls for them.

The implications of this research have generally discouraged teachers from our previous focus on subskills of reading and writing, such as grammar and vocabulary, and encouraged us to focus on cognitive strategies that imitate those of proficient L1 readers and writers. Classrooms have turned toward teaching the processes of reading and writing.

Yet, oddly enough, until recently little in the L2 research literature has addressed reading and writing together, and despite the parallels between research findings in these domains and despite commonsense views that reading and writing have a reciprocal effect on each other, including the notion that good writers learn to write well in part by reading a great deal (see, however, Flahive & Bailey, this volume), adult ESL classrooms are only beginning to consider how to effectively integrate both reading and writing. We know that reading builds knowledge of various kinds to use in writing and that writing consolidates knowledge in a way that builds schemata to read with (Bereiter & Scardamalia, 1987; Sternglass, 1988). We also know that, for example, biology professors learn to write articles the way biology professors do by reading articles that biology professors have written. We do not have courses that teach biology professors to write like biology professors. Yet we continue to separate ESL reading courses from ESL writing courses.

This anomaly probably results from several causes. First, reading researchers themselves have urged that reading be taught in its own right and not be thought of as merely a skill in support of other language skills (Grabe, 1986). That is, reading should be thought of as more than merely a prompt for discussion or writing.

Second, writing pedagogy of the 1980s has also made the role of reading material in the ESL classroom unclear. In the past, readings that appeared in ESL writing textbooks were used as model texts; classes analyzed the structure of these texts, and students were instructed to pattern their own writing after those model structures (Raimes, 1986; Reid, this volume). Influenced by process approaches to writing instruction, teachers became reluctant to continue the use of texts as models because of the implication that form pre-exists content, that to write well students needed only to pour their content into the model forms exemplified in the reading passages. The role of reading in the writing classroom became somewhat uncertain. Were readings to be used as source material for student writing, as stimulus for ideas? How were writing teachers to treat those reading texts? Were writing teachers being asked to teach reading at the same time as writing? (See Kroll, this volume, for the argument that L2 writing teachers must also be reading teachers.) No systematic approach or consensus on how to use nonfiction readings in ESL writing classrooms has yet emerged. Up to now, discussion in the literature on using reading in writing classrooms has primarily revolved around making a case for teaching fiction (Gajdusek, 1988; Mlynarczyk, 1992; Spack, 1985).

A third reason functioning to keep reading instruction out of the advanced ESL writing classroom is related to the structure of higher education in this country. Although native English speakers take courses in freshman composition (often without readings in support of writing), reading courses are considered remedial for native students (Bartholomae & Petrosky, 1986) and as a result are typically also unavailable for nonnatives except in language institutes.[3] It is assumed that ESL students at advanced levels are already reading well independently. (See Blanton, this volume, on the error of this view.) After all, these students are reading a great deal in other content-area classes. But difficulty and inefficiency in reading are easily dissimulated. This effort is hidden from us and from our content-area colleagues. While we see and hear about our students' problems in writing, their reading problems may remain invisible, implying no problem exists.

Finally, however problematic, exit exams in writing are quite common in colleges and universities, prompting the development of writing courses to prepare students for them; this is not the case in reading.[4] As a result, we have advanced ESL writing courses but do not typically teach reading beyond the level of language institutes despite the fact that ESL students report a greater need for proficiency in reading than in any other English language skill at the university level (Carrell, 1988a; Christison & Krahnke, 1986).

The unfortunate separation of reading and writing has impoverished instruction in both domains. Without readings in ESL writing classrooms, teachers tend to rely heavily on expressivist writing assignments based on personal experience or previous knowledge (Bazerman, 1980; Horowitz, 1986b; Spack, 1988). While this form of writing is valuable, it is limited and not the type of writing typically required from ESL students in higher education (Horowitz, 1986a; Johns, 1981; Reid, 1987). Reading, a major source of new knowledge, is ignored, and students are not called upon to develop the ability to select and integrate new knowledge with knowledge and information they already possess and with their analyses and reactions to that new knowledge and information. It is this ability to integrate or internalize new information in writing that undergirds the notions both of knowledge-transforming (Bereiter and Scardamalia, 1987) and of critical literacy (Flower et al., 1990) and may in fact be what we actually mean when we speak of comprehension of a text.

Writing pedagogy in the 1980s and 1990s has remained fairly closely in line with writing research, having undergone an enormous change in the 1980s, a virtual paradigm shift, as teachers abandoned remedial models of writing instruction and incorporated research insights into the classroom. While L2 reading research has produced insights as far-reaching as those of writing research, its impact on textbooks and classrooms has been less noticeable (Grabe, 1986). Schema theory and the notion of top-down processing of text did inspire the successful incorporation of pre-reading activities into many reading classrooms (Anderson & Pearson, 1984; Carrell & Eisterhold, 1983; Goodman, 1976). But to judge by textbooks and pedagogical articles on reading in the 1980s, researchers' exploration of the notion of the interactive nature of reading (Rummelhart, 1977; Stanovich, 1980) has had an almost negligible impact (Grabe, 1986). As a result, the unfortunate effect of teaching reading and writing in separate courses has had dramatic consequences on reading instruction, robbing reading of its natural purpose and ignoring its social dimensions. The rest of this chapter will explore the implications of this situation, touching on a number of themes that will be taken up again more specifically in the subsequent chapters of this book.

Isolated Reading Classes: Reading for No Real Reason

The research literature in L2 emphasizes the importance of purpose in both writing and reading (Eskey, 1986; Kroll, 1991). In recent writing instruction, purpose for writing has become a central focus. Many classrooms now include, for example, unevaluated writing journals in which students can freely explore topics of personal interest to them and from which they may select entries to develop into full essays (Blanton, 1987; Spack & Sadow, 1983). Writing on topics selected in this manner goes a long way toward ensuring the kind of internal motivation for writing which presumably results in the commitment to task which, in turn, is thought to help writing and language improve. But the immediate purpose for writing about a particular subject is neither language nor even writing improvement. It is, rather, a more natural purpose, i.e., communication with a reader about something of personal significance to the writer. The emphasis on publishing student writing grows from the same belief in the importance of purpose; if a piece is to be published, a student has far more reason to feel intellectually committed to the writing, to both the content and form of the text. Finally, the entire thrust of writing instruction within an English for Specific Purposes context rests on the belief that students should learn to write what they will need to write and in the way they will need to write within the academic disciplines they have chosen (Horowitz, 1986a; Reid, 1987).

The literature on reading has also pointed out that readers read for different purposes and that those purposes affect what is attended to and with what intensity (Eskey, 1986). This concern with purpose has emerged in the L2 reading classroom most clearly in pre-reading questions intended to lend direction to reading by giving students something to read for. But this understanding of purpose is extremely narrow. Certainly, having a purpose for reading a text should make that text easier to read, but that avoids the real question: Why is this text being read in the first place? While it is axiomatic that our L2 students learn to read by reading, it appears that in L2 reading classes this axiom has been inappropriately reversed: the reason for reading a text is to learn to read. Yet as Flower et al. (1990) point out,

> Literacy, as Richardson, Vygotsky, and others have defined it, is not syn-
> onymous with the ability to read (decode) or write (transcribe) per se.
> Rather it is a "goal-directed, context-specific" behavior, which means
> that a literate person is able to use reading and writing in a transac-
> tional sense to achieve some purpose in the world at hand. . . . (p. 4)

The failure to provide real purposes for reading suggests that in iso-
lated L2 reading classes (i.e., ones in which students are not reading to write), students are not reading but merely practicing reading. This "reading practice" is evident in reading selections and in pedagogical focuses in L2 reading classrooms.

Text Selection

The reading material used in many ESL reading classes both reveals and furthers the distortion of the reading class into the reading prac-
tice class. Since isolated reading classes serve no other purpose than to teach reading, there is no particular reason to read one text rather than another. In line with that reasoning, then, most readings in L2 reading classes are short texts on a variety of topics that are thought to be of high interest to our students: pollution, friendship, language, cultural differences, education, the role of women in various cultures.[5]

Short texts are selected because they conveniently fit into our class periods better than long texts, they take less time to read, and they are thought to be easier to read than longer texts. But short texts are, in fact, likely to be more difficult to read since students never read enough about the subject to build the knowledge about it that would allow them to read with ease and pleasure. (See Sternglass, 1988, on the issue of knowledge building for the purpose of knowledge making.) Like our students, we allow our intuitions to lead us astray — when our students have trouble reading, they slow down and try to decode the text word for word, operating locally, microscopically, and hoping that by simplifying and separating, they will later be able to add up all the pieces and understand. When confronted with students having difficulties reading, we have the same reaction: to break up the reading, go microscopic, and give students shorter, "easier" texts to read (Bartholomae & Petrosky, 1986).

Furthermore, we select a variety of subject matters to maintain student interest and motivation and, ostensibly, to focus attention on content. We hope that by using a shotgun approach to subject matter we will eventually hit upon at least one subject of interest to each of our students. That may or may not happen, but the result of constant shifts in subject matter is once again the same: The texts are harder to read because the students must gear up for a new subject with each reading selection. This approach to reading material also denies our students the eye-opening experience readers have when they return to a text read earlier with new knowledge structures born of reading other texts on the same subject (see Spack, this volume). The original text now literally means something new to the reader; the meaning of sections of text previously blurred by misunderstanding is clarified through the lens of new knowledge. But the possibility for such growth is eliminated by asking students to switch their attention from pollution to animal behavior to education with each new chapter.

Finally, there is the question of high interest. It is possible to argue that the subjects typically covered in ESL readers are of high interest to teachers and textbook writers, but not particularly to L2 students. The topics *might* be of high interest if these students could already read them as easily as *we* read them. But L2 reading is a struggle, and these subjects are unlikely to be of high enough personal interest to our students to compensate for the burden created by asking students to read a hodge-podge of subjects for no particular reason except to learn to read English better. (See Kroll, this volume, for a glimpse into a classroom using such an approach.) This approach to teaching reading resembles writing classes of ten years ago, when teachers struggled to divine what might be interesting, motivating topics for students to write on and came up with such assignments as "Describe your most embarrassing moment." Even if we locate high interest readings, as Bartholomae & Petrosky (1990) maintain, the issue is less what students read (i.e., the discovery of the perfect text) than what they then do with what they read, how we ask them to engage that text.

Pedagogical Practices

One source of the problems in isolated reading classes is confusion about what we can accomplish. If we are convinced by evidence that pleasure reading contributes to L2 reading and writing proficiency (Elley & Mangubhai, 1983; Hafiz & Tudor, 1989; Krashen, 1988, 1984; van Naerssen, 1985), one goal of a reading class might be to promote pleasure reading. Unfortunately, this goal is unrealistic; for all but the most proficient of our students, L2 reading is too difficult a chore to be engaged in simply for pleasure (Janopoulos, 1986), and to build proficiency in reading strictly through pleasure reading takes time our ESL students may not have.

Our goal then becomes to attempt to preempt reading difficulties by teaching generic strategies for reading *any* text. Our teaching strategy has been to examine the cognitive processes of proficient readers, those who presumably do read a great deal for pleasure, to isolate the strategies they use, and to teach these strategies to our students. We find that proficient readers do not read all texts in an invariable, plodding pace from word to word, dictionary in hand, as some of our less proficient students do. Instead, they skim some texts or sections of text, they scan, they read in chunks rather than word for word, they note cohesion markers, they guess vocabulary meaning from context, and they read fast (Grabe, 1986). So we direct our students to imitate these behaviors and practice skimming, scanning, guessing, and chunking texts; we tell them not to use dictionaries; we give them practice recognizing cohesion markers; and we push them to read fast (Eskey & Grabe, 1988).

The problem with teaching these cognitive strategies is that even if our students accomplish these goals, they are still not learning reading; they are learning strategies for reading, which can at best be only imitations of reading behaviors, like children turning the pages of books they cannot yet read. We seem to have assumed that these strategies are the causes of proficiency in reading. But these strategies are the *result* not the cause of reading proficiency; good readers read fast because they can. They are able to comprehend incoming text quickly. If our students use dictionaries and read slowly with an even amount of attention to every word, they do this because this is all they *can* do. They do *not* comprehend; they do not know which words are essential to meaning and which may be passed over.[6] If proficient readers skim some texts, they do so because the text, as they themselves judge it for their own internally motivated purposes, merits no more careful reading. The answer to the question of which texts should be skimmed, which scanned, which words looked up in the dictionary, or which texts abandoned altogether is determined by the reader's purpose in reading. If the purpose in reading is only to practice reading, there can be no internally motivated answers to these questions. With no purpose for reading, then skimming, scanning, or any of the other strategies we teach all become no more than artificial exercises. By taking over control of their reading through post-reading exercises and telling our students which texts to skim, which information to scan for, and how fast to read, we are preventing the very grappling with meaning that would allow students to develop their own strategies for rapid and accurate text processing. (See Devine, this volume, for discussion of the interaction between goal setting, or purpose, and metacognition.)

The problems inherent in teaching strategies to improve reading devoid of any true purpose for reading are exacerbated by textbooks that direct students to practice these techniques thoroughly, that is, with every, or nearly every, text in the book. Despite the research findings that good readers read for varying purposes and with varying degrees of attention, isolated reading courses tend in fact to direct students to do the opposite, to regard each reading selection addressed in class as equally important and eligible for similar analysis. Again we see clear parallels with the kinds of discredited writing instruction practices in which every text students write is taken to be a final draft and then corrected and evaluated.

Another nearly universal pedagogical practice in L2 reading classrooms is post-reading comprehension checks, often aimed, like standardized reading tests, at checking comprehension by asking students to identify the main idea of a text or passage. But this enterprise is problematic. First, knowing the main idea of a text does not mean understanding the text. Second, questioning students about the main idea does absolutely nothing to *show* students how to achieve comprehension, whether or not they can successfully spot the same main idea we spot. Finally, pointing out that our students' version of the main idea is or is not the same as ours, far from helping our students achieve understanding, does not even help our students identify the main idea! It is not clear that we even know exactly how we determine what the main idea of a text is. (See Parry, 1987 for an interesting discussion of factors that may have influenced a group of West African students in their construction of the meaning of a text.) If we do not know how we ourselves recognize the main idea of a text, we cannot teach it to our students and end by merely mystifying them. Yet there seems to be almost an obsession with main ideas in reading pedagogy and testing that is reminiscent of the previous exaggerated interest in topic sentences in writing and that represents a reductionist view of reading. By relying so heavily and confidently on comprehension and main idea questions, we seem to be defining — and encourage our students to define — text comprehension as correct responses to comprehension questions. Yet, many would argue that

> the only way to demonstrate comprehension is through extended discourse where readers become writers who articulate their understandings of and connections to the text in their responses. Response is, then, an expression and explanation of comprehension; and comprehension means using writing to explicate the connections between our models of reality — our prior knowledge — and the texts we recreate in light of them. (Petrosky, 1982, pp. 24–25, discussing David Bleich)

Typical comprehension checks also imply that the meaning of a text resides in the text and that the students' goal is to ferret out the meaning the author put there. This implication is out of tune with the notions, so pervasive in current reading research, of reading as the construction, not the deciphering, of meaning and of reading as interaction between reader and text, in which meaning depends as much on what the reader brings to the text as what the text brings to the reader. The usual comprehension check denies the role of the reader in constructing meaning. Yet Tierney & Pearson (1983) assert that "there is no meaning on the page until a reader decides there is" (p. 569).

Furthermore, exactly what do our students gain by correctly identifying the main idea in an ESL textbook article on dreams or friendship? What difference does it make if the student correctly or incorrectly identifies the same main idea as the teacher? In natural reading contexts, proficient and even less skilled readers reading for a real-world purpose not only skim, scan, or chunk for their own purposes, but they also choose to privilege either main ideas or details of a text, again depending on their purpose in reading. In a given text read by a specific reader in a real-world context, the main idea may or may not be significant. The reader may retain only a striking image or line of reasoning, or even, as is often the case with academic readers, only a citation or reference to another text. But if the purpose for reading a text is to practice reading, then students have no basis on which to privilege main ideas or details. By persistently imposing a check for comprehension of main ideas, we may in fact be training our students to read in ways characteristic of poor readers, bound to the text and lacking the purpose that would allow them to skip over information they themselves judge uninteresting or unnecessary.

Thus on one hand, a leveling process takes place such that all the texts read are given equal attention and therefore equal weight, and on the other hand, a selection process occurs whereby someone besides the reader decides what should be salient to the reader. If that which resonates for the student does not match the main idea of the text, the importance of the student's encounter with the text is undermined and the student's reading is dismissed as a failure to understand.

Attempting to Teach What Cannot Be Taught

Perhaps one difficulty with the entire enterprise of teaching the construction of meaning, whether in reading or in writing, is that although it can be learned, in some important, very real sense, it cannot be taught (see Eskey, 1986). Perhaps we are unwilling to believe this. Perhaps it is because we feel we need to teach *something* in isolated reading classes that we have typically turned to teaching not reading, not text comprehension or meaning construction, but reading strategies and study skills.

One of the complaints in the early 1980s against traditional approaches to teaching L2 writing was that students were not really writing but rather manipulating language, not using language to communicate but rather to practice grammar or to practice larger components of written texts, such as rhetorical patterns (Kroll, 1991). In traditional approaches to teaching writing, we assumed that by teaching students to write a topic sentence, to select and explain three examples, and to write a conclusion, we had given students all the building blocks necessary to create virtually any expository text (Kroll, 1991).

Don't we see the same kinds of narrowly focused aims in current traditional reading courses, aims of learning vocabulary by studying prefixing and suffixing, aims of identifying main idea and supporting details, aims of recognizing discourse features? Certainly, the ability to recognize discourse features and a large number of vocabulary items helps make reading easier, but if these abilities are set as the goals for the course rather than as a means of facilitating the reading of specific texts selected for a real purpose, we are back to teaching skills. More sophisticated ones, to be sure, but for all their sophistication, they still do not get to the heart of the question of how to help L2 students read.

Ironically, it may be that both proficient and less skilled L2 readers already have and can make use of the entire gamut of skills that we teach in reading classes but use these skills to different degrees in L2 reading (Sarig, 1987). L2 reading classes may not even need to teach skills, which L2 readers may already possess, but could provide the opportunity for L2 readers to discover *through meaningful contact with L2 texts* which combination of skills works best for them in L2.

In the 1980s, we recognized that if the purpose of writing in a writing class is to practice writing in order to get ready for "real" assignments, students were being seriously handicapped in the development of their ability to decide what to write and how to write it. As long as reading classes have no other purpose than to develop skills, to practice reading, or to learn language, attempts to get students to read with real direction are similarly doomed. The reading class becomes a hothouse, self-referential and solipsistic, in which students spend all their time rehearsing and never performing, getting ready to read while real reading is deferred. (See Blanton, this volume, on reading as performance.) When we teach a reading or writing course as a skills course, we act as though real reading and writing will come later, once our students know where to look for the main idea of a text or how to write a topic sentence. But it makes no sense to defer real reading and writing until students are adequately prepared, because adequate preparation is itself a result of a purposeful plunge into the struggle with meaning.

Reading researchers, paralleling writing researchers, have for years indicated that reading instruction must be more concerned with meaning and less with skills. For over twenty years in the literature on teaching reading to native speakers, researchers have been calling for a focus on meaning (Goodman, 1976; Smith, 1971); for ten years in the L2 literature (Carrell, 1983a; Hudson, 1982), researchers have emphasized the importance of text content over reading skills. Yet as lately as the December 1989 *TESOL Quarterly*, Carrell, Pharis, &

Liberto must again call for approaches to teaching reading, including semantic mapping and ETR, which will aid students not in developing skills and strategies with which to confront *any* text, but in comprehending specific texts.[7] Hudson (1991) makes a similar plea for ESL reading. Isolated L2 reading classes seem to have allowed us to get lost in details, not of decoding skills as in the past, but of main idea hunting and learning word suffixes and prefixes, and to lose sight of reading as a purposeful, real-world activity.

The benefits of integrating L2 reading and writing in the same classroom thus seem undeniable and, since reading and writing draw upon the same cognitive text world (Carson, this volume; Kucer, 1985), reciprocal. The chapters of this book detail the ways in which reading in the composition classroom sustains writing.

But writing, even beyond providing a purpose for reading, clearly also enhances reading. Anticipating in writing the content of a text, i.e., writing before reading (Spack, 1990), primes schemata and thereby facilitates reading a text. Interacting with the content of a text by annotating and engaging the text in dialogue brings home more clearly the reader's own understanding of the text, for it is often through the pressure of new or opposing ideas that our own ideas may become clear to us, just as it is often by expressing the ideas of others in our own words (in effect, translating them), that these other or new ideas begin to have meaning. Writing is a way of reading better "because it requires the learner to reconstruct the structure and meaning of ideas expressed by another writer. To possess an idea that one is reading about requires competence in regenerating the idea, competence in learning how to write the ideas of another" (Squire, 1983, cited in Sternglass, 1986, p. 2). (See Zamel, 1992, for a further discussion of writing to read.) Furthermore, as a student engages a reading text by responding or reacting to it in writing, in effect communicating with the writer through text, the essentially social nature of literacy becomes unmistakable.

Social Acts of Reading and Writing

Research on cognitive processes has had tremendous influence on reading and writing theory, on writing pedagogy, and to some degree on reading classroom practice. But writing classrooms have counterbalanced this emphasis on cognitive processes with an awareness of the social dimension of writing. Writing classrooms have, for example, been much concerned with audience, the discourse communities into which we hope to initiate our students as writers. The recognition of the social dimension of writing has also become commonplace in writing classrooms in the form of peer responding, which has helped to break down the isolation of the individual author and to work against the very notion of individual authorship (Allaei & Connor, 1990; Leki, 1990b; Mittan, 1989).

Like writing, reading is not only a cognitive process. It is intricately bound up in a social, historical, and cultural network, one we are only beginning to explore (Carson, 1992). As readers, we are members of discourse communities formed primarily through reading the same texts. It is this broad social dimension of reading that allows us teachers and textbook writers to agree on the main idea of a text, for example, and to make assertions about textual misinterpretations we think our students make. If we agree on the main idea of a text, it is not because the main idea mechanically signals itself in the text (it is obviously not always the last sentence of the introduction or the first sentence of some fixed paragraph), but because we share the writer's discourse community. An important key to helping our students read better may also lie in clearer classroom recognition of this social dimension of reading.

But reading is also an essentially social activity in the more immediate sense that the text is where a specific reader and writer meet. Reader response theory describes text as the locus of struggle over meaning, suggesting the importance not of the text (where meaning does *not* reside) but of the encounter between individual human beings mediated through the text (Dasenbrock, 1991; Fish, 1980; Nystrand, 1989; Robinson, 1991; Rubin, 1988). L2 reading research, particularly in an interactive view of reading, also does not locate meaning in the text and has shown us repeatedly that the meaning of a given text depends on who is reading it (Anderson et al., 1977; Carrell, 1983a; Parry, 1987; Steffenson & Joag-Dev, 1984). Each reader's reading of a text is somewhat different. Different readings are created not only by different readers but also over time. Thus the Shakespeare we read today is not and cannot be the same work that people read in Shakespeare's time. (See Dasenbrock, 1991 for the L1 debate about the ontological status of historical texts.) In fact, we count on that very fluidity of meaning over time when we advise students to leave a draft aside for a few days before rereading it for revision.

Yet despite this recognition of the instability of meaning, we often seem to entertain only in theory the idea that meaning does not reside in the text. In practice, our insistent privileging of cognitive strategies betrays our view of the text as a puzzle. If meaning did reside in the text, then well-honed cognitive strategies would be sufficient to unravel meaning. But a text is not a puzzle or a dictator; it is a partner in a dialogue, in a negotiation. Yet little is done to give students practice in negotiating meaning mediated by text or to foster the notion that meaning is created by the interaction of a specific reader and a text. In our reading classes a single, privileged interpretation of a text dominates, as is made clear by post-reading comprehension checks with their predetermined answers, ones that the teacher knows and the students must guess.

Ironically, this cognitive bias may be increased by reading theory's current view of reading as interactive, locating meaning in the interaction between the reader and the text, but with no clear role for the writer. The interactive view does, however, leave room for a social dimension in terms of the individual reader's formation as a social being. Schema theory, on which interactive views of reading are based, clearly views schema formation as the result of individual experience *within* a social context. (See, for instance, Anderson et al., 1977; Flynn, 1983; Kintsch & Greene, 1978; and Steffenson & Joag-Dev, 1984 for descriptions of different stances taken before texts by different genders and sociocultural groups.)

Nevertheless, we seem consistently to ignore the social dimension of reading. The usual practice in our reading classrooms, for example, has worked against the idea of the classroom as an interpretive community and instead often sends our students home to read, alone, already published texts, by authors they do not know, writing about settings with which they are not familiar. Significantly, it is only when they return to class that they learn, from the teacher, how well their personal struggle with the text went. Certainly, the struggle with meaning is internal, and cognitive, but this struggle can also be made external, public, and social. By so doing, we can balance the action of individual cognition with the power of social interaction to shape and restructure meaning.

On the Brink of a Change: The Transactional Reading/Writing Classroom

While the attitudes and activities described above persist in reading classes, we seem now to be on the brink of a shift in reading pedagogy similar to the one that occurred in writing over the last ten years and at least partly occasioned by the growing interest, of which this volume is evidence, in bringing reading systematically into writing classrooms. If we use reading and writing reciprocally in L2 classrooms, focusing less on teaching language, reading, or writing and more on allowing students to engage intellectually with text, this engagement with text fosters a view of reading and writing as active construction of meaning. The text can now legitimately be read with varying degrees of attention since the text has peaks and valleys of importance for the reader; comprehension of each section of the text is no longer necessary; the significance of main ideas and details becomes clearer as the student determines which ones further his or her purposes; structures of knowledge are built that can be used to read/write other texts on the same subject; and the student reader/writer must come to terms with the transformation of old knowledge and incorporation of new knowledge into existing schemata (Bereiter & Scardamalia, 1987). Most importantly, teaching reading in the composition classroom no longer defers real reading until the future; reading is done for present, legitimate purposes.

Reading in composition classrooms may also give reading a social dimension that we have ignored by operating as though reading can only be individual and by directing our students to read at home alone and then answer questions about the text. Our students' facility in reading need not improve only through reading published texts. By reading each other's texts in a reading/writing class, students directly confront the elusive, slippery nature of meaning. A writer intends a meaning; a reader perceives something else. When the reader and writer are face to face (especially with the support of a teacher's expert guidance), a real negotiation over meaning can take place.

If we are convinced by an interactive view of reading, we need to permit and encourage our students to become more active in reading — not merely to be led by the text, but to make it their own by responding to whatever is salient *to them* rather than merely pursuing the writer's meaning. This means that for some texts, the author's main idea may be entirely irrelevant to the reader's purpose and will play no role in the reader's use of the text. In this way we might see the metaphor of interactive as extending beyond its cognitive dimension, i.e., beyond the idea that both top-down and bottom-up strategies interact in reading. In a reading/writing class, interactive takes on a transactional meaning, implying an essential interface of reading and writing (Sternglass, 1986), by which we understand (1) that reading and writing interact, or function reciprocally; (2) that the reader can interact more actively with the text by viewing reading as dialogic and by writing to the text (responding to it, for example, with notes in the margin or in a reading journal); and (3) that in reading, the reader is also interacting with a writer who wrote for genuine purposes of communication.

In many writing classrooms these days, students read each other's writing and respond to it to help the writer improve that draft. In a reading/writing classroom, this activity can take on a new role, not only the one of various kinds of text repair or editing but of students using each other's writing as sources for their own writing, considering and addressing their classmates' points of view, and citing each other, not only published work, in their bibliographies.

Even with published texts, by reading them together in groups and interpreting as they go, students witness competing meanings and clarify their own understandings through discussion, debate, and the need to translate their understandings into their own words. By ultimately forming joint interpretations of their readings rather than learning from the teacher what the meaning of a text is, students experience the social dimension inherent in communicating through a text, a dimension too long neglected in ESL reading instruction. By making reading social, we externalize the process and demonstrate, or allow students to demonstrate to each other, that reading is meaning construction, that competing meanings are generated by texts read by different people or even by the same people at different times. (See Section III of this volume, on Social Perspectives, for further examples of ESL reading instruction that aims at these goals.)

The notion of meaning as negotiation and text as the locus of struggle suggests another insight that current views on writing may have to offer reading specialists. In post-reading comprehension questions, reading classrooms maintain an emphasis on error that many writing classrooms have chosen to downplay. Writing research has emphasized the futility and the negative, stifling effect of marking all the errors L2 students make in writing (Leki, 1990a; Zamel, 1985). As writing specialists tried to come to terms with the problem of errors in L2 students' writing, it became increasingly clear that it makes more sense to focus on what students can do well, rather than constantly reminding them of what they know they cannot do well, and to intervene in their writing process to help them do what they cannot do. In many writing classes these days, students show their drafts to others, including the teacher, as the drafts are developing in order to get guidance and feedback on their writing. Most writing teachers are convinced of the value of that kind of intervention. How might such an attitude be adopted in reading instruction in order to promote the goals of helping L2 students learn to read with ease, pleasure, and understanding? How can we intervene in our students' reading processes?

In a first step, again by analogy to procedures in writing classes in which teachers refuse to appropriate their students' writing, reading teachers might consider refraining from appropriating the meaning of the texts their students read. In other words, in helping students read, the question should not be "What is the author saying here? What is the author's main idea?" but rather "What did you get out of this? What do you make of this part? How does it happen that different class members understand this text differently?" While students lose little by not getting the main idea of an ESL reading passage about dreams or animal behavior, they gain a great deal if they are able to make some portion of that text their own, linguistically, rhetorically, or conceptually.

A de-emphasis of error also implies our acceptance of the idea that our students cannot understand everything they read and that they do not need to. They need to read actively and selectively, picking out what they can use to advance their own agendas. Furthermore, since any individual act of understanding is a reconstruction and in that sense necessarily a misreading (see Bartholomae, 1986), we must also accept that our students will not interpret texts the same way we do.[8] But negotiating through their understandings of a text with other students requires the struggle with meaning that leads to the ability to engage in constructing meaning with power and confidence.

We can also make our struggle with meaning visible by letting students see our reading processes. Many writing teachers write with their students and share their drafts to demonstrate their writing processes (Spack, 1984). In teaching reading we might consider doing more reading out loud in our classes and doing so in a way that demonstrates our reading processes, thinking aloud as we read, as subjects are asked to do in protocol analyses (Davey, 1983). Rather than only giving individual students individual exercises in chunking, we might show them by reading out loud how we ourselves chunk groups of words together, how we use intonation to get us through heavy embedding, how we backtrack when we have lost the thread of the text, how we ignore incongruities or puzzling words for as long as possible before interrupting the flow of our reading, and, most importantly, how we work to tie the incoming text to patterns of information we already know. To help our students read faster, instead of timing them and pushing them to read faster individually, by reading out loud we keep them to a brisker pace than they might normally adopt when reading silently, and yet through intonation, pauses, and backtracking we also give them additional cues on how we are interpreting a text. By the same token, like writing conferences, reading conferences in which individual students reveal and demonstrate their reading processes to us may also uncover unproductive or self-defeating approaches to reading and allow us to intervene directly in the students' construction of meaning from a text.

Conclusion

While the research findings in reading and writing echo each other, teaching practices have not kept pace with each other, especially not in helping advanced ESL students read. The separation of reading from writing may be the result of our natural inclination to divide things up in order to deal with them, or it may be that the inclination to divide language up is a legacy of the ALM days, but, as this volume demonstrates, the time seems to have come for a new reintegration of reading and writing classrooms rather than a division of language into atomized, learnable bits or skills. The fact that reading and writing processes can be isolated does not mean that teaching those isolated processes is the best way to help our students read and write with greater ease. The construction of meaning, whether through reading or writing, is a messy, organic, and holistic task, perhaps less amenable to generic attempts to preempt problems than we once thought. Bringing the world of text together in one classroom gives every promise of enhancing our ESL students' ability to both read and write English through the cross-fertilization of reading and writing pedagogy, research, and theory.

Notes

1. Evidence from studies of inefficient L1 readers also shows the opposite tendency, excessive and inaccurate guessing about the meaning of a text without enough bottom-up information (Kimmel & MacGinitie, 1984).
2. The picture is actually more complex than this. L1 studies consistently show this pattern of allotting attention (Bereiter & Scardamalia, 1987; Perl, 1979), but at least one L2 study shows that even less-proficient writers also attend to meaning (Raimes, 1985).
3. Among the odd historical divisions within higher education in this country, we might also mention the division in English departments between literature and writing instruction, in certain ways analogous to the division between writing and reading courses: the first in each pair considered more prestigious and more appropriately a concern of higher education.
4. This is not to suggest in any way that there should be exit exams in reading. The wisdom of exit exams in writing is already questionable enough.
5. ESP, adjunct, and sheltered writing courses are the exceptions to this pattern.
6. In the same way, excessive attention to details in inexperienced writers is the symptom, not the cause, of difficulty with the task.
7. These techniques have been used for some time to teach reading to native English-speaking children. For more information on these techniques, see Heimlich & Pittelman (1986), Stahl & Vancil (1986), and Au (1979).
8. It is interesting to note that in certain domains, such as in reading literature, idiosyncratic readings are often prized as more illuminating than pedestrian interpretations of a text. What we admire in the best literary critics and the best scientists is not that they understand texts well but that they extend our understanding of the meaning of a text by moving beyond the standard interpretation rendered by the discourse community for which it is intended.

Works Cited

Allaei, S. K. & Connor, U. M. (1990). Exploring the dynamics of cross-cultural collaboration in writing classrooms. *The Writing Instructor, 10,* 19–28.

Anderson, R. C. & Pearson, P. D. (1984). A schema-theoretic view of basic processes in reading comprehension. In P. D. Pearson (Ed.), *Handbook of reading research* (pp. 255–87). New York: Longman.

Anderson, R. C., Reynolds, R. E., Schallert, D. L., & Goetz, E. T. (1977). Frameworks for comprehending discourse. *American Educational Research Journal, 14,* 367–81.

Arndt, V. (1987). Six writers in search of texts: A protocol-based study of L1 and L2 writing. *ELT Journal, 41,* 257–67.

Au, K. H.-P. (1979). Using the experience-text-relationship method with minority children. *The Reading Teacher, 32,* 677–79.

Bartholomae, D. (1986). Wanderings: Misreadings, miswritings, misunderstandings. In T. Newkirk (Ed.), *Only connect: Uniting reading and writing* (pp. 89–118). Upper Montclair, NJ: Boynton/Cook.

Bartholomae, D. & Petrosky, A. (1990). *Ways of reading.* New York: Bedford/St. Martin's.

Bartholomae, D. & Petrosky, A. (1986). *Facts, artifacts, and counterfacts: A reading and writing course.* Upper Montclair, NJ: Boynton/Cook.

Bazerman, C. (1980). A relationship between reading and writing: The conversational model. *College English, 41,* 656–61.

Bereiter, C. & Scardamalia, M. (1987). *The psychology of written composition.* Hillsdale, NJ: Erlbaum.

Blanton, L. (1987). Reshaping students' perceptions of writing. *ELT Journal, 41,* 112–18.

Carrell, P. L. (1988a). Introduction. In P.L. Carrell, J. Devine, & D. Eskey (Eds.), *Interactive approaches to second language reading* (pp. 1–7). New York: Cambridge University Press.

Carrell, P. L. (1988b). Some causes of text-boundedness and schema interference in ESL reading. In P. L. Carrell, J. Devine, & D. Eskey (Eds.), *Interactive approaches to second language reading* (pp. 101–13). New York: Cambridge University Press.

Carrell, P. L. (1983a). Some issues in studying the role of schemata, or background knowledge, in L2 comprehension. *Reading in a Foreign Language, 1,* 81–92.

Carrell, P. L. (1983b). Three components of background knowledge in reading comprehension. *Language Learning, 33,* 183–205.

Carrell, P. L., Devine, J., & Eskey, D. E. (Eds.). (1988). *Interactive approaches to second language reading.* New York: Cambridge University Press.

Carrell, P. L. & Eisterhold, J.C. (1983). Schema theory and ESL reading pedagogy. *TESOL Quarterly, 17,* 553–73.

Carrell, P. L., Pharis, B.G., & Liberto, J.C. (1989). Metacognitive training for ESL reading. *TESOL Quarterly, 23,* 657–78.

Carson, J. G. (1992). Becoming biliterate: First language influences. *Journal of Second Language Writing, 1,* 53–76.

Christison, M. A. & Krahnke, K. (1986). Student perceptions of academic language study. *TESOL Quarterly, 20,* 61–81.

Clarke, M. (1979). Reading in English and Spanish: Evidence from adult ESL students. *Language Learning, 29,* 121–150.

Cohen, A., Glasman, H., Rosenbaum-Cohen, P. R., Ferrara, J., & Fine, J. (1979). Reading for specialized purposes: Discourse analysis and the use of student informants. *TESOL Quarterly, 13,* 551–64.

Cumming, A. (1989). Writing expertise and second language proficiency. *Language Learning, 39,* 83–141.

Cziko, G. (1978). Differences in first- and second-language reading: The use of syntactic, semantic and discourse constraints. *Canadian Modern Language Journal, 34,* 473–89.

Dasenbrock, R. W. (1991). Do we write the text we read? *College English, 53,* 7–18.

Davey, B. (1983). Think-aloud: Modeling the cognitive processes of reading comprehension. *Journal of Reading, 27,* 219–24.

Devine, J. (1988). A case study of two readers: Models of reading and reading performance. In P. Carrell, J. Devine, & D. Eskey (Eds.), *Interactive approaches to second language reading* (pp. 127–39). New York: Cambridge University Press.

Devine, J., Carrell, P. L., & Eskey, D. E. (Eds.). (1987). *Research in reading in English as a second language.* Washington, DC: TESOL.

Dubin, F., Eskey, D.E., & Grabe, W. (Eds.). (1986). *Teaching second language reading for academic purposes*. Reading, MA: Addison-Wesley.

Elley, W.B. & Mangubhai, F. (1983). The effect of reading on second language learning. *Reading Research Quarterly, 19,* 53–67.

Eskey, D.E. (1986). Theoretical foundations. In F. Dubin, D.E. Eskey, & W. Grabe (Eds.), *Teaching second language reading for academic purposes* (pp. 3–21). Reading, MA: Addison-Wesley.

Eskey, D.E. & Grabe, W. (1988). Interactive models of second language reading: Perspectives on instruction. In P.L. Carrell, J. Devine, and D. Eskey (Eds.), *Interactive approaches to second language reading* (pp. 223–38). New York: Cambridge University Press.

Fish, S. (1980). *Is there a text in this class? The authority of interpretive communities*. Cambridge: Harvard University Press.

Flower, L., Stein, V., Ackerman, J., Kantz, M.J., McCormick, K., & Peck, W.C. (1990). *Reading to write: Exploring a cognitive and social process*. New York: Oxford University Press.

Flynn, E.A. (1983). Gender and reading. *College English, 45,* 236–53.

Gajdusek, L. (1988). Toward wider use of literature in ESL: Why and how. *TESOL Quarterly, 22,* 227–57.

Goodman, K. (1976). Reading: A psycholinguistic guessing game. In H. Singer & R. Ruddell (Eds.), *Theoretical models and processes of reading* (2nd ed.) (pp. 497–505). Newark, DE: International Reading Association.

Grabe, W. (1986). The transition from theory to practice in teaching reading. In F. Dubin, D.E. Eskey, & W. Grabe (Eds.), *Teaching second language reading for academic purposes* (pp. 25–48). Reading, MA: Addison-Wesley.

Hafiz, F.M. & Tudor, I. (1989). Extensive reading and the development of language skills. *ELT Journal, 43,* 1–13.

Hall, C. (1990). Managing the complexity of revising across languages. *TESOL Quarterly, 24,* 43–60.

Hatch, E., Polin, P., & Part, S. (1970). Acoustic scanning or syntactic processing. Paper presented at the meeting of the Western Psychological Association, San Francisco.

Heimlich, J.E. & Pittelman, S.D. (1986). *Semantic mapping: Classroom applications*. Newark, DE: International Reading Association.

Horowitz, D. (1986a). Essay examination prompts and the teaching of academic writing. *English for Specific Purposes, 5,* 107–20.

Horowitz, D. (1986b). Process, not product: Less than meets the eye. *TESOL Quarterly, 20,* 141–44.

Hosenfeld, C. (1984). Case studies of ninth grade readers. In J.C. Alderson & A.H. Urquhart (Eds.), *Reading in a foreign language* (pp. 231–44). New York: Longman.

Hudson, T. (1991). A content comprehension approach to reading English for science and technology. *TESOL Quarterly, 24*(1), 77–104.

Hudson, T. (1982). The effect of induced schemata on the "shortcircuit" in L2 reading: Non-decoding factors in L2 reading performance. *Language Learning, 32,* 1–31.

Janopoulos, M. (1986). The relationship of pleasure of reading and second language writing proficiency. *TESOL Quarterly, 20,* 763–68.

Johns, A. (1981). Necessary English: A faculty survey. *TESOL Quarterly, 15,* 51–57.

Johnson, D.M. & Roen, D.H. (Eds.). (1989). *Richness in writing: Empowering ESL students*. New York: Longman.

Jones, S. & Tetroe, J. (1987). Composing in a second language. In A. Matsuhashi (Ed.), *Writing in real time* (pp. 34–57). New York: Longman.

Kimmel, S. & MacGinitie, W.H. (1984). Identifying children who use a preservative text processing strategy. *Reading Research Quarterly, 19,* 162–72.

Kintsch, W. & Greene, E. (1978). The role of culture-specific schemata in the comprehension and recall of stories. *Discourse Processes, 1,* 1–13.

Krapels, A. (1990). An overview of second language writing process research. In B. Kroll (Ed.), *Second language writing* (pp. 37–56). New York: Cambridge University Press.

Krashen, S.D. (1988). Do we learn to read by reading? The relationship between free reading and reading ability. In D. Tannen (Ed.), *Linguistics in context: Connecting observation and understanding* (pp. 269–98). Norwood, NJ: Ablex.

Krashen, S.D. (1984). *Writing: Research, theory, and applications.* Oxford: Pergamon.

Kroll, B. (1991). Teaching writing in the ESL context. In M. Celce-Murcia (Ed.), *Teaching English as a second or foreign language* (2nd ed.) (pp. 245–63). New York: Newbury House.

Kroll, B. (Ed.). (1990). *Second language writing.* New York: Cambridge University Press.

Kucer, S. (1985). The making of meaning: Reading and writing as processes. *Written Communication, 2,* 317–36.

Leki, I. (1990a). Coaching from the margins: Issues in written response. In B. Kroll (Ed.), *Second language writing* (pp. 57–68). New York: Cambridge University Press.

Leki, I. (1990b). Potential problems with peer responding in ESL writing classes. *CATESOL Journal, 3,* 5–19.

McLaughlin, B. (1987). Reading in a second language: Studies of adult and child learners. In S.R. Goldman & H.T. Trueba (Eds.), *Becoming literate in English as a second language* (pp. 57–70). Norwood, NJ: Ablex.

Mittan, R. (1989). The peer review process: Harnessing students' communicative power. In D.M. Johnson & D.H. Roen (Eds.), *Richness in writing: Empowering ESL students* (pp. 207–19). New York: Longman.

Mlynarczyk, R. (1992). Student choice: An alternative to teacher-selected reading material. *College ESL, 1*(2), 1–8.

Nystrand, M. (1989). A social-interactive model of writing. *Written Communication, 6,* 66–85.

Parry, K.J. (1987). Reading in a second culture. In J. Devine, P.L. Carrell, & D.E. Eskey (Eds.), *Research in reading in English as a second language* (pp. 59–70). Washington, DC: TESOL.

Perl, S. (1979). The composing processes of unskilled college writers. *Research in the Teaching of English, 13,* 317–36.

Petrosky, A. (1982). From story to essay: Reading and writing. *College Composition and Communication, 33,* 19–37.

Radecki, P.M. & Swales, J.M. (1988). ESL students' reaction to written comments on their written work. *System, 16,* 355–65.

Raimes, A. (1986). Teaching ESL writing: Fitting what we do to what we know. *The Writing Instructor, 5,* 153–66.

Raimes, A. (1985). What unskilled writers do as they write: A classroom study. *TESOL Quarterly, 19,* 229–58.

Reid, J. (1987). ESL Composition: The expectations of the academic audience. *TESOL Newsletter, 21,* 34.

Rigg, P. (1977). The miscue-ESL project. In H.D. Brown, C.A. Yorio, & R.H. Crymes (Eds.), *Teaching and learning ESL: Trends in research and practice. On TESOL '77* (pp. 106–18). Washington, DC: TESOL.

Robinson, D. (1991). Henry James and euphemism. *College English, 53,* 403–27.

Rubin, D.L. (1988). Introduction: Four dimensions of social construction in written communication. In B.A. Rafoth and D.L. Rubin (Eds.), *The social construction of written communication* (pp. 1–33). Norwood, NJ: Ablex.

Rummelhart, D. (1977). Toward an interactive model of reading. In S. Dornic (Ed.), *Attention and performance,* vol. 6 (pp. 573–603). New York: Academic Press.

Sarig, G. (1987). High-level reading and the first and foreign language: Some comparative process data. In J. Devine, P.L. Carrell, & D.E. Eskey (Eds.), *Research in reading in English as a second language* (pp. 105–20). Washington, DC: TESOL.

Silva, T. (1990). ESL composition instruction: Developments, issues and directions. In B. Kroll (Ed.), *Second language writing* (pp. 11–23). New York: Cambridge University Press.

Smith, F. (1971). *Understanding reading: A psycholinguistic analysis of reading and learning to read,* 1st ed. New York: Holt, Rinehart, and Winston.

Spack, R. (1990). *Guidelines: A cross-cultural reading/writing text.* New York: St. Martin's.

Spack, R. (1988). Initiating ESL students into the academic discourse community: How far should we go? *TESOL Quarterly, 22,* 29–51.

Spack, R. (1985). Literature, reading, writing, and ESL: Bridging the gaps. *TESOL Quarterly, 19,* 703–26.

Spack, R. (1984). Invention strategies and the ESL college composition student. *TESOL Quarterly, 18,* 649–70.

Spack, R. & Sadow, C. (1983). Student-teacher working journals in ESL freshman composition. *TESOL Quarterly, 17,* 575–94.

Stahl, S.A. & Vancil, S.J. (1986). Discussion is what makes semantic maps work in vocabulary instruction. *The Reading Teacher, 40,* 62–67.

Stanovich, K.E. (1980). Toward an interactive-compensatory model of individual differences in the development of reading fluency. *Reading Research Quarterly, 16,* 32–71.

Steffensen, M.S. & Joag-Dev, C. (1984). Cultural knowledge and reading. In J.C. Alderson & A.H. Urquhart (Eds.), *Reading in a foreign language* (pp. 48–61). New York: Longman.

Sternglass, M. (1988). *The presence of thought: Introspective accounts of reading and writing.* Norwood, NJ: Ablex.

Sternglass, M. (1986). Introduction. In B. Petersen (Ed.), *Convergences: Transactions in reading and writing* (pp. 1–11). Urbana, IL: NCTE.

Tierney, R.J. & Pearson, P.D. (1983). Toward a composing model of reading. *Language Arts, 60,* 568–69.

van Naerssen, M. (1985). Relaxed reading in ESP. *TESOL Newsletter, 19,* 2.

Zamel, V. (1992). Writing one's way into reading. *TESOL Quarterly, 26,* 463–85.

Zamel, V. (1985). Responding to student writing. *TESOL Quarterly, 19,* 79–101.

Zamel, V. (1983). The composing processes of advanced ESL students: Six case studies. *TESOL Quarterly, 17,* 165–87.

Classroom Activities

One of the most critical "reciprocal themes" that Leki draws from ESL reading and writing is the social nature of these processes and the importance of small-group work for reading as well as for writing. As she suggests, "By making reading social, we externalize the process and demonstrate, or allow students to demonstrate to each other, that reading is meaning construction, that competing meanings are generated by texts read by different people or even by the same people at different times." With this in mind, invite students to read and interpret together a text that they choose as a group (perhaps a reading from a newspaper, a textbook, or a section from a longer book). Students can develop their own purposes for reading this text together (to gain inspiration for writing a paper, perhaps, or to develop their understanding of a current event or other relevant topic), and then work together on reaching their own interpretations of the text ("making meaning"). If students already collaborate in peer response groups for writing, it would be helpful for them to note the similarities and differences in working in peer response groups for reading as well.

You can also foster students' involvement in text by having them read their peers' work. Leki points out, "By reading each other's texts in a reading/writing class, students directly confront the elusive, slippery nature of meaning. [. . .] When a reader and writer are face to face (especially with the support of a teacher's expert guidance), a real negotiation over meaning can take place." You may want to go a step beyond peer response and ask students to use each other's writing as source material for their own essays (making sure to use proper citation, of course). When students respond to and build on each other's ideas, they will better understand the concept of reading and writing as a purposeful means of communication between a writer and an audience.

Thinking about Teaching

Leki notes that many teachers already share their writing processes with students and suggests that a similar strategy would be appropriate for demonstrating reading processes. If you decide to engage in this activity, keep track of your own reading processes in your teaching journal. What do you notice about yourself as a reader? How do you create meaning from words on the page? Then demonstrate your reading processes to students by reading aloud to the class. Provide them with a copy of the text or project it onto a screen using a computer or an overhead projector. Think aloud as you read, and give students the opportunity to take notes on the processes you use to construct meaning from the text. Then have students read to each other and think aloud in pairs, taking notes on one another's processes. Students can share these notes with each other, and then share their work in a whole-class discussion that emphasizes the importance of reading purposefully and of making meaning from language in order to engage their own internal motivations for reading.

5

Approaches to Grammar Instruction

Teaching grammar remains a contentious issue in many college and university English departments. Though a number of studies have addressed the question of whether grammar instruction leads to improved writing, there has been little consensus, and teachers of composition still find themselves embroiled in debate as they define their programs and plan their courses. The debate is particularly relevant to the teaching of developmental writers, who some argue suffer simply from a lack of foundation in grammar, usage, and mechanics. The writers in this chapter acknowledge the politicization of the issue. They move, however, to a middle ground: Grammar instruction should be an effective transfer of the rules to students' own writing; in this way, students become more aware of their options as writers. "Practice of forms improves usage," Janice Neuleib and Irene Brosnahan suggest, citing Henry Meckel, "whereas memorization of the rules does not." Constance Weaver, meanwhile, suggests directed activities for teaching grammar in the context of students' own writing.

Teaching Grammar to Writers

Janice Neuleib and Irene Brosnahan

Janice Neuleib and Irene Brosnahan situate their ideas within contemporary arguments about whether or not to teach grammar. In this article, first published in 1987 in the Journal of Basic Writing, *they examine*

*findings from research and address the need to teach grammar to under-
graduate students, especially those who are studying to be writing teachers. In their classrooms, Neuleib and Brosnahan have observed the ineffectiveness of having students simply memorize grammar concepts,
especially students' "inability to apply grammar to editing problems." To
ameliorate such difficulties, they believe it is important to teach students
to recognize patterns of errors, "to understand how language works."*

At a recent workshop for high school and community college teachers, an earnest young high school teacher explained forcefully to
an experienced community college teacher that grammar was of no
use in teaching writing. The high school teacher cited the now-famous
Braddock, Lloyd-Jones, and Schoer quotation. She said that knowing
grammar had no effect on writing ability, insisting that "all the
research" counterbalanced any intuitive and experiential evidence the
older teacher might have to offer. The young teacher had, however,
misquoted the passage; it says: "the teaching of *formal* [emphasis
ours] grammar has a negligible or, because it usually displaces some
instruction and practice in composition, even a harmful effect on the
improvement of writing."

Taking the words *teaching of formal grammar* to mean *knowing
grammar* is a serious mistake. What the research cited by Braddock
et al. indicates is that instruction in traditional grammar over a limited period of time (a semester or less in the research studies being
discussed) showed no positive effect on students' writing. In fact, several research studies and much language and composition theory
argue for certain types of grammar instruction, when effective methods are used for clearly defined purposes. When writers learn grammar, as opposed to teachers merely "covering" it, the newly acquired
knowledge contributes to writing ability.

In separate essays on grammar, both Kolln (139) and Neuleib
(148) point out that the often-quoted passage in Braddock et al. was
preceded by "Uncommon, however, is carefully conducted research
which studies composition over an extended period of time" (37). Few
people seem to pay attention to the qualification, however. Also,
another 1963 study, one that Kolln reviews, has attracted much less
notice than *Research in Written Composition.* Yet that other study, by
Meckel, is more extensive and thorough in its conclusions and recommendations than is the Braddock work. Meckel's work shows that
major questions still existed in 1963 about the teaching of grammar.[1]

Meckel points to three crucial issues (981): First, none of the
grammar studies up to 1963 extended beyond one semester — "a time
span much too short to permit development of the degree of conceptu-
alization necessary for transfer to take place." Second, none of the
studies had to do with editing or revising, that is "with situations in

which pupils are recasting the structure of a sentence or a paragraph." Finally, none of the studies makes comparisons between students who had demonstrated knowledge of grammar and those of equal intelligence who had none.

Meckel's recommendations indicate that studies with systematic grammatical instruction ran too short a time or that the research involved presentation of rules without assured student comprehension. Meckel offers several important conclusions (981): (1) Although grammar has not been shown to improve writing skills, "there is no conclusive evidence, however, that grammar has *no* transfer value in developing composition skill." (2) More research is needed to be done on "the kind of grammatical knowledge that may reasonably be expected to transfer to writing."[2] (3) Sometimes *formal grammar* has meant grammar without application; grammar should be taught systematically with applications. (4) "There are more efficient methods of securing *immediate* [Meckel's emphasis] improvement in the writing of pupils, both in sentence structure and usage, than systematic grammatical instruction." (5) Practice of forms improves usage whereas memorization of rules does not.

In spite of Meckel's work being little known, trends in the profession were confirming his conclusions. The years following 1963 were filled with sentence-combining research that showed statistically significant results on methods that relied on practice with forms (e.g., Mellon; O'Hare). This research culminated in the 1978 study by Daiker, Kerek, and Morenberg in which college students made significant progress in writing, including surface structure and punctuation, without any kind of instruction except in sentence-combining exercises and essay writing. Sentence combining, a method of teaching grammar without explicit grammar instruction, fits with Meckel's earlier conclusion on the effectiveness of practice of forms as opposed to the learning of rules.

Shaughnessy in her 1977 *Errors and Expectations* developed a new method of helping students with writing by using grammar. Working with open-admissions students, she developed a form of grammar instruction that has since been called error analysis. Error analysis fits with Meckel's recommendation that students work only on the errors in their own writing and not on rules external to that writing. Teachers gear instruction only to the needs of the students. Shaughnessy shows many error patterns which teachers can use to understand each student's needs. Shaughnessy offers an approach to error excluding formal grammar instruction, but including grammar at every step.

D'Eloia in the *Journal of Basic Writing* explained the reason for the grammatical approach to basic writing instruction introduced by Shaughnessy: ". . . something was radically wrong with the research design [of earlier studies which rejected grammar instruction] or with the instruction in grammar itself. . . . They [basic writing teachers] cannot bring themselves to believe that units combining the analysis of a grammatical principle with well-structured proofreading, imitation, paraphrase, and sentence consolidation exercises, and with directed writing assignments could fail to produce more significant results in both fluency and error control" (2). D'Eloia then offers applied grammar activities effective with basic writers similar to those in Shaughnessy's book.

More recently, Bartholomae in "The Study of Error" shows how instructors can discover error-producing language patterns in student writing. He shows that correcting these patterns requires special insight on the part of teachers. Says Bartholomae, "An error . . . can only be understood as evidence of intention. . . . A writer's activity is linguistic and rhetorical activity; it can be different but never random. The task for both teacher and researcher, then, is to discover the grammar of *that* [Bartholomae's emphasis] coherence. . . ." (255).

Harris demonstrates this error-analysis approach to a specific problem. She shows that the fragmented free modifier can indicate linguistic growth. Rather than being a case for the red pencil, the fragmented free modifier is often a chance for a teacher to encourage growing linguistic strength. Being able, however, to recognize such indication of growth and using it to help a student develop requires sophisticated grammatical knowledge on the part of the teacher.

Student-centered approaches similar to those illustrated by Harris and Bartholomae demonstrate how grammar can be effectively used in teaching. Of course, merely covering grammar from a workbook would detract from student achievement. Teaching grammar from a traditional grammar text would be worse. DeBeaugrande explains why grammar texts do not teach students either grammar or writing. He argues that teachers need to understand grammar if they are to help improve students' writing. He attacks grammar textbooks, though, saying that they are written for and by grammarians who find the concepts easy since they "know what the terms mean" (358). He calls for a "learner's grammar" taught by techniques that are accurate, workable, economical, compact, operational, and immediate (364). He illustrates some of the techniques, many of which expand and extend Shaughnessy's and D'Eloia's patterns.

Shaughnessy, D'Eloia, Bartholomae, Harris, and DeBeaugrande all illustrate how grammar instruction improves writing skills. Teachers, however, need grammatical knowledge to use the methods illustrated. To analyze errors and to discover language patterns, teachers need to do more than "cover" grammar. They need to be able to work out exercises of the types illustrated by Shaughnessy and D'Eloia, exercises patterned to students' individual language problems.

Yet, received knowledge in the profession seems to legislate in another direction. A few years ago, every time we did a workshop in the schools, teachers were shocked when we said that studies showed that teaching traditional grammar would not improve students' abilities as writers. More recently we have found many teachers too ready to assume that they can omit grammar instruction because it will not help students to write better. These assumptions are reinforced by journal articles which reject formal grammar instruction.[3]

This dismissal of grammar teaching is unfortunate not only because practice has shown that teachers must know grammar to analyze student errors but also because many questions regarding grammar instruction are worth studying. Fundamental questions concern what kind of grammar is being taught, how it is being taught, and what the rationale for that teaching is. Finally, we as a profession need to ask if we understand grammar and the nature of language.

In our opinion, the preparation of teachers is the crucial issue in teaching effectiveness. A confused teacher increases student perplexity. Arguing against the teaching of grammar in the lower grades, Sanborn tells of a teacher who was confused about the difference between a participle and a gerund: The teacher said "being" in "Being accused of something I didn't do made me mad" was a participle (73). Of course, traditional grammar is replete with ambiguities in its terminology. The term *participle* is ambiguous in that it is both a form term (for a verb) and a function term (modifying a noun, another ambiguity), and the term *gerund* is a function term (functioning in a nominal position) with an implied form (a verb form ending in -*ing*). If our profession had prepared the teacher well, she would have been aware of the ambiguities in the grammar. If some teachers want to teach eight parts of speech in English, for instance, they need to know that the parts of speech are defined neatly, sensibly, and logically by inflectional forms in Latin but that they are defined inconsistently and illogically by mixing form and function in English. Unless teachers are informed about the imperfections of traditional grammar, students will fail to understand it and thereby to learn and retain it.

Superficial retention became painfully obvious to us in a recent survey we conducted in an English grammar course required of upper-class students seeking teacher certification in English. At the beginning of the course, the prospective teachers filled out a questionnaire and took a test in grammar. The questionnaire asked when the prospective teachers had been taught grammar, what kind of grammatical activities they had had, and how they rated themselves on various types of grammatical knowledge. Of the twenty-four participants in the study, twenty-three reported having studied grammar at two or more levels of schooling (elementary school, junior high, high school, college), and fifteen at three or more levels. All reported having learned grammar through a variety of activities such as diagramming sentences, memorizing grammatical terms and labeling parts of speech, identifying and correcting grammatical errors, writing sentences and paragraphs with grammatical forms indicated, and so on. They also rated themselves rather high (mostly 3 or above on a scale of 1 to 5) in most grammatical skills listed, particularly in knowing names of and identifying parts of speech and parts of sentences, standard grammatical usage, and correct punctuation rules and applications.

The results of the grammar test, given with the questionnaire, however, indicated little retention of formal grammatical knowledge and an inability to apply grammar to editing problems. Only three out of twenty-four prospective teachers could accurately name the eight parts of speech — most of them could name four or five (usually noun, verb, adjective, adverb), but function terms like subject and object were mixed in. Most participants could name the two important parts of a sentence and count the number of sentences in a given passage taken from Warriner (58), but no one could accurately count the number of clauses in the paragraph. Some participants even counted fewer clauses than sentences. Although most of these prospective teachers knew what a verb was, only half the group could pick out a transitive verb, and no one could identify an intransitive verb. Only six could find the solitary passive verb in the passage. A prepositional phrase was easily identified, but only two participants correctly picked out an adverbial clause, and only four found an adjective clause. Quite a few people labeled phrases as clauses, apparently not knowing the difference between phrases, clauses, and sentences. Thus, an obvious discrepancy existed between the prospective teachers' perceptions of their formal grammar knowledge and their demonstrated knowledge.

The grammar test also contained two sentences which the participants were to punctuate. They also had to explain their reasons for using each punctuation mark as they did:

1. Please turn off the light its much too bright

2. I was anxious to go shopping but my mother who is usually so organized was taking her time today.

Only seven participants, less than a third of the group, could punctuate sentence 1 correctly; many either used a comma to separate the two clauses and/or neglected the apostrophe for *its*. With sentence 2, almost everyone separated the nonrestrictive clause with a pair of commas, and thirteen of them put a comma before *but*. As for providing the rules of punctuation, only three participants could explain the punctuation in sentence 1 in appropriate grammatical terms, and only one participant could do so for sentence 2. A number of the participants offered explanations involving pauses and meaning, while others misused grammatical terms. For the majority of these prospective teachers, therefore, punctuation rules had not been learned at the conscious operational level. Of course, we realize that the performance of this group of prospective teachers cannot be generalized to all students who have studied grammar, but having taught grammar to similar upperclass students in the last fifteen years, we can say that their lack of formal grammatical knowledge is typical.

We would like to suggest that the first step in increasing teachers' understanding of grammar is to develop a clear definition of the term. Theorists as disparate as Kolln and Hartwell stress the confusion in the definition of grammar. Kolln points out that the Braddock et al. report did not define "formal grammar," so conclusions could not be confirmed. In addressing this need for definition, Hartwell builds upon W. Nelson Francis's 1954 "Revolution in Grammar" to define five grammars: Grammar 1 is intrinsic knowledge of language rules and patterns that people use without knowing they use them; Grammar 2 is the linguistic science that studies the system of Grammar 1; Grammar 3 merely involves linguistic etiquette, such as calling "he ain't" bad grammar; Grammar 4 is "school grammar," the system that is oversimplified in traditional handbooks and workbooks; Grammar 5, stylistic grammar, uses grammatical terms to teach prose style, in the manner of Lanham, Williams, Christensen, and Strunk and White (Hartwell 109–10). Hartwell stresses that these five grammars often do not match. They are pieces of puzzles that fit into different pictures or that overlap untidily in the same picture. Without being aware of the mismatch between Grammar 4, "school grammar," and Grammar 1, intuitive grammar, many teachers teach Grammar 4 as if it made perfect sense.

We strongly feel that writing teachers need to study the historical background of grammar, be well-acquainted with better descriptions of language (that is, with Grammar 2, linguistic studies, as well as Grammar 5, stylistic grammar), and appreciate relations among different grammars. Still, teachers should not begin to teach linguistics in their writing classes. College level linguistics is not the solution for junior and senior high school students. Rather, when teachers understand how language works, they can make the description of the language accessible to students.

The challenge now is in the area of teacher training and retraining. At the end of the semester, the prospective teachers described in the study above had been exposed to the history of language study and to many of the concepts reviewed here. They went on to learn that to work with basic writers at any level, teachers have to do the hard part. They have to understand stylistic choices, and they have to analyze errors so that they can show students how language works. When teachers do more than "cover" grammar, writers will improve their writing by using the grammar they have learned.

Notes

1. For a thorough review of the research, see Meckel; for a summary of Meckel's findings, see Kolln.

2. Sentence-combining research represents at least one kind of grammatical knowledge that has proved to be transferable to writing. See Neuleib for a summary of sentence-combining research through that date.
3. Hartwell's "Grammar, Grammars, and the Teaching of Grammar" illustrates the sort of dismissal of grammar that encourages this attitude in teachers. Hartwell does mention error analysis, but in his conclusion he calls for a halt to all grammar research. The message teachers often carry from such an article is to abandon grammar instruction of any type.

Works Cited

Bartholomae, David. "The Study of Error." *College Composition and Communication* 31 (1980): 253–69.

Braddock, Richard, Richard Lloyd-Jones, and Lowell Schoer. *Research in Written Composition.* Urbana, IL: National Council of Teachers of English, 1963.

Christensen, Francis. "A Generative Rhetoric of the Sentence." *College Composition and Communication* 14 (1963): 155–61.

Daiker, Donald, Andrew Kerek, and Max Morenberg. "Sentence-Combining and Syntactic Maturity in Freshman English." *College Composition and Communication* 29 (1978): 36–41.

DeBeaugrande, Robert. "Forward to the Basics: Getting Down to Grammar." *College Composition and Communication* 35 (1984): 358–67.

D'Eloia, Sarah. "The Uses — and Limits — of Grammar." *Journal of Basic Writing* 1 (1977): 1–48.

Francis, W. Nelson. "Revolution in Grammar." *Quarterly Journal of Speech* 40 (1954): 299–312.

Harris, Muriel. "Mending the Fragmented Free Modifier." *College Composition and Communication* 32 (1981): 175–82.

Hartwell, Patrick. "Grammar, Grammars, and the Teaching of Grammar." *College English* 47 (1985): 105–27.

Kolln, Martha. "Closing the Book on Alchemy." *College Composition and Communication* 32 (1981): 139–51.

Lanham, Richard. *Revising Prose.* New York: Scribner's, 1979.

Meckel, Henry. "Research on Teaching Composition and Literature." *Handbook of Research on Teaching.* Ed. Nathaniel L. Gage. Chicago: Rand, 1963.

Mellon, John. *Transformational Sentence Combining: A Method for Enhancing the Development of Fluency in English Composition.* Urbana, IL: National Council of Teachers of English, 1966.

Neuleib, Janice. "The Relation of Formal Grammar to Composition." *College Composition and Communication* 23 (1977): 247–50.

O'Hare, Frank. *Sentence-Combining: Improving Student Writing Without Formal Grammar Instruction.* Urbana, IL: National Council of Teachers of English, 1971.

Sanborn, Jean. "Grammar: Good Wine Before Its Time." *English Journal* 75 (1986): 72–80.

Shaughnessy, Mina. *Errors and Expectations.* New York: Oxford UP, 1977.

Strunk, William, and E. B. White. *The Elements of Style,* 3rd ed. New York: Macmillan, 1979.

Warriner, John E., John H. Treanor, and Sheila Y. Laws. *English Grammar and Composition 8*. Rev. ed. New York: Harcourt, 1965.

Williams, Joseph. *Style: Ten Lessons in Clarity and Grace*. Glenview, IL: Scott, 1981.

Classroom Activities

Develop a questionnaire for basic writing students similar to the one that Neulcib and Brosnahan provided for their own students (preservice student teachers). The purpose of the questionnaire is for students to reflect not only on how much grammar knowledge they have retained, but also on how they have studied grammar throughout their schooling. A similar questionnaire for developing writers would provide interesting results for both students and teachers. Students could describe their experiences with the study of grammar or list rules they have learned over the years. You may approach class discussion of the results of these self-assessments by comparing your own experiences with grammar instruction to those described by students.

Thinking about Teaching

Neuleib and Brosnahan suggest error analysis as an appropriate means of teaching grammar to basic writers. If students are able to recognize patterns of error, they will become more adept at editing their work. In this context, it may be useful to collaborate with colleagues to determine which errors are the most common among your population of students. Create a rubric based on categories suggested by Neuleib and Brosnahan. Then exchange student papers and diagnostic tests and proofread for categories of error that seem most prevalent. After this exchange, discuss the kinds of errors that predominate and the best ways to approach such editing difficulties with your students.

Teaching Style through Sentence Combining and Sentence Generating

Constance Weaver

In Teaching Grammar in Context *(1996), Constance Weaver argues that the most effective form of grammar instruction does not have students memorize rules. Instead, it teaches grammar in connection with real writing, which includes material written by students themselves. The following selection, taken from that book, presents several creative strategies that will help students add variety to their sentences and develop a more sophisticated writing style. Throughout the mini-lessons presented here, Weaver emphasizes the potential for creativity in grammar instruction and demonstrates her enthusiasm for playing with language and ideas.*

Teachers who need more background in grammar to adapt and expand [the following] lessons or develop their own might find Diana Hacker's *A Writer's Reference* (1995) particularly useful. More realistic in its assessment of how the language is really used by educated people is *The Right Handbook: Grammar and Usage in Context,* by Belanoff, Rorschach, and Oberlink (1993). Both of these would also be excellent references for students at the high school and college levels.

Usually, it works well for the teacher to make transparencies for the concepts being taught, and to use different colored transparency pens to clarify particular constructions, marks of punctuation, and so forth. I prefer to use examples from students' own writing or examples from literature, such as the many published examples in Scott Rice's *Right Words, Right Places* (1993); in practice, though, I all too often find myself concocting short examples that can easily be printed by hand on a transparency. All these lessons can be taught to the entire class or to a smaller group of students, but follow-up application commonly needs to be guided individually. Or to put it bluntly, without further guidance, such lessons will not necessarily transfer to students' own writing any better than traditional grammar book exercises have done; they simply reflect a more efficient use of time than the traditional practice exercises and tests. Students will inevitably need guidance in applying these concepts during revision and editing.

Most of these lessons I have taught with students in various classes at the college level, but particularly with the preservice and inservice teachers in my Grammar and Teaching Grammar class. In working with those enrolled in this course, I have usually had a dual or triple aim: to teach something that could benefit them as writers themselves; to suggest and exemplify something that they might profitably teach to their students, at least in simplified form; and to model possible ways of teaching grammar in context. Here, these suggestions often look like rather formal lesson plans, with goals indicated and the reader addressed as "you." But to emphasize the fact that these lessons represent ongoing experimentation, some lessons or parts of them have been written in a more conversational tone — to share what I have done as a teacher at the college level and sometimes to make suggestions for how my experiments might be modified to achieve goals at other levels. This, I hope, will also emphasize the fact that adaptations will usually be necessary as well as desirable: that we must all to some extent reinvent the wheel of effective instruction in our own classrooms, even while we share our efforts with each other, collaborate with one another, and benefit from others' experiences.

1. Introducing Participial Phrases

GOALS   To help writers see the effectiveness of using present participle phrases, when used as free modifiers. In addition, to help writers see that they can sometimes move such phrases for greater effectiveness, as they revise. Such lessons are most appropriate for writers who provide few narrative and descriptive details in their writing, or writers who provide such details in separate sentences, instead of appropriately subordinating some details in modifying phrases.

BACKGROUND   One of the constructions that most distinguishes professional writers from student writers is the participial phrase used as a free modifier — that is, as a modifier that is not absolutely essential to the sentence and therefore is set off by punctuation — usually by commas in prose, but sometimes just by line divisions in poetry (Christensen and Christensen, 1978). The present participle phrase commonly conveys action, whether it is used in poetry, fiction, or nonfiction. Such free modifiers most commonly occur at the end of the clause, even if they modify the subject of that clause. The second most common position is before the subject-predicate unit. Least common is a participial free modifier occurring between the subject and the predicate.

Possible Procedures

1. Put some examples on transparencies and discuss them with the students. For example:

I watched the flashing past of cotton fields and cabins, *feeling that I was moving into the unknown.*   — Ralph Ellison, *Invisible Man* (1952)

"I wish we could get wet," said Lily, *watching a boy ride his bicycle through rain puddles.*   — Amy Tan, *The Moon Lady* (1992)

Father,
All these he has made me own,
The trees and the forests
Standing in their places.
          — Teton Sioux, *The Trees Stand Shining* (H. Jones, 1993)

Still laughing, Mama bustled about the kitchen until her masterpiece was complete.   — Phil Mendez, The Black Snowman (1989)

Far below, a sea of purple and orange clouds churned, *dashing like waves in slow motion against the mountain's green forests and reddish-brown volcanic rock.*
> — Tom Minehart, "On Top of Mount Fuji, People Hope for Change" (July 17, 1993)

The river that used to surge into the Gulf of California, *depositing ruddy-colored silt that fanned out into a broad delta of new land at its mouth,* hardly ever makes it to the sea anymore.
> — Paul Gray, "A Fight over Liquid Gold" (1991)

2. Discuss the placement of the participial phrases. In most cases, the participial phrase is probably most effective as is. However, what about putting the participial phrase before the subject in the second example?

Watching a boy ride his bicycle through rain puddles, Lily said, "I wish we could get wet."

Is this order perhaps as good as the original, even though the focus has changed? By thus discussing the effects and effectiveness of placing modifiers differently, students develop a sense of style and an ability to suit the grammar to the sense of what they are writing.

3. You might also discuss examples like the following sentences from Richard Wright's poem "Between the World and Me" (1935), wherein two past tense verbs are followed by a present participle phrase:

The dry bones stirred, rattled, lifted, *melting themselves into my bones.*

And then they had me, stripped me, *battering my teeth into my throat till I swallowed my own blood.*

Why might the poet have switched from past tense verbs to present participle phrases at the ends of these sentences? How is the effect different?

ADDITIONAL MINI-LESSONS   Students may benefit from follow-up lessons in which they listen to or read more literary excerpts making effective use of present participle phrases. The teacher can encourage the students to find and share examples themselves. Another kind of mini-lesson can involve taking a bare-bones sentence from a student's paper and brainstorming together about details that might be added in free modifying -ING phrases. Similarly, one can demonstrate how to combine already written sentences during revision. See also the following lessons in this category.

2. Using Present Participle Phrases as Free Modifiers

POSSIBLE PROCEDURE   Suggest to writers the option of writing "I am" poems (see Figure 1) in which they equate themselves metaphorically with things that reflect their interests, suit their personalities, suggest their goals. Emphasize the possibility of using present participle free modifiers by sharing examples in which the writer has used them effectively.

3. Creating Participial Phrases and Absolutes through Sentence Combining

GOAL   To encourage writers to use participial phrases (both present and past) and absolute constructions in their writing. Also, to consider the stylistically effective placement of these free modifiers.

Possible Procedures

1. Put the sets of sentences shown in Figure 2 on transparencies, leaving plenty of room to write the changes that the students suggest. It may be helpful to provide a copy of the activity for each student, so that students can more easily focus on the task and keep a record of the sentences they have created. Adapted from Allyn & Bacon's *The*

Figure 1.   Example of an "I am" poem, in which the writer uses participial phrases as free modifiers.

I am "Four Strong Winds" and the "Moonlight Sonata,"
    melancholy yet serene.
I am a Bilbo's pizza with whole wheat crust,
    tomato bubbly and cheese gooey.
I am 5 a.m., a nun
    greeting the morning solitude,
    grateful for the absolution of a new day.
I am a midnight lover,
    cherishing and tender,
    tracing a smile in the dark
    with my fingertips.
I am a whitewater raft,
    sturdy yet flexible,
    bouncing over hidden rocks
    to rest beyond the whirlpool.
Connie Weaver

Writing Process, Book 9 (1982), the sentences describe a short nonverbal motion picture titled *Dream of the Wild Horses.*

2. Explain that, for now, you want the sentences in each set combined into a single sentence, with the sentence in capitals remaining untouched and the others reduced to parts of sentences (free modifiers), but kept in the same order. Do the first two or three with the students. If the students reorder the parts of the resultant sentence or choose a different original sentence to leave unchanged (which is common), you can accept these variations but, whenever possible, discuss which version works better in the flow of the narrative. Don't worry, for now, about examining the structure of the newly created parts of sentences; that can be done after the narrative is created.

3. After creating a satisfying narrative, you can call students' attention to the three kinds of free modifiers they have created:

> *Running dreamily,* the herd fades into the distance, *leaving sea and shore undisturbed.* [present participle phrase. The *-ing* in these free modifiers shows that the phrases are present participles. They are verb phrases functioning as modifiers.]
>
> The herd stampedes, *panicked by an inferno.* [past participle phrase] *Singed by the flames and choked by the smoke,* the herd plunges desperately into the sea. [past participle phrase. The *-ed* forms in these free modifiers show that the phrases are past participles. They, too, are verb phrases functioning as modifiers.]
>
> *Their fears forgotten,* the horses frolic in the waves. [absolute phrase. The absolute has a subject and retains the essence of the verb phrase. Often, the absolute can be restored to a complete sentence by adding *am, is, are, was,* or *were,* as in *Their fears were forgotten.*]
>
> The horses gallop in slow motion, *their manes suspended in twilight, their hooves tracing deliberate patterns in the sand.* [The first absolute consists, in effect, of a subject plus a past participle phrase. The second absolute has a subject followed by a present participle phrase. The addition of *were* would restore each absolute to a complete sentence.]

As these examples illustrate, the participial phrase is essentially a verb phrase functioning like an adjective, to modify a noun. The present participle phrase typically connotes present action, while the past participle phrase connotes completed action or description. The absolute construction is effective for conveying descriptive detail, without giving it the full weight of a grammatically complete sentence.

Teacher Resources

Christensen, F., and B. Christensen. *Notes toward a New Rhetoric: Nine Essays for Teachers.* 2nd ed. New York: Harper & Row, 1978. These essays

Figure 2.   Sentences for creating participial phrases and absolutes.

---

1. A HERD OF WILD HORSES RACES ALONG A BEACH.
   Their hoofbeats carve patterns in the sand.
   Their hoofbeats churn the surf.
   [A herd of wild horses races along a beach, their hoofbeats carving patterns in the sand and churning the surf.]

2. Manes are flying
   Legs are flailing
   THE HORSES SURGE FORWARD INTO A DEEPENING MIST.
   [Manes flying, legs flailing, the horses surge forward into a deepening mist.]

3. THE THUNDERING HERD ALMOST DISAPPEARS.
   The herd is veiled by a blue haze.
   [The thundering herd almost disappears, veiled by a blue haze.]

4. Two stallions emerge suddenly.
   TWO STALLIONS BEGIN TO FIGHT.
   [Suddenly emerging, two stallions begin to fight.]

5. THEY REAR ON THEIR POWERFUL HIND LEGS.
   They circle each other in a deadly dance.
   [They rear on their powerful hind legs, circling each other in a deadly dance.]

6. The stallions have fought to a stalemate.
   THE STALLIONS RACE TO THE FRONT OF THE HERD.
   [Having fought to a stalemate, the stallions race to the front of the herd.]

7. THE HERD STAMPEDES.
   The herd is panicked by an inferno.
   [The herd stampedes, panicked by an inferno.]

8. The herd is singed by the flames.
   The herd is choked by the smoke.
   THE HERD PLUNGES DESPERATELY INTO THE SEA.
   [Singed by the flames and choked by the smoke, the herd plunges desperately into the sea.]

9. Their fears are forgotten.
   THE HORSES FROLIC IN THE WAVES.
   They dive into the depths.
   They surface again.
   [Their fears forgotten, the horses frolic in the waves, diving into the depths, then surfacing again.]

10. The horses are restored.
    THE HORSES MOVE BACK TOWARD THE SHORE.
    [Restored, the horses move back toward the shore.]

Figure 2. (continued)

---

11. THE SHORE IS NOW SOFTENED BY TWILIGHT.
    The shore is tinted with muted pinks and lavenders.
    [The shore is now softened by twilight, tinted with muted pinks and lavenders.]
12. THE HORSES GALLOP IN SLOW MOTION.
    Their manes are suspended in twilight.
    Their hooves trace deliberate patterns in the sand.
    [The horses gallop in slow motion, their manes suspended in twilight, their hooves tracing deliberate patterns in the sand.]
13. The herd runs dreamily.
    THE HERD FADES INTO THE DISTANCE.
    The herd leaves sea and shore undisturbed.
    [Running dreamily, the herd fades into the distance, leaving sea and shore undisturbed.]

---

by Francis Christensen are valuable in helping us understand some of the characteristics of today's prose style.

Daiker, D. A., A. Kerek, and M. Morenberg. *The Writer's Options: Combining to Composing.* 4th ed. New York: Harper & Row, 1990. Intended as a text at the college level, this book is also especially valuable to teachers interested in implementing sentence-combining activities that draw upon the research of Christensen and others.

Killgallon, D. *Sentence Composing: The Complete Course.* Portsmouth, NH: Boynton/Cook, 1987. Excellent book for students, especially at the high school level. . . .

4. Appreciating and Using Absolute Constructions

GOALS To help writers appreciate the absolute construction as a means of conveying descriptive detail, and to help them become sufficiently aware of the absolute construction to use it in their writing.

NOTE . . . Technically the absolute is a phrase, because it's not quite grammatically complete as a sentence. Because the absolute has a "subject" and the *essence* of a verb, it can also be described as a near-clause.

Possible Procedures

1. Locate some effective absolutes from literature. The references cited in the lesson immediately above are good resources, as is Scott Rice's *Right Words, Right Places* (1993). The absolute construction is

particularly common in narrative fiction and poetry — even in many picture books for children. Here are some further examples:

> I saw the giant bend and clutch the posts at the top of the stairs with both hands, bracing himself, *his body gleaming bare in his white shorts.*
> — Ralph Ellison, *Invisible Man* (1952)

> Before me, in the panel where a mirror is usually placed, I could see a scene from a bullfight, *the bull charging close to the man and the man swinging the red cape in sculptured folds so close to his body that man and bull seemed to blend in one swirl of calm, pure motion.*
> — Ralph Ellison, *Invisible Man* (1952)

> A sudden blow: *the great wings beating still*
> *Above the staggering girl, her thighs caressed*
> *By the dark webs, her nape caught in his bill,*
> He holds her helpless breast upon his breast.
> — W. B. Yeats, "Leda and the Swan" (1924)

Notice how the three absolutes in the Yeats excerpt keep the reader suspended before the main clause, as Zeus in the form of a swan approaches and then claims the girl.

2. As a follow-up, encourage students to experiment with absolutes in their own writing. As a preparatory activity, you might encourage "boast" poems like this:

> My car is a sleek gray cat,
>   its paws leaping forward the instant I accelerate,
>   its engine purring contentedly.

3. Often in students' narrative writing, one finds simple sentences like *My car is a sleek gray cat,* sentences that could benefit from including more descriptive detail in absolute phrases. When writers are ready to revise at the sentence level, the teacher can help them consider ways of expanding some sentences through absolutes that convey descriptive detail. Past participle phrases can also add descriptive detail, while present participle phrases are often effective in conveying narrative detail.

Classroom Activities

At the end of the mini-lesson on introducing participial phrases, Weaver suggests: "Students may benefit from follow-up lessons in which they listen to or read more literary excerpts making effective use of present participle phrases. The teacher can encourage the students to find and share examples themselves." Have students locate interesting examples from texts that you are reading in class. Then ask students, working individually or in small groups, to find as many phrases as they can. Have students write their favorite examples on the board; then, as a class, try moving the participial phrases around to experiment with word order. Does the placement of the participial phrase make a difference to the sense of the sentence, or to the power of the language?

Thinking about Teaching

In Figure 1, Weaver provides yet another inventive example of using participial phrases in context, the "I am" poem. Consider beginning a meeting or writing workshop for teachers by having each person write his or her own version of an "I am" poem. You can decide as a group which particular version of the participial phrase you would like to try. Share the poems in small groups or with the whole group, or publish them in a small booklet or electronically. You may also wish to try this activity with students, writing along with them in class and reading the results aloud. Weaver asks us as teachers of writing to pay attention to the many ways language can work so that we can experience the benefits of teaching and studying grammar in the context of reading and writing. The "I am" poems are a creative means of working toward this end.

6

Learning Differences

Developing writers arrive in our classrooms with complex sets of needs generated by their varied learning differences, learning styles, previous access to education, and current educational support systems. In a fruitful learning environment, varied teaching methods can work to support both the individual and collective needs of our students. Similarly, the selections in this chapter offer varied perspectives for approaching teaching and learning through diverse strategies and suggestions. Patrick L. Bruch demonstrates the connections between social justice work and universal instructional design. Bruch also discusses how the theory of universal instructional design works in practice and offers a writing assignment that features inclusive participation for students with (and without) apparent learning differences.

Linda Feldmeier White argues that "we can be more effective teachers and advocates for students with LD if we separate the idea of learning disability . . . from the positivistic discourse that dominates LD research and pedagogy." She further examines the implications of her position for the composition classroom. Both of these writers offer methods for teaching and empowering students with learning differences and suggest that all students, whatever their needs, may benefit from instruction that addresses a wide range of learning practices.

Interpreting and Implementing Universal Instructional Design in Basic Writing

Patrick L. Bruch

In his study, Universal Design: Inclusive Post Secondary Education for Students with Disabilities, Patrick L. Bruch envisions strong interconnections between universal instructional design and social justice work, especially in basic writing courses for students with (and without) apparent learning differences. Universal instructional design takes its name from the architectural concept of universal design; for instance, the use of ramps rather than stairs creates legally mandated access to buildings for people in wheelchairs and serves "universal" needs as well for children in strollers, people with backpacks on wheels, and so on.

However, Bruch suggests that in composition studies, "universal" access often implies the goal of assimilation to the status quo, rather than toward social justice for all students. In order to work for social justice, Bruch argues, we need to make our pedagogy as equitable as possible and to consider "universality" as a process rather than an outcome. Bruch describes how these theories work in practice, providing examples of how students can be involved in shaping activities and assignments, leading to more equitable conditions for students in basic writing courses.

In a society that values equality and diversity, the concept of a universally designed curriculum captures a broadly shared ideal. Indeed, education scholarship in the United States might be read as an ongoing debate about our successes and failures in creating neutral, universal curricular contexts in which different people can learn together. Ideals of universality have typically assumed that curricula can escape the relations of power and privilege that shape public life. Dominant strands of current social theory and political philosophy challenge this way of thinking about what we should be working for as we design curricula and policy. In this chapter, I offer an interpretation of Universal Instructional Design (UID) informed by this contemporary thinking about justice. I then highlight the implications of this interpretation of UID for the teaching of writing, discussing my own effort to implement a writing curriculum compatible with UID.

Contemporary Social Theory

In her recent study of political philosophy, Iris Marion Young (1991) highlights transformations in ideas of justice that have resulted from the social theories and group movements that emerged in the 1960s and 1970s. For Young, feminist, anti-racist, gay rights, disability rights, and other movements drew attention to the shortcomings of those definitions of justice that were understood to be universal in the sense of being timeless and independent of specific contexts. As an alternative to pursuit of "a self-standing rational theory . . . independent of actual social institutions and relations" (p. 4), the social group movements highlighted the need for understandings of justice that were able to recognize and address unintended consequences of seemingly or actually neutral policies and practices. As Young explains, rather than searching for a universality good for all people and all times, contemporary critical theories see justice as rooted in specific social and historical contexts. Here, rather than be an abstract principle that stands outside of experience, justice depends upon "hearing a cry of suffering or distress or feeling distress oneself" (p. 5). Where more traditional theories valued detachment and distance, current theories like Young's are participatory and process oriented.

Building on Young's arguments about the need for a more contextual and processual understanding of universal justice, Fraser (1997) has recently drawn attention to the dynamic relationship between two domains, the material and the cultural, in the current social and historical context. For Fraser, listening to the experiences and voices of marginalized social groups suggests that injustice operates in different ways on these two conceptually distinguishable, though overlapping planes. The first understanding of injustice is material. Here, attention to injustice focuses on unequal distribution of things like income, property ownership, access to paid work, education, health care, leisure time, and so on. The second understanding of injustice is cultural and symbolic. Here, injustice refers to "cultural domination . . . nonrecognition . . . and disrespect" (Fraser, p. 14). These forms of injustice often overlap. Physical disability, for instance, is often related to economic disenfranchisement. But the conceptual distinction is useful because it helps draw attention to the fact that economic enfranchisement may not, alone, remedy the unjust relations attached to disability in current institutions. Persons labeled as disabled may still be culturally marginalized, misrecognized, and disrespected.

What is useful about disentangling these overlapping planes of injustice, then, is that by doing so we are equipped with a more robust vocabulary for talking about injustice and suffering in our midst. Thus equipped, we are better able to recognize the need for multiple and perhaps seemingly contradictory remedies for injustice. For, as Fraser highlights, where emphasis on the material view leads people to appreciate injustices rooted in the political-economic structure of society and encourages them to advocate for material equality — remedying injustice by *redistributing* goods and abolishing group difference — the cultural view recognizes the injustice of misrecognition and disrespect and thus leads its proponents to advocate remedying injustice through *recognition* and revaluation of group specificity. Contending with both material and cultural obstacles to equal treatment within significant public contexts like schooling, an adequate conceptual foundation for transforming curriculum must bring together redistribution and recognition.

Summarizing the essential insight that these movements have helped to generate, Catherine Prendergast (1998) has recently argued that, in order to overcome injustices such as White privilege and male privilege, "it will not be simply enough to add women and people of color and stir. Without significant changes to the profession and pedagogy, women and people of color will continue to wind up on the bottom" (p. 50). What is needed are redefinitions of what it means to participate in social practices like work and schooling so that part of the purpose of participating in such practices is to change the practice itself. Within such a view, the universality and thus justness of our practices becomes participatory — they are always in the process of being redefined as we continuously learn more about how our practices relate to material or cultural injustice. Instead of creating a system that applies to any situation, universality means working within concrete contexts to enable more people to participate more fully in defining inequities and better alternatives.

Although Prendergast's (1998) recognition of the need for transformation of "the profession and pedagogy" (p. 50) usefully applies current thinking about justice to the educational context, she concludes her study by explicitly refusing to address classroom issues, pointing to the compromises that, within accepted educational discourses, such attention demands. She concludes that although "at this point articles dealing with composition generally incline toward some pedagogical imperatives," in order to be true to her evidence "[that] not only is an agenda of socialization insufficient for enfranchisement but that it might be detrimental to enfranchisement" (p. 50), she can only reemphasize that "we need to recognize that our rhetoric is one which continually inscribes our students as foreigners" (p. 51). If school curricula are to put into practice recent theories of multicultural justice, they must be transformed to provide marginalized groups meaningful opportunities to participate in and transform educational and other institutions. Our curricula will have to provide a means for expressing and valuing cultural difference in ways that make group difference one of the purposes of knowledge forms like literacy, rather than the foreign element that pollutes literacy. In the absence of such respect and recognition, redistribution fails to fulfill its promise.

Universal Instructional Design

Fulfilling the promise of redistributive measures will involve more fully connecting such remedies to culturally oriented remedies. Growing out of architecture, a field of knowledge in which the connections between material and cultural issues are uniquely visible, Universal Design (UD), in its affirmation of critical revisionary feedback, potentially responds well to our need for new models of participating in knowledge. Universal Design as a professional movement grew out of emerging awareness within architecture of unintended consequences of design features that were thought to be impartial. Specifically, persons with disabilities made building designers aware that their designs were unjust both in terms of the material access they made available and in terms of the cultural and symbolic messages they sent to persons with disabilities and to those temporarily able bodied. Buildings with stairs at each entrance, with doorknobs or other mechanisms that require particular kinds of dexterity not possessed by all, or other features that make the buildings very difficult for some persons to use, materially obstruct equal access. Additionally, such structures and cultural messages about who is expected to participate in public life and who is capable of citizenship, messages that unjustly misrecognize and disrespect certain persons.

Universal Design holds great promise when translated to curriculum design if we remain aware of the central critical capacity that, in practice, UD has placed at the center of the design process — listening to the experiences of those who use the structure, observing the degree to which the structure facilitates equal participation, and continuously revising. In this sense, I see Universal Design as operationalizing a contingent understanding of the term "universal" consistent with the political philosophies I described in the previous section of this chapter. Universal names an ideal and a process rather than a realized outcome or a fixed state of affairs. Seeing universality as a process values participation and discourages those privileged by current structures from ignoring the obligation to listen, learn, and revise. That revisions responsive to particular undesirable effects of designs also enhance the usability of structures in unintended ways is a bonus effect that should help counter arguments against constant revision.

In my view, Universal Design offers educators a chance to design curricula from the position of listener rather than all knowing expert. As Young (1997) has argued, listening plays an important role in identifying and transforming injustice:

> with careful listening able-bodied people can learn to understand important aspects of the lives and perspective of people with disabilities. This is a very different matter from imaginatively occupying their standpoint, however, and may require explicit acknowledgment of the impossibility of such a reversal. (p. 42)

The lesson here for me is that at its best, the design of structures aspires to universal access through listening and learning about how different people understand their experiences in them. With respect to this important process, it seems that curricular designers may have an advantage over building designers because our structures are much more flexible and easily revisable. Thus, there is no reason that curricula need to replicate the situation where buildings meet the letter of laws mandating access but fail to fulfill the spirit of equity.

Connecting UID to Composition Studies: Redefining Writing as Literacy Work

So far, I have offered an understanding of UID as a way of applying the insights of contemporary theories of justice to education. This connection provides a way to practically extend resources developed over the past 30 years within composition studies. It holds promise for addressing issues familiar to compositionists and for broadening attention to issues of access that compositionists have largely ignored. At the heart of the emerging attention to disability is a recognition on the part of composition scholars that assumptions about the physical, emotional, and cognitive norm have negatively impacted the structures we design — our curricula, our profession, and pedagogies.

But composition teachers have tended to separate issues of distribution from issues of recognition. Scholars have recently concentrated attention on the overall failure of redistributive pedagogies that narrowly conceived universality as universal access to a valued set of conventions. Prendergast's (1998) characterization of such efforts as potentially "detrimental to enfranchisement" (p. 50) and Fox's (1993) recent argument that "access through language pedagogy . . . is an unqualifiable failure" (p. 42) both draw attention to the professional tendency to theorize about recognition while emphasizing assimilation in the classroom. The injustice of redistributive pedagogies is less about the limitations of a valued dialect to provide the economic access it promises, though there is that. Additionally, the emphasis on assimilating valued conventions creates an educational context of disrespect in which those who are the beneficiaries of conventions are able to go on without questioning the ways that the structures they are operating within unjustly privilege them. Transforming the teaching of writing in ways that implement the kind of UID I have discussed holds promise for better serving students with disabilities as well as all others, because all are, ultimately, underserved by curricula that concentrate solely on either issues of distribution or issues of recognition.

Applying UID to the teaching of writing means transforming the curriculum to ameliorate cultural and material obstacles to educational equity. Materially, I am speaking of how the class itself operates — the physical layout of activities, the material design of handouts, texts, the environment of the classroom, how much time is spent in different ways, and so on. Culturally, I am referring to questions about the identities students are assumed to have or expected to inhabit by the curricula of the class. As a conceptual framework, UID draws attention to the interrelation of these cultural and material issues.

They both become the focus of critical reflection and potential revision in pursuit of the goal of equity.

The practice of UID has resulted in changes in the way that I understand what I want students to learn, in the assignments that I gave, and in the classroom activities through which we work on assignments. UID provides a framework for shifting our attention from literacy as a stable skill that we want to import to a more participatory formulation of writing as a matter of simultaneously doing and shaping in pursuit of equality and difference. A term that, for me, names this understanding of what students learn in writing classes is literacy work. In writing classes students learn to participate in and reflect on the various kinds of work that literacy does. They learn to appreciate that language use is a practice of relating to others and to reflectively navigate those relationships.

Applying the insights of UID to writing classes, the idea of literacy work defines writing as a reflective and revisionary practice. That is, when one writes one simultaneously accomplishes the immediate concrete goal of communicating in a particular context and at the same time, one expresses ideas about communication in that context. As one student, Asante, phrased this insight in a paper for a recent class, "by me writing this paper in this way, I am communicating my thoughts about communication to you, but yet a lot of people may not see it this way at first." In other words, writing includes both participation according to current conventions and reflection on those conventions and the relations of equality and difference they are part of.

As mentioned earlier, a key principle that UID offers to writing teachers is critical participation and revision. The material and cultural issues faced when serving any group are so multifaceted and complex, and the ways that students receive and interpret teachers' messages are so unpredictable, that no design for a class can address all issues and concerns beforehand. Instead, the message of UID is multiple formats supplemented by participatory feedback and redefinition. No single curricular mode can achieve universality and serve all students equally, so classes must be built to work towards contingent universality of serving the students that are actually there.

The role of student feedback is essential here. In one recent class, for example, I learned an important lesson about my practices for introducing new assignments. My method was to extensively describe the new essay assignment on paper, including a discussion of the rhetorical practices I wanted students to recognize and work on, why and how. My introduction to the summary assignment read like this:

> Academic writing is a set of practices for participating in conversation with others. One of the most important of these practices is summarizing. This first project is focused on reading carefully and writing good, strong, summaries. Strong summaries tell your readers what others in

the "conversation" you are joining have been saying. Strong summaries convince readers that your view of the conversation has some merit. A strong summary convinces readers that you should be listened to and creates a context for you to add your piece to the conversation.

In an effort to appeal to a broad audience, I contextualized the assignment by linking something I thought students would identify with, conversation, to academic writing. I also offered an in-class overview and provided students with examples to use as models of successful responses that could inspire them in thinking about how they might respond to the assignment. When I asked students for questions, there were none.

When I requested feedback from students on their progress after about a week, one student reported that she had been stuck because she wasn't sure if she understood the assignment "correctly." Although concerns with "giving the teacher what he wants" influence all students, the fact that this student had a learning disability that required a very direct and linear understanding of tasks like writing had made the situation paralyzing for her. In our discussion, I asked her what she thought about the assignment and she said that she thought she could take the authors one at a time and tell readers what they say. We discussed what she thought each of the authors was trying to say and made notes about why she understood them as she did. When I assured her that her understanding was fine she was relieved and said that she was thrown off by my introductory discussion.

I responded to this problem by redesigning the way I introduce new assignments to be much more focused on how the students understand the assignment rather than how I understand it. I now include much more student-generated discussion of how they understand what they are being asked to do and how they anticipate getting to work. One activity that has been very helpful in this regard is simply taking five minutes to let students write the assignment in their own words and then share them. Because I want students to think about the cultural work involved in writing as well as the practical work, I have broken down this process so that students begin by sharing their versions of the assignment in a small group with two or three others. I ask them to share their versions and to talk not so much about who's right or wrong, but about the different kinds of cultural work done by the different kinds of writing that each in the group imagine doing. My role as teacher while these conversations are happening evolves over the course of the term. Early on in the semester I circulate in the groups helping students develop a vocabulary for talking about the work writing does, the consequences of writing in different ways. As students develop confidence in addressing this issue, my role shifts towards helping groups maintain focus and work out difficulties that arise. As a classroom practice, the exercise teaches that rather than being right or wrong, different kinds of writing do different kinds of work. Some of these kinds of work, such as stating and defending an opinion, are more highly valued in some contexts than others.

In addition to operating as material transformations that provide broader and fuller access, such curricular redesigns that evolve from student participation in the design of the class raise and contend with cultural obstacles to equitable access as well. On one level, an activity like the one described above creates a context of greater recognition for students like the one who inspired the change, but also for many others. It creates an opportunity for each student to make an understanding of the assignment that recognizes their needs. Further, it creates a context for beginning to grapple with the cultural work that writing does. For example, in one of the groups I sat in on as students were discussing their understandings of the "strong summary" assignment, two students began to disagree when one African American student compared her understanding of the assignment to another, White, student's understanding by saying that she wanted to make her opinion "plain rather than hidden." The other student responded that a summary shouldn't have an opinion at all. To which the first responded that, for her, a summary is "my view of how I see them." At this point, I intervened to remind the students that the object of sharing was not to decide who in the group was right or wrong, but to try and clarify different understandings and the different kinds of work they do. This encouraged the two students to share their views of the work that their own and each others' interpretations do. Martha explained that she believed her way of understanding a summary would let readers decide how to understand the texts she discussed, using her opinion or not. Mary explained that she believed her way would let readers decide by leaving herself out and just saying what the authors said. Another student here joined in to add that Mary's would, then, be what Mary believed the authors said, which both Mary and Martha agreed to. The value that I hope comes of such exchanges is making each of the students more familiar with how two fundamentally different ways of understanding writing understand themselves and each other. It clarified that one kind of work writing strives to do is to help readers make informed decisions for themselves and that there are different opinions of how best to facilitate this. It provided a basis for each of the students to read and write in a more informed way.

An unexpected outcome of this new activity was that allowing students to take a significant hand in interpreting the assignment required that I clarify for myself the learning objectives and acceptable parameters of responses. In other words, the activity made me more fully reflect on multiple ways of demonstrating learning. In a writing class, flexibility is restricted by the fact that students must write. But the form of that writing is a point of negotiation with profound material and cultural implications. Sarah was most comfortable using writing to communicate stable meanings. Other students I have encountered find that trying to limit themselves to one way of understanding what are invariably complex texts or issues is constraining and demands they limit their writing to acceptable partial versions. In negotiating with students about the range of fully credible responses to the summary assignment, I have had to think about what abilities I want students to work on and demonstrate. For me, what matters is that students learn to read carefully and to help readers see both how they interpret texts and why they think their interpretations are credible in an academic setting. This means linking their summaries directly to what authors say. I think that if students do that, their writing will serve them well in many academic and public situations. As I have learned from student suggestions of how they understand and approach the assignment, this does not demand a thesis based, paragraph oriented, linear, traditional school essay.

An option that one student suggested for herself has become a formal alternative on my assignment sheet. This student was uncomfortable with the idea that she was being asked to be an expert on the various positions making up a conversation that she was previously unfamiliar with. She decided to write out a conversation between the authors that would show readers how she understood their positions. For her, the imaginary context would tell her readers that she was offering one, tentative interpretation of how the authors' opinions related to each other. My assignment sheet now suggests two broad options for completing the assignment as follows:

> Option 1: Find a common thread that emerges across the conversation we've been reading and write an essay in which you present and discuss this common thread by summarizing how at least 3 of the sources relate to it. Feel free to bring in your own experiences or your own senses of the issues, but be sure to concentrate on offering a substantial review of the perspectives offered by each of the authors you discuss, explaining how they each relate to the common thread.

> Option 2: Write a dialogue between four of the authors we've read in which they continue the conversation that their essays are a part of. Incorporate into what each author says your understanding of their view of the issues. Have each speaker use some direct quotes from their pieces to explain what they mean. In the dialogue, each person should talk at least three times, each time speaking at least 85 words. Try to capture some of the voice and style of each of the speakers in what you have them say.

Overall, these curricular transformations shift the emphasis from simple assimilation of conventions to a participatory recognition of the contingency of those conventions and their effects. I say "participatory" in order to call attention to the essential insight of Universal Design that those who inhabit structures have important roles to play in remaking those structures. In terms of a writing class that implements this concept in its instructional design, students are expected to learn that part of the purpose of writing is to call attention to aspects of the structure of writing that "many people may not see" as Asante, my previously quoted student, phrased it. They are learning as well that as writers part of their job is to participate in creating alternative designs for texts. Students in such a class are learning about literacy work by doing the work of literacy. They are interanimating redistributive and recognition-oriented remedies to educational injustice.

References

Fox, T. (1993). Standards and access. *Journal of Basic Writing, 12*(1), 37–45.
Fraser, N. (1997). *Justice interruptus: Critical reflections on the "postsocialist" condition.* New York: Routledge.
Prendergast, C. (1998). Race: The absent presence in composition studies. *College Composition and Communication, 50*(3), 36–53.
Young, I. M. (1991). *Justice and the politics of difference.* Princeton, NJ: Princeton University Press.
Young, I. M. (1997). *Intersecting voices: Dilemmas of gender, political philosophy, and policy.* Princeton, NJ: Princeton University Press.

Classroom Activities

In order to facilitate an equitable classroom environment, Bruch negotiates course assignments with students in basic writing courses. "The role of student feedback is essential here," Bruch states. To further extend the use of student feedback, he describes the process he and the students undertake after he distributes the initial assignment:

> I now include much more student-generated discussion of how they understand what they are being asked to do and how they anticipate getting to work. One activity that has been very helpful is this regard is simply taking five minutes to let students write the assignment in their own words and then share them.

Students continue this process by working in small groups, and Bruch initially "circulate[s] in the groups helping the students develop a vocabulary for talking about the [cultural] work that writing does, the consequences of writing in different ways." This process, he explains, facilitates more independence as the course progresses.

The result, Bruch suggests, is that students assist in reshaping the assignment so that he must "clarify for [himself] the learning objectives and acceptable parameters of responses," creating more accessible pedagogy for students with (and without) apparent learning differences and invaluable opportunities for self-reflection for students and teachers. Consider implementing this process in your own classroom, offering students a role in negotiating the assignment with their own critically engaged feedback.

Thinking about Teaching

Bruch's article is included in the collection *Curriculum Transformation and Disability (CTAD): Implementing Universal Design in Higher Education,* edited by Jeanne L. Higbee. This collection is published by the Center for Research on Developmental Education and Urban Literacy (CRDEUL) at the University of Minnesota and is available on the Web at <http://www.myacpa .org/sc/scd/CTAD/ctad-a.pdf>. Take another look at Bruch's article in context with the others in the CTAD collection and, based on your own observations and discussions with students and colleagues, consider the implications for universal instructional design at your own institution and in your own classroom. Reflect on your ideas in your teaching journal with the goal of conceiving equitable access for students with (and without) apparent learning differences. Share your ideas with students and colleagues in class and at meetings and consider revising your work for conference presentations and publication.

From Learning Disability, Pedagogies, and Public Discourse

Linda Feldmeier White

In these excerpts from a longer article first published in College Composition and Communication (CCC) *in 2002, Linda Feldmeier White analyzes the social construction of learning disabilities research and teaching methods "from the perspective of disability studies." In particular, she interrogates the notion of "overcoming" used to support a behaviorist pedagogy of remediation and the teaching of "fragmented skills." In addition, White examines the implications of social class and race in the diagnosis of learning disabilities as she argues for a constructivist pedagogy that will address the needs of all students.*

n a 1995 speech titled "Disabling Education: The Culture Wars Go to School," Boston University (BU) historian Jon Westling told a story about a student he called "Somnolent Samantha." Samantha approached him on the first day of class with a letter from the disability services office requesting accommodation for a learning disability (LD) involving "auditory processing": she would need extra time on tests, a separate room for testing, a seat in the front row, and help from her professor if she missed information because she could not help falling asleep during his lectures. Though Samantha is clearly a parody of students with LD, the satire is pointed and the intent is serious. Samantha represents Westling's argument, expounded in several speeches, that the LD movement, an egregious instance of political correctness, tries to replace academic rigor with excuses ("We are taught not that mathematics is difficult for us but worth pursuing, but that we are ill.") and common sense with double talk ("LDU [Learning Disabled University] is trying to keep LD philosophy students safe from the perplexities of Aristotle, to accommodate foreign language majors who have foreign language phobia, and to comfort physics students who suffer from dyscalculia, which is, of course, the particular learning disablement that prevents one from learning math" [Strosnider A38; Westling, "Government"]). To challenge these "myths," Westling, as provost, began to deny accommodations to students at BU. He enforced policies requiring students to have disabilities recertified every three years, denied requests for services, and refused to allow course substitutions for foreign language requirements. Ten students with LDs brought a class-action suit against the university, arguing that Westling violated their civil rights and was guilty of discrimination.

Westling's anti-LD salvos misfired. When Judge Patti Saris ruled on the case in 1997, by which time Westling was BU's president, six students were awarded damages, more stringent requirements for recertifying disabilities were removed, and BU was instructed to establish a committee to examine its policy on course substitutions. Saris's ruling focused on the Samantha speech as evidence of Westling's bias, an indication that he had made decisions about students on the basis of stereotypes — a violation since the law requires that decisions be "based on actual risks and not on speculation, stereotypes, or generalizations about disabilities." Saris noted that Westling had admitted that Samantha was not a real student, and that both Westling and his assistant, Craig Klafter, had

> expressed certain biases about the learning disabilities movement and stereotypes about learning disabled students. Westling and Klafter indicated repeatedly that many students who sought accommodations on the basis of a learning disability were lazy or fakers (e.g., "Somnolent

Samantha"), and Klafter labeled learning disabilities evaluators "snake oil salesmen." If not invidiousness, at the very least, these comments reflect misinforced stereotypes. . . . (*Guckenberger et al. v. Boston University*)

Saris also faulted Westling for becoming involved in reviewing accommodation requests, since he had "no expertise in learning disabilities and no training in fashioning reasonable accommodations for the learning disabled."[1]

The story of Samantha, Westling, and Saris raises issues that are not often discussed in composition studies.[2] Like Saris, most composition specialists see LD as the province of experts whose special training enables them to diagnose and treat the condition and whose judgments should not be questioned. I find this deference to medical constructions of learning problematic: If we think that students with LD are beyond our expertise, then we marginalize them as essentially different from "normal" students. The current public discourse on LD offers only two positions: either LD is a neurological condition that only experts understand, or LD is a myth, a euphemism for lack of intelligence. Questioning the first view allies one with the second. But there are other ways to look at LD — new ways to see problems are emerging, among both LD professionals and their critics, that composition specialists should be aware of. In this article, I examine LD from the perspective of disability studies. Though my reading of the LD literature has led me, like Westling, to question the concept of LD, my position is different from his. I critique LD, but not because I want to exclude students with LD from higher education. My argument is that we can be more effective teachers and advocates for students with LD if we separate the idea of learning disability — that school failure subjects students to the same kinds of oppression that characterize other disabilities — from the positivist discourse that dominates LD research and pedagogy.

Historically, the LD movement won support for some students who have difficulty with schooling by establishing LD as a neurological impairment. According to this argument, it is because their learning problems are biologically based that LD students deserve accommodation; without neurological impairment, they would be no different from other poor students. Within this framework, arguments about the social construction of LD are easily conflated with arguments that LD is a fraud. But it is important to recognize that LD, like all disabilities, is socially constructed. Further, it is possible to do so without aligning oneself with Westling's campaign to keep students with LD out of higher education — indeed, as I discuss later, LD professionals who focus on neurological impairment are more closely allied with conservatives like Westling than with supporters of inclusive admissions policies, in both epistemology and pedagogical theory.

If we bracket the question of whether a physical impairment exists, LD is no less real. Its growth as a diagnosis since the mid-1960s is inarguable. For LD to have gained its current popular, disciplinary, and legal status in only a few decades, our culture must have been primed to understand learning problems as "an invisible handicap," perhaps because the consequences and the stigma of school failure are so similar to those attached to physical impairments. A school child discovered to have "congenital word blindness" who, therefore, changes status from "dunce" to "cripple-brained" (an early twentieth-century term for LD) or from "slow learner" to "learning disabled" or "dyslexic" is not taking a very big step.[3] [. . .]

Epistemology and Pedagogy

In this section, I use spelling instruction as an illustration of the differences between LD pedagogy and holistic models of language teaching. Spelling pedagogies are revealing because spelling appears to be one of the most unambiguously mechanical literate behaviors but is actually heavily influenced by semantic knowledge. Comparing LD spelling pedagogy with whole-language spelling pedagogy provides clear examples of the limitations of behaviorist theory in explaining the perception of language.

Cognitive psychologists outside of special education are exploring relationships between culture and perception. Indeed, in "Shared Cognition: Thinking as Social Practice," Lauren Resnick maintains that constructivism is now "a pervasive assumption" of cognitive psychology. Research into "situated cognition" or "shared cognition" is based on the premise that knowledge is always an interpretation of experience. Conclusions drawn from earlier experiments are being revised by researchers aware that laboratory learning experiments can be misleading if the lab setting is assumed to be neutral, since no setting is neutral. Perception is affected by schema: "The empiricist assumption that what we know is a direct reflection of what we can perceive in the physical world has largely disappeared" (1). The collection of conference papers in which Resnick's statement appears, which includes work by Jean Lave, James Wertsch, Shirley Brice Heath, Barbara Rogoff, and Michael Cole, were published in 1991 by the American Psychological Association and is in its third printing. But, as Mike Rose notes in a 1988 *CCC* article, "cognitive reductionism," the tendency "to see singular, unitary cognitive explanations for broad ranges of poor school performance," though it is often challenged, is "surprisingly resilient" and re-emerges (267). Nowhere is this resiliency more evident than in learning disability research and pedagogy.

The dominant paradigm of the LD field is summarized by one of its founding fathers, William Cruickshank: "Neurological dysfunction leads to perceptual processing deficits which, in turn, result in a variety and complexity of learning disabilities" (xiv). In Cruickshank's scheme, there is no space between deficit and disability, no mediation that needs to be accounted for. Learning is acquiring knowledge through repetition and practice, and teaching is placing information in the brain, where knowledge and ability are quantities most reliably measured by standardized tests. Thus, in *Learning Disabilities and Brain Function,* William Gaddes and Dorothy Edgell analyze learning to spell as a matter of creating engrams (altering neural tissue to constitute a memory). The causes of spelling deficit are "brain lesions in the language circuits." Spelling disability is an "impaired or undeveloped behavioral skill" and remediation requires "the exercise of neuromuscular *movement*" (410, emphasis in original). Gaddes directs the diagnostician who wants to help a learning disabled child learn to spell to conduct a series of forty-two tests in order to discover deficits so that the appropriate remedial drills can be selected. There are seventeen questions about "auditory processes and aphasic signs in oral speech" (e.g., "Is hearing normal on an audiometric test?"); thirteen questions about "visual processes" (e.g., "Can the child look at pictures of common objects and match them with a similar picture?"); six questions about "tactile processes" ("Can the child write while blindfolded or with his hand obscured?"); and six questions about "motor-expressive processes" (e.g., "What is the child's finger-tapping speed for each hand? Are they both normal?") (411–13). Multisensory teaching methods (writing letters on the child's back or asking him to write the letters in damp sand while sounding them phonetically) are recommended in order to "build engrams linking the occipital, temporal, parietal, and motor strip areas that are crucial to correct writing." But despite his assertion that this diagnostic battery is needed to plan remediation, Gaddes devotes little space to making connections between diagnosis and teaching: "Once a clearly defined diagnostic understanding of the child's strengths and weaknesses is made available to the special teacher, a suitable battery of remedial techniques can be selected. Any experienced teacher already has an armamentarium of teaching skills to draw from" (413).

Disciplinary isolation is evident here, as it is in most LD pedagogy. Though the text, published in 1994, is in its third edition (the first was in 1980), there is no recognition of the limits of behaviorism. LD specialists are determined to keep meaning making out of their tent, as they must be, since paying attention to meaning would turn the enterprise of manipulating and measuring behavior into a much different field of investigation. The diagnostic questions Gaddes asks keep him from seeing others. He is uninterested in questions about language, a variable whose nature he assumes he understands. When he asserts that "the phonetic inaccuracy of a person's spelling is a reliable measure that discriminates LD from normal groups" (413–14), Gaddes is unaware that our ideas about phonetic accuracy are constructions. He is not thinking of phonetically (in)accurate correct spellings like "jumped" or "gives" or "sign" or "neuropsychological" or of the phonetic (in)accuracy of these children's misspellings: "groceriss," "mistiufus," "emidietly," "pachont," "feachure," "plesher," "nolage," "marvales" (Hughes and Searle 98, 115).

Even when empirical evidence fails to confirm the effectiveness of behaviorist teaching strategies, LD researchers often seem unaware that there might be relevant research in other disciplines. Thomas Oakland and his colleagues report a controlled experiment with the Dyslexia Training Program (DTP), an adaptation of the Orton-Gillingham Alphabetic Phonics method of multisensory instruction. In the DTP, the lessons begin with letter recognition and "extend sequentially to sophisticated levels of linguistic knowledge," like the syllabication of polysyllabic words. "As they progress through the curriculum, students are taught an extensive vocabulary to apply to their language learning, code marks that indicate speech sounds, symbols plus abbreviations related to word decoding, and formulas for syllable division and spelling" (141). The experimental program the researchers studied consisted of 350 one-hour lessons, five days a week, for ten months a year, for two years. (In some cases, the DTP was delivered via videotape, to test the feasibility of using the curriculum with students whose teachers lack the training to administer the program. Videotape was equally effective.) At the end of the program, DTP students had made "clinically significant" gains in reading ability, which the researchers note were "relatively modest . . . given the intensity and duration of the intervention." Students' spelling performance had not improved, and the researchers note that the failure of the DTP to improve spelling had already been well documented in "more than 2,000 children using the DTP in Texas schools." In explaining this result, although they notice that spelling is a complex skill requiring "morphological and semantic" knowledge, they don't question their methods. Their explanation is that spelling is complex and "rarely mastered by individuals with severe reading disability" (Oakland et al. 146).

If they looked at research in other fields, LD specialists would find a richer and more useful picture of language and learners. Margaret Hughes and Dennis Searle's work provides a good contrast. Theirs is an eight-year longitudinal study of children from three elementary schools, from kindergarten to sixth grade. They do not attempt to prove that one and not the other of the methods used by the teachers whose students they followed produce uniformly good spellers. Their research produces a different kind of knowledge, a narrative about how correct spelling develops from presound logic, to phonemic spelling, to the use of nonsound features characteristic of correct spelling. Among their findings are that children who reached correct spelling did so in different ways; that some whose development stalled in an early grade made progress later on; that good spellers approached spelling with the assumption that it had order that they could make sense of, while poor spellers saw it as arbitrary; that poor spellers judged correctness by assessing the act of production rather than the appearance of the word — if they found a word difficult to produce, they weren't certain it was correct, but they were adamant that words they found easy to spell were correct, even when they were wrong (Hughes and Searle, 103, 125). [. . .]

Overcoming and Maintaining Standards

While Westling was battling LD, other proponents of "academic standards" were publishing arguments that attacked a different group of students similarly judged to be illiterate and recipients of undeserved accommodation in open admissions programs. The opponents of remediation at CUNY have been more successful (see Sternglass 296–302). Arguments like Traub's *City on a Hill* accomplish what Westling failed to achieve: a convincing representation of students whose differences matter so much that their presence compromises higher education. Though we recognize students with LD as different from basic writers, it is important to notice that the same person can have both identities. Westling recognizes the similarity of the LD and basic writer identities when he attacks LD as political correctness. As recipients of legal protection on college campuses, the students of "LDU" are tainted by their association with other minorities who refuse to stay in their places. But there are problems with the fit between LD and political correctness. Westling can't pursue his criticism of LD diagnosis too seriously without challenging philosophies congenial to conservative views. Problems with LD diagnosis are too closely tied to problems with IQ and standardized tests to be explored. The attack on LD has been less successful than the attack on basic writing because conservatives and LD researchers share key beliefs in the certainty and objectivity of empirically produced knowledge and in the inevitability of hierarchical structures.

Both the learning disabled and the basic writer occupy sites at the intersection of conflicting stories about learning and schooling. Bruce Horner has analyzed ways that the texts constituting basic writing, in responding to the dominant public discourse on open admissions without challenging its binaries, established an academic field as it also reinscribed basic writers as marginal to the university (201–2). Writers with LD are more privileged than basic writers; "learning disabled" is a middle-class, white identity. But writers with LD are marginalized; their presence in higher education is always a concession, recognized as privilege and not invisible as normal. For students with LD, marginalization is maintained by the trope of overcoming.[4] When

Westling focused on Samantha's somnolence, he made it easy for Judge Saris to accuse him of misrepresentation. Being a hard worker is a crucial part of the LD identity. Dudley-Marling, and Dippo hypothesize that the concept of LD supplements the conventional beliefs about schooling that are needed to justify inequality in a democratic society: that public education allows everyone who works hard to succeed, in proportion to their genetic endowment of intelligence. LD provides an explanation for failure, failure that is "unexpected" and, therefore, doesn't require social change. In the LD narrative, school failure is always an anomaly and always a prelude to later success — often extraordinary success. The metaphors of discrepancy and reversal are crystallized in another element of LD culture, the idea that LD is the "affliction of geniuses." Lists of famous people who have been diagnosed or retrospectively diagnosed (Einstein, Edison, Hans Christian Anderson, William Butler Yeats, among others) grow ever longer. But if, as Westling notes, LD provides "comforting illusions," these are not without a price. It is cold comfort to a student who is not doing well that her disability is the affliction of geniuses. She might doubt that she is a genius; the burden of failure remains with the individual.

This focus on overcoming is, in fact, pervasive. LD is a media staple, and the conservative jeremiad is less common (and perhaps less harmful) than the interlocking narratives of scientific progress and overcoming that organize this discourse. A recent feature story on LD in *Newsweek,* whose cover announces "New Hope for Kids Who Can't Read," is similar to many others. The story of revolutionary new discoveries is familiar:

> Until recently, dyslexia and other reading problems were a mystery to most teachers and parents. As a result, too many kids passed through school without mastering the printed page. Some were treated as mentally deficient; many were left functionally illiterate, unable to ever meet their potential. But in the last several years, says Yale researcher Sally Shaywitz, "there's been a revolution in what we've learned about reading and dyslexia." Scientists like Shaywitz and Berninger are using a variety of new imaging techniques to watch the brain at work. Their experiments have shown that reading disorders are most likely the result of what is, in effect, faulty wiring in the brain — not laziness, stupidity, or a poor home environment. (Kantrowitz and Underwood 74)

No mention is made in the article of alternative views of emergent literacy.

Accompanying this narrative is a series of then-and-now case studies. Eleven-year-old Jason Nicholas was assigned in first grade "to special education classes with three mildly retarded children." Now, after a summer program for dyslexic boys at the University of Washington, "he'll never be a great speller. He still stumbles over new words in a text. But he's an honors student in his sixth-grade class" (74). Jean Urban (pictured examining MRI images of her own brain) couldn't grasp phonics in the first grade. "With special training Urban, now ten and in fifth grade, is making progress and says she's 'pretty good at reading.' She is part of a study at Yale that will see whether the special training is actually changing how her brain works" (73). Matthew Schafir "finally got help, thanks to his mother, Peggy." They lived in a tent in order for him to receive "intensive intervention" at a reading clinic seven hours away from their home. "His reading level went from second to fifth grade in six weeks" (74). "Discount broker Charles Schwab struggled in school with reading. At Stanford, he flunked English 'once or twice' and failed French. He never knew his problem was dyslexia, though, until his son was diagnosed with it" (75). John Corcoran was a social studies teacher but couldn't read. "At forty-eight, he registered for a public library literacy program. That was a start, but the real improvement came when he began treating the dyslexia explicitly" (78). Harvard MBA Susan Hall quit her job in order to help her son Brandon, who "finally made a breakthrough" when she took him to the Lindamood Clinic in California (78). A full page is devoted to Stephen J. Cannell, who is "so dyslexic he barely made it through school" but now "one of TV's most prolific writer-producers and a successful novelist" (79).

The emphasis is relentless. Overcoming is so necessary a part of the LD story we are willing to make public, that, after I had read research studies and popular accounts of LD for many years, my perceptions of LD changed dramatically when I read Gerber and Reiff's *Speaking for Themselves: Ethnographic Interviews with Adults with Learning Disabilities*. Gerber and Reiff chose nine subjects for their study, to represent a range of adult outcomes. Of their three least successful subjects, none finished high school. Even the most successful adults —a dentist, a lawyer, and a counselor — have less than glowing stories to tell. The longitudinal studies Gerber and Reiff review, from 1968 as well as from 1985, indicate that successful adults with LD are those with less severe impairments, from affluent families, who had a positive educational experience (often in private schools) (Gerber and Reiff 5–12). Within the narrative of scientific progress, there is no place for this story or, for that matter, for stories about mothers who don't solve their children's problems.[5]

Implications for the College Writing Classroom

The research that I have done on LD was first motivated by my questions about how to work with students with LD. That research led to a second question: I then wanted to know why teaching fragmented skills was so often recommended for students with LD, when all that I knew about teaching writing had led me away from these methods.

I think that the foregoing discussion answers the second question and also suggests how to answer the first. The answers to questions about teaching given by "learning disability" — those that have evolved from trying to tie pedagogy directly to empirical research on neurological dysfunction — offer false hope that scientific progress will cure what is wrong. But the broader field of learning disability — the insights and strategies that have evolved as education has become more inclusive — has much to offer. As Brueggemann, Cheu, Dunn, Heifferon, and I have argued in an earlier *CCC* article, disability provides a better position than (temporarily) able ones from which to question what is normal. The accommodations that have developed for students with LD often reveal features of schooling that serve to invent or increase differences among students. We can create better assignments and assessments if we use the lens provided by LD to examine whether teaching practices that require accommodations are really necessary.[6]

In working with students with LD, it is important to try to create a classroom that offers the pleasures of academic writing (getting to explain and having others listen to one's explanations) and reading (the joy of changing one's mind). Teaching that attempts to "remediate" by focusing on what is wrong with the way students are reading and writing only emphasizes their disability. When Rosalie Fink interviews successful adults with dyslexia, she finds that they have been able to learn to read. All are professionals who have careers that require sophisticated reading and writing abilities. Despite continuing difficulty with phonetic decoding, they all as children became avid readers but at a later age than usual, often when they were ten or eleven. They started to read because there were things that they wanted to know. Reading in a particular area of interest (e.g., chemistry, airplanes, love stories), they developed enough knowledge to be able to make sense of words they couldn't decode. When Fink administered a battery of tests to her study's participants, they all scored well on reading comprehension. Some were also able to read quickly, and some had also developed subskills (like oral reading accuracy, spelling, and word recognition), while others had not. Their experiences parallel those of Christopher Lee. He says that when his teachers worked hard to teach him how to decode, he never did get past "first base." It was only later that he realized he could get to home plate (comprehension) without necessarily touching all the bases. He finally began to understand reading in his sophomore English class in college, when he had a teacher who was good at making the readings she assigned interesting. She didn't confine reading to just working with print; she played music, showed films, had students role play: "Although there were pages of reading requirements, the class was never about reading; it was about meaning — transporting ourselves from the classroom right into the story. . . . Even the most complex material would come clear to me. For the first time, I was able to talk intelligently about these stories" (Lee and Jackson 30–31). Lee learned the basics of writing in a high school English class by observing fellow students' reactions to his and others' weekly papers; he developed confidence in his sense of audience and that strength led to the practice and discipline he needed to become a writer (52–53). For teachers who work with students with LD, the most important teaching skills are those that work with all students.

I end with a story to counter Westling's. I was teaching a first-year writing class in which my attempts to enact critical pedagogy were more successful than they usually are. This class had become a community of learners in which my role was important but no longer central. At about mid-semester, a student who had been turning in very carefully edited papers turned in an essay that had noticeable mistakes in spelling and punctuation. He came to me after class to explain why. His girlfriend had edited the other papers, and this was the first one he hadn't asked her to do for him. He turned in what he was able to do on his own because he decided it was worthwhile to work on editing, and he wanted to know how well he was doing. I wish that I had more stories like this to tell. Students become skilled at dealing with the classrooms they have lived in, where not learning is often a better, safer bet than learning. I have met — at times I have been — the student Westling remembered when he represented her as "Somnolent Samantha." I don't believe that Samantha is just a fiction but that a better reader of classrooms and students would see that she learned to sleepwalk in school.

Notes

1. Westling claimed during the trial that he had been misunderstood and "was not attacking individuals who have or believe they have disabilities" — a disingenuous defense. It is clear that he was looking for politically correct excesses to attack. In a speech to the Heritage Foundation, he joked that having denied students accommodations, he was waiting to be sued, "as intrepidly as a brewer of hot coffee" ("Getting Government Out of Higher Education"). Though Saris ruled against BU on the most significant issues, the damage awards were not large — they ranged from $1 in nominal damages to $13,000, and totaled $30,000 (Wolinsky and Whelan 290). BU eventually prevailed on the course substitution issue. When the BU committee that Saris instructed to study course substitutions met, it recommended that foreign language requirements not be waived. In a subsequent ruling in 1998, Saris then upheld the university's right to refuse course substitutions, since the university could now demonstrate that it had considered the accommodation but had a legitimate curricular reason for denying it (Selingo "Judge Says Boston U. Can Require Learning Disabled to Meet Language Requirement"; Sparks and Ganschow 285). Accounts of the trial are available in *The Chronicle of Higher Education,* which reprints the judge's ruling at its Web site. (See *Guckenberger et al. v.*

Boston University et al.; Kim Strosnider "Boston U. Chief Admits He Made
Up Story of Disabled Student"; Jeffrey Selingo "Judge Says Boston U.
Violated Rights of Learning Disabled.") Most national newsmagazines also
covered the trial, e.g., Joseph Shapiro "The Strange Case of Somnolent
Samantha." The *Journal of Learning Disabilities* devotes its July 1999
issue to the BU case with articles by BU attorneys Lawrence Elswit, Erika
Geetter, and Judith Goldberg; and plaintiffs' attorneys Sid Wolinsky and
Amy Whelan as well as LD specialists' reflections on the implications of the
decision. A more recent (1999) Supreme Court decision on the ADA curtails
protections for those whose disabilities have been mitigated by treatment.
This decision makes LD students' rights to accommodations in higher education less certain. After making its ruling, the Supreme Court directed a
federal appeals court to reconsider its judgment in favor of Marilyn
Bartlett. Bartlett, who is learning disabled but has a Ph.D. in educational
administration, had sued the New York bar examination board when they
refused her request for accommodations in the administration of the bar
exam. The law board argued that Bartlett was no longer disabled since she
had learned to compensate for her deficits. (Hebel; *Bartlett v. NY State
Board of Law Examiners*).

2. Patricia Dunn's *Learning Re-Abled,* which provides an extensive review of LD
research and critiques of that research, is the only extended treatment of the
relationship between LD and composition studies. Dunn reviews the small
amount of previous literature on LD in composition studies, noting that "the
LD field is a bottomless ocean into which composition specialists have rarely
ventured" (48–57). She points out that theories underlying the discourse of LD
and the discourse of composition studies are incompatible. Making the leap
means negotiating different paradigms, with different language, common
knowledge, and assumptions — at times, it has seemed to me, different realities. Dunn's resolution of these conflicts is more sympathetic to LD theory
than mine is. Learning Re-Abled and her more recent *Talking, Sketching,
Moving: Multiple Literacies in the Teaching of Writing* describe ways of teaching composition that recognize and build upon diversity.

3. Eileen Simpson, author of a well-known autobiography about dyslexia, recognized the connection long before she was diagnosed. Speculating on why
one of her elementary school teachers chastises other students for reading
poorly but doesn't punish her when she cannot read at all, she recognizes
her kinship with another disabled body:

> It must be that whatever was the matter with me — and surely it
> was something grave if all the others could make words out of the
> letters, and, even more remarkable, string the words together so that
> they told a story — it must be that whatever was the matter with me
> was beyond punishment. I searched for an explanation, and found
> one. Often when we had gone on outings to the nearby village, we
> had seen an ill-tempered dwarf who made rude and incomprehensi-
> ble remarks as we passed by the bench where he sat. The nuns had
> taught us not to stare at him. We were to avert our eyes and say
> silently, "God bless the mark!" Mother Cecilia had averted her eyes.
> She must silently have said the prayer for me. (8)

4. Simi Linton explains the implications of overcoming: "The ideas imbedded in the *overcoming* rhetoric are of personal triumph over a personal condition. The idea that someone can *overcome* a disability has not been generated within the community; it is a wish fulfillment from the outside" (18).

5. The NIMH brochure, in its "case studies" of Susan, Dennis, and Wallace, does recount a story in which difficulties in school are predictive of later failure. Wallace had problems in school, dropped out in the tenth grade, and "spent the next twenty-five years working as a janitor" (15). Significantly, Wallace went to school during the early 1960s, so his LD went undiagnosed. Susan and Dennis are doing well because someone diagnosed their problem and they were able to get help. "Wallace, sadly, was a product of his time, when learning disabilities were more of a mystery and often went unrecognized" (16). In order for diagnosis to be hopeful, being undiagnosed is the only possibility for failure that can be recognized.

6. The controversy over whether students with LD should be allowed to have extra time on tests is a good example. Stanovich ("Sociopsychometrics" 358) and Kelman and Lester (161–80) examine this issue and conclude that there is usually no or very little explicit rationale for making tests speeded. They argue that if speed is genuinely important for some real-world performance, then speed should be a factor for everyone who takes the test, even if he or she has dyslexia. If it isn't, then speed shouldn't be a requirement for anyone.

Works Cited

American Psychiatric Association. *Diagnostic and Statistical Manual of Mental Disorders.* 4th ed. Washington, DC: American Psychiatric Association, 1995.

Bartlett v. NY State Board of Law Examiners. U.S. Court of Appeals. Docket No. 97-9162. 14 September 1998. Rpt. in *U.S. Court of Appeals for the Second Circuit Decisions* 27 May 2000 <http://www.law.pace.edu/lawlib/legal/us-legal/judiciary/search-second.html>.

Brueggemann, Brenda Jo, Linda Feldmeier White, Patricia A. Dunn, Barbara A. Heifferon, and Johnson Cheu. "Becoming Visible: Lessons in Disability." *CCC* 52 (2001): 368–98.

Cruickshank, William. Foreword to the First Edition. *Learning Disabilities and Brain Function: A Neuropsychological Approach.* 3rd ed. By William H. Gaddes and Dorothy Edgell. New York: Springer-Verlag, 1994. xii–xv.

Dudley-Marling, Curt, and Don Dippo. "What Learning Disability Does: Sustaining the Ideology of Schooling." *Journal of Learning Disabilities* 28 (1995): 408–14.

Dunn, Patricia. *Learning Re-Abled: The Learning Disability Controversy and Composition Studies.* Portsmouth, NH: Boynton/Cook, 1995.

———. *Talking, Sketching, Moving: Multiple Literacies in the Teaching of Writing.* Portsmouth, NH: Boynton/Cook, 2001.

Fink, Rosalie. "Literacy Development in Successful Men and Women with Dyslexia." *Annals of Dyslexia* 48 (1998): 311–46.

Gaddes, William H., and Dorothy Edgell. *Learning Disabilities and Brain Function: A Neuropsychological Approach.* 3rd ed. New York: Springer-Verlag, 1994.

Gerber, Paul J., and Henry B. Reiff. *Speaking for Themselves: Ethnographic Interviews with Adults with Learning Disabilities.* Ann Arbor: U of Michigan P, 1991.

Hebel, Sara. "New Supreme Court Rulings Could Impede Disability-Bias Suits against Colleges." *Chronicle of Higher Education* 2 July 1999: A31.

Horner, Bruce. "Discoursing Basic Writing." *CCC* 47 (1996): 199–222.

Hughes, Margaret, and Dennis Searle. *The Violent E and Other Tricky Sounds: Learning to Spell from Kindergarten through Grade 6.* York: Stenhouse, 1997.

Kantrowitz, Barbara, and Anne Underwood. "Dyslexia and the New Science of Reading." *Newsweek* 22 November 1999: 72–79.

Kelman, Mark, and Gillian Lester. *Jumping the Queue: An Inquiry into the Legal Treatment of Students with Learning Disabilities.* Cambridge: Harvard UP, 1997.

Lee, Christopher, and Rosemary Jackson. *What About Me? Strategies for Teaching Misunderstood Learners.* Portsmouth, NH: Heinemann, 2001.

Linton, Simi. *Claiming Disability: Knowledge and Identity.* New York: New York UP, 1998.

National Institute of Mental Health (NIMH). *Learning Disabilities.* By Sharon Neuwirth. Washington, DC: GPO, 1993.

Oakland, Thomas, et al. "An Evaluation of the Dyslexia Training Program: A Multisensory Method for Promoting Reading in Students with Reading Disabilities." *Journal of Learning Disabilities* 31 (1998): 140–47.

Resnick, Lauren. "Shared Cognition: Thinking as Social Practice." *Perspectives on Socially Shared Cognition.* Ed. Lauren B. Resnick, John M. Levine, and Stephanie D. Teasley. Washington, DC: American Psychological Association, 1991. 1–20.

Rose, Mike. "Narrowing the Mind and Page: Remedial Writers and Cognitive Reductionism." *CCC* 39 (1988): 267–302.

Selingo, Jeffrey. "Judge Says Boston U. Can Require Learning Disabled to Meet Language Requirement." *Chronicle of Higher Education* 12 June 1998: A42.

———. "Judge Says Boston U. Violated Rights of Learning Disabled." *Chronicle of Higher Education* 5 September 1997: A65.

Shapiro, Joseph. "The Strange Case of Somnolent Samantha." *U.S. News & World Report* 14 April 1997: 31.

Simpson, Eileen. *Reversals: A Personal Account of Victory over Dyslexia.* 1979. Rev. ed. New York: Noonday–Farrar, Straus and Giroux, 1991.

Sparks, Richard L., and Leonore Ganschow. "The Boston University Lawsuit: Introduction to the Special Series." *Journal of Learning Disabilities* 32 (1999): 284–85.

Spear-Swerling, Louise, and Robert J. Sternberg. "The Sociopsychometrics of Learning Disabilities." *Journal of Learning Disabilities* 32 (1999): 350–61.

Stanovich, Keith E. "The Sociopsychometrics of Learning Disabilities." *Journal of Learning Disabilities* 32 (1999): 350–61.

Sternglass, Marilyn S. *Time to Know Them: A Longitudinal Study of Writing and Learning at the College Level.* Mahwah, NJ: Lawrence Erlbaum, 1997.

Strosnider, Kim. "Boston U. Chief Admits He Made Up Story of Disabled Student." *Chronicle of Higher Education* 18 April 1997: A38.

Traub, James. *City on a Hill: Testing the American Dream at City College.* Reading: Addison-Wesley, 1995.

Westling, Jon. "Getting Government Out of Higher Education." The Heritage Foundation Lectures and Seminars 3 May 1995 and 6 July 1998 <http://www.heritage.org/library/categories/education/lect533.html>.

Wolinsky, Sid, and Amy Whelan. "Federal Law and the Accommodation of Students with LD: The Lawyers Look at the BU Decision." *Journal of Learning Disabilities* 32 (1999): 286–91.

Classroom Activities

White suggests: "In working with students with LD, it is important to try to create a classroom that offers the pleasures of academic writing (getting to explain and having others listen to one's explanations) and reading (the joy of changing one's mind)." She also cites studies that indicate that struggling students make the most significant gains when they find a subject of critical interest to them and are given the chance to study it in depth.

In this regard, consider giving students the opportunity to complete extended study of a topic or issue that they find particularly compelling. At the beginning of the semester, work with the class to come up with a list of topics that they would like to examine in depth over the course of the semester. Have each student choose the topic or issue that most interests him or her and then organize the class into small groups according to their choices. Work with each group to develop appropriate reading and writing assignments for the semester.

Thinking about Teaching

White argues that "comparing LD spelling pedagogy with whole-language spelling pedagogy provides clear examples of the limitations of behaviorist theory in explaining the perception of language." Behaviorist theory, White further suggests, can be linked to the standards movement in education and to the emphasis on phonics (as opposed to meaning-making) in reading instruction.

With this in mind, consider familiarizing yourself with the No Child Left Behind Act of 2001 (see <http://www.ed.gov/offices/OESE/esea/>). The act mandates that all states implement accountability systems relying on annual standardized tests in reading and math. In light of White's article, how do you feel about the act's emphasis on standardized tests and "programs that use scientifically proven ways of teaching children to read," including phonics instruction as a key component of reading pedagogy? (No Child Left Behind stresses mastery of five key components of reading: phonemic awareness, phonics, fluency, vocabulary, and comprehension.) Does this emphasis on teaching and assessing fragmented reading skills shape K–12 accountability tests in your state? Does your state also require successful completion of standardized tests in order to matriculate to or graduate from a college or university? As you investigate these questions, consider your own perspectives on the issues involved, as well as the implications for access to higher education for students with learning differences. You may wish to share White's article with colleagues and discuss how it affected your views on standardized testing, whole-language pedagogy, and strategies for teaching students with learning disabilities.

7

Writing and Adult Learners

As more adult learners and students of "nontraditional" ages (beyond the usual demographic of eighteen- to twenty-four-year-olds) decide to begin or return to college, many of us will see a shifting population in our basic writing classrooms. Such adult learners may well have different needs and purposes for attending college than their younger counterparts. Balancing child care and other family responsibilities with full-time jobs and college course work can be a critical concern for this population. At the same time, many adult learners, as well as their teachers, report a more pronounced sense of commitment to their education and a more direct sense of purpose than they see in younger students. The presence of adult learners in the classroom can certainly enhance the learning environment for all of our students, as the following arguments demonstrate, often using the writing of returning adult students as evidence.

Many of us have wondered how to create a stronger connection between our course and the lives of our students. The voices of adult learners that speak in the following selections reinforce the notion of the writing process as an everyday problem-solving activity. Adrienne Rich, Sarah Nixon-Ponder, and Barbara Gleason describe pedagogies that grow out of the real-world experiences of adult learners. Throughout this section, each of the writers offers suggestions that can stimulate the learning environment (both in the classroom and beyond) for all of our students.

Teaching Language in Open Admissions

Adrienne Rich

First published in 1972 and informed by the political struggles of its era, feminist poet and essayist Adrienne Rich's article "Teaching Language in Open Admissions" is a testimony to the necessities and possibilities of teaching students in basic writing. With a nod toward the liberatory philosophies of Paulo Freire and Jean-Paul Sartre, Rich analyzes both the philosophical and the practical issues of teaching open-admissions students at the City College of New York in the late 1960s and early 1970s — the same time and place in which Mina Shaughnessy began the inquiry that would lead to Errors and Expectations. *"Teaching Language in Open Admissions," dedicated to Shaughnessy, stands as a companion piece to the foundational work of* Errors and Expectations.*

To the memory of Mina Shaughnessy, 1924–1978

I stand to this day behind the major ideas about literature, writing, and teaching that I expressed in this essay. Several things strike me in rereading it, however. Given the free rein allowed by the SEEK program (described in the text of the essay) when I first began teaching at the City College of New York, it is interesting to me to note the books I was choosing for classes: Orwell, Wright, LeRoi Jones, Lawrence, Baldwin, Plato's *Republic*. It is true that few books by black women writers were available; the bookstores of the late sixties were crowded with paperbacks by Frederick Douglass, Malcolm X, Frantz Fanon, Langston Hughes, Eldridge Cleaver, W. E. B. Du Bois, and by anthologies of mostly male black writers. Ann Petry, Gwendolyn Brooks, June Jordan, Audre Lorde, I came to know and put on my reading lists or copied for classes; but the real crescendo of black women's writing was yet to come, and writers like Zora Neale Hurston and Margaret Walker were out of print. It is obvious now, as it was not then (except to black women writers, undoubtedly) that integral to the struggle against racism in the literary canon there was another, as yet unarticulated, struggle, against the sexism of black and white male editors, anthologists, critics, and publishers.

For awhile I have thought of going back to City College to ask some of my former colleagues, still teaching there, what could be said of the past decade, what is left there of what was, for a brief time, a profound if often naively optimistic experiment in education. (Naively optimistic because I think the white faculty at least, those of us who were most committed to the students, vastly underestimated the psychic depth and economic function of racism in the city and the nation, the power of the

---

*See Halasek and Highberg (xvi), who provide a similar context for "Teaching Language in Open Admissions." Halasek, Kay, and Nels P. Highberg. Introduction: Locality and Basic Writing. *Landmark Essays on Basic Writing*. Landmark Essays Vol. 18. Ed. Kay Halasek and Nels P. Highberg. Mahwah, New Jersey: Lawrence Erlbaum Associates, 2001. xi–xxix.

political machinery that could be "permissive" for a handful of years only to retrench, break promises, and betray, pitting black youth against Puerto Rican and Asian, poor ethnic students against students of color, in an absurd and tragic competition for resources which should have been open to all.) But it has seemed to me that such interviews could be fragmentary at best. I lived through some of that history, the enlarging of classes, the heavy increase of teaching loads, the firing of junior faculty and of many of the best and most dedicated teachers I had known, the efforts of City College to reclaim its "prestige" in the media; I know also that dedicated teachers still remain, who teach Basic Writing not as a white man's — or woman's — burden but because they choose to do so. And, on the corner of Broadway near where I live, I see young people whose like I knew ten years ago as college students "hanging-out", brown-bagging, standing in short skirts and high-heeled boots in doorways waiting for a trick, or being dragged into the car of a plumed and sequined pimp.

Finally: in reprinting this essay I would like to acknowledge my debt to Mina Shaughnessy, who was director of the Basic Writing Program at City when I taught there, and from whom, in many direct and indirect ways, I learned — in a time and place where pedagogic romanticism and histrionics were not uncommon — a great deal about the ethics and integrity of teaching.

This essay was first published in *The Uses of Literature,* edited by Monroe Engel (Cambridge, Mass.: Harvard University, 1973).

My first romantic notion of teaching came, I think, from reading Emlyn Williams's play *The Corn Is Green,* sometime in my teens. As I reconstruct it now, a schoolteacher in a Welsh mining village is reading her pupils' essays one night and comes upon a paper which, for all its misspellings and dialect constructions, seems to be the work of a nascent poet. Turning up in the midst of the undistinguished efforts of her other pupils, this essay startles the teacher. She calls in the boy who wrote it, goes over it with him, talks with him about his life, his hopes, and offers to tutor him privately, without fees. Together, as the play goes on, they work their way through rhetoric, mathematics, Shakespeare, Latin, Greek. The boy gets turned on by the classics, is clearly intended to be, if not a poet, at least a scholar. Birth and family background had destined him for a life in the coal mines; but now another path opens up. Toward the end of the play we see him being coached for the entrance examinations for Oxford. I believe crisis strikes when it looks as if he has gotten one of the village girls pregnant and may have to marry her, thus cutting short a career of dazzling promise before it has begun. I don't recall the outcome, but I suspect that the unwed mother is hushed up and packed away (I would be more interested to see the play rewritten today as *her* story) and the boy goes off to Oxford, with every hope of making it to donhood within the decade.

Perhaps this represents a secret fantasy of many teachers: the ill-scrawled essay, turned up among so many others, which has the mark of genius. And looking at the first batch of freshman papers every semester can be like a trip to the mailbox — there is always the possibility of something turning up that will illuminate the weeks ahead. But behind the larger fantasy lie assumptions which I have only gradually come to recognize; and the recognition has to do with a profound change in my conceptions of teaching and learning.

Before I started teaching at City College I had known only elitist institutions: Harvard and Radcliffe as an undergraduate, Swarthmore as a visiting poet, Columbia as teacher in a graduate poetry workshop that included some of the best young poets in the city. I applied for the job at City in 1968 because Robert Cumming had described the SEEK program to me after Martin Luther King was shot, and my motivation was complex. It had to do with white liberal guilt, of course; and a political decision to use my energies in work with "disadvantaged" (black and Puerto Rican) students. But it also had to do with a need to involve myself with the real life of the city, which had arrested me from the first weeks I began living here.

In 1966 Mayor John Lindsay had been able, however obtusely, to coin the phrase "Fun City" without actually intending it as a sick joke. By 1968, the uncollected garbage lay bulging in plastic sacks on the north side of Washington Square, as it had lain longer north of 110th Street; the city had learned to endure subway strikes, sanitation strikes, cab strikes, power and water shortages; the policeman on the corner had become a threatening figure to many whites as he had long been to blacks; the public school teachers and the parents of their pupils had been in pitched battle. On the Upper West Side poor people were being evicted from tenements which were then tinned-up and left empty, awaiting unscheduled demolition to make room for middle-income housing, for which funds were as yet unavailable; and a squatter movement of considerable political consciousness was emerging in defiance of this uprooting.

There seemed to be three ways in which the white middle class could live in New York: the paranoiac, the solipsistic, and a third, which I am more hesitant to define. By the mid-sixties paranoia was visible and audible: streets of brownstones whose occupants had hired an armed guard for the block and posted notices accordingly; conversations on park benches in which public safety had replaced private health as a topic of concern; conversion of all personal anxieties into fear of the mugger (and the mugger was real, no doubt about it). Paranoia could become a life-style, a science, an art, with the active collaboration of reality. Solipsism I encountered first and most concretely in a conversation with an older European intellectual who told me he liked living in New York (on the East Side) because Madison

Avenue reminded him of Paris. It was, and still is, possible to live, if you can afford it, on one of those small islands where the streets are kept clean and the pushers and nodders invisible, to travel by cab, deplore the state of the rest of the city, but remain essentially aloof from its causes and effects. It seems about as boring as most forms of solipsism, since to maintain itself it must remain thick-skinned and ignorant.

But there was, and is, another relationship with the city which I can only begin by calling love. The city as object of love, a love not unmixed with horror and anger, the city as Baudelaire and Rilke had previsioned it, or William Blake for that matter, death in life, but a death emblematic of the death that is epidemic in modern society, and a life more edged, more costly, more charged with knowledge, than life elsewhere. Love as one knows it sometimes with a person with whom one is locked in struggle, energy draining but also energy replenishing, as when one is fighting for life, in oneself or someone else. Here was this damaged, self-destructive organism, preying and preyed upon. The streets were rich with human possibility and vicious with human denial (it is breathtaking to walk through a street in East Harlem, passing among the lithe, alert, childish bodies and attuned, observant, childish faces, playing in the spray of a hydrant, and to know that addiction awaits every brain and body in that block as a potential killer). In all its historic, overcrowded, and sweated poverty, the Lower East Side at the turn of the century had never known this: the odds for the poor, today, are weighted by heroin, a fact which the middle classes ignored until it breathed on their own children's lives as well.

In order to live in the city, I needed to ally myself, in some concrete, practical, if limited way, with the possibilities. So I went up to Convent Avenue and 133rd Street and was interviewed for a teaching job, hired as a poet-teacher. At that time a number of writers, including Toni Cade Bambara, the late Paul Blackburn, Robert Cumming, David Henderson, June Jordan, were being hired to teach writing in the SEEK program to black and Puerto Rican freshmen entering from substandard ghetto high schools, where the prevailing assumption had been that they were of inferior intelligence. (More of these schools later.) Many dropped out (a lower percentage than the national college dropout rate, however); many stuck it out through several semesters of remedial English, math, reading, to enter the mainstream of the college. (As of 1972, 208 SEEK students — or 35 to 40 percent — have since graduated from City College; twenty-four are now in graduate school. *None* of these students would have come near higher education under the regular admissions programs of the City University; high-school guidance counselors have traditionally written off such students as incapable of academic work. Most could not survive economically in college without the stipends which the SEEK program provides.)

My job, that first year, was to "turn the students on" to writing by whatever means I wanted — poetry, free association, music, politics, drama, fiction — to acclimate them to the act of writing, while a grammar teacher, with whom I worked closely outside of class, taught sentence structure, the necessary mechanics. A year later this course was given up as too expensive, since it involved two teachers. My choice was to enlarge my scope to include grammar and mechanics or to find a niche elsewhere and teach verse writing. I stayed on to teach, and learn, grammar — among other things.

The early experience in SEEK was, as I look back on it, both unnerving and seductive. Even those who were (unlike me) experienced teachers of remedial English were working on new frontiers, trying new methods. Some of the most rudimentary questions we confronted were: How do you make standard English verb endings available to a dialect-speaker? How do you teach English prepositional forms to a Spanish-language student? What are the arguments for and against "Black English"? The English of academic papers and theses? Is standard English simply a weapon of colonization? Many of our students wrote in the vernacular with force and wit; others were unable to say what they wanted on paper in or out of the vernacular. We were dealing not simply with dialect and syntax but with the imagery of lives, the anger and flare of urban youth — how could this be *used,* strengthened, without the lies of artificial polish? How does one teach order, coherence, the structure of ideas while respecting the student's experience of his or her thinking and perceiving? Some students who could barely sweat out a paragraph delivered (and sometimes conned us with) dazzling raps in the classroom: How could we help this oral gift transfer itself onto paper? The classes were small — fifteen at most; the staff, at that time, likewise; we spent hours in conference with individual students, hours meeting together and with counselors, trying to teach ourselves how to teach and asking ourselves what we ought to be teaching.

So these were classes, not simply in writing, not simply in literature, certainly not just in the correction of sentence fragments or the redemptive power of the semicolon; though we did, and do, work on all these. One teacher gave a minicourse in genres; one in drama as literature; teachers have used their favorite books from *Alice in Wonderland* to Martin Buber's *The Knowledge of Man;* I myself have wandered all over the map of my own reading: D. H. Lawrence, W. E. B. Du Bois, LeRoi Jones, Plato, Orwell, Ibsen, poets from W. C. Williams to Audre Lorde. Sometimes books are used as a way of learning to look at literature, sometimes as a provocation for the students' own writing, sometimes both. At City College all Basic Writing teachers have been free to choose the books they would assign (always keeping within the limits of the SEEK book allowance and considering the fact that non-SEEK students have no book allowance at all, though their financial need may be as acute.) There has never been a set curriculum or a required reading list; we have poached off each others' booklists, methods, essay topics, grammar-teaching exercises, and anything else that we hoped would "work" for us.[1]

Most of us felt that students learn to write by discovering the validity and variety of their own experience; and in the late 1960s, as the black classics began to flood the bookstores, we drew on the black novelists, poets, and polemicists as the natural path to this discovery for SEEK students. Black teachers were, of course, a path; and there were some who combined the work of consciousness-raising with the study of Sophocles, Kafka, and other pillars of the discipline oddly enough known as "English." For many white teachers, the black writers were a relatively new discovery: the clear, translucent prose of Douglass, the sonorities of *The Souls of Black Folk,* the melancholy sensuousness of Toomer's poem-novel *Cane.* In this discovery of a previously submerged culture we were learning from and with our students as rarely happens in the university, though it is happening anew in the area of women's studies. We were not merely exploring a literature and a history which had gone virtually unmentioned in our white educations (particularly true for those over thirty); we were not merely having to confront in talk with our students and in their writings, as well as the books we read, the bitter reality of Western racism: we also found ourselves reading almost any piece of Western literature through our students' eyes, imagining how this voice, these assumptions, would sound to us if we were they. "We learned from the students" — banal cliché, one that sounds pious and patronizing by now; yet the fact remains that our white liberal assumptions were shaken, our vision of both the city and the university changed, our relationship to language itself made both deeper and more painful.

Of course the students responded to black literature; I heard searching and acute discussions of Jones's poem "The Liar" or Wright's "The Man Who Lived Underground" from young men and women who were in college on sufferance in the eyes of the educational establishment; I've heard similar discussions of *Sons and Lovers* or the *Republic.* Writing this, I am conscious of how obvious it all seems and how unnecessary it now might appear to demonstrate by little anecdotes that ghetto students can handle sophisticated literature and ideas. But in 1968, 1969, we were still trying to prove this — we and

---

[1]What I have found deadly and defeating is the anthology designed for multiethnic classes in freshman English. I once ordered one because the book stipends had been cut out and I was trying to save the students money. I ended up using one Allen Ginsberg poem, two by LeRoi Jones, and asking the students to write essays provoked by the photographs in the anthology. The college anthology, in general, as nonbook, with its exhaustive and painfully literal notes, directives, questions, and "guides for study," is like TV showing of a film — cut, chopped up, and interspersed with commercials: a flagrant mutilation by mass technological culture.

our students felt that the burden of proof was on us. When the Black and Puerto Rican Student Community seized the South Campus of C.C.N.Y. in April 1969, and a team of students sat down with the president of the college and a team of faculty members to negotiate, one heard much about the faculty group's surprised respect for the students' articulateness, reasoning power, and skill in handling statistics — for the students were negotiating in exchange for withdrawal from South Campus an admissions policy which would go far beyond SEEK in its inclusiveness.

Those of us who had been involved earlier with ghetto students felt that we had known their strength all along: an impatient cutting through of the phony, a capacity for tenacious struggle with language and syntax and difficult ideas, a growing capacity for political analysis which helped counter the low expectations their teachers had always had of them and which many had had of themselves; and more, their knowledge of the naked facts of society, which academia has always, even in its public urban form, managed to veil in ivy or fantasy. Some were indeed chronologically older than the average college student; many, though eighteen or twenty years old, had had responsibility for themselves and their families for years. They came to college with a greater insight into the actual workings of the city and of American racial oppression than most of their teachers or their elite contemporaries. They had held dirty jobs, borne children, negotiated for Spanish-speaking parents with an English-speaking world of clinics, agencies, lawyers, and landlords, had their sixth senses nurtured in the streets, or had made the transition from southern sharehold or Puerto Rican countryside to Bedford-Stuyvesant or the *barrio* and knew the ways of two worlds. And they were becoming, each new wave of them, more lucidly conscious of the politics of their situation, the context within which their lives were being led.

It is tempting to romanticize, at the distance of midsummer 1972, what the experience of SEEK — and by extension, of all remedial freshman programs under Open Admissions — was (and is) for the students themselves. The Coleman Report and the Moynihan Report have left echoes and vibrations of stereotypical thinking which perhaps only a first-hand knowledge of the New York City schools can really silence. Teaching at City I came to know the intellectual poverty and human waste of the public school system through the marks it had left on students — and not on black and Puerto Rican students only, as the advent of Open Admissions was to show. For a plain look at the politics and practices of this system, I recommend Ellen Lurie's *How to Change the Schools,* a handbook for parent activists which enumerates the conditions she and other parents, black, Puerto Rican, and white, came to know intimately in their struggles to secure their children's right to learn and to be treated with dignity. The book is a photograph of the decay, racism, and abusiveness they confronted, written not as muckraking journalism but as a practical tool for others like themselves. I have read little else, including the most lyrically indignant prose of radical educators, that gives so precise and devastating a picture of the life that New York's children are expected to lead in the name of schooling. She writes of "bewildered angry teenagers, who have discovered that they are in classes for mentally retarded students, simply because they cannot speak English," of teachers and principals who "behaved as though every white middle-class child was gifted and was college material, and every black and Puerto Rican (and sometimes Irish and Italian) working-class child was slow, disadvantaged, and unable to learn anything but the most rudimentary facts." She notes that "81 elementary schools in the state (out of a total of 3,634) had more than 70 percent of their students below minimum competence, and 65 *of these were New York City public schools*!" Her findings and statistics make it clear that tracking begins at kindergarten (chiefly on the basis of skin color and language) and that nonwhite and working-class children are assumed to have a maximum potential which fits them only for the so-called general diploma, hence are not taught, as are their middle-class contemporaries, the math or languages or writing skills needed to pass college entrance examinations or even to do academic-diploma high-school work.[2] I have singled out these particular points for citation because they have to do directly with our students' self-expectations and the enforced limitation of their horizons years before they come to college. But much else has colored their educational past: the drug pushers at the school gates, the obsolete texts, the punitive conception of the teacher's role, the ugliness, filth, and decay of the buildings, the demoralization even of good teachers working under such conditions. (Add to this the use of tranquilizing drugs on children who are considered hyperactive or who present "behavior problems" at an early age.)

To come out of scenes like these schools and be offered "a chance" to compete as an equal in the world of academic credentials, the white-collar world, the world beyond the minimum wage or welfare, is less romantic for the student than for those who view the process from a distance. The student who leaves the campus at three or four o'clock after a day of classes, goes to work as a waitress, or clerk, or hash-slinger, or guard, comes home at ten or eleven o'clock to a crowded apartment with TV audible in every corner — what does it feel like to this student to be reading, say, Byron's "Don Juan" or Jane Austen for a class the next day? Our students may spend two or three hours in the subway going to and from college and jobs, longer if the subway

---

[2]Ellen Lurie, *How to Change the Schools* (New York: Random House, 1970). See pp. 31, 32, 40–48.

system is more deplorable than usual. To read in the New York subway at rush hour is impossible; it is virtually impossible to think.

How does one compare this experience of college with that of the Columbia students down at 116th Street in their quadrangle of gray stone dormitories, marble steps, flowered borders, wide spaces of time and architecture in which to talk and think? Or that of Berkeley students with their eucalyptus grove and tree-lined streets of bookstores and cafés? The Princeton or Vassar students devoting four years to the life of the mind in Gothic serenity? Do "motivation" and "intellectual competency" mean the same for those students as for City College undergraduates on that overcrowded campus where in winter there is often no place to sit between classes, with two inadequate bookstores largely filled with required texts, two cafeterias and a snack bar that are overpriced, dreary, and unconducive to lingering, with the incessant pressure of time and money driving at them to rush, to get through, to amass the needed credits somehow, to drop out, to stay on with gritted teeth? Out of a graduating class at Swarthmore or Oberlin and one at C.C.N.Y., which students have demonstrated their ability and commitment, and how do we assume we can measure such things?

Sometimes as I walk up 133rd Street, past the glass-strewn doorways of P.S. 161, the graffiti-sprayed walls of tenements, the uncollected garbage, through the iron gates of South Campus and up the driveway to the prefab hut which houses the English department, I think wryly of John Donne's pronouncement that "the University is a Paradise; rivers of Knowledge are there; Arts and Sciences flow from thence." I think that few of our students have this Athenian notion of what college is going to be for them; their first introduction to it is a many hours' wait in line at registration, which only reveals that the courses they have been advised or wanted to take are filled, or conflict in hours with a needed job; then more hours at the cramped, heavily guarded bookstore; then perhaps, a semester in courses which they never chose, or in which the pace and allusions of a lecturer are daunting or which may meet at opposite ends of an elongated campus stretching for six city blocks and spilling over into a former warehouse on Broadway. Many have written of their first days at C.C.N.Y.: "I only knew it was different from high school." What was different, perhaps, was the green grass of early September with groups of young people in dashikis and gelés, jeans and tie-dye, moving about with the unquenchable animation of the first days of the fall semester; the encounter with some teachers who seem to respect them as individuals; something at any rate less bleak, less violent, less mean-spirited, than the halls of Benjamin Franklin or Evander Childs or some other school with the line painted down the center of the corridor and a penalty for taking the short-cut across that line. In all that my students have written about their high schools, I have found bitterness, resentment, satire, black humor; never any word of nostalgia for the school, though sometimes a word of affection for a teacher "who really tried."

The point is that, as Mina Shaughnessy, the director of the Basic Writing Program at City, has written: "the first stage of Open Admissions involves *openly admitting* that education has failed for too many students."[3] Professor Shaughnessy writes in her most recent report of the increase in remedial courses of white, ethnic students (about two-thirds of the Open Admissions freshmen who have below-80 high school averages) and of the discernible fact, a revelation to many, that these white students "have experienced the failure of the public schools in different ways from the black and Puerto Rican students." Another City College colleague, Leonard Kriegel, writes of this newest population: "Like most blue-collar children, they had lived within the confines of an educational system without ever having questioned that system. They were used to being stamped and categorized. Rating systems, grades, obligations to improve, these had beset them all their lives. . . . They had few expectations from the world-at-large. When they were depressed, they had no real idea of what was getting them down, and they would have dismissed as absurd the idea that they could make demands. They accepted the myths of America as those myths had been presented to them."[4]

Meeting some of the so-called ethnic students in class for the first time in September 1970, I began to realize that: there *are* still poor Jews in New York City; they teach English better to native speakers of Greek on the island of Cyprus than they do to native speakers of Spanish on the island of Manhattan; the Chinese student with acute English-language difficulties is stereotyped as "nonexpressive" and channeled into the physical sciences before anyone has a chance to find out whether he or she is a potential historian, political theorist, or psychologist; and (an intuition, more difficult to prove) white, ethnic working-class young women seem to have problems of self-reliance and of taking their lives seriously that young black women students as a group do not seem to share.

There is also a danger that, paradoxically or not, the white middle-class teacher may find it easier to identify with the strongly

[3]Mina P. Shaughnessy, "Open Admissions — A Second Report," in *The City College Department of English Newsletter,* vol. II, no. 1., January 1972. A. R., 1978: See also Shaughnessy's *Errors and Expectations: A Guide for the Teacher of Basic Writing* (New York: Oxford, 1977), a remarkable study in the methodology of teaching language.

[4]"When Blue-Collar Students Go to College," in *Saturday Review,* July 22, 1972. The article is excerpted from the book *Working Through: A Teacher's Journal in the Urban University* (New York: Saturday Review Press, 1972). Kriegel is describing students at Long Island University of a decade ago; but much that he says is descriptive of students who are now entering colleges like C.C.N.Y. under Open Admissions.

motivated, obviously oppressed, politically conscious black student than with the students of whom Kriegel has written. Perhaps a different set of prejudices exists: if you're white, why aren't you more hip, more achieving, why are you bored and alienated, why don't you *care* more? Again, one has to keep clearly in mind the real lessons of the schools — both public and parochial — which reward conformity, passivity, and correct answers and penalize, as Ellen Lurie says, the troublesome question "as trouble-making," the lively, independent, active child as "disruptive," curiosity as misbehavior. (Because of the reinforcement in passivity received all around them in society and at home, white women students seem particularly vulnerable to these judgments.) In many ways the damage is more insidious because the white students have as yet no real political analysis going for them; only the knowledge that they have not been as successful in school as white students are supposed to be.

Confronted with these individuals, this city, these life situations, these strengths, these damages, there are some harsh questions that have to be raised about the uses of literature. I think of myself as a teacher of language: that is, as someone for whom language has implied freedom, who is trying to aid others to free themselves through the written word, and above all through learning to write it for themselves. I cannot know for them what it is they need to free, or what words they need to write; I can only try with them to get an approximation of the story they want to tell. I have always assumed, and I do still assume, that people come into the freedom of language through reading, before writing; that the differences of tone, rhythm, vocabulary, intention, encountered over years of reading are, whatever else they may be, suggestive of many different possible modes of being. But my daily life as a teacher confronts me with young men and women who have had language and literature *used against* them, to keep them in their place, to mystify, to bully, to make them feel powerless. Courses in great books or speed-reading are not an answer when it is the meaning of literature itself that is in question. Sartre says: "the literary object has no other substance than the reader's subjectivity; Raskolnikov's waiting is my waiting which I lend him. . . . His hatred of the police magistrate who questions him is my hatred, which has been solicited and wheedled out of me by signs. . . . Thus, the writer appeals to the reader's freedom to collaborate in the production of his work."[5] But what if it is these very signs, or ones like them, that have been used to limit the reader's freedom or to convince the reader of his or her unworthiness to "collaborate in the production of the work"?

[5]Jean-Paul Sartre, *What Is Literature?* (New York: Harper Colophon Books, 1965), pp. 39–40.

I have no illuminating answers to such questions. I am sure we must revise, and are revising, our notion of the "classic," which has come to be used as a term of unquestioning idolatry instead of in the meaning which Sartre gives it: a book written by someone who "did not have to decide with each work what the meaning and value of literature were, since its meaning and value were fixed by tradition."[6] And I know that the action from the other side, of becoming that person who puts signs on paper and invokes the collaboration of a reader, encounters a corresponding check: in order to write I have to believe that there is someone willing to collaborate subjectively, as opposed to a grading machine out to get me for mistakes in spelling and grammar. (Perhaps for this reason, many students first show the writing they are actually capable of in an uncorrected journal rather than in a "theme" written "for class.") The whole question of *trust* as a basis for the act of reading or writing has only opened up since we began trying to educate those who have every reason to mistrust literary culture. For young adults trying to write seriously for the first time in their lives, the question "Whom can I trust?" must be an underlying boundary to be crossed before real writing can occur. We who are part of literary culture come up against such a question only when we find ourselves writing on some frontier of self-determination, as when writers from an oppressed group *within* literary culture, such as black intellectuals, or, most recently, women, begin to describe and analyze themselves as they cease to identify with the dominant culture. Those who fall into this category ought to be able to draw on it in entering into the experience of the young adult for whom writing itself — as reading — has been part of the not-me rather than one of the natural activities of the self.

At this point the question of method legitimately arises: How to do it? How to develop a working situation in the classroom where trust becomes a reality, where the students are writing with belief in their own validity, and reading with belief that what they read has validity for them? The question is legitimate — How to do it? — but I am not sure that a description of strategies and exercises, readings, and writing topics can be, however successful they have proven for one teacher. When I read such material, I may find it stimulating and heartening as it indicates the varieties of concern and struggle going on in other classrooms, but I end by feeling it is useless to me. X is not myself and X's students are not my students, nor are my students of this fall the same as my students of last spring. A couple of years ago I decided to teach *Sons and Lovers,* because of my sense that the novel touched on facts of existence crucial to people in their late teens, and my belief that it dealt with certain aspects of family life, sexuality, work, anger, and jealousy which carried over to many cultures. Before the students

[6]Ibid., p. 85.

began to read, I started talking about the time and place of the novel, the life of the mines, the process of industrialization and pollution visible in the slag heaps; and I gave the students (this was an almost all-black class) a few examples of the dialect they would encounter in the early chapters. Several students challenged the novel sight unseen: it had nothing to do with them, it was about English people in another era, why should they expect to find it meaningful to them, and so forth. I told them I had asked them to read it because I believed it was meaningful for them; if it was not, we could talk and write about why not and how not. The following week I reached the classroom door to find several students already there, energetically arguing about the Morels, who was to blame in the marriage, Mrs. Morel's snobbery, Morel's drinking and violence — taking sides, justifying, attacking. The class never began; it simply continued as other students arrived. Many had not yet read the novel, or had barely looked at it; these became curious and interested in the conversation and did go back and read it because they felt it must have something to have generated so much heat. That time, I felt some essential connections had been made, which carried us through several weeks of talking and writing about and out of *Sons and Lovers,* trying to define our relationships to its people and theirs to each other. A year or so later I enthusiastically started working with *Sons and Lovers* again, with a class of largely ethnic students — Jewish, Greek, Chinese, Italian, German, with a few Puerto Ricans and blacks. No one initially challenged the novel, but no one was particularly interested — or, perhaps, as I told myself, it impinged too dangerously on materials that this group was not about to deal with, such as violence in the family, nascent sexual feelings, conflicting feelings about a parent. Was this really true? I don't know; it is easy to play sociologist and make generalizations. Perhaps, simply, a different chemistry was at work, in me and in the students. The point is that for the first class, or for many of them, I think a trust came to be established in the novel genre as a possible means of finding out more about themselves; for the second class, the novel was an assignment, to be done under duress, read superficially, its connections with themselves avoided wherever possible.

Finally, as to trust: I think that, simple as it may seem, it is worth saying: a fundamental belief in the students is more important than anything else. We all know of those studies in education where the teacher's previously induced expectations dramatically affect the learning that goes on during the semester. This fundamental belief is not a sentimental matter: it is a very demanding matter of realistically conceiving the student where he or she is, and at the same time never losing sight of where he or she *can* be. Conditions at a huge, urban, overcrowded, noisy, and pollution-soaked institution can become almost physically overwhelming at times, for the students and for the staff: sometimes apathy, accidia, anomie seem to stare from the faces in an overheated basement classroom, like the faces in a subway car, and I sympathize with the rush to get out the moment the bell rings. This, too, is our context — not merely the students' past and my past, but this present moment we share. I (and I don't think I am alone in this) become angry with myself for my ineffectualness, angry at the students for their apparent resistance or their acceptance of mediocrity, angriest at the political conditions which dictate that we have to try to repair and extend the fabric of language under conditions which tend to coarsen our apprehensions of everything. Often, however, this anger, if not driven in on ourselves, or converted to despair, can become an illuminating force: the terms of the struggle for equal opportunity are chalked on the blackboard: this is what the students have been up against all their lives.

I wrote at the beginning of this article that my early assumptions about teaching had changed. I think that what has held me at City is not the one or two students in a class whose eyes meet mine with a look of knowing they were born for this struggle with words and meanings; not the poet who has turned up more than once; though such encounters are a privilege in the classroom as anywhere. What has held me, and what I think holds many who teach basic writing, are the hidden veins of possibility running through students who don't know (and strongly doubt) that this is what they were born for, but who may find it out to their own amazement, students who, grim with self-depreciation and prophecies of their own failure or tight with a fear they cannot express, can be lured into sticking it out to some moment of breakthrough, when they discover that they have ideas that are valuable, even original, and can express those ideas on paper. What fascinates and gives hope in a time of slashed budgets, enlarging class size, and national depression is the possibility that many of these young men and women may be gaining the kind of critical perspective on their lives and the skill to bear witness that they have never before had in our country's history.

At the bedrock level of my thinking about this is the sense that language is power, and that, as Simone Weil says, those who suffer from injustice most are the least able to articulate their suffering; and that the silent majority, if released into language, would not be content with a perpetuation of the conditions which have betrayed them. But this notion hangs on a special conception of what it means to be released into language: not simply learning the jargon of an elite, fitting unexceptionably into the status quo, but learning that language can be used as a means of changing reality.[7] What interests me

---

[7]Compare Paulo Freire: "Only beings who can reflect upon the fact that they are determined are capable of freeing themselves." *Cultural Action for Freedom*, Monograph Series No. 1 (Cambridge, Mass.: Harvard Educational Review and Center for the Study of Development and Social Change, 1970).

in teaching is less the emergence of the occasional genius than the overall finding of language by those who did not have it and by those who have been used and abused to the extent that they lacked it.

The question can be validly raised: Is the existing public (or private) educational system, school, or university the place where such a relationship to language can be developed? Aren't those structures already too determined, haven't they too great a stake in keeping things as they are? My response would be, yes, but this is where the *students* are. On the one hand, we need alternate education; on the other, we need to reach those students for whom unorthodox education simply means too much risk. In a disintegrating society, the orthodox educational system reflects disintegration. However, I believe it is more than simply reformist to try to use that system — while it still exists in all its flagrant deficiencies — to use it to provide essential tools and weapons for those who may live on into a new integration. Language is such a weapon, and what goes with language: reflection, criticism, renaming, creation. The fact that our language itself is tainted by the quality of our society means that in teaching we need to be acutely conscious of the kind of tool we want our students to have available, to understand how it has been used against them, and to do all we can to insure that language will not someday be used by them to keep others silent and powerless.

Classroom Activities

Rich discusses the readings that her open-admissions students often found meaningful, including literary works by Richard Wright, William Carlos Williams, Henrik Ibsen, and Audre Lorde. She also mentions authors whose works she wishes had been available to her students, such as Zora Neale Hurston and Margaret Walker. Consider bringing excerpts from these writers' works (as well as your own favorite texts — and works recommended by the students) to class to facilitate reading and writing opportunities for students. As an extended assignment, students can choose to read an entire text (such as Margaret Walker's *For My People* or Henrik Ibsen's *A Doll's House*) and respond with analytic and/or creative writing of their own.

Thinking about Teaching

The problems that Rich poses in her essay are still as much a part of the discussion of teaching basic writing today as they were in the late 1960s and early 1970s. Rich lists questions that grew out of her early experience in teaching basic writing, an experience that she found both "unnerving and seductive":

- How do you make standard verb endings available to a dialect speaker?

- How do you teach English prepositional forms to a Spanish-language student?

- How does one teach order, coherence, the structure of ideas while respecting the student's experience of his or her thinking or perceiving?

- How do you develop a working situation in the classroom where trust becomes a reality, where students are writing with belief in their own validity, and reading with belief that what they read has validity for them?

In your teaching journal, respond to some of these questions. Do they continue to hold relevance today for your own classroom? You may want to share the approaches you use to address the needs and desires of today's generation of basic writing students with colleagues. What impact has the composition theory and practice of the past thirty years had on your own methods? What similarities and differences do you find between your own classrooms and the ones that Rich describes? How do you deal with new issues (such as the decline of equal-access education and open-admissions universities and the rise of standardized testing) not addressed in Rich's essay? How would you update Rich's essay to address contemporary concerns of students in basic writing?

Using Problem-Posing Dialogue in Adult Literacy Education

Sarah Nixon-Ponder

In the following article, first published in 1995 in the journal Adult Learning, *Sarah Nixon-Ponder considers the needs of adult learners as she presents the activity of problem-posing, which "begins by listening for students' issues" and which "can build confidence and self-esteem in [students'] abilities to think critically." This student-centered classroom structure provides opportunities for even the most reticent students to begin to speak. Nixon-Ponder proposes a set of discrete steps that engage "adult learners [who] need the initial structure." Not only do these steps create a real-world framework; they also reflect aspects of the writing process. Students work collaboratively to "describe the content" of a given text, dialogue, picture, or orally presented story, to "define the problem," to "personalize the problem," to "discuss the problem," and to "discuss alternatives (solutions) to the problem." Such collaborative work strengthens real-world skills in solving problems and imagining alternative solutions — skills implicit in the writing process.*

A group of women are gathered around a table, deep in discussion. Spreadsheets with schedules, open notebooks with lists, copies of government documents, and a diagram with measurements of a living space are spread before them. The women are discussing several options, looking earnestly at the pros and cons of each, and speaking in detail on specific aspects of one option. While two women are searching for a specific reference in the government documents, another is rapidly taking notes on the discussion at hand. In all aspects this appears to be a professional business planning meeting, right? Close, but not quite. This is a group of women in an adult literacy class who have arrived at a solution to their childcare situation by using a process called problem-posing dialogue.

Problem-posing is a tool for developing and strengthening critical thinking skills. It is an inductive questioning process that structures dialogue in the classroom. Problem-posing dialogue is noted in the works of Dewey and Piaget who were strong advocates for active, inquiring, hands-on education that resulted in student-centered curricula (Shor, 1992). Freire expanded on the idea of active, participatory education through problem-posing dialogue, a method that transforms the students into "critical co-investigators in dialogue with the teacher."

Learners bring to adult education programs a wealth of knowledge from their personal experiences, and the problem-posing method builds on these shared experiences. By introducing specific questions, the teacher encourages the students to make their own conclusions about the values and pressures of society. Freire (1970) refers to this as an "emergence of consciousness and *critical intervention* in reality."

So how is this done? What does it look like? What is the final outcome? Let's take a look at these questions as we walk through the process of problem-posing.

How to Conduct Problem-Posing Dialogue

Problem-posing begins by listening for students' issues. During breaks, instructors should listen to students' conversations with one another and make notes about recurring topics. Based on notes from these investigations, teachers then select and bring the familiar situations back to the students in a codified form: a photograph, a written dialogue, a story, or a drawing. Each situation contains personal and social conflicts that are of deep importance to the students.

Teachers begin by asking a series of inductive questions (listed below) that moves the discussion of the situation from the concrete to the analytical. The problem-posing process directs students to name the problem, understand how it applies to them, determine the causes of the problem, generalize to others, and finally suggest alternatives or solutions to the problem. The "responsibility of the problem-posing teacher is to diversify subject matter and to use students' thought and speech as the base for developing critical understanding of personal experience, unequal conditions in society, and existing knowledge" (Shor, 1992).

Five Steps of Problem-Posing

Auerbach (1990) has simplified the steps of problem-posing. Problem-posing is a means for teaching critical thinking skills, and many adult learners need the initial structure these steps provide in order to build confidence and esteem in their ability to think critically. When beginning to problem-pose, it is important to spend time on each step, for these are all essential components in learning how to critically think about one's world.

Describe the Content

The teacher presents the students with a *code*. Codes are a vital aspect of problem-posing. They *must* originate from the students' concerns and experiences, which makes them important to the students and their daily lives. According to Wallerstein (1983), codes can be

- written dialogues, taken from a variety of reading materials, that directly pertain to the problem being posed.

- role-plays adapted from written or oral dialogues.

- stories taken from the participants' lives and experiences.

- text from newspapers, magazines, community leaflets, signs, phone books, welfare or food stamp forms, housing leases, insurance forms, school bulletins.

- pictures, slides, photographs, collages, drawings, photo-stories, or cartoons.

After the students have studied the code, the teacher begins by asking questions, such as: What do you see in the picture (photograph, drawing, etc.)? What is happening in the picture (photograph, drawing, etc.)? or What is this dialogue (story, article, message) about? What is happening in the dialogue (story, article, message)?

Define the Problem

The students uncover the issue(s) or problem(s) in the code. Teachers may need to repeat the following questions: What is happening in the picture (photograph, drawing, etc.)? What is happening in the dialogue (story, article, message)? Students may identify more than one problem. If this occurs, the teacher should ask the students to focus on just one problem (especially with beginning problem-posers), using the other problem(s) for a future problem-posing idea. Students may identify two problems or issues that cannot be separated and must be dealt with together. This, too, is acceptable just as long as it is the students' decision to work with the two problems together.

Personalize the Problem

At this point, the teacher becomes the facilitator of the discussion, thus guiding the students to talk about how this problem makes them feel and what the problem makes them think about, so that they can internalize the problem. Through discussion, the students will relate the issue(s) or problem(s) to their own lives and cultures. The facilitator should assure that all students are given the chance to share their experiences, understanding as well that some may choose not to share. No one should be made to speak if she/he does not feel comfortable doing so. Learning that others have been in similar situations is very important; this experience will serve as an affirmation to their experiences, lives, and cultures; as an esteem builder; and as a means for bonding with other learners and the facilitator.

Discuss the Problem

The facilitator guides the students toward a discussion on the social/economic reasons for the problem by asking them to talk about why there is a problem and how it has affected them. During this step, it is critical for the facilitator *not* to expound upon personal and political beliefs. This temptation may be very strong during problem-posing dialogue, but resistance to do so is absolutely vital to the growth of the students. Because students' beliefs may differ greatly from those of the facilitator's, students will be more apt to take risks and openly share their beliefs if they believe that this is *their* dialogue and they have ownership in its process.

Discuss Alternatives to the Problem

The facilitator should coach the students into suggesting possible solutions to the problem, and discuss the consequences of the various courses of action. Through discussion, adult students become aware that they have the answers to their problems, especially when they approach their problems and concerns through a cooperative, group effort. Facilitators need to urge the students to search for several alternatives to the problem or issue at hand; the solutions need to be those that can be achieved.

Problem-posing delves deeply into any issue or problem, demonstrating the extent of its social and personal connections. Problem-posing "focuses on power relations in the classroom, in the institution, in the formation of standard canons of knowledge, and in society at large" (Shor, 1992). It challenges the relationship between teacher and student and offers students a forum for validating their life experiences, their cultures, and their personal knowledge of how their world works. Problem-posing is dynamic, participatory, and empowering.

Problem-posing is more than a technique that teaches critical thinking; it is a philosophy, a way of thinking about students and their ability to think critically and to reflect analytically on their lives. Eduard Lindeman, one of America's founding fathers of adult education, firmly believed that the responsibility of adult education was to teach learners how to think analytically and critically; this, too, is the role of problem-posing.

Problem-Posing in Action: Two Case Studies

So what does this look like in an adult literacy education (ABE) program? Let's take a look at two examples from actual literacy programs.

Case 1: An ABE Literacy Class

As an ABE instructor, I was always on the lookout for methods that would promote critical thinking in my class. The students in the program were bright and resourceful adults, and I felt the need to challenge their abilities and push them to question the surrounding world view. I spent many hours listening to my students talk about their lives, experiences, and cultures. Living in the Southwest and being an Anglo woman (many times the only Anglo) among the Latinas/Latinos and Native Americans made me very aware of our differing cultures and lifestyles, but more importantly, it made me see the similar problems that all of us encountered and experienced as people and as women. This awareness made me seek out the problem-posing method.

In one class, in particular, the subject of childcare was always on the women's minds; they discussed the topic before, during, and after class. I introduced this issue in "codes" for problem-posing. Because the topic was extremely relevant to their everyday lives and came from them, not me (as I informed them), it was emotionally charged and personal. They worked through the first three steps quickly and with ease. They related to the pictures I brought in, the short story and newspaper articles that we read, and the story that I shared about my divorced sister and her two children. They brought in relevant reading materials and shared their own stories on the problem of childcare — some of them funny and happy, most of them full of frustration and sadness. Their discussions on the reasons for this lack of good affordable childcare ranged from money issues, to unreliable (or no) transportation, to physical isolation from others, to cultural beliefs about who is qualified to care for someone else's children.

For weeks we worked on this topic. Writing assignments arose naturally as the women wrote their feelings about the discussions in dialogue journals, sharing these with others, and their oral histories became written testaments of their lives. They researched different laws on childcare facilities and they learned about co-operatives, thus reading materials on varying levels of difficulty. They answered their problem by taking this issue into their own hands — into their own control — and discussed reasonable alternatives to this overwhelming problem. Their solution was to organize a system for childcare on their own by sharing their resources. They planned schedules for taking care of each others' children, and those with reliable transportation arranged for carpools. They planned meals for their children and the care keeper(s) using arithmetic to figure amount of food and cost. They discussed discipline problems, and they organized a system for funding their project. They had a problem, and they found the solution for it.

This is problem-posing in action. It is exciting and educational; it is cross-cultural and multicultural because it draws from all of the students' cultures. Additionally, problem-posing builds confidence and community among learners. When I initiated problem-posing dialogue into my ABE class, I had no idea exactly where it would take us. But I believed that my students were able to work through this process and arrive at tangible solutions to their childcare dilemma. All of the basic skills were used. They read different types of materials on different reading levels; they wrote journal entries, oral histories, and letters; they planned schedules, organized carpools, and figured budgets. They learned that they had the answers to their problems, and they learned the steps to take in order to arrive at solutions.

Case 2: A GED Writing & Social Studies Class

In *Empowering Education: Critical Teaching for Social Change,* Ira Shor (1992) discusses different ways to tie problem-posing into all classes: science, health, computers, writing, literature, media, engineering, architecture, and sociology. He begins each class "in a partic-

ipatory and critical way by posing the subject matter itself as a problem." He asks his students to investigate their knowledge about the
subject matter and to think critically about it in an active and
reflective way. So, how is this achieved?

I practiced this form of problem-posing in my GED classes. I began
by asking the students to think about a specific issue (e.g., What is correct writing? Who sets the standards for correct writing? or What is
history? Why should history be studied?). Then I would ask them to
write their feelings about this issue, keeping in mind the following
questions: What do you think about it? How does it make you feel?
Why do you feel this way? What are your personal experiences with
this? After the students had time to reflect, we began discussing the
topic. If no one volunteered to be the first to share with the class, I
would start by talking about my experiences. This would get the dialogue flowing, and others soon willingly volunteered to talk about
their feelings and experiences.

Next, I asked small groups of students to compare their responses
and explore the similarities or differences in each other's experiences.
As a class, we talked about the differences or similarities, what we
could learn from them, and how their beliefs could be applied to the
class. We tried to figure out ways to make the class materials relevant
and meaningful to their studies and their lives. We brought outside
materials into the class. We talked about how to make the class theirs
— how the curriculum, materials, and instruction could reflect their
interests and preferences.

Problem-Posing as a New Concept

This was a new concept for most of my students. Some students had a
difficult time with the nontraditional format of the class structure.
Most were not used to being asked their opinions or beliefs. They did
not believe in themselves; they did not believe that they were capable
of helping to build the curriculum of a class, of their class. And of
course, a few grasped this idea wholeheartedly and ran with it from
the beginning. They became leaders, and they accepted the challenge
to change their education. They also helped the others to see the
benefits of problem-posing dialogue and the importance of learning to
think critically.

As the instructor, I had to learn the art of facilitating the discussions and the cooperative groups. I had to learn to let go of power and
control and turn it over to my students, thus becoming a facilitator
who guides, shares, and coaches. Problem-posing taught me to trust
students, to trust in their abilities, to rely on their resourcefulness and
experiences, and to make learning meaningful to them.

Problem-posing enables students to bring to the program their experiences, cultures, stories, and life lessons. Their lives are reflected in the thoughtful, determined, and purposeful action that defines problem-posing dialogue. Moreover, problem-posing is a dynamic, participatory, and empowering philosophy that teaches students how to think critically and examine analytically the world in which they live.

Works Cited

Auerbach, Elsa R. *Making Meaning, Making Change: Participatory Curriculum Development for Adult ESL and Family Literacy.* Boston: University of Massachusetts, 1990.

Freire, Paulo. *Pedagogy of the Oppressed.* New York: Seabury, 1970.

Shor, Ira. *Empowering Education: Critical Teaching for Social Change.* Chicago: University of Chicago Press, 1992.

Wallerstein, Nina. *Language and Culture in Conflict: Problem-Posing in the ESL Classroom.* Reading, MA: Addison-Wesley, 1983.

Classroom Activities

Adult learners have a variety of concerns that connect their lived experiences to the world of the classroom. Students can work through the process that Nixon-Ponder describes by selecting a reading or working on a community problem that captures their collective interest, and then following the steps of problem-posing to create connections between the classroom and the "real world." Such an approach may also work as the first step of a research project. For instance, students concerned about welfare reform might consult an article in a local newspaper or from the Internet. Following Nixon-Ponder's steps, students would work together to "describe the content" of the article, "define the problem" suggested by the article, "personalize the problem" in terms of their own communities, "discuss the problem," and "discuss alternatives to the problem." While each step suggests a writing assignment (personalizing a problem, for instance, could lead to a narrative essay), students could work through the entire process collaboratively to gain a fuller perspective of the problem. Each student could then write his or her own researched essay exploring the proposed alternatives. Which solutions are feasible? Which solutions probably will not work? As they complete their research and compose their essays, students should be encouraged to evaluate solutions in terms of the needs and concerns in their communities. This sort of approach creates a realistic purpose for writing, since students use problem-posing to confront problems and to propose action concerning issues that are crucial in their own lives and in the world outside their classroom.

Thinking about Teaching

Adult learners approach the study of writing and reading with varying expectations about education and from the perspective of many different learning styles. Problem-posing dialogue depends on active class discussion to consider the issues at hand. Nixon-Ponder suggests that during the problem-posing process "it is critical for the facilitator not to expound upon personal and political beliefs." However, as Nixon-Ponder acknowledges, even the most fascinating lesson plan may not generate significant discussion. You may wish to discuss with colleagues the appropriateness of presenting personal experiences and opinions as part of the classroom conversation. Consider how students might respond. Will some students automatically accept the teacher's position? Will others automatically rebel against it? Will students think that their own opinions are being stifled and become afraid to speak? Or, in conveying your own ideas to students, is it possible to demonstrate respect for all opinions presented in the classroom, even if they are significantly different from your own? Try using problem-posing dialogue as a way to discuss these issues and to create alternative solutions to the problem. This discussion might take place within an electronic discussion group for a broader geographic representation. You may also wish to pose this problem to students as part of class discussion.

Returning Adults to the Mainstream: Toward a Curriculum for Diverse Student Writers

Barbara Gleason

In the following article, Barbara Gleason writes:

> *I endorse the position that remediation is inappropriate for adults who are returning to college after a five-, ten-, or even twenty-year hiatus. Far preferable are courses that have been designed to meet the specific needs of working adults, needs that are best understood not by analyzing placement test scores but by understanding these students' diversity in areas such as age, gender, family, educational history, culture, social class, sexual orientation, and employment.*

To further articulate her position, Gleason describes such a course, provides examples of student writing, and includes sample case studies of two very different adult students. These case studies are particularly effective in demonstrating how Gleason translates theory into practice. By studying the progress of these two students throughout the course,

*Gleason illustrates the success of a particular assignment sequence —
"(1) a language/literacy autobiography, (2) a storytelling and story writing multitask project, (3) a student interview report, and (4) an ethnographic research writing project" — and suggests the necessity of a specialized curriculum that builds on the diverse strengths that adult students bring to the classroom. Although Gleason argues for mainstreaming adult writers and draws on her experiences teaching a full-credit-bearing, mainstreamed course, the pedagogy she describes can certainly benefit students in a basic writing classroom as well.*

The phenomenon of working adults returning to college has generated a great deal of interest and curricular experimentation since the 1970s. In *Second Shift: Teaching Writing to Working Adults,* Kelly Belanger and Linda Strom describe innovative approaches to writing instruction in five worker education programs affiliated with colleges or universities. Issues associated with remediation must inevitably be confronted by such programs, where the prevailing view is that non-credit remedial courses are inappropriate for mature adults returning to college. At Youngstown State University and Swingshift College, for example, Kelly Belanger and Linda Strom developed a mixed ability writing course addressing the needs of the working students who belong to a steelworkers' union (72–84).

I endorse the position that remediation is inappropriate for adults who are returning to college after a five-, ten-, or even twenty-year hiatus. Far preferable are courses that have been designed to meet the specific needs of working adults, needs that are best understood not by analyzing placement test scores but by understanding these students' diversity in areas such as age, gender, family, educational history, culture, social class, sexual orientation, and employment. By reading students' personal narratives and autoethnographies of home, neighborhood, and work communities, teachers can learn about their students to better assist them in entering the culture of college. Similarly, students' analyses of their own home and community languages can help pave the way for their acquisition of academic literacies (Groden, Kutz, and Zamel; Kutz, Groden, and Zamel). As Terry Dean argues in "Multicultural Classrooms," composition courses offer a valuable and much-needed space in which students can focus on learning academic culture and, in many cases, "mainstream" culture as well.[1]

For the past three years, I have been teaching "remedial" and "college-level" returning adult students in one introductory writing course offered by a worker education bachelor's degree program within the City College of New York (CCNY).[2] Since its inception in 1981, this program — The Center for Worker Education (CWE) — has offered only full-credit college courses in its regular curriculum: the program's founders believed that all CWE students should enroll in full-credit bearing courses, regardless of placement test scores. As a teacher of writing in this program, I have been learning about how the particular needs and interests of these students can dovetail with a curriculum for a mainstreamed writing course.

Understanding the "Diversity" of Returning Adults

To encourage students to become acquainted, I ask that they introduce themselves to one other student during the first class meeting. The homework assignment for that week is for each student to write a letter to a peer about the challenges, joys, and fears of returning to college. By following up on initial introductions in class with an exchange of letters, each student learns about the cultural background, educational history, and special concerns of one other person in the class. As they develop friendships, these older adult students often form support networks and encourage each other academically. In addition, this initial assignment enables me to begin to know my students, for I read these letters as well.

I also ask my students to complete a questionnaire about their educational, language, and cultural backgrounds. By learning about my students' educational histories, I am far better equipped to assist them in entering an academic community with specialized forms of communication. I view my role as one of intervening in a lifelong process of literacy development, a conceptual frame for writing instruction best articulated by Louise Wetherbee Phelps:

> But what is it, then, that teaching teaches? Not literally writing as a discursive practice. . . . *Teaching teaches writing to developing persons within concrete life situations* [emphasis added]. Thus it teaches the development of literacy, addressing itself not simply to particular discourse events and texts but to the whole life process by which literacy — and reflection — become habitual, skilled, mature, and subject to self-understanding. . . . (71)

With each passing semester, I learn more about the "concrete life situations" of these students and, as a result, more fully appreciate the issues that are likely to concern them. For example, I only recently realized that earning a General Equivalency Diploma (rather than completing high school) may represent an important accomplishment or a sense of educational failure — or both. Reading students' commentaries on their literacies and educational histories allows me to begin assisting them individually early in the semester.

The completed questionnaires of the twenty-four students who had registered for my spring 1999 CWE writing class reveal the high level of diversity common to introductory CWE classes. As has been true of all my CWE classes, this group was highly heterogeneous in every way except for one: gender. Twenty-one students (86 percent) were women and three were men — a proportion that has remained constant throughout the six semesters that I have taught in this program. In all other respects, this class was notable for its diversity. Students' ages ranged from twenty to fifty, with an average age of thirty-six. Ten of these twenty-four students were immigrants, all but one coming from countries in the Caribbean, Central America, or South America. English was the primary language of sixteen students, six were bilingual in Spanish and English, and two were actively learning English as a second language. Eight of the fourteen U.S.-born students were African-American women.

These students were just as diverse academically as they were culturally. Ten had earned a General Equivalency Diploma and fourteen, a high school diploma. Of these fourteen, five had earned a high school diploma in a country outside the U.S.; that means that only nine in a class of twenty-four students had earned a high school diploma within the U.S.[3] This variability in high school backgrounds is matched by these students' City University of New York (CUNY) skills test scores and their college grade point averages. Of the twenty-two students who completed the course, twelve had no test scores listed in the CCNY student database, either because they had not taken the tests or because their scores had not yet been recorded. Of the ten students whose test scores were recorded, four had failed either the reading or the writing test, and six had passed both the reading and the writing test. As for their grade point averages, four students' transcripts indicate that they had GPAs below 2.0 and seven students had GPAs of 3.0 or higher.

From the standpoint of curriculum, there are two ways in which these students' cultural and educational diversity is important. First, these students have a great deal to teach me and each other about their social and cultural worlds; and second, nearly all of these students are struggling at some level to enter into an unfamiliar world of expectations, attitudes, ways of knowing, and styles of communicating. This is even more likely to be true for students enrolled in an elective writing class due to educational insecurities, low grades, or failing test scores. Unlike many middle class, native English-speaking people, these students do not usually experience college as a natural extension of their home communities or even of high school.

Jacqueline Jones Royster refers to this home-school culture gap in an analysis of her own experiences as an African-American woman who routinely crosses discourse boundaries: "Like [W. E. B.] Du Bois, I've accepted the idea that what I call my 'home place' is a cultural community that exists still quite significantly beyond the confines of a well-insulated community that we call the 'mainstream'" (34). One important consequence of this gap, Royster goes on to explain, is that it "narrows the ability [of educators] to recognize human potential" (34). Those of us who function as gatekeepers, however reluctantly, by virtue of teaching entry-level writing courses understand that academic styles of communicating are generally only partially familiar — if familiar at all — to "nonmainstream" students (Bartholomae; Bizzell).

The older adult students who enter CWE have often been observed by their teachers to be remarkably capable conversationalists and oral presentors whose writing skills frequently belie their intellectual and verbal capacities. These students — most of them women — are likely to have raised families and held full-time jobs while maintaining close ties to extended families, which is to say that they have been negotiating complex verbal exchanges for many years. However, many of these students begin learning in college classes before having acquired "essayist literacy" — the generalized academic style of communicating that is characterized by "straightforward, objective, specially organized representations of reality rather than personally authored, socially embedded discourse" (Farr 9). Despite this, many of these students are expert communicators in the oral traditions of their home cultures, a phenomenon that presents special opportunities for teachers in multicultural classrooms.

A Curriculum for Mainstreaming

My CWE writing curriculum comprises a sequence of four assignments that move students from an initially inward focus on their own literacies and languages to a progressively outward focus on the literacies and communication practices of others.[4] The four assignments are (1) a language/literacy autobiography, (2) a storytelling and story writing multitask project, (3) a student interview report, and (4) an ethnographic research writing project. All of these assignments involve students in practicing academic forms of knowing, persuading, and communicating while reflecting on their own literacy experiences and examining the languages and literacies of other people.

The first formal essay assignment is a language/literacy autobiography, which students prepare for by writing a letter to a classmate about combining work with school and returning to college at a mature age. These letters are followed by a more formal autobiographical essay assignment that invites students to examine their formal and informal literacy learning as children, adolescents, and younger adults. Very often, recalling these memories and recording them in writing is painful, for the very events being remembered may account for students' having decided not to pursue higher education earlier. On the other hand, most have successful work histories that bolster their self-esteem and provide the self-discipline and everyday habits necessary to succeed in college. These positive aspects of students' lives can be usefully examined in self-reflective, autobiographical writing.

The second assignment involves a sequence of four successive tasks. Students begin by telling each other brief conversational stories during class and then writing down these same stories. They later transcribe their audiotaped recordings, producing a transcript of an oral story that can then be compared to the written story. In the final phase of the project, students write a comparative analysis of the oral story and the written story, examining differences in story structure, content, and language. At the end of the project, students generally report that they prefer their written stories, and that these stories benefited from the absence of pressure associated with conversational situations and from the opportunity to revise. With this finding comes a new respect for their own writing and a resolve on the part of most students to improve their speaking and storytelling competencies (Gleason "Something of Great Constancy").

Students then move on to writing reports on interviews they conduct with one another about writing. This interview assignment, which I explain more fully below, functions to prepare students for the ethnographic research project — which I view as the capstone assignment of this course. A key value of the ethnographic writing project is its multitask feature: it offers such a wide array of reading, speaking, research, and writing activities that every student can experience some forms of success while stronger writers are always challenged by the analytical and rhetorical demands of writing an ethnographic essay.

In the remainder of this chapter, I will describe the interview assignment and the ethnographic research project, and establish a rationale for their use in a mainstreamed writing course for returning adults.

Capitalizing on Conversational Competencies

To introduce students to ethnographic research strategies, I begin with a student-student interview on the subject of writing outlined by Peter Elbow and Pat Belanoff in *A Community of Writers* (153–65). The two stated purposes of this interview are (1) for students to learn about writing and writers in a general sense, and (2) for each student to inquire about the specific experiences, attitudes, and aspirations of one writer. An unstated goal of this assignment is for students to get to know each other and form mutually supportive bonds that are sorely needed by commuter students who work full time while attending college. Well over one half of these students reported to me later in the semester that they have formed new friendships during the course of their initial and follow-up interviews (on the phone and in class).

To prepare students for interviewing, I distribute a short written explanation of the importance of scripting a list of questions beforehand, remaining flexible during the interview, audiotaping, and note-taking. We talk in class about the value of ice-breaker questions, being sensitive to privacy issues, and staying focused as an interviewer.[5] For nearly all students, this is the first interview they have ever conducted, it is anticipated with some trepidation, and it turns out to be a surprisingly pleasurable and memorable learning experience. One fall 1999 student succinctly sums up her perception of this assignment's value: "My best work is my interview with Maria. This is the exercise that taught me the most new skills. I interviewed, recorded, transcribed, summarized, and analyzed. I was very pleased with the final draft." Others report listening, asking questions, and incorporating quotes into their writing as particularly important skills that they practiced while interviewing and writing the interview report.

Most students say they value the relationships formed with their peers as well as the research and writing skills they practiced, often for the first time, while working on their interview projects. As much as I value these two dimensions of this project, I prize even more its use of conversational expertise as a resource for developing writers. Many of these students' communication styles differ from the topic-centered, "get-to-the-point" styles common to mainstream American speakers, and their language (oral and written) may therefore be subject to negative evaluation by teachers; nonetheless, these students' communication styles tend to serve them well in conversational situations. Moreover, as Peter Elbow reminds us, we teach to strength by "capitalizing on the oral language skills students already possess and helping students apply those skills immediately and effortlessly to writing" ("The Shifting Relationships" 290).

By inviting them to conduct interviews with one another during class, I encourage students to use their existing language forms as a bridge to acquiring academic styles of thinking, talking, and writing. Students may, for example, speak to one another in both Spanish and English; or they may use a narrative style that seems to "meander from the point and take on episodic frames" — suggested by Akua Duku Anokye as the preferred narrative style of some African Americans (48); others make particularly effective use of humor and joke-telling while conversing with each other. These culturally and personally preferred communication styles are then folded into the student interviewer's written report to illustrate an interviewee's particular style of speaking and as evidence for the student writer's claims. Two features central to academic writing are "the giving of reasons and evidence rather than just opinions, feelings, [and] experience" and the ability to "step outside one's own narrow vision" (Elbow "Reflections on Academic Discourse" 140). Reporting on an interview requires a writer to consider and represent an interviewee's point of view by means of summary, paraphrase, and quotes in a prose style that blends narrative and exposition as well as personal and public forms of writing.

Presenting Ethnographic Research Strategies
to Student Writers

In *The Professional Stranger,* Michael H. Agar explains that ethnography refers to both a research process and a written product (1–2). Agar describes ethnographic research as a process that "involves long-term association with some group, to some extent in their own territory, with the purpose of learning from them their ways of doing things and viewing reality" (6). With this general definition in mind, I present ethnography to students as a process that initially entails gaining entry to a community of people and then observing that group's daily routines, rituals, traditional customs, and communicative practices. I go on to explain that an ethnographer records these observations by writing descriptive "fieldnotes" and soon begins searching for recurring themes or topics that will form the basis of an analysis. To further introduce ethnography to students, I rely on *Fieldworking,* an innovative textbook that builds an entire curriculum on the foundation of reading and writing strategies commonly employed by ethnographers (Chiseri-Strater and Sunstein).

To illustrate the forms of writing that I am assigning, I distribute samples of former students' ethnographic essays along with excerpts from a professionally written ethnography. By reading good examples of ethnographic writing, students gain substantial insight into the task they are now being asked to undertake. When we discuss these writing samples in class, I elicit their explanations for why these texts exemplify successful writing: not surprisingly, there are some in every group who already know "what makes writing good" (Coles and Vopat). Such discussions also allow me to demystify the approach I take to evaluating and grading students' final products.

I frequently hand out in class copies of a student's ethnographic essay entitled "You Wanna Play with Me?" The author, Marthe, created a title that gives voice to the children in the Head Start program she was studying and at the same time alludes to her thesis: that children learn through playing.[6] This thesis appears in her introduction, is developed with examples of children's behaviors all through her essay, and reappears quite persuasively in Marthe's conclusion. After describing the classrooms, the teachers, and the children in this Head Start program, Marthe begins building her argument by presenting and commenting on children playing:

> Everything young children do is a learning experience. In one of my observations of this classroom, I observed how Jade, a happy, confident, assertive little girl took some building blocks and asked me "you wanna play with me?" I explained to her that I came to watch the children play and I asked her if she minded. She answered, "No, but you gonna play with me after?" I answered, "Maybe, if I had time." She then said, "Can you make me a box?" I asked her to try. "I can't try," she whined. As I

continued my observation she began to stack the blocks and join them together. After a while she said, "Look, I made a box." From this one attempt Jade did not only strengthen her problem solving skills and develop language, but she also learned how to make a box which in turn helped her develop her self esteem and made her confident in her abilities. Since Jade is very verbal, she also developed her reasoning skills and her social interaction with adults.

A major strength of Marthe's essay is her successful use of narrative and descriptive writing to construct an argument. Her essay exemplifies two points made by Donna Dunbar-Odom: ethnographic research methods offer students the opportunity (1) to "'own' their research," and (2) to learn that constructing an argument is far more complex than "merely taking and supporting one side of a binary argument" (20).

Because of her enthusiasm for working with small children, Marthe was highly motivated by her research, as she explains in her portfolio cover letter:

> The one assignment I enjoyed the most was my ethnographic research, "You Wanna Play with Me?" I enjoyed this the most because I studied and observed a group of individuals I hold dear to my heart, children. Not only are children unique and remarkable individuals, but they are also the group of individuals that society has put at the end of their list.

Marthe's testimonial on her engagement as a writer aligns closely with the feelings of many other student ethnographers: selecting a community for their research generally allows students to spend time with people they want to know better or to study a place of special interest to them. A woman with an emerging awareness of animal rights produced a remarkably fine report on an animal shelter; another woman interviewed several co-workers in her office and analyzed the reasons for a pervasive morale problem; and an immigrant from the Dominican Republic wrote about one of the family-owned stores, or *botanicas,* that sells products associated with *Santería,* which she describes as a "system of common belief among Dominican and other Caribbean people" that "mixes African and Catholic religions." As their teacher, I am continuously learning about the special interests, workplaces, and cultural communities that my students report on, just as they learn from one another by reading their work-in-progress and discussing these research projects with each other in class.

In addition to distributing samples of other students' ethnographic writing, I usually invite students to read an excerpt from Barbara Myerhoff's *Number Our Days,* after which we view her thirty-minute film by the same name. Through her descriptive and narrative writing about a community of elderly Jewish immigrants, Myerhoff develops an argument that agism is a pervasive problem in contemporary U.S.

society. An unusual feature of her writing is her hybrid style: literary language is combined with a social scientist's purpose. Developing a writing style is not a prominent feature of most introductory writing classes; however, more advanced students often take pleasure in noticing and imitating other writers' styles. In every writing course I have taught, there are some students, usually the most proficient writers, who want to focus on stylistic issues. By closely reading the prose of authors such as Barbara Myerhoff, these students can pursue their interests in developing their own prose styles.

To illustrate the potential that this project holds for diverse student writers, I will describe the cases of two returning adults — one classified as "remedial" and the other as "college-level" by their scores on the City University of New York (CUNY) Writing Assessment Test. I have chosen to underscore the mainstreaming challenge to teachers by selecting two extreme examples of students who are enrolled in the same class. The two students whose cases I cite as "Joan" (age thirty-three) and "Liam" (age thirty-six).

Joan and Liam both withdrew from high school without graduating and later earned their GEDs. Not surprisingly, these two students recall early school failures in the literacy autobiographies that they wrote at the beginning of our course. Educational insecurities and writing anxieties had led both Joan and Liam to register for my elective introductory writing course. But here is where their similarities end. Joan's writing efforts are significantly burdened by a complex learning disorder — a diagnosis she received while enrolled in my writing class. Liam, on the other hand, brings to his college education nineteen years of avid reading and a substantial history of political activism that includes crafting political messages for publication in the broadcast and print media.

Joan

Having left her Brooklyn high school without graduating, Joan had had "to go on public assistance" to support her infant daughter. While her daughter was still very young, Joan worked as a waitress and then as a file clerk in a car wash company. Reflecting back on that period of her life, Joan recalled that she enjoyed working as a file clerk because there was "little reading and no writing" required of her.

At the age of eighteen, Joan first attempted to earn her General Equivalency Diploma. She was to fail the exam four times before passing on her fifth attempt six years later. Knowing that many others would have given up after failing, one, two, or possibly three times, I asked Joan what had induced her to persist in taking and retaking her GED exam until she finally passed. "I wanted to go to college," she explained. "I wanted to better myself," she continued, going on to say that being on public assistance had motivated her to consider attending college. Joan married at twenty-two and gave birth to a second daughter two years later. Childcare responsibilities would further delay Joan's pursuit of a college education.

At thirty-two, Joan began her college career at the Center for Worker Education. One semester later, she enrolled in the mainstreamed college writing course that I was teaching. When Joan was casting about for a community to focus on for her field research project, I asked her what she particularly wanted to learn about. Joan replied that she was interested in college and in learning about being a college student. I suggested that she focus her research on her own college environment. For Joan, this interest in college was no small matter; it represented her struggle to overcome substantial obstacles to learning, literacy, and formal education.

Despite the obvious difficulties Joan experienced with reading and writing on her GED exams and in a chef's school that she attended for eighteen months, and despite her deliberate avoidance of jobs that required reading and writing, Joan did not believe that she had problems with reading and writing. Thus, when she failed her CUNY writing assessment test, Joan attributed her poor performance to "test-taking anxiety."

In August of 1998, Joan passed the CUNY reading assessment test but failed the math and writing tests. Had she registered at our college's main campus, or at any of CUNY's other sixteen colleges, Joan would have been placed into remedial writing — which in most colleges would have prevented her from being eligible for college composition or for core curriculum courses. However, Joan chose to enter the City College Center for Worker Education, where there are no remedial courses.

Joan's Writing

I first encountered Joan's writing when she responded to a questionnaire that I distributed during the second week of class. Here are four of the questions and her written answers:

- **Why did you enroll in this writing course?**
  So I can learn how to ~~right~~ ^{writing} better
  How to use better words. I Drop out of H.S.

- **What concerns do you have about your writing?**
  That Sometimes I loose my train of thought.
  What I want to say does not come out on papper.

- **Do you feel comfortable speaking during class discussions? Please explain your answer.**
  Sometime I do and sometime I don't. depends on what is discuss.

- **Do you have any concerns about your language use (speaking or writing)?**
  My *Fear* is when people see my writing they may not understand what I am talking about

These four written responses, as well as the other comments Joan wrote on this questionnaire, portray a student with a history of difficulties in school as well as severe frustrations with writing. Joan's difficulties as a writer were expressed both by the content of her messages and by the forms of her language: sentence fragments, misspelled words, and punctuation errors appeared in nearly every statement she wrote, diminishing only slightly after she acquired some proofreading strategies. However, unlike the writing of most "basic writers" I have encountered, Joan frequently embeds metaphors in her prose, as she does in this passage from her literacy autobiography: "Diaries, stories, letters and poems: I have them all. I enjoy writing, because it lets me be me. I enjoy free writing a lot more. It is like letting the pen and paper do their dance." All through the semester, Joan continued to employ metaphorical language in her expository prose, exhibiting a verbal competency that seemed oddly out of sync with her other competencies as a writer.

While enrolled in her humanities course the previous semester, Joan had learned from her instructor that she would have to improve her writing significantly to remain in college. In an interview conducted after our writing class had ended, she talked about her experiences in that humanities course:

> My first professor . . . pulled me aside the second week of class and told me to drop out before 'cause . . . she thought I had PROBLEMS and she wanted me to get tested [for dyslexia] . . . she came up to me and said "your work is the last work I read out of everybody in all my classes" and I asked her why and she said "I dread reading your work — It's really painful" — and I asked her why — she goes "your fragments your sentence structure" um she says "your writing is atrocious" and those were her exact words and it was like a dagger in my heart and in my pride and I held them back and I bit my lip and I said "ok — I'm still not dropping your class — I'm going to do my best."

Joan did complete her humanities class, earning a passing grade at the end of the term. She also took her instructor's advice to heart and enrolled in my elective college writing course the following semester. As for the passing grade she had earned for the humanities course, Joan believed it to be a "sympathy grade" — a gift from her teacher because her mother had passed away that semester.

The number of spelling errors that I observed in Joan's writing was unusually high, even in the context of a basic writing class. In fact, Joan's unedited writing closely resembles that of a person who is "dysgraphic," that is, a person who has a great deal of trouble producing written language (McAlexander et al. 25–26). A high frequency of errors and unusual errors are two indications of dysgraphia (McAlexander et al. 26). A third signal is writing in which letters are frequently missing/dropped from words, a condition that suggests an "inability to relate sounds to spelling" (28). All three of these conditions apply to Joan's writing. As it turned out, I was the fourth CWE teacher to recommend that Joan be tested for dyslexia. This she did arrange to do.

At midsemester, Joan learned for the first time, at the age of thirty-three, that she had a learning disorder. It is described in her evaluation report as "a combination of inattentiveness, auditory processing, organizational delays, and emotional factors" — all of which are "contributing to Joan's short-term memory deficits and delays in language processing."[7] Almost as soon as she learned of this herself, Joan called me at home to inform me of the diagnosis. From this point on, I read and evaluated Joan's writing with this newly diagnosed learning disorder in mind.

Joan's Ethnographic Research Writing

In the seventh week of our fifteen-week semester, Joan began her ethnographic research project. She had decided to study her own college community to further her goal of becoming a successful college student. The first assignment Joan completed for this project was a short research proposal.

In a one-page essay, Joan describes the community she will study and several questions she plans to use to frame her observations and interviews. An early draft (labeled "second draft") that she turned in to me begins with the following paragraph:

> As a student at CWE I got the change to observe the students, professors and the receptionists. How the students and professors inter act with the receptionists. How the receptionists get any work done? What is there a different between the day shift and the night shift? Do they realized that the students and Staffs depend on them for the information and services. How do they feel about their job?

In this draft, Joan conveyed the direction her research would take and posed several useful questions. I encouraged Joan to begin proofreading. With the assistance of writing tutors and her computer's software program toolbox, Joan was able to produce a third draft that more closely aligns with the expectations of college teachers. Here is her revision of the paragraph cited above:

As a student at Center for Worker Education I have the chance to observe the students, professors, the receptionists. I will observe how the students and professors deal with the receptionists. How the receptionists interact with the high demand of students and professors. I wonder if the receptionists get any work done? Is there a different between the day shift and the night shift? How do they do their job? These are some of the questions that I seek answers for as I observed the desk for several weeks.

In this proposal essay, Joan succeeds in identifying the place and the people that she will investigate while posing several questions that she will use to guide her observations. Joan had developed these questions during a conference in which she and I discussed her research plans.

By learning to revise, to proofread, and to request responses from readers, Joan made substantial progress in overcoming her writing anxieties and began to function far more effectively as a student writer. Her newly acquired writing process allowed Joan to stay afloat in class and to manage an intensive six-week project that entailed writing a research proposal, writing descriptive fieldnotes, interviewing at least one person, and writing a final research report. In addition to talking to me about her learning and her writing, Joan talked to CWE writing tutors, sometimes two or three times per week.

Joan wrote her descriptive fieldnotes during the course of three days. She focused her observations on the reception desk, where students, advisors, administrators, and faculty all approach CWE receptionists to request assistance. Once she got home, Joan wrote out and typed her notes, producing ten double-spaced pages of writing — in itself a substantial accomplishment for an insecure and inexperienced writer. Here is an excerpt from the notes Joan wrote on her second day of observing:

Friday, April 16, 1999
4:30pm
Wow! They must be at least 50 students here this is too much for me. Z, Mr. O, Mr. L, Mr. H, and J W working for their pay to day. So many student. Some look good and some are wearing jean and dress and suits. Some of the students have the hair done nice. I wonder what they are all here for. I can not hear to much anymore., because all the student are talking to each other and my bench is now filled with people sitting on it. There is so much happening around here today

4:45pm
There is a student talking to Z not so nice, but Z is smiling and been nice to her. Z is now telling student to put there name on the list and they will be call next. Wow! She control all those students and put them in there place. . . .

Her observations on this day, in conjunction with interviews she conducted with receptionists and a program administrator, led Joan to conclude that these receptionists respond very effectively to the many requests that come their way. In addition, Joan began noticing the heavy demands placed on CWE receptionists, particularly during evening hours when classes are in session. In her ethnographic essay, Joan concluded that the CWE receptionists play a centrally important though sometimes underrecognized role in maintaining a smooth flow of communications among students, teachers, advisors, and administrators. By reading Joan's report and fieldnotes, I found myself developing a new respect for these receptionists and for their roles in this college community.

When writing her ethnographic essay, Joan successfully narrowed the focus of her research to these CWE workers' experiences and the reception desk as a central gathering place for students and staff. Although the five-page essay that Joan ultimately wrote would not be considered a good example of successful college writing by most of my colleagues, I concluded that, for Joan, the act of completing a five-page written report of her own research was a highly significant achievement in her development as a writer. Moreover, this essay clearly documents Joan's learning about academic culture generally and, more specifically, about the Center for Worker Education receptionists and the reception area as a central meeting place. Equally important, Joan's essay demonstrates her newly acquired abilities to segment discourse into paragraphs, to ask and answer research questions, to write an essay introduction, and to use quotes to support general assertions and observations. Joan's collected ethnographic writing includes a total of sixteen (typed) final draft pages: a one-page research proposal, ten pages of fieldnotes, and a five-page ethnographic essay. The sheer volume of writing that Joan produced during the six weeks that she worked on this project represented a milestone in her writing life.

Liam

Liam grew up in a rural Irish farming community that lacked electricity and television in his early years. On winter nights, Liam and his family would visit neighbors, playing cards and telling stories for entertainment. In his literacy autobiography, Liam describes his father as a man with "a flare for storytelling" and his mother as an avid letter writer. Liam's mother corresponded regularly with relatives overseas, reading the letters she received to her family "aided by only a single gaslight hanging from the ceiling." When he wasn't farming, Liam's father wrote local news for community publications.

Liam recalls learning to read both English and Gaelic in a "small two-room country school." Between the ages of eight and twelve, he often missed classes to help his aging father with farmwork. When Liam entered secondary school at the age of twelve, he left a class of only three students for a class of sixty. He learned right away that his primary school education had not prepared him to compete academically: "It hit me that I was indeed in at the deep end. I did not recognize many of the subjects the teachers were talking about, nor did I have any knowledge of them." After three years of lagging behind his contemporaries and earning low exam grades, Liam left high school without graduating. Today, he looks back on his secondary school experience as a "bad dream."

When he emigrated to England as a young man, Liam hungrily read the *Irish Post,* a newspaper that reported the news from Ireland and addressed topics of interest to Irish immigrants. It was then that Liam developed a keen interest in learning about Ireland and, perhaps as a consequence, he became a voracious reader. A political awakening accompanied Liam's newly acquired reading habit. But writing was another matter. Liam continued to feel deeply insecure about his writing abilities.

In November of 1997, Liam took and passed the three CUNY skills tests in reading, writing, and math. During his first semester at CWE, Liam enrolled in an introductory humanities course that I happened to be teaching. Liam's performance in the class was impressive: in addition to earning an A for his coursework, he ultimately published a literacy autobiography entitled "A Reading Road: From Mayo to Manhattan" in a CWE student journal, *City at the Center.* However, Liam felt extremely anxious about writing and believed himself underprepared as a college writer. I advised Liam to address his concerns by enrolling in a college composition course, but instead he chose to enroll in a remedial writing course at another college. Liam believed that the low stress and low stakes of a remedial course would best serve his needs. After completing this remedial writing class, Liam expressed to me his satisfaction with his progress. He then enrolled in the mainstreamed writing course that I was teaching.

Liam's Writing

I had first seen Liam's writing in the humanities course he had enrolled in one year earlier. I knew Liam to be a proficient student writer who could one day publish his essays or stories. In addition to being an avid reader, Liam is an easy conversationalist and a good listener. And, like his father, Liam is a good storyteller. Having tried many different lines of work, Liam had discovered bartending to best suit his temperament and his talents. Bartending has allowed Liam to meet a wide range of people, from compulsive gamblers to "the Romeos, who conquered Beauty Queens from Manhattan to Miami but end up looking for an invitation to someone's house for Christmas or Thanksgiving." Liam is also a sharp observer of people.

When asked to complete a questionnaire at the beginning of his writing class, Liam expressed confidence about his oral communication skills but insecurities about his writing:

- **What concerns do you have about your writing?**
  Writers Block, Critical Writing, Essays, Grammar

- **Do you feel comfortable speaking during class discussions? Please explain your answer.**
  Yes Very Comfortable, Lots of Encouragement from my Professor

- **Do you have any concerns about your language use (speaking or writing)?**
  Not any about Speaking. Writing — (Grammar is a task)

Unlike Joan, who reported being told by a former teacher that her writing was "atrocious" and "painful" for her teacher to read, Liam recalls being encouraged and cites that encouragement as a reason for enrolling in this writing course. In fact, I had found Liam an easy student to encourage; and he had received similarly positive responses from the three teachers who had selected his writing for publication in the CWE student journal.

Liam's Ethnographic Research Writing

As an immigrant from Ireland, Liam takes a particularly strong interest in Irish-American organizations and publications. At the conclusion of our humanities course, Liam had given me a gift subscription to a magazine called *Irish America* and a book on the recent Irish peace accords. It came as no surprise, then, that Liam would want to focus his research on the Union Students of Ireland Travel, an organization that provides services for Irish and U.S. students who are traveling back and forth between these two countries.

In the opening of his research proposal, Liam asserts his view that Ireland should create a "national service of sorts": a program that would bring Ireland's youth to the United States to "broaden their horizons." He goes on to describe an organization that facilitates travel between the U.S. and Ireland for college students of both countries. Here is the second half of that proposal:

> The U.S. work and travel program which is sponsored by USIT has been in operation for over thirty years. Every year, students from third level colleges in Ireland travel to the U.S. to be part of this program. USIT helps Irish students to spend up to four months living, working, and traveling throughout the United States. For those students who come

here, if only for a short summer stay, it gives them an opportunity to learn about the American way of life.

The staff at the USIT office has already given me the approval to visit one day and monitor their office procedures. The following is information that I would like to find out. How do USIT select what students are accepted into their program, and what students are rejected? How much does it cost a participant? Must all participants be currently in the third level education? How is the program administered here, and in Ireland? How many students come to the U.S. each year? Is employment pre arranged, is this a major task? Is there a support network on the ground here for the students when they arrive, and for the summer? What are the student's opinion of USIT, and the U.S.A.?

I am looking forward to this research assignment, not just because I am Irish immigrant. I was always interested in Irish immigration issues, and I successfully campaigned for a change in the 1965 Immigration Act, as it had unfairly discriminated against Immigrants from Western Europe. I will see first hand how USIT prepares students for America.

A clear strength of Liam's writing is his ability to inform and also persuade his readers with an ethical appeal. In this proposal, Liam establishes his credibility as a writer by making three claims: (1) that he himself is an Irish immigrant, which means he can draw on personal experiences as a source of knowledge; (2) that he strongly advocates travel by Irish youth to the U.S., indicating a sincere interest in an organization that provides services to U.S.-Irish travelers; and (3) that he already understands international travel and immigrants' experiences well enough to ask informed questions. Finally, Liam asserts a type of moral authority by referring to his successful efforts at participating in a campaign against unjust laws affecting immigrants.

Liam conducted his research during the week of his spring break, spending several days at the American Youth Hostel in Manhattan — where the USIT offices are housed. In the course of his research, Liam recorded his observations of people's movements and communications, he interviewed employees and student travelers, and he collected the brochures and pamphlets that USIT provides. By interviewing employees, Liam gained access to the results of a survey questionnaire designed to gauge student travelers' satisfaction with USIT's services. USIT employees also shared with Liam the unsolicited letters that they had received from Irish students.

At the end of the semester, Liam reported on the pleasure he had taken from his observations of the people who worked at USIT and of those passing through the offices of this Irish-American organization. I had distributed a list of questions about field research experiences and asked students to respond in writing. Here is Liam's response to one question:

Question: How easy or difficult was this assignment for you?

Liam: This assignment was not as difficult as it seemed to be, when first I read the assignment. I enjoyed observing and writing the field notes. Spending mornings and afternoons at the American Youth Hostel (AYH) was exciting. Interviewing was easy for me as the students were in New York during my research. I felt the notes were very helpful when I was writing my report. My notes were essential to my report.

At the conclusion of his fieldwork experience, Liam had gathered enough specific information to write a substantive ethnographic essay. As is often true of more and less proficient writers, Liam produced a ten-page essay, twice the length of Joan's.

The report that Liam completed portrays the USIT offices, the USIT workers, and the student travelers who come looking for assistance. Embedded in Liam's descriptions are telling details that are informative but also suggestive of more than has been told:

A three-foot high black gridiron rail separates the general public from the American Youth Hostel (AYH) property. Between the gridiron and the AYH building there are a number of benches, round tables and chairs. The tables have umbrellas to provide shade from the morning sun. Most of the seats are occupied by people in their late teens or early 20's, who are sitting around smoking cigarettes, drinking coffee, and bottles of water. It is a scene reminiscent of a Paris sidewalk café. These young people are speaking foreign languages, with the occasional American voice rising above the others. The luggage they have with them tells a geographic story of its own. One tall young man with his hair down to his shoulders, has a travel bag that promotes Argentina, while a young lady, with a punk style hair do and some tattoos, has Norway stamped in bold lettering on her backpack. The T-shirts being worn by these travelers tell a story of where they have been traveling, from the Hard Rock Café in Los Angeles to Miami Beach Florida.

In this passage, Liam uses his descriptions to portray people and also to imply questions about where they have come from and where they are going. One of the more challenging aspects of ethnographic writing is to learn how to use descriptive writing purposefully — to communicate an idea or present an argument. It is usually the stronger student writers who manage to use description for a rhetorical purpose.

On the sixth page of his essay, Liam sums up an experience common to many of the young Irish travelers: "Homesickness and loneliness are two of the most frequent problems the students suffer from when they are in the U.S." With this general assertion, Liam introduces the contents of many thank-you letters that Irish students have mailed to the USIT employees after returning home. Liam cites the volume of this mail and quotes from one such letter as evidence of the positive response of Irish students to USIT and the importance of the services it provides:

> It is obvious from the amount of thank you mail that the staff at the USIT office receive each year from students when they return to Ireland, that their support role means a lot to the visiting students. One of the many letters Maire has on file is from a student who went through a period of loneliness while in New York last year. The thank you letter, which is almost two pages in length, states "Your concern and help took a massive weight off my shoulders. The time taken by you and the manner in which you dealt with me will not be forgotten." So wrote Mary Walsh from County Kerry in Ireland.

Liam's use of textual sources sets him apart from the majority of these student ethnographers. Using printed documents as primary or secondary sources involves transcending the fundamental requirements of the ethnographic writing assignment that I have conceived for an introductory writing class. For more advanced writers, however, citing sources is often a desirable challenge. Marthe, whose work I use to model a student's ethnographic writing, has integrated a secondary source into her text and appended a bibliography to her report.

The ethnographic essay that Liam completed bears many of the hallmarks of "good writing" noted by contributors to Coles and Vopat's *What Makes Writing Good*. Liam's text is a narrative that has a sense of being complete (143); his writing exhibits his commitment to his writing task, and his willingness to share his values with his readers (137). Liam creates an interplay between the particular and the general, reaching from concrete details toward abstract ideas (137); he knows how to create artful beginnings and how to use "attention-getting introductory tactics" (131); he uses a conversational tone that he knows how to translate into writing, avoiding a dull, institutional voice (126). In short, Liam's ethnographic essay exhibits many of the qualities that well-known writing teachers value.

Conclusion

Conventional college writing assignments generally fall under one of four categories: (1) personal narrative, (2) expository essay, (3) textual analysis, and (4) library research. For assignments that involve textual analysis and library research, students must first engage in critically reading new and unfamiliar types of texts and then write in a style that relies on logical reasoning and the use of evidence. For inexperienced or "basic" writers, this entire process involves a sudden immersion in academic forms of knowing and communicating and therefore a daunting challenge. As Marilyn Sternglass points out in *Time to Know Them*, these students will acquire academic language forms and writing abilities over time, especially when provided with appropriate instruction. However, they are unlikely to experience success as college writers when they begin by writing textual analyses and library research reports. Instead, they may fail to complete their assignments adequately or, when they do complete them, receive negative evaluations of their writing from teachers. This happened to Joan, who enrolled in Humanities 1 (an introductory literature course) during her first semester of college, and learned from her teacher that her writing was "atrocious" and "painful" to read.

The curriculum that I have outlined here offers one primary advantage to inexperienced writers: it enables them use "the oral [to] sustain the literate" (Brandt 7). Students begin their interviewing and ethnographic projects by using oral language in conversational situations to create two types of primary sources: transcripts of spoken language and fieldnotes. These are forms of writing that the most inexperienced and hesitant writer can dive into without fear of failure or negative evaluation from teachers: although I do comment on the content of these texts — and, very occasionally, make suggestions on how to improve them, I do not grade students' transcripts or fieldnotes. They function primarily as resources for more formal writing assignments.

More experienced student writers, such as Liam — who had passed a placement test prior to entering my writing class, still need to practice analytical thinking, research writing, and many other cognitive and rhetorical skills. All of the assignments in this curriculum require students to go beyond descriptive and narrative writing toward interpretation, inferencing, and analysis. When writing the ethnographic essay, students may choose to cite sources with in-text referencing and a bibliography. This is an appropriate challenge for the more proficient writers and one they frequently accept.

There are many possible avenues toward successful curricula for mainstreamed writing courses. The one I have been experimenting with relies on assignments with two key features: (1) the use of oral language and conversational competencies as resources for developing writers, and (2) sequenced multitask assignments comprising more and less difficult tasks. In addition to well-constructed assignments, there are still many other issues that must be addressed for mainstreamed writing classes: grading practices, support for teachers (for example, workshops and meetings), and support for students (for example, classroom tutors and class size).

In worker education classes, successfully mainstreamed writing courses take on a special significance. Slowing down student progress with noncredit remedial courses runs counter to a primary aim of these programs: they generally accelerate students' academic progress with classes conveniently scheduled in the evenings and on weekends, long class meetings that are held once a week, full-credit bearing courses, and the offer of college credits for life experiences. At the

Center for Worker Education, students' academic progress is even further accelerated by four-credit courses in place of the three-credit courses commonly offered in the regular City College curriculum.

Most of the working adult students I have met in my classes are highly motivated to learn and to perform well in their college classes. They bring with them many resources that strengthen their chances of academic success, for example, workplace literacies, conversational competencies, bilingualism, self-discipline, determination, and the confidence so often born of maturity. They nevertheless enter college filled with the anxiety of this being their "last chance saloon."

Returning adult students can increase their odds for success in college by using their existing languages and literacies to negotiate their learning of new discourses and literacies. However, "students in basic writing classes . . . should not be treated differently from students in so-called regular composition courses" (Sternglass 296–97). All students entering college, regardless of writing placement test scores, benefit from immediate engagement with assignments that foster critical reasoning, interpretive reading, analytical as well as narrative writing, and persuasion. A well-designed writing course curriculum for students of highly mixed abilities will meet the dual challenge of allowing underprepared students to experience success while encouraging stronger students to expand the limits of their existing literacies.

Acknowledgments

I would like to thank Edward Quinn for many useful responses to several drafts of this essay, Karl Malkoff and Barbara Comen for their suggestions and support, and Gerri McNenny for her insightful editing.

Notes

1. As Terry Dean points out in "Multicultural Classrooms, Monocultural Teachers," various different theoretical models explain how students can mediate home and school cultures. Shirley Brice Heath is particularly well known for advocating ethnography as a venue for classroom learning about home and school cultures. This interactive, reciprocal approach to pedagogy allows for developing shared understanding and negotiation of the various languages and literacies that appear in a classroom community. In contrast to Heath's negotiation model, Paulo Freire calls for students from non-main-stream cultural enclaves to transform mainstream culture rather than being absorbed into it (*Pedagogy* 28). These issues are also addressed extensively in *Writing in the Multicultural Settings* (Severino, Guerra, and Butler).

2. The City College of New York (CCNY) is one of seventeen junior and senior colleges that comprise the City University of New York (CUNY).

3. For a useful discussion of the issues faced by immigrants who are attending college, see Hirvela.

4. This writing curriculum is one I first used as a teacher in a mainstreamed writing course for younger adult students on City College's main campus. The course formed the heart of a pilot project supported by the Fund for Improvement in Post-Secondary Education. For overviews of this program's curriculum and its evaluation, see Soliday and Gleason, and see Gleason, "Evaluating Writing Programs in Real Time."

5. Two useful resources for learning about interviewing are *People Studying People* by Robert A. Georges and Michael O. Jones and "Ch. 7: Interviewing," in *Fieldworking* by Bruce Jackson.

6. The names of all students whose writing appears in this essay have been changed. Their writing is presented here with their permission and in the form in which I received it as their teacher.

7. Joan included her evaluation report in her writing portfolio and has granted permission for its use here.

Works Cited

Agar, Michael H. *The Professional Stranger: An Informal Introduction to Ethnography.* New York: Academic Press, 1980.

Anoke, Akua Duku. "Oral Connections to Literacy: The Narrative." *Journal of Basic Writing* 13.2 (1994): 46–60.

Bartholomae, David. "Inventing the University." *When a Writer Can't Write.* Ed. Mike Rose. New York: Guilford, 1985. 134–65.

Belanger, Kelly, and Linda Strom. *Second Shift: Teaching Writing to Working Adults.* Portsmouth, NH: Boynton/Cook Heinemann, 1999.

Bizzell, Patricia. "What Happens When Basic Writers Come to College?" *College Composition and Communication* 37 (1986): 294–301.

Brandt, Deborah. *Literacy as Involvement: The Acts of Readers, Writers, and Texts.* Carbondale: Southern Illinois UP, 1990.

Chiseri-Strater, Elizabeth, and Bonnie Stone Sunstein. *Fieldworking: Reading and Writing Research.* Upper Saddle River, NJ: Prentice Hall, 1997.

Coles, William E., Jr., and James Vopat. *What Makes Writing Good: A Multiperspective.* Lexington, MA: D.C. Heath, 1985.

Dean, Terry. "Multicultural Classrooms, Monocultural Teachers." *College Composition and Communication* 40 (1989): 23–37.

Dunbar-Odom, Donna. "Speaking Back with Authority: Students as Ethnographers in the Research Writing Class." *Attending to the Margins: Writing, Researching, and Teaching on the Front Lines.* Ed. Michelle Hall Kells and Valerie Balester. Portsmouth, NH: Boynton/Cook Heinemann, 1999. 7–22.

Elbow, Peter. "Reflections on Academic Discourse: How It Relates to Freshmen and Colleagues." *College English* 53.2 (1991): 135–56.

———. "The Shifting Relationships Between Speech and Writing." *College Composition and Communication* 36.3 (1985): 283–303.

Elbow, Peter, and Pat Belanoff. *A Community of Writers: A Workshop Course in Writing.* 2nd ed. New York: McGraw-Hill, 1995.

Farr, Marcia. "Essayist Literacy and Other Verbal Performances." *Written Communication* 10 (1993): 4–38.

Freire, Paulo. *Pedagogy of the Oppressed.* New York: Continuum, 1982.

Georges, Robert A., and Michael O. Jones. *People Studying People: The Human Element in Fieldwork.* Berkeley: U of California P, 1980.

Gleason, Barbara. "Evaluating Writing Programs in Real Time: The Politics of Remediation." *College Composition and Communication* 51.4 (2000): 560–88.

——. "Something of Great Constancy: Storytelling, Story Writing, and Academic Literacy." *Attending to the Margins: Writing, Researching, and Teaching on the Front Lines.* Ed. Michelle Hall Kells and Valerie Balester. Portsmouth, NH: Boynton/Cook Heinemann, 1999. 97–113.

Groden, Suzy, Eleanor Kutz, and Vivian Zamel. "Students as Ethnographers: Investigating Language Use as a Way to Learn Language." *The Writing Instructor* 6 (1987): 132–40.

Heath, Shirley Brice. *Ways with Words: Language, Life, and Work in Communities and Classrooms.* New York: Cambridge UP, 1983.

Hirvela, Alan. "Teaching Immigrant Students in the College Writing Classroom." *Attending to the Margins: Writing, Researching, and Teaching on the Front Lines.* Portsmouth, NH: Boynton/Cook Heinemann, 1999. 150–64.

Jackson, Bruce. "Ch. 7: Interviewing." *Fieldworking.* Urbana: U of Illinois P, 1987. 70–102.

Kutz, Eleanor, Suzy Q. Groden, and Vivian Zamel. *The Discovery of Competence: Teaching and Learning with Diverse Student Writers.* Portsmouth, NH: Boynton/Cook Heinemann, 1993.

McAlexander, Patricia J., Ann B. Dobie, and Noel Gregg. *Beyond the "SP" Label: Improving the Spelling of Learning Disabled and Basic Writers.* Urbana: NCTE, 1992.

Myerhoff, Barbara. *Number Our Days.* New York: Simon and Schuster, 1978.

Phelps, Louise Wetherbee. *Composition as a Human Science: Contributions to the Self-Understanding of a Discipline.* New York: Oxford UP, 1988.

Royster, Jacqueline Jones. "When the First Voice You Hear Is Not Your Own." *College Composition and Communication* 47 (1996): 29–40.

Severino, Carol, Juan C. Guerra, and Johnnella E. Butler, eds. *Writing in Multicultural Settings.* New York: MLA, 1997.

Soliday, Mary, and Barbara Gleason. "From Remediation to Enrichment: Evaluating a Mainstreaming Project." *Journal of Basic Writing* 16.1 (1997): 64–78.

Sternglass, Marilyn S. *Time to Know Them: A Longitudinal Study of Writing and Learning at the College Level.* Mahwah, NJ: Lawrence Erlbaum, 1997.

Classroom Activities

Developing writers often encounter many challenges as they learn how to incorporate quotations into their academic writing. One of the advantages of the interview assignment that Gleason presents as part of her four-assignment sequence is the opportunity for students to practice citing interview sources as part of their writing. Students also have a chance to create critical thinking questions and to practice note taking. Most significantly, as Gleason suggests, "I prize even more its use of conversational expertise as a resource for developing writers." Consider presenting this assignment to students in your basic writing class, perhaps as an introduction to an additional ethnographic assignment later in the term.

Thinking about Teaching

Gleason's article is particularly helpful in that it demonstrates ethnographic methods (by presenting case studies of students, for instance) as it describes ethnographic writing assignments for returning adult students. Take a closer look at Gleason's ethnographic approach and consider writing an ethnographic study of your own. As Gleason suggests, the late anthropologist Barbara Myerhoff's *Number Our Days* (New York: Simon and Schuster, 1980) is a fine example of an ethnographic study that would be worth reading as you consider an appropriate subject and approach for your own ethnographic work.

Critical Thinking

M any developing writers enter our classrooms with little awareness of their own thinking and learning processes. With practice,
however, developmental students can improve their evaluative and
analytic skills, and the writers in this chapter show that the basic
writing classroom affords a wide array of opportunities for such practice. Nancy Lawson Remler urges teachers to consider active learning
strategies, reasoning that students who are actively involved in a lesson will develop stronger critical thinking skills than those who passively absorb information, and Glynda Hull and Mike Rose take a
close look at the critical thinking processes of Robert, a basic writing
student at UCLA. Collectively, these writers help demystify the teaching of critical thinking by providing strategies that take into account
the needs — and build on the strengths — that students bring to the
basic writing classroom.

The More Active the Better:
Engaging College English Students
with Active Learning Strategies

Nancy Lawson Remler

*Using Charles Bonwell and James Eison's definition of active learning
and Benjamin S. Bloom's taxonomy of educational objectives, among
other theories of critical thinking, Nancy Lawson Remler illustrates her
own means of encouraging student engagement in college English
courses. In Remler's suggestions for providing students with leadership
roles in the classroom, developmental writing instructors will find many*

useful applications for their classrooms. Remler's strategies — which will attract developing writers' interests and build on their skills — are designed to foster critical thinking, writing, and reading. This article orig- inally appeared in Teaching English in the Two-Year College *in 2002.*

Among Arthur Chickering and Zelda Gamson's "seven principles of good practice" in undergraduate education are "active learning techniques" (3). These instructional strategies are popular, and evi- dence supporting the benefits of active learning is "too compelling to ignore" (Sutherland and Bonwell 5). In fact, Sutherland and Bonwell go so far as to say that "active learning is necessary for achieving many college course objectives" and that "all faculty can and should use it in their teaching" (83). I do. In fact, I believe that active learn- ing not only helps students meet course objectives and grasp impor- tant concepts; it also helps students "*become aware* of strategies for learning and problem solving" (McKeachie, Pintrich, Lin, and Smith 1). Moreover, active learning facilitates enthusiasm in the classroom, enthusiasm that possibly reaps other, long-term benefits: with active learning "students may be more likely to view their college experience as personally rewarding" (Braxton, Milem, and Sullivan).

Even though active learning reinforces students' understanding of course concepts, the varied types of active learning strategies differ in how actively students participate in the learning process. Charles Bonwell and James Eison define active learning as "anything that involves students in doing things and thinking about the things they are doing" (2). They further narrow the definition by attributing to it these characteristics:

- students are involved in more than listening

- less emphasis is placed on transmitting information and more on developing students' skills

- students are involved in higher-order thinking (analysis, synthe- sis, evaluation)

- students are engaged in activities (reading, discussing, writing)

- greater emphasis is placed on students' exploration of their own attitudes and values (2)

Even with such characteristics in mind, active learning strategies could vary in the extent to which students engage in the learning process. Class discussion, for instance, may allow some of the more verbose students to dominate the conversation while quieter students remain in the background. Minute papers, lecture summaries, and other short writing assignments do engage students in more than lis- tening, and they facilitate exploration of attitudes and values

(Bonwell and Eison 13–19). However, they could still allow the professor to dominate classroom activity.

My preference is that student work dominate class activities. Students are, after all, the people having to grasp the concepts. I also want all students to participate in class activities, not just those with more vivacious personalities. My assumption is that the more active students are in the lesson (with appropriate scaffolding, of course), the more engaged they will be in the subject matter and the better opportunity they will have to learn and apply course concepts. My experiences, as well as student reactions to class activities, seem to validate this assumption.

Active Learning in College English Classrooms

Many English classes have revolved around active learning strategies since the 1960s, as the process approach gained popularity and inspired workshop composition classes (Villanueva 1). However, process writing isn't the only means of fostering students' active participation in composition and literature courses. They can also learn actively as they analyze their peers' writing, examine reading selections, and practice concepts of Standard English. In my composition and literature courses, I facilitate active learning by switching places with my students, a technique invoking Jeanne Gerlach's collaborative learning and Bonwell and Eison's peer-teaching theories, as well as Lois Rubin and Catherine Herbert's collaborative peer-teaching method. As students take the teacher's role by generating questions and guiding discussions, they not only have the most active role in the classroom, but they also boost their enthusiasm and confidence by revealing to the class (and themselves) their knowledge of the concepts they're studying. They also act responsibly as they realize the intellectual investment (as well as the time investment) required to lead a class. Several active learning strategies facilitate this student-as-teacher role.

Generating Questions for Discussion

Questioning is a good technique for fostering students' participation in class discussion. Bonwell and Eison provide several helpful guidelines for composing and asking such discussion questions. However, some professors find the technique challenging because they might ultimately be unable to avoid dominating the discussion, either from enthusiasm about the topic or because students do not discuss as actively as professors had hoped. I also value the questioning method but have modified it so that students generate their own discussion questions. Often they find this task daunting at first and ask questions inviting recall of facts. To help them in the question-writing process, I use what many scholars of active learning propose: Bloom's taxonomy, a categorization of thinking skills ranging from factual knowledge at the lower end to evaluative thinking at the higher end. Together the class reads a children's text (or several) and compose questions about that text, working at all six of Bloom's levels of thinking. Then, also using Bloom's taxonomy, we generate questions about a work of literature commonly taught in college classes. During subsequent literary discussion, I have students write questions about what they've read, stipulating that questions generate critical thinking above the knowledge level. Usually students' questions generate hearty discussions of the assigned reading because they have an intellectual investment not only in the assignment but also in the class plan. They can also discuss issues they find important rather than focusing on ideas the teacher wants to talk about.

A great example of this strategy is a recent discussion of W. E. B. Du Bois's *The Souls of Black Folk*. Students had read the introductory note and the forethought to that book. Before our discussion, I gave students the following instructions: "Pretend that you are teaching the class. You want to give your students a quiz on today's assigned material. Write three questions you would include on that quiz. The questions should generate thinking above the knowledge level, and they should indicate that you have read and understand these selections." Examples of students' questions were, "What does Du Bois mean by 'the problem of the Color Line'?" "What does Du Bois mean by 'the Veil'?" and "How is Du Bois's ancestry important to the purpose of this book?" The questions were the same ones I would have asked them had I led the class. But I didn't tell them that; instead, we discussed the questions enthusiastically, and students seemed to acquire a firm understanding of those concepts before reading subsequent chapters in the book. By forming the questions themselves, students established ownership in the class and were able to plan the class discussion.

Group Work in Discussing Standard English

When teaching usage of Standard English, I always fear the glazed look in my students' eyes. Even though they recognize the importance of making subjects and verbs agree or avoiding comma splices and fused sentences, the traditional mode of teaching such concepts — an explanation and subsequent drill exercise — bores them. What's more, drill exercises are often so irrelevant to students' own writing that they rarely transfer such concepts to their own essays. To get my students involved in learning these concepts, I trade places with them by putting them in small groups and assigning them a concept to explain to the class. For instance, if the day's lesson is avoiding run-ons when combining independent clauses, I'll have one group explain how to join two independent clauses using the semicolon and conjunctive adverb, while another group explains subordination of one clause, and another group explains using the period or the semicolon. As each group explains its technique, the students in the group must refer to guidelines in the textbook; they must also demonstrate the technique to the class with their own examples instead of those provided in the textbook. Leading the class makes students responsible for knowing one portion of the chapter thoroughly and referring to other portions for guidance as they write. My students corroborate John Bargh and Yaacov Schul's finding that teaching results in "an increase in the organization and/or elaboration of the specific subject matter that was taught" (594). By composing their own examples, students not only apply their knowledge, but they also make the concepts relevant to their own work, thereby increasing the likelihood of retaining those concepts. Leading the class motivates teamwork in ascertaining accuracy of examples and explanations.

As each group conducts its lesson, I sit in a student's desk and take a student's role. If I notice an omitted concept, I'll raise my hand and ask questions students usually ask me: "Is a conjunctive adverb the same kind of word that starts a dependent clause?" "Do you always put a semicolon before *however*?" If the students leading the lesson can answer my questions correctly, they've grasped the concept.

Some concepts of Standard English are more difficult than others, and students often hesitate to lead the class if they're uncertain of their assigned content. To relieve pressure, I assure students before they present their lessons that they're free to admit, "This is the part we didn't understand." When they identify their trouble spots, I step back into my teacher role and help them out. If students inadvertently explain a concept incorrectly, I also revert to my teacher role to redirect the group's thinking or to explain the concept to them. These small-group activities facilitate a learning community as we all take leadership and learner roles. Furthermore, learning processes are explicit as students demonstrate publicly what they do and do not comprehend. Finally, as they identify confusing concepts and ask for my assistance, they exhibit the necessity of making mistakes as they learn.

Group Work in Teaching Literature

In literature classes, students generally appreciate some choice of the works they read. With active learning strategies, I give them that choice. Students work in groups of four or five. Each group chooses a work of literature, subject to my approval, and they work during the semester on a lesson plan about that work. I provide guidelines for this assignment, and I confer with them during the planning process, advising them to consider their objective: what is it they want the class (me included) to learn? I also require their lesson to facilitate class discussion. Again, they use Bloom's taxonomy as a guide, and they consult secondary sources to support their claims about their chosen work. At the same time, they use their creativity to plan an informative and engaging lesson. Recently one group taught a lesson on oral versus written poetry; another group arranged the classroom as a coffee house (juice and doughnuts included) to discuss various ways to interpret poetry. With appropriate scaffolding, these student groups led provocative discussions about literature of their choice, thereby claiming some ownership in the course. Simultaneously, they exhibited their constructed knowledge culminating from mostly independent work.

Conclusion

Although active learning strategies are numerous, one effective way to engage students and foster enthusiasm — for the course and possibly for college overall (Braxton, Milem, and Sullivan) — is to give them a leadership role in the class. Although such a strategy may not work for every class in higher education, it certainly works well in my first-year composition and sophomore literature classes. I believe these strategies could also work in other humanities or social science courses. Not only do students apply their new skills; they also participate in a learning community as they and I interchange roles. Furthermore, as students engage in the concepts of composition and literature, they simultaneously work as teams. The more active students are in the learning process, the better.

Works Cited

Bargh, John A., and Yaacov Schul. "On the Cognitive Benefits of Teaching." *Journal of Educational Psychology* 72 (1980): 593–604.

Bloom, Benjamin S., ed. *Taxonomy of Educational Objectives: The Classification of Educational Goals.* New York: Longman, 1956.

Bonwell, Charles C., and James A. Eison. *Active Learning: Creating Excitement in the Classroom.* ASHE-ERIC Higher Education Report 1. Washington: George Washington U, School of Education and Human Development, 1991.

Braxton, John M., Jeffrey F. Milem, and Anna Shaw Sullivan. "The Influence of Active Learning on the College Student Departure Process." *Journal of Higher Education* 7.5 (2000): 569–90. Education Full Text. Wilson Web. 30 Oct. 2001 <http://vweb.hwwilsonweb.com>.

Chickering, Arthur W., and Zelda Gamson. "Seven Principles for Good Practice in Undergraduate Education." *AAHE Bulletin* 39 (1987): 3–7.

Du Bois, W. E. B. *The Souls of Black Folk.* New York: Dover, 1994.

Gerlach, Jeanne M. "Is This Collaboration?" *Collaborative Learning: Underlying Processes and Effective Techniques.* Ed. K. Bosworth and S. Hamilton. San Francisco: Jossey, 1994. 5–14.

McKeachie, Wilbert J., Paul R. Pintrich, Lin Yi-Guang, and David A. F. Smith. *Teaching and Learning in the College Classroom: A Review of the Research Literature.* Ann Arbor: U of Michigan, 1986.

Rubin, Lois, and Catherine Herbert. "Model for Active Learning: Collaborative Peer Teaching." *College Teaching* 46.4 (1998): 26–30. Education Full Text. Wilson Web. 1 Nov. 2001 <http://vweb.hwwilsonweb.com>.

Sutherland, Tracey E., and Charles C. Bonwell, eds. *Using Active Learning in College Classes: A Range of Options for Faculty.* San Francisco: Jossey, 1996.

Villanueva, Victor. "The 'Given' in Our Conversations: The Writing Process." *Cross-Talk in Comp Theory: A Reader.* Ed. Victor Villanueva. Urbana, IL: NCTE, 1997. 1–2.

Classroom Activities

Remler's suggestions in the section "Group Work in Teaching Literature" help to foster students' critical literacy skills by demonstrating "their constructed knowledge culminating from mostly independent work." Consider creating a project for developing writers based on Remler's suggestions. Provide students with a list of books (or textbook readings) that they are assigned to teach to the class. As Remler indicates, choice is a key component of active learning, so student groups should have some degree of choice in their reading for this project. Remler asks students, as a second step, to decide "what [. . .] they want the class (me included) to learn." Have students plan and teach a lesson and lead a class discussion.

Thinking about Teaching

Throughout her article, Remler frequently refers to Bloom's taxonomy of educational objectives. In order to create, revise, and refresh your classroom assignments for developing writers, consider using Bloom's taxonomy to plan your own assignment sequence. A helpful Web site that presents key terms for Bloom's taxonomy can be found on the University of Minnesota's Center for Teaching and Learning Services Web site at <http://www1.umn.edu/ohr/teachlearn/syllabus/bloom .html>. Consider how Bloom's "scaffolding" of intellectual development in the cognitive domain (in ascending order: knowledge, comprehension, application, synthesis, and evaluation) is an appropriate model of critical thinking for your own writing classroom.

"This Wooden Shack Place": The Logic of an Unconventional Reading

Glynda Hull and Mike Rose

Glynda Hull and Mike Rose bring unique perspectives to basic writing and to the American system of education in general. Their search for solutions to systemic problems leads them to value the unconventional in the processes of reading, interpreting, and critical thinking. Yet these teachers also understand the necessity of student and teacher working together to arrive at shared meaning, as they demonstrate in the case of one student named Robert. "Robert's interpretation" of a poem he is studying "will cause his teacher to modify his reading, and the teacher's presentation of his interpretation will help Robert acquire an additional approach to the poem." In this article, first published in College Composition and Communication *in 1990, Hull and Rose examine Robert's "unconventional" reading in detail, allowing the reader to follow along as Robert reveals how social class and cultural background affect his critical thinking and close reading.*

This is a paper about student interpretations of literature that strike the teacher as unusual, a little off, not on the mark. When we teachers enter classrooms with particular poems or stories in hand, we also enter with expectations about the kind of student responses that would be most fruitful, and these expectations have been shaped, for the most part, in literature departments in American universities. We value some readings more than others — even, in our experience, those teachers who advocate a reader's free play. One inevitable result of this situation is that there will be moments of mismatch between what a teacher expects and what students do. What interests us about this mismatch is the possibility that our particular orientations and readings might blind us to the logic of a student's interpretation and the ways that interpretation might be sensibly influenced by the student's history.

The two of us have been involved for several years in a study of remedial writing instruction in American higher education, attempting to integrate social-cultural and cognitive approaches to better understand the institutional and classroom practices that contribute to students being designated remedial (Hull and Rose). One of the interesting things that has emerged as we've been conducting this research is the place of reading in the remedial writing classroom, particularly at a time when composition professionals are calling for the integration of reading and writing while affirming, as well, the place of literature in remedial instruction (Bartholomae and Petrosky; Salvatori, "Reading and Writing"). As this integration of reading, and particularly the reading of literature, into the remedial writing classroom continues, composition teachers will increasingly be called on to explore questions of interpretation, expectation, and background knowledge — particularly given the rich mix of class and culture found in most remedial programs. We would like to consider these issues by examining a discussion of a poem that was part of a writing assignment. Specifically, we will analyze a brief stretch of discourse, one in which a student's personal history and cultural background shape a somewhat unconventional reading of a section of a poem. We will note the way the mismatch plays itself out in conversation, the logic of the student's reading and the coherent things it reveals about his history, and the pedagogical implications of conducting a conversation that encourages that logic to unfold.

The stretch of discourse we're going to analyze comes from a conference that immediately followed a classroom discussion of a poem by the contemporary Japanese-American writer Garrett Kaoru Hongo. The class is designated as the most remedial composition class at the University of California; it is part of a special program on the Los Angeles campus (the Freshman Preparatory Program) for students determined by test scores to be significantly at risk. (The SAT verbal scores of this particular section, for example, ranged from 220 to 400.) Mike Rose taught the class at the time he was collecting data on remedial writing instruction at the university level, and though his class was not the focus of his research, he did keep a teaching log, photocopy all work produced by the class, and collect sociohistorical and process-tracing data on several students and tape record selected conferences and tutorial sessions with them. For reasons that will shortly be apparent, a student named Robert was one of those Rose followed: he will be the focus of this paper. Let us begin this analysis with the poem Robert and the others in the class read; the discussion took place during the third week of the fall quarter:

And Your Soul Shall Dance

for Wakako Yamauchi

Walking to school beside fields
of tomatoes and summer squash,
alone and humming a Japanese love song,
you've concealed a copy of *Photoplay*
between your algebra and English texts.
Your knee socks, saddle shoes, plaid dress,
and blouse, long-sleeved and white
with ruffles down the front,
come from a Sears catalogue
and neatly complement your new Toni curls.
All of this sets you apart from the landscape:
flat valley grooved with irrigation ditches,

a tractor grinding through alkaline earth,
the short stands of windbreak eucalyptus
shuttering the desert wind
from a small cluster of wooden shacks
where your mother hangs the wash.
You want to go somewhere.
Somewhere far away from all the dust
and sorting machines and acres of lettuce.
Someplace where you might be kissed
by someone with smooth, artistic hands.
When you turn into the schoolyard,
the flagpole gleams like a knife blade in the sun,
and classmates scatter like chickens,
shooed by the storm brooding on your horizon.

— Garrett Kaoru Hongo

The class did pretty well with "And Your Soul Shall Dance." They followed the narrative line, pictured the girl, and understood the tension between her desires (and her dress) and the setting she's in. The ending, with its compressed set of similes and metaphors, understandably gave them some trouble — many at first took it literally, pictured it cinematically. But, collaboratively, the class came to the understanding that the storm meant something powerful and disquieting was brewing, and that the girl — the way she looks, her yearning for a different life — was somehow central to the meaning of the storm. The class was not able, however, to fit all the pieces together into one or more unified readings. And during the discussion — as members of the class focused on particular lines — some students offered observations or answers to questions or responses to classmates that seemed to be a little off the mark, unusual, as though the students weren't reading the lines carefully. Rose wondered if these "misreadings" were keeping the students from a fuller understanding of the way the storm could be integrated into the preceding events of the poem. One of these students was Robert.

A brief introduction. Robert is engaging, polite, style-conscious, intellectually curious. His father is from Trinidad, his mother from Jamaica, though he was born in Los Angeles and bears no easily discernible signs of island culture. His parents are divorced, and while he spends time with both, he currently lives with his mother in a well-kept, apartment-dense area on the western edge of central Los Angeles. Robert's family, and many of their neighbors, fall in the lower-middle-class SES bracket. He was bused to middle and high school in the more affluent San Fernando Valley. His high-school GPA was 3.35; his quantitative SAT was 410, and his verbal score was 270. In class he is outgoing and well-spoken — if with a tinge of shyness — and though his demeanor suggests he is a bit unsure of himself, he volunteers answers and responds thoughtfully to his classmates.

During the last half hour of the class on the Hongo poem, the students began rough drafts of an interpretive essay, and in his paper Robert noted that his "interpretation of this poem is that this girl seems to want to be different from society." (And later, he would tell his teacher that Hongo's poem "talked about change.") Robert clearly had a sense of the poem, was formulating an interpretation, but he, like the others, couldn't unify the poem's elements, and Rose assumed Robert's inability was caused by his misreading of sections of the poem. Here is Rose's entry in his teacher's log:

> Robert was ok on the 1st third of the poem, but seemed to miss the point of the central section. Talk with the tutor — does he need help with close reading?

Rose decided to get a better look, so he moved his regularly scheduled conference with Robert up a week and tape-recorded it. In the three-minute excerpt from that conference that follows, Robert is discussing the storm at the poem's conclusion — the foreboding he senses — but is having some trouble figuring out exactly what the source of this impending disruption is. Rose asks Robert if — given the contrast between the farming community and the girl's dreams and appearance — he could imagine a possible disruption in her not-too-distant future. We pick up the conversation at this point. To help clarify his own expectations, Rose replayed the stretch of tape as soon as Robert left, trying to recall what he intended in asking each of his questions.

1a *Rose:* What do you think . . . what, you know, on the one hand what might the reaction of her parents be, if she comes in one day and says, "I, I don't like it here, I want to leave here, I want to be different from this, I want to go to the city and . . ." [*Expectation:* Robert will say the parents will be resistant, angry — something rooted in the conservative values associated with poor, traditional families.]

1b *Robert:* Um, that would basically depend on the wealth of her family. You'd wanna know if her parents are poor . . . [*mumbling*] . . . they might not have enough money, whereas they can't go out and improve, you know . . . [Responds with a *qualification* that complicates the question by suggesting we need to know more. This further knowledge concerns the family's economic status, something Rose had assumed was evident.]

2a *Rose:* OK. OK. [*Acknowledges with hesitation*] From what we see about the background here and the times and the look, what can . . . can we surmise, can we imagine, do you think her parents are wealthy or poor? [*Focuses* on the poem, asking for a conjecture. *Expectation:* Robert's attention will be drawn to the shacks, the hand laundering, the indications of farm labor.]

2b   *Robert:*   I wouldn't say that they're wealthy but, again, I wouldn't say that they are poor either. [Responds with a *qualification*]

3a   *Rose:*   OK. [*Acknowledges with hesitation*] And why not? [Requests elaboration. *Expectation:* Robert will provide something from the poem, some line that explains the ambiguity in his answer.]

3b   *Robert:*   Because typical farm life is, you know, that's the way that you see yourself, you know, wear jeans, just some old jeans, you know, some old saddle shoes, boots or something, some old kinda shirt, you know, with some weird design on the shoulder pad . . . [Responds by creating a *scenario*]

3c   *Rose:*   Uh huh . . . [*Unsure about direction,* but *acknowledges*]

3d   *Robert:*   . . . for the guys. And then girls, probably wear some kind of plain cloth skirt, you know, with some weird designs on it and a weird shirt. I couldn't really . . . you really wouldn't know if they're . . . whether they were rich or not. Cause mainly everyone would dress the same way . . . [Continues *scenario* leading to an observation]

4a   *Rose:*   Yeah. [Sees the purpose of the scenario] That's right, so you wouldn't be able to tell what the background is, right? [*Confirms* Robert's observation and *reflects back*] Let's see if there's anything in the poem that helps us out. (pause) "All of this sets you apart . . ." this is about line twelve in the poem, "All of this sets you apart from the landscape: / flat valley grooved with irrigation ditches, / a tractor grinding through alkaline earth, / the short stands of windbreak eucalyptus / shuttering the desert wind / from a small cluster of wooden shacks / where your mother hangs the wash." [*Focuses* on poem] Now if she lives with her mother in a wooden shack, a shack . . . [*Begins line of reasoning*]

4b   *Robert:*   OK. OK. Oh! [*interrupts*] Right here — is it saying that she lives with her mother, or that she just goes to this wooden shack place to hang her clothes? [*Challenges* teacher's line of reasoning]

4c   *Rose:*   Oh, I see. So you think that it's possible then that her mother . . . [*Reflects back*]

4d   *Robert:*   [*picks up thought*] washes her clothes probably at home somewhere and then walks down to this place where the wind . . . the wind . . . so the eucalyptus trees block this wind, you know, from . . . [*Elaborates*]

4e   *Rose:*   [*picks up thought*] so that the clothes can dry.

4f   *Robert:*   Right. [*Confirms*]

5a   *Rose:*   Well, that's certainly possible. That's certainly possible. [*Confirms*] Um, the only thing I would say if I wanted to argue with you on that would be that that's possible, but it's also the only time that this writer lets us know anything about where she might live, etc. . . . [*Begins to explain his interpretation* — an interpretation, we'd argue, that is fairly conventional: that the family is poor, and that poverty is signaled by the shacks, the place, most likely, where the family lives]

Certainly not all of Robert's exchanges — in classroom or conference — are so packed with qualification and interruption and are so much at cross purposes with teacher expectation. Still, this stretch of discourse is representative of the characteristics that make Robert's talk about texts interesting to us. Let us begin by taking a closer look at the reasoning Robert exhibits as he discusses "And Your Soul Shall Dance." To conduct this analysis, we'll be intersecting socioeconomic, cognitive, and textual information, bringing these disparate sources of information together to help us understand Robert's interpretation of sections of "And Your Soul Shall Dance," explicating not the poem, but a particular reading of it in a particular social-textual setting.

Here are a few brief comments on method:

Our data comes from the stretch of discourse we just examined, from other sections of the same conference, from a stimulated-recall session (on an essay Robert was writing for class) conducted one week prior to the conference,[1] and from a follow-up interview conducted four months after the conference to collect further sociohistorical information.

To confirm our sense of what a "conventional" reading of this section of the poem would be, we asked six people to interpret the lines in question. Though our readers represented a mix of ages and cultural backgrounds, all had been socialized in American literature departments: two senior English majors — one of whom is Japanese-American — two graduate students — one of whom is African-American — and two English professors — one of whom is Mexican-American. Regardless of age or cultural background, all quickly offered the same interpretation we will be suggesting is conventional.[2]

Analysis

1a–1b

1a *Rose:* What do you think . . . what, you know, on the one hand what might the reaction of her parents be, if she comes in one day and says, "I, I don't like it here, I want to leave here, I want to be different from this, I want to go to the city and . . ."

1b *Robert:* Um, that would basically depend on the wealth of her family. You'd wanna know if her parents are poor . . . (*mumbling*) . . . they might not have enough money, whereas they can't go out and improve, you know . . .

Robert claims that the reaction of the girl's parents to "I want to leave here . . . [and] go to the city . . ." would "depend on the wealth of her family." This qualification is legitimate, though the reasoning behind it is not quickly discernible. In the follow-up interview Robert elaborates: "[If she goes to the city] she's gonna need support . . . and if they're on a low budget they won't have that much money to be giving to her all the time to support her." The social context of Robert's reasoning becomes clearer here. He comes from a large family (eleven siblings and half-siblings), some members of which have moved (and continue to move) across cultures and, to a degree, across class lines. It is the parents' obligation to help children as they make such moves, and Robert is aware of the strains on finances such movement brings — he is in the middle of such tension himself.

2a–4f

This segment includes Robert's qualified response to "do you think her parents are wealthy or poor?" his farm fashion scenario, and his perception of the "small cluster of wooden shacks." As we've seen, we need to understand Robert's perception of the shacks in order to understand his uncertainty about the parents' economic status, so we'll reverse the order of events on the transcript and deal first with the shacks.

> 4a   *Rose:*   Yeah. That's right, so you wouldn't be able to tell what the background is, right? Let's see if there's anything in the poem that helps us out. (pause) "All of this sets you apart . . ." this is about line twelve in the poem, "All of this sets you apart from the landscape: / flat valley grooved with irrigation ditches, / a tractor grinding through alkaline earth, / the short stands of windbreak eucalyptus / shuttering the desert wind / from a small cluster of wooden shacks / where your mother hangs the wash." Now if she lives with her mother in a wooden shack, a shack . . .
>
> 4b   *Robert:*   OK. OK. Oh! Right here — is it saying that she lives with her mother, or that she just goes to this wooden shack place to *hang* her clothes?

Those of us educated in a traditional literature curriculum, and especially those of us trained in an English graduate program, are schooled to comprehend the significance of the shacks. We understand, even if we can't readily articulate them, the principles of compression and imagistic resonance that underlie Hongo's presentation of a single image to convey information about economic and historical background. Robert, however, isn't socialized to such conventions, or is only partly socialized, and so he relies on a model of interpretation Rose had seen him rely on in class and in the stimulated-recall session: an almost legalistic model, a careful, qualifying reasoning that defers quick judgment, that demands multiple sources of verification. The kind of reasoning we see here, then, is not inadequate. In fact, it's pretty sophisticated — though it is perhaps inappropriately invoked in a poetic world, as Rose begins to suggest to Robert in 5a. We'll come back to this momentarily, but first we want to address one more issue related to Robert's uncertainty about the income level of the girl's parents.

We would like to raise the possibility that Robert's background makes it unlikely that he is going to respond to "a small cluster of wooden shacks" in quite the same way — with quite the same emotional reaction — as would a conventional (and most likely middle-class) reader for whom the shacks might function as a quickly discernible, emblematic literary device. Some of Robert's relatives in Trinidad still live in houses like those described in the poem, and his early housing in Los Angeles — further into central Los Angeles than where he now lives — was quite modest. We would suggest that Robert's "social distance" from the economic reality of poor landscapes isn't as marked as that of the conventional/middle-class reader, and this might make certain images less foreign to him, and, therefore, less emotionally striking. This is certainly *not* to say that Robert is naive about his current position in American society, but simply to say that the wooden shacks might not spark the same dramatic response in him as in a conventional/middle-class reader. The same holds true for another of Hongo's indicators of economic status — the hanging of the wash — for Robert's mother still "likes to wash her clothes by hand." Paradoxically, familiarity might work against certain kinds of dramatic response to aspects of working-class life.

In line with the above assertion, we would like to consider one last indicator of the girl's economic status — the mention of the Sears catalogue. The Sears catalogue, we believe, cuts two ways in the poem: it suggests lower-income-level shopping ("thrifty," as one of our readers put it) and, as well, the importing of another culture's garments. But the catalogue also carries with it an ironic twist: it's not likely that conventional readers would consider a Sears catalogue to be a source of fashion, so there's a touch of irony — perhaps pity mixed with humor — in this girl fulfilling her romantic dreams via Sears and Roebuck. We suggest that Robert's position in the society makes it difficult for him to see things this way, to comply with this conventional reading. He knows merchandise from Sears is "economical" and "affordable," and, to him, there's nothing ironic, pitiable, or humorous about that. When asked if he sees anything sad or ironic about the girl buying there he responds, "Oh, no, no," pointing out that "some of the items they sell in Sears, they sell in other stores." He then goes on to uncover an interesting problem in the poem. He uses the Sears catalogue to support his assertion that the family isn't all that poor (and thus doesn't necessarily live in those shacks): "She couldn't be really poor because she has clothes from the Sears catalogue." Robert knows

what real poverty is, and he knows that if you have enough money to
buy at Sears, you're doing OK. He goes on to speculate — again with
his careful, qualifying logic — that if she is as poor as the shacks suggest, then maybe the Sears clothes could be second-hand and sent to
her by relatives, in the way his family sends clothes and shoes to his
relatives in Trinidad. Hongo's use of the Sears catalogue is, in some
ways, undercut by other elements in his poem.

> 3b *Robert:*   Because typical farm life is, you know, that's the way that
> you see yourself, you know, wear jeans, just some old jeans, you
> know, some old saddle shoes, boots or something, some old kinda
> shirt, you know, with some weird design on the shoulder pad . . .
>
> 3c *Rose:*   Uh huh . . .
>
> 3d *Robert:*   . . . for the guys. And then girls, probably wear some kind
> of plain cloth skirt, you know, with some weird designs on it and a
> weird shirt. I couldn't really . . . you really wouldn't know if they're
> . . . whether they were rich or not. Cause mainly everyone would
> dress the same way . . .

Now we can turn to the farm fashion scenario. Given that the "small
cluster of wooden shacks" doesn't seem to function for Robert as it
might for the conventional reader, he is left more to his own devices
when asked: "do you think her parents are wealthy or poor?" What
begins as a seeming non sequitur — and a concrete one at that — does
reveal its purpose as Robert plays it out. Though Robert has a frame of
reference to understand the economics of the scene in "And Your Soul
Shall Dance" and the longing of its main character, he is, after all, a city
boy, born and raised in central Los Angeles. What he does, then, when
asked a question about how one determines the economic background
of people moving across a farm landscape is to access what knowledge
he does have about farm life — things he's read or heard, images he's
gleaned from movies and television shows (e.g., *Little House on the
Prairie*) — and create a scenario, focusing on one indicator of socioeconomic status: fashion. (And fashion is a sensible criterion to use here,
given the poem's emblematic use of clothing.) Classroom-observational
and stimulated-recall data suggest that Robert makes particularly
good use of visual imagery in his thinking — e.g., he draws pictures
and charts to help him comprehend difficult readings; he rehearses
sentences by visualizing them before he writes them out — and here
we see him reasoning through the use of scenario, concluding that in
certain kinds of communities, distinctions by readily discernible indicators like dress might not be all that easy to make.

> 4d *Robert:*   washes her clothes probably at home somewhere and then
> walks down to this place where the wind . . . the wind . . . so the
> eucalyptus trees block this wind, you know, from . . .

4e *Rose:*   so that the clothes can dry.

4f *Robert:*   Right.

This section also involves the wooden shacks, though the concern here is Robert's assertion that the mother doesn't have to live in the shacks to hang the wash there. Robert's reasoning, again, seems inappropriately legalistic. Yes, the mother could walk down to this place to hang her clothes; the poem doesn't specify "that [the girl] lives with her mother, or that [the mother] just goes to this wooden shack place to *hang* her clothes." But to Rose during the conference this seemed like a jurisprudential rather than a poetic reading. In the follow-up interview, however, Robert elaborated in a way that made Rose realize that Robert might have had a better imagistic case than his teacher first thought — for Rose missed the full visual particulars of the scene, did not see the importance of the "tractors grinding through the alkaline earth." Robert elaborates on "this place where . . . the eucalyptus trees block this wind." He describes this "little shack area where the clothes can dry without being bothered by the wind and dust . . . with all this . . . the tractor grinding through the earth. That brings up dust." Robert had pictured the surrounding landscape — machines stirring up grit and dust — and saw the necessity of trees to break the dust-laden wind so that wash could dry clean in the sun. The conventional reader could point out that such a windbreak would be necessary as well to protect residents, but given Robert's other interpretations, it makes sense, is coherent, to see the shacks — sheds of some kind perhaps or abandoned housing — as part of this eucalyptus-protected place where women hang the wash. What's important to note here is that Robert was able to visualize the scene — animate it, actually — in a way that Rose was not, for Rose was focusing on the dramatic significance of the shacks. Robert's reading may be unconventional and inappropriately jurisprudential, but it is coherent, and it allows us — in these lines — to animate the full landscape in a way that enhances our reading of the poem.

Conclusion

We hope we have demonstrated the logic and coherence of one student's unconventional reading. What we haven't addressed — and it could certainly now be raised — is the pedagogical wisdom of encouraging in a writing classroom the playing out of such unconventional readings. Reviewing the brief stretch of Rose's and Robert's discourse, we see how often teacher talk is qualified, challenged, and interrupted (though not harshly), and how rarely teacher expectations are fulfilled. If the teacher's goals are to run an efficient classroom, cover a set body of material, and convey certain conventional reading and writing strategies to students who are on the margin of the academic community, then all these conversational disjunctions are troubling.

What we would like to suggest, though, is that the laudable goal of facilitating underprepared students' entry into the academic community is actually compromised by a conversational pattern that channels students like Robert into a more "efficient" discourse. The desire for efficiency and coverage can cut short numerous possibilities for students to explore issues, articulate concerns, formulate and revise problems — all necessary for good writing to emerge — and can lead to conversational patterns that socialize students into a mode of interaction that will limit rather than enhance their participation in intellectual work.[3] We would further suggest that streamlined conversational patterns (like the Initiation-Comment-Response pattern described by Mehan) are often reinforced by a set of deficit-oriented assumptions about the linguistic and cognitive abilities of remedial students, assumptions that are much in need of examination (Hull et al.; Rose, *Lives*).

We would pose instead a pedagogical model that places knowledge-making at its center. The conversational techniques attending such a model are not necessarily that demanding — Robert benefits from simple expressions of encouragement, focusing, and reflecting back — but the difference in assumptions is profound: that the real stuff of belonging to an academic community is dynamic involvement in generating and questioning knowledge, that students desperately need immersion and encouragement to involve themselves in such activity, and that underprepared students are capable — given the right conditions — of engaging in such activity. We would also underscore the fact that Robert's reading (a) does bring to light the problem with the Sears catalogue and (b) animates the landscape as his teacher's reading did not do. Finally, we would suggest that engaging in a kind of "social-textual" reading of Robert's reading moves us toward deeper understanding of the social base of literary interpretation (cf. Salvatori, "Pedagogy").

In calling for a richer, more transactive model of classroom discourse, we want to acknowledge that such a model removes some of the control of teacher-centered instruction and can create moments of hesitance and uncertainty (as was the case with Rose through the first half of the transcript). But hesitancy and uncertainty — as we all know from our own intellectual struggles — are central to knowledge-making. Furthermore, we are not asking teachers to abandon structure, goals, and accountability. A good deal of engineering still goes on in the transactive classroom: the teacher focusing discussion, helping students better articulate their ideas, involving others, pointing out connections, keeping an eye on the clock. Even in conference, Rose's interaction with Robert is clearly goal-driven, thus Rose's reliance on focusing and reflecting back. Rose operates with a conventional reading in mind and begins moving toward it in 5a — and does so out loud to reveal to Robert the line of such reasoning. Robert's interpretation, though, will cause his teacher to modify his reading, and the teacher's presentation of his interpretation will help Robert acquire an additional approach to the poem. (In fact, the very tension between academic convention and student experience could then become the focus of discussion.) This, we think, is the way talk and thought should go when a student seems to falter, when readings seem a little off the mark.[4]

Notes

1. In stimulated recall, a student's writing is videotaped and, upon completion, replayed to cue recall of mental processes occurring during composing. For further discussion of the procedure and its advantages and limitations, see Rose, *Writer's Block.*
2. Frankly, we had trouble arriving at a way to designate the readings we're calling conventional and unconventional. And we're not satisfied yet. Certain of Robert's responses seem to be influenced by class (e.g., his reaction to the wooden shacks and Sears), and we note that, but with reluctance. We don't want to imply that class is the primary determiner of Robert's reading (vs., say, socialization into an English department — which, we realize, would correlate with class). We also don't want to imply that middle-class readers would, by virtue of class, automatically see things in a certain way, would have no trouble understanding particular images and allusions. One of the people who read this paper for us, Dennis Lynch, suggested that we use Wayne Booth's notion of "intended audience" — that Robert is simply not a member of the audience for whom the poem was written, thus he offers a reading that differs from the reading we're calling conventional. The notion of intended audience makes sense here, and fits with our discussion of socialization. Hongo, like most younger American poets, honed his craft in an English department and an MFA program, places where one's work is influenced by particular audiences — fellow poets, faculty, journal editors, etc. But, finally, we decided not to use the notion of intended audience, for it carries with it a theoretical framework we're not sure does Robert or Hongo full justice here. We use words like "conventional" and "middle-class," then, with reserve and invite our readers to help us think through this problem.
3. For two different but compatible perspectives on this claim see Shor; Tharp and Gallimore.
4. We would like to thank Linda Flower, Kay Fraser, Marisa Garrett, Jonathan Lovell, Dennis Lynch, Sandra Mano, Cheryl Pfoff, Mariolina Salvatori, Melanie Sperling, and Susan Thompson-Lowry for their comments on this paper. We benefited from a discussion at a meeting of the directors of the California Writing Project, and we would also like to acknowledge three anonymous *CCC* reviewers who gently guided us toward an understanding of the gaps and blunders in the essay. This work has been supported by grants from the McDonnell Foundation Program in Cognitive Studies for Educational Practice and the Research Foundation of the National Council of Teachers of English.

Works Cited

Bartholomae, David, and Anthony Petrosky, eds. *Facts, Counterfacts and Artifacts: Theory and Method for a Reading and Writing Course.* Upper Montclair, NJ: Boynton, 1986.

Hongo, Garrett Kaoru. "And Your Soul Shall Dance." *Yellow Light.* Middletown, CT: Wesleyan UP, 1982. 69.

Hull, Glynda, and Mike Rose. "Rethinking Remediation: Toward a Social-Cognitive Understanding of Problematic Reading and Writing." *Written Communication* 6 (Apr. 1989): 139–54.

Hull, Glynda, Mike Rose, Kay Losey Fraser, and Marisa Garrett. "The Social Construction of Remediation." The Tenth Annual Ethnography in Education Forum. Univ. of Pennsylvania, Feb. 1989.

Mehan, Hugh. *Learning Lessons.* Cambridge: Harvard UP, 1979.

Rose, Mike. *Lives on the Boundary: The Struggles and Achievements of America's Underprepared.* New York: Free Press, 1989.

———. *Writer's Block: The Cognitive Dimension.* Carbondale: Southern Illinois UP, 1984.

Salvatori, Mariolina. "Pedagogy: From the Periphery to the Center." *Reclaiming Pedagogy: The Rhetoric of the Classroom.* Ed. Patricia Donahue and Ellen Quandahl. Carbondale: Southern Illinois UP, 1989. 17–34.

———. "Reading and Writing a Text: Correlations between Reading and Writing Patterns." *College English* 45 (Nov. 1983): 657–66.

Shor, Ira. *Empowering Education: Critical Teaching for Social Change.* Chicago: Chicago UP, 1992.

Tharp, Roland G., and Ronald Gallimore. *Rousing Minds to Life.* New York: Oxford UP, 1989.

Classroom Activities

Hull and Rose ask readers to think critically about the class and cultural backgrounds of their students. Extend this inquiry by asking students to think critically about the class and cultural backgrounds of their audience for a specific writing task. Focusing on the audience will help them answer such questions as the following: What does my audience already know about this topic? What is the attitude of my audience toward this topic? What background information do I need to supply to help the audience understand my point of view? Such an activity can help students frame their purposes more concisely; it can also serve as a journal entry or prewriting exercise.

Thinking about Teaching

Hull and Rose discuss how their interpretation of Garrett Kaoru Hongo's poem is influenced by what they call a "conventional middle-class reading." It might be interesting to spend some time discussing what constitutes a conventional middle-class reader or writer. Such an activity could lead to a better understanding of how class differences may play out in the classroom. Recall, for example, an assignment that you presented in class that elicited a very different response from what you had expected, with varied responses among the students themselves. Perhaps differences in social class conventions or expectations account for the variety of interpretations, as Hull and Rose maintain. Discussing such incidents with other teachers may help you draw connections between classroom experiences and real life and could provide insights into teaching the processes of critical thinking and writing.

9

Collaborative Learning

Many of us have attempted to use collaborative learning strategies in our classes and have been discouraged or dissatisfied with the results. In the revision stage of the writing process, for example, students often seem afraid to critique their peers and are not willing to trust other students to critique their writing, since they see this task as belonging strictly to the teacher. Group members may fall off task or have difficulty communicating with each other because of cultural or other differences. Yet many teachers continue to revise their strategies and expectations because they see the potential benefits: increased communication among students, better problem solving, and better critical thinking skills. The selections in this chapter highlight the use of teamwork as part of a comprehensive plan for the writing classroom and present two interesting experiments.

Peter Elbow provides step-by-step collaborative learning activities that may appeal to students who are not normally comfortable working in groups. His collage activity will be helpful to instructors interested in trying out new approaches to collaborative learning. Richard Raymond writes about a collaborative learning community he helped create with teachers of Speech Communications and Anthropology at the University of Arkansas–Little Rock. A class of entering first-year students took linked courses in these disciplines, as well as Raymond's course in composition. Raymond documents the collaboration that took place as teachers and students came together as a community of learners.

Using the Collage for Collaborative Writing

Peter Elbow

Peter Elbow, whose work on freewriting has heavily influenced today's process-oriented basic writing courses, presents in this article the metaphor of collage as a means for practicing a variety of collaborative writing activities. He begins by outlining the strengths and weaknesses of collaborative writing, and then presents the notion of collage as a way of building on the strengths of collaboration and addressing its weaknesses. In addition, Elbow suggests how collaborative writing can incorporate both individual and group work. The collage, as Elbow shows, helps students understand the benefits of collaborative work, while facilitating an opportunity for them to strengthen their individual writing. This article was originally published in Composition Studies *(formerly* Freshman English News) *in 1999.*

P lenty of people have celebrated collaborative writing (e.g., Ede and Lunsford; LeFevre), so I can invoke the medieval trope of *occupatio:* I will *not* give all the reasons why collaborative writing is a good thing; I will *not* talk about how frequently it occurs in the world and therefore how our students should learn to use it; nor about the collaborative dimension of writing we think of as private; nor about how collaborative writing helps students learn better because of all the pooling of information, ideas, and points of view; nor about the students who have hated writing because it makes them feel lonely and helpless but who come to *like* it when they write with others; nor will I cite the much-cited Harvard research showing how students who study together get better grades (Light).

But I will mention in passing one interesting benefit of collaborative writing that I've noticed but found undercelebrated. When people write alone, they make countless simple and complex writerly decisions *tacitly,* instinctively — without articulating the reasons for them (e.g., to start with this idea, or to move that point later in the paper, or to change a word or phrase to modify the voice or the relationship to the reader). And that's as it should be: tacit decisions are quicker and the writer is going by feel, by ear. As Polanyi reminds us, our tacit knowledge always outstrips our conscious and articulate knowledge. But the process of writing with someone else forces us to put many of these decisions into words. If I say to my partner, "Let's start with this point," I usually have to say why — especially if I am proposing a change. And if my partner disagrees with me, he or she will naturally give reasons for the resistance. In short, the process of collaborative writing forces students to become more conscious and articulate about rhetorical decision making.

But what I find underrepresented in our professional literature about collaborative writing are the *problems*. First, collaborative writing is difficult and often unpleasant. When I used to force students to write pieces in pairs or groups, at least half of them would say at the end that it was the worst experience of the semester. And when I gave them the choice, relatively few took it. Collaborative writing may be jolly and social, but it takes a long time and leads to disagreements. Is there anyone who has not vowed never again to engage in a piece of committee writing?

Second, the writing that results from collaboration is often pretty bad. It is likely to be bland because the parties have to agree and they can only agree on lowest-common-denominator thinking. And there is often a dead, "committee" voice — no energy or presence. The surest proof of the existence of God is the King James translation of the Bible: only divine intervention could have permitted a committee to produce such wonderful prose.

Third, the collaborative process often silences weaker, minority, or marginal voices. The assertive and entitled tend to carry the day. Whenever there is a need for consensus in group work, there is great danger of silencing weaker voices (see Clark and Ede; Trimbur).

In order to deal with this perplexity — that collaborative writing is at once so valuable, so important, and yet so problematic — I've come to use the collaborative collage. Where the solo collage can serve as a bridge to regular essays, the collaborative collage can serve as a bridge to full collaboration. But like the solo collage, the collaborative collage is valuable in its own right. It can be as nice to stand on the bridge as on the other shore. (Readers not familiar with written collages will probably get a pretty good picture from what follows. But for a full and direct description of written collages, see "Collage: Your Cheatin' Art" in this volume,* and also the first workshop in Elbow and Belanoff.)

The procedure for creating a collaborative collage is so easy and simple that it will make some people nervous. Let me lay out the directions I give to pairs or small groups working together.

- Individually, write as much as you can about the topic. Write your own thoughts. It's fine to use rough, exploratory writing. Try to exploit the insights, language, and energy that come from moving fast and getting caught up in your thinking and feeling.

- There is an alternative first step you can use if you prefer. Each person writes for ten or fifteen minutes — however he or she wants to start. Then people switch papers for the next piece of

---

*Peter Elbow. *Everyone Can Write: Essays Toward a Hopeful Theory of Writing and Teaching Writing.* New York: Oxford UP, 2000. [Editor's note]

writing so that what is written is some kind of response to what the first person wrote. And so on. This method adds more of the quality of dialogue — thought answering thought. But by the same token, it can reduce the amount of sheer diversity in the collage, because the writers are much in touch with each other. In the first, nondialogical method, writers might well be in entirely different ball parks — which can be a genuine advantage.

- Individually, go back over what you yourself have written and choose the bits and sections you like most. Some might be a page or more, others very short. Choose at least twice as much material as you'll need for your contribution to the finished collage. Clean them up enough to share, but there's no need to spend too much time on the job.

- Together in your pair or group, read your individual pieces to each other. (Or share them through silent reading.)

- Together, agree on which pieces should be chosen for the collage. (Ground rule: no fair leaving anyone out — or letting anyone dominate the final version.)

- Together, give some feedback and suggestions in response to those pieces you have chosen. But there's no need for agreement in your responses. Just let everyone throw in their two cents. (You'll also have to agree on whether the final revising and polishing of bits should be done by the original authors or by means of trading pieces with each other.)

- Together, decide on a sequence for all the pieces you've chosen.

- Together, as part of this discussion about sequence, you may well decide you need some new pieces. Good new ideas might have come up in discussion; or you might realize that something important is missing.

- Individually, write any necessary new pieces; and revise and polish the chosen pieces.

- Together, look at what you have produced and decide whether to call it finished or to carry on with more work: for example, reordering of parts; revising of parts; writing new parts. This decision is collaborative, but further work can be individual.

Note that some of these tasks require agreement, but many do not. That is, there is genuine collaboration going on here — but only to a limited degree. This makes it much easier on participants than full collaboration and gives them a good bridge from individual work to group work. That is, participants *don't* have to agree on their ideas, thinking, conclusion, or thesis. They *don't* have to agree on language, wording, or phrasing. There are none of those awful tippy-toe discussions or time wasting arguments about how to phrase something. Nor about the voice or tone. At every moment, individuals are entirely in charge of every piece of writing with respect to thinking, wording, and voice — though of course these decisions are often influenced by comments and feedback from others.

Yet genuine collaboration is also going on — in fact two levels of collaboration:

- *Weak collaboration:* members read their writing to each other and give and receive individual responses from each other, and thereby *influence* each others' thinking and writing; this collaboration has a substantive effect on the final outcome. Yet this degree of collaboration is easy and nonstressful because participants don't have to agree.

- *Strong collaboration:* participants have to agree on which blips to use; they have to agree on what order to put them in; they have to agree on who does the revising; they have to agree on whether more revising is needed or whether to call it finished. Strong collaboration is harder because it requires agreement or consensus. But the scope of what people have to agree on is pretty limited.

Thus the collaborative collage speaks to the first problem of collaboration: difficulty or unpleasantness. But can it deal with the other two problems — weak or bland writing and the stifling of minority ideas and voices? Obviously, it can.

The collaborative collage invites all participants to stay entirely in charge of their own writing, and as a result, the final product is richer and more complex than most collaborative writing. (Even if members decide to revise each other's pieces, single individuals are in charge of thinking and language at any given moment.) The final product contains multiple points of view, multiple voices, multiple styles — and as a result, more tension and energy. Minority ideas and thinking have not been left out. In a collage, contrasts are a benefit, a source of energy that stimulates thinking in readers. The collaborative collage is a gathering of pieces each written from an "I" point of view — for the sake of a "we" enterprise.

The process I've described so far usually results in an open collage — a collage with multiple and conflicting points of view. If the students need to produce a *focused* collage, they must carry their partial collaboration a few steps further. They needn't leave out any of the conflicting material, but they need to spend additional time discussing the thinking in their open collage and find a way to agree on a conclusion or at least a common point of view. And then they need to write, add, arrange, or revise bits — again not taking away any of the contradictory material — in order to make the whole collage end up saying or implying their collaborative conclusion or point of view. They can even stop short of full agreement if they can agree on where they disagree and articulate that meta-agreement — further spelling out the implications of the various views and explaining what would need to be decided in order to settle their disagreement. But it's important for students to realize that even though they reach ultimate agreement on a conclusion or point of view, the focused collage still can and really ought to contain wildly divergent and contradictory pieces.

Learning to Make Space for Other Voices

Let me briefly suggest three additional methods for helping solo writers begin to get comfortable collaborating with other writers. These activities can serve as a bridge or introduction even to the mild collaboration I've already described.

1. The student writes a draft alone, but then shares that draft with one or more others and invites them to write out some of their own thoughts in response: new thoughts on the topic itself or thoughts about what the writer has said — perhaps even how it was said. These responses go to the original writer who then gets to incorporate some passages from them into his or her piece. The writer can put these passages in quotation marks, or in a different typeface, or even in a separate column running alongside the writer's own text. Thus the single writer stays in complete charge of his or her text — but incorporates the voices of others.

2. The student is writing about a topic while also doing lots of reading or interviewing about it. The student is asked to produce not a conventional, connected research or documented essay, but a collage that contains extensive and extended quotations from the reading or interviews. Again, the interjected material might be in long block quotations, in separate typefaces, or in a parallel column or two. The goal here is to help students "place" their own thoughts and voices in authoritative dialogue with the voices of others, especially of published writers. That is, this procedure can help prevent two common problems in research or documented essays by students: (a) essays where the writer says almost nothing and merely wholesales the ideas and voices of others; (b) essays where the writer brings in nothing but perfunctory "quotes" to back up what is essentially his or her own monologue.

3. Students work in pairs (or trios) and start by writing a "real time" dialogue: they simply pass a sheet of paper back and forth to each

other so each can write a response to the previous turn. (The process is even easier in an online classroom.) If they want to avoid one writer having to wait while the other one is writing, they can get two dialogues going on two different topics. This procedure can seem odd and artificial at first, but students get comfortable pretty quickly if we help them see that they are simply putting on paper what they do naturally and comfortably in spoken conversation. They usually benefit from being encouraged to let the dialogue go where it wants to go, even if it wanders. It's a voyage of thinking and discovery. Then the students read over what they have created, and they collaborate on revising it into a satisfying and coherent dialogue. This doesn't mean the organization or sequence of ideas has to be neat and tidy. Think about Plato! Thus the students have to agree about what the main line or direction should be, which parts to keep and discard, and how to arrange or rearrange. But they each get to revise their own contributions.

These three processes help students get used to making good texts out of multiple thoughts and voices.

Using the Collaborative Collage as a Bridge Back to Better Solo Writing

The collaborative collage can guide students not only toward better full collaboration, but also toward better solo writing. That is, the experience of writing and sharing collaborative collages — and seeing the unexpected virtues of them — can help students learn to get into their solo pieces some qualities that are rare and precious in writing: conflicting ideas, multiple points of view, perplexity, tension, and complexity of structure. The larger principle of learning that operates here (as articulated by Vygotsky and Mead) is that we eventually learn to do by ourselves what we first learned to do socially in interaction with others. We internalize the social process.

That is, much *solo* writing suffers from the same weakness that is found in much collaborative writing. Many student writers, feeling a pressure always to have a clear "thesis," end up settling for the lowest-common-denominator point that the various parts of the self can agree on. They are tempted to stop writing when they feel perplexed or come across conflicting feelings and ideas — nervously sweeping complications under the rug. Students have somehow been led to think that writing should always "flow" — a favorite word of praise — and thus that the texture should be seamless. They don't realize the pleasure and energy that comes from *bumps*. In truth, most good solo writing represents a single writer having some internal dialogue with herself — having more than one point of view and using more than one voice. Writing needs the drama of thinking and the performance of voices.

All these virtues can be summed up in the catchword that we've taken from Bakhtin's mouth: "dialogic." Fair enough. But it's fruitful to encourage some notes of overt *dialogue* into solo writing: passages where the writer actually breaks out into a different voice and point of view. It's not hard to create such passages by using launching pads like these: "Notice the complications we must consider, however, when we listen to the thoughts of someone who disagrees: '. . .'" or, "There are some serious objections, however, to what I have just been saying: '. . .'" Or, "But wait a minute. Let's look at this issue from a contrasting point of view: '. . .'" In each case, the writer can carry on for a paragraph or longer speaking in a different voice from a different point of view. Of course it's hard to get full rhetorical control over multiple voices and points of view, but even when students don't handle the richness and complexity so well, they almost always gain powerful benefits to their thinking. (Teachers have often found ways to give better grades to papers that fall down — when their downfall stems from the attempt to deal with complex thinking — than to seamless papers that settle for simple, obvious thinking.)

I'm fascinated by the literal ability to talk to oneself — to give voice to the multiple views and consciousnesses that inhabit us. The ability to have thoughtful dialogues with oneself may be one of the most important goals of schooling. It is surely the mark of educated or developed persons to be able to engage in thinking and dialogue when there are no others around who are interested in their topic or interested in talking to them. One of the biggest difficulties for adolescents, in particular, is that they feel so vulnerable to their peers and therefore find it hard to delve very far into issues or feelings or points of view that their peers ignore or scorn as weird. One of the main things I want to teach my students is that they can pursue their ideas, even when they feel alone and can't get others to listen.

To sum up. My goal in this teaching activity is to make collaborative writing not only easier and more inviting, but also more complex and conflicted. And in the end, the most lasting goal may be to get richer thinking and more voices into solo writing as well.

Works Cited

Clark, Suzanne, and Lisa Ede. "Collaboration, Resistance, and the Teaching of Writing." *The Right to Literacy.* Ed. Andrea Lunsford, Helene Moglen, and James Slevin. New York: Modern Language Association, 1990. 276–87.

Ede, Lisa, and Andrea Lunsford. *Singular Texts / Plural Authors: Perspectives on Collaborative Writing.* Carbondale, IL: Southern Illinois UP, 1990.

Elbow, Peter, and Pat Belanoff. *A Community of Writers: A Workshop Course in Writing.* 3rd ed. New York: McGraw-Hill, 1999.

LeFevre, Karen Burke. *Invention as a Social Act.* Carbondale, IL: Southern Illinois UP, 1987.

Light, Richard J. *Harvard Assessment Seminar: Explorations with Students and Faculty about Teaching and Learning and Student Life.* Cambridge: Harvard Graduate School of Education, 1990.

Mead, George H. *Mind, Self, and Society.* Chicago: U of Chicago P, 1934.

Polanyi, Michael. *Personal Knowledge: Toward a Post-Critical Philosophy.* New York: Harper and Row, 1958.

Trimbur, John. "Consensus and Difference in Collaborative Learning." *College English* 51 (Oct 1989): 602–16.

Vygotsky, Lev. *Mind in Society: The Development of Higher Psychological Processes.* Ed. M. Cole, V. John-Steiner, S. Scribner, and E. Souberman. Cambridge: Harvard UP, 1978.

Classroom Activities

Elbow provides a variety of activities for teaching collage and for facilitating collaborative learning among students. Consider choosing one or more of these activities based on student need and level of development in the writing process. As Elbow suggests, one of the most important benefits of collaborative writing may be "better solo writing. That is, the experience of writing and sharing collaborative collages — and seeing the unexpected virtues of them — can help students learn to get into their solo pieces some qualities that are rare and precious in writing: conflicting ideas, multiple points of view, perplexity, tension, and complexity of structure."

In particular, Elbow focuses on the need for multiple points of view in solo writing, a strategy that may be especially tricky for developing writers to negotiate. Building on the benefits of the collage activities, Elbow lists several "launching pad" sentence openers that students can employ to acknowledge multiple voices, including: "Notice the complications we must consider, however, when we listen to the thoughts of someone who disagrees: '. . .'" You may want to create and distribute a handout of such openers and invite students to use them in their writing. After students have worked on collaborative learning activities with peers and are experimenting with this method of engaging multiple voices in their solo writing, remind them of the connections between the conversations of collaborative learning and the dialogue that the individual writer conducts with his or her own thoughts.

Thinking about Teaching

To illustrate the problems of collaborative writing, Peter Elbow asks the rhetorical question: "Is there anyone who has not vowed never again to engage in a piece of committee writing?" Although Elbow presents collage exercises as a way of mitigating collaborative writing problems for students, clearly these activities have applications for instructors as well. Elbow provides ten bullet-point steps for creating a collaborative collage that he believes are "so easy and simple that it will make some people nervous." With a colleague or other writing partner, follow the ten steps that Elbow suggests. To reflect further on this activity, write in your teaching journal about your own process of completing the steps, and decide whether Elbow's activity would be worth using at a committee meeting to stimulate the group's thinking.

Building Learning Communities on Nonresidential Campuses

Richard Raymond

In the following article, which won TETYC's nineteenth annual best article award for 1999, readers will find a clearly written narrative of how three teachers at Richard Raymond's institution created a successful learning community at a primarily nonresidential campus. In addition, Raymond offers pragmatic suggestions and assignments for fostering collaborative learning and critical thinking in the writing classroom — and for drawing connections among a linked, interdisciplinary series of three courses that his entering first-year students were required to take. With help from a university grant and support from the administration and from teachers of composition, speech communication, and anthropology, they all worked together inside and outside of the classroom to create an innovative collaborative learning environment for students. Raymond also includes entries from his teaching journal, comments from a student assessment of the program conducted outside the classroom, and an excerpt from a student paper in order to document the progress that students made throughout the semester.

Introduction

Over the last three decades, I have taught in a rural two-year college and in two urban universities; all three schools have been dormless or nearly so. In each of these institutions, I have worked with writing teachers who shared my dismay when we learned of a first- or second-year student transferring elsewhere, having found no community, no place to live and learn, no core as she accumulated credits in the "core." We grieved, too, over students lost not to other schools but to learning. Sometimes, these students dropped out; others stayed, writing just well enough to pass the state Regents' essay, but not well enough to connect ideas in and among other disciplines.

Over these same years, "learning communities" have emerged, with program designers and administrators hoping that clustered classes would shore up enrollment, the first concern described above. But they have claimed a more high-minded motive as well: to help students form a site where — through writing — they feel connected even as they connect what they learn. According to recent comprehensive studies of learning communities, promises of enduring friendships and enriched learning have been kept (Matthews et al.; Tinto, Goodsell-Love, and Russo). Major universities — including BYU, Wisconsin, Washington, UC Berkeley, and SUNY — have kept these promises with interdisciplinary explorations of a common theme such as "World Hunger." Four-year and two-year colleges, notably Evergreen State in Washington and La Guardia Community College in New York, have done likewise, "clustering" courses in composition, social science, and humanities around topics like "Work, Labor, and Business in American Life" (Matthews et al. 460). Assessment of these programs consistently confirms that students have found not only a place to stay but also a way to learn, constructing knowledge through reading and writing, listening and speaking (Matthews et al. 469).

In fall semester 1997, encouraged by this history of success, I joined two colleagues in starting a learning community at the University of Arkansas at Little Rock (UALR). Our community linked my section of Comp I with Carol Thompson's section of speech communication and Julie Flinn's section of cultural anthropology. Naturally, we hoped to help solve the retention problem at UALR, where 59 percent of the first-year students never see a second year, having dropped out or having transferred to the cheaper Pulaski Technical College, to the residential, less urban University of Central Arkansas thirty miles away, or to the more fashionable University of Arkansas at Fayetteville, the state system's flagship institution. We also wanted to help twenty-five students to connect these core courses by exploring themes of acculturation, the role of language in finding one's place.

In addition to the studies mentioned above, we found decades of literature on structuring learning communities to help us set up the thematically linked courses. However, we quickly saw an obstacle faced only by the nonresidential schools mentioned in the literature: lack of student residents. UALR, an urban university of some eleven thousand students, has just one five-story dormitory; most of the non-resident students, averaging twenty-seven years of age, work part- or full-time off campus. Such students — even the traditional eighteen-year-olds — come to campus for back-to-back classes and then leave for work. With this student profile, we could not promise the bonding that would come with living as a community in a dorm, nor could we promise regular student-faculty meals, a selling point in some programs.

Below I describe a solution to this problem, one that roots in demographics but that finds solutions in expressivist, cognitive, and social constructionist pedagogies (White 59). The narrative, I hope, will honestly expose the errors — strategic and pedagogical — as well as ground our feelings of success. I hope, too, that this story will encourage the many four- and two-year colleges whose non-residential campuses make learning communities seem improbable consider developing them.

This story begins with crucial preliminaries: letter-writing, securing the help of administrators and registrars, coordinating schedules, and linking syllabi thematically. Moving then to the teaching of the community, the narrative relates first-day activities, the linking of assignments and communal learning, then discusses assessment.

Preliminaries

Julie, Carol, and I wanted to see if a learning community could help average students connect core curriculum courses and, in so doing, help them find their place as learners. Therefore, in collaboration with the dean, we decided to aim the promotional letter at *all* entering first-year students eligible for Composition 1, that is, those who had scored a quite modest 19 or higher on the ACT, a pool of some seven hundred students. The letter stressed communal learning, even though we had no dormitory and regular meals to offer (see Appendix A).

Stressing connected, communal learning, the letter apparently addressed a need that both students and parents recognized. Within five working days, we had accepted thirty students, begun a waiting list, and mailed a follow-up letter inviting the students to one of the advising and registration sessions.

Prior to mailing the letters, we three teachers met twice with Dr. Thea Hoeft, Director of Undergraduate Advisement, deans, the head registrar, and the vice-chancellor for student activities, all of whom we needed to make the community happen:

- The vice-chancellor, head of UALR's First-Year Experience program, promoted the learning community in his oral and written recruiting efforts.

- The registrar approved listing the three courses as "restricted" to ensure that we would have only volunteers in the community. He also approved cross-listings in the university course schedule, including a "comment line" instructing the students to call any of the three instructors for further information.

- The dean of the College of Arts, Humanities, and Social Sciences, Deborah Baldwin, agreed to pay for mailing the letters and to receive all the response cards. She also has taken every opportunity to promote this and subsequent learning communities before the college faculty.

- Thea Hoeft gave up five hours of her time to conduct the two advisement sessions.

Such collaboration between faculty and administrators builds a professional community that doesn't exist on every campus; more to the point here, this teamwork proved critical to starting and sustaining the learning community.

We also received help from the associate vice-chancellor, whose committee on curriculum development grants approved our proposal for financial support. The grant provided each teacher $1,950 as compensation for developing the courses over the summer. We also happily accepted an additional $400 to pay for assessment materials and for food we would share with the students on the first day and during assessment sessions (see discussion below).

As each teacher developed a syllabus over the summer, we met three times — twice over coffee, once over lunch — to find and synchronize the thematic links, a process made possible by reading each other's texts. Eventually, we settled on the following interrelated anthropological themes, each taken up at approximately the same time in each class:

- Coming into a Culture,

- Making Words and Making a Living,

- Gender and Marriage,

- Social Ranking and Stratification, and

- Government, Religion, and Justice.

Using Jack Selzer's thematic reader *Conversations* in a Comp I class, I easily found selections that would help the students explore the concepts they were learning in anthropology.[1] While they learned about ethnocentrism in anthropology, for example, the students read Alice Walker's "Everyday Use" in Comp I to find distinctions between ethnocentrism and legitimate racial pride. Similarly, the students read and discussed Sizer's *Horace's Compromise* to understand the difference between teaching that produces conformists and teaching that acculturates thinkers. They explored Rodriguez's "Aria" and Darrow's "Address to the Prisoners" to contemplate the causes of exclusion from cultures, Glaspell's "Trifles" to learn what happens when marriage stifles individualism, Orwell's "A Hanging" and Koch's "Death and Justice" to understand the causes and effects of capital punishment, and King's "Birmingham Jail" to see the roles of government and churches in making justice a dream deferred.

Speaking, Reading, and Writing in the Learning Community

With the syllabi thematically linked, we teachers met one more time to plan strategy for the first day of class. Wanting to assess the learning that occurred in the community, we thought of devoting the first session to an in-class essay on a "Doonesbury" cartoon depicting a jaded lecturer and his mindless students (Selzer 95). We would then ask for another essay on this same cartoon on the last day, hoping to see not only better writing but also better understanding of the traditional classroom as a potentially destructive site of acculturation.

The need for assessment data notwithstanding, we quickly realized the deadening effect of such an opener, one that would intimidate most students and do nothing to establish community. We therefore moved the "Doonesbury" essay to a first homework assignment (see discussion of assessment below), focusing instead on community-building activities. First, we decided that all three teachers as well as the assessment expert, Dr. Kathy Franklin, should attend my 8:00 A.M. composition class, where we would reintroduce ourselves as their learning community teachers — we had already met at the advisement sessions mentioned above — and invite the students to enjoy the donuts and coffee provided by the grant budget.

Wanting learning as well as pastries to characterize the first day, we also borrowed a "birth order" workshop from the National Writing Project to stimulate thought on the influence of early discourse communities in shaping the ways we learn and interact. Appendix B displays the guidelines we distributed to move from pleasantries to active learning for all the Older Children, Middle Kids, Babies, and Onlies in the class.

As each student stood by his or her birth order poster and reported the group's findings, predictably celebrating the group's virtues — leadership, flexibility, patience — while playfully demonizing the Other, the Bossy Big Sisters, the Spoiled Little Brothers, we quickly saw the value of this one-hour workshop.

- First, we had broken the ice, with instructors participating in the appropriate birth order group, underscoring implicitly the idea of students and teachers as peers in learning.

- We also moved from conversation to writing (posters), then to public speaking and listening, modeling thereby the interconnectedness of speech and composition.

- We introduced the role of family in acculturating students, a central theme in the anthropology class.

- We bonded with laughter, a far stronger glue than donuts when it comes to holding communities together.

Having bonded on day one, we devoted the next two weeks to readings and writings on families and education to explore further the anthropological theme of "coming into a culture" (header in Comp I syllabus, weekly schedule). To help the students read anthropologically, I first assigned Alice Walker's story "Everyday Use" and asked them to answer the questions in Figure 1 in their journal.

Questions one through six introduced the students to close reading and helped them understand the term "ethnocentrism," the first word they would learn in anthropology; question seven helped them to understand journaling as a reflective process, a way of moving from "what happened?" to "what does the text mean?" At the same time, answering these questions prepared the students for class discussion and for writing their first papers on one of the ethnocentrism topics in Appendix C.

While the essay assignment does restrict students to the "conversation" started by Walker — thereby fostering responsible reading — it also encourages the students to find their own topics (Murray; Graves). In addition, the assignment allows students to interpret Walker's text in anthropological terms or to respond to her story with an anthropological story of their own.

Reinforcing the concept of community, I scheduled a writing group day, when each student shared her first draft with two peers, who then responded orally and in writing, using guidelines I provided. After this community-building experience, the students conferred individually with me, then revised their papers and submitted the draft and the revision. Having received my written responses to the second draft, the students revised a second time, then submitted the piece again for further comment and a grade (see discussion below on further revision in portfolio assignment). Then to underscore the *ongoing* nature of dialogue in any learning community, I scheduled a reading day, when four volunteers read their papers to the whole class and invited responses.

During the two-and-a-half-week period devoted to the writing of this paper in response to Walker, the students continued their reading and journaling on the anthropological theme of "coming into a culture." Focusing now on nonfiction pieces — Gardner's "A Nation at Risk," Rich's "Claiming an Education," and others — students examined the roles of schools and teachers in effecting — or stifling — healthy acculturation.

Moving next to a related theme concurrently studied in the anthropology class, "making words and making a living," the students continued these same rhythms of study — reading, journaling, discussing — exploring such pieces as Smitherman's "White English in Blackface, or Who Do I Be?" and Rodriguez's "Aria: a Memoir of a Bilingual Childhood." Such work led to a second essay (Appendix D), one asking students to narrate their experiences being brought into their cultures by teachers.

Figure 1. Questions on Walker's "Everyday Use"

Walker, *"Everyday Use,"* pp. 74–82

1. In paragraphs 1–6, what actions and details reveal the narrator's (mother's) view of Dee?
2. How has the fire (2, 10) affected Maggie's personality?
3. How does Dee's education affect her view and her treatment of her mother and her sister Maggie (11, 22, 25–27, 36)? What is the nature of her **ethnocentrism?**
4. Why does Dee want the churn top and the quilts (53, 66)?
5. Why does the mother return the quilts to Maggie?
6. Find five similes (or metaphors) in the narrative and explain what each comparison reveals about the character described.
7. What inference can you draw from this narrative that will answer the question at the top of p. 74, "What's college for?"

Having moved through the drafting-responding-revising process on this assignment, I held a second communal reading day, then broke new anthropological ground with the themes "gender and marriage" and "social ranking and stratification," featuring not only Glaspell's "Trifles," as mentioned above, but also Steele's "A Negative Vote on Affirmative Action" and Wilkins's "Racism Has Its Privileges."

To help students probe more deeply into the connection between these readings and the textbook material in anthropology, all three teachers periodically asked students to write in class in their reflective journals (a journal separate from the one they kept for Comp I), noting points of anger, confusion, or enthusiasm as they learned of placement and displacement in cultures, both American and Other. Also, Kathy Franklin, the assessment expert, began meeting with a student focus group. Having lured volunteers with pizza (paid for by the grant) to meet with her outside of class, Kathy asked them to practice the collaborative techniques they learned in speech to examine their experiences — negative as well as positive — learning in a community. They spoke of teachers allowing too little time for journaling, of students having no time to meet as study groups outside of class, of peers who seem unprepared for response sessions, of students and teachers who talk too much; they also admitted — now — to seeing their peers as friends, their teachers as fellow learners, and the classroom far less stratified than those they had experienced in high school or in college.

Having received this midterm assessment from Dr. Franklin, we resolved to allow more writing/reflecting time in class and to draw out the less talkative students by inviting them to read from their journals. We also resolved to bite our lips more often, sharing our views as community members but not dominating any conversation. Though duly chastened by the students' negative remarks, we teachers enjoyed hearing that the students shared our perception of a growing community that had learned how to learn.

Buoyed by a shared sense of community, we continued reading, talking, and writing, focusing now on the themes that would round out the students' course in cultural anthropology: "Government, Religion, and Justice." In addition to the pieces by Orwell, Koch, and Dr. King noted above, we read Weisberg's "This Is Your Death." The students journaled as always to monitor their responses to these controversial texts; in so doing, they also prepared for class, where I asked them to mediate arguments on crime and punishment, on order and justice. These discussions, usually quite lively, generated healthy peer exchanges over drafts and mainly successful essays.

In helping the students find their topics, I did not require them to confront an adversary, to strike the militant Aristotelian stance of one who seeks to vanquish a foe rather than to build community (Lamb). Instead, I asked them to enter an ongoing conversation, using the text — whether the fictional text of Glaspell, the nonfiction texts of Steele, Koch, or King, or the "text" of the learning community — to present readings designed to keep readers talking, encouraging healthy dissensus as well as mediated consensus (Bruffee; Trimbur).

As the end of the semester approached, I wanted to give the students a chance to position themselves as individuals within the community. To facilitate this finding of place, I asked each student to focus on a text(s) and a conversation she or he had found most compelling. Appendix E shows this invitation to critical analysis.

The first topic invited students to respond to an ethnographic text read in anthropology, either the exotic story of Eskimo life recorded in *Never in Anger* or the story of RVing in America, *Over the Next Hill.* The second topic encouraged students to return to a conversation in Comp I, choosing a text worthy of response and of rhetorical analysis; the third offered the same encouragement but took students beyond the texts we had read in the community. Whatever the student's choice, each wrote on the nature of living in communities and the challenge of doing so as an individual, as one voice responding to many voices.

Assessing the Nonresidential Learning Community

Naturally, we will need to accumulate years of data to show conclusively that the learning communities have performed as well as their predecessors on other campuses in achieving the two objectives: to retain students and to improve learning. However, we have been encouraged by the early results, as generated by the following instruments of assessment (Franklin):

- Pretest: The "Doonesbury" essay, given as the first night's homework, showed some understanding of learning theory and the potentially stupefying effect of lecturing. However, nearly all the essays lacked development, offering little or no textual support for the inferences drawn. I returned the papers, with comments but no grade, and asked the students to file them in their journals. They did so and promptly forgot the exercise.

- Posttest: We asked the students to write about the same cartoon again, this time as a final exam, counting ten percent of the grade in Comp I. Many complained loudly, a reaction I anticipated, given their weariness by the end of the semester. Their objections notwithstanding, I stuck with the requirement, not wanting to sabotage the assessment plan. In addition, I saw the analysis of the cartoon as a way to see what they had learned about its imbedded anthropological themes. Of course, in assessing the results, we factored in their low motivation on the pretest (no grade) and the high motivation on the posttest (grade). Nevertheless, we were pleased by the papers: they showed more sophisticated understanding of the cartoon as an example of misacculturation; also, unlike the pretests, all but two of the essays showed facility in using examples to support generalizations.

- Attitude Survey: This lengthy questionnaire, prepared by Dr. Franklin, provided qualitative data suggesting that students generally endorse the idea of learning communities. However, they more frequently praised the linked courses for increasing their number of friends rather than for helping them learn anthropology, failing to see the connection between the "fun, comfortable environment" of the community and the depth and range of their learning. Predictably, too, some said that "learning community" means "more work, less credit."

- Focus Group: This group of eight students echoed the voices in the survey, praising the "comfort," the new friendships, wishing for more time to meet outside of class, objecting to having to do "more work" than other first-year students do in unlinked classes. As mentioned above, they also complained of too little time for journal writing in class and of too much teacher talk. Having purged these complaints, they recognized, too, the connectedness of writing and speaking as ways to learn anthropology; consequently, they hoped to take more linked courses at higher levels in and beyond the core curriculum.

- Portfolio: The students' sense of "belonging" to the learning community — and the learning generated, at least in part, by that sense of connectedness — were born out in most of the portfolios. Determining forty percent of the course grade in Comp I, the portfolio included a piece from Comp I, from speech (an outline or text of a speech), and from cultural anthropology; it also included an artifact symbolizing their work in the learning community (or their life in the family), their reflective journal (not graded, just required), and the metacognitive cover essay.

- Grades on the Portfolio: Seven of the students earned an *A* on the portfolio, twelve a *B,* three a *C,* one a *D.* No one received an *F.* These high grades resulted primarily from cover essays that showed the metacognitive ability to analyze the strengths and weaknesses of a piece of writing and to place each piece in a larger picture of struggle and growth.

- Faculty Reflective Journals: All three faculty kept a reflective journal, as did the students. For both students and teachers, the reflective journal provided a place to complain without fear of penalty of too little time, of annoying or uncooperative peers, of having to meet unrealistic expectations. More important, this journal also invited a healthy looking back, attempting to see where and how learning happened or collapsed.

To provide admittedly selective evidence of these claims of partial success, I share some remarks from my reflective journal, then move to a sample of student writing strong enough — particularly in contrast to writing in recent unlinked writing classes — to motivate me to try the learning community again.

Reflective Journal Entries

September 18

Before class begins each day, the students grow ever more rowdy. I complimented them today for their noise: they seem comfortable with one another, joking as well as talking — quite a contrast to the beginning of the semester.

September 25

Class got off to a rocky start today; sleepy faces, no show of interest. But Heather Rainey read from her thoughtful journal; her remarks challenging Darrow's view of the causes of crime led to some rich discussion, some honest talk about access to the American Dream.

December 9

Just finished reading the portfolios. I'm pleased. After all their stewing about artifacts, they came through with photos of family members, pictures of the tools of our community, ritual necklaces made in anthropology. My favorite portfolio is that of Sarah Martin. Using her photographic skills, she composed a 9″x12″ portrait of the ethnographies, The Easy Access Handbook, a CD, and owl candles — all really quite striking. Sarah's cover piece offers sophisticated reflection on her growth as writer and learner. While Sarah's cover piece may be the best, it is not atypical. As far as I'm concerned, these portfolios tell us what we need to know to assess the educational value of learning communities. The case of Zhang Bing-wen confirms this view. In the beginning, Zhang, an Asian student, begged to drop the LC. He just knew he would fail anthropology and lose "face" at school and at home. His older sister phoned me to beg for his release. Instead of granting their request, I urged Zhang to give us three teachers a chance; I also referred him to Carol and Julie, invoking our "talk first" policy. It worked. He stayed, earned a *B* on the first anthro test. With his head no longer bowed in silence, he went on to become one of the most talkative students in the class. He earned a *B* in Comp and *B*s in the other courses as well. In short, he learned and we retained him!

Excerpt from Student Writing

This excerpt comes from a student who early in the course confessed her American ethnocentrism. In this passage, written near the end of the semester, she expresses tolerance, even appreciation, for the Other, suggesting that she has achieved an objective of the community: to value difference:

> From a Comp I essay on the anthropological ethnography, *Never In Anger*: [The Utku Eskimos] show a great amount of affection to a child before he or she acquires ihmuma, reason. . . . Ihuma is developing when a child begins to respond to the social world, to recognize people . . . to understand and talk . . . to participate in useful social games . . . used to tease the child into doing what is right. In America, we have do's and don'ts for our children, but the Utku just wait for the child to conform. One example occurs when Saarak had to quit nursing from her mother because a new baby was born. Saarak screamed and slapped at her mother and sister, but Saarak's mother only said, "Don't hurt her" . . . Many Americans believe the best way to get a child to conform to society is by using strict discipline. The Utku culture has showed, however, that a child without discipline can decide his or her own progress without spoiling society.
>
> — Heather Rainey,
> "The Utka Acculturation"

Impressions

While we lack sufficient data to make any conclusive claims about the value of learning communities on a primarily nonresidential campus,

I can describe two strong impressions shared by me and my two colleagues, as well as by Dr. Franklin, the assessment chief.

- Having spent hours together in designing and teaching the linked courses, we teachers have transformed ourselves from professional acquaintances to professional friends. Clearly, we should expect our students to experience the hollowness of the curricular core if we work in isolation from our colleagues across campus. A fragmented faculty will almost certainly teach a fragmented curriculum.

- Most first-year students can write and think metacognitively in thematically linked courses.

Two-thirds of the students shared these impressions, valuing their deeper capacities for independent thought as well as their new friends. The following comment from a student's reflective journal speaks for many in the group:

> The connections of these courses taught me not only the use of the skills, but also how to use those skills to connect smaller things in my life to form a larger picture, a broader spectrum, of what the world actually looks like. . . . [The teachers have] taught me to take off my ethnocentric lenses and to look at the world in a new light.

Such sentiments bode well for using learning communities not only to facilitate this connected learning but also to retain students. Though five withdrew before the semester began, the result of conflicts with work or family responsibilities, only one student dropped the learning community after it had formed. Typically, core composition classes lose at least five students over the course of the semester.

Teaching in this learning community has also convinced me that we can overcome the inherent obstacles to linked courses on nonresidential campuses. True, we have far less time to meet, eat, and talk outside of class, compared to that time available on residential campuses. But we knit the students together by relying on social constructionist theory in all three classes, using small group work to interpret texts and to respond to writers, collaborating in the making of community knowledge. We also encouraged the students to develop and heed individual voices in the community. We did so by using the reader-response journal as a cognitive prewriting activity; by encouraging expressivist writing — freewrites, narratives — and by holding reading days that celebrate individual voices.

Last fall I taught a Comp I linked to courses in ethics and in personal awareness — the newest learning community. This spring, my colleagues offered communities linking Comp II with ethics and religious world views, Comp I with earth science, and Comp II with

Civilization II. As other ideas for linkages percolate across campus, we have begun to see the campus's single dorm as the reason why we must build learning communities, not as the reason why we can't.

Appendix A

Invitation Letter

Dear _____:

Congratulations on your admission to UALR! We're looking forward to your studying here with us. We're also eager to help you make those choices that will shape your life — socially, academically, and professionally — during and after your years at UALR.

With this letter, we invite you to make that first choice: to consider enrolling in our **Learning Community,** a new program for eligible first-year students. And you're eligible!

Here's how the Learning Community works: You will enroll in a "block" of **three core courses: Rhetoric 1311.19, Composition I,** 8:00–9:15, Tuesday and Thursday; **Speech Communication 1300.17,** 9:25–10:40, Tuesday and Thursday; **Cultural Anthropology 2316.02,** 10:50–12:05, Tuesday and Thursday.

Consider the advantages of enrolling in this block of back-to-back courses:

- Preferred Scheduling: You'll be first to register. Also you'll have Tuesday and Thursday afternoons free for study, for part-time work on or off campus, or for other courses.

- Study Groups: You'll be part of a Community of Learners studying and working together in all three courses. Such support from trusted peers will help you do well in these three courses and foster habits of collaborative learning that will carry you far in your academic and professional lives. And study partners often become good friends!

- Making Connections: You will reinforce your learning by connecting each class to the other two. For example, some of your compositions and speeches will ask you to respond to readings from cultural anthropology. In turn, your anthropology class will give you further practice in writing and speaking as means of learning the material.

Please let us know if you're interested in joining our Learning Community by returning the enclosed card. We will select twenty-five students, filling the slots as we receive the cards, so please don't delay!

After we have chosen our Community members, we will invite you to campus to get acquainted and to complete your academic advisement for fall semester. We look forward to hearing from you!

Dr. Juliana Flinn, Professor of Anthropology
Dr. Carol Thompson, Associate Professor of Speech
Dr. Rich Raymond, Professor of Rhetoric and Writing

Appendix B

Collaborative Learning Task: Birth Order

Directions:

1. Pull your chairs together with others of your birth order group.

2. Appoint a person to read through the task before you go any further.

3. Agree on another person to record the views expressed by the group and the decisions the group makes collectively.

4. Choose a person to speak for the group.

5. Read and discuss the following questions:

   a. How did your position in the family affect your behavior in the family?

   b. How might that family history affect your behavior in a group within the learning community?

6. Review the recorder's notes to see that they accurately express the views of the group. List your findings on the poster paper provided; tape your paper to the wall.

Source: Pat Fox and the Coastal Georgia Writing Project; the Little Rock Writing Project.

Appendix C

Essay Assignment on "Ethnocentrism"

First Essay: Ethnocentrism

Please write an essay on one of the following topics. Be sure that your paper presents a **thesis** that addresses your **purpose** and your **audience.** Because you must present examples and explanations to support your thesis, your essay will probably be 2–3 pages long (double-spaced, 12 point type). Your final draft, **due Tuesday, September 2,** must be word processed. I will return your essay on Thursday, September 4; the **revision** will be due on **September 9.**

1. Use Wangeroo Leewanike (Dee) in Walker's story: "Everyday Use," to illustrate the meaning of "ethnocentrism." *Audience:* Parents or friends who have heard you use the term "ethnocentrism" but aren't sure what you mean. *Purpose:* to make sure that your audience understands the difference between healthy ethnic pride and ethnocentrism.

2. Describe two or three artifacts cherished by your family. *Audience:* Members of your learning community. *Purpose:* to explain the "everyday use" of each artifact (it need not be valuable in monetary terms) and the reasons for cherishing each object.

3. Devise your own topic in response to Walker's story. You might focus on brother/sister rivalries as students, or on the role of parents as teachers, or on your reasons for attending college. *Audience:* Members of your writing group and, potentially, the whole class. *Purpose:* to introduce yourself as an individual shaped as a learner by your experience as a family member.

Appendix D

Narrative Assignment

Your essay should explore at least three episodes in your life in which a teacher or teachers have shaped your attitudes toward learning, toward formal education, and toward your local, state, or national culture. Your essay should reach a conclusion on what conditions foster — and stifle — your sense of place, of belonging in American culture.

Appendix E

Critical Analysis

For your fourth assignment, please compose a critical essay on a text or texts that have some anthropological significance. The word "critical" does not mean "to find fault"; rather, it means to analyze and interpret your chosen text(s).

Suggested Topics

1. Focusing on *Never in Anger* or on *Over the Next Hill,* discuss one of the author's conclusions about the subculture examined in the ethnography. The possibilities are endless: sources of entertainment, distribution of work, gender roles, attitudes toward the Other (outsiders, dominant culture), methods of subsistence, language, contributions to dominant culture. *Audience:* Members of the learning community for spring semester, all of whom dread having to read an ethnography.

2. The title of your reader, *Conversations,* implies that reading and writing involve an **exchange,** a "conversation" between writer and reader. Focusing on one of the essays (five pages or longer) that we have read, discuss the **techniques** the author uses to draw us into the conversation on the anthropological issue at hand (education and acculturation, gender roles, ethnocentricity, capital punishment, social justice, and the roles of church and state). Your essay should explain to what extent the author made you respond, lured you into conversation. Your **audience** doubts that any "freshman reader" is worth the paper it's printed on.

3. Design your own topic. *Guidelines:* Your topic must relate to one of the anthropological themes printed in your Comp I syllabus. Your paper must also respond to a "text" — a book, a novel, an essay, a film. You must aim your paper at a particular audience, people who need to hear what you have to say.

Note

1. For a copy of the Comp I syllabus — and any other pedagogical or assesment tool mentioned in this article — send an e-mail message to rcraymond @ualr.edu.

Works Cited

Bruffee, Kenneth. "Collaborative Learning and the 'Conversation of Mankind.'" Villanueva 393–414.

Franklin, Kathy K. "Making Connections: Evaluation of the 1997 Learning Community Pilot." Univ. of Arkansas at Little Rock, July 10, 1998.

Graves, Richard L. "What I Learned from Verle Barnes: The Exploratory Self in Writing." *Rhetoric and Composition: A Sourcebook for Teachers and Writers.* 3rd ed. Ed. Richard L. Graves. Portsmouth, NH: Heinemann, 1990. 132–36.

Lamb, Catherine E. "Beyond Argument in Feminist Composition." *College Composition and Communication* 42 (1991): 11–24.

Matthews, Roberta S., Barbara Leigh Smith, Jean MacGregor, and Faith Babelnick. "Creating Learning Communities." *Handbook of the Undergraduate Curriculum.* Ed. J. G. Gaff and J. L. Ratcliff. San Francisco: Jossey, 1997. 457–75.

Murray, Donald. "Teach Writing as a Process Not Product." Villanueva 3–6.

Selzer, Jack. *Conversations.* 3rd ed. New York: St. Martin's, 1997.

Tinto, Vincent, Anne Goodsell-Love, and Pat Russo. "Freshman Interest Groups and the First-Year Experience: Constructing Student Communities in a Large University." *Journal of the Freshman Year Experience* 6.1 (1994): 7–28.

Trimbur, John. "Consensus and Difference in Collaborative Learning." Villanueva 439–56.

Villanueva, Victor. ed. *Cross-Talk in Comp Theory: A Reader.* Urbana: NCTE, 1997.

White, Charles R. "Placing Community-Building at the Center of the Curriculum." *Metropolitan Universities: An International Forum.* Baltimore: Towson U, 1998. 55–62.

Classroom Activities

In Appendix B, Raymond provides a collaborative learning task on birth order (from Pat Fox and the Georgia Coastal Writing Project and the Little Rock Writing Project) that was used as a first-day icebreaker for students in the composition course and was a key element of the collaborative learning community. An important purpose of this activity was to build community in the classroom from the very beginning as students divided themselves into groups and followed a set of directions based on birth order ("Older Children, Middle Kids, Babies, and Onlies"). Teachers also participated in this activity, "underscoring implicitly the idea of students and teachers as peers in student learning." Consider participating in this collaborative learning task with your own students, either as a first-day exercise or later in the term when the class may need support and continued focus in the benefits of creating a learning community. You may want to give more emphasis to writing by changing steps 5a and 5b to include an in-class writing component that students can then read aloud to other members of their group. Another way to build writing into this task would be to assign students to write a journal entry or short summary that evaluates the success of this collaborative learning task on birth order.

Thinking about Teaching

Although the learning community that Raymond helped to build was designed for students who were eligible for first-year composition, successful learning communities have also been created for students in developmental studies. To find out more about how these collaborative learning groups work at other colleges and universities, consult an Internet search engine such as <www.google.com> and do a search using the term *learning communities*. You will then have access to several Web pages that describe learning communities for colleges and universities that serve a variety of populations, including "virtual" learning communities located on the World Wide Web. From this selection, and from the details included in Raymond's article, you can begin to create your own idea of what a learning community for developmental learners might look like at your own institution. Consult with other teachers across disciplines to discern interest, and share your thoughts with administrators.

10

Technology

Over the last two decades, many basic writing programs have implemented the use of computer labs and classrooms as well as distance learning and other forms of computer-mediated instruction. Many teachers have recognized the advantages of electronic media in helping students become better communicators, more skillful problem solvers, and more engaged members of their communities. However, access to technology can be a volatile political issue, drawing attention to problems of student privilege and institutional financial solvency. If many students in basic writing come to class well acquainted with computers and electronic media, others lack even the most basic keyboarding skills. How do we productively engage the first group of students while not ignoring or limiting access to the second?

In this chapter, Catherine Matthews Pavia offers case studies of two students in basic writing with limited access to computers outside of the classroom. Pavia documents changes that she made to her pedagogy based on the findings of her teacher research; she also describes the "technology narrative" that she assigns. Martha Clark Cummings writes about her experiences in Japan with computer-mediated instruction and EFL students who are enrolled in a basic writing course taught entirely in English. Cummings discusses how she created an online version of this course and presents an Internet-based assignment that develops students' skills in reading, writing, and communicating in English. Both of these articles provide the opportunity to consider the benefits and challenges surrounding computer-mediated instruction in our classrooms and online.*

Issues of Attitude and Access: A Case Study of Basic Writers in a Computer Classroom

Catherine Matthews Pavia

Previous research on students in basic writing and computer classrooms, Catherine Matthews Pavia suggests, accentuated positive outcomes for a majority of students who generally had sufficient access to technology. Pavia's research takes a different approach. She focuses on those students with limited access to computers outside the classroom, providing case studies of two students. Matt grew up in Lawrence, Massachusetts, in a low-income neighborhood and Maria grew up in the Dominican Republic and attended high school in Dorchester, Massachusetts. Based on this teacher research, Pavia states, she made significant changes in her pedagogy, including assigning a technology narrative. Drawing on the work of Moran and Duffelmeyer, Pavia invites students to write a narrative that asks them to think critically about technology. Like its counterpart, the literacy narrative, the technology narrative "allows [the instructor] to discover what students bring with them to writing and computer use."

It's Monday, 10:10 a.m., and our basic writing class begins. The twenty students start their daily ten-minute freewrite — or freetype — on the personal computers in front of them while I roam around the room, making sure that all of the computers are working. Some students already have two paragraphs typed as I walk by, and with fingers flying, are on their way to a one-page journal entry. But a few students have barely managed three sentences and sit, typing slowly and looking intently at the keyboard. I give the class an extra five minutes to write because some seem to have just started, but I know that this will only allow the slower students to type a few more sentences, while others will produce another half of a page. I wonder how I should account for students' different abilities with and knowledge of computers.

Most of the research on computer use in basic writing classrooms does not acknowledge scenarios such as this. The early literature from the 1980s on computers and basic writing students tends to present

---

*For a critical perspective on access to technology, see Cynthia Selfe's Technology and Literacy in the Twenty-First Century: The Perils of Not Paying Attention (Carbondale, IL: Southern Illinois UP, 1999).

computers as a saving grace for basic writers. Researchers praise computers for increasing students' motivation and enjoyment of writing (Moberg 47; Rodrigues 337), for increasing the amount of text produced by basic writers (Etchison 39), and for leading students towards better revision practices (McAllister and Louth 417; Daiute 137; Dalton and Hannifin 340).

Twenty years later, research on computer use in college and the benefits of basic writing computer classes still tends to paint an idealistic picture. The recent Pew Internet and American Life Project enthusiastically portrays college students as having easy access to computers and much experience with computers. It reports that 20 percent of college students began their computer use between ages five and eight, and that 85 percent have their own computer (Jones 6). However, this portrayal of the majority's connection with and access to computers glosses over the students who did not grow up around computers because of their economic or cultural situations. Similar idealism prevails in recent literature regarding computer use in basic writing. In their nationwide survey of developmental writing teachers, Stan and Collins report that "positive evaluations of using technology overwhelmingly outweighed the neutral or negative ones" (32). And Kish presents computers as the answer to basic writing students' difficulties with writer's block.

Some research, however, has begun to question the overwhelming amount of praise for computers in writing classrooms. Gay was one of the first to argue that computers alone do not empower writers (63). Dowling similarly argues that computers do not necessarily facilitate writing (234). Moreover, Agnostina and Varone found that teachers in computer classrooms tend to intervene with basic writing students during their writing process, which is not always a positive or welcome experience, particularly if it distracts writers from their writing (46). But the caution signs raised by these articles and others like them have not been glaring enough to slow the technological bandwagon from picking up more basic writing programs and teachers in the name of progress. My own experiences teaching in the basic writing computer classroom point to the need for more research into the computer experience; attitudes; genealogies, which Sloane defines as an individual's memory, understandings, and prior experiences with writing, reading, and technology; and overall technological complexities that basic writers may bring to the computer classroom (50). More needs to be learned about this subject, particularly given the speed with which computer technology and our relationships to it are changing.

In their nationwide survey, Stan and Collins uncovered some contradictions and disparities between what writing instructors had to say about using computers in basic writing. I feel those contradictions in my own teaching: I could discuss many positive aspects of teaching in a computer classroom, among which are pedagogical variety, student interest, expanded audiences, a broader definition of "writing," and so forth. But I also need to consider individually the students in my classes who struggle with the computers. I feel that there is personal and pedagogical value in doing so and harmful repercussions for these students in failing to do so.

In an attempt to do just that and to address some of these issues in my own teaching, I began conducting teacher research with basic writers in my computer classroom during fall semester 2002. I wanted to explore the following questions: What do some basic writers bring to the computer classroom that could complicate their interactions with technology and their ability to write with technology? And how can I, as a teacher, account pedagogically for differences I see in students' abilities to write with technology?

After detailing my methodology, I present two case studies of basic writers and discuss the importance of attitude and access, two key issues that emerged from my case studies. I conclude with a reflection on three ways I have changed my own pedagogy as a result of my teacher research and case studies.

Methodology

I chose to conduct teacher research with four of the twenty students in one of my basic writing classes. Ruth Ray defines teacher research as "systematic and intentional inquiry" performed by teachers (173). She further defines "systematic" as research that "implies methodical data gathering, analyzing, and reporting" (173). According to Ray, teacher research differs from other composition research because of its "collaborative spirit; its emphasis on the interrelationship between theory and practice; and its interest in bringing about change . . . *from within the classroom*" (183, italics in original). I chose to conduct teacher research not only because my questions arose from my teaching but also because my purpose for conducting the research matched Ray's words exactly: I wanted to bring about change from within my classroom.

I also chose a case study approach in part because of Sloane's work in "The Haunting Story of J." In this article Sloane addresses the need for individual genealogies of students in computer writing classrooms because our experiences with technology are always influenced by memory, learned responses, previous experiences with writing, reading, and communicative technology, and by our individual and cultural genealogies (50). As Sloane says, "Writing is also an intellectual and emotional activity of splicing together prior selves, understanding, and experiences" (52). Because of their detailed focus on individual students, case studies allow researchers to access these "prior selves, understanding, and experiences." My case study differs from Sloane's in its focus. Sloane looks at a student's genealogy to discover the motivation behind his composition choices, whereas I focus on the influence of students' genealogies on their interactions with computers and on their ability to write using computers.

The four freshmen, Valerie, Tom, Matt, and Maria,[1] who agreed to participate in my case study, were placed into basic writing based on their performance in a one-hour essay placement test, which was read and scored by a minimum of two readers. The stated goal of English 111, the basic writing class at the University of Massachusetts, Amherst, is to help students develop reading and writing abilities that they will need to be successful in their university careers. English 111 classes are capped at twenty students and are held in computer writing classrooms stocked with a computer for each student and a printer for the class as a whole. Each class meets twice a week for two hours and five minutes for each class period. Throughout the course, the students write three drafts of five essays of at least 750 words, numerous shorter "exploratory writings," in-class freewrites, and grammar assignments, and produce a final magazine collection of their essays.

As their basic writing teacher, I observed Tom, Valerie, Matt, and Maria throughout the semester and collected and read all of their exploratory writings, two drafts of each paper, and occasional freewrites and in-class assignments. I also spoke with each individually about each paper. In my capacity as a researcher (which does overlap some in data-gathering with my capacity as a teacher), I took notes on each student's writing and computer concerns after meeting with them for each paper, I asked them to write a letter to me about their computer experience in the class, and I interviewed each formally and extensively towards the end of the semester to ask open-ended questions about their family, class, and cultural backgrounds; their experiences with writing in general; their experiences with computers in general; and their experiences with and attitudes about writing with computers in our classroom and elsewhere.

Although I asked each student to participate in my research for different reasons (outlined below), all demonstrated aspects of their writing process with the computers that intrigued me. Tom, an African-American student, had talked with me and written frequently about his experiences growing up in a violent, inner-city environment. I suspected that Tom didn't have much access to computers in his dorm because he produced the smallest amount of writing both in class and in the final draft of each of his papers. I asked Valerie to participate because, as a hearing-impaired ESL student, she worked with two computers during class; on one, Valerie communicated with her interpreter, who typed everything that was said in class, and on the other, Valerie did class work. I wondered what kind of effect, if any, the multiple uses of computers had on her. Matt, a Caucasian freshman, always came to class early to work on the computers. Only once during the entire semester was Matt not already present in the computer classroom when I arrived, usually thirty minutes before class started in the morning. I wondered why Matt would opt for computer time rather than sleep, a choice not made by many freshmen! I also observed that Matt didn't get as much writing done in class as many of the other students. Maria, a Hispanic and ESL student, was the only student who turned in handwritten drafts of her papers. I wondered if this was by necessity or by choice, and if the latter, what her reasons were for choosing to write without the computer.

Although I collected data from all four students, the findings I present in this article are based only on data gathered from Matt and Maria, primarily because of space issues in the article, but also because I gathered the most data and conducted more extensive interviews with Matt and Maria. Tom and Valerie both struggled extensively with writing in the course, and the times we arranged to discuss their papers and for formal interviews were spent working on specific pieces of writing rather than discussing writing and computers in general. As I worked with Tom and Valerie, my role as teacher took priority over my role as researcher. Plus, meetings with Valerie required a sign language interpreter to be present, which resulted in almost no informal meetings and formal meetings bound by the time constraints of the interpreter.

Portraits of Two Basic Writers in a Computer Classroom

Matt

Matt was born and grew up in Lawrence, Massachusetts, in a low-income neighborhood, which he described in detail in one of his essays and in our informal discussion about the essay. Both of his parents work, but he does not know exactly what they do, although he does know that his mom works on computers as part of her job.

While growing up, Matt did not have a computer in his home; his parents got their first computer when he was in high school, but he told me that he still never used it much because he "never learned how to use a computer." It seems that Matt's home computer goes unused most of the time, since he reported that his parents also rarely use the home computer. Matt's first time using a computer was on the family's home computer. He used AOL to go online. Matt told me that his high school did have computers and that all students were required to take typing, but the school computers were "Apple and old." Until he came to college, Matt used computers mainly to type essays for high school classes. Now he uses computers "for stuff on campus — essays, looking stuff up. I have a lot of online quizzes from classes." He also e-mails occasionally, but said that he doesn't e-mail or chat "like other people do."

Matt also doesn't have much practice with writing. In his high school, they did "a lot of oral presentations and stuff like that," but did not write much. Matt told me that if he didn't have to write, he wouldn't; it's not something he likes to do.

Despite his dislike of writing and his relative inexperience with computers, three different times in our formal interview, Matt emphasized his desire to learn how to type. He also said that writing on the computer is currently more difficult for him than writing by hand. "I like typing," he said, "but I just think it's easier to write something. I just want to learn how to type quicker." This desire may stem from Matt's feelings of inadequacy on the computer: "I know how to *use* it [the computer]," he said. "But I think I might need more time in class, just cause, . . . I type slower than I would write . . . so I think I really need a little bit more time."

Although he feels inadequate and uncomfortable with his typing ability, Matt likes computers and wishes he knew more about them because, as he told me, "you're going to need to learn how to use them, to use them good when you get a job and stuff, so that's why . . . I like to use them." Matt is particularly concerned that he needs to learn how to use the computers for his future job (he wants to go into business).

Matt likes having computers in our writing classroom because they provide an opportunity for him to use computers without distraction. "At home I get distracted," he said, whereas in the computer classroom, "I get a lot more done. It's easier in class cause everyone else is doing it too, so you don't get distracted." His tendency to get distracted in his dorm is the reason Matt comes to class early to work on his papers. He also comes in at 8 o'clock in the evening to work, even though he has access to friends' computers in the dorm. "The lab's open 8 to 10," he said. "Sometimes the dorm's too loud and the library's usually packed at night." For Matt, our classroom computer lab provided him with a place he could come to write without distraction and a means of improving skills he will need in the future, even though the computers require more time for him when writing in class.

Maria

Maria grew up in the Dominican Republic, the youngest of three children and the only girl. Her aunt raised her because the family's poverty forced Maria's parents to travel. Maria's father enlisted with the Dominican air force, which required that he travel from city to city, and her mother traveled regularly to Venezuela to buy clothing that she would resell in the Dominican Republic. Maria's two older brothers immigrated to Dorchester, Massachusetts, when she was 13. In high school Maria began living with her brothers during the school year and returning to the Dominican Republic in the summer. Maria's first language is Spanish, but she speaks English well and someday wants to be an immigration lawyer.

Because of their poverty, Maria's family did not have a computer while she was growing up, but her brothers bought her a used computer when she turned 16 in response to her complaints that "there was never time to use [the school computer]." When I commented on her brothers' generosity, Maria laughed and said that they had their own motives: It turned out that they used it to play video games. "So where is the homework? They used it more than I did. They said, 'Hey, we paid for this.' I said, 'But it was for me!'" Maria told me that her parents' reaction to the computer was negative. When she showed her parents her computer, her mom said, "Get that away from me!" and she still "doesn't even touch it."

Two years later, Maria is using the same computer, which is now even more outdated. "It's sooooo slow," she said. "It takes it like 5 minutes to download a picture." The computer's speed is why she writers her essays first on paper. When I asked about her handwritten drafts, she said, "Just forget about it. I write all of my drafts on paper." She also tells me that it's too expensive to print her drafts on campus, so she waits to type them until her final draft. Plus, she said, "It's easier for me to write them down, to think, instead of just typing up whatever's in my head. . . . Computers are easier, but if you want to think about it, then it's pencil and paper I think is easier." Maria told me that she's trying to talk her brothers into getting her a new computer, but "they say they need a computer [first]."

Although she writes a lot of papers for her classes — sometimes twice a week for her anthropology class — Maria calls herself a "slacker" when it comes to writing. She doesn't write e-mails, although she thinks it's "really fun" to get e-mail. She told me, "My friends say, 'Why don't you ever answer me?' I say, 'We talk on the phone. What's the point?'" She also complained to me during one of our informal meetings about her cousin in the Dominican Republic, who e-mails because it's their only way of communicating. She gets tired of having to respond to his e-mails: "I hate writing back," she said.

Despite her dislike for writing e-mails and papers on computers, Maria feels comfortable with her knowledge of computers, with one exception: She explained that when she types, "I have to look at the keyboard. . . . I think it's so annoying. Other people type without looking at the keyboard. That's the only thing that's so not fair." And, as I noticed in class, Maria enjoys computers. She stayed after class to surf the Internet, to find "cool" sites, and to ask my advice about making online purchases. When I asked her how she feels about computers in general, Maria stopped complaining about her slow computer and the cost of printing and instead emphasized the convenience of computers for research and for presenting finished versions: "I do love computers," she said. "It's so much easier. It beats going to the library. No books. And it looks better when you type something up than when you hand it in written down. I love my slow computer!"

Discussion of Case Studies

Of the many interesting issues that arose in my observations of and discussions with Matt and Maria, I've chosen the two that I see as the most intriguing and important in their effect on my pedagogy. My observations of and discussions with Matt and Maria helped me realize that I need to provide the basic writing students in my class with a balanced perspective and pedagogy in regard to computer use. The two areas that I will discuss are students' attitudes toward computers and students' access to computers.

Students' Attitudes: "Cause You're Going to Need to Know How to Use Them"

As can be seen in the earlier portrayals, neither Matt nor Maria likes to write in general. Matt likes writing only when he can choose something that interests him or that relates to him, but told me, "I don't think of myself as a writer. If I didn't have to write, I don't think I would write. If it wasn't required . . . it's not something I'd like to do." When I asked Maria if she likes to write, she said, simply, "No." Maria calls herself "a slacker cause I just write enough to get by." She told me that she does like to write poems about things she's passionate about, like sexism and bilingual education. She often wrote poems during freewriting when I did not provide a writing prompt.

In contrast to their negative attitudes towards writing, both Maria and Matt like computers in general and like having them in our classroom. In fact, even though Maria frequently complained about her slow computer in our informal discussions and our formal interview, she ended the interview by telling me, "I love my slow computer!" Matt explained his positive attitude toward computers by referring to his future — that he'll eventually "need to know how to use them." Matt's responses seem common, according to Stan and Collins. They note that students tend to see computers as a "useful tool" and "feel they are learning the technology of the future" when they use computers (32). Matt and Maria's positive attitudes toward computers reflect society's positive and idealistic views about computers and the benefits of computer literacy. Although Sloane argues that students' attitudes toward computers echo their parents' attitudes (57), I saw society as having the biggest influence on Matt and Maria's attitudes about computers and about writing with computers. Both students' comments fit well with Selfe's discussion that society perceives computer literacy as a means of ensuring economic success.

Matt and Maria's positive attitudes toward computers do not transfer to their attitudes toward writing with computers. Neither enjoys writing with the computer — Maria even hates to write e-mails on the computer, as discussed earlier. This dislike of writing with computers seems natural, given both students' dislike of writing in general, but it does not conform to the larger research studies on students' attitudes in relation to writing with computers. Gay found students' attitudes toward writing improved with computer use (68), and Stan and Collins report that this finding is consistent across research and "has been generally accepted as a first step toward subsequent writing improvement" (24).

Both students seem to feel empowered and positive about the presence of computers in the classroom, particularly given their perceptions about the importance technology will have in their futures, and yet both feel hesitant or inferior when it comes down to their abilities to use and write with the machines. Matt doesn't know how to type well and wants to "know more about them [computers]," and when I asked Maria if she was comfortable with the computers, she compared her abilities with those of other students, pointing out her shortcomings. When speaking with me, Matt referred primarily to "typing" when he discussed writing or composing on the computer, whereas he referred to writing with pen and paper as "writing."

Batschelet and Woodson argue that this distinction between writing with computers and computers as machines/technology is made only by beginning writers and does not exist with experienced writers (qtd. in Stan and Collins 23–24). As a writing instructor, I am used to writing with computers and see writing as necessarily connected to computers, but the students in my classes may not always connect writing with computers and may need pen and paper writing assignments until they become accustomed to writing solely with computers. As a basic writing teacher, then, I need to be aware that students may have negative attitudes about writing with computers even when they have positive attitudes towards having the computers in class. If one of my goals is to help students enjoy writing and become more confident in their writing, I need to help students overcome feelings of inadequacy and hesitation about using the computers to write.

Students' Access: "Other People Type Without Looking . . . That's So Not Fair"

For basic writers, writing is an unfamiliar and often complex territory to be navigated with caution. Stan and Collins agree, defining basic writers as lacking self-confidence and "unpracticed and unskilled in composing specific forms of texts valorized traditionally by faculty" (22, 20). For Shaughnessy, the definition of basic writers as inexperienced beginners who "must, like all beginners, learn by making mistakes," explained many of the reasons why basic writers write the way they do: "Some writers, inhibited by their fear of error, produce but a few lines an hour or keep trying to begin" (7). Shaughnessy's descriptions are increasingly relevant when we add computers into the mix of basic writing classrooms. What happens in a computer classroom when basic writers, who by definition lack experience in writing, also lack experience with computers?

Both Matt and Maria's abilities to write with a computer and their access to computers directly reflect their family, class, and cultural backgrounds. Neither student had used a computer or owned a computer until they were in high school. Even after receiving access to home computers, neither student used computers regularly or saw their parents using computers at home. Maria's brothers used her computer, but only to play video games.[2]

Both Matt and Maria continue to have difficulties with computer access. Matt is grateful for the access afforded him by the classroom computer lab, because "the dorm's too loud and the library's usually packed." Yet, as Moran discusses, this allows Matt "institutional access," which still disadvantages him when compared with students with "home access" (218–19). And although Maria has access to a computer, its age and speed, combined with her economic situation and inability to afford printing, limit that access to such an extent that she handwrites her papers.

I found Faigley and Porter's definitions of "access" to be helpful when analyzing Matt and Maria's situations. Faigley says that "information literacy" requires more than just speaking of access as equipment and technical skill (135). Porter's definition is similar, but threefold: access includes (1) infrastructure (money and machines), (2) literacy (education and training), and (3) community acceptance (freedom to speak online) (99). According to the first part of both Faigley's and Porter's definitions of access as equipment and machines, our classroom computer lab has provided Matt and Maria with more access to technology by providing them with the opportunity to use the machines for their writing, an opportunity that is harder for them to come by than for other students. In their comments to me, it's evident that Matt and Maria both see the computers in our classroom as empowering — Matt gets to practice his typing, and Maria gets to present me with an occasional in-class draft that, because she wrote it using the computers in class, looks better than her handwritten drafts. Maria has the opportunity to use the classroom computers after class to surf the Web, and Matt finds writing on the computer during class easier — "cause everyone else is doing it too." Many researchers claim that computers in the classroom are distractions for students because of anxiety over the text's visual appearance or because of the physical disruptions of the keyboard and computer environment (Sharples 94; Crafton 272; Dowling 232, 228), but in Matt's case the computer classroom provides him with access to computers without the distractions he finds in other places of institutional and dorm access.

However, when referring to the second part of both Faigley's and Porter's definitions of access as "information literacy" and "education and training," the "access" that the computer classroom provides Matt and Maria is more problematic. The basic writing class pedagogy at my university, as outlined earlier, does not encompass any education or training with computers until students assemble their final portfolios the last week of class. Then, they are given a handout on formatting their papers to look less like student essays. Our basic writing program pedagogy focuses instead on the drafting and revising process of writing, not on training in word processing or practice typing. Yet we usually assume students have a certain degree of this second type of computer access, education and training in computer use, which is a poor assumption when our classes include students such as Matt and Maria. Although Matt and Maria's cases may be exceptional, they do show the importance of addressing individual circumstances in our pedagogies.

For me, having computers in the classroom seems to be a "Catch-22" when viewed in terms of equity. Olson says schooling ought to be a "maker of opportunities" (204). Basic writing computer classrooms can be viewed as makers of opportunities — the basic writing classroom becomes a place to give all students the opportunity to write with technology, an opportunity students like Matt and Maria do not readily have. Yet, even as computers in the classroom create opportunities, they may accentuate differences in opportunity. As mentioned in the introduction to this paper, as I roamed around the classroom each day while students wrote, the differences between those who had the opportunity to learn to write with computers early and those who didn't were very clear. Unfortunately, as Conway says, marginalization and alienation can result from "even the most well-intentioned attempts to empower 'at-risk' populations" (91).

We therefore need to be careful when we make arguments that computer classrooms provide students with more access. For example, as co-director of a basic writing program, Grabill decided that a need of basic writing is to "introduce sophisticated writing technologies to our students for reasons of access — students could not be successful at our university without access to these technologies" (94). It's unclear if Grabill is referring to access to the machines only or also to the information literacy and training in use of the machines. But Grabill's conclusion is clear: "In effect, we provided our students with an advantage" (100). Yet this claim of advantage and Grabill's justification for requiring basic writing to be taught using computers takes a more long-term approach to issues of success and access, defining "advantage," "access," and "success" within the context of the university, not within the context of the basic writing class itself.

For the two students I followed and interviewed, writing on computers in the classroom did not lead to more empowerment when viewed from a more short-term focus on the class itself. Both Matt and Maria struggled with writing on the computer. Matt, in particular, wrote significantly less in class than most other students. For example, Microsoft Word's word count feature allowed me to see that Matt freewrites (15 minutes of writing in response to open-ended prompts) for the entire semester averaged 113 words per freewrite, compared to the class average of 190 words per freewrite. The two students who sat next to Matt averaged 224 and 273 words per freewrite, which may have contributed to Matt's awareness of his slow typing and his self-comparisons to other students. Maria also struggled, although not to this extent, averaging 147 words per freewrite. Maria was also very conscious of the fact that "other people type without looking at the keyboard. . . . That's so not fair."[3]

In their nationwide survey of basic writing teachers, Stan and Collins found that students "just plain write more — more words, more pages" when computers were added to the basic writing classroom (33). Even if it is the case for the majority of students, those without access and extensive computer experience are further disadvantaged in the writing classroom because other students write even more, while they, in turn, write even less.[4] Of course, Matt and Maria's typing struggles and lower word counts may be a result of their struggles with writing in general and not solely a result of their struggle with writing on computers. But for students such as Matt and Maria, the computer may add "complexity to an already complex process," as Crafton says (322). Crafton believes that we tend to see computers as "labor-saving" devices, but if they do complicate writing or the writing process for some students, students might actually need more time when we ask them to write with the computer, a fact that Matt was well aware of and spoke about in our interview.

Moreover, Nichols found that writers who were unsure of the word processing system or who weren't excellent typists experienced many interventions and complexities in composing that negatively affected their short-term and long-term memory and interrupted their focus on their writing plans and goals, a focus that Perl and Flower and Hayes found so crucial in distinguishing between beginning and expert writers. Using the example of Gina, whom he defines as a "better" writer, Nichols suggests that better writers than basic writers are more likely to use a word processing system to their advantage (92). I have observed in my teaching that it's not necessarily *better* writers who can use the computers to their advantage, but in the case of producing more writing at one time, it takes *computer-experienced* writers. The extra tasks involved when writing with computers require more time for some writers than what they would otherwise need to write with pen and paper.

Without knowing individual students' genealogies, we may easily overlook the difficulties that lack of computer experience produces for some students in computer writing classrooms. Stan and Collins record that almost all instructors in their survey agreed that students with minimal or no computer skills presented a problem in class, mainly because the instructors had to teach them the necessary word processing commands and uses (37). From Stan and Collins's article, it doesn't seem that many instructors recognized any long-term problems this lack of access and experience presented for students. Stan and Collins report that most instructors thought these problems disappeared as the semester progressed, with one exception: students who lacked typing skills, they found, were at a "decided disadvantage" (37). Stan and Collins conclude this section of their report with a quote and a question from one instructor surveyed: "A small handful of students . . . fall way behind. . . . Should knowledge of word processing be a requirement for entry into a basic writing course?" (34).

When addressing questions such as these, we need to remember, as Thomas says, that "before anything else [basic writers] need to learn hope and self-confidence" (59). Being enrolled in a writing class in a computer lab when they do not have much computer knowledge may lead students to doubt their abilities when what they really need is confidence. In their presentation of some of the problems and contradictions in computer use in basic writing classes, Stan and Collins argue, "Technology can serve to alleviate or even transform a basic writer's anxiety about writing — or it can erode still further a basic writer's confidence" (22).

After struggling with issues such as these while working with and interviewing Matt, Maria, and students like them, I am convinced that "providing access" is a much more complex concept than just providing the machines. Access issues run deeper than computers, programs, availability, and use in a writing classroom — they stem from and encompass students' family, culture, and class genealogies that affect their interactions with the classroom component in the overall picture of access.

There are plenty of research studies showing that computers can help basic writing students, and I've seen this in my own classes. But in some cases, computers can also further disadvantage students, and I need to take this into consideration in my pedagogy. I therefore believe that *the option* to write with computers is a good one for basic writers. Without the availability of computers in classrooms, students with less access to machines may not be able to make the decision to write with them, while students with home access always have that option. In this sense, computer classrooms do provide students with *access to choice*. Perhaps we need to combine Grabill's long-term definition of "access" and "success" with a short-term definition based on success in the writing class. The following section outlines three ways in which I have altered my pedagogy in an attempt to balance providing access to computers without further disadvantaging some students.

Alterations to My Pedagogy

First, I have adopted Moran's and Duffelmeyer's suggestions to have students write technology narratives at the beginning of the semester. In this technology narrative, Duffelmeyer asks students about their attitudes about technology; the influences of their parents, friends, teachers, schools, and society in general on their attitudes and uses of technology; and their individual chronologies with computers (295). Moran suggests that these technology autobiographies will not only help us learn about students' connections, or lack thereof, to the technology we are asking them to use, but are also the first step in helping students become "reflective and critical users" of the technology (220). Technology narratives allow me to discover what students bring with them to writing and to computer use.

I now assign these technology narratives before establishing a firm plan for my course so that, if needed, I can change my approach and assignments to account for individual students' access issues and genealogies. I have at times added computer instruction to lesson plans, allowed individual students more time with assignments, accepted handwritten drafts from individual students, and, most successfully, have held office hours in the computer classroom in response to technology narratives. The smaller writing class gives me a unique opportunity to tailor my curriculum for the students. Students will probably not get this flexibility and attention to their individual genealogies in larger classes.

My second pedagogical change is striving for a balanced approach to using computers in the classroom. Even in a class with computers available, I now assign writing without the computers. I required a balanced portion of the writing in the class to be done with pen and paper for those students who aren't empowered by computers and for whom complexities added by the computer might take away from the focus and time needed to put their thoughts and ideas in writing. Despite what students may think, the existence of the machines in the classroom does not necessarily give them access to knowledge about computers, to stellar typing abilities, to future success in jobs, or to prolonged access and contact with computers in the future. What it does give is access to choice and to the opportunity to write with computers if students choose to do so. I therefore try to present the computers as a choice instead of deciding for students that all writing in the class — or even the majority of writing in the class — will be done on computers.

Third, I try to follow Kish's statement when planning assignments: "Computers are tools to aid students in the writing process; they should not subsume writing as a priority" (154). I have decided to avoid assignments in basic writing classes that might subsume writing by involving technology in the writing process in even more complicated ways than word processing does. Stan and Collins report of a variety of uses of software in basic writing classes, including Web page projects. In their article, they quote Jeffrey Maxson, who defends assigning Web pages in basic writing classes using the following rationale: "students already possess expertise in understanding and interpreting images, sounds. . . . Hypermedia authorship can thus serve to introduce them to academic literacy through means with which they are familiar" (28–29). Although I have assigned Web page writing and creation to students before, after my teacher research, I have decided not to assign Web page authorship in basic writing because producing and supplementing writing with images and designs does add complexity, regardless of students' familiarity with reading images. Given the definition of basic writers discussed earlier, I use computers only for word processing in my basic writing classes.

Above all, as basic writing teachers, we need to avoid making assumptions about our students' computer knowledge and about the effects of computers in our classrooms and instead make active inquiries into these issues. This requires us not only to research issues surrounding computer use in basic writing classrooms, but also to get to know our students better so we can see the attitudes and genealogies that they are bringing with them to the computer classroom. We also need to carefully consider our goals for our students' learning and make decisions regarding the use of technology in our classrooms based on these goals. Let's not jump on the technology bandwagon wholeheartedly if it causes individual students in our classes to fall further behind in their journey as writers.

Notes

1. Students' names have been changed.
2. Olson says that this use of computers as a "personal video arcade" is common in lower-class homes because users are only required to know how to load the program, whereas in middle-class homes, computer use more typically involves sophisticated programming and interaction with the computer (202).
3. The computers in our classroom are not equipped with any typing tutorials. I should have looked into this possibility for Matt. Instead, I offered to be in the classroom at additional times in case he wanted to come in and type or write. He continued to come to class early and came only one additional time outside of class time.
4. Conway's study of four basic writers in a computer classroom also presents a perspective different from Stan and Collins's report, perhaps because Conway is also looking at individual students instead of conducting larger, more general research. Conway argues that computer classrooms may lead to more alienation for some students as they did for the four students she observed, three of whom, she argues, actually became "nonwriters" in the course of the class. Like Matt and Maria, the students Conway followed did

not produce more writing or become more confident in their writing as they wrote on computers in class (80).

Works Cited

Agnostina, Karen Nilson, and Sandra D. Varone. "Interacting with Basic Writers in the Computer Classroom." *Computers and Composition* 8.3 (1991): 39–50.

Conway, Glenda. "What Are We Doing Today? High School Basic Writers Collaborating in a Computer Lab." *Computers and Composition* 12.1 (1995): 79–95.

Crafton, Robert E. "Promises, Promises: Computer-Assisted Revision and Basic Writers." *Computers and Composition* 13.3 (1996).

Dalton, David W., and Michael J. Hannafin. "The Effects of Word Processing on Written Communication." *Journal of Educational Research* 80 (1987): 338–42.

Daiute, Collette A. "The Computer as Stylus and Audience." *College Composition and Communication* 34 (1983): 134–45.

Dowling, Carolyn. "Word Processing and the Ongoing Difficulty of Writing." *Computers and Composition* 11.3 (1994): 227–35.

Duffelmeyer, Barbara Blakely. "Critical Computer Literacy: Computers in First-Year Composition as Topic and Environment." *Computers and Composition* 17.3 (2000): 289–307.

Etchison, Craig. "Word Processing: A Helpful Tool for Basic Writers." *Computers and Composition* 6.2 (1989): 33–43.

Faigley, Lester. "Beyond Imagination: The Internet and Global Digital Literacy." *Passions, Pedagogies, and 21st Century Technologies.* Ed. Gail E. Hawisher and Cynthia L. Selfe. Logan, UT: Utah State UP, 1999. 129–39.

Flower, Linda, and John R. Hayes. "A Cognitive Process Theory of Writing." *Cross-Talk in Comp Theory.* Ed. Victor Villanueva, Jr. Urbana, IL: NCTE, 1997. 251–75.

Gay, Pamela. "Questions and Issues in Basic Writing and Computing." *Computers and Composition* 8.3 (1991): 63–81.

Grabill, Jeffrey T. "Technology, Basic Writing, and Change." *Journal of Basic Writing* 17:2 (1998): 91–105.

Jones, Steve. "The Internet Goes to College: How Students Are Living in the Future with Today's Technology." Pew Internet and American Life Project. 15 September 2002. <http://www.pewinternet.org>.

Kish, Judith Mara. "Breaking the Block: Basic Writers in the Electronic Classroom." *Journal of Basic Writing* 19.2 (2000): 141–59.

McAllister, Carole, and Richard Louth. "The Effect of Word Processing on the Quality of Basic Writers' Revisions." *Research in the Teaching of English* 22 (1988): 417–27.

Moberg, Goran. "Remedial Writing on Computers: Evaluation by Students and Faculty of a Pilot Project." *Computers and Composition* 4.3 (1987): 35–51.

Moran, Charles. "Access: The 'A' Word in Technology Studies." *Passions, Pedagogies, and 21st Century Technologies.* Ed. Gail E. Hawisher and Cynthia L. Selfe. Logan, UT: Utah State UP, 1999. 205–20.

Nichols, Randall G. "Word Processing and Basic Writers." *Journal of Basic Writing* 5.2 (1986): 81–97.

Olson, C. Paul. "Who Computes?" *Critical Pedagogy and Cultural Power.* Ed. David W. Livingstone. Granby, MA: Berger and Garvey, 1987. 179–204.

Perl, Sondra. "The Composing Processes of Unskilled College Writers." *Cross-Talk in Comp Theory.* Ed. Victor Villanueva, Jr. Urbana, IL: NCTE, 1997. 17–42.

Porter, James E. "A Rhetorical Ethics for Internetworked Writing." *New Directions in Computers and Composition Studies.* Ed. Gail E. Hawisher and Cynthia E. Selfe. Greenwich, CT: Ablex, 1998.

Ray, Ruth. "Composition from the Teacher-Research Point of View." *Methods and Methodology in Composition Research.* Ed. Gesa Kirsch and Patricia A. Sullivan. Carbondale and Edwardsville, IL: Southern Illinois UP, 1992. 172–89.

Rodrigues, Dawn. "Computers and Basic Writers." *College Composition and Communication* 36 (1985): 336–39.

Selfe, Cynthia. *Technology and Literacy in the Twenty-First Century: The Importance of Paying Attention.* Carbondale and Edwardsville, IL: Southern Illinois UP, 1999.

Sharples, Mike. "Computer Support for the Rhythms of Writing." *Computers and Composition* 11.3 (1994): 217–26.

Shaughnessey, Mina. *Errors and Expectations: A Guide for the Teacher of Basic Writing.* New York: Oxford UP, 1977.

Sloane, Sarah J. "The Haunting Story of J: Genealogy as a Critical Category in Understanding How a Writer Composes." *Passions, Pedagogies, and 21st Century Technologies.* Ed. Gail E. Hawisher and Cynthia L. Selfe. Logan, UT: Utah State UP, 1999. 49–65.

Stan, Susan, and Terence G. Collins. "Basic Writing: Curricular Interactions with New Technology." *Journal of Basic Writing* 17.1 (1998): 18–41.

Thomas, J. C. "Observations on a New Remedial Language Arts Course." *Writing at Century's End: Essays on Computer-Assisted Composition.* Ed. L. Gerrard. New York: Random House, 1987. 55–63.

Classroom Activities

Consider assigning a technology narrative in your own writing course. Pavia cites Duffelmeyer's suggestions for creating a technology narrative, including "ask[ing] students about their attitudes about technology; the influences of their parents, friends, teachers, schools, and society in general on their attitudes and uses of technology; and their individual chronologies with computers" (Duffelmeyer 295).

As an introductory activity to this assignment, students can reflect on their experiences via e-mail or an electronic discussion board available on Blackboard, WebCT, or another classroom management system. If students have limited access to electronic media, consider assigning this reflection as a letter, freewriting, or journal entry to share with the instructor, or with the class in small or large group discussion.

Thinking about Teaching

Pavia makes a persuasive case for questioning rather than assuming uncritically that technology access is universally available. In your teaching journal, consider access to technology at your institution. Does everyone (including part-time and commuting students and contingent faculty) have equal access to computers and to computer-mediated instruction? If not, what barriers to access seem to be in place? How can those barriers be changed or at least ameliorated? Compare notes with other teachers to broaden your perspective, and to decide on an equitable course of action.

"Because We Are Shy and Fear Mistaking": Computer-Mediated Communication with EFL Writers

Martha Clark Cummings

Martha Clark Cummings investigates how computers facilitate learning for EFL students in Japan who are enrolled in her English-language basic writing course. Cummings's colleagues had categorized these students as "passive, unmotivated, and possibly resistant to studying English." However, when Cummings offered her class online instead of face-to-face, she found that her students' interest and participation strongly increased. Online conversations were especially fruitful for these EFL students, "transform[ing] English from a dead language to be memorized for the purpose of passing examinations into a communication tool it was possible to have fun with."

Also in this selection, Cummings presents a scaffolded assignment employing electronic media. This assignment provides opportunities for engaged Internet use with clear audiences and purposes, and includes some instruction in avoiding plagiarism.

For a writing teacher who envisions herself building a safe community in a classroom where interaction and collaboration blossom and thrive, where meaningful and achievable language learning goals are articulated and enacted, where risks are taken, and time is invested in and outside the class, my first face-to-face meetings with my university students in Japan hit me with the force of a blow to the solar plexus. I'm sure that for my students it was no less painful.

These students, university sophomores, had passed a rigorous entrance examination to gain admittance to one of the top 100 (out of 500 or so) universities in Japan. Their performance on this examination demonstrated their proficiency in English grammar, knowledge of vocabulary, and reading comprehension. However, since they had learned English through the traditional *yakudoku* (grammar/translation) method, their knowledge of English was similar to an American high school student's knowledge of Latin. They could not understand me when I spoke to them and, in fact, did not expect me to address them in English. They struggled to speak a few words of English and were shocked that I knew no Japanese. They had very little experience writing essays, in Japanese or in English. My course was called Academic Writing Two.

I had been warned by my colleagues that because this is a specialized university, with majors in Computer Science and Computer Engineering only, these students tended to be "geeks," loosely defined as people who prefer working with computers and mathematical formulas to working with people. This turned out to be an understatement, as an early entry in my journal illustrates. Note that it also illustrates my extreme culture shock. I include this slightly hyperbolic description because it demonstrates so vividly how utterly unsuited for each other my students and I seemed to be, at the outset.

> At this particular university, classrooms are male places. Young male places. These boys have been forced to wear uniforms and keep their hair short and uncolored and now they can wear whatever the hell they want and do whatever the hell they want with their hair and stop washing.
>
> When the boys come to my class it is a miserable time of day for them. Sometimes I am there waiting and sometimes I come in after they do, depending how much I dread seeing them that day. They all push in at once, rushing toward their seats, the furthest from me they can find, running, some of them, to the seats in the last row, the seats near the windows. They gallop to their seats, see me, abruptly avert their eyes and sit down where they are standing, as if the sight of me has turned them to stone. Each student sits in exactly the same seat each time if he can. I know which seat they consider theirs by the horrified look on their faces when someone else is occupying it.
>
> They are crammed, jammed into their too-small seats, their oversized pants and untied shoes like prison wear, their hair a uniform orange — the color their hair gets when it is bleached — and hanging in slender threads across their eyes. In October, the classroom is a cold place with only the heat of our bodies to warm us.
>
> The boys slide into their seats, shivering as the cold of the plastic seeps through the thin fabric of their jeans. They don't know each other

yet, so they do not talk. They have already had two other classes and lunch before they get to my class, so one of my biggest jobs is keeping them awake. I do this by trying to get them to talk to each other.

Even when I ask them to, they cannot turn away from the front of the classroom to face each other, as if their heads were locked in place, like cows in stanchions. "Turn your heads," I tell them, smiling. "Turn toward the person next to you." It is as if they were made of glass and their necks would snap. "Say hello," I tell them. Then say, "Listen to this," and read your freewriting aloud. They shudder. I may as well have told them to take a giant pair of pliers and start pulling out their own teeth.

What does a Western teacher do with a group of Japanese students who may very well believe that their days applying themselves to studying English are over? I had also been warned by my colleagues that my students, recently recovering from *shiken jihoku,* or examination hell, would be passive, unmotivated, and possibly resistant to studying English. In Japan, every student who attends a university must pass the university's entrance examination. High school students usually spend a great deal of time, energy, and family resources — for tutoring — to pass these examinations (Brown and Yamashita). Once they have entered a university, however, they become the teacher's responsibility. Teachers are expected to pass their students, and if they don't, they are blamed for their students' failure. To further complicate matters, students can get jobs after attending a university regardless of their grades (Hadley and Evans).

My teaching experience had been primarily ESL (English as a Second Language) rather than EFL (English as a Foreign Language) in New York and California, where there was a heterogeneous, immigrant population with a wide variety of attitudes and motivations toward learning English. In Japan, I started by considering what I *did* know about my students. They were all majoring in Computer Engineering and Computer Science. There were enough computers at the university for every student and every instructor to be working at one at all times. We were all extremely uncomfortable in each others' physical presence. Perhaps teaching them via Computer-Mediated Communication (CMC) was a way to begin. This move was also inspired in part by a very positive reaction to CMC I had had previously from one very quiet Japanese student who was in a class I taught in California. She described her experience as follows:

I don't miss my turn anymore! I realized today that I don't have to worry about turn-taking when communicating online. I can finally say something in class without hesitation. Turn-taking in class has been a stressful and unpleasant experience for me since I started studying in California. I always miss my turn when I have something to say. And

when I have nothing to say, I get the floor. I sometimes feel so dumb just sitting in class listening to people talking. What is wrong with me? What is it that stops me from participating like the others in class? I have been asking myself these questions even though I had known that some factors such as cultural differences, my personality, and my English proficiency level would prevent me from speaking up in class. I was thinking how many times I spoke during the first half of this class. Probably a few times. I don't know how many times I have posted my comments since the online segment started, but I feel like I am saying a lot more than before. I don't think I have missed my turn yet!
(Cummings et al.)

Much has been written about intercultural clashes between Western teachers and their Japanese students, with students being described as silent, unmotivated, and hostile, and teachers as overeager to impose their values and as making inappropriate demands on the students (Akimoto-Sugimori; Cohen; Miyoshi; Paul). I did not want to fall into the trap, where, according to Baumann, "whatever any 'Asian' informant was reported to have said or done was interpreted with stunning regularity as a consequence of their 'Asianness,' their 'ethnic identity,' or the 'culture' or their 'community'" (1). Feeling some trepidation, I moved out of the physical classroom and into CMC, to see if our intercultural clashes and inhibitions might be reduced there.

This article describes the road toward communication through writing for a group of basic writers and their teacher in the deep north of Japan. It is action research in that I perceived and wanted to reflect on a problem in my own classroom. For whatever reasons, my students and I were silencing each other. I had one potential solution at my fingertips — I was a trained, experienced CMC writing teacher, and my students were majoring in Computer Engineering and Computer Science. The action I decided to take was to try teaching them through CMC for a semester and see if the situation improved. My student writers were familiar with the conventions of CMC text display, could navigate using computer keyboards and mice, and understood — better than I did — the workings of software, operating systems, and web pages. They could work with different forms of texts, such as multimedia documents and hyperlinks, which they occasionally included in their submissions for the class. I reasoned that a good starting place for addressing what seemed to be a major teaching problem might be Computer-Mediated Communication, since it was a place where the students felt at least as competent as I did.

Review of the Relevant Literature

This review of the literature includes four strands. In recent years, much has been written about the importance of interaction in language learning in general and writing in particular, about the importance of motivation in language learning, and about the kinds of interaction available in Computer-Mediated Communication and whether this interaction enhances language learning. Finally, in reference to this study, the link between literacy and CMC will be examined.

Sociocultural Theory, Interaction, and Communities of Practice

For Vygotsky, learning, even learning to think, starts with interaction. He argued that the role of schools was to help learners develop their thought processes through collaboration with others. Collaborative learning leads us to create knowledge through interaction, and writing is learned through collaboration, problem-solving, and the expression of our own ideas (Bruffee). Learning a language also entails the development of a new identity through "negotiated experience [in which we] define who we are by the way we experience ourselves through participation" (Wenger 149). Pavlenko and Lantolf suggest that we "reconceptualise L2 learning as an intrinsically social — rather than simply cognitive — process of socialisation into specific communities of practices, also referred to as 'situated learning'" (157) (see also Lave and Wenger). In describing academic writing, Casanave uses the game metaphor to describe the importance of students' participation in the communities of practice they wish to become members of. That is, players must understand the rules of the game from the inside, as participants, rather than from the outside, as spectators. She also emphasizes that "[f]irst-hand accounts" give us "vivid description of social practice" spotlighting "the diversity and unpredictability of individual experience" (15).

Attitude and Motivation

The literature in this domain is vast. Motivation has been studied in psychology and education (Dörnyei *Teaching*), probably because there is a commonsense relationship between student motivation and success in school (Dörnyei "New Themes"). In the field of second language acquisition, motivation has been viewed via Gardner's socioeducational model (Gardner and MacIntyre), arguing that "Teachers, instructional aids, curricula, and the like clearly have an effect on what is learned and how students react to the experience" (9). In other words, there are things we can do in the classroom that will influence student motivation. This depends, of course, on the context in which one is working. Critics of Gardner's model (Crookes and Schmidt; Dörnyei *Teaching*) have pointed out that it more accurately describes learners in an ESL rather than an EFL context. Dörnyei and Ottó suggest that for second-language students motivation is "dynamically changing" and "initiates, directs, coordinates, amplifies, terminates, and evaluates the cognitive and motor processes whereby initial wishes and desires are selected, prioritised, operationalised and (successfully or unsuccessfully) acted out" (65). This is a much more thorough definition albeit less subject to a teacher's influence. Students in Japan, who have had English hammered into them in order to pass entrance examinations, may find themselves in the position described by Deci: "When people feel pressured, compliance or defiance results. Compliance produces change that is not likely to be maintained, and defiance blocks change in the first place" (196). That is, they may have caved in to the pressure enough to pass the exam and subsequently refuse to learn more. In reporting the findings of a number of research studies, Deci states that "students who learned in order to put the material to active use displayed considerably greater conceptual understanding of the material than did students who learned in order to be tested" (47).

Computer-Mediated Communication

Computer-Mediated Communication (CMC), for example, using computers to facilitate interaction between people, has become increasingly common in higher education (Nunan). CMC has been credited with increasing student motivation, enhancing cooperation and collaboration between students, and changing the nature of turn-taking in courses (Bowers; Cummings et al.). It is seen as a powerful way "to link learners" (Warschauer "Computer-Mediated" 477). CMC has been described as a bridge between speaking and writing and as an enabling and empowering tool that combines expression, interaction, reflection, problem-solving, critical thinking, and collaboration (Egbert and Hanson-Smith; Chapelle). In addition, CMC, accessible 24 hours a day, 7 days a week, increases opportunities for communication (Warschauer "Computer-Mediated"; Gonglewski, Meloni, and Brant). Furthermore, CMC is interactive, promoting dialogue (Warschauer "Computer-Mediated") while at the same time encouraging more complex language than face-to-face communication (Matsuda et al.). CMC is less face threatening than face-to-face interaction, allowing students to voice opinions more freely (Cummings et al.). According to Nunan, "good" online courses promote interaction (i.e., are student-centered rather than teacher-led), are conducted by a professor who responds rapidly and thoroughly to student needs as they are expressed online, and foster a climate in which all students are encouraged to respond.

Research has demonstrated that students express more complex thoughts and feelings in CMC than in other forms of written composition (Warschauer, Shetzer, and Meloni). Participation increases because pragmatic aspects of conversation such as turn-taking and interrupting are irrelevant (Cummings et al.; Sullivan and Pratt). In addition, Gonglewski, Meloni, and Brant found that motivation was higher among learners who communicated with people they did not know and whom they knew they would not meet.

Literacy, Writing Development,
and Computer-Mediated Communication

First, in Computer-Mediated Communication, everyone has more time to work. Not everyone chooses to take advantage of it, but writers have time to compose (Sullivan and Pratt) and teachers have time to demonstrate processes (Day and Batson). CMC provides a variety of audiences for student writers instead of just one, the teacher (DiMatteo; Warschauer "Motivational"). Possibly, the CMC environment is less intimidating because the audience, including the teacher, is invisible (Cummings et al.). Students who are shy or who have other reasons for not wanting to participate in face-to-face classrooms may find CMC classes easier to participate in (Scattergood).

Design and Scope of the Study

My goal, in moving away from the face-to-face classroom was to increase interaction and motivation, which in turn, I hoped, would increase second-language acquisition, enhancing student writing. To do this, I looked for ways to lower my students' and my own inhibitions, which included moving to an environment that was familiar to all of us, CMC. The value of Computer-Mediated Communication in general and with relevance to literacy and the teaching of writing pertains directly to this study.

Nunan's description of his study could well describe this one:

> The aim of the study was to generate insights rather than to test hypotheses. . . . In keeping with recent approaches to case study in educational research, this study is particularistic and descriptive, adopts a heuristic approach to data, and relies heavily on inductive reasoning. (53)

Following Warschauer ("On-line"), I set out to investigate how the use of CMC could alleviate stress and improve the quality and quantity of the written communication between these basic writers and me. In addition to our already mentioned inability to communicate aurally/orally, the stress of our time together was compounded by two other facts. First, our time together was limited. We met for 90 minutes, once a week for fourteen weeks. Second, we had so much to accomplish. In three short years (approximately 80 hours of writing instruction), students were to begin doing original research that would lead to the writing and presentation of their graduation theses in English. Granted, the thesis was only 4–6 pages. But for most of these students, it would require an effort of monumental proportions.

Through this action research, I hoped to answer the following questions: Would moving this particular group of students away from face-to-face interaction into Computer-Mediated Communication do any of the following: 1) increase interaction, 2) lower inhibition, 3) increase motivation, 4) increase awareness of audience, or 5) enhance the teaching and learning of writing? Previous experience and a review of the literature had led me to believe that the answers to these questions might be yes.

I set up an asynchronous Internet classroom using http://www.nicenet.org and also communicated with the students through the campus e-mail system. After the first two class meetings, we did not see each other again until the last class, in the fourteenth week.

At my university, students are required to take ten semesters of English, including two courses in listening and speaking, one in pronunciation, and two in technical reading. There are four writing courses: Academic Writing One and Two, Technical Writing, and Thesis Writing. The course described in this article is Academic Writing Two (see Appendix A for the syllabus). The obvious difference from typical academic writing courses is the online nature of the course. To the best of my knowledge, at the time of the study no one else at the university was teaching a course exclusively online.

A total of 50 college sophomores in two classes participated in this study. Most of the students (90% of them) participated actively, completing between 85 and 100% of the written assignments. Almost all of the learners were under 20 years old and 90% of them were male. The writing ability of the students was basic (see Appendix B for pretest samples). One unusual feature of this study was that the students, because of their very busy schedules, usually met together in the designated computer lab at the regularly scheduled time, but without the instructor. This is not the way online instruction usually happens (Warschauer "On-line").

Procedure and Data Collection

Students were required to read and respond to eight readings over approximately fourteen weeks. In this course I piloted materials that were later adapted for *Inspired to Write* (Withrow, Brookes, and Cummings). Students submitted their weekly assignments to nicenet.org. In addition, they answered questions in two questionnaires about their experiences with and attitudes toward English, writing in general, and this course in particular.

At the beginning of the course, students answered a set of "First Day Questions" adapted from Mlynarczyk and Haber (see Appendix C). Relevant answers to these questions include the following. In answer to question 5, "What do you hope to do after you graduate?" only three students mentioned the possibility of studying more English, and only one said he wanted to get a job using English. In answer to questions 6 and 7, asking for good and bad past experiences with writing, most of the answers were about writing in Japanese; bad experiences far outnumbered good. In 32% of the responses, the concept of shame was included, as in "I am ashamed about mistaking word." The students' technological interests were reflected in other answers about bad experiences with writing. They described instances of writing an e-mail that was not sent due to technical difficulties, or pushing the wrong key on a mobile phone when trying to send an e-mail message. Several typical responses are given below. These responses indicate that students saw the value of writing as a tool for personal interaction, and a heuristic device for memorization. They also suggest that students remember what they are praised for.

In response to "Describe a good experience you have had with writing," students wrote:

- When I was high school student, I have a girl friend. We wrote each together. It was much fun for me! I thought it was interesting to write a letter then.

- I was sometimes praised at my English writings at my English class in junior high school (though I wasn't praised at my Japanese writings. . .). So I made an efforts. And my English grade was good. I think I didn't hate English thanks to this.

- It is difficult to memorize things only by seeing. We can memorize things by writing. Moreover we can say freely by writing. Example it is Email and so on.

Bad experiences with writing mentioned by students included failing the English section examination (although there is no writing required on the examination), disliking writing in general (even writing in Japanese), experiencing difficulty mastering Chinese characters (one of the three alphabets used in Japanese writing), and being perceived as a messy writer (I think that we can safely translate "dirty" as "messy" and that possibly messiness is considered proof of incompetence):

- I failed in the entrance examination at twice because I had no knowledge of English writing and reading.

- Basically, I don't like write. I couldn't write a Japanese essay well. So my Japanese test score with essay was generally low. Homework of a composition also worried me.

- When I was 10 years old, I was punished by teacher. And that teacher forced me to write KANJI 3600 words. I don't want to remember it.

- Because I often mistake to write a character, I was got angry by parents. When writing an English sentence, I am worry. I mistake a character in Japanese or English.

These sample responses suggest, that for these students, writing is an activity that leads to punishment, shame, and revelations of incompetence.

One salient difference between face-to-face classes and this online class is that the online students asked many more personal questions and offered more personal information than in face-to-face classes, where most students wrote "Nothing" in answer to questions 13 ("What questions do you have right now?") and 14 ("What else would you like to tell me about yourself?"). A few students in the face-to-face course asked questions about my grading policy and why there were no final exams, but most had no questions and nothing to tell. On the other hand, at the beginning of the CMC class, it seemed that students were responding to the lack of restraint and possibly emboldened by reading one another's responses. For whatever reasons, the quality and quantity of the responses were different.

In answer to question 13 ("What questions do you have right now?"), I received responses like the following.

About language learning:

- Have you ever studied foreign language? If so, would you tell me a key to making progress quickly?

- Aren't you studying Japanese? And if you are studying Japanese, how are you studying?

- When I will be able to feel actually I make progress?

About American culture (not always entirely serious, I think):

- I heard that Manhattan's people don't have umbrella. Any shop sales no umbrella. Is it really?

About places where their lives and mine might intersect:

- Nowadays I exercise with my friends in SRLU (University weight room). Don't you exercise with us?

Questions like these gave me the sense that the students were genuinely interested in improving their English skills and saw me as someone who might be able to provide them with guidance on how to proceed. But amid these friendly voices came one anxious voice:

- I'm afraid why do you use this online lecture system? Does the system completely safe? I'm afraid do you really read all sent documents by students? Can the system identify students completely?

This response shows a mix of knowledge and distrust of the computer-mediated world we were entering. I responded to this student by reassuring him with what I did know about the system and asking questions in order to allow him to demonstrate his expertise.

In response to question 14 ("What else would you like to tell me about yourself?"), students told me what they liked:

- I like the movie. The most favorite movie is "Brave heart". Please see, if you like a movie.

- I like punk rock. But I can't play electric guiter. I want to play, but I think that I can't. And I like movie. I like acter – Michel Douglas, Robert De Niro, Jodie Foster, Tea Leoni-

And also expressed their fears:

- I am very afraid of writing because I don't have confidence my grammar power. I am afraid of getting bad score in writing test.

I reminded this student that there were no tests in my course, and that if he did his best, he would pass. The point is that in a face-to-face class no student had ever expressed such a fear.

During the course, because of the students' previous experience with studying English through rote memorization for the sole purpose of passing an examination, it seemed important to make the transition to using English for interaction with native speakers of English. Therefore, the key assignment of the course was to interview, via e-mail, a native speaker of English in their chosen field who lived outside of Japan and to write an essay describing that person. This assignment was based on what I learned from Mlynarczyk and Haber as well as Rafoth. In order to prepare for the interview, students worked in teams, investigating websites that described professions, finding appropriate interviewees, and then writing lists of possible questions. To begin the assignment, they read and responded to two essays based on interviews, "The Model Medic" and "No Laughing Matter," both now published in *Inspired to Write* (Withrow, Brookes, and Cummings). In reading these two example essays, I wanted the students to see that other people's writing could be used as a model without resorting to plagiarism. I strongly support Pavlenko and Lantolf's notion that "the initial step toward . . . reconstruction of a self [in a new language] . . . is the appropriation of others' voices . . ." (167).

One of the convenient features of many Internet classrooms, including nicenet.org, is that hyperlinks may be created, allowing students to access interesting and appropriate web pages with one click of the mouse. Setting up the links took quite a bit of time, but eventually I had a page of hyperlinks that I thought would be helpful to the students and could be re-used the following semesters (although links to web pages must always be checked to make sure they are still active).

The steps in the interview assignment, which were conducted by teams of four students, were as follows:

1. Investigate one or more websites describing careers until you find a career that interests you (for example, http://www.bls .gov/oco/oco1002.htm).

2. Investigate one or more of the websites describing companies that employ people in the career you are interested in (for example, http://www.allgraphicdesign.com/jobs/html).

3. Find the name and e-mail address of a person doing the job you are interested in.

4. Find out all you can about the person by studying his/her home-page and/or looking him/her up on Google.com or a similar search engine.

5. Write a list of questions you would like to ask this person.

6. Post your questions to our website and ask another team and Professor Martha to comment on your questions (Are they interesting? Clear? Grammatically correct?).

7. Send a very polite and apologetic e-mail explaining the assignment to your prospective interviewee, including a tentative deadline for his/her response. [I provided a template for this message, then decided that in future semesters I will ask students to compose this politely intrusive message themselves as it is a useful writing task.]

8. Wait one week. If you do not get a reply, politely remind the recipient of your request.

9. Wait two weeks. If you still have no reply, go back to the hyperlinks and choose another potential interviewee. Start the process again.

10. When you get a reply, draft an essay modeled on one of the two examples.

The reader may cringe at the thought of these e-mail requests for interviews going out into the world, both for the sake of the students (What if the students don't get a reply?) as well as for the sake of the recipients (Imagine receiving such an e-mail request from a group of students in another country. How tempted you would be to delete it! How guilty you would feel if you did!)

Once the assignment was fully understood, it created considerable tension in our CMC classroom, but it was the tension of anticipation rather than anxiety. The high point of the semester was when the first team of students posted the message, "We got a reply!" with the details of who they had written to and what the person had said. For most of these students, this was their first contact with a native speaker of English they didn't know personally. While two teams never received replies from anyone, ten others had thoughtful and generous replies from computer scientists all over the world, providing them with material from which they were able to compose enjoyable and well-written essays (see Appendix D for an example).

Results of the Online Course

I cannot state that the students' written work was measurably better during and after the 14-week CMC course compared to similar courses I was teaching and have taught face to face. Their essays were not longer, more developed, more unified, more coherent, or generally more free from error than those of their face-to-face counterparts. What did seem to change, however, were the students' attitudes: toward writing, learning English, accuracy, and communicating with each other, their instructor, and native speakers of English in general.

By the middle of the semester, in response to my assignments, students were beginning to write more than was required of them. When I asked them to react to what one person had written in response to a reading, often an online conversation would ensue, as in the following example:

> *Student A:* When I read your essay, I remember some thing. My family proceed one year to eat "sukiyaki," not to eat "tosikosisoba," this tradition is success from my grandfather to my father, but . . . I don't like it so much, before it, would I have a familly?

> *Student B:* I want to eat sukiyaki too. I think sukiyaki is very very delicious!! Specially saying, I want to eat sukiyaki which my father cook. My father is master of coffee lounge. So my father is very nice cook. This writing makes me hungry too!! How about your father's cooking?

Student C: I wanna eat them too. I agree with your theory that the meal which is made by one's family is very delicious. I wanna eat my mother's dishes too.

Student D: I want to eat my mother's dishes too. When I was my home, I thought I can cook dishes more good than my mother. But it was wrong. Nowaday, I think that my mother's dishes may be best deshes for me. Someone said the most important thing of cooking is love. I didn't agree it, but I can agree it now. How do you think, A?

Student A responded and the conversation continued. I was delighted. This may not seem like much to those who are used to working with native speakers of English, but for these students, engaging in this kind of banter in English was accomplishing two enormous tasks. First, it was transforming English from a dead language to be memorized for the purpose of passing examinations into a communication tool it was possible to have fun with. Second, it was transforming the students, in my eyes, from sullen, silent, frightened, noncommunicative young men and women into real people with whom I had a great deal in common.

In addition to communicating with each other, these students began to communicate with me. Again, keeping in mind that not once in two years did a student ask me a question in a face-to-face class, I was surprised and pleased to be receiving e-mails like these:

Hello! I'm X from your Academic Writing 2 class. I have some question. The homework that was written in your Email "The Model Medic." I don't know what to do. Your e-mail told me to write the first draft of my interview and use "The Model Medic" as a model for this essay. I think "The Model Medic" is an essay. And this 200 words homework makes me easy to think I should write an essay. Should I write the first draft of my interview or an essay? Could you tell me detailed what to do?

I was even more gratified to receive this request:

I'm in your Thursday, third period, Academic Writing student. By the way, I have posted free writing in Conferencing Topics "Freewriting 4/22-5/6" about twenty times. These days I have had a question. Would you tell me if the box of "Freewriting 4/22-5/6" have limit to be posted, or not? And if there is the limit, Could I continue to post my free writing? See you.

I quickly replied that there was no limit, and that the student was welcome to write as much and as often as he liked, reassuring him that I would respond to all of his freewriting. During the second half of the semester, this student and another challenged each other to freewrite every day, and this one actually succeeded.

The net result of these interactions was twofold. The students realized that knowing how to use English to communicate in writing got them results. I realized that the students were eager to participate in the course, fulfill the requirements, and communicate with me and with other native speakers.

At the end of the semester, the students completed two questionnaires, one for me and one for the university, evaluating the course. I was particularly interested in what they perceived as the benefits of CMC versus the benefits of face-to-face instruction, so I asked them to comment on each. To keep the process completely anonymous, I created a new Internet classroom for the sole purpose of completing these evaluations. The students, overloaded with preparation for final exams in their computer courses and realizing that I would have no way of knowing who had responded and who hadn't, answered briefly, if at all. Based on these anonymous responses, the benefits of computer-mediated instruction can be divided into three categories:

Learning from each other:

- I read other student writing! I learned much diversity of grammar and words. As we are beginner, we tend to use the same words and the same grammar again and again. That is not a good thing. If you don't force us to give a feedback to partners, maybe we will not read other's writing, so this is good assignment.

- Each people have diferent opinion. So, from this I notice that I don't ever notice things. [Meaning, I think, I noticed things I hadn't ever noticed.]

Communicating with native speakers:

- We can learn a great deal ONLINE. The way of writing a letter and contacting with a foreigner.

- There will not be differentiation between Japanese and foreigner in future. I will have to use English. Then, it will be useful what I learned in this class.

- I don't have experience to send a foregn man E-mail. I was very excited.

Communicating with the instructor:

- By writing E-mail, I asked to professor question or displeasure that I have. It was pleasure for me that I could communicate with professor.

On the other hand, students seemed to be saying that they missed some of the benefits of face-to-face instruction such as companionship, seeing others' facial expressions, and the motivation of having a "live" person to be accountable to:

- I don't want to not meet Professor Cummings.

- I would like to be able to discuss with people face to face.

- It has good tension.

- We can tell our opinion in direct.

- We can see people's expressive.

- We will take the course more serious.

In the students' anonymous evaluations of the course required by the university, in addition to giving the course the highest numerical evaluations one of my courses at this university had received so far, 4.6 and 4.8 out of 5, on a scale from 1 to 5, some students wrote optional comments. Most did not. Perhaps they felt they had already commented enough. However, to the question, "Would you recommend this course to your friends?" one strongly negative comment appeared here and nowhere else: "I don't think this is a class. Are we in the deep mountain? You should explain this in advance. I have been discouraged."

This was certainly a justifiable complaint. This gregarious student felt cheated of the opportunity for face-to-face interaction with his peers and teacher. After reading what he wrote, I went to the head of my program to ask if the course could be listed as a Computer-Mediated Communication course in the university catalog, but he was quick to remind me that students at this university do not have the opportunity to choose which section of a course they want to take, but are assigned to courses in alphabetical blocks.

Despite this one negative voice, in this online course for EFL writers, attitudes, motivation, and relationships changed. Students learned from each other, communicated with each other and native speakers of English, and grew to see English as a tool for communication with the world. As the instructor, I learned that behind the silent façade in the face-to-face classroom, there were people with the same yearnings for fulfillment and for a sense of competence that I had. Perhaps this is enough.

Implications for Research and Teaching

There is much to discover about ways that EFL writers can change their perceptions of English writing from being a boring school subject, a trap, a tedious chore imposed from the outside to becoming a tool for international communication. If the size of the sample had been larger, surely the findings could be stated more persuasively. If different groups of EFL writers from different settings were compared with these native speakers of Japanese in rural Japan, we could learn still more. Also of interest would be a longitudinal study of EFL writers involved in Computer-Mediated Communication designed to study how their attitudes and actual writing abilities evolved over a period of several years.

One unexpected outcome of the study was the impact that it had on me, the instructor. I found out things about my students that I would not have learned in the face-to-face classroom, causing my attitude toward them to change. I learned that they were in fact motivated, lively, curious about me and my culture, eager to share their culture, as well as their hopes and dreams, with me. These were not passive, unmotivated survivors of grueling entrance examinations with no energy left to give to learning to write in English. Knowing this gave me back my own motivation to interact and collaborate with these young, enthusiastic, vulnerable student writers.

Since this was a case of action research involving my own students and me, I would be interested in studying other instructors teaching groups of students they found particularly stressful to deal with face to face, to see if working with them in a CMC environment relieved some of the stress and/or gave the teachers a different perspective on their students.

Perhaps one of the most promising avenues for further research that emerges from this study is the need to analyze the ways in which CMC allows teachers and students to develop relationships with or attitudes toward each other that they would not otherwise have developed and to find out if these attitudes are maintained toward the next groups of students or instructors they meet.

This inquiry confirms what we already know but often forget. There is more to EFL writers than meets the eye. They have a lot to say and great difficulty in saying it. Computer-Mediated Communication, standing halfway between speech and writing, might provide a place for interaction to begin.

Works Cited

Akimoto-Sugimori, Noriko. "An ALT-JTE Relationship Which Failed." *Japanese Schools: Reflections and Insights*. Ed. M. Wada and A. Cominos. Kyoto, Japan: Shugakusha, 1996. 161–67.

Baumann, Gerd. *Contesting Culture*. Cambridge, UK: Cambridge UP, 1996.

Bowers, Paul. "Discovery-Based Learning: Lessons in Wireless Teaching." *Syllabus* 14.6 (2001): 38–39.

Brown, James Dean, and Sayoka Okada Yamashita. "English Language Entrance Examinations at Japanese Universities: What Do We Know About Them?" *JALT Journal* 17.1 (May 1995): 7–30.

Bruffee, Kenneth. *A Short Course in Writing: Composition, Collaborative Writing, and Constructive Reading.* 4th ed. New York: Longman/Pearson Education, 1997.

Casanave, Christine Pearson. *Writing Games: Multicultural Case Studies of Academic Literacy Practices in Higher Education.* Mahwah, NJ: Lawrence Erlbaum, 2002.

Chapelle, Carole. *Computer Applications in Second Language Acquisition.* Cambridge, UK: Cambridge UP, 2001.

Cohen, Andrew. "Student Processing of Feedback on Their Compositions." *Learner Strategies in Language Learning.* Ed. Anita Wenden and Joan Rubin. London: Prentice Hall International, 1987. 57–69.

Crookes, Graham, and Richard Schmidt. "Motivation: Reopening the Research Agenda." *Language Learning* 41 (1991): 469–512.

Cummings, Martha Clark, Chigusa Katoku, Jon Nichols, and Jen Russell. "Meeting the Challenges of Web-Based Instruction." International TESOL Conference, St. Louis, MO: March 2001.

Day, Michael, and Trent Batson. "The Network-Based Writing Classroom: The ENFI Idea." *Computer Mediated Communication and the Online Writing Classroom, Volume Two: Higher Education.* Ed. Marie Collins and Zane Berg. Cresskill, NJ: Hampton Press, 1995. 15–46.

Deci, Edward L., with Richard Flaste. *Why We Do What We Do: Understanding Self-Motivation.* New York: Putnam, 1995.

DiMatteo, Anthony. "Under Erasure: A Theory for Interactive Writing in Real Time." *Computers and Composition* 7 (April 1990): 71–84.

Dörnyei, Zoltan. "New Themes and Approaches in Second Language Motivation Research." *Annual Review of Applied Linguistics* 21 (2001): 43–59.

———. *Teaching and Researching Motivation.* Harlow, UK: Pearson Education, 2001.

———, and István Ottó. "Motivation in Action: A Process Model of L2 Motivation." *Working Papers in Applied Linguistics.* Vol. 4. London: Thames Valley University, 1998. 43–69.

Egbert, Joy, and Elizabeth Hanson-Smith, eds. *CALL Environments: Research, Practice, and Critical Issues.* Alexandria, VA: TESOL, 1999.

Gardner, Robert, and Peter MacIntyre. "A Student's Contribution to Second Language Learning. Part II: Affective Variables." *Language Teaching* 26 (1993): 1–11.

Gonglewski, Margaret, Christine Meloni, and Jocelyne Brant. "Using E-mail in Foreign Language Teaching: Rationale and Suggestions." *Internet TESL Journal* 7.3 (2001). Retrieved August 7, 2003 <http://iteslj.org/Techniques/Meloni-Email.html>.

Hadley, Gregory, and Chris Evans. "Constructions Across a Culture Gap." *Action Research.* Ed. Julian Edge. Alexandria, VA. TESOL, 2001. 129–43.

Lave, Jean, and Etienne Wenger. *Situated Learning: Legitimate Peripheral Participation.* New York: Cambridge UP, 1991.

Matsuda, Paul Kei, A. Suresh Canagarajah, Linda Harklau, Ken Hyland, and Mark Warschauer. "Changing Currents in Second Language Writing

Research: A Colloquium." *Journal of Second Language Writing,* 12.2 (2003): 151–79.

Miyoshi, Masao. "Culture Bumps and Icebergs." *Japanese Schools: Reflections and Insights.* Ed. M. Wada and A. Cominos. Kyoto, Japan: Shugakusha, 1996. 195–99.

Mlynarczyk, Rebecca, and Steven Haber. *In Our Own Words.* 3rd ed. New York: Cambridge UP, 2005.

Mynard, Jo. "Using Synchronous Computer-Mediated Communication with First Year Female Emirati University Students." *Using Information Technology in the Language Classroom: A Practical Guide for Teachers and Students.* Ed. P. A. Towndrow and M. Vallence. Singapore: Pearson Prentice Hall (2004).

Nunan, David. "A Foot in the World of Ideas: Graduate Study through the Internet." *Language Learning and Technology* 3.1 (July 1999): 52–74.

Paul, David. "Why Are We Failing?" *The Language Teacher* 20 (1996): 29–30, 39.

Pavlenko, Aneta, and James P. Lantolf. "Second Language Learning as Participation and the (Re)construction of Selves." *Sociocultural Theory and Second Language Learning.* Ed. James P. Lantolf. Oxford, UK: Oxford UP, 2000. 155–77.

Rafoth, Ben. "Interviewing." *The Subject Is Research.* Ed. Wendy Bishop and Pavel Zemliansky. Portsmouth, NH: Boynton/Cook-Heinemann, 2001. 82–91.

Scattergood, Ellen. "A Community of Practice: Language Learners Participating in English through Journals, E-Mail, and Weblogs." Unpublished MA Project, Teachers College Japan, 2004.

Sullivan, Nancy, and Ellen Pratt. "A Comparative Study of Two ESL Writing Environments: A Computer-Assisted Classroom and a Traditional Oral Classroom." *System* 29.4 (1996): 491–501.

Vygotsky, Lev. *Thought and Language.* Cambridge, MA: MIT Press, 1986.

Warschauer, Mark. "Computer-Mediated Collaborative Learning: Theory and Practice." *The Modern Language Journal* 81.4 (1997): 470–81.

———. "Motivational Aspects of Using Computers for Writing and Communication." *Telecollaboration in Foreign Language Learning: Proceedings of the Hawai'i Symposium* (Technical Report #12). Honolulu: University of Hawai'i Teaching and Curriculum Center, 1996. 29–46.

———. "On-line Learning in Second Language Classrooms: An Ethnographic Study." *Network-Based Language Teaching: Concepts and Practice.* Ed. Mark Warschauer and Richard Kern. New York: Cambridge UP, 2000.

———. Christina Meloni and Heidi Shetzer. *Internet for English Teaching.* Alexandria, VA: TESOL, 2000.

Wenger, Etienne. *Communities of Practice: Learning, Meaning and Identity.* Cambridge, UK: Cambridge UP, 1998.

Withrow, Jean, Gay Brookes, and Martha Clark Cummings. *Inspired to Write.* New York: Cambridge UP, 2004.

Appendix A

Course Syllabus

Course Goals

This course will help you improve your fluency in the kinds of reading and writing that will be required at this university. Reading and writing are not discrete skills, studied and learned separately. They are linked and best learned together. Through this course, you will become a more proficient reader and writer in English and you will learn to enjoy reading and writing more.

In this course we will review the basic components of good writing, that is, prewriting, planning, writing and revising drafts, paragraph structure, unity and coherence, kinds of logical order, and patterns of organization. We will also study and apply the techniques of professional writers, both fiction and non-fiction, to make our writing more powerful and meaningful to our readers.

In this course you will learn to write, critically evaluate your own writing, then get feedback from both your classmates and from your instructor. In addition, we will cover how to use outside references and how to use the Internet to do research. Depending on the needs of the group, we may also review sentence-level grammar.

Instructional Procedures

Each week, you will receive your assignments and submit them via the Internet. After the first class meeting, we will meet online only.

Here is the website for our course. Please go to http://www.nicenet.org and click on "join a class." You will go to a window where there is a box that says "Class Key." Please enter this number in the box:

[Number deleted; the course still exists.]

Go to the next window and give yourself a username and password. Don't forget your password! Please fill in your e-mail address and your name. I have posted the first assignment under "documents." Please post your answers to the First Day Questions in Conferencing: First Day Questions. I strongly recommend that you write your responses in your favorite word processing program first, then cut and paste them into the response box in the conference.

Sometimes you will have short reading assignments selected by the professor. You will find these in the "Documents" section. You will read the assignment and write in your response in the "Conferencing" section.

Evaluation and Grading Policy

Your writing will be evaluated on how much time and effort, how much thought, and how much care you put into it.

You will get a B in this course if you:

- Submit each assignment by the day and time the class would normally meet

- Participate in class by completing all tasks and assignments

- Help your classmates with their writing (I will show you how)

- Read and write all required reading and writing, giving the task your full attention

- Proofread and spell-check all final drafts

If you make an exceptional effort and do excellent work, you will get an A.

If you do less than everything on the above list, you will get a C.

If you do less than half of the work, you will fail the course.

Appendix B

Academic Writing 2: Pretest

Prompt
"Recently the quality of life has been improving in Japan." Write an essay agreeing or disagreeing with the above statement. You have 30 minutes to complete your essay. Do not use a dictionary.

Student One
I disagree this statement because it have been increasing some people which can not work. So, the quality of life has not been improving in Japan. And, Japan became dangerous by war and BSE [mad cow disease]. So, life didn't become safe in Japan, and I afraid future. I hope peace in the world.

Student Two
I disagree with. What is the quality of life? I think it decides on that how much stress we feel. We have studied and worked to be happier, more productive, more intelligent, and more peaceful. But we have made new many problemes, so human beings

Student Three
I disagree recently the quality of life in Japan. I think president Kiozumi is fool. He said, Now Japan better than that Japan, but Japan is NO CHANGING! I don't say "Recently the quality of life has been improving in Japan." I'm disappointed. Recently, Japan is poor, therefore decrease jobs. Can not work, therefore can not get money, people are hard. The Japan is little chaos now.

Appendix C

First Day Questions
Spring 2003
Academic Writing Two

Post your answers in the Conferencing Topic called "First Day Questions." Write at least 4 sentences for questions 4, 6, 7, 8, 9, 10, 11, and 12.

1. Name and number

2. E-mail address

3. Place of birth

4. What do you hope to learn in this class?

5. What will you do after you graduate?

6. Write about a good experience you had with writing, in English or in Japanese.

7. Write about a bad experience you had with writing.

8. Have you ever done any writing for yourself only — journals, diaries, poems, stories? If so, explain how this writing was different from the writing you did for school.

9. What is your image of a person who likes to write a lot? In other words, close your eyes and picture someone who loves to write. What do you see?

10. What suggestions would you make for how to teach writing to a class like this one?

11. What do you think is good about your writing? (Don't say "nothing." There is something! Think!)

12. What do you think is bad about your writing?

13. What questions do you have right now?

14. What else would you like to tell me about yourself?

Appendix D

Sample Student Essay Based on an Online Interview

Lindsay Shippee is Systems Analyst in the University of Arizona. We got interested in the fields of computer science and information technology, and took contact to him this time.

A Systems Analyst is responsible for designing, building, testing, and implementing computer systems. This includes analyzing client business requirements, writing system specifications, programming and unit testing application programs, system testing, putting systems into production, and training system users. Sometimes a large project can take several years to complete, and involve hundreds, even thousands, of programs. Lindsay once worked on a five-year systems project with a team of 186 programmers and analysts.

He became a systems analyst by accident. He attended college to become a history teacher, but when he could not find a job. So he studied for a year at a technical college and learned several computer programming languages. When he applied for work, his first employer thought he would make a good systems analyst, and offered him a job. That was how it began.

The most fun he ever had programming was when he wrote a series of complex mathematical programs for a large insurance company. They were at the heart of a big system Lindsay and other building, but nobody else on the team wanted to write them. They were too difficult. So he worked a lot of extra hours to make them work properly, and he was very proud when they were finished.

Recently, he helps maintain about 400 desktop computers and servers for the College of Humanities at the University of Arizona. He loves working in a university environment. Because, it is fun to work with professors and students, and he is learning a lot.

We got a message from Lindsay, most programmers in large business corporation work in team. When we become a senior programmer-analyst, we are often offered the position of team leader, and we must coordinate and plan the work of other team members according to the project. We are responsible to getting the work done on time, yet most of the work is being done by other people. It is not easy to be a good leader. But it is a very challenging job. We thought we are the University of . . . student studying some programming and high level computer sciences. So we will be team leader of programmers. We should get more skills of computer science to success our futures.

Classroom Activities

If you teach online or with a classroom management system such as Blackboard or WebCT, consider giving students an assignment similar to the one described in the essay. However, keep in mind, as Cummings acknowledges, that some students are not enthusiastic about online instruction. As one student wrote, "I would be able to discuss with people face-to-face" if the students worked together in the classroom.

In order to continue thinking critically about technology, consider initiating a discussion with students on the positive and negative consequences of electronic communication. How is electronic communication similar to and different from other modes of communication? Are audience expectations different for electronic and face-to-face communication? How can you convey in an e-mail (or in a text message or in an online social networking site such as facebook.com) the tone you would use when communicating in person? Also consider the differences between posing these questions as part of a face-to-face classroom discussion and an electronic conversation.

Thinking about Teaching

Cummings states that she assigned "two example essays [because] I wanted students to see that other people's writing could be used as a model without resorting to plagiarism." In this regard, Cummings appears to view plagiarism as a conceptual problem for students. Students plagiarize, especially from online sources, because they may still be learning how to incorporate outside sources into their own essays. As a solution, Cummings offers model texts that demonstrate how other writers use sources without plagiarizing.

In your teaching journal, reflect on the plagiarism issues that you may have encountered. If the plagiarism seems to be conceptual, consider how you can provide models for students — and practice in incorporating quotations, paraphrases, and summaries (see Chapter 4 for ideas about summaries). If you have encountered plagiarism that does not seem conceptual, consider how you might create a writing activity that invites students to reflect on ethics and writing — and the responsibilities of the writer in developmental and college composition courses. Discuss your reflections and ideas with colleagues and also initiate a discussion with students on these issues.

11

Engaging Difference

How do we meet the challenges of culturally diverse classrooms? What are ways of interrogating our own positions as teachers when our race, social class, gender, and sexual orientation may be different from the majority of our students? Often the classroom is a microcosm of the community outside its doors — where race, social class, gender, sexual orientation, age, ethnicity, and language differences create fear and conflict rather than understanding and harmony among our students. Moreover, based on past experiences with those who openly displayed prejudices or held inappropriate stereotypes or deficit models of student achievement, students may perceive teachers as representatives of alien cultures. How can we facilitate a classroom in which differences are not denied but engaged? The challenge is to create a learning environment in which all students feel valued and appreciated for who they are and who they are becoming, an environment in which students can grow intellectually as writers prepared to immerse themselves in college-level literacies.

By demonstrating the interconnections of language and culture, the writers in this chapter document the persistence of racism, classism, sexism, and homophobia, and the challenges of working for social justice and engaging difference through teaching and writing. In an excerpt from her groundbreaking book *Borderlands/La Frontera: The New Mestiza*, Chicana-tejana lesbian feminist poet, fiction writer, and teacher Gloria Anzaldúa reflects on coming of age in the borderlands of the Rio Grande Valley in South Texas, and the inseparable intersections of language and culture. June Jordan presents a teaching narrative that argues for the power and persistence of Black English in a society that valorizes the cultural practices of

Standard (white) English. Jordan's article includes excerpts from student texts on Black English, ending with a compelling statement of purpose written by her student, Willie Jordan. Kay Thurston writes about challenges facing students at Navajo Community College. In describing the cultural background of her students, she also challenges white composition teachers to confront their own Western ethnocentrism and to begin to envision a more inclusive course design that would "mitigate barriers" between Eurocentric ideas of education and a Navajo approach. Confronting the reader with real-life situations in school and beyond, Anzaldúa, Jordan, and Thurston provide thoughtful explorations of potentially transforming cultural practices that have critical implications for our students and for ourselves.

How to Tame a Wild Tongue

Gloria Anzaldúa

Gloria Anzaldúa writes, "So, if you want to really hurt me, talk badly about my language. Ethnic identity is twin skin to linguistic identity — I am my language. Until I can take pride in my language, I cannot take pride in myself." As a Chicana / tejana lesbian feminist poet, fiction writer, and teacher, she explores the implications of growing up on the "borderlands" of the Mexican and American cultures in Texas. In her preface to Borderlands/La Frontera *(1987), Anzaldúa clarifies her terms: "[B]orderlands are not particular to the Southwest. In fact, borderlands are physically present when two or more cultures edge each other, where people of different races occupy the same territory, where under, lower, middle, and upper classes touch, where the space between two individuals shrinks with intimacy." Such cultural space sounds not unlike many of our classrooms.*

In this selection, a chapter from Borderlands/La Frontera, *Anzaldúa recounts how growing up Chicana continues to shape her life, especially in terms of language. She writes in "Spanglish," a combination of Spanish and English, both to help the reader understand the rich cultural conditions of the borderlands and to demonstrate to Anglo and non-Spanish-speaking readers what it means to be the "other" — outside of so-called mainstream language and culture. Certainly, many ESL students may have shared Anzaldúa's childhood experience of the teacher who did not care to understand how Anzaldúa pronounced her name. "'If you want to be American, speak "American,"' her teacher tells her. In this essay, Anzaldúa reminds us that there are many ways of speaking American.*

"We're going to have to control your tongue," the dentist says, pulling out all the metal from my mouth. Silver bits plop and tinkle into the basin. My mouth is a motherlode.

The dentist is cleaning out my roots. I get a whiff of the stench when I gasp. "I can't cap that tooth yet, you're still draining," he says.

"We're going to have to do something about your tongue," I hear the anger rising in his voice. My tongue keeps pushing out the wads of cotton, pushing back the drills, the long thin needles. "I've never seen anything as strong or as stubborn," he says. And I think, how do you tame a wild tongue, train it to be quiet, how do you bridle and saddle it? How do you make it lie down?
Who is to say that robbing a people of
its language is less violent than war?

— Ray Gwyn Smith[1]

remember being caught speaking Spanish at recess — that was good for three licks on the knuckles with a sharp ruler. I remember being sent to the corner of the classroom for "talking back" to the Anglo teacher when all I was trying to do was tell her how to pronounce my name. "If you want to be American, speak 'American.' If you don't like it, go back to Mexico where you belong."

"I want you to speak English. *Pa'hallar buen trabajo tienes que saber hablar el inglés bien. Qué vale toda tu educación si todavía hablas inglés con un* 'accent,'" my mother would say, mortified that I spoke English like a Mexican. At Pan American University, I and all Chicano students were required to take two speech classes. Their purpose: to get rid of our accents.

Attacks on one's form of expression with the intent to censor are a violation of the First Amendment. *El Anglo con cara de inocente nos arrancó la lengua.* Wild tongues can't be tamed, they can only be cut out.

Overcoming the Tradition of Silence

Abogadas, escupimos el oscuro,
Peleando con nuestra propia sombra
el silencio nos sepulta.

En boca cerrada no entran moscas. "Flies don't enter a closed mouth" is a saying I kept hearing when I was a child. *Ser habladora* was to be a gossip and a liar, to talk too much. *Muchachitas bien criadas,* well-bred girls don't answer back. *Es una falta de respeto* to talk back to one's mother or father. I remember one of the sins I'd recite to the priest in the confession box the few times I went to confession: talking back to my mother, *hablar pa' 'tras, repelar. Hocicona, repelona, chismosa,* having a big mouth, questioning, carrying tales are all signs of being *mal criada.* In my culture they are all words that are derogatory if applied to women — I've never heard them applied to men.

The first time I heard two women, a Puerto Rican and a Cuban, say the word "*nosotras*," I was shocked. I had not known the word existed. Chicanas use *nosotros* whether we're male or female. We are robbed of our female being by the masculine plural. Language is a male discourse.

And our tongues have become
dry   the wilderness has
dried out our tongues   and
we have forgotten speech.

— Irena Klepfisz[2]

Even our own people, other Spanish speakers *nos quieren poner can-
dados en la boca.* They would hold us back with their bag of *reglas de
academia.*

Oyé como ladra: el lenguaje de la frontera

Quien tiene boca se equivoca.

— Mexican saying

"*Pocho,* cultural traitor, you're speaking the oppressor's language by
speaking English, you're ruining the Spanish language," I have been
accused by various Latinos and Latinas. Chicano Spanish is considered by the purist and by most Latinos deficient, a mutilation of
Spanish.

But Chicano Spanish is a border tongue which developed naturally. Change, *evolución, enriquecimiento de palabras nuevas por
invención o adopción* have created variants of Chicano Spanish, *un
nuevo lenguaje. Un lenguaje que corresponde a un modo de vivir.*
Chicano Spanish is not incorrect, it is a living language.

For a people who are neither Spanish nor live in a country in
which Spanish is the first language; for a people who live in a country
in which English is the reigning tongue but who are not Anglo; for a
people who cannot entirely identify with either standard (formal,
Castillian) Spanish nor standard English, what recourse is left to
them but to create their own language? A language which they can
connect their identity to, one capable of communicating the realities
and values true to themselves — a language with terms that are neither *español ni inglés,* but both. We speak a patois, a forked tongue, a
variation of two languages.

Chicano Spanish sprang out of the Chicanos' need to identify ourselves as a distinct people. We needed a language with which we could
communicate with ourselves, a secret language. For some of us, language is a homeland closer than the Southwest — for many Chicanos
today live in the Midwest and the East. And because we are a complex,
heterogeneous people, we speak many languages. Some of the languages we speak are:

1. Standard English

2. Working-class and slang English

3. Standard Spanish

4. Standard Mexican Spanish

5. North Mexican Spanish dialect

6. Chicano Spanish (Texas, New Mexico, Arizona and California have regional variations)

7. Tex-Mex

8. *Pachuco* (called *caló*)

My "home" tongues are the languages I speak with my sister and brothers, with my friends. They are the last five listed, with 6 and 7 being closest to my heart. From school, the media, and job situations, I've picked up Standard and working-class English. From Mamagrande Locha and from reading Spanish and Mexican litera-ture, I've picked up Standard Spanish and Standard Mexican Spanish. From *los recién llegados,* Mexican immigrants, and *braceros,* I learned the North Mexican dialect. With Mexicans I'll try to speak either Standard Mexican Spanish or the North Mexican dialect. From my parents and Chicanos living in the Valley, I picked up Chicano Texas Spanish, and I speak it with my mom, younger brother (who married a Mexican and who rarely mixes Spanish with English), aunts, and older relatives.

With Chicanas from *Nuevo México* or *Arizona* I will speak Chicano Spanish a little, but often they don't understand what I'm saying. With most California Chicanas I speak entirely in English (unless I forget). When I first moved to San Francisco, I'd rattle off something in Spanish, unintentionally embarrassing them. Often it is only with another Chicana *tejana* that I can talk freely.

Words distorted by English are known as anglicisms or *pochismos.* The *pocho* is an anglicized Mexican or American of Mexican origin who speaks Spanish with an accent characteristic of North Americans and who distorts and reconstructs the language according to the influence of English.[3] Tex-Mex, or Spanglish, comes most naturally to me. I may switch back and forth from English to Spanish in the same sentence or in the same word. With my sister and my brother Nune and with Chicano *tejano* contemporaries I speak in Tex-Mex.

From kids and people my own age I picked up *Pachuco. Pachuco* (the language of the zoot suiters) is a language of rebellion, both against Standard Spanish and Standard English. It is a secret lan-guage. Adults of the culture and outsiders cannot understand it. It is made up of slang words from both English and Spanish. *Ruca* means girl or woman, *vato* means guy or dude, *chale* means no, *simón* means yes, *churro* is sure, talk is *periquiar, pigionear* means petting, *que gacho* means how nerdy, *ponte águila* means watch out, death is called *la pelona.* Through lack of practice and not having others who can speak it, I've lost most of the *Pachuco* tongue.

Chicano Spanish

Chicanos, after 250 years of Spanish/Anglo colonization, have developed significant differences in the Spanish we speak. We collapse two adjacent vowels into a single syllable and sometimes shift the stress in certain words such as *maíz/maiz, cohete/cuete.* We leave out certain consonants when they appear between vowels: *lado/lao, mojado/mojao.* Chicanos from South Texas pronounce *f* as *j* as in *jue (fue).* Chicanos use "archaisms," words that are no longer in the Spanish language, words that have been evolved out. We say *semos, truje, haiga, ansina,* and *naiden.* We retain the "archaic" *j,* as in *jalar,* that derives from an earlier *h* (the French *halar* or the Germanic *halon* which was lost to Standard Spanish in the sixteenth century), but which is still found in several regional dialects such as the one spoken in South Texas. (Due to geography, Chicanos from the Valley of South Texas were cut off linguistically from other Spanish speakers. We tend to use words that the Spaniards brought over from Medieval Spain. The majority of the Spanish colonizers in Mexico and the Southwest came from Extremadura — Hernán Cortés was one of them — and Andalucía. Andalucians pronounce *ll* like a *y,* and their *d's* tend to be absorbed by adjacent vowels: *tirado* becomes *tirao.* They brought *el lenguaje popular, dialectos y regionalismos.*)[4]

Chicanos and other Spanish speakers also shift *ll* to *y* and *z* to *s.*[5] We leave out initial syllables, saying *tar* for *estar, toy* for *estoy, hora* for *ahora (cubanos* and *puertorriqueños* also leave out initial letters of some words). We also leave out the final syllable such as *pa* for *para.* The intervocalic *y,* the *ll* as in *tortilla, ella, botella,* gets replaced by *tortia* or *tortiya, ea, botea.* We add an additional syllable at the beginning of certain words: *atocar* for *tocar, agastar* for *gastar.* Sometimes we'll say *lavaste las vacijas,* other times *lavates* (substituting the *ates* verb endings for the *aste).*

We use anglicisms, words borrowed from English: *bola* from ball, *carpeta* from carpet, *máchina de lavar* (instead of *lavadora*) from washing machine. Tex-Mex argot, created by adding a Spanish sound at the beginning or end of an English word such as *cookiar* for cook, *watchar* for watch, *parkiar* for park, and *rapiar* for rape, is the result of the pressures on Spanish speakers to adapt to English.

We don't use the word *vosotros/as* or its accompanying verb form. We don't say *claro* (to mean yes), *imagínate,* or *me emociona,* unless we picked up Spanish from Latinas, out of a book, or in a classroom. Other Spanish-speaking groups are going through the same, or similar, development in their Spanish.

Linguistic Terrorism

> *Deslenguadas. Somos los del español deficiente.* We are your linguistic
> nightmare, your linguistic aberration, your linguistic *mestisaje,* the sub-
> ject of your *burla.* Because we speak with tongues of fire we are cultur-
> ally crucified. Racially, culturally, and linguistically *somos huérfanos* —
> we speak an orphan tongue.

Chicanas who grew up speaking Chicano Spanish have internalized
the belief that we speak poor Spanish. It is illegitimate, a bastard language. And because we internalize how our language has been used
against us by the dominant culture, we use our language differences
against each other.

Chicana feminists often skirt around each other with suspicion
and hesitation. For the longest time I couldn't figure it out. Then it
dawned on me. To be close to another Chicana is like looking into the
mirror. We are afraid of what we'll see there. *Pena.* Shame. Low estimation of self. In childhood we are told that our language is wrong.
Repeated attacks on our native tongue diminish our sense of self. The
attacks continue throughout our lives.

Chicanas feel uncomfortable talking in Spanish to Latinas, afraid
of their censure. Their language was not outlawed in their countries.
They had a whole lifetime of being immersed in their native tongue;
generations, centuries in which Spanish was a first language, taught
in school, heard on radio and TV, and read in the newspaper.

If a person, Chicana or Latina, has a low estimation of my native
tongue, she also has a low estimation of me. Often with *mexicanas y
latinas* we'll speak English as a neutral language. Even among
Chicanas we tend to speak English at parties or conferences. Yet, at
the same time, we're afraid the other will think we're *agringadas*
because we don't speak Chicano Spanish. We oppress each other trying to out-Chicano each other, vying to be the "real" Chicanas, to speak
like Chicanos. There is no one Chicano language just as there is no one
Chicano experience. A monolingual Chicana whose first language is
English or Spanish is just as much a Chicana as one who speaks several variants of Spanish. A Chicana from Michigan or Chicago or
Detroit is just as much a Chicana as one from the Southwest. Chicano
Spanish is as diverse linguistically as it is regionally.

By the end of this century, Spanish speakers will comprise the
biggest minority group in the U.S., a country where students in high
schools and colleges are encouraged to take French classes because
French is considered more "cultured." But for a language to remain
alive it must be used.[6] By the end of this century English, and not
Spanish, will be the mother tongue of most Chicanos and Latinos.

So, if you want to really hurt me, talk badly about my language.
Ethnic identity is twin skin to linguistic identity — I am my language.

Until I can take pride in my language, I cannot take pride in myself. Until I can accept as legitimate Chicano Texas Spanish, Tex-Mex, and all the other languages I speak, I cannot accept the legitimacy of myself. Until I am free to write bilingually and to switch codes without having always to translate, while I still have to speak English or Spanish when I would rather speak Spanglish, and as long as I have to accommodate the English speakers rather than having them accommodate me, my tongue will be illegitimate.

I will no longer be made to feel ashamed of existing. I will have my voice: Indian, Spanish, white. I will have my serpent's tongue — my woman's voice, my sexual voice, my poet's voice. I will overcome the tradition of silence.

> My fingers
> move sly against your palm
> Like women everywhere, we speak in code . . .
> — Melanie Kaye/Kantrowitz[7]

"Vistas," corridos, y comida: My Native Tongue

In the 1960s, I read my first Chicano novel. It was *City of Night* by John Rechy, a gay Texan, son of a Scottish father and a Mexican mother. For days I walked around in stunned amazement that a Chicano could write and could get published. When I read *I Am Joaquín,*[8] I was surprised to see a bilingual book by a Chicano in print. When I saw poetry written in Tex-Mex for the first time, a feeling of pure joy flashed through me. I felt like we really existed as a people. In 1971, when I started teaching High School English to Chicano students, I tried to supplement the required texts with works by Chicanos, only to be reprimanded and forbidden to do so by the principal. He claimed that I was supposed to teach "American" and English literature. At the risk of being fired, I swore my students to secrecy and slipped in Chicano short stories, poems, a play. In graduate school, while working toward a Ph.D., I had to "argue" with one advisor after the other, semester after semester, before I was allowed to make Chicano literature an area of focus.

Even before I read books by Chicanos or Mexicans, it was the Mexican movies I saw at the drive-in — the Thursday night special of $1.00 a carload — that gave me a sense of belonging. *"Vámonos a las vistas,"* my mother would call out and we'd all — grandmother, brothers, sister, and cousins — squeeze into the car. We'd wolf down cheese and bologna white bread sandwiches while watching Pedro Infante in melodramatic tearjerkers like *Nosotros los pobres,* the first "real" Mexican movie (that was not an imitation of European movies). I remember seeing *Cuando los hijos se van* and surmising that all

Mexican movies played up the love a mother has for her children and what ungrateful sons and daughters suffer when they are not devoted to their mothers. I remember the singing-type "westerns" of Jorge Negrete and Miquel Aceves Mejía. When watching Mexican movies, I felt a sense of homecoming as well as alienation. People who were to amount to something didn't go to Mexican movies, or *bailes* or tune their radios to *bolero, rancherita,* and *corrido* music.

The whole time I was growing up, there was *norteño* music sometimes called North Mexican border music, or Tex-Mex music, or Chicano music, or *cantina* (bar) music. I grew up listening to *conjuntos,* three- or four-piece bands made up of folk musicians playing guitar, *bajo sexto,* drums and button accordion, which Chicanos had borrowed from the German immigrants who had come to Central Texas and Mexico to farm and build breweries. In the Rio Grande Valley, Steve Jordan and Little Joe Hernández were popular, and Flaco Jiménez was the accordian king. The rhythms of Tex-Mex music are those of the polka, also adapted from the Germans, who in turn had borrowed the polka from the Czechs and Bohemians.

I remember the hot, sultry evenings when *corridos* — songs of love and death on the Texas-Mexican borderlands — reverberated out of cheap amplifiers from the local *cantinas* and wafted in through my bedroom window.

Corridos first became widely used along the South Texas/Mexican border during the early conflict between Chicanos and Anglos. The corridos are usually about Mexican heroes who do valiant deeds against the Anglo oppressors. Pancho Villa's song, *"La cucaracha,"* is the most famous one. *Corridos* of John F. Kennedy and his death are still very popular in the Valley. Older Chicanos remember Lydia Mendoza, one of the great border *corrido* singers who was called *la Gloria de Tejas.* Her *"El tango negro,"* sung during the Great Depression, made her a singer of the people. The everpresent *corridos* narrated one hundred years of border history, bringing news of events as well as entertaining. These folk musicians and folk songs are our chief cultural mythmakers, and they made our hard lives seem bearable.

I grew up feeling ambivalent about our music. Country-western and rock-and-roll had more status. In the fifties and sixties, for the slightly educated and *agringado* Chicanos, there existed a sense of shame at being caught listening to our music. Yet I couldn't stop my feet from thumping to the music, could not stop humming the words, nor hide from myself the exhilaration I felt when I heard it.

There are more subtle ways that we internalize identification, especially in the forms of images and emotions. For me food and certain smells are tied to my identity, to my homeland. Woodsmoke curling up to an immense blue sky; woodsmoke perfuming my grandmother's clothes, her skin. The stench of cow manure and the yellow patches on the ground; the crack of a .22 rifle and the reek of cordite. Homemade white cheese sizzling in a pan, melting inside a folded *tortilla*. My sister Hilda's hot, spicy *menudo, chile colorado* making it deep red, pieces of *panza* and hominy floating on top. My brother Carito barbequing *fajitas* in the backyard. Even now and three thousand miles away, I can see my mother spicing the ground beef, pork, and venison with *chile*. My mouth salivates at the thought of the hot steaming *tamales* I would be eating if I were home.

Si le preguntas a mi mamá, "¿Qué eres?"

> Identity is the essential core of who
> we are as individuals, the conscious
> experience of the self inside.
>
> — Kaufman[9]

Nosotros los Chicanos straddle the borderlands. On one side of us, we are constantly exposed to the Spanish of the Mexicans, on the other side we hear the Anglos' incessant clamoring so that we forget our language. Among ourselves we don't say *nosotros los americanos, o nosotros los españoles, o nosotros los hispanos.* We say *nosotros los mexicanos* (by *mexicanos* we do not mean citizens of Mexico; we do not mean a national identity, but a racial one). We distinguish between *mexicanos del otro lado* and *mexicanos de este lado.* Deep in our hearts we believe that being Mexican has nothing to do with which country one lives in. Being Mexican is a state of soul — not one of mind, not one of citizenship. Neither eagle nor serpent, but both. And like the ocean, neither animal respects borders.

> *Dime con quien andas y te diré quien eres.*
> (Tell me who your friends are and I'll tell you who you are.)
> — Mexican saying

Si le preguntas a mi mamá, "¿Qué eres?" te dirá, "Soy mexicana." My brothers and sister say the same. I sometimes will answer *"soy mexicana"* and at others will say *"soy Chicana"* o *"soy tejana."* But I identified as *"Raza"* before I ever identified as *"mexicana"* or "Chicana."

As a culture, we call ourselves Spanish when referring to ourselves as a linguistic group and when copping out. It is then that we forget our predominant Indian genes. We are seventy to eighty percent Indian.[10] We call ourselves Hispanic[11] or Spanish-American or Latin American or Latin when linking ourselves to other Spanish-speaking peoples of the Western hemisphere and when copping out. We call ourselves Mexican-American[12] to signify we are neither Mexican nor

American, but more the noun "American" than the adjective "Mexican" (and when copping out).

Chicanos and other people of color suffer economically for not acculturating. This voluntary (yet forced) alienation makes for psychological conflict, a kind of dual identity — we don't identify with the Anglo-American cultural values and we don't totally identify with the Mexican cultural values. We are a synergy of two cultures with various degrees of Mexicanness or Angloness. I have so internalized the borderland conflict that sometimes I feel like one cancels out the other and we are zero, nothing, no one. *A veces no soy nada ni nadie. Pero hasta cuando no lo soy, lo soy.*

When not copping out, when we know we are more than nothing, we call ourselves Mexican, referring to race and ancestry; *mestizo* when affirming both our Indian and Spanish (but we hardly ever own our black ancestry); Chicano when referring to a politically aware people born and/or raised in the U.S.; *Raza* when referring to Chicanos; *tejanos* when we are Chicanos from Texas.

Chicanos did not know we were a people until 1965 when Cesar Chavez and the farmworkers united and *I Am Joaquín* was published and *la Raza Unida* party was formed in Texas. With that recognition, we became a distinct people. Something momentous happened to the Chicano soul — we became aware of our reality and acquired a name and a language (Chicano Spanish) that reflected that reality. Now that we had a name, some of the fragmented pieces began to fall together — who we were, what we were, how we had evolved. We began to get glimpses of what we might eventually become.

Yet the struggle of identities continues, the struggle of borders is our reality still. One day the inner struggle will cease and a true integration take place. In the meantime, *tenémos que hacer la lucha. ¿Quién está protegiendo los ranchos de mi gente? ¿Quién está tratando de cerrar la fisura entre la india y el blanco en nuestra sangre? El Chicano, si, el Chicano que anda como un ladrón en su propia casa.*

Los Chicanos, how patient we seem, how very patient. There is the quiet of the Indian about us.[13] We know how to survive. When other races have given up their tongue, we've kept ours. We know what it is to live under the hammer blow of the dominant *norteamericano* culture. But more than we count the blows, we count the days the weeks the years the centuries the eons until the white laws and commerce and customs will rot in the deserts they've created, lie bleached. *Humildes* yet proud, *quietos* yet wild, *nosotros los mexicanos-Chicanos* will walk by the crumbling ashes as we go about our business. Stubborn, persevering, impenetrable as stone, yet possessing a malleability that renders us unbreakable, we, the *mestizas* and *mestizos,* will remain.

Notes

1. Ray Gwyn Smith, *Moorland Is Cold Country,* unpublished book.
2. Irene Klepfisz, *"Di rayze aheym*/The Journey Home," in *The Tribe of Dina: A Jewish Women's Anthology.* Melanie Kaye/Kantrowitz and Irena Klepfisz, eds. (Montpelier, VT: Sinister Wisdom Books, 1986), 49.
3. R. C. Ortega, *Dialectologia Del Barrio,* trans. Hortencia S. Alwan (Los Angeles, CA: R. C. Ortega Publisher & Bookseller, 1977), 132.
4. Eduardo Hernandéz-Chávez, Andrew D. Cohen, and Anthony F. Beltramo, *El Lenguaje de los Chicanos: Regional and Social Characteristics of Language Used by Mexican Americans* (Arlington, VA: Center for Applied Linguistics, 1975), 39.
5. Hernandéz-Chávez, xvii.
6. Irena Klepfisz, "Secular Jewish Identity: Yidishkayt in America," in *The Tribe of Dina,* Kaye/Kantrowitz and Klepfisz, eds., 43.
7. Melanie Kaye/Kantrowitz, "Sign," in *We Speak in Code: Poems and Other Writings* (Pittsburgh, PA: Motheroot Publications, Inc., 1980), 85.
8. Rodolfo Gonzales, *I Am Joaquin/Yo Soy Joaquin* (New York, NY: Bantam Books, 1972). It was first published in 1967.
9. Gershen Kaufman, *Shame: The Power of Caring* (Cambridge, MA: Schenkman Books, Inc., 1980), 68.
10. John R. Chávez, *The Lost Land: The Chicano Images of the Southwest* (Albuquerque, NM: University of New Mexico Press, 1984), 88–90.
11. "Hispanic" is derived from *Hispanis (España,* a name given to the Iberian Peninsula in ancient times when it was a part of the Roman Empire) and is a term designated by the U.S. government to make it easier to handle us on paper.
12. The Treaty of Guadalupe Hidalgo created the Mexican-American in 1848.
13. Anglos, in order to alleviate their guilt for dispossessing the Chicano, stressed the Spanish part of us and perpetrated the myth of the Spanish Southwest. We have accepted the fiction that we are Hispanic, that is Spanish, in order to accommodate ourselves to the dominant culture and its abhorrence of Indians. Chávez, 88–91.

Classroom Activities

Anzaldúa suggests that there are many languages that Chicanos speak; she lists them as follows:

1. Standard English

2. Working-class and slang English

3. Standard Spanish

4. Standard Mexican Spanish

5. North Mexican Spanish dialect

6. Chicano Spanish (Texas, New Mexico, Arizona, and California have regional variations)

7. Tex-Mex

8. *Pachuco* (called *caló*)

Like Anzaldúa, students can also list the languages they speak and write as well as discuss how language usage may change, depending on such variables as audience, purpose, and occasion. We as teachers might use Anzaldúa's work to help us think about what it means to "speak American"; furthermore, what does it mean for our students? Do these definitions continue to change in relation to cultural shifts?

Thinking about Teaching

The cultural conflicts between students, and between teachers and students, often mirror the actual problems in our communities — and sometimes the difficulties seem insurmountable. Yet Anzaldúa's work offers a vision of how change might be enacted. With other teachers, you may wish to read and discuss the issues Anzaldúa presents in *Borderlands / La Frontera,* including how language is implicated in the formation of identity and culture. How do Anzaldúa's ideas figure in your teaching? What are the social and political implications for basic writing and ESL courses, at your school and across the country?

Nobody Mean More to Me Than You[1] and the Future Life of Willie Jordan

June Jordan

For the late writer and teacher June Jordan, language and literacy issues remained inseparable from social justice work. In the following essay, first published in her collection On Call: Political Essays *(1985), Jordan chronicles her experiences with teaching Black English to undergraduates at SUNY–Stony Brook. Intertwined with Jordan's narrative is the story of her student Willie Jordan, who struggles with events surrounding the murder of his brother by New York City police officers. Throughout the essay, Jordan intersperses examples of student writing, such as the "Guidelines to Black English" on which her class collaborated, and Willie Jordan's end-of-semester essay on "racism, poverty, and the abuse of power." Noting that "Willie's writing needed the kind of improvement only intense practice will yield," Jordan looked forward "to see[ing] what happened when he could catch up with himself, entirely,*

*and talk back to the world." The story of Willie's progress — as well as
the stories of the writing processes of Jordan's students in the Black
English course as they struggled with questions of audience and purpose
— make for compelling reading and pose many questions about the political and cultural implications of language.*

B lack English is not exactly a linguistic buffalo; as children, most of
the thirty-five million Afro-Americans living here depend on this
language for our discovery of the world. But then we approach our
maturity inside a larger social body that will not support our efforts to
become anything other than the clones of those who are neither our
mothers nor our fathers. We begin to grow up in a house where every
true mirror shows us the face of somebody who does not belong there,
whose walk and whose talk will never look or sound "right," because
that house was meant to shelter a family that is alien and hostile to
us. As we learn our way around this environment, either we hide our
original word habits, or we completely surrender our own voice, hoping to please those who will never respect anyone different from themselves: Black English is not exactly a linguistic buffalo, but we should
understand its status as an endangered species, as a perishing, irre-
placeable system of community intelligence, or we should expect its
extinction, and, along with that, the extinguishing of much that constitutes our own proud, and singular identity.

What we casually call "English," less and less defers to England
and its "gentlemen." "English" is no longer a specific matter of geography or an element of class privilege; more than thirty-three countries
use this tool as a means of "intranational communication."[2] Countries
as disparate as Zimbabwe and Malaysia, or Israel and Uganda, use it
as their non-native currency of convenience. Obviously, this tool, this
"English," cannot function inside thirty-three discrete societies on the
basis of rules and values absolutely determined somewhere else, in a
thirty-fourth other country, for example.

In addition to that staggering congeries of non-native users of
English, there are five countries, or 333,746,000 people, for whom this
thing called "English" serves as a native tongue.[3] Approximately 10
percent of these native speakers of "English" are Afro-American citizens of the U.S.A. I cite these numbers and varieties of human beings
dependent on "English" in order, quickly, to suggest how strange and
how tenuous is any concept of "Standard English." Obviously, numerous forms of English now operate inside a natural, an uncontrollable,
continuum of development. I would suppose "the standard" for English
in Malaysia is not the same as "the standard" in Zimbabwe. I know
that standard forms of English for Black people in this country do not
copy that of whites. And, in fact, the structural differences between
these two kinds of English have intensified, becoming more Black, or

less white, despite the expected homogenizing effects of television[4] and other mass media.

Nonetheless, white standards of English persist, supreme and unquestioned, in these United States. Despite our multi-lingual population, and despite the deepening Black and white cleavage within that conglomerate, white standards control our official and popular judgments of verbal proficiency and correct, or incorrect, language skills, including speech. In contrast to India, where at least fourteen languages co-exist as legitimate Indian languages, in contrast to Nicaragua, where all citizens are legally entitled to formal school instruction in their regional or tribal languages, compulsory education in America compels accommodation to exclusively white forms of "English." White English, in America, is "Standard English."

This story begins two years ago. I was teaching a new course, "In Search of the Invisible Black Woman," and my rather large class seemed evenly divided between young Black women and men. Five or six white students also sat in attendance. With unexpected speed and enthusiasm we had moved through historical narratives of the nineteenth century to literature by and about Black women, in the twentieth. I had assigned the first forty pages of Alice Walker's *The Color Purple,* and I came, eagerly, to class that morning:

"So!" I exclaimed, aloud. "What did you think? How did you like it?"

The students studied their hands, or the floor. There was no response. The tense, resistant feeling in the room fairly astounded me.

At last, one student, a young woman still not meeting my eyes, muttered something in my direction:

"What did you say?" I prompted her.

"Why she have them talk so funny. It don't sound right."

"You mean the language?"

Another student lifted his head: "It don't look right, neither. I couldn't hardly read it."

At this, several students dumped on the book. Just about unanimously, their criticisms targeted the language. I listened to what they wanted to say and silently marvelled at the similarities between their casual speech patterns and Alice Walker's written version of Black English.

But I decided against pointing to these identical traits of syntax; I wanted not to make them self-conscious about their own spoken language — not while they clearly felt it was "wrong." Instead I decided to swallow my astonishment. Here was a negative Black reaction to a prize-winning accomplishment of Black literature that white readers across the country had selected as a best seller. Black rejection was aimed at the one irreducibly Black element of Walker's work: the language — Celie's Black English. I wrote the opening lines of *The Color*

Purple on the blackboard and asked the students to help me translate these sentences into Standard English:

> *You better not never tell nobody but God. It'd kill your mammy.*
> Dear God,
>   I am fourteen years old. I have always been a good girl. Maybe you
> can give me a sign letting me know what is happening to me.
>   Last spring after Little Lucious come I heard them fussing. He was
> pulling on her arm. She say it too soon, Fonso. I aint well. Finally he
> leave her alone. A week go by, he pulling on her arm again. She say,
> Naw, I ain't gonna. Can't you see I'm already half dead, an all of the
> children.[5]

Our process of translation exploded with hilarity and even hysterical, shocked laughter: The Black writer, Alice Walker, knew what she was doing! If rudimentary criteria for good fiction include the manipulation of language so that the syntax and diction of sentences will tell you the identity of speakers, the probable age and sex and class of speakers, and even the locale — urban/rural/southern/western — then Walker had written, perfectly. This is the translation into Standard English that our class produced:

> *Absolutely, one should never confide in anybody besides God. Your secrets
> could prove devastating to your mother.*
> Dear God,
>   I am fourteen years old. I have always been good. But now, could you
> help me to understand what is happening to me?
>   Last spring, after my little brother, Lucious, was born, I heard my
> parents fighting. My father kept pulling at my mother's arm. But she
> told him, "It's too soon for sex, Alfonso. I am still not feeling well."
> Finally, my father left her alone. A week went by, and then he began
> bothering my mother, again: Pulling her arm. She told him, "No, I won't!
> Can't you see I'm already exhausted from all of these children?"

(Our favorite line was "It's too soon for sex, Alfonso.")

Once we could stop laughing, once we could stop our exponentially wild improvisations on the theme of Translated Black English, the students pushed me to explain their own negative first reactions to their spoken language on the printed page. I thought it was probably akin to the shock of seeing yourself in a photograph for the first time. Most of the students had never before seen a written facsimile of the way they talk. None of the students had ever learned how to read and write their own verbal system of communication: Black English. Alternatively, this fact began to baffle or else bemuse and then infuriate my students. Why not? Was it too late? Could they learn how to do it, now? And, ultimately, the final test question, the one testing my sincerity: Could I teach them? Because I had never taught anyone Black

English and, as far as I knew, no one, anywhere in the United States, had ever offered such a course, the best I could say was "I'll try."

He looked like a wrestler.

He sat dead center in the packed room and, every time our eyes met, he quickly nodded his head as though anxious to reassure, and encourage, me.

Short, with strikingly broad shoulders and long arms, he spoke with a surprisingly high, soft voice that matched the soft bright movement of his eyes. His name was Willie Jordan. He would have seemed even more unlikely in the context of Contemporary Women's Poetry, except that ten or twelve other Black men were taking the course, as well. Still, Willie was conspicuous. His extreme fitness, the muscular density of his presence underscored the riveted, gentle attention that he gave to anything anyone said. Generally, he did not join the loud and rowdy dialogue flying back and forth, but there could be no doubt about his interest in our discussions. And, when he stood to present an argument he'd prepared, overnight, that nervous smile of his vanished and an irregular stammering replaced it, as he spoke with visceral sincerity, word by word.

That was how I met Willie Jordan. It was in between "In Search of the Invisible Black Woman" and "The Art of Black English." I was waiting for Departmental approval and I supposed that Willie might be, so to speak, killing time until he, too, could study Black English. But Willie really did want to explore Contemporary Women's Poetry and, to that end, volunteered for extra research and never missed a class.

Towards the end of that semester, Willie approached me for an independent study project on South Africa. It would commence the next semester. I thought Willie's writing needed the kind of improvement only intense practice will yield. I knew his intelligence was outstanding. But he'd wholeheartedly opted for "Standard English" at a rather late age, and the results were stilted and frequently polysyllabic, simply for the sake of having more syllables. Willie's unnatural formality of language seemed to me consistent with the formality of his research into South African apartheid. As he projected his studies, he would have little time, indeed, for newspapers. Instead, more than 90 percent of his research would mean saturation in strictly historical, if not archival, material. I was certainly interested. It would be tricky to guide him into a more confident and spontaneous relationship both with language and apartheid. It was going to be wonderful to see what happened when he could catch up with himself, entirely, and talk back to the world.

September, 1984: Breezy fall weather and much excitement! My class, "The Art of Black English," was full to the limit of the fire laws. And, in Independent Study, Willie Jordan showed up, weekly, fifteen minutes early for each of our sessions. I was pretty happy to be teaching, altogether!

I remember an early class when a young brother, replete with his ever present pork-pie hat, raised his hand and then told us that most of what he'd heard was "all right" except it was "too clean." "The brothers on the street," he continued, "they mix it up more. Like 'fuck' and 'motherfuck.' Or like 'shit.'" He waited. I waited. Then all of us laughed a good while, and we got into a brawl about "correct" and "realistic" Black English that led to Rule 1.

Rule 1: *Black English is about a whole lot more than mothafuckin.*

As a criterion, we decided, "realistic" could take you anywhere you want to go. Artful places. Angry places. Eloquent and sweetalkin places. Polemical places. Church. And the local Bar & Grill. We were checking out a language, not a mood or a scene or one guy's forgettable mouthing off.

It was hard. For most of the students, learning Black English required a fallback to patterns and rhythms of speech that many of their parents had beaten out of them. I mean *beaten.* And, in a majority of cases, correct Black English could be achieved only by striving for *incorrect* Standard English, something they were still pushing at, quite uncertainly. This state of affairs led to Rule 2.

Rule 2: *If it's wrong in Standard English it's probably right in Black English, or, at least, you're hot.*

It was hard. Roommates and family members ridiculed their studies, or remained incredulous, "You *studying* that shit? At school?" But we were beginning to feel the companionship of pioneers. And we decided that we needed another rule that would establish each one of us as equally important to our success. This was Rule 3.

Rule 3: *If it don't sound like something that come out somebody mouth then it don't sound right. If it don't sound right then it ain't hardly right. Period.*

This rule produced two weeks of compositions in which the students agonizingly tried to spell the sound of the Black English sentence they wanted to convey. But Black English is, pre-eminently, an oral/spoken means of communication. *And spelling don't talk.* So we needed Rule 4.

Rule 4: *Forget about the spelling. Let the syntax carry you.*

Once we arrived at Rule 4 we started by fly because syntax, the structure of an idea, leads you to the worldview of the speaker and reveals her values. The syntax of a sentence equals the structure of your consciousness. If we insisted that the language of Black English adheres to a distinctive Black syntax, then we were postulating a profound difference between white and Black people, *per se.* Was it a difference to prize or to obliterate?

There are three qualities of Black English — the presence of life, voice, and clarity — that testify to a distinctive Black value system that we became excited about and self-consciously tried to maintain.

1. Black English has been produced by a pre-technocratic, if not anti-technological, culture. More, our culture has been constantly threatened by annihilation or, at least, the swallowed blurring of assimilation. Therefore, our language is a system constructed by people constantly needing to insist that we exist, that we are present. Our language devolves from a culture that abhors all abstraction, or anything tending to obscure or delete the fact of the human being who is here and now/the truth of the person who is speaking or listening. Consequently, *there is no passive voice construction possible in Black English.* For example, you cannot say, "Black English is being eliminated." You must say, instead, "White people eliminating Black English." The assumption of the presence of life governs all of Black English. Therefore, overwhelmingly, *all action takes place in the language of the present indicative.* And every sentence assumes the living and active participation of at least two human beings, the speaker and the listener.

2. A primary consequence of the person-centered values of Black English is the delivery of voice. If you speak or write Black English, your ideas will necessarily possess that otherwise elusive attribute, voice.

3. One main benefit following from the person-centered values of Black English is that of *clarity.* If your idea, your sentence, assumes the presence of at least two living and active people, you will make it understandable because the motivation behind every sentence is the wish to say something real to somebody real.

As the weeks piled up, translation from Standard English into Black English or vice versa occupied a hefty part of our course work.

> Standard English (hereafter S.E.): "In considering the idea of studying Black English those questioned suggested — "
> (What's the subject? Where's the person? Is anybody alive in there, in that idea?)
> Black English (hereafter B.E.): "I been asking people what you think about somebody studying Black English and they answer me like this:"

But there were interesting limits. You cannot "translate" instances of Standard English preoccupied with abstraction or with nothing/nobody evidently alive, into Black English. That would warp the language into uses antithetical to the guiding perspective of its community of users. Rather you must first change those Standard English sentences, themselves, into ideas consistent with the person-centered assumptions of Black English.

Guidelines for Black English

1. Minimal number of words for every idea: This is the source for the aphoristic and/or poetic force of the language; eliminate every possible word.

2. Clarity: If the sentence is not clear it's not Black English.

3. Eliminate use of the verb *to be* whenever possible. This leads to the deployment of more descriptive and therefore, more precise verbs.

4. Use *be* or *been* only when you want to describe a chronic, ongoing state of things.

   > He *be* at the office, by 9. (He is always at the office by 9.)
   > He *been* with her since forever.

5. Zero copula: Always eliminate the verb *to be* whenever it would combine with another verb, in Standard English.

   > S.E.: She is going out with him.
   > B.E.: She going out with him.

6. Eliminate *do* as in:

   > S.E.: What do you think? What do you want?
   > B.E.: What you think? What you want?

   Rules number 3, 4, 5, and 6 provide for the use of the minimal number of verbs per idea and, therefore, greater accuracy in the choice of verb.

7. In general, if you wish to say something really positive, try to formulate the idea using emphatic negative structure.

   > S.E.: He's fabulous.
   > B.E.: He bad.

8. Use double or triple negatives for dramatic emphasis.

   > S.E.: Tina Turner sings out of this world.
   > B.E.: Ain nobody sing like Tina.

9. Never use the *–ed* suffix to indicate the past tense of a verb.

   > S.E.: She closed the door.
   > B.E.: She close the door. Or, she have close the door.

10. Regardless of intentional verb time, only use the third person singular, present indicative, for use of the verb *to have,* as an auxiliary.

    S.E.: He had his wallet then he lost it.
    B.E.: He have him wallet then he lose it.
    S.E.: We had seen that movie.
    B.E.: We seen that movie. Or, we have see that movie.

11. Observe a minimal inflection of verbs. Particularly, never change from the first person singular forms to the third person singular.

    S.E.: Present Tense Forms: He goes to the store.
    B.E.: He go to the store.
    S.E.: Past Tense Forms: He went to the store.
    B.E.: He go to the store. Or, he gone to the store. Or, he been to the store.

12. The possessive case scarcely ever appears in Black English. Never use an apostrophe ('s) construction. If you wander into a possessive case component of an idea, then keep logically consistent: *ours, his, theirs, mines.* But, most likely, if you bump into such a component, you have wandered outside the underlying worldview of Black English.

    S.E.: He will take their car tomorrow.
    B.E.: He taking they car tomorrow.

13. Plurality: Logical consistency, continued: If the modifier indicates plurality then the noun remains in the singular case.

    S.E.: He ate twelve doughnuts.
    B.E.: He eat twelve doughnut.
    S.E.: She has many books.
    B.E.: She have many book.

14. Listen for, or invent, special Black English forms of the past tense, such as "He losted it. That what she felted." If they are clear and readily understood, then use them.

15. Do not hesitate to play with words, sometimes inventing them: e.g. "astropotomous" means huge like a hippo plus astronomical and, therefore, signifies real big.

16. In Black English, unless you keenly want to underscore the past tense nature of an action, stay in the present tense and rely on the overall context of your ideas for the conveyance of time and sequence.

17. Never use the suffix *–ly* form of an adverb in Black English.

    S.E.: The rain came down rather quickly.
    B.E.: The rain come down pretty quick.

18. Never use the indefinite article *an* in Black English.

> S.E.: He wanted to ride an elephant.
> B.E.: He want to ride him a elephant.

19. Invariant syntax: in correct Black English it is possible to formulate an imperative, an interrogative, and a simple declarative idea with the same syntax:

> B.E.: You going to the store?
> You going to the store.
> You going to the store!

Where was Willie Jordan? We'd reach the mid-term of the semester. Students had formulated Black English guidelines, by consensus, and they were now writing with remarkable beauty, purpose, and enjoyment:

> *"I ain hardly speakin for everybody but myself so understan that."*
>
> — Kim Parks

Samples from student writings:

> "Janie have a great big ole hole inside her. Tea Cake the only thing that fit that hole . . .
> "That pear tree beautiful to Janie, especial when bees fiddlin with the blossomin pear there growin large and lovely. But personal speakin, the love she get from starin at that tree ain the love what starin back at her in them relationship." (Monica Morris)

> "Love is a big theme in, *They Eye Was Watching God*. Love show people new corners inside theyself. It pull out good stuff and stuff back bad stuff . . . Joe worship the doing uh his own hand and need other people to worship him too. But he ain't think about Janie that she a person and ought to live like anybody common do. Queen life not for Janie." (Monica Morris)

> "In both life and writin, Black womens have varietous experience of love that be cold like a iceberg or fiery like a inferno. Passion got for the other partner involve, man or woman, seem as shallow, ankle-deep water or the most profoundest abyss." (Constance Evans)

> "Family love another bond that ain't never break under no pressure." (Constance Evans)

> "You know it really cold/When the friend you/Always get out the fire/Act like they don't know you/When you in the heat." (Constance Evans)

> "Big classroom discussion bout love at this time. I never take no class where us have any long arguin for and against for two or three day. New to me and great. I find the class time talkin a million time more interestin than detail bout the book." (Kathy Esseks)

As these examples suggest, Black English no longer limited the students, in any way. In fact, one of them, Philip Garfield, would shortly "translate" a pivotal scene from Ibsen's *A Doll House,* as his final term paper.

> *Nora:* I didn't gived no shit. I thinked you a asshole back then, too, you make it so hard for me save mines husband life.
>
> *Krogstad:* Girl, it clear you ain't any idea what you done. You dont exact what I once done, and I losed my reputation over it.
>
> *Nora:* You asks me believe you once act brave save you wife life?
>
> *Krogstad:* Law care less why you done it.
>
> *Nora:* Law must suck.
>
> *Krogstad:* Suck or no, if I wants, judge screw you wid dis paper.
>
> *Nora:* No way, man. (Philip Garfield)

But where was Willie? Compulsively punctual, and always thoroughly prepared with neatly typed compositions, he had disappeared. He failed to show up for our regularly scheduled conference, and I received neither a note nor a phone call of explanation. A whole week went by. I wondered if Willie had finally been captured by the extremely current happenings in South Africa: passage of a new constitution that did not enfranchise the Black majority, and militant Black South African reaction to that affront. I wondered if he'd been hurt, somewhere. I wondered if the serious workload of weekly readings and writings had overwhelmed him and changed his mind about independent study. Where was Willie Jordan?

One week after the first conference that Willie missed, he called: "Hello, Professor Jordan? This is Willie. I'm sorry I wasn't there last week. But something has come up and I'm pretty upset. I'm sorry but I really can't deal right now."

I asked Willie to drop by my office and just let me see that he was okay. He agreed to do that. When I saw him I knew something hideous had happened. Something had hurt him and scared him to the marrow. He was all agitated and stammering and terse and incoherent. At last, his sadly jumbled account let me surmise, as follows: Brooklyn police had murdered his unarmed, twenty-five-year-old brother, Reggie Jordan. Neither Willie nor his elderly parents knew what to do about it. Nobody from the press was interested. His folks had no money. Police ran his family around and around, to no point. And Reggie was really dead. And Willie wanted to fight, but he felt helpless.

With Willie's permission I began to try to secure legal counsel for the Jordan family. Unfortunately Black victims of police violence are truly numerous while the resources available to prosecute their killers are truly scarce. A friend of mine at the Center for Constitutional Rights estimated that just the preparatory costs for bring the cops into court normally approaches $180,000. Unless the execution of Reggie Jordan became a major community cause for organizing, and protest, his murder would simply become a statistical item.

Again, with Willie's permission, I contacted every newspaper and media person I could think of. But the William Bastone feature article in *The Village Voice* was the only result from that canvassing.

Again, with Willie's permission, I presented the case to my class in Black English. We had talked about the politics of language. We had talked about love and sex and child abuse and men and women. But the murder of Reggie Jordan broke like a hurricane across the room.

There are few "issues" as endemic to Black Life as police violence. Most of the students knew and respected and liked Jordan. Many of them were from the very neighborhood where the murder had occurred. All of the students had known somebody close to them who had been killed by police, or had known frightening moments of gratuitous confrontation with the cops. They wanted to do everything at once to avenge death. Number One: They decided to compose personal statements of condolence to Willie Jordan and his family written in Black English. Number Two: They decided to compose individual messages to the police, in Black English. These should be prefaced by an explanatory paragraph composed by the entire group. Number Three: These individual messages, with their lead paragraph, should be sent to *Newsday*.

The morning after we agreed on these objectives, one of the young women students appeared with an unidentified visitor, who sat through the class, smiling in a peculiar, comfortable way.

Now we had to make more tactical decisions. Because we wanted the messages published, and because we thought it imperative that our outrage be known by the police, the tactical question was this: Should the opening, group paragraph be written in Black English or Standard English?

I have seldom been privy to a discussion with so much heart at the dead heat of it. I will never forget the eloquence, the sudden haltings of speech, the fierce struggle against tears, the furious throwaway, and useless explosions that this question elicited.

That one question contained several others, each of them extraordinarily painful to even contemplate. How best to serve the memory of Reggie Jordan? Should we use the language of the killers — Standard English — in order to make our ideas acceptable to those controlling the killers? But wouldn't what we had to say be rejected, summarily, if we said it in our own language, the language of the victim, Reggie Jordan? But if we sought to express ourselves by abandoning our language wouldn't that mean our suicide on top of Reggie's murder? But if we expressed ourselves in our own language wouldn't that be suicidal to the wish to communicate with those who, evidently, did not give a damn about us/Reggie/police violence in the Black community?

At the end of one of the longest, most difficult hours of my own life, the students voted, unanimously, to preface their individual messages with a paragraph composed in the language of Reggie Jordan. *"At least we don't give up nothing else. At least we stick to the truth: Be who we been. And stay all the way with Reggie."*

It was heartbreaking to proceed, from that point. Everyone in the room realized that our decision in favor of Black English had doomed our writings, even as the distinctive reality of our Black lives always has doomed our efforts to "be who we been" in this country.

I went to the blackboard and took down this paragraph, dictated by the class:

> "... YOU COPS!
> WE THE BROTHER AND SISTER OF WILLIE JORDAN, A FELLOW STONY BROOK STUDENT WHO THE BROTHER OF THE DEAD REGGIE JORDAN. REGGIE, LIKE MANY BROTHER AND SISTER, HE A VICTIM OF BRUTAL RACIST POLICE, OCTOBER 25, 1984. US APPALL, FED UP, BECAUSE THAT ANOTHER SENSELESS DEATH WHAT OCCUR IN OUR COMMUNITY. THIS WHAT WE FEEL, THIS, FROM OUR HEART, FOR WE AIN'T STAYIN' SILENT NO MORE:"

With the completion of this introduction, nobody said anything. I asked for comments. At this invitation, the unidentified visitor, a young Black man, ceaselessly smiling, raised his hand. He was, it so happens, a rookie cop. He had just joined the force in September and, he said, he thought he should clarify a few things. So he came forward and sprawled easily into a posture of barroom, or fireside, nostalgia:

"See," Officer Charles enlightened us, "Most times when you out on the street and something come down you do one of two things. Over-react or under-react. Now, if you under-react then you can get yourself kilt. And if you over-react then maybe you kill somebody. Fortunately it's about nine times out of ten and you will over-react. So the brother got kilt. And I'm sorry about that, believe me. But what you have to understand is what kilt him: Over-reaction. That's all. Now you talk about Black people and white police but see, now, I'm a cop myself. And (big smile) I'm Black. And just a couple months ago I was on the other side. But see it's the same for me. You a cop, you the ultimate authority: the Ultimate Authority. And you on the street, most of the time you can only do one of two things: over-react or under-react. That's all it is with the brother: Over-reaction. Didn't have nothing to do with race."

That morning Officer Charles had the good fortune to escape without being boiled alive. But barely. And I remember the pride of his smile when I read about the fate of Black policemen and other collaborators, in South Africa. I remember him, and I remember the shock and palpable feeling of shame that filled the room. It was as though that foolish, and deadly, young man had just relieved himself of his foolish, and deadly, explanation, face to face with the grief of Reggie Jordan's father and Reggie Jordan's mother. Class ended quietly. I copied the paragraph from the blackboard, collected the individual messages and left to type them up.

Newsday rejected the piece.

The Village Voice could not find room in their "Letters" section to print the individual messages from the students to the police.

None of the tv news reporters picked up the story.

Nobody raised $180,000 to prosecute the murder of Reggie Jordan.

Reggie Jordan is really dead.

I asked Willie Jordan to write an essay pulling together everything important to him from that semester. He was still deeply beside himself with frustration and amazement and loss. This is what he wrote, un-edited, and in its entirety:

"Throughout the course of this semester I have been researching the effects of oppression and exploitation along racial lines in South Africa and its neighboring countries. I have become aware of South African police brutalization of native Africans beyond the extent of the law, even though the laws themselves are catalyst affliction upon Black men, women and children. Many Africans die each year as a result of the deliberate use of police force to protect the white power structure.

"Social control agents in South Africa, such as policemen, are also used to force compliance among citizens through both overt and covert tactics. It is not uncommon to find bold-faced coercion and cold-blooded killings of Blacks by South African police for undetermined and/or inadequate reasons. Perhaps the truth is that the only reasons for this heinous treatment of Blacks rests in racial differences. We should also understand that what is conveyed through the media is not always accurate and may sometimes be construed as the tip of the iceberg at best.

"I recently received a painful reminder that racism, poverty, and the abuse of power are global problems which are by no means unique to South Africa. On October 25, 1984, at approximately 3:00 p.m. my brother, Mr. Reginald Jordan, was shot and killed by two New York City policemen from the 75th precinct in the East New York section of Brooklyn. His life ended at the age of twenty-five. Even up to this current point in time the Police Department has failed to provide my family, which consists of five brothers, eight sisters, and two parents, with a plausible reason for Reggie's death. Out of the many stories that were given to my family by the Police Department, not one of them seems to hold water. In fact, I honestly believe that the Police Department's assessment of my brother's murder is nothing short of ABSOLUTE BULLSHIT, and thus far no evidence had been produced to alter perception of the situation.

"Furthermore, I believe that one of three cases may have occurred in this incident. First, Reggie's death may have been the desired outcome of the police officer's action, in which case the killing was premeditated. Or, it was a case of mistaken identity, which clarifies the fact that the two officers who killed my brother and their commanding parties are all grossly incompetent. Or, both of the above cases are correct, i.e., Reggie's murderers intended to kill him and the Police Department behaved insubordinately.

"Part of the argument of the officers who shot Reggie was that he had attacked one of them and took his gun. This was their major claim. They also said that only one of them had actually shot Reggie. The facts, however, speak for themselves. According to the Death Certificate and autopsy report, Reggie was shot eight times from point-blank range. The Doctor who performed the autopsy told me himself that two bullets entered the side of my brother's head, four bullets were sprayed into his back, and two bullets struck him in the back of his legs. It is obvious that unnecessary force was used by the police and that it is extremely difficult to shoot someone in his back when he is attacking or approaching you.

"After experiencing a situation like this and researching South Africa I believe that to a large degree, justice may only exist as rhetoric. I find it difficult to talk of true justice when the oppression of my people both at home and abroad attests to the fact that inequality and injustice are serious problems whereby Blacks and Third World people are perpetually short-changed by society. Something has to be done about the way in which this world is set up. Although it is a difficult task, we do have the power to make a change."

— Willie J. Jordan Jr.
EGL 487, Section 58, November 14, 1984

It is my privilege to dedicate this book to the future life of Willie J. Jordan Jr.
August 8, 1985

Notes

1. Black English aphorism crafted by Monica Morris, a Junior at S.U.N.Y. at Stony Brook, October 1984.
2. *English Is Spreading, But What Is English?* A presentation by Professor S. N. Sridahr, Dept. of Linguistics, S.U.N.Y. at Stony Brook, April 9, 1985: Dean's Conversation Among the Disciplines.
3. Ibid.

4. *New York Times,* March 15, 1985, Section One, p. 14: Report on study by Linguistics at the University of Pennsylvania.
5. Alice Walker, *The Color Purple* (1982), p. 11, Harcourt Brace, N.Y.

Classroom Activities

Developing writers of all cultural backgrounds can benefit substantially from reading teaching and literacy narratives, especially stories that deal with social justice and struggles with the languages of community and school. In this regard, consider reading "Nobody Mean More to Me Than You and the Future Life of Willie Jordan" with your students. Invite your students to create critical thinking questions for discussion that focus on language, writing, and rhetoric.

Example questions to stimulate students' thinking might include the following: How would you explain this statement: "The syntax of a sentence equals the structure of your consciousness" (Rule 4 in "Guidelines for Black English")? How would you describe the three qualities of Black English that Jordan lists ("the presence of life, voice, and clarity")? What struggles with audience did Jordan's students face, and how did they address those struggles? Who was Jordan's audience for this essay, and what were her purposes for telling these particular stories about her teaching? Give students the opportunity to discuss their questions in small groups and to develop their responses in their journals or in a longer paper. You might also ask students to write a literacy narrative — an essay in which they reflect on their own experiences with language and explore how various communities have shaped the way they speak, write, and read.

Thinking about Teaching

Jordan's essay, first published in the mid-1980s, presents compelling insights into the intersections of teaching writing and issues of social justice. Consider your reading of Jordan's essay as an opportunity to reflect on such issues both locally and globally in your teaching journal — and perhaps in an essay of your own. Jordan's work also can be a catalyst for a group discussion with other teachers. This discussion could be a starting point in considering the implications of education for social justice as it pertains to basic writing programs at the local, regional, or national level. Faculty may have questions or suggestions about how or whether to include social justice content in a writing course. Moreover, a forum for sharing ideas may lead to curricular and institutional changes. Faculty across the curriculum may want to share syllabi and assignments; guest speakers could also be arranged.

Mitigating Barriers to Navajo Students' Success in English Courses

Kay Thurston

Kay Thurston won TETYC's (Teaching English in the Two-Year College) *1998 Best Article Award for this description of "the tremendous barriers to success in colleges and universities" that Navajo students face. She draws on her experiences teaching writing and literature at Navajo Community College, a two-year tribal college in the center of the Navajo, or Diné, nation. Ninety-six percent of the students are Navajo, the majority of whom live in poverty. Thurston does a thorough job of describing the geographic isolation of her students and the rich cultural heritage with which they arrive in the composition classroom. Rather than blaming the victim or the culture for "the high failure rate" experienced by her students, Thurston suggests that we look at more global factors, which she sees as applicable to "students from radically different cultures." Thurston describes in detail five major barriers that her students encounter: "financial difficulty, family obligations, prescriptive attitudes toward Standard American English, instructor/faculty ethnocentrism, and ambivalence toward Western education." Thurston also presents thoughtful solutions that challenge the reader to examine his or her own values and prejudices.*

Introduction

Navajos, or the Diné, are one of four hundred Native American tribes currently recognized by the U.S. government. Of the 150,000 people living on the Navajo reservation despite its isolation and intense poverty, many are struggling to retain their traditional ways — their language, spiritual beliefs and ceremonies, and a culture completely unlike that of white, middle-class Americans.

Navajo Community College (NCC), the first tribally controlled college, was built in 1968 by tribal leaders and medicine men on a sacred site between the Chuska Mountains, Tsaile Lake, and Canyon de Chelly in northeastern Arizona. NCC is located in the center of the Navajo Nation, which is, in many ways, like a third-world country, about the size of West Virginia. To buy groceries, NCC staff, faculty, and students make a 60-mile round trip to Chinle, Arizona, a town of seven thousand. To shop at K-Mart, a hardware store, or to see a movie, they make a 180-mile round trip past pine-covered mountains, red-orange Navajo sandstone towering above rugged piñon and juniper, and sheep, cows, and horses scattered among clumps of sage to Gallup, New Mexico.

Of the 550 students who attend NCC's main campus annually, 96 percent are Navajo. NCC's mission is to take these Navajo students, most of whom grew up on the reservation (some in very traditional families, and others in families that have been influenced, to varying degrees, by dominant society), and make them bicultural so that they can function effectively in both the Western and Navajo worlds. NCC succeeds because it focuses on Navajo culture, tradition, and beliefs; it addresses Navajo students' unique needs; and its faculty, knowing that most Navajo dropouts are not academic failures, accept part of the blame for the high Navajo failure and attrition rate. Still, these students face tremendous barriers to success in colleges and universities, and it seems to me that the barriers take five major forms: financial difficulty, family obligations, prescriptive attitudes toward Standard American English, instructor/faculty ethnocentrism, and ambivalence toward Western education.

Financial Difficulty

Probably the number one reason for the high attrition rate of Navajo students is financial. While it would, of course, be incorrect to suggest that every Navajo student struggles financially, the fact is that poverty on the Navajo reservation is so widespread it's the norm. According to the Navajo Nation's 1990 Census Report, only 44.8 percent of those over sixteen are employed in the labor force — for males sixteen and over, the unemployment rate is 30.3 percent. In 1989, the Navajo Nation's median household income was $10,433, and per capita income was $4,106, putting 56.1 percent of the Navajos living on the reservation below the poverty level. Half the homes are without water and electricity — it is disconcerting to see hogans (traditional round dwellings made of wood and earth) without power standing beneath massive systems of power lines strung from the reservation's coal-generating plants to meet energy consumption needs in distant cities in California. Many commuting students live in traditional hogans with earthen floors and can't make it to class after heavy rains that turn their roads into slippery mud. Most cannot call for a missed assignment, either, as 77.5 percent of the homes on the Navajo Nation are without telephone service.

For me, the reality of the students' extreme level of poverty was hammered home recently when I required students to use the college's computers to type their writing assignments. Two weeks later, two students were still turning in handwritten assignments because they had been unable to find one dollar for a disk. To ameliorate students' financial burdens, I allowed some class time each semester for a student services or financial aid representative to counsel students. I also considered the cost of the textbooks I selected, put texts and articles on reserve in the library, and remained flexible about requiring typed assignments. I learned to ask questions and then to make exceptions, for example, for the single parent who has returned to school and is trying to feed four children on food stamps. Though computer and typewriter use may be free, child care is not. To middle-class faculty, this level of poverty may seem inconceivable, but I assure you it is real, and it is a factor with which many, if not most, Navajo students struggle continuously.

Family Obligations

A second serious obstacle the Navajo student faces is the faculty member who doesn't understand or won't acknowledge the importance and time-consuming nature of family responsibilities. Many of us, probably, would raise an eyebrow at a student who tells us that she missed a week of classes because her grandfather had a stroke, but to a traditional Navajo's way of thinking, this problem is not only legitimate but imperative. The student and her family would first take the stroke victim to a diagnostician to determine what healing ceremony (or ceremonies) needed to be performed. If the diagnostician calls for a Lightning Way or Wind Way ceremony, the student's presence will be required for four or five days; if the grandfather should pass on, then for four days, her presence would be required to help her grandfather's spirit travel on to the fifth world. Since most reservations are located far from urban centers and universities, and since most ceremonies last from two to nine days, the student is likely to be out of town for seven to ten days. If her English teacher's absence policy drops students after three or four absences, but the student's family requires her presence for a ceremony that will enable her grandfather to walk again, chances are high that the student will drop the class, especially if the family needs the grandfather out of the nursing home as quickly as possible to care for the livestock that constitute the economic base for the entire extended family.

The family ties of Native American students are usually strong and can never be underestimated. Navajo students, for example, introduce themselves not by telling what they do for work, but by naming their four clans. When, in developmental writing courses, I ask students to write a paragraph describing their best friend, most describe a parent, grandparent, uncle, aunt, brother, sister, or cousin. In the Navajo kinship system, cousins are more akin to brothers and sisters, and aunts and uncles more like mothers and fathers. The Navajo word for paternal uncle, in fact, means "little father," and for maternal aunt, "little mother": these terms reflect the Navajo relatives' assumption of far more responsibility than Anglos for the welfare of their nieces and nephews. Such relationships lend an urgency that an Anglo instructor may not understand to a student's attendance at his niece's Kinaaldá — a female puberty ceremony lasting four days, held when a niece begins menstruation — a family duty that cannot be put off, for example, until spring break. A traditional Navajo student with strong family ties, when forced to choose between honoring a teacher's absence policy and his "little daughter's" entrance into womanhood, will probably choose the latter. Other ceremonies require the participation of the entire community: the Jemez Pueblo people of New Mexico, for example, have feast days and dances, most lasting about a week. For instance, late in November, Jemez Pueblo students attending the University of New Mexico return home for three to five days to pray and fast, clean the Pueblo village, replaster houses, prepare food for the guests, and perform ceremonial dances.

The holidays scheduled at mainstream institutions — Columbus Day, the Fourth of July, President's Day, and Christmas — do not hold special significance for Navajos. Therefore, Anglo instructors follow the lead of Native American instructors who, because they are more likely to understand and respect Native American students' need for family contact and involvement, are generally more flexible with absence policies and more willing to accommodate students with family responsibilities.

Prescriptive Attitude toward Standard American English

A third problem that Navajo students encounter in the English classroom is that an Anglo instructor often has little or no knowledge of Native American language conventions. Such instructors (1) assume in students a level of familiarity with Standard American English (SAE) that a middle class Euro-American would have; (2) are untrained and unaware of dialect or second language difficulties, regarding conventional Indian English as "wrong," and expecting students to "clean up" the English they have spoken and heard their entire lives; and (3) expect students to replace their Navajo English dialect with SAE in fifteen to sixteen weeks.

When 82 percent of the adults on the Navajo reservation speak Navajo, and only 21 percent of the 131,229 Navajos five years and older speak English only, it's unreasonable to expect Navajo students to be as familiar with SAE as Anglo students.[1] Navajo English is quite different from SAE. Let me illustrate with three examples. Navajo students, in general, have difficulty with plural formation, verb tenses, and rhetorical style. In Navajo, animate nouns are made plural not by adding an "-s" but by adding a variety of other endings. "Boy," in Navajo, is *ashkii;* "boys" is *ashiike.* No affix is attached to inanimate nouns; instead, the plural is indicated by changes in the verb associated with the noun in question. As a result, Navajo students will write that they have one ball, "two ball," and "many ball scattered about the field." Or "Many of my relative live in Shiprock." Navajo English forms plurals by adding "-s," but also contains words such as "elderlies," "sheeps," "cattles," "firewoods," "mens," "womens," and "childrens." Another example illustrates the special difficulties of bilingual or nonstandard dialect. In Navajo, verb tense is shown by the position of the verb in a sentence, not by a change in its ending. In Navajo English, although the position of the verb does not change, past tense endings are often omitted, as in "I hear him sing yesterday." Irregular verbs pose problems as well — often, after learning to form the regular past tense, students create words like "hurted" and "eated."

Recognition that Native American students are often bilingual and speak a nonstandard American English dialect has led to two strategies at NCC:[2] first, ESL, bilingual, and nonstandard American English speakers, as well as students from historically oral cultural backgrounds require more than one or two semesters to establish and refine college-level writing skills. For this reason, NCC instructors offer three developmental English courses. About 96 percent of the students complete at least one of them before moving on to first-year composition, and many work their way through all three. In the first level are students who cannot write a complete, coherent sentence. The second and third levels of developmental English deal not only with the nuts and bolts of English usage and Western rhetorical styles, but also with problems specific to Navajo and Navajo English speakers. NCC faculty members are in the process of designing a textbook for these classes — an English textbook specifically for Navajo students, one that uses Navajo themes in its sample writings and exercises and that addresses the kinds of errors bilingual Navajo students are most likely to make.

In addition, maximum enrollment in developmental English courses at NCC is limited to fifteen so that students can receive the individual attention and the specific instruction they require to become proficient in written SAE. Finally, composition instructors at NCC approach SAE as one dialect, not superior to Navajo English, but the one required for success in the world beyond the Navajo Nation's four sacred mountains.

Instructor/Faculty Ethnocentrism

Anglo instructors' (often unconscious) ethnocentrism and almost total ignorance about Native American cultures constitute a fourth barrier to Navajo students' success in English courses. I believe this ethnocentrism is caused primarily by gaps in our education: even though we understand that to be effective teachers, in Hap Gilliland's words, we "must understand and accept as equally valid, values and ways of life different from our own," we know little about others' cultures, histories, and educational philosophies. Gilliland adds that when "the teacher does not know, understand, and respect the culture of the students, then the students are at a disadvantage *in that teacher's class*" (4).

Such ethnocentrism or ignorance causes us to lose far more Native American students than we realize. During the second week of teaching a composition course at the University of New Mexico, I used an essay by Jessica Mitford on embalming; the next day, the three Navajos enrolled in the class dropped it. Later, I discovered that in Navajo culture, talking or writing about death is taboo. By requiring the students to discuss death and then write about it, I had offended and alienated them. Patricia Clark Smith had a similar experience teaching on the Navajo reservation. When she once brought an owl she'd fashioned out of scrap cloth to a class, the students "literally recoiled." "I learned too late," she writes, "that owls and images of owls are just something you do not mess with if you are Navajo" (287). Owls, in Navajo culture, are messengers warning a person to be alert and careful, especially for the next four days.

But instructor ethnocentrism does more than cause instructors inadvertently to alienate Native American students; it also leads to failure to acknowledge and validate different rhetorical styles. The Navajo rhetorical style differs considerably from the European linear style. In an unpublished paper, Navajo English instructor Della Toadlena writes that "Navajo is an oral language in which much story telling takes place," and that this tradition explains why Navajo students do better with narrative essays that follow chronological order than with expository essays (5). "An English speaker wastes no time in stating his argument right off and then brings in details to support his idea. Unlike his Anglo counterpart, a Navajo brings out detail after detail and eventually arrives at the point he wants to make" (Toadlena 13). For Navajos, it is important not to offend the audience they are addressing by coming right to the point. To illustrate the more indirect communication style of Navajo people, Toadlena discusses a typical visit from relatives. First, greetings are exchanged, and then the welfare of each family and its members is discussed. Next, food is served while weather, livestock, and crops are discussed. Only after all this exchange is the real reason for the visit brought out by the visitors — the relatives, in this case, were sponsoring an Enemy Way Ceremony and needed some help (13–14).

Use of the Western rhetorical style is, therefore, awkward and difficult for some Navajo students. When Anglo instructors ask students to state their thesis at the beginning of an essay, they're asking students to go against their cultural conventions — and asking them to be bad storytellers. Most composition instructors fail "thesis-less" papers, or papers that make their point in a roundabout or indirect way near the conclusion, when instead, we should be learning, promoting, and assigning equal value and legitimacy to the various rhetorical styles of all cultures. Here in the Southwest, then, effective instructors would teach both the Western and the Navajo rhetorical styles, privileging neither, and would explain the necessity of taking audience and purpose into account when choosing a particular rhetorical strategy.

Instructor ethnocentrism also manifests itself in the tendency to gear courses and methods toward the Anglo student, with little or no consideration for others. Navajo educators criticize Western education for its lack of relevance, saying that it fails to tie schoolwork to anything real; that course content is not connected to everyday life — to family, community, and nation. This criticism is legitimate. Too often, the texts in the composition classroom speak only to the experiences and cultural backgrounds of Anglo students. Textbook publishers' efforts to include multicultural readings in texts have not gone unnoticed at tribal colleges. Still, instructors must supplement those texts with others and explore issues impacting students' lives today, such as the Navajo/Hopi land dispute, Anglo appropriation of Native American rituals and spirituality, the American Indian Religious Freedom Act, the use of peyote in the Native American Church, and autobiographical narratives. And here at NCC, some instructors are successfully experimenting with portfolios that include community projects like writing letters for illiterate community members, making videos, recording oral histories, and so forth.

Although the traditional Navajo way of life is based on sharing and cooperation, and not on acquiring and competing, English instructors often expect work to be performed individually, with little (if any) collaboration. Those teaching Navajos need to place less focus on the individual and more on community — to lecture less, plan more collaborative and small group work, and try to build "learning communities."

Finally, I've noticed that the discussion styles of Navajo and Anglo students are a bit different. Navajo students typically take more time to consider a response to a question — a few seconds longer than most Anglo instructors are willing to wait. The Navajo method of discussion takes more time, is more thorough, and more in depth. I expect students to be open and expressive — and some are — but, as Toadlena writes, "that is not the proper way Navajos are taught to deal with strangers" (8). I like the way Northern Cheyenne elder Grover Wolf Voice explains the "delay" in responding. He says, "Even if I had a quick answer to your question, I would never answer immediately. That would be saying that your question was not worth thinking about" (Gilliland 32).

Patricia Clark Smith's experience teaching on the reservation illustrates the Navajo discussion style. She writes:

> I had to get used to the fact that when I asked a question, I would not see several hands waving competitively in the air. Instead, there'd usually be a silence — sometimes a long silence. Then someone might say something. And after a while, someone else. And then another person. It wasn't that there were never heated exchanges and wild laughter; there were, especially as the class came to trust me and one another more.

But for the most part the class felt not so much like a tennis match with questions and answers volleyed back and forth from the teacher's side to the students' side as like a circle slowly drawing together in consensus. The actual result was that a larger percentage of the people in that class eventually spoke up than during an average class on campus, where the most persistent handwavers often shut down other students. (286)

In order to eradicate ethnocentrism and ignorance about Navajo cultures, Navajo Community College formally educates its instructors so that they become familiar with Navajo students' cultural backgrounds and the historical context within which they teach. In two mandatory semester-long courses, faculty learn about the Navajo creation stories — or at least the first of twelve levels of understanding the stories. The first level seems like a fairy tale, myth, or religion, with Holy People and insect people, Father Sky and Mother Earth, monsters, and the Twins who slay the monsters. Instructors learn that the stories represent a historical charter between the Holy People and the Diné and that relating course material to traditional creation stories will inspire and motivate traditional Navajo students. Instructors also learn about Navajo history, for example, that the United States government paid fifty dollars for each scalp (or, sometimes, an ear) of a dead Navajo. They learn that the Diné — as well as Native Americans of almost every tribe — were "relocated" or forced from their homelands and contained within reservations on less desirable land. They learn that Kit Carson, who is portrayed as an American hero in Anglo school books, led the United States Army in hunting down resisting Navajos and forcing their surrender by destroying their shelters, livestock, and crops. After four years' incarceration in Ft. Sumner, New Mexico, a location so barren that self-sufficiency was impossible, the Diné were allowed to return to their traditional homeland, only to find that 90 percent had been taken by settlers, ranchers, and mining interests. In return for the loss of land, and for agreeing to accept reservations, tribes were offered annuities and education. Navajo leaders thought they were agreeing to an education that would combine the best of both the Navajo and Western worlds — one that would allow the Diné to keep their own traditional ways and values. What they got was something very different.

Often well-meaning educators (both Anglo and Navajo) saw Native Americans' cultural customs as "stumbling blocks" and set out to destroy them. They tried to eradicate Navajos' language, dress, and traditions, including their complex healing ceremonies. Educators went to reservations also determined to negate Navajo ways of knowing, such as crystal-gazing and hand trembling; and to negate Navajo ways of doing — it is said, for example, that before white people came and the knowledge was lost, Navajos could travel from one place to another by means of prayer. Navajos had, too, an advanced judicial system in which perpetrators of crimes, rather than being locked up or banished, were brought back into balance through participation in certain ceremonies and by making restitution to the victim or victim's family. White educators tried to eradicate the Navajos' completely different way of viewing the world, one that, rather than being based on separation and difference, is circular and cyclic, one that sees things in terms of patterns in nature.

To "civilize" Indians, the United States government created off-reservation boarding schools designed not to provide a real education, but to assimilate Native Americans into the dominant culture and to train them for menial positions in the labor force. A 1950s Bureau of Indian Affairs (BIA) program report from Riverside, California, for example, describes in glowing terms the successful training of four bus boys. Anglo educators considered that a laudable achievement. Navajo leaders did not agree and were also deeply troubled that Navajo children placed in BIA boarding schools were separated from their parents for three to five years, even throughout the summers, when they were placed with area families; were paddled or forced to clean toilets for speaking Navajo instead of English; were punished for refusing to worship a Christian god or for participating in traditional Navajo religious practices like praying with corn pollen to the Holy People at dawn; and were one hundred times more likely to commit suicide than white teenagers. Most Navajo students at any institution have either attended BIA boarding schools or have close relatives who did, and today, many traditional Navajos blame the rise in domestic violence and alcoholism on the trauma experienced by students at BIA boarding schools. Knowing the history of Navajo experience of Western education helps NCC faculty understand why some students' grandparents discourage them from attending college (among traditional people, some students tell me, education still has a "bad, bad name").

Ambivalence toward Western Education

Often what instructors interpret as poor or lackluster performance, lack of ability, or lack of motivation by Navajo students is actually ambivalence toward Western education. Historical, philosophical, and practical reasons for this ambivalence toward Western education exist that have far more to do with failure and attrition rates than have been acknowledged. In teaching English, we deny or negate the students' own tribal languages. Toadlena writes that for Navajo students, "English often represents more than the usual freshman irritant. It is a symbol of oppression and, as such, is a formidable stumbling block" (1). "Even today," she adds, there is no choice about learning English. While for most Americans learning a second language is not a requirement for economic survival, for the Navajo student, it is a must. It is not a cultural imposition suggesting that the individual give up something of who he is in order to survive. For the Navajo students, surviving has to do with being able to operate adequately within a different value system foreign to them. (1)

The goals of Navajo education are actually broader than our own: they include a deeper understanding of and appreciation for Western as well as Navajo history, culture, language, and literacy; an understanding of the importance of the Navajo values of equality, balance, sharing, cooperation, kinship, and high ethical standards; and the building of students' self-confidence and inner strength. Self-confidence and inner strength are important to Navajo people because they believe that before individuals can go out and build or contribute to their community, they must build their own centers. Only after building a strong personal foundation can they focus on livelihood, and only then on building community or nation. Also considered absolutely essential to a quality education is the application of knowledge. Clearly, Navajos raised to believe that this is the nature of a quality education will be disillusioned when they enter institutions of higher education that negate, deny, or exclude their native values and beliefs.

Navajo students may be ambivalent about Western education for practical reasons, too. Success in college can cost the student a great deal in terms of family and culture, and it is not hard to understand why they might not be especially eager to pay the price. Success in a Western institution, too often, means leaving home and traditional ways behind. It means assimilation into a dominant culture that values materialism, and that, to many Navajos' way of thinking, focuses on technological development at the expense of other equally or more important ends.

How should educators address students' ambivalence toward Western education? I'm not sure, but it is my opinion that as long as the ambivalence remains hidden or unstated, it constitutes an obstacle to students' success. It helps when the instructor understands his or her place in the larger historical context and when the instructor understands the reasons for his or her students' ambivalence. Perhaps if we acknowledge up front that the United States education system has been used as a tool for all-out assimilation and affirm that that is not our purpose, emphasize that SAE can be used as a tool to resist assimilation and preserve Navajo tradition, and show students how writing skills can help students meet the needs of their families, communities, and nations, we can make a difference. On a practical level, this might mean having Navajo students use reading skills to analyze and interpret government documents for community members at

Chapter Houses and then use their Navajo literacy skills to translate government documents from English into Navajo. Students could also be taught to use their English skills to write letters to newspaper editors, members of Congress, and other public officials to express their views. If we can make English writing skills relevant, perhaps we can retain more Navajo students.

Conclusion

Navajos and other Native Americans have a great deal to contribute to their own communities and to the larger society.[3] But are we doing enough to mitigate the barriers between Navajos and a college degree? Statistics indicate that we are not: five years ago, the Native American high school student dropout rate, at 35.5 percent, was over twice that of Euro-American students and higher than that of any other United States ethnic or racial group; and according to the Navajo Nation's 1990 Census Report, 56.5 percent of the adults living on the reservation do not have high school degrees, and only 5.5 percent have a bachelor's degree or higher. In 1993, an unpublished study of composition courses at the University of New Mexico conducted by the Orality/Literacy Committees[4] found that Native Americans are two and a half times more likely to drop or fail those courses than their Anglo counterparts — and because it is the only course required of all college graduates at many institutions, failure to pass composition means failure to attain a degree.

It is time for English instructors, when faced with students from radically different cultural backgrounds and whose needs differ from those of mainstream students, to stop blaming the high failure and attrition rates solely on bilingualism, substandard schooling, low self-esteem, lack of familiarity with SAE, and/or lack of motivation — it is time to look beyond these factors and work to mitigate all the barriers that all minority culture students face.

Notes

1. This situation is not unique to the Navajo people: 221 different Indian languages are known today, and before European colonization, the number was as high as 2,000 (Snipp 41).
2. Mainstream institutions in the Southwest (including the University of New Mexico, Northern Arizona University, and Arizona State University, where the Native American student populations are relatively high), have established composition sections specifically for Native American students. Typically taught by instructors familiar with Native American students' cultures and their dialects, most of these sections use readings and create assignments geared toward Indians and issues that affect them. Problems associated with this strategy include first the assumption of the existence of the "Native American," when the term actually refers to four hundred

different Native American peoples in the United States alone, each with different customs, beliefs, languages, and English dialects. Second, each student comes to college with different levels of traditionalism and assimilation into dominant culture, and the more assimilated often don't need or want to enroll in a special section of composition.

3. What impact, for example, would the Native American belief that before a decision is made, its impact on the next seven generations must be considered have on, say, the development or use of nuclear power? The federal deficit? The stockpiling of nuclear weapons?

4. An interdisciplinary group of interested University of New Mexico faculty and graduate students organized the Orality/Literacy Committee in 1992 to explore the causes and to devise appropriate responses to a perceived high failure rate for Native Americans in UNM composition courses.

Works Cited

Gilliland, Hap. *Teaching the Native American.* 2nd ed. Dubuque, IA: Kendall, 1992.

Navajo Nation Government. 1990 Census: Population and Housing Characteristics of the Navajo Nation. Scottsdale, AZ: Printing, 1993.

Smith, Patricia Clark. "Icons in the Canyon." *The New Criticism and Contemporary Literary Theory: Connections and Continuities.* Ed. William J. Spurlin and Michael Fischer. New York: Garland, 1995. 275–95.

Snipp, C. Matthew. *American Indians: The First of This Land.* New York: Sage, 1989.

Toadlena, Della. "Why Navajo Students Have Problems with Writing." Unpublished manuscript, 1989.

Classroom Activities

Many developing writers from a variety of cultural backgrounds have had to deal with cultural issues and concerns about assimilation in regard to learning Standard American English. Thurston suggests that instructors "acknowledge up front that the United States education system has been used as a tool for all-out assimilation." In this way, instructors can begin to recognize their students' concerns and "ambivalence toward Western education." However, Thurston advises, we need to go even further, to "show students how writing skills can help students meet the needs of their families, communities, and nations. . . ." Classroom activities that inspired Thurston's pedagogy include translating government documents for those who cannot read or write in English (which uses both Navajo and English literacy skills) and writing "letters to newspaper editors, members of Congress, and other public officials to express their views." Most communities have immediate, if often hidden needs, for those with literacy skills, and opportunities exist for developing writers to intervene in purposeful ways. Ask students to research what kinds of literacy issues exist in their home communities. Students can work together to make lists and brainstorm ideas for service learning projects. If your college or university also has a service learning or volunteer services office, invite a representative from that office to speak to your class on the literacy needs in your community — and on how students can help. Students can keep journals of their service learning work and can complete research-oriented tasks related to their service learning projects. Thurston's letter-writing project would also work well in conjunction with this activity.

Thinking about Teaching

Thurston suggests that teachers need to confront their own "often unconscious" ethnocentrism, which may include the privileged Eurocentric and Western notions of the teaching of writing and reading. One means of doing this work is to learn as much as you can about your students' cultural backgrounds. Students should not be expected to do this work for their teachers (especially since many students are still engaged in the lifelong process of learning more about their own cultural heritage); rather, teachers can take on this task themselves, either individually or in groups. In addition, you and your colleagues may wish to examine your views concerning stereotypes. What can be done to help us face our fears, intolerance, impatience, or lack of understanding of students from cultural, racial, religious, or class backgrounds different from our own — and to create an environment in which we internalize and then model tolerance, cultural appreciation, and community?* All of these goals, Thurston offers, go a long way toward promoting a positive learning climate for students and for increasing retention. Reflect on these issues in your teaching journal, and share your ideas with other instructors and students.

---

*I am indebted to Susan Peterson and Lynne Shivers, English department faculty at the Community College of Philadelphia, who ran workshops on confronting stereotypes for students and instructors when I was a junior faculty member at the College in the mid-1990s. Participating in forums that gave people of many backgrounds the opportunity to speak and listen openly with each other is an experience that has inspired my teaching ever since. [Editor's note]

12

Teaching ESL and Generation 1.5 Students

E SL and Generation 1.5 students come from a great diversity of backgrounds, as the Alternative Table of Contents for this edition of *Teaching Developmental Writing: Background Readings* indicates. English language learners may be international students; refugees; immigrant residents; and students who were born and raised in the United States but who are multilingual, speaking languages other than English in their home communities. This chapter accounts for some of this diversity by focusing on pedagogies that value a range of students' experiences with learning English as a second language. The focus here is not on the "grammatical correctness" of English language learners' writing; instead, readers will encounter pedagogies that emphasize student-centered learning and writing as a means of gaining fluency in English.

Yu Ren Dong asks students to write literacy autobiographies about their experiences with writing and reading in their first language so that students can understand the continuum of the writing process. Throughout this article the voices of Dong's students speak clearly and poignantly about their experiences with literacy in their countries of origin. Beth Hartman and Elaine Tarone, in excerpts from a longer article, examine the intersections of high school and college writing for Generation 1.5 learners whose first language is Vietnamese; they offer a set of best practices and recommendations for facilitating the high school-to-college transition for these English language learners. Together these essays demonstrate a pedagogy that focuses on English language fluency and that values the whole student. The student voices and the recommendations of teachers represented in these selections help to tell an important part of the story.

The Need to Understand ESL Students' Native Language Writing Experiences

Yu Ren Dong

"Teachers are quick to recognize ESL students' grammatical errors in their writing," writes Yu Ren Dong, "but often they are slow to get to know these students, who differ widely in their expectations of schooling, their views of the roles of teacher and students, their reading and writing experiences back home, their learning style preferences, and how all of these impact their learning to read and write in English." To ameliorate this situation in her own classroom, Dong invites students to write about "how they learned to write in their native language . . . and about the differences they perceived when comparing writing in their native language to writing in English." Her article, first published in Teaching English in the Two-Year College *in 1999, documents her study of twenty-six first-year students at a four-year university who had come from a wide variety of backgrounds, had had extensive training in reading and writing in their first language, and had also attended New York City public high schools. Throughout the article, the voices of Dong's students speak clearly and poignantly about their experiences with literacy in their native countries. For instance, a student from Russia writes: "I had one great teacher. . . . She gave us such nice topics that everyone wanted to write. The teacher told us: 'You think you are students? No! You are writers!'" Dong's strategies for understanding students' literacy histories will certainly benefit native English speakers as well as ESL students.*

Introduction

I remember a high school assignment that I dreaded. I had to write about my experiences in life and how they influenced my life. I thought to myself "What real experience did I have in my life?" I sat down for days without anything. But a week later I started to write a list of things that I did when I was young back in my home country, and soon I began to see that there were a lot of things on the list. I began to write my paper and was surprised to see how wonderfully it turned out. This was the most satisfying assignment that I had ever done. This was because I found out something about myself that influenced me tremendously in my life. From that I learned that when writing you can find out more about yourself.

Like the above first-year ESL student, many non-English-speaking students come to college composition with rich home cultural, educational, language, and literacy backgrounds. In particular, some have acquired sophisticated literacy skills in their native languages. Research on second language acquisition in academic settings done by Cummins and Collier has shown that students with native literacy skills often acquire English language skills faster than those without native literacy skills. Unfortunately, these students' native language and literacy learning experiences are often not considered when planning instruction.

Teachers are quick to recognize ESL students' grammatical errors in their writing, but often they are slow to get to know these students, who differ widely in their expectations of schooling, their views of the roles of teacher and students, their prior schooling, their reading and writing experiences back home, their learning style preferences, and how all of these impact their learning to read and write in English. As composition instructors encounter more and more linguistically and culturally diverse students in their classrooms, they must attempt to learn about these students' literacy backgrounds and to develop strategies to make good use of what the students learned back home in order to accelerate their learning of English reading and writing skills. Such knowledge is particularly important not only for these students to succeed in American schools, but also for building a classroom environment where diverse educational, cultural, and literacy backgrounds are valued and become resources rather than problems.

Method

In order to investigate ESL students' native literacy learning experiences, I invited twenty-six first-year college students at a four-year college in New York City to write autobiographies describing how they learned to write in their native language. I wanted to find out how these students learned to read and write in their native countries, what writing assignments they liked, and what the differences in writing were between their native language and English. The twenty-six students who participated in the research project had all had extensive schooling in their home countries before coming to America. Most of them had acquired a high level of native language literacy skills and, therefore, were competent readers and writers in their native languages, which included Chinese, Korean, French/Creole, Hebrew, Italian, Russian, Polish, and Spanish. The majority of them also attended and graduated from New York City public high schools. Their average American educational experience was about two-and-a-half years. Therefore, they were able to compare two educational systems and two sets of language and literacy learning experiences, native and United States.

In order to elicit students' responses, I wrote a letter to these students with a series of probing questions (see Appendix). I asked them specifically about how they learned to write in their native language, about the first things they remember writing, about the most satisfying piece of writing in their native language, and about the differences they perceived when comparing writing in their native language to writing in English.

Students were more responsive about their learning experiences with writing in the following three major areas:

- writing instruction in their native languages,

- most satisfying writing assignments in their native languages,

- differences between writing in their native language and in English.

Writing Instruction in Native Languages

Despite a wide range of native literacy learning experiences noted by these twenty-six students, a common theme emerged: students all had had some kind of native language writing instruction before coming to the United States. Very often this instruction began in the elementary school, as one student wrote:

> I was only four year old when I started to go to school in my country, Peru. When I went to the first grade, my teacher began to teach us the vowels and then the consonants of the alphabet. Then the teacher proceeded to teach the class how to form simple words like: mama and papa and then Mi mama me mima, which means my mother cares for me. In the second grade, I was taught to read simple stories and later my teacher taught the class components of a sentence. We learned about the verb, the subject, and the predicate. It was a bit hard for most seven year old, including me to learn these grammar rules. . . . By the time I finished the third grade, I knew how to form complicated sentences and how to construct paragraphs that made sense. I was also able to read books that were more complex, the newspapers and signs in the street that once I wondered what they meant. In my fourth grade, my teacher taught the class words that were similar in meanings and I learned a variety of words quickly and also learned how to use them in sentences too.

Reflecting on their native literacy learning experiences, many students revealed the distinctive ways that their teachers back home used to teach them how to write in their native languages. For example, the student from Haiti recalled writing instruction in his schooling like this:

> I learned speak Creole first, but went to school learning French. Some of the first things that I remember writing were about my family. I was about five year old then. The teacher asked us to describe my family and

the games that I played. . . . The teachers in my country (Haiti) would have me recite what I had written for homework. Haitian teachers are also very strict. Some would have me rewrite word-for-word what I had to read the previous day. If I could not write and remember, I would be beaten or be sent to detention. Sometimes a teacher would sent a student to stand in the corner on one foot for fifteen minutes in order to get students to do their work.

Several Russian students revealed a strong focus on language and structure in native writing instruction, for example:

Usually teachers in Russia paid more attention to the grammar mistakes. Therefore they helped us how to use correct words. We had some special orthographic rules. Teachers helped us to combine sentences and spelling. . . . At school back in Russia, we had a lot of homework and sometimes the teachers gave us the permission so that we could stay behind and study in the afternoon. The classmates who had excellent marks helped us to do better work by tutoring. . . . Some of the teachers who didn't have families stayed with us and gave extra help.

One Russian student noted the excitement of learning to write in Russian and the high expectations that her teacher maintained for the students:

In Russia, students write a lot. In my middle school years, we used to write compositions for ten to fifteen pages. I had one great teacher. She did not give us any unusual techniques, but she explained to each and every student any mistakes he or she made, and told us how to write better. She gave us such nice topics that everyone wanted to write. The teacher told us: "You think you are students? No! You are writers!"

Students also described a range of writing tasks assigned by their teachers back home. These assignments included: diary/journal, literature responses, research papers, aesthetic prose, and essays. A Korean student recalled a progression from diary writing to writing a book report in her schooling back in Korea and how the teacher motivated the students to write:

I began to write in Korean when I was about nine year old. I had to write my diary as homework. I wrote almost everyday, and my teacher looked over and gave me some comments. When I was a middle school student, I used to write about my impression of certain books that we read. There were two or three contests about this type of writing on certain books every month. The teacher gave a prize to a student who was the best writer of the month.

A Polish student wrote about a variety of writing assignments given by her teachers and the expectation of how to write a literary analysis in her high school:

> I started to learn how to write in Polish, my native language, during the last few years in the elementary school. The teacher gave us a lot of freedom in our writing. Our assignments could be a letter, a dialogue, a monologue, or defending a position. Later we had to write what the authors point in the writing the book was and what the main characters and ideas in the book were and how we could compare it to our lives and our experiences and what our personal opinion was about the book.

A Russian student described a kind of research-oriented essay assignment in his high school experience:

> In my high school days back home, we were assigned to write essays. The essays in Russian were usually much longer and complicated. For example, we wrote a book about the life of Tolstoy, a famous Russian writer. It was about twenty-one pages long and very complicated. I had to say a lot of different information from different sources like encyclopedias.

A Chinese student confirmed the similar writing assignments that she had back home and in the United States. However, she mentioned a different type of writing that she was taught to write:

> Back in China at middle school and high school, we learned how to write a kind of prose, we called san wen, an interpretation of a natural scenery using your own voice. This was a literary genre created by classical Chinese writer Zhu Zi Qing. Reading his writing, for example his masterpiece "The moonlight over the lotus pond," I had this (transactional) feeling with the writer and enjoyed the way the writer put the words on the paper. It was beautiful.

Several students noted a close connection between reading and writing when talking about their progression in learning how to write in their native language. These students said that they were taught to use literature for vocabulary development and imitating certain styles of writing. A strong emphasis on reading to write was shown in these students' reflections as shown in the following Chinese student's autobiography:

> Reading is important because it lets you know how a nice piece should be like. You can't write down something nice without knowing what is nice. It's easy to read some stories as entertainment, but it's not easy to catch the ways that how these good writers wrote. My teachers back in China helped us know how these writers wrote by explaining their ideas and how they chose words with similar meanings.

Reading was closely related to writing. Several students noted the importance of reading to write and imitating the style of the writers:

When I was more proficient in Spanish, my native language, I was taught to read the famous authors' works like Miguel de Cervantes and other famous Spanish novelists works. They influenced me a lot in my style of writing. I fell in love with the way they used the words in their novels. Since then, I started to use complex sentence structures in Spanish with a great many fancy words. Thanks to them I gained a vast knowledge of the Spanish vocabulary.

A Bangladeshi student recalled how he took trouble to bring books to America to use reading to refresh his reading and writing skills:

Now I write letters to my friends back home and I also read novels in my native language. The best writing practice of my language is to read novels. When I came over here, I brought about two hundred books with me and now I am rereading them again and again since I don't have more books to read. By doing that, I can still feel about my country and keep up with my writing.

Most Satisfying Writing Assignments in Their Native Languages

Reading through these students' writing autobiographies, I noticed a consistency. Though many of these students might not be verbal in class or perform well in English, they were already successful writers in their native languages. Many of them continued writing in their native languages after coming to the United States. Students told stories of how the most satisfying piece of writing that they wrote made a difference in their perception of writing and motivated them to become successful writers. For example, a Polish student recalled:

I still remember my first favorite book on love and the assignment based on that book back home in Poland. It was an old Celtic myth "Tristan and Tholdo" and "Tristan 1964". My writing was read in front of the class, that made me feel like a really good writer. When I finished elementary school, I already knew that I liked to write and my papers were pretty good. According to that I chose a high school with a special writing program. I wrote a lot, especially poetry. One of my poems "Angel" got the first award in school poetry contest.

A Russian student wrote about competing in a writing contest:

When I was twelve, I read a story and I hated the end of it. So, I rewrote the end of the story and made it a happy one. There was a writing contest among all the school students of the Soviet Union. I sent in my story. I was not among the first winners, but I still got a prize of one hundred rubles. It was big money for me, a small girl who have never had more than a ruble.

A Chinese student revealed how he used writing to express his feelings and passion to win his girlfriend back:

> I love to write a lyric prose. My most satisfying school assignment came when I was in the secondary school back in Hong Kong. I had a girlfriend back then and we had wonderful days together. But we broke up after a while. I was so hurt. One day, my Chinese teacher asked us to write a letter to someone we love. I wrote about my ex-girlfriend and I didn't know how to stop or did not even want to stop. I said all the words that I wanted to say to her and I listened to my feelings from my heart. Finally this composition was marked a highest grade in class and my teacher encouraged me to send it to the newspaper and I did. A few weeks later, my writing was printed on the prose section of the newspaper. My girlfriend was so touched by all this that we went back together. From writing that piece I learned how powerful writing is and I liked to express myself in writing.

The most satisfying writing assignment was also remembered by many students as the most challenging assignment. The challenge stimulated their interest and motivated them to achieve, as shown in the following:

> The most satisfying school assignment that I can remember was when I had to do a research project in my high school back home. The project was about some of the pre-Inca cultures in my country. In the field research I had to go to some ruins in the mountains with my fellow students. The trip was fun and the ruins were a nice place to visit with lots of tourists around. In my group I had to be the leader because I was the one with more background about the subject. At the end our research paper was about forty pages long, full of graphs and pictures.

Differences between Writing in a Native Language and Writing in English

Home literacy stories told by these students also revealed their struggles with writing in English. Besides learning a different language and writing system, students indicated that often the differences between their native language and English baffled them and created more barriers in learning to write in English. For example, comparing her writing in Korean and writing in English, Kim talked about her struggle with the whole process of writing in English:

> It is quite different to write in Korean and in English. When I write in Korean, I do not worry about my grammar or vocabularies. I just write in papers what I think in my head. Some grammar makes me confused, but I don't think it twice because I know that I can express my thought anyway. However, writing in English takes long time because I have to think about grammar and vocabulary. Every time I write, I have trouble

with some sentences because I can't express my thoughts in well organized sentences. So I rewrite three or four times. Also grammar in Korea and in English is different. For example, in Korea, a verb comes after an object. There isn't a subject-verb agreement.

In addition to language differences and rhetorical and stylistic differences in writing, especially the impact of writing instruction on students' perceptions of what was judged as a piece of good writing, teacher expectations varied from culture to culture. For example, a Polish student wrote:

> There are a lot of things similar but there are a lot of things different too between the two languages. Sometimes when I write, I like to write it in general not specific. . . . In Polish, we wrote papers, we didn't have to give statistics or write sentences specific, what happened first and then the next, and examples. We were supposed to just give clues rather than being specific in Polish. A lot of times we had to write about our own opinions in Polish. So our own opinions should be counted as good too. But here I had to write about in more specific ways, especially when I don't know how to pick examples from a lot of things. I didn't think of it when I first came to America, because I thought Americans should write the same way as Polish people do. What can be different? But right now I am really seeing the difference.

A Chinese student recalled something considered in American schools as taboo but in her culture a common practice for developing writing skills:

> In my high school years, my Chinese teacher used to talking about three parts of essay writing, my opinion, proving it and the conclusion. It looked like writing in English, but it doesn't require a lot of examples or details and we can use other's words without stating where they come from because they are something everyone knows.

Another Chinese student further commented on writing instruction she received in China and how that influenced her learning to write in Chinese:

> My Chinese teachers back in high school asked us to use strong supporting details from old times. For example, if you want to write: The soldiers who are not ambitious are not good soldiers. This topic demands you give historical examples to show your point, such as Napoleon and many Chinese historical figures to illustrate that those who did not have high goals in their lives, cannot succeed anything. Very often you don't remember the exact words such as what Napoleon said, but the teacher did not look for those details. In Chinese, good writing often begins with a historical background information from the past to the present. Then the writer leads the reader into the thesis.

Conclusion/Implications

Even though the scale of this native literacy investigation was small, the findings reveal something worth noticing and exploring. Stories coming from students' own voices were telling. They offered a glimpse into the educational systems and cultural values from these students' perspectives. The findings, especially in cross-cultural writing differences, confirmed some results obtained from second language writing research done by Ballard and Clanchy, Carson, and Matalene. The students' insights into their native writing instruction, such as the use of sources for learning to write, the methods used in teaching students how to write, and the ways of motivating students to write, give composition teachers information about different ways of learning and viewing literacy in different cultures. Instead of treating these different ways of knowing as deficient or ignoring the impact of these ways of knowing on students' learning to write in English, we need to, as Matalene suggests, "try to understand and appreciate, to admit the relativity of our own rhetoric, and to realize that logics different from our own are not necessarily illogical" (806). It is only by doing so that we can begin to understand ESL students and to design instruction that is responsive to their needs.

First, in dealing with nonnative students, composition instructors need information about students' native literacy learning in order to tailor their instruction. In getting to know the students and their home literacy backgrounds, teachers send the message that ESL students' home literacy backgrounds are acknowledged and valued rather than dismissed or ignored. This sharing can be used as an activity of cross-cultural literacy awareness for both the teacher and the students in the classroom. Such sharing is crucial in building a community of learners so that students who are outsiders can play the roles of insiders whose native literacy and native cultural backgrounds are considered rich resources and not obstacles.

Second, differences in writing and in writing instruction across languages and cultures challenge teachers to expand their teaching repertoire and to diversify teaching strategies when dealing with diverse students. Composition instructors can pinpoint areas for more focused and individualized instruction according to each individual student's needs and background. For example, the Polish student's native literacy instruction is different from the Chinese student's. As Matalene argues, composition teachers need to be aware of not only students' ways of knowing, but also the social, cultural, historical, and educational contexts where students' schooling has been situated. In doing so, teachers can gain deeper understanding of the students' worlds of learning to write, such as their perceptions of the role of memory, the nature of writing, and the issues of authenticity and ownership of the text. Teachers need to incorporate such knowledge into their teaching, helping students to be consciously aware of the differences in writing between their native language and English and to understand the need to adapt to a new discourse in the new culture.

Third, students from different educational and cultural systems often bring with them a whole set of expectations, including anticipated teacher behaviors and preferences for literacy learning in the new culture. Therefore, teachers need to find ways to accommodate students' needs and make good use of students' strengths. For example, giving students choices in reading and writing assignments and allowing students to use their native language in writing at the initial stage can ease the transition and build confidence on the part of learners.

Fourth, one difficulty identified by these ESL students in their autobiographies was their lack of basic working vocabulary and knowledge about the English language. This points to the need for providing ESL students the time and the opportunity to learn new English vocabulary and to use it in their writing. Effective ways of teaching vocabulary might be keeping a reading vocabulary journal, teaching reading for contextual clues, designing language awareness activities focusing on major language points in reading and writing, and training in dictionary and thesaurus skills. All these provide the language assistance which ESL students desperately need.

Fifth, in the reading and literature oriented curriculum, the purposes and functions of reading need to be expanded to address a wide range of demands and needs, such as reading for pleasure, reading for aesthetic appreciation, reading for comprehension, reading for learning and critical thinking, and reading for writing. Writing needs to be brought into the reading curriculum. Teachers need to make explicit connections between reading and writing.

As indicated by the majority of these ESL students' autobiographies, the students would like their American teachers to understand their struggle with learning the new language, literacy skills, and academic content at the same time. One way of building the understanding is for teachers to learn about the students' native language and literacy backgrounds. The more teachers know, the better they can serve ESL students.[1]

Appendix

Writing Prompt for Native Writing Experience

Dear Student,

Thank you very much for having written a composition on your journey to become a writer in English at the beginning of this semester. I was impressed by your achievement in English, especially in learning to write in a language that is not your native language. Your writing makes me want to know more about your writing, specifically, about your native language writing. In your writing, please try to answer the following questions:

What is your native language?

How did you learn to write in your native language?

What writing assignments did your teacher back home assign to you?

How did your teacher go about teaching you how to write in your native language?

What are the differences in writing in English and in your native language?

Do you write in your native language now? If so, what do you write about and to whom?

Note

1. I would like to thank Kevin Birth, Sue L. Goldhaber, and Norman Lewis for their help with this project, and the students who participated in the study. I am also grateful for valuable input from Judith Summerfield in the course of the research process and to Myra Zarnowski in the course of writing this article.

Works Cited

Ballard, Brigid, and John Clanchy. "Assessment by Misconception: Cultural Influences and Intellectual Traditions." *Assessing Second Language Writing in Academic Contexts.* Ed. Liz Hamp-Lyons. Norwood: Ablex, 1990. 19–36.

Carson, Joan G. "Becoming Biliterate: First Language Influences." *Second Language Writing* 1 (1992): 37–60.

Collier, Virginia Patricia. "Age and Rate of Acquisition of Second Language for Academic Purposes." *TESOL Quarterly* 21 (1987): 617–41.

Cummins, James. "The Role of Primary Language Development in Promoting Education Success for Language Minority Students." *Schooling and Language Minority Students: A Theoretical Framework.* Ed. California State Department of Education. Los Angeles: California State University, Evaluation, Dissemination, and Assessment Center. 1981. 3–49.

Matalene, Carolyn. "Contrastive Rhetoric: An American Writing Teacher in China." *College English* 47 (1985): 789–808.

Classroom Activities

Have students write a narrative on "their native learning literacy experiences." First they can brainstorm a list of important features of their first language (Does their first language include articles? How many letters does the alphabet have? Are there masculine and feminine forms of words?) and of their cultural background (political situations in their homelands, celebration of holidays and rites of passage, favorite foods and activities). In discussing these lists, ask students to describe the relationships they see between language and culture and to explain how language is a medium of expression for culture. After reflecting on these ideas, students can begin to draw connections between language as a form of identity and how they learned to write in their native language.

Thinking about Teaching

Not all ESL students have attained written fluency in their language of origin. This concern may be especially important for students who have experienced interruptions in their education, for a variety of reasons. Students in this situation may share a great deal with native speakers of English who have not attained written fluency in English and who are often enrolled in classes for developing writers. If you already teach native speakers of English, note in your teaching journal the similarities and differences that you see as these students grapple with written fluency in English. If you teach exclusively in an ESL program, consider initiating discussions with teachers in a basic writing program. Similarly, basic writing teachers may want to begin speaking on a regular basis with teachers of ESL students. Work together to create shared conversations on issues of common concern. Keep track of similarities and differences in approaches to pedagogy. Make sure to hold the literacy narratives of your students clearly in mind as you work together to discuss solutions. Share the results of these conversations with students so that you can have their input as well.

From **Preparation for College Writing**

Beth Hartman and Elaine Tarone

In these excerpts from a longer article (first published in Generation 1.5 Meets College Composition*), Beth Hartman and Elaine Tarone demonstrate the disconnects in the teaching practices of ESL teachers, mainstream English teachers, and mainstream content-course teachers at a public high school. They compare and contrast these practices with the academic expectations of college-level writing courses and then offer pedagogical suggestions to support students' transitions from high school to college. While Hartman and Tarone studied teaching practices, they kept the needs of students at the forefront.*

The teachers in this study worked with students whose first language was Vietnamese and whom Hartman and Tarone describe as "limited English proficient (LEP) students . . . [who] are moving through U.S. pub-

*lic high schools and entering institutions of higher education" (99) —
elsewhere identified as Generation 1.5. The purpose of their study is to
"obtain a snapshot of the teaching practices that existed in the school at
the time of the study, and use this information to help inform college and
university teachers attempting to help LEP students coming from similar
public school experiences to become more academically proficient in the
area of writing" (103). Hartman and Tarone conclude with a set of recommended teaching practices that challenge us to facilitate intellectually
challenging environments for English language learners.*

Importance of Teaching the Writing Process

The ESL teachers described very little process writing in the ESL
classes, even at the upper levels, and even then this was usually just
one draft that was corrected and revised. This lack of quantity of
process writing contrasted sharply with the situation in the mainstream English classes, where teachers reported using the process
approach, including prewriting exercises and multiple revisions, routinely at all grade levels.

A particularly important step in the writing process is prewriting.
Zamel (1982) reviewed case studies of successful college-level ESL
writers and noticed that all of those students talked about the value
of classroom discussion of a particular composition topic before they
were asked to write about it. She stresses that this is a crucial aspect
of teaching composition, and notes that methods based on the traditional read–analyze–write model ignore this step. However, although
mainstream English classes did stress prewriting activities, these did
not appear to be of primary importance in either the ESL classes or in
mainstream content classes. Mainstream content teachers indicated
in their comments that they did not have the time to give these students the attention they needed in prewriting, and we have already
noted that the concentration of ESL writing instruction on the controlled end of the continuum seemed to preclude much process writing, including prewriting activity.

The ESL classroom would be a particularly good place for the use
of prewriting activities, because in these activities the students can
get the help they need in clarifying their ideas, learning culturally
appropriate ways of expressing them, and developing suitable vocabulary — in other words, in prewriting discussions, students have the
opportunity to learn the values and assumptions of the culture of the
mainstream classroom, and strategies for communicating successfully
in writing in that culture, and ESL teachers are particularly good
resources for that learning.

The revision aspect of process writing was also quite different in the
ESL classes and the mainstream English classes. The ESL teachers
appeared to be focused on grammatical and structural errors in asking

students to revise their writing, rather than on teaching writing revision as a process of discovering meaning or learning to couch their message in more culturally appropriate forms. From the comments made by the ESL teachers in the interviews, revision was apparently viewed more as a correction process than a learning one, a process focused primarily upon identification of error. Taylor (1981) says:

> A major result of a writing program which focuses primarily on form is an insufficient emphasis on content which would create the opportunity for students to experience the process of discovering meaning and then of struggling to give it form through revision. (p. 9)

Kroll (1991) points out that editing or correcting grammar errors on the first draft can be a counterproductive activity, possibly exacerbating whatever insecurities students might have about their writing and drawing their attention away from other kinds of revision work such as communication of ideas and organization. She recommends correcting grammar errors on the final draft after the content has been corrected. When teachers view revision as primarily a process of error correction, the students may develop the idea that revision is a punishment for failure to do it right the first time rather than learn that revision is a valuable process in learning to write.

Writing as a way of discovering meaning and revision as a method of learning to express it more clearly is especially valuable to LEP students. Feedback during the revision process can provide L2 learners with valuable input as they plan and organize their writing at the conceptual level, learning new cultural models for expressing their thoughts. Indeed, Leki (1992) suggests that LEP writers need more work with writing (i.e., idea expression) than they do with accuracy of language forms. She stated that native-speaker students need a concept- and strategy-focused stage in the revision process to help them become socialized to the majority culture's norms and values for academic mainstream classes.

> the self-reflection taught in process approach classes functions in part to socialize young native students into their own society, to help them situate themselves in current social and political debates, and thereby to prepare them to take up various roles in this society. (p. 7)

We suggest that immigrant students could also benefit from such self-reflection.

The Role of Academic Content in Writing Assignments

Although it is important that immigrant students learn the writing process, it is also important that they be exposed to authentic writing tasks from the content areas so they become aware of the schemata, purposes, and rhetorical conventions these classes assume (Reid, 1992). In this survey, the teachers in the mainstream content classes indicated that there was a variety of writing styles LEP students needed to be able to use in their classes. These included short-answer questions for tests, comparison and contrast, critiques, and term papers. Mainstream content teachers also indicated that they did not teach these writing styles.

Current ESL pedagogy stresses the importance of using content material in the ESL classroom. However, only one ESL teacher in our interviews indicated that she used content material in the teaching of writing in her ESL class, and she noted that this is where these students seemed to have the most difficulty.

More efforts to teach writing in ESL classes by using content material from mainstream classes would probably help to shift the focus on form to more concern with the communication of ideas and the knowledge of subject matter that these students need to be able to demonstrate in their mainstream classes. LEP students may have problems writing for these classes because of poor language skills or lack of knowledge about content material. However, even if students have strong language skills and content knowledge, they may still have a "limited or skewed perception" of what is expected of their writing in mainstream classes. The problem of communicating successfully may be due to their lack of familiarity with the culturally accepted forms or modes of academic prose (Reid, 1992). In this survey, one of the mainstream English teachers notes the difficulty Southeast Asian American students have with writing in a "logical mode," and feels this may be due to cultural differences (cf. Atkinson, 1997, for a discussion of the nature of "critical thinking skills" and the pitfalls involved in trying to teach them).

Mainstream teachers commented that LEP students were hesitant to speak up in class. However, an ESL teacher stated that her students always spoke up in class quite readily. Possibly small homogeneous groups gave these students more confidence to speak up in ESL class. Possibly the ESL class allowed them to develop their English proficiency in a less competitive setting. Such an opportunity to express themselves on academic subjects would be an important factor in the development of writing skills (Miramontes, 1993). Adamson (1993) urges ESL teachers to teach language through content while these students are still in ESL so they may gain the confidence they need to become more active participants in mainstream classrooms.

An effective way to teach language through content might be by providing adjunct courses for upper level LEP students (Murie, 1998). In an adjunct course, LEP students are concurrently enrolled in ESL and content courses. The ESL and content teachers work together to coordinate a program based on the language requirements of the LEP students in content courses. The activities of the language classes are then determined by the requirements of the content courses. Such courses would provide ESL teachers with a more accurate notion of what students are struggling with in mainstream classes, and provide the opportunity for a wider range of contextualized writing assignments.

Variety of Types of Writing

The ESL teachers stated that in ESL classes students were exposed primarily to descriptive or narrative writing, and little if any argumentative or analytical writing. According to mainstream teachers, in mainstream English classes and mainstream content classes, students are required to do comparison–contrast, analytical, definitional, cause–effect, and even some research project type writing.

At the university level, a focus on critical writing and thinking skills appears to be a top priority in the language curriculum according to a survey by Snow (1988). ESL teachers in secondary schools such as the one studied here should provide learners with more exposure to a wider range of types of writing. Here again, it is possible that students would need to spend more time in ESL classes and adjunct ESL/content classes in order to be exposed to this wider range of writing instruction.

Role of One-on-One Tutoring in Writing

When mainstream teachers were asked to make recommendations for improving the writing skills of the Southeast Asian American students, the most common recommendation of these mainstream teachers was one-on-one tutoring for the students, possibly with some of the better senior class students. It is interesting that none of the ESL teachers made this recommendation.

To our knowledge, there is very little research on the use of native-speaking peers in assisting LEP students in learning written language skills. Adamson (1993), in his review of the successful academic strategies of LEP learners, found that learners benefited greatly from peer interaction. With one student, it was the most important factor in his learning. In a study of peer interaction and the oral language proficiency of Spanish-speaking elementary children, Johnson (1983) found that interethnolinguistic peer tutoring increased students' verbal interaction in English and resulted in increased vocabulary comprehension — but this was oral, not written, second language development. However, if one area where these LEP writers need help is with vocabulary and concepts (in addition to grammar and mechanics), then one-on-one peer interaction might help with this area during the process of writing, particularly in the prewriting phase. Such interaction might be of less help with the final draft, where issues of grammatical accuracy would come to the forefront, and where the ESL teacher input might be necessary.

Use of the Native Language in Teaching Writing

Some teachers mentioned situations where use of the native language was an especially effective learning strategy for the Southeast Asian American students. The use of the native language as a helpful tool in learning a second language is well supported by other studies. Auerbach (1993), in a survey of ESL literacy studies, looks at the positive results achieved when use of the native language is allowed in the ESL classroom, and calls on the field to give up the idea that instruction must be entirely in English. Perhaps we should look at the advantages of native speaking instructors or tutors and a more bilingual approach to literacy at the secondary level. Being able to discuss vocabulary and concepts in the native language is a strategy that Adamson (1993) found to be very successful in one of his case studies and is also noted by Saville-Troike (1984) as a tactic used by those students who performed best in content areas.

Implications for Teaching

Based on the patterns in the teacher responses that we have outlined we believe there are clear implications for the teaching of writing to nonnative speakers of English (particularly Southeast Asian Americans) at the secondary and at the college or university level.

1. Allow and encourage LEP students to spend more time in ESL classes to develop their literacy skills to higher levels before being mainstreamed. A consistent theme for all the ESL teachers was that they did not have enough time to teach students to write well. This would have gone far in enriching the academic proficiency of the Southeast Asian American students in the study and helped them perform better and become more active participants in their mainstream classes. At the advanced level, as LEP students are ready to move to mainstream classes, provide a bridge for the transition by offering very advanced adjunct ESL courses designed in cooperation with content area teachers.

2. Spend more time on the problems these students have with organization and content in their writing. These are the areas with which mainstream teachers are most concerned. If possible, the teaching of grammar should be integrated into all areas of the students' learning.

3. Include more process writing in the ESL writing instruction. This method of teaching writing can be valuable as a way of learning language and discovering meaning. Students need to be

encouraged to see it in that light rather than solely as a correction process. Rather than teaching writing skills prescriptively by presenting models first, allow the students to build from their own ideas and show them the models and language forms to use as they are writing to help them express their ideas.

4. In ESL classes, if a controlled to freewriting model continues to be used, move more quickly from the controlled end of the teaching continuum to the freewriting end, giving the students more opportunities to learn organizational and thinking skills by drawing from their own ideas in writing.

5. In teaching writing in ESL, use content material that the LEP students are likely to encounter in mainstream classes. Teaching writing through content with the use of simplified texts on high-interest topics will likely result in more attention paid to content and organization and on grammar in context than on grammar and structure out of context. An adjunct course provides an excellent setting for teaching writing through content.

6. LEP students need to be able to present their ideas in a logical manner not just in descriptive writing, but in a wider variety of complex rhetorical modes such as comparison–contrast, cause–effect, and argumentation in order to be ready for their mainstream writing assignments.

7. Consider using peer tutors in roles that make sense. Many of the mainstream teachers in this survey seemed to think one-on-one tutoring would be very helpful. With some organization and selection, it might be good to use native-speaker students within the school to help nonnatives, especially with the prewriting phase of a process writing assignment; such native tutors might prove an economical resource and possible a rewarding experience for the students.

8. Allow and encourage wherever possible the use of the native language. A specific example is the use of writing techniques like "reformulation."[1] Reformulation gives the learner a more active role in comparing his or her own writing with that of specific target equivalents while permitting the use of the native language. In general, the strategic use of the native language appears to be beneficial in helping ESL students understand language and concepts and this is essential for the development of academic competence.

---

[1]Gilbert (1996) provided a description of the use of the technique of reformulation in learning low intermediate writing skills in a second language. In this technique, there is a principled role for the use of the native language in combination with specific target language models.

Acknowledgments

We are grateful to Kimberly Taylor Townsend, the graduate research assistant who conducted interviews, gathered and transcribed the data that we analyzed in the chapter. We would like to thank Andrew Cohen, Bill Johnston, and the editors of this volume for their constructive comments and suggestions. Any problems, inconsistencies, or clarity issues that remain are our responsibility.

References

Adamson, H. D. (1993). *Academic competence. Theory and classroom practice: Preparing ESL Students for content courses.* New York: Longman.

Atkinson, D. (1997). A critical approach to critical thinking in TESOL. *TESOL Quarterly, 31(1),* 71–94.

Auerbach, E. (1993). Reexamining English only in the ESL classroom. *TESOL Quarterly, 27(1),* 9–13.

Johnson, D. M. (1983). Natural language learning by design: A classroom experiment in social interaction and second language acquisition. *TESOL Quarterly, 17,* 55–68.

Kroll, B. (1991). Teaching writing in the ESL context. In M. Celce-Murcia (Ed.), *Teaching English as a second or foreign language* (pp. 245–63). Boston: Heinle and Heinle.

Leki, I. (1992). *Understanding ESL writers.* Portsmouth, NH: Boynton/Cook.

Miramontes, O. (1993). ESL policies and school restructuring: Risks and opportunities for language minority students. *The Journal of Educational Issues of Language Minority Students, 12,* 77–96.

Murie, R. (1998). Strengthening the bridge: A high school–university partnership. *MinneTESOL/WiTESL Journal, 15,* 1–11.

Reid, J. (1992). Helping students write for an academic audience. In P. Richard-Amato & M. Snow (Eds.), *The multicultural classroom* (pp. 210–21). Reading, MA: Addison-Wesley.

Saville-Troike, M. (1984). What really matters in second language learning for academic achievement. *TESOL Quarterly, 18,* 199–219.

Snow, M. (1988). Content-based language instruction: Investigating the effectiveness of the adjunct model. *TESOL Quarterly, 22,* 553–74.

Taylor, B. (1981). Content and written form: A two-way street. *TESOL Quarterly, 15,* 5–13.

Zamel, V. (1982). Writing: The process of discovering meaning. *TESOL Quarterly, 16,* 195–209.

Classroom Activities

Hartman and Tarone recommend that teachers of U.S.-educated ESL (and Generation 1.5) students teach less "prescriptively," so that students learn to see writing as a process that "draw[s] from their own ideas." Eschewing a singular focus on grammar correction or writing from models, Hartman and Tarone suggest that students write more analytic and argumentative essays, skills that they will need for mainstream college-level English courses. In this vein, Hartman and Tarone also state that LEP (limited English proficient) students need to move beyond narrative and descriptive writing in order to learn a variety of complex patterns of organization.

To practice this skill, invite students to reread a narrative or descriptive essay that they have composed earlier in the course. Ask them to make a list of possible analytic and persuasive topics inspired by their earlier writing which they might write about further. For example, invite students to write a narrative about their transition from high school (or other previous life experience) to college. Then, assign students to write an essay that analyzes the transition from a more persuasive context, such as equitable access to higher education, financial aid issues, or differing instructional or social practices or some other aspect of the transition of interest to students. Moving from narrative to persuasive writing facilitates students' practice with the complex organizational skills that come from analyzing and synthesizing their own ideas.

Thinking about Teaching

Hartman and Tarone suggest teaching practices that may at first seem to be contradictory: keeping LEP students in ESL classes for longer periods of time, while also making sure that the students work with peers who speak English as a first language. At the same time, Hartman and Tarone offer the concept of "reformulation," in which LEP students use their first language in order to reformulate their ideas in the "target" language.

In your teaching journal, record your initial impressions of Hartman and Tarone's suggested practices, or write down your classroom observations if you already employ these practices or have used them in the past. In addition, you may want to explore local conditions of the high school-to-college transformation and investigate teaching practices of ESL and mainstream English teachers in the feeder high schools in your area. You also may want to consider ongoing conversations or other collaborations between your institution and the high schools in your region. With this information you can fashion a classroom practice that builds on what your students already know — and that challenges students to reflect on their own goals and processes in learning academic English.

13

Assessment

" $\underset{\text{authors}}{M}$ ore than many issues within the field of composition," write the authors of the Conference on College Composition and Communication position statement, "writing assessment evokes strong passions." Many of us continue to struggle to define and refine our own assessment strategies. We continue as well to search for the most effective ways of assessing in our discipline — that is, measuring, judging, evaluating — our students' writing proficiency. The three articles in this chapter revisit many of the issues that spark debate, including proficiency criteria, exit assessment, the writing process, portfolio review, and the impact of K–12 standardized testing implemented as a result of federal and state legislation.

This chapter begins with the CCCC Position Statement on Assessment. In 1993, the Executive Committee of the Conference on College Composition and Communication charged the CCCC Committee on Assessment with developing "an official position statement" that would help writing teachers explain assessment in composition courses to administrators and other stakeholders. This document, adopted in 1995, presents assessment in hypothetical (if not utopian) terms. The other two selections offer case studies that illustrate the material realities of assessment for both teachers and students. Kay Harley and Sally I. Cannon contend that much assessment deals with what a writer doesn't do, how his or her writing doesn't measure up, rather than with the incipient strengths of the writing, such as the developing personal voice of the writer. To explore the notion of assessment, they present a case study of Mica, a student enrolled in a pilot program that combined basic and first-year writing courses. Mica's voice resonates throughout the article, arguing for a reconsideration of what it means to be identified as a "basic writer." In excerpts from an article first published in the *Journal of Basic Writing* in 2004, Susan Naomi Bernstein examines the impact of state-mandated accountability testing on students transitioning from high school standards-based writing to college basic writing. She provides a case study of Noah, a student identified as an English language learner. Noah's testimony documents the challenges of learning English in Texas urban public schools that focus on preparation for state-mandated accountability tests. This testing system would eventually serve as a model for the No Child Left Behind Act of 2001.

CCCC Position Statement

For several years, the Conference on College Composition and Communication Committee on Assessment worked to create "an official position statement . . . that would help [writing teachers] explain writing assessment to colleagues and administrators and secure the best assessment options for students." Because teachers and administrators often seem to be at cross-purposes in defining the means and ends of writing assessment, the CCCC position statement attempts to help all parties involved reach some sort of consensus. The statement lists ten assumptions regarding writing assessment that should be considered when creating new policies and implementing new classroom practices. The rest of the document illustrates these assumptions, as the writers list how assessment implicates students, faculty, administrators, and legislators. The CCCC Committee on Assessment is forceful in its argument that institutional assessment measures should involve neither an exploitation of students and faculty nor a compromise of pedagogical integrity.

In 1993, the CCCC Executive Committee charged the CCCC Committee on Assessment with developing an official position statement on assessment. Prior to that time, members of CCCC had expressed keen interest in having a document available that would help them explain writing assessment to colleagues and administrators and secure the best assessment options for students.

Beginning in 1990 at NCTE in Atlanta, Georgia, open forums were held at both NCTE and CCCC conventions to discuss the possibility of a position statement: its nature, forms, and the philosophies and practices it might espouse. At these forums, at regular meetings, and through correspondence, over one hundred people helped develop the current document.

An initial draft of the statement was submitted to the CCCC Executive Committee at its March 1994 meeting, where it was approved in substance. The Executive Committee also reviewed a revised statement at its November 1994 meeting. An announcement in the February 1995 issue of CCC invited all CCCC members to obtain a draft of the statement and to submit their responses to the Assessment Committee. Copies of the draft statement were mailed to all 1995 CCCC Convention preregistrants, and the final draft was presented in a forum at the 1995 CCCC Convention in Washington, D.C. Changes based on discussions at that session, and at a later workshop, were incorporated into the position statement, which was subsequently approved for publication by the CCCC Executive Committee.

The CCCC Committee on Assessment acknowledges the contributions of the cochairs of the previous [1994] CCCC Committee on Assessment, Edward Nolte and Sandra Murphy. In addition, Donald Daiker provided substantial assistance as a former member of the committee.

Members of the [1995] CCCC Committee on Assessment [were]: Kathleen Blake Yancey, Chair; Arnetha Ball, Pat Belanoff, Kathleen Bell, Renee Betz, Emily Decker, Christine Farris, Thomas Hilgers, Audrey Roth, Lew Sayers, and Fred Thomas.

More than many issues within the field of composition studies, writing assessment evokes strong passions. It can be used for a variety of appropriate purposes, both inside the classroom and outside: providing assistance to students; awarding a grade; placing students in appropriate courses; allowing them to exit a course or sequence of courses; and certifying proficiency, to name some of the more obvious. But writing assessment can be abused as well: used to exploit graduate students, for instance, or to reward or punish faculty members. We begin our position statement, therefore, with a foundational claim upon which all else is built; it is axiomatic that in all situations calling for writing assessment in both two-year and four-year institutions, the primary purpose of the specific assessment should govern its design, its implementation, and the generation and dissemination of its results.

It is also axiomatic that in spite of the diverse uses to which writing assessment is put, the general principles undergirding writing assessment are similar:

> Assessments of written literacy should be designed and evaluated by well-informed current or future teachers of the students being assessed, for purposes clearly understood by all the participants; should elicit from student writers a variety of pieces, preferably over a period of time; should encourage and reinforce good teaching practices; and should be solidly grounded in the latest research on language learning.

These assumptions are explained fully in the first section below; after that, we list the rights and responsibilities generated by these assumptions; and in the third section we provide selected references that furnish a point of departure for literature in the discipline.

Assumptions

All writing assessments — and thus all policy statements about writing assessment — make assumptions about the nature of what is being assessed. Our assumptions include the following.

First, *language is always learned and used most effectively in environments where it accomplishes something the user wants to accomplish for particular listeners or readers within that environment.* The assessment of written literacy must strive to set up writing tasks, therefore, that identify purposes appropriate to and appealing to the particular students being tested. Additionally, assessment must be contextualized in terms of why, where, and for what purpose it is being undertaken; this context must also be clear to the students being assessed and to all others (i.e., stakeholders/participants) involved.

Accordingly, there is no test which can be used in all environments for all purposes, and the best "test" for any group of students may well be locally designed. The definition of "local" is also contextual; schools with common goals and similar student populations and teaching philosophies and outcomes might well form consortia for the design, implementation, and evaluation of assessment instruments even though the schools themselves are geographically separated from each other.

Second, *language by definition is social.* Assessment which isolates students and forbids discussion and feedback from others conflicts with current cognitive and psychological research about language use and the benefits of social interaction during the writing process; it also is out of step with much classroom practice.

Third, *reading — and thus, evaluation, since it is a variety of reading — is as socially contextualized as all other forms of language use.* What any reader draws out of a particular text and uses as a basis of evaluation is dependent upon how that reader's own language use has been shaped and what his or her specific purpose for reading is. It seems appropriate, therefore, to recognize the individual writing program, institution, consortium, and so forth as a community of interpreters who can function fairly — that is, assess fairly — with knowledge of that community.

Fourth, *any individual's writing "ability" is a sum of a variety of skills employed in a diversity of contexts, and individual ability fluctuates unevenly among these varieties.* Consequently, one piece of writing — even if it is generated under the most desirable conditions — can never serve as an indicator of overall literacy, particularly for high stakes decisions. Ideally, such literacy must be assessed by more than one piece of writing, in more than one genre, written on different occasions, for different audiences, and evaluated by multiple readers. This realization has led many institutions and programs across the country to use portfolio assessment.

Fifth, *writing assessment is useful primarily as a means of improving learning.* Both teachers and students must have access to the results in order to be able to use them to revise existing curricula and/or plan programs for individual students. And, obviously, if results are to be used to improve the teaching-learning environment, human and financial resources for the implementation of improvements must be in place in advance of the assessment. If resources are not available, institutions should postpone these types of assessment until they are. Furthermore, when assessment is being conducted solely for program evaluation, all students should not be tested, since a representative group can provide the desired results. Neither should faculty merit increases hinge on their students' performance on any test.

Sixth, *assessment tends to drive pedagogy.* Assessment thus must demonstrate "systemic validity"; it must encourage classroom practices that harmonize with what practice and research have demonstrated to be effective ways of teaching writing and of becoming a writer. What is easiest to measure — often by means of a multiple choice test — may correspond least to good writing, and that in part is an important point: *choosing a correct response from a set of possible answers is not composing.* As important, just because students are asked to write does not mean that the "assessment instrument" is a "good" one. Essay tests that ask students to form and articulate opinions about some important issue, for instance, without time to reflect, to talk to others, to read on the subject, to revise, and so forth — that is, without taking into account through either appropriate classroom practice or the assessment process itself — encourage distorted notions of what writing is. They also encourage poor teaching and little learning. Even teachers who recognize and employ the methods used by real writers in working with students can find their best efforts undercut by assessments such as these.

Seventh, *standardized tests, usually developed by large testing organizations, tend to be for accountability purposes, and when used to make statements about student learning, misrepresent disproportionately the skills and abilities of students of color.* This imbalance tends to decrease when tests are directly related to specific contexts and purposes, in contrast to tests that purport to differentiate between "good" and "bad" writing in a general sense. Furthermore, standardized tests tend to focus on readily accessed features of the language — on grammatical correctness and stylistic choice — and on error, on what is wrong rather than on the appropriate rhetorical choices that have been made. Consequently, the outcome of such assessments is negative: students are said to demonstrate what they do "wrong" with language rather than what they do well.

Eighth, *the means used to test students' writing ability shapes what they, too, consider writing to be.* If students are asked to produce "good" writing within a given period of time, they often conclude that all good writing is generated within those constraints. If students are asked to select — in a multiple choice format — the best grammatical and stylistic choices, they will conclude that good writing is "correct" writing. They will see writing erroneously, as the avoidance of error; they will think that grammar and style exist apart from overall purpose and discourse design.

Ninth, *financial resources available for designing and implementing assessment instruments should be used for that purpose and not to pay for assessment instruments outside the context within which they are used.* Large amounts of money are currently spent on assessments that have little pedagogical value for students or teachers. However, money spent to compensate teachers for involvement in assessment is also money spent on faculty development and curriculum reform since inevitably both occur when teachers begin to discuss assessment which relates directly to their classrooms and to their students.

Tenth, and finally, *there is a large and growing body of research on language learning, language use, and language assessment that must be used to improve assessment on a systematic and regular basis.* Our assumptions are based on this scholarship. Anyone charged with the responsibility of designing an assessment program must be cognizant of this body of research and must stay abreast of developments in the field. Thus, assessment programs must always be under review and subject to change by well-informed faculty, administrators, and legislators.

Assessment of writing is a legitimate undertaking. But by its very nature it is a complex task, involving two competing tendencies: first, the impulse to measure writing as a general construct; and second, the impulse to measure writing as a contextualized, site and genre-specific ability. There are times when re-creating or simulating a context (as in the case of assessment for placement, for instance) is limited. Even in this case, however, assessment — when conducted sensitively and purposefully — can have a positive impact on teaching, learning, curricular design, and student attitudes. Writing assessment can serve to inform both the individual and the public about the achievements of students and the effectiveness of teaching. On the other hand, poorly designed assessments, and poorly implemented assessments, can be enormously harmful because of the power of language: personally, for our students as human beings; and academically, for our students as learners, since learning is mediated through language.

Students who take pleasure and pride in using written language effectively are increasingly valuable in a world in which communication across space and a variety of cultures has become routine. Writing assessment that alienates students from writing is counterproductive, and writing assessment that fails to take an accurate and valid measure of their writing even more so. But writing assessment that encourages students to improve their facility with the written word, to appreciate their power with that word and the responsibilities that accompany such power, and that salutes students' achievements as well as guides them, should serve as a crucially important educational force.

Students should:

1. demonstrate their accomplishments and/or development in writing by means of composing, preferably in more than one sample written on more than one occasion, with sufficient time to plan, draft, rewrite, and edit each product or performance.

2. write on prompts developed from the curriculum and grounded in "real-world" practice.

3. be informed about the purposes of the assessment they are writing for, the ways the results will be used, and avenues of appeal.

4. have their writing evaluated by more than one reader, particularly in "high stakes" situations (e.g., involving major institutional consequences such as getting credit for a course, moving from one context to another, or graduating from college).

5. receive response, from readers, intended to help them improve as writers attempting to reach multiple kinds of audiences.

Faculty should:

1. play key roles in the design of writing assessments, including creating writing tasks and scoring guides, for which they should receive support in honoraria and/or release time; and should appreciate and be responsive to the idea that assessment tasks and procedures must be sensitive to cultural, racial, class, and gender differences, and to disabilities, and must be valid for and not penalize any group of students.

2. participate in the readings and evaluations of student work, supported by honoraria and/or release time.

3. assure that assessment measures and supports what is taught in the classroom.

4. make themselves aware of the difficulty of constructing fair and motivating prompts for writing, the need for field testing and revising of prompts, the range of appropriate and inappropriate uses of various kinds of writing assessments, and the norming, reliability, and validity standards employed by internal and external test-makers, as well as share their understanding of these issues with administrators and legislators.

5. help students to prepare for writing assessments and to interpret assessment results in ways that are meaningful to students.

6. use results from writing assessments to review and (when necessary) to revise curriculum.

7. encourage policy makers to take a more qualitative view toward assessment, encouraging the use of multiple measures, infrequent large-scale assessment, and large-scale assessment by sampling of a population rather than by individual work whenever appropriate.

8. continue conducting research on writing assessment, particularly as it is used to help students learn and to understand what they have achieved.

Administrators and higher education governing boards should:

1. educate themselves and consult with rhetoricians and composition specialists teaching at their own institutions, about the most recent research on teaching and assessing writing and how they relate to their particular environment and to already established programs and procedures, understanding that generally student learning is best demonstrated by performances assessed over time and sponsored by all faculty members, not just those in English.

2. announce to stakeholders the purposes of all assessments, the results to be obtained, and the ways that results will be used.

3. assure that the assessments serve the needs of students, not just the needs of an institution, and that resources for necessary courses linked to the assessments are therefore available before the assessments are mandated.

4. assure opportunities for teachers to come together to discuss all aspects of assessments; the design of the instruments; the standards to be employed; the interpretation of the results; possible changes in curriculum suggested by the process and results.

5. assure that all decisions are made by more than one reader.

6. not use any assessment results as the primary basis for evaluating the performance of or rewards due a teacher; they should recognize that student learning is influenced by many factors such as cognitive development, personality type, personal motivation, physical and psychological health, emotional upheavals, socioeconomic background, family successes and difficulties which are neither taught in the classroom nor appropriately measured by writing assessment.

Legislators should:

1. not mandate a specific instrument (test) for use in any assessment; although they may choose to answer their responsibility to the public by mandating assessment in general or at specific points in student careers, they should allow professional educators to choose the types and ranges of assessments that reflect the educational goals of their curricula and the nature of the student populations they serve.

2. understand that mandating assessments also means providing funding to underwrite those assessments, including resources to assist students and to bring teachers together to design and implement assessments, to review curriculum, and to amend the assessment and/or curriculum when necessary.

3. become knowledgeable about writing assessment issues, particularly by consulting with rhetoricians and composition specialists engaged in teaching, on the most recent research on the teaching of writing and assessment.

4. understand that different purposes require different assessments and that qualitative forms of assessment can be more powerful and meaningful for some purposes than quantitative measures are, and that assessment is a means to help students learn better, not a way of unfairly comparing student populations, teachers, or schools.

5. include teachers in the drafting of legislation concerning assessments.

6. recognize that legislation needs to be reviewed continually for possible improvement in light of actual results and ongoing developments in writing assessment theory and research.

Selected References

Belanoff, Pat, and Marcia Dickson, eds. *Portfolios: Process and Product.* Portsmouth, NH: Boynton, 1991.

Black, Laurel, Donald Daiker, Jeffrey Sommers, and Gail Stygall, eds. *New Directions in Portfolio Assessment: Reflective Practice, Critical Theory, and Large Scale Scoring.* Portsmouth, NH: Boynton, 1994.

Cooper, Charles, and Lee Odell, eds. *Evaluating Writing: Describing, Measuring, Judging.* Urbana, IL: NCTE, 1977.

CCCC Committee on Assessment. "A Selected Bibliography on Postsecondary Writing Assessment, 1979–91." *College Composition and Communication* 43 (1992): 244–55.

Elbow, Peter. "Ranking, Evaluating, and Liking: Sorting Out Three Forms of Judgment." *College English* 55 (1993): 187–206.

Gordon, Barbara. "Another Look: Standardized Tests for Placement in College Composition Courses." *WPA: Writing Program Administration* 10 (1987): 29–38.

Greenberg, Karen. "Validity and Reliability: Issues in the Direct Assessment of Writing." *WPA: Writing Program Administration* 16.1–2 (1992): 7–22.

Greenberg, Karen, Harvey Wiener, and Richard Donovan, eds. *Writing Assessment: Issues and Strategies.* New York: Longman, 1986.

Huot, Brian. "Reliability, Validity, and Holistic Scoring: What We Know and What We Need to Know." *College Composition and Communication* 41 (1990): 201–13.

Moss, Pamela. "Can There Be Validity without Reliability?" *Educational Researcher* 23.2 (1994): 5–12.

———. "Validity in High Stakes Writing Assessment: Problems and Possibilities." *Assessing Writing* 1.1 (1994): 109–28.

Odell, Lee. "Defining and Assessing Competence in Writing." *The Nature and Measurement of Competency in English.* Ed. Charles Cooper. Urbana, IL: NCTE, 1981: 95–139.

White, Edward. "Issues and Problems in Writing Assessment." *Assessing Writing* 1.1 (1994): 11–29.

———. *Teaching and Assessing Writing.* 2nd ed. San Francisco: Jossey, 1994.

Wiggins, Grant. *Assessing Student Performance: Exploring the Purpose and Limits of Testing.* San Francisco: Jossey, 1993.

———. "Assessment: Authenticity, Context, and Validity." *Phi Delta Kappan* 75.3 (1993): 200–14.

Williamson, Michael, and Brian Huot, eds. *Validating Holistic Scoring for Writing Assessment.* Cresskill, NJ: Hampton, 1993.

Yancey, Kathleen Blake, ed. *Portfolios in the Writing Classroom: An Introduction.* Urbana, IL: NCTE, 1992.

Classroom Activities

The writers of the CCCC document argue that "the means used to test students' writing ability shapes what they, too, consider writing to be." Consider this assumption in the context of your basic writing curriculum. Near the beginning of the course, ask students to reflect in their journals about how their placement test seems to define writing ability. Then, near the end of the course (and especially if the writing program includes an end-of-course assessment measure), have students reflect on what they have learned about writing ability. How do students define *good writing?* Have their assumptions changed or remained the same? Why? How are these ideas implicated in the end-of-term assessment? Asking students to reflect on the content of the course, the assessment process, and their own success as learners further encourages them to use their critical thinking skills.

Thinking about Teaching

The sixth assumption of the CCCC document states: "assessment tends to drive pedagogy." With this statement in mind, examine the assessments used in your writing program; what is driving your pedagogy? With other teachers, consider evaluating your institution's assessment strategy in light of the CCCC recommendations. Determine which guidelines your program already includes and which aspects of your program are in need of reevaluation and revision. Also consider how the assessment of basic writing students may be driven by institutional or legislative goals. Are such goals congruent with your goals for the course? With students' goals?

You may wish to suggest faculty review of assessment tools and processes, if such a review does not already exist. The CCCC position statement suggests that faculty affected by (but not responsible for designing) an assessment should demand an explication of its theoretical base.

Failure: The Student's or the Assessment's?

Kay Harley and Sally I. Cannon

First published in 1996 in the Journal of Basic Writing, *the following article by Kay Harley and Sally I. Cannon is powerful and poignant. Both a "good read" and pedagogically provocative, the article presents a case study of Mica, a student in a pilot program at Saginaw Valley State University that combined basic and first-year English courses. Harley and Cannon use this study to explore the notion of assessment.*

The writers acknowledge the ongoing struggle to define and redefine academic discourse related to assessment. For instance, most assessment instruments look at a sample as an isolated text instead of reading a piece of writing contextually and intertextually. That is, much assessment deals with what a writer doesn't do, how his or her writing doesn't measure up. Such criteria often fail to recognize current controversies in composition studies, such as the role of personal voice in academic writing. After considering these and other controversial issues, Harley and Cannon conclude that assessment practices need further evolution. Moreover, Mica's voice resonates throughout this article, arguing for a reconsideration of what it means to be a basic writing student.

The issue, then, is not who misses the mark but whose misses matter and why.

— Bartholomae ("Margins" 68)

Being in an college english class I felt I was final going to learn something about this word call english. . . . I knew I was going to learn everything I always want to learn it made me feel good.

— Mica

Overview

In some ways, Mica was like other underprepared, basic writers who
enrolled in the pilot program for developmental writers at our mid-
western state university. Acknowledging her checkered academic past
and resolved to start afresh, Mica was attracted to our pilot program.
Instead of taking the traditional sequence of a three-hour, noncredit,
basic writing course followed by a two-semester freshman writing
course, students like Mica, whose placement essay exam indicated the
need for developmental work in writing, could enroll in our program,
which combined the developmental and the first semester freshman
English courses. The pilot provided intensive support through
increased contact time with faculty, collaboration with peers, and
tutoring from upper class students who focused on improving students' writing and on assisting the freshmen in negotiating their ways
into the university community. We used Mike Rose's *Lives on the
Boundary* as a focal text to foreground issues of language and learning, access and denial, power and education, supplemented by brief
articles from local and national sources.

The pilot program gave another option to students like Mica, a
young African American, nineteen years old, and a single mother of a
young child. Her high school performance garnered a 2.7 GPA but was
interrupted by the emotional and physical demands of a pregnancy
during her junior year. She scored in the fourth percentile on the
Nelson-Denny reading test (equivalent to an upper elementary student) which placed her in the university's developmental reading
course. She felt unsure about herself and her writing, and, in her own
words, went through high school worried that "someone knew my
secret and they were calling me dumb behind my back." She was a student "at risk" whose success at the university was a gamble. In addition, Mica found herself at a preponderantly white university, where
300 African American students often feel isolated in a university population of about 7,000. The university's demographics were mirrored
in our pilot population; Mica was one of three African Americans out
of a total of forty-five enrolled in the Fall 1992 pilot.

However, Mica stood apart from her peers because she was a student whom our best teaching and assessment strategies did not serve.
She forced us to rethink just about everything we did. Her writing continually challenged our expectations and ways of reading. Mica was
also often vocal and forthright, letting us know what she was thinking, and not afraid of challenging us: "Why are you teaching us this?";

"What do you mean?"; "You said this yesterday and today you're telling us this!" Then, increasingly as the semester wore on, she became sullen and silent, defensive about our response to her writing. We had often praised her writing for its strong content and lively voice. At the same time, however, we would note the structural and grammatical problems that plagued every draft. She seemed confused about what she perceived as our ambivalence toward her writing.[1]

At the end of the semester, Mica failed the pilot program. We, however, asked ourselves how we had failed Mica, specifically in our assessment of her work. With over 80 percent of the students passing the combined course with a "C" or better, it became particularly important to analyze reasons for Mica's failure.

The assessment practice we used is widely considered one of the best to date in the discipline: a holistically scored portfolio, judged pass/fail by English faculty both within and external to the pilot. Nonetheless, as we've reflected upon our assessment of Mica, we have come to believe that a mismatch exists between our portfolio criteria and the texts Mica produced, even texts that had been revised over the semester with our criteria in mind. We now doubt that current assessment criteria and practices can "read" Mica's work adequately, or the work of other culturally diverse students whom our institutions are publicly committed to educating. Jay Robinson and Patti Stock in "The Politics of Literacy" have written, "if we would be literate, and help others to become so, it is time for thoughtful listening to those voices that come from the margins; it is time for reflective reading of texts that inscribe those voices as centrally human ones" (313). While many of us have made progress in learning to listen to others' voices, this progress is not embodied adequately in our assessments.

While the profession discusses writing as embedded in a context, we represent writing in our assessments as uniform and monolithic. We may call for multiple samples by which to evaluate performance, but during the portfolio evaluation itself, we read each paper largely as an isolated text, not contextually or intertextually. And while we may specify different genres, the criteria we use for evaluation fail to acknowledge the blurring of genres that is evident in much writing both within and outside the academy today. Further, our criteria fail to recognize the current controversies over the role of personal voice in academic writing and argument. They also privilege linear forms of organization. In short, our assessments penalize students for "missing the mark" in ways that may be incompatible with our profession's evolving notions of the socially contextualized nature of writing and discourse.

This paper, then, explores what we now see as our failure in assessing Mica's work and speculates on how we might reconceptualize the assessment of writing, particularly the writing of culturally diverse students.

Assessment and the Pilot Program

Briefly, our assessment required the students to submit a portfolio of four pieces selected from writing they had done during the course. While we urged students to incorporate ideas or examples from early papers in later ones or revise versions of early ones as their thinking on issues was deepened by the reading, writing, and discussions in the course, the requirements for the portfolio didn't describe or reflect this. Rather they read quite conventionally:

a. Personal Reflective piece: This essay should demonstrate your ability to use details effectively to narrate/describe; it should have a focus, a point.

b. Expository piece: This essay should demonstrate your ability to create a thesis and support it with evidence — personal examples, examples of others, material from the coursepack or Rose.

c. Synthesis paper: This essay should demonstrate your ability to synthesize (make connections between) ideas from the coursepack, Rose, and your own thinking about education and work, to focus them in a thesis, and to present them in an organized and coherent fashion.

d. In-class/Impromptu paper: This essay should demonstrate your ability to write a clear and organized essay under timed conditions and without the opportunity to revise.

The criteria we shared with students and used as a department in the pass/fail evaluations of student portfolios also reflected traditional rubrics.

A Pass portfolio should demonstrate the ability to:

a. write fluently

b. grapple with a topic; develop and explore the implications of ideas and insights

c. provide a focus, generally through an explicit thesis statement

d. support ideas with reasons and/or examples from personal experience and/or outside sources

e. organize ideas into clear paragraphs

f. avoid multiple grammatical mistakes, particularly sentence boundary problems.

Challenges of Reading and Assessing Mica's Writing

The following essay, Mica's first of the semester, illustrates the difficulty we had in assessing her writing. The assignment asked the students to describe an experience or moment in their lives in which they learned something. By establishing a clear focus and drawing upon sensory details, they were to narrate the experience so that their readers could relive the moment with them and reflect upon what that experience taught them. Mica decided to write about the birth of her child. The first two paragraphs of her essay, entitled "Ready or Not," are reprinted below:

> Waking up saying good-bye to everyone "Bye Mama, Beebee, and Chris". Oh well I'm left here in this empty house again no one to talk to. Don't anybody care that I'm 9-1/2 months pregnant and my stomach is as big as a beach ball, and that I wobble like a weeble when I walk.
>
> I remember whimpering as if I was a two years old. Mica get a whole to yourself stop whimpering for your eyes get puffy. Baby, why don't you come out. All my friend have had their babies. What are you waiting on to come out of there; sweetie your mama is tired of being pregnant. I can remember being so angry that if anybody would have came over here I would have chewed them up alive. Oh! I got to get out of here before I go crazy. Running up and down the stairs, I figure if I jiggle you up then maybe you will come out. Doing this for five minutes and nothing happen. Just huffing and puffing like a dog sitting in the hot summer sun. Well, I guess I'll take me a shower. Getting undress and guess what the telephone rang, Oh, Oh, somebody cares about me. The Mrs. Know-it-all-mother-in-law, the bat. Hello, "Mica what are you doing?" "I replied," nothing, I was about to get into the shower, can you call me back?" Yeah, bye bye. Wicked witch I never thought she cared. Oh well back to the shower. In the shower the water running on my stomach I can feel you in there come out of there my stomach began making the gesture like the baby was trying to really come out.

For most readers of freshman English essays, this paper misses the mark. It isn't "correct." Yet, we want to argue, these notions of "correctness" — correctness not only in terms of surface features but also of acceptable styles, genres, and organization — though deeply embedded in our thinking and assessment criteria are often unstated and not fully examined. Mica's paper jars and challenges, yet it handles language in complex ways. It shifts from direct to indirect discourse; from Mica as narrator, to Mica as a character thinking aloud, to Mica speaking directly to other characters or her unborn child. But we dismiss this complexity and judge through the lens of "error." The direct discourse is often unmarked. Sentences are sometimes fragmented or fused. Tense shifts occur seemingly at random. The missing tense markers, particularly "d" or "ed," and copula ("to be") deletions reflect

Black English Vernacular (BEV). Further, her organization contains nothing explicit.

Mica's writing did not include any of the distancing and reflecting that were part of our expectations for a personal reflective essay. In "Reflections on Academic Discourse: How It Relates to Freshmen and Colleagues," Peter Elbow explores how academic discourse assumes "that we can separate the ideas and reasons and arguments from the person who holds them" (140).[2] Mica was unable or refused to squelch the personal — to separate the message from the messenger — to adopt a disinterested, objective stance. Her preference for situating her ideas in personal terms is seen in several other essays discussed later in this paper.

Rather than reading Mica's text for what it doesn't do, it can be read for what it is achieving. Robert Yagelski, for example, suggested in his 1994 CCCC presentation that we might evaluate a student text like this as personal testimony. Mica's writing does render the immediacy of her experience of labor with her first child. It is filled with strong details. The storying patterns, oral resonances, and rich rhythm give the piece its poignancy and power. These reflect a mode of discourse prevalent in Black English that Geneva Smitherman in *Talkin and Testifyin: The Language of Black America* defines as tonal semantics. One feature of tonal semantics, Smitherman notes, is the use of repetition, alliterative word play, and a striking and sustained use of metaphor, something seen throughout Mica's work (134). Mica writes about a jumbled, chaotic, and intensely personal time that demands a strong emotive voice. That Mica has achieved such a voice is a mark, not of a basic writer, but of an accomplished one.

Features similar to those in Mica's personal essay appeared in all of her subsequent writing in the course, including her summaries and explanatory essays. More clearly in those papers did we see how personal anecdotes are acceptable in academic discourse only when framed by generalizations. It is the framing that appears indispensable, for if a student like Mica offers a personal example without a corresponding generalization, the personal doesn't qualify as support.

David Bartholomae has noted that all errors are not created equal.

> The errors that count in the work of basic writers have no clear and absolute value but gain value only in the ways that they put pressure on what we take to be correct, in the ways that these errors are different from acceptable errors. The work that remains for the profession is to determine the place of those unacceptable styles within an institutional setting, within an institution with its own styles of being right, its own habitual ways of thinking and writing ("Margins" 68–69).

Mica's paper challenged our habitual ways of assessing writing and left us questioning whether the "unacceptable" in Mica's writing might have a rightful place in a freshman writing course and in academic discourse more generally. Can the boundaries of academic discourse be broadened so that "personal testimony" or an "emotive voice" or "tonal semantics" might find a place? In suggesting this, we are not suggesting that a student like Mica cannot or should not learn the dominant academic discourse, including what some describe as the "superficial features" of grammar, style, and mechanics. Nor are we suggesting that our job as teachers is not to help all students to do so, giving them access to many voices and styles. Nonetheless, we are suggesting that the writing of students like Mica may also call us to transform academic discourse and the assessment practices which support it.

Unpacking Metaphors of Exclusion: Deficiency, Foreignness, and Monogeneric Papers

Bartholomae demonstrates that we sort out and label "on the assumption that basic writers are defined by what they don't do (rather than by what they do), by the absence of whatever is present in literate discourse: cognitive maturity, reason, orderliness, conscious strategy, correctness" ("Margins" 67). While we immediately recognized a power and immediacy in Mica's writing, our early diagnoses of her work focused on deficits — the lack of reason, orderliness, conscious strategy, and correctness that Bartholomae (and our assessment guides) enumerate. These quick notes made for ourselves, for example, focus on what Mica failed to do in an expository essay exploring the distinction between child abuse and discipline, a paper that drew upon a time when she was accused of abusing a toddler at a day care center at which she worked:

> — problems framing the experience and/or moving between her frames/generalizations and her examples — movement is a key problem, transitions — abruptly inserts dictionary definitions of discipline and child abuse — moves directly into 1st person narrative example with no lead in and a complete shift in style — ends with question posed to reader rather than restatement (or even direct statement) of main point of paper — multiple tense marker errors and other BEV features —

While these notes exemplify error analysis and try to move beyond a simple recording of errors ("her moves show an awareness of what is needed"), they nonetheless show that we read Mica's essay primarily in terms of its deficits: it lacks conventional features of academic prose.

Here is the opening of the essay:

Ten years ago if you told your child "don't do that," and they did it any way you would spank them for not listening to you. Back then the way you discipline your child was your business. Now days its everybodys business the way you discipline your child.

Child Abuse vs. Discipline

When do you know its child abuse? And when do you know it simply discipline.

DISCIPLINE is defined as training especially training of the mind.

CHILD ABUSE is defined as mistreatment of a child by parents or guardians.

It's Thursday, I said to myself, I have one more day before I can rest, rest, rest. Dealing with 20-5 kids a day really takes a lot out of you. . . .

It was 10:05 and all the kids had arrived. We sang good morning to each other then split up in groups. We had a full load and that was about 25 kids so that made us have five kids a piece. As the day went along it was time for coloring. I caught one of my kids putting crayons in his mouth. "David get the crayons out of your mouth. They're not to eat, but to color," I said. He didn't have anything to say back. But as soon as I turned my head he had them back in his mouth. We went through this about four times. The fourth time I got up and tapped him on his hand — Not hit, or smack but tapped him on his hand. He didn't cry, he just took the crayons out of his mouth and continued coloring.

If, instead of assessing Mica's essay in terms of its deficits, we set it alongside some of the reading we were doing and asked students to do, Mica's style does not look so foreign or lacking. Her abrupt shifts and lack of transitions are not altogether dissimilar to those of Mike Rose in his opening of *Lives on the Boundary,* the book used in our course.

Rose moves from description of students and of the university campus, to a carefully recorded observation of a teacher drawing out students' knowledge about the renaissance, to a pictorial image of the medieval goddess Grammatica which then functions metaphorically, to statistics about changing enrollment patterns in American universities — all of which create a rich and multifaceted collage. No explicit transitions mark the movements, only white space on the page.

Rose's style is quite different from directly stated thesis and support pattern that guides much of our instruction and assessment of basic writers. He interweaves precise objective description, vivid image, significant anecdote, personal experience, quotes from official documents, general statement, and reflection. Mica's child abuse paper parallels Rose in significant ways. Her essay is full of ideas and passion as she explores the damaging consequences of mistaking discipline for child abuse and the difficulties of clearing your name, particularly if you are a single mother from a minority group, when charges of abuse have been leveled. She offers personal testimony, clearly conveys the events/examples, includes detail and dialogue to place the reader in the scene, and writes with a strong sense of conviction. While not using many of the devices of academic argument, she is nonetheless making a claim: that discipline should not be mistaken for child abuse. She elaborates upon her points and shows the harm that mistaking discipline for child abuse can cause. She writes to effect change.[3]

To take another example, David Bartholomae has demonstrated how a careful look at the writing of Patricia Williams, an African American legal scholar and author of *The Alchemy of Race and Rights,* can cause us to question the way we read the prose of basic writers. Williams, like Rose, upsets our conventional expectations of academic prose. "Williams' writing is disunified: it mixes genres; it willfully forgets the distinctions between formal and colloquial, public and private; it makes unseemly comparisons. In many ways, her prose has the features we associate with basic writing, although here those features mark her achievement as a writer, not her failure" ("Tidy House" 11). We do not, Bartholomae suggests,

> read "basic writing" the way we read Patricia Williams' prose, where the surprising texture of the prose stands as evidence of an attempt to negotiate the problems of language . . . She is trying to do something that can't be conventionally done. To say that our basic writers are less intentional, less skilled, is to say the obvious . . . It is possible . . . that when we define Williams-like student writing as less developed or less finished . . . we are letting metaphors of development or process hide value-laden assumptions about thought, form, the writer, and the social world ("Tidy House" 19).

Errors in Our Expectations

Two papers Mica wrote later in the course again show her defying our expectations about the appropriate form and content. In one, we had asked students to select an article, summarize it, and respond. Mica chose a collection of brief interviews concerning women and work entitled "Is Success Dangerous to Your Health?" She opens as follows:

> In reading the interview article, "Is Success Dangerous to your Health," none of the three interviewees in their interview explain or answer the question ask in the title of the interview, Is Success Dangerous to your Health? I couldn't grasp what the author was try to do however, what I did find in the article is "RESPECT". All of the three interviewees felt they were not respect. The title of the article pull me right into the paper. However, I was very disapointed not to find what I was looking for. Will my career affect my health in anyway.

Mica had written guidelines, model opening sentences, and class assistance on how to write a summary and response. However, she sets these aside (perhaps largely unconsciously) to pursue her own frustration with the title, a point she returns to in her conclusion where she unabashedly makes suggestions to the author about how to answer the question the title posed. Her "back talk" to the author is a significant rhetorical move, yet it and her use of first person belie the expectations for an objective summary. Again, our immediate response to Mica's summary/response is to dismiss it as not meeting the terms of the assignment. And, indeed, it does not. However, her gutsy move in challenging the author surely demonstrates critical thinking as well as a critical engagement with the text, something our assessment practices sometimes overlook in favor of acceptable genre features. Consider, for example, the "safe" and predictable but totally unengaged five paragraph theme that passes without question. The paper passes, no doubt, because it can demonstrate the surface features and stylistic conventions of academic discourse: the clear structure, the explicit signposting, etc. But content — which we continually maintain is the most important feature when assessing any kind of prose — is often overlooked. Is this a "fair" and accurate assessment of either writer?

The last assignment of the semester was a synthesis paper which asked students to bring together their thinking about education or work, the two themes of the class. Students were to create a fresh look at the topic by making connections among the different readings from the course and integrating those with their views, experience, and writing done in earlier papers and in their journal.

Mica chose to write about education, specifically her experience in the pilot project. Our initial assessment of Mica's paper was that it failed to do what was expected. In our minds it did not "read" as a synthesis. The paper never established a focus in the form of a thesis statement, it failed to smoothly link specific examples and personal experience to generalizations, and it made little use of quotations from the reading as support. Instead, Mica recounted her experience from the beginning of the semester to the end with no immediately apparent synthesis or reflection, as these first two paragraphs suggest:

> It's first day in college, and I'm excited I drove around the hold campus to find a policeman so, I can get direction to my class. Finally I found one he and looked like he was hiding behind the trees waiting to give someone a ticket. I drove over to him, and rolled down my window. "Can I help you?," He said, Yes you can I need help trying to find my class the room number z204. "O.K. young lady you keep straight on this street we one and turn right, Then you see this building a lot of people will be coming in and out of it." Thank you very much sir. I seen this big building about as half big as a major hotel like the Marriot Hotel. I entered

the building, Everyone was walking so fast like they were in a marathon.

Finally, I found room z204 I walk in; it was pretty full. I sat by the window so I could look out of it since no one was talking. Being in a college English class I felt I was final going to learn something about this word call english. All through high school I felt so insure about writing, I always felt someone knew my secret and they were calling me dumb behind my back. I felt a little dumb but, I knew someday I will learn were to put a period, comma, and a semicolon without feel unsure about it. So, in college I felt this is when every thing is going to change. I knew I was going to learn everything I always want to learn it made me feel good.

The paper adopts a narrative stance from which it never departs, thus defying our expectations for a synthesis paper. However, if we temporarily put aside those expectations to read differently, the paper does synthesize Mica's experience in the pilot course. She captures the confusion and anxiety of a new student coming to a college campus for the first time, likening the campus buildings and the policeman's behavior to the closest thing she knows: the city. She compares our modern buildings to a Marriot hotel. That comparison, coupled with her admission of her "secret" about feeling "dumb," suggests how much strength it actually took to walk in the doors of our institution.

The paper shows Mica as a beginning writer, new to the university and its expectations, negotiating her way into academic discourse, just as she seeks to find her way physically into the academic campus. She explores issues of anxiety about writing, the pitfalls of peer response groups, and power relations in the classroom. This reading acknowledges a focus, which our initial reading could not because, limited by predetermined portfolio requirements and paper features, it linked focus with thesis. Now we realize that the focus was there: it was Mica's — her story of her first semester college English experience. The narrative mode was her way of shaping her experience, of telling her story.

Carolyn Heilbrun in *Writing a Woman's Life* discusses the ways female literary figures write to organize and make sense of their lives. While Heilbrun is discussing works of fiction, not academic discourse, Jane Tompkins and other scholars writing academic discourse do directly call upon their personal experience to enrich and organize their understanding of professional concepts. If Tompkins, why not Mica? Certainly the profession is expanding its notion of what is acceptable in its own academic discourse. And while Mica's writing is far from model prose, and she does not have conscious control over the strategies she uses, her writing has made us realize that the time is ripe for a reconsideration of what is "acceptable" in student discourse as well.

Locating Oneself in the Privileged
Discourse of the Academic World

Clearly, Mica is a student whose style betrays her and sets her apart from the mainstream at our — and most — college campuses. Perhaps, then, we need to assess Mica's work as her attempt to locate herself in the privileged discourse of the academic community. This would lead us to view her writing problems not as internal or cognitive, but rather as ones of appropriation. Mica's work throughout the course was marked by styles that clashed with our deeply embedded notions of academic discourse represented in our assignment and evaluation constructs. In assessing her, we judged these as deficits. Consistently rich in details, we said, but she could not control them. Our assignments called for the person, the details, yet our assessments demanded that these be "controlled," that specifics be framed, that thesis and generalization be tied to example. If her status in coming to the university is deeply divided, fragmentary, how can we expect a central point, a main idea?

David Bartholomae suggests

> if we take the problem of writing to be the problem of appropriating the power and authority of a particular way of speaking, then the relationship of the writer to the institutions within which he writes becomes central (the key feature in the stylistic struggle on the page) rather than peripheral (a social or political problem external to writing and therefore something to be politely ignored) ("Margins" 70).

Our assessment criteria didn't allow us to read Mica's prose as an attempt to negotiate the problems of language. Rather, the assessment criteria were presented as objective and uniform. Such criteria may protect us and the university community at large from looking critically at the mismatch between the rhetoric of our policies and programs for ethnically underrepresented and academically underprepared students and the realities of their struggles to make sense of an unfamiliar social dialect.[4]

Grammar Is Not Neutral

Mica describes quite poignantly her purpose in voluntarily enrolling in our pilot program: "I was final going to learn something about this word call english." She suggests an academic history fraught with insecurity, afraid that someone would find out her "secret." Interestingly, Mica views that secret and the solution to her problem as a mechanical one: "I knew someday I will learn were to put a period, comma, and a semicolon." This characterization of writing in terms of grammar, of course, is not unusual. Many writers (and teachers) conflate the two. (Consider the numbers of people who, when told that you are an English teacher, respond with a comment about "watching their grammar.") As we continued to study Mica's writing and reflect upon our work with her long after the semester ended, we began to understand how strongly Mica held to her belief in the power of punctuation. We realized that learning correct grammar was Mica's agenda. As Mina Shaughnessy noted, "grammar still symbolizes for some students one last chance to understand what is going on with written language so that they can control it rather than be controlled by it" (11).

Carolyn Hill discusses how grammar is a political issue to basic writers: "Grammar is not a neutral 'thing' to them, rather a completely socialized representative of those authorities who seem to students to be outside themselves" (250). Later in her synthesis paper, Mica constructs her instructors' point of view and appears suspicious of our motives in not focusing dominantly upon grammatical issues. She writes:

> I enjoy every bit of writing I did in the class but, I felt disappoint cause I didn't learn what I want to learn in the class. . . . I really felt that we should have discuss more of what I believe she saw going on in the class. Since, she mentioned it herself that she was having a problem with grammer, fused sentence, tense sentences, and fragments. We did work on this for a couple of days but i felt it wasn't enough.

In saying "we should have discuss more of what *I believe she saw going on in the class*" Mica seems to feel that we were unjustly withholding information that she believes could solve her writing problems and eliminate her "secret." That intensive one-on-one tutoring from peers and instructors, diagnostic analyses of her patterns of error, comparisons of her own patterns to typical nonstandard patterns of Black English Vernacular, and extensive opportunities for revision did not help Mica gain greater power over spelling, punctuation, and syntax remains one of our greatest puzzles.

Mica's sentence points to power relations in the classroom. Mica frames the teacher/student relationship as a struggle between two people with two competing solutions to her writing problems. She is indignant (perhaps rightfully so) that her solution, more grammar instruction, is being ignored. In retrospect, we suspect that our actions are well described by Hill: "Ostensibly I wanted to give up authority, help students to be self-starters. Covertly, the institution and I collaborated to see to it that students be quickly notified if that start did not place them in the proper arms of Standard English, focused and controlled" (78).

Mica wanted to gain control over her writing and her errors; she wanted access to the social power identified with academic discourse. Yet neither she nor her instructors confronted this agenda centrally.

Her relationship to the institution within which she wrote, her very placement in a basic writing course, the value placed by the university and those exercising influence in the society on copy editing, correctness, and conventional styles were peripheral concerns. Correctness was thought of as context-free. That is something the English profession can no longer afford to assume. Perhaps that is why we saw such little change in these areas of Mica's writing.

Rethinking Assessment

Reexamining and questioning our assessment of Mica's portfolio has left us with more questions than answers. As we now critique our portfolio assessment we see that we inadvertently worked to keep intact the boundaries and borders by which basic writing is institutionally defined, ironically the very boundaries our pilot project meant to collapse.

Thus, while we endorse and encourage more courses like ours, courses which collapse borders and work to eliminate notions of basic writers as "foreigners,"[5] we realize that our assessment practices must evolve significantly as well.

First, we need to understand that assessment is complexly situated, and different audiences may require different evaluations. In reviewing our guidelines for a passing portfolio we would now ask, "For whom are we evaluating Mica's work?" During the portfolio reading, who is the primary audience? Is it Mica? Is our purpose to reveal to her where she has succeeded or failed in meeting the standards set for an introductory university writing course? Is the primary audience her future college instructors? If so, what do they need to learn about writing as a deeply embedded cultural and social act, about the time needed to acquire new discourse practices, and about current challenges to hierarchical patterns of organization if they are to determine what should constitute "passing" work in an introductory writing course which enrolls culturally diverse students? Or is the audience the local, state, or national community? The needs and interests of these groups differ; our assessments need to reflect this.

In addition, we need to devise ways to read student texts contextually and intertextually not only in the classroom setting but in evaluation sessions. Our prespecified portfolio requirements pressured us into reading each paper as an individual entity. What we now want to strive for is a more intertextual reading of the portfolios, an assessment practice that views the essays in a portfolio as interrelated and recursive. Read as a whole, Mica's papers have a surprising unity, both in content and approach. We wonder what would happen if during the portfolio evaluation we actively read Mica's work as her ongoing exploration of the issues that were central to her views of education, work, and mastery of written English. All of them contain strong narrative elements; all have a directness in confronting the issues she's chosen as her topics; all fail to clearly and explicitly link example to generalization, provide direct transitions, or follow a linear order; and all demonstrate a lack of control of surface features including spelling, word ending, person and tense inflections, and punctuation.

We need to resist (or read against) our unconscious notions of academic discourse as monolithic and standard. It's a myth that all synthesis papers will look like some imagined prototype of a synthesis paper. Yet, when evaluating portfolios holistically, we often operate under this myth. Papers that contain the expected features of a particular assignment pass without question, while quirky papers that don't easily correspond to a genre or mode — even if particularly rich in content — are often failed. Narrative strategies are undervalued, even when they are deeply reflective. In professional conferences and articles, we repeatedly remind ourselves to avoid false dichotomies, yet too often we fall back into simplistic either/or formulations in evaluation. Our assessment criteria suggest an essay is either personal reflection or exposition, either narrative or argument. The language is either academic discourse or not. The thesis/generalization is either directly stated or it cannot be credited. We need to immerse students in a variety of discourses, being careful not to limit students like Mica to only one voice. We do well to remember the frustration of feminist writer, bell hooks, with teachers who "did not recognize the need for African American students to have access to many voices" (qtd. in Delpit 291).

Finally, we need to understand errors, not as deficits, but as attempts at appropriating the discourses of other communities. This shift would allow us to recognize and extend rather than automatically penalize these attempts at appropriation. Matters of syntax and usage are not neutral as our portfolio criteria imply. We need to become sensitive to the power relationships implicit in all language use and to the political implications of judgments of error as "nonstandard," particularly as higher education opens itself to an increasingly diverse student body.

We have no clear answer to the question raised in our title. Was the failure Mica's or that of our assessment procedures? We suspect the failure rests on both sides. We did fail Mica: we failed to read her texts contextually; we failed to assess her portfolio in light of her attempts to appropriate a new discourse; we failed by oversimplifying the nature of academic discourse; we failed by setting her work against some constructed "mythical" portfolio demonstrating competence; we failed by not seeing the power relations involved in any attempts to work on nonstandard usages. The answer, however, is also complex — as complex, perhaps, as Mica's writing and as Mica herself. At times she appeared evasive and angry; at times bewildered; at times fiercely proud and determined.

Would we pass Mica's portfolio today? No. However, Mica's writing has challenged our notions of what is good and acceptable written discourse in introductory academic settings, and we think it should challenge others in the English profession, the university, and society.

Mica did not meet our expectations. Her writing continues to intrigue and frustrate us. Yet it may be the Micas — those students who do not meet our expectations — who shed the strongest light on our practices.

Notes

1. Some ambivalence was undoubtedly present, both on our part and on Mica's. In working with Mica, we probably at times exemplified "a certain sense of powerlessness and paralysis" that Lisa Delpit has described "among many sensitive and well-meaning literacy educators who appear to be caught in the throes of a dilemma. Although their job is to teach literate discourse styles to all of their students, they question whether that is a task they can actually accomplish for poor students and students of color. Furthermore, they question whether they are acting as agents of oppression by insisting that students who are not already a part of the 'mainstream' learn that discourse" (285). Mica also may have been deeply ambivalent, caught in the conflicts between her home discourses and the discourses of the university, and feeling torn between institutions and value systems in ways that Keith Gilyard documents. Thus, she may have been choosing to resist or "not learn" as Herb Kohl describes it, rather than learn that which she perceived as denying her a sense of who she was. While issues such as these are important to our thinking, this paper looks more specifically to the implications of current assessment practices.
2. Elbow makes the good point that "it's crazy to talk about academic discourse as one thing" (140). However, we often teach and assess academic discourse as if it were. We believe that many teachers of writing (perhaps unconsciously) hold a collective, monolithic view of academic discourse, which poses problems to assessment, particularly the assessment of students at risk. This monolithic view of academic discourse is defined primarily by its stylistic and mechanical surface features, features such as mapping or signposting, explicitness, objectivity, and formal language (Elbow 144–46).
3. Smitherman discusses a characteristic use of narrative as a persuasive tool in Black English: "The relating of events (real or hypothetical) becomes a black rhetorical strategy to explain a point, to persuade holders of opposing views to one's own point of view, and in general, to 'win friends and influence people'" (147–48).
4. Anne DiPardo explores this issue in *A Kind of Passport* when she examines the "patterns of tension" in an institution's commitment to educational equity, looking particularly at the "good intentions and enduring ambivalence" embedded in the language of the basic writing curricula.
5. See Bruce Horner for a recent discussion of this and other metaphors used to characterize basic writers.

Works Cited

Bartholomae, David. "The Tidy House: Basic Writing in the American Curriculum." *Journal of Basic Writing* 12.1 (1993): 4–21.

———. "Writing on the Margins: The Concept of Literacy in Higher Education." *A Sourcebook for Basic Writers*. Ed. Theresa Enos. New York: Random House, 1987. 66–83.

Delpit, Lisa D. "The Politics of Teaching Literate Discourse." *Freedom's Plow: Teaching in the Multicultural Classroom*. Ed. T. Perry and J. W. Fraser. New York: Routledge, 1995. 285–95.

DiPardo, Anne. *A Kind of Passport: A Basic Writing Adjunct Program and the Challenge of Student Diversity*. Urbana, IL: National Council of Teachers of English, 1993.

Elbow, Peter. "Reflections on Academic Discourse: How It Relates to Freshmen and Colleagues." *College English* 53.2 (1991): 135–55.

Gilyard, Keith. *Voices of the Self*. Detroit: Wayne State UP, 1991.

Heilbrun, Carolyn. *Writing a Woman's Life*. New York: Ballantine Books, 1988.

Hill, Carolyn Ericksen. *Writing from the Margins: Power and Pedagogy for Teachers of Composition*. New York: Oxford UP, 1990.

Horner, Bruce. "Mapping Errors and Expectations for Basic Writing: From the 'Frontier Field' to 'Border Country.'" *English Education* 26.1 (Feb. 1994): 29–51.

Kohl, Herb. *I Won't Learn From You! The Role of Assent in Education*. Minneapolis, MN: Milkweed Editions, 1991.

Robinson, Jay, and Patti Stock. "The Politics of Literacy." *Conversations on the Written Word: Essays on Language and Literacy*. Ed. Jay Robinson. Portsmouth, NH: Boynton/Cook, 1990. 271–317.

Rose, Mike. *Lives on the Boundary*. New York: Free Press, 1989.

Shaughnessy, Mina. *Errors and Expectations*. New York: Oxford UP, 1977.

Smitherman, Geneva. *Talkin and Testifyin: The Language of Black America*. Boston: Houghton Mifflin, 1977.

Williams, Patricia. *The Alchemy of Race and Rights*. Cambridge: Harvard UP, 1991.

Yagelski, Robert P. Speech. "Writing Assessment and the Challenges of Cultural Diversity." Conference on College Composition and Communication. Nashville, March 1994.

Classroom Activities

Mica writes: "I enjoy every bit of writing I did in the class but, I felt disappoint cause I didn't learn what I want to learn in the class." Harley and Cannon identify Mica's concern as wanting "to gain control over her writing and her errors; she wanted access to the social power identified with academic discourse. Yet neither she nor her instructors confronted this agenda centrally." Such an agenda seems difficult to confront; nonetheless, it may be worthwhile to stage such a confrontation with students to allow them "to gain control" over their progress in the course. The goals and reasons for institutional assessment can be presented not only to discuss these tools but also to challenge them.

Moreover, students can learn to chart their own improvement when you replicate the conditions of institutional writing assessment on a small scale. At the beginning of the semester, have students write a timed essay in response to a question or prompt. Collect the essay, but do not mark or grade it. Instead, put this writing away until the end of the semester, at which time students can complete a timed in-class essay based on a prompt or question similar to the initial assignment. Have students compare and contrast their writing from the beginning and the end of the semester. What has changed? Where do students see improvements? If you use writing portfolios in your course, this reflective response can be a valuable addition to each student's portfolio.

Thinking about Teaching

If our pedagogy continues to change to include more diverse student voices, Harley and Cannon affirm, so also must our assessment procedures and policies "evolve significantly." Harley and Cannon urge us to consider that assessment is "complexly situated" and that we need to look not only at the texts we are assessing but also at the multiple audiences for whom the assessment is intended.

Such reflection introduces the notion of standards as a political issue. Assessment practices tend to privilege correctness, orderliness, reason, distance, and formula, mirroring the value placed on these categories by administrators and employers, if not by ourselves and our students, as markers of good writing. Yet at the same time, we emphasize in our classes that rhetorical maturity, risk taking, and critical engagement are also important goals in a basic writing course. If these practices and emphases need not contradict each other in the classroom, then perhaps they also need not be at cross-purposes in assessment. Such issues may be critical starting points for an important discussion among teachers and administrators evaluating the assessment needs of their students in writing courses.

From Teaching and Learning in Texas: Accountability Testing, Language, Race, and Place

Susan Naomi Bernstein

This case study of Noah, a Mexican American student enrolled in basic writing, is excerpted from Susan Naomi Bernstein's longer article in the

Journal of Basic Writing. *In the original article, Bernstein focuses on Texas state education law and state-mandated accountability testing. The Texas system served as a model for the No Child Left Behind law of 2001. In particular, Bernstein is interested in the impact of education law and accountability testing on former students, the majority of whom were English language learners (ELL) who had attended urban public schools in Texas. Bernstein presents a teaching narrative of a fall-semester linked course in basic writing and reading against the backdrop of controversies surrounding accountability testing and attrition rates in urban Texas public schools which her students had attended.*

One student, Noah, repeated the basic writing course the following semester and enrolled in an American Studies course linked to the basic writing course. Bernstein writes, "Rather than paint Noah as a victim of circumstance, however, I document Noah's own metamorphosis as he moved from public high school experiences to college basic writing" (5). Noah, a visual artist, tells the story of his own transformations and describes how his experiences as an artist helped to facilitate his matric-ulation to college. At the same time, he also recounts a story of attending under-funded urban schools and the long-term effects that state-mandated tests have had on his writing. Noah's description of schooling in the service of state-mandated assessment is unfortunately all too com-mon in the literacy narratives of Generation 1.5 students and other stu-dents educated in economically distressed public school systems bound by state and federal accountability measures. Yet in this case study, Noah begins to speak back to a system that defined him by his deficits rather than by his evident strengths.

Learning: The Story of Noah

In order to investigate my perceptions of this course in more detail, I followed the progress of another student from the fall semester class, Noah, who struggled all semester with reading and writing. Although Noah would need to repeat the writing portion of the course with me in the spring semester, his goals remained constant and clear. As our case study developed, I shared research and drafts of this article with Noah. In particular, I emphasized the question that grounded my inquiry: how might students make sense of their own subject positions as English language learners within an urban public school system that emphasized state-mandated accountability testing?

As seen through the lens of practitioner-inquiry research, Noah's story was particularly interesting to me because it provided an oppor-tunity to investigate "how teachers and students co-construct teaching and learning across classrooms and across contexts" (Cochran-Smith and Lytle 44). As Cochran-Smith and Lytle suggest, "When teachers redefine their own relationships to knowledge about teaching and learning, they often begin to reconstruct their classrooms and to offer different invitations to their students to learn and to know" (52).

Noah was a first-year college student of traditional age whose first language was Spanish; he moved to the United States from a small town in Mexico at the age of nine, just before fourth grade. Like the other students in the fall semester, Noah was part of the first generation in his family who had an opportunity to attend college, and he contemplated becoming a teacher himself. Having graduated from high school in the top ten percent of his class, however, Noah now felt frustrated by his lack of adequate preparation for college. At the same time, as he read and thought about the assignments, he began to recognize his own experiences in the context of the course readings.

Because Noah's US schooling took place in Texas urban public schools, his situation seemed even more complicated than that of the typical English language learner. Valencia, Villareal, and Salinas cite considerable research to discuss how education for English language acquisition is delivered to Texas public school students who are identified as English language learners (ELL). Initially, these researchers suggest, most children are assigned to "transitional bilingual education (TBE)":

> In Texas, for example, ELL children in bilingual programs are classified as "English-proficient" when they demonstrate *oral fluency* by obtaining a score at the 40th percentile or higher on a standardized English language assessment measure. (Texas Education Code, 1999, 275)

Nonetheless, "TBE programs last only about two to three years," Valencia, Villareal, and Salinas recount, noting that exit criteria for such programs are based on oral proficiency, rather than proficiency in academic English. Using oral proficiency alone as the sole measure of English language acquisition tends, not unexpectedly, to have a negative impact on students' development of reading and writing skills, which will be required not only for future tests but also — and even more critically—for success in further education.

After encountering this research as part of our case study, Noah noted in our discussions that the conditions of schooling described by Valencia, Villareal, and Salinas clearly illustrated his own circumstances. As Noah related, he was not punished for or forbidden from speaking Spanish in school, as previous generations of US-educated Latino children had been (Anzaldúa, Valencia). However, as a student who did not yet speak English, Noah found that there were other difficult consequences for entering a school system focused on accountability testing. [. . .]

Noah received no assistance in dealing with language issues as he began fourth grade (Valdés). Although the school told Noah that he would be enrolled in a program to learn English, this program never materialized. In fourth grade, Noah's language arts classes were taught in Spanish, while the teacher would speak in English to the other teachers in the school, if not to her students. Fourth grade math was conducted entirely in English, which Noah did not yet understand. As a result, he found it difficult to pay attention and often fell asleep in class.

In fifth grade, an Anglo teacher who spoke only in English to the students (but in Spanish to their parents) taught Texas history using only books written in English, which many of the students still had difficulty understanding. The Spanish translation of the Texas history textbook remained off limits to students. By sixth grade, Noah reported that, since he did not speak much English, his teacher initially tried to help him. However, his teacher's assistance was not consistent and Noah was often sent down to the lower grades to help take care of the younger students. At the time, Noah stated, he was happy about the situation, but "it wasn't good overall because if I'd stayed [in the sixth grade] I would have learned more English." In addition, because Noah's neighborhood in Houston had a high crime rate, his parents were afraid to allow him to play outside, which Noah understood as yet another lost opportunity to learn English.

At this juncture, Noah's story seems to follow the pattern described in Kozol's *Savage Inequalities,* rife with the lost opportunities and the silences endured by students who do not conform to state-mandated standards, students that Schemo describes as "push[ed] out the back door." However, in high school, Noah made a remarkable discovery. He described himself as "a student who likes to try different things," who, perhaps because of the challenges he faced in learning English, understood that he needed to be "alert and pay attention to what's going on." He was especially fascinated by "how things worked" and this interest led him to try his hand at skills such as carpentry, electronics, and art. An art teacher at Noah's high school eventually hired Noah to help renovate an old shed into an art studio in the art teacher's backyard, thus drawing together many of Noah's interests.

Noah's art teacher soon became his mentor. Since advanced classes were closed to students who were not identified as meeting high English proficiency standards, Noah enrolled in art classes. Noah found that "art helped to relieve stress and express emotions." Art was also a means of learning English for Noah, as his mentor continually emphasized. Because becoming an artist meant creating a portfolio, Noah's mentor suggested that "art is writing as well as painting."

By the fall of 2003, when he first enrolled at the university, Noah understood that "if I didn't go to college, I wouldn't have the opportunity to express my feelings and nothing would change about my life." In that first semester, he felt often that college was too hard for him and that he "didn't know how college worked." In addition, Noah was depressed by the difficulties that he continued to have with English. However, by the spring semester of 2004, Noah related that he knew that he would need to "be strong and keep fighting for my education — keep working, keep fighting, keep going."

Noah expressed relief that he was not alone in his struggles to learn English in Texas public schools. Nonetheless, Noah also noted his disappointment that the problem continues to be so widespread. Perhaps such discussions might seem dispiriting for students caught up in the mechanisms of inequitable public schooling in Texas, and yet when these issues were exposed as systemic problems rather than individualized notions of "success" or "failure," Noah's investment in his own education grew that much stronger.

Noah enrolled in a second semester of basic writing, this time linked with an introductory American Studies course that offered a cultural studies perspective. This six-hour course was designed for students who need to repeat the basic writing course, usually for reasons of English language acquisition and proficiency. In this second course, he discovered the work of Howard Zinn who, in *A People's History of the United States,* defamiliarizes the study of United States history by presenting a more inclusive point of view. Noah used this opportunity to continue to fill in the gaps in an education that had focused more on readiness for standardized testing rather than on preparation for college study.

In the brief samples that follow, I include writing from two of Noah's essays, one from each of the two semesters in which he has been my student. In a late semester essay for the fall 2003 linked reading and basic writing course, Noah wrote about the implications of Jean Anyon's study "Social Class and the Hidden Curriculum of Work" for his own schooling. In his essay written at midterm for the spring semester linked American studies and basic writing course, Noah focused on Howard Zinn's presentation of the history of Christopher Columbus' voyages to the Caribbean. Noah's essay contrasted Zinn's version of Columbus' voyages with more traditional versions as presented in high school (and earlier) and in reading prompts for state-mandated standardized tests. Following are excerpts from those essays:

November 2003

In my high school I think that we didn't have some of the resources because we use to borrow the cafeteria and library from a middle school next to my high school. We used to cross a bridge every day to eat. When it was time to do big projects we would cross the street to go at the library or if you were looking for a book for your reading classes, even though we use the cafeteria to do our test (TAAS). It was very cold inside and students were complained. In my English class I saw that boxes in my classroom arrived, but they stayed for two weeks without being opened, but when the teacher finally opened them we saw that they were books. I remember we didn't use them all the school season.

When I read this quote from Anyon's article "available textbooks are not always used" (Anyon 177). It attracted me because it brought memories from my high school. The teachers only ordered books just to have nice bookshelf, instead of giving them to the students so that they could learn. I think that Anyons tries to say that teachers' work based on what they think they know, but I believe that a classroom should be book based. Such that the students work to what the book say. What Anyon says about a Working-Class Schools, is true . . .

March 2004

Public schools give us the TAAS test, which seems to include material that I think is not beneficial for College. In the reading section of the TAAS tests there were stories about Christopher Columbus. One of the stories was not making sense by knowing the real story as when I read "Columbus, the Indians, and Human Progress" Columbus said "they would make fine servants" (Zinn 3). This is a quote where students are not going to find on these readings on the TAAS Test, so I think if we give them a well-rounded acknowledgement of Columbus would benefit students more. They would be better prepared in their education. That would be given the ability to interpret Columbus in their own way . . .

I do not know why public schools hide many things as history like Christopher Columbus, but working as a teacher I would do every thing to help students to get a better understanding on history and know more about history. When is time to be on the next level (college), students can be prepare to do a big step and move forward without difficulties.

What stands out for me in these samples of Noah's writing is his growing awareness of how his reading and writing were shaped by standardized testing. In his fall semester essay, Noah identifies how the problems of education for test preparation interfered with his schooling, especially in terms of reading. As Noah continued to think through this interference, he considered how students were not given full or accurate information about history. Since the state accountability tests focus on short reading passages, there is neither time nor space enough to allow for multiple perspectives. As Noah suggests, this truncated version of the Columbus story is presented to students as "history."

In his conversations with me in the spring semester, Noah speculated that one of the reasons that students described their schoolwork as "boring" might be "because their reading level in English was low." He noted that as a result of a more concentrated focus in reading and critical thinking, his interest and comprehension in reading in English had improved considerably since beginning college.

As a result of his own evolving processes, in the second semester, Noah's writing focused on the problematic nature of the reading section of the state-mandated test. The readings for the test were generally short and did not allow for interrogation or discussion. Test preparation followed the same pattern, with much focus on systematically responding to questions and how to identify correct answers. Critical analysis of the reading was rarely, if ever, a subject of classroom inquiry.

Noah perceived the problem as one of instructional focus. He had discovered in his first year of college that his professors placed more value on critical thinking, analytic reading, and persuasive writing than on "finding the right answer." In that regard, he suggested that students needed solid preparation for college that focused on more intellectual aims, rather than on preparation for testing. Rather than conclude in despair, Noah grounded his reflections in advocacy for future generations of students in his community. As Noah challenged himself to make sense of his reading in order to fashion his thoughts into writing, he also considered the necessity of changing the content of schooling in order to achieve a more felicitous outcome.

Closing Concerns

Goodman suggests (and Noah concurred) that:

> development [of quantitatively measured standard usage conventions] does not follow a straight line from one writing episode to the next. . . . Development reflects the growing experience of the writers and their personal histories within a specific cultural context as they begin to control written language to express their meaning. (Vygotsky 1986, 200)

This articulation of the development of the writing process illustrates yet another concern expressed by Noah and his peers. The written product of a single standardized test might not necessarily reflect the most accurate measure of student progress or success in writing. Yet this written product (as well as standardized tests in additional subject areas) had determined whether or not students would graduate from high school. As students found their own situations reflected in Schemo's *New York Times* articles, they related stories of friends and relatives who had dropped out of high school in part because of continued test failure.

As Noah's story suggests, literacy develops within a specific cultural context rather than in isolation. Bored by reading and frustrated by writing, Noah and his peers reported that they had not usually read novels or book-length nonfiction narratives in high school and had very rarely written essays that had allowed them to explore their own interpretations of a longer text. When expected to complete such tasks as part of their college course work, the students were at a loss as to how to respond.

Because the focus of their education was preparation for accountability testing, Noah and his classmates recognized that they were not provided with the opportunity to develop the literacy skills necessary for writing, reading, and critical thinking (Hillocks; McNeil; McNeil and Valenzuela). Yet these students eventually discovered that they could in fact succeed and progress when they had access to a variety of approaches to learning, rather than one standardized methodology that was meant to apply to all students regardless of their needs and desires.

Learning self-advocacy and self-efficacy can benefit students as they face the transitions between moving away from standards-based education to the intellectual challenges and long-term goals of becoming fluent in academic discourse (Sternglass). Such fluency is more than acculturation to college demands, but rather a means of speaking back to a system that has been shown to limit the educational horizons of students in greatest need. In this way, students who are survivors of such systems can re-create their own subject positions as advocates for their communities rather than as victims of the powers that be.

Moreover, as Siegel and Fernandez suggest, "critical approaches to the study of literacy education examine the ways in which literacy instruction participates in the production of these persistent inequalities but also how literacy instruction may become a site for contesting the status quo" (73). As we encounter more and more students who have been impacted by the ramifications of No Child Left Behind, we need not give in to our own frustrations and despair (Meyer).

Instead, we can use our own positions as teachers and researchers to not only challenge systemic inequalities as they are written into education law, but to advocate for change as well. As a transplanted Northerner who found myself living and working in the swamps of southeast Texas, I was inspired by the resilience of my students in the face of the hurdles that they encountered throughout their education. In light of their dreams, I owed them nothing less.

Acknowledgments

I would like to thank my student "Noah" for his willingness to participate in this case study, as well as for reading and commenting on drafts of this article. My fall semester 2003 students in basic writing also generously shared their thoughts and essays as part of this research. The Learners Community at University of Houston-Downtown offered the space for teaching experimental basic writing classes in the 2002–03 and 2003–04 school years, and a Title V Faculty Leadership Program grant gave helpful time to write in spring 2004. Bonne August, Shannon Carter, Stephen Cormany, and Ann E. Green read and provided invaluable comments on the manuscript at various stages. Drue McClure, Nancy Mize, Ardell Siegel, and Patricia Shepherd shared inspiring conversation as I talked through many of the ideas presented here. I would also like to thank Houston's Writers in the Schools program for additional support.

Works Cited

Anyon, Jean. From "Social Class and the Hidden Curriculum of Work." In *Rereading America: Cultural Contexts for Critical Thinking and Writing.* 5th ed. Eds. Gary Columbo, Robert Cullen, and Bonnie Lisle. Boston/New York: Bedford/St. Martin's, 2001. 174–90.

Anzaldúa, Gloria. *Borderlands/La Frontera: The New Mestiza.* 2nd ed. San Francisco, CA: Aunt Lute Books, 1999.

Bernstein, Jake. "The Hammer Drops: Democrats Define the Case Against the Republicans Redistricting Map." *The Texas Observer.* 18 July 2003. <http://www.texasobserver.org/showArticle.asp?ArticleID=1402>.

———. "Test Case." *The Texas Observer.* 30 August 2002. <http://www.texasobserver.org/showArticle.asp?ArticleFileName=020830f1.htm>.

Blalock, Glenn, and Richard Haswell. "Student Views of TAAS." February 2003. <http://comppile.tamucc.edu/TAAS/index.html>.

Blanton, Linda Lomon. "Classroom Instruction and Language Minority Students: On Teaching to 'Smarter' Readers and Writers." In Harklau, Losey, and Siegal, 119–42.

CLEAR English Language Arts Curriculum. *English Language Arts Grade 3: Model Lessons, Unit 6, Fantasy (Training Document).* Houston Independent School District, November, 2003.

Cochran-Smith, Marilyn, and Susan Lytle. *Inside/Outside: Teacher Research and Knowledge.* New York/London: Teachers College Press, 1993.

Coleman, Garnet F. Texas State Representative, District 147. Personal Communication. 6 February 2004.

Comfort, Carol, Ed. *Breaking Boundaries.* Upper Saddle River, NJ: Prentice Hall, 2000.

Delpit, Lisa D. *Other People's Children: Cultural Conflict in the Classroom.* New York: New Press, 1995.

Farris, Sara. "Your Textbook Is in the Library: Go Find It." Fifty-Fifth Annual Convention of the Conference on College Composition and Communication. San Antonio, Texas. March 2004.

Flag Pledge. Texas State Library. 18 April 2004. <http://www.tsl.state.tx.us/ref/abouttx/flagpledge.html>.

Gillespie, Spike. "Reading, Writing, and Pledging." *The Texas Observer* 24 October 2003: 30–31.

Goodman, Yetta. "The Writing Process." *Notes from a Kidwatcher: Selected Writings of Yetta Goodman.* Ed. Sandra Wilde. Portsmouth, NH: Heinemann, 1996. 191–206.

Guerrero, Michael D. "Research in Bilingual Education: Moving Beyond the Effectiveness Debate." In Valencia (Ed.), 170–91.

Harclau, Linda, May M. Losey, and Meryl Siegal, Eds. *Generation 1.5 Meets College Composition: Issues in the Teaching of Writing to U.S.-Educated Learners of ESL.* Mahwah, NJ: Erlbaum, 1999.

———. "Linguistically Diverse College Students: What Is Equitable and Appropriate?" In Harklau, Losey, and Siegal, 1–14.

Hillocks, George. *The Testing Trap: How State Assessments Control Learning.* New York/London: Teachers College Press, 2002.

Houston Independent School District. *Facts and Figures.* January 2004. <http://www.houstonisd.org/vgn/images/portal/cit7634/22560382004Facts Figures.pdf>.

Katz, Susan Roberta. "Does NCLB Leave the U.S. Behind in Bilingual Teacher Education?" *English Education* 36.2 (January 2004): 141–52.

Kozol, Jonathan. *Savage Inequalities: Children in America's Schools.* New York: HarperCollins, 1992.

Language Arts 11th Grade. 23 May 2004. <http://www.roundrockisd.org/academics/alignedcurriculum/200304/Langarts/Secondary/11thgrade.doc>.

LaCelle-Peterson, Mark. "Choosing Not to Know: How Assessment Policies and Practices Obscure the Education of Language Minority Students." *Assessment: Social Practice and Social Product.* Ed. Ann Filer. London/New York: Routledge, 2000. 27–42.

McNeil, Linda M. *Contradictions of School Reform: Educational Costs of Standardized Testing.* New York: Routledge, 2000.

———, and Angela Valenzuela, "The Harmful Impact of the TAAS System of Testing in Texas: Beneath the Accountability Rhetoric." In *Raising Standards or Raising Barriers? Inequality and High Stakes Testing in Public Education,* edited by Gary Orfield and Mindy Kornhaber. 2001. <http://caracas.soehd.scufresno.edu/whatsnew/valenzuela/Valenzuela1%20.pdf>.

Metcalf, Stephen. "Reading Between the Lines." *Nation.* 10 January 2002. <http://www.thenation.comdoc.mhtml?i=20020128&s=metcalf&c=>.

Meyer, Richard. "Shifting to Political Action in Literacy Research and Teacher Education." *English Education* 36.2 (January 2004): 134–40.

Released Tests. Texas Education Agency. 18 April 2004. <http://www.tea.state.tx.us/student.assessment/resources/release/#2003>.

Schemo, Diana Jean. "For Houston Schools, College Claims Exceed Reality." *New York Times.* 28 August 2003. <http://www.nytimes.com>.

———. "Questions on Data Cloud Luster of Houston School." *New York Times.* 11 July 2003. <http://www.nytimes.com>.

Shor, Ira. *Empowering Education: Critical Teaching for Social Change.* Chicago/London: University of Chicago P, 1992.

Siegel, Marjorie, and Susana Laura Fernandez. "Critical Approaches." *Methods of Literacy Research: The Methodology Chapters from The Handbook of Reading Research.* Vol. 3. Ed. Michael L. Kamil, Peter B. Mosenthal, P. David Pearson, and Rebecca Barr. Mahwah, NJ: Erlbaum, 2002. 65–75.

Steele, Claude M. "Not Just a Test." *Nation.* 15 April 2004. <http://www.thenation.com/doc.mhtml?i=20040503&c=1&s=steele>.

Sternglass, Marilyn. *Time to Know Them: A Longitudinal Study of Writing and Learning at the College Level.* Mahwah, NJ: Erlbaum, 1997.

Texas Education Agency. Press Release. 30 May 2003. <http://www.tea.state.tx.us/press/takscores03.html>.

Texas Education Agency. Student Assessment Division. *TAKS: Texas Assessment of Knowledge and Skills, Information Booklet 11 Exit Level English Language Arts.* 2002. <http://www.tea.state.tx.us/studentassessment/taks/booklets/>.

Texas Higher Education Coordinating Board. "Success Initiative." *Summary of Sunset Legislation: 78th Legislative Session*. July 2003. <www.thecb.state.tx.us/cfbin/ArchBottom.cfm?DocID=620&Format=Word>.

Valdés, Guadalupe. *Learning and Not Learning English: Latino Students in American Schools*. New York: Teachers College Press, 2001.

Valencia, Richard R., Ed. *Chicano School Failure and Success: Past, Present, and Future*. 2nd ed. London/New York: Routledge, 2002.

———. "The Plight of Chicano Students: An Overview of Schooling Conditions and Outcomes." In Valencia, Ed., 3–51.

———, Bruno J. Villareal, and Moises F. Salinas. "Educational Testing and Chicano Students: Issues, Consequences, and Prospects for Reform." In Valencia, Ed., 253–309.

Ybarra, Raul. "Cultural Dissonance in Basic Writing Courses." *Journal of Basic Writing* 20.1 (2001): 37–52.

Zancanella, Don, and Elizabeth Noll. "Teaching Education in Language Arts and Literacy in the Era of 'No Child Left Behind.'" *English Education* 36.2 (January 2004): 101–03.

Zinn, Howard. *A People's History of the United States*. Abridged Teaching Edition Revised and Updated. New York/London: The New Press, 2003.

Classroom Activities

Elsewhere in this book, it is suggested that students write personal narratives about their development as readers and writers (Dong, Chapter 12) and about their computer literacy experiences (Pavia, Chapter 10). In order to move from narrative reflection to persuasive analysis, ask students to revise their narratives to analyze the cultural contexts of their personal stories. Students can ask themselves and each other questions about the local and global conditions that informed their schooling and can propose changes and improvements to the current system, as well as ideas for strengthening successful programs.

Invite students to consider a congressional representative or other civic leader as the audiences for their essays, and to send their essays, written as letters, to those leaders or to a local or national newspaper. Students also can post their essays to a class or other Web site or to a blog.

Thinking about Teaching

For this article, Bernstein researched the education laws of her state, as well as how the laws were enacted in the local urban public school system from which many of her students enrolled in basic writing had graduated. In this way, she was able to learn about the ways in which writing instruction was conceptualized as preparation for state-mandated accountability testing. As a result, she designed a pedagogy to address the transition from high school to college-based writing.

Consider taking a look at the No Child Left Behind law (available at <http://www.ed.gov/nclb/landing.jhtml?src=pb>) and investigating your own state's mandates for accountability testing. In addition, find out how these mandates translate into writing instruction for students in local and regional public schools. What, if any, differences are there in standards for high school and college writing? What are the pedagogical possibilities for reframing college writing to move beyond the formulaic structures presented by state-mandated tests? Record your findings in your teaching journal and discuss your ideas with colleagues at your institution and in professional settings.

14

Basic Writing and the Writing Center

In this final chapter, Gregory Shafer and Anne DiPardo discuss the ways in which writing centers can contribute to the education of developing writers. Shafer refers to the work of Brazilian educator Paulo Freire as he articulates the purposes of the writing center as a site of democratic education and critical pedagogy. DiPardo studies the interactions of two young female students of color, a Navajo student who is enrolled in basic writing and an African American student who works as a peer tutor in the writing center. Together these two articles present the satisfactions and challenges of writing center work for developing writers and their tutors.

Negotiating Audience and Voice in the Writing Center

Gregory Shafer

"Back in the writing center," writes Gregory Shafer, "composition is too often about imposed power, about learning to write for one's teacher, about learning a prefabricated, immutable form. It is too often about following orders." In the following article, originally published in Teaching English in the Two-Year College *in 1999, Shafer attempts to negotiate basic writing students' struggles with voice, with instructors' emphases on teaching five-paragraph themes and other "basic skills" in a typical developmental writing curriculum. Included in this selection are the inspired voices of four developing writers, whose compelling stories could*

not be confined to the strictures of the five-paragraph essay. Using the ideas of Freire and hooks, as well as those of Elbow and Shaughnessy, Shafer attempts to evolve a pedagogy that values both audience and voice as he and students work together in the writing center.

Introduction

Each day they trudge into the writing center with the same familiar look of consternation and anger. Sometimes it's because their instructor has failed to address the content of their essays, but more often it's simply about voice and control. Within their classes, a kind of power struggle ensues as each writer attempts to transcend the mechanical and prescribed prose that has become a staple of the five-paragraph theme. They are developmental writers, but they want to use elements of their dialect, include their culture and diction, and pepper their narratives with the occasional obscenity when it accurately captures the heart of their story.

Marcus, a husky African American student, slides into the seat next to me and gingerly lays his paper in front of my eyes. "She says I can't use the word 'thug-ass' to describe my cousin," he says as he wipes the sweat from his forehead and lowers his backpack to the floor. Marcus's essay is a character paper about his cousin, a man who has comic aspirations to be a big-time criminal. Thus, Marcus, in his smartly sarcastic style, has given the appellation of "My Thug-Ass Cousin" to his paper. Quickly, I read it over again, only I already know the content and style. Marcus is a wonderfully fluid writer. His style is unrestrained and honest. His detailed description of his cousin chronicles both the humor and pathos in a young man who has romanticized the "gangster" image. Marcus's approach to his paper is both personal and racial. He wants to make his audience laugh while helping them to see the continuing blight of racism and the concrete way it affects real people. And yet, through all of the raw honesty and pathetic humor, he is being told to "eliminate the obscenities" because they are "inappropriate in an academic setting." "So what am I supposed to do?" he asks me with his big, undaunted smile. "She's not gonna let me use 'ass' in my paper."

Silence. I sit and contemplate the things I'd like to say to his instructor. The way she is blunting and effacing the voice of a talented young writer seems unethical, unconscionable, but I can't sacrifice his grade so I can make a statement. "Let me talk to her," I say. "Leave the paper as it is," I add with reassurance. "It's beautiful and thoughtful. It makes your audience think. I like it a lot!" Marcus smiles and shakes his head. Now the hard work begins as I think about talking to his instructor about voice and a very special talent.

Each week, my work in the writing center presents me with at least a couple of the dilemmas that I describe with Marcus. I have come to call them questions of autonomy and voice, since their implications go well beyond issues of "appropriateness" or academic format. Indeed, they touch upon the basic freedom we are willing to extend to basic and minority writers. With all of the talk about empowerment and hegemony in our profession, are we really willing to elevate genuine expression above petty, egocentric worries about academic protocol? In the same way, is our hesitance about "obscenities" more about academics or culture? Are we jittery about "nasty language" because it symbolizes an unharnessed and angry political voice? And finally, are we truly doing our job, if we censor the uninhibited writer simply because he doesn't fit into the narrow parameters of what has come to be called safe "academic discourse"? Who, in the end, are we serving when we shape and limit unconventional students? In this essay, I hope to answer some of these questions.

Another Example

Polly is twenty-five, but her experience and wisdom make her seem much older. As she strolls confidently into the writing center, she personifies bell hooks's description of the student who is adamant about receiving a "liberatory education" while feeling "terribly wounded" (19) by the dearth of true freedom she receives from her instructors. As with Marcus, Polly is engaged in a very riveting, flesh-and-blood experience concerning her ex-husband. As I read over her paper, I'm shocked and moved by her vivid description of the beatings, the verbal abuse, the cavalier use of intimidation. "This is real — right?" I ask her with an incredulous look. Quickly, she smiles and shakes her head, yes. Polly is reliving her marriage and the emotional scars it left. As I read more, the dialogue, the detail of the beatings seem more and more authentic and dramatic. I stop and take a deep breath.

It is, put simply, a paper that exposes the brutality that is lamentably a part of too many marriages. Its style is unreserved, unbridled. Polly isn't holding back: "He scratched me with his long nails. He was doing more than hurting me now. He wanted to leave a scar, to leave his mark on my face."

Finally I reach her instructor's comments and recognize the focus of Polly's frustration. The evaluation seems detached and unrelated to the paper. Somehow, the instructor has washed away the emotion and violence that oozes from the writing and has limited her observations to questions of form and usage. Her comments are professional, surgical. She has taken a personal drama and reduced it to insipid comments on rules and form: "Your form is good, but you sometimes deviate from the thesis. Remember, you're writing a comparison/contrast paper. Don't lose that focus. You might consider a review of fragments too. They pop up quite frequently. Well done!"

"What do you think of my paper?" asks Polly. "Because this doesn't tell me nothing!" she fumes with obvious anger. Again, as with Marcus's work earlier, I see what seems to be a stripping away of the meat and blood of a paper. Each instructor seems unsure or unwilling to deal with the topics that transcend the "academic community." Lost in both of their evaluations is the need for writers to be heard, to bring a piece of their lives, culture, and social context into the writing they do. The struggle, while simmering beneath the surface, is very real and raises serious questions about the role of college writing instruction. Is it our job to assist students in becoming models of academic discourse, replete with properly placed commas and standard white English, or rather, is it our job to help them unleash the clamor and discord that rumbles inside their heads, a cacophony that can enliven their papers if it is allowed to become part of their discourse?

The Practice of Academic English

Most scholarship I have read seems to suggest that we should be guardians of civilized English, that we should quiet writers by molding them into "academic scholars," into people like us. David Bartholomae's "Inventing the University" talks candidly about the cumbersome but necessary task a college student faces in trying to approximate the jargon and style of the academic community. His message is that the academy's first job is to prescribe a style that mirrors itself. Forget about individualism, our role is to make students more like us. "I am continually impressed with the patience and good will of our students," writes Bartholomae in describing the daunting task of learning academic prose. The students are "appropriated by a specialized discourse," which requires them to "speak our language," or "carry the bluff" (273). In short, then, the most difficult but important role of the college composition instructor is to help writers become more like the university, to shed their cultural personas and learn to embrace a foreign and rather stiff language, one that serves them in few ways beyond the context in which they use it.

Little is said about self-actualization, expression, or fulfillment. Indeed, it is an ironic aspect of our profession that we extol the democratic and strive for student autonomy while forcing students to write in a contrived discourse that serves to exult the academic community over the students it is supposed to empower. Is this what students would call a paradox if they were in Literature 101?

Marcus and Polly are certainly left empty and alienated by the practice. Neither have aspirations of being scholars or academics, but that doesn't prevent their instructors from compelling them to learn the specific style and expectations that academic discourse entails. Should we then wonder why students feel that college composition is less about them and their lives than the foreign register of their instructor, who stands at the front of the class loaded with answers? In the same way, should we feel surprised or upset when our students crank out the plastic, apocryphal prose that is too often a part of first-year composition? We cry for voice and power. We preach liberation. And then we require the fabricated prescriptions that embody nothing of the person behind the words.

Working with students like Marcus and Polly helps highlight the importance of a curriculum that transcends this egocentric, self-aggrandizing approach. Both demonstrate an extremely deft and vivid eye for their world and the significance of their experiences. Marcus writes about his "Thug-Ass Cousin" as both a parody on the romanticism some youths have toward a violent world and a dramatic statement on the limitations placed on African Americans:

> He sits in front of this bank, getting himself up for a big-time bank robbery that's ain't ever gonna happen. He could have and probably should have gone to work that day. But minimum wage doesn't get him out of bed the way it should. And it probably never will.

The writing is poetic, almost song-like. The wisdom and message are profound. Marcus doesn't write like any university or college professors I know, and this is perhaps one of the reasons his prose is so dramatic and riveting. The challenge for us as a scholarly community is what to do with this forever emerging and organic voice. Do we define a liberatory education as shaping our students to be like us, or do we celebrate a mosaic of new styles and voices radiating from our classrooms — voices and styles that are troubling and difficult because they are not part of our formal education? There is a kind of arrogance in Bartholomae's message, and it hasn't been lost on the academic community that enforces it. Instead of reaching out to the dialects and cultures outside the ivy-covered walls of the college, it defines success as a labor of mimicry.

Support from Freire and bell hooks

I have often felt that the sentiments of Paulo Freire and bell hooks better reflect the ideas of a truly emancipatory education. Rather than advocating an experience that exults the power and inherent goodness of the academic world, it seems clearly revolutionary and rebellious. Marcus and Polly, I am virtually certain, would be better served by their inclusive political pedagogy. In particular, bell hooks seems in touch with the power of "transgressing" and the implications of such an education. "I have been most inspired," writes hooks, "by those teachers who have had the courage to transgress those boundaries that would confine each pupil to a rote, assembly-line approach to learning" (13). She writes about the dichotomy between an education of "active participation" and one that embraces the "passive consumer" (14). In other words, students become most alive and empowered when they are personally creating, actively evaluating their world in a style that reflects and changes that world. Marcus tells his story through not only the content but the style as well. The pathos and violence of his life is reflected in his use of double negatives, in his deviations from standard English.

To eliminate this component from his essay is to rip out its viscera and leave it as little more than an assembly line replica of what too many first-year students think is effective writing. How often have I heard college instructors lament such spiritless writing? And yet, how often have I seen these same instructors practice a prescription that takes the pen out of their students' hands?

Many professors should ask themselves if they are afraid or threatened by a truly emancipatory education, one that begins with students and transcends the safe haven of the college theme. Many, I believe, are intimidated by the idea that their students might force them to think, that prose like that of Marcus's might compel them to redefine and broaden the concept of acceptable writing — forcing them into unknown territory. Indeed, when I asked Marcus's instructor why it was "wrong" or "inappropriate" to use "gonna" or a double negative, she fell safely back on the assertion that it is not part of "academic writing." Really? Would this instructor, I silently wondered, be surprised to read some of the work of Geneva Smitherman or bell hooks? Is the premise that such writing is "inappropriate" an arbitrary way of precluding new voices, as many attempt to do in the field of canonical literature? Clearly, this instructor, while seeming to want the best for Marcus, was acting as an oppressor.

Such instructors hooks calls "benevolent dictators," those who are more interested in maintaining their authority "within their mini-kingdom, the classroom" (17) than in self-actualization. Within such a system, few people grow, learn, or change, as a static and immutable form of discourse is inculcated to its passive subjects. The key, adds hooks, is to promote risk-taking and to embrace it as a part of learning for both teacher and student. "Professors must practice being vulnerable in the classroom, being wholly present in mind, body, and spirit," she contends (21). The alternative, she later adds, is a curriculum that "reinforces systems of domination," that perpetuates a smug and lifeless status quo. "Empowerment cannot happen if we refuse to be vulnerable while encouraging students to take risks" (21), she reminds us.

For Paulo Freire, such risks are key to humanistic education. In his classic *Pedagogy of the Oppressed,* he labels passive, top-down approaches to learning as a "banking system of education," one that relegates students to the role of receptacle. For Freire, true, humanistic education emanates from a pedagogy that promotes problem-posing and dialogue over transferals of information and "domestication" (71). In considering the plight of both Marcus and Polly, we can quickly see his point. In a composition class that seeks to deposit information in a linear, static way, there is simply no room for thought, dialogue, or growth. In such a scenario, students become little more than robots who obediently learn and memorize the single, instructor-endorsed way to success. Without dialogue or debate, the instruction is narrative in form, flowing from teacher to student and devoid of action and reflection. The task becomes one of pursuit, chasing the instructor and trying to unlock the keys to success.

For Polly and Marcus, the process is also demoralizing because it leaves them as something less than human. Indeed, how can we consider ourselves thinking and vital individuals when our culture and language is being expunged without critical discussion? Again Freire speaks to this in his distinction between animal and human. For Freire, the animal is primarily a being that lives without reflection, a being that adapts without considering implications or meaning. "Animals," writes Freire, "are beings in themselves" (87). They do not, in other words, step away from their lives to contemplate the significance of why and how they exist. It is not, in short, a critical, introspective life.

In contrast, truly human beings are able to step back and analyze their lives and values. They can ascribe meaning to actions and synthesize events to make conclusions about their feelings and ethics. In short, they construct reality rather than simply respond to it. They, to use Freire's words, "infuse the world with their creative presence" (88). They become active partners in their education.

Polly and Marcus both find themselves being treated as passive beings that are expected to learn the routine in much the same way a dog learns tricks. With the context being bereft of dialogue or active problem-posing, the learning is more akin to rote memorization. The students are irrelevant, voiceless. Again, Freire addresses this with eloquent prose: "Animal activity, which occurs without praxis, is not creative; man's transforming activity is" (91).

In the end, then, we must ask ourselves who is really being served in a pedagogy that elevates prescription over critical dialogue. Is it the developmental writer, who, according to many of my colleagues, needs close instruction because of a lack of experience? Or is it really the instructor, who finds it both easier and safer to disseminate rules and forms over an organic process of learning? My experience in the writing center would clearly indicate that the instructor is the main beneficiary of a top-down education. While such a pedagogy instills students with a formula for organization and usage, it negates the fundamental act of thinking, of learning through a heuristic, personal process.

After our second meeting, Marcus is ready to change his essay to "what will ever make my instructor happy," while Polly is resigned to the limited comments she receives. Both, lamentably, have come to see the context as being despotic and impersonal. "I'm just worried about my grade in the end," says Marcus later in the semester. "I'll do what makes her happy. It's her class."

Solutions and Alternatives

Writing Is Social

On Tuesday, Sally wheels herself into the writing center, surveying the room as she maneuvers her wheelchair to the computer and timidly touches the keys. She is a fifty-eight-year-old student who has returned to school to take writing classes and get out of the house.

"Think you could take a look at this?" she asks me in a deferential tone. Her essay is titled "My Old Brown Coat," and as I read it over, I'm immediately touched by the quaint voice as well as the short, simple sentences. Her paper is nostalgic and filled with a curious affection for a piece of apparel:

> The old brown coat I owned was not like any coat I owned. After it was torn, it became a disaster. It lost its shape and style. It was tattered. The coat was ten years old. It was so special.

"This is nice," I say with a smile. However, as I continue to reread, I become increasingly aware of the jerky sentences, and I wonder how her audience will respond to the lack of fluidity. I begin to think of strategies to help her connect sentences and assist her audience in reading and enjoying her paper. "You know," I say to her as I look away from the computer screen, "we could work on the flow of your prose. I like your paper, but as I read it, I want you to combine some of your sentences — so I don't have to work so hard as a reader."

My work with Sally begins to provide me with ideas for how to empower other students, students like Marcus and Polly who are struggling with demands of audience. All three, it seems to me, highlight the social character of writing. When we sit down to write a paper, we are not simply writing for ourselves but for a group of subjective people. The content and style, then, must reflect a cooperative effort to express our views without alienating readers.

In the case of Marcus and Polly, decisions must be made as a negotiation. Teachers must ask themselves what is essential in terms of diction, organization, and style, while writers must consider both their readers and the goals of their writing. For Polly and Marcus, the value of their cultural lexicon must be weighed along side audience expectations. For Sally, integrity of voice must be weighed against the demand for more melodic sentences.

Similar questions, it seems to me, must be asked in response to non-standard dialects. Both writers and instructors must consider the transaction between reader and writer (Rosenblatt) — the social dynamic of communication — and come to a collaborative decision as to what is acceptable in a certain context. Such a democratic approach includes students and helps illuminate the realities of writing for an audience. At the same time, it eliminates a linear caveat from teacher to student, resulting in a class that stresses obedience over construction.

This vision is especially important as I begin to work with Kathy. Her essay on how she contracted a socially transmitted disease is poignant and moving. However, it is rife with the most offensive array of gratuitous obscenities I have ever read in a student paper. And then, there is the request from her teacher to place the thesis statement at the end of the introduction.

Kathy is the consummate example of why it is important to protect the integrity of the writer's voice while fulfilling the demands of one's audience. Indeed, as I read over her writing, I am plunged into the chaos of the doctor's examination table. And yet, the obscenities seem to intrude more than enhance:

> I winced as the assistant rolled in a tray of metal gadgets. There was no little speculum this time. This man was wielding what looked like a fucking shoehorn. I cried out when he shoved it between my legs. He then chided me, telling me it didn't hurt. Like he had a god damn clue [. . .].

I finish reading, take a deep breath, and smile. "This is wonderful," I assure her. "I'm wondering, however, if we could respond to your teacher's concerns about language and thesis. Do the obscene words contribute to your message or divert attention from it?"

Later, as we begin to reconsider the essay, we work together to capture the essence of this personal experience while respecting the concerns of readers. It is always a collaborative experience, a negotiation. There are ways, we find, to respect the visions of author and teacher. Writing is about more than either a monolithic model of the university essay or a personal vision of what the author has planned.

Writing Is a Process

Much has been written about alternatives to the traditional composition class. Many of these suggestions have centered on the importance of process, development, and autonomy as integral parts of learning as one writes. Little debate exists as to the need for time as one constructs and designs a piece of writing. We know, for instance, that composition is not a clean, linear act but one that is recursive, messy, social, and cooperative. While more and more instructors allow for this freedom and process in the college composition class, fewer are willing to extend this same autonomy to basic writers, who are often perceived as unable to generate prose without careful and direct instruction. This, I believe, gives rise to the benevolent despot, the instructor, who, in his/her attempt to help the basic writer, actually stymies any generative process. "These students come from deprived backgrounds," an instructor once told me. "They simply need more help from us."

That help, I would contend, begins with process and the journey of discovery that every writer experiences as he/she begins to write. It does not begin with a prescriptive, emasculating set of caveats but enough freedom so that the student has the opportunity to "cook and grow" as Peter Elbow would say. Basic writers, argued Mina Shaughnessy, must "learn by making mistakes" (5). The process, as with other writers, is one of gradual, evolutionary construction. While it is filled with errors, it is also a time of learning through direct experience. "The writer understands that writing is a process, not a rigid procedure. He continually rediscovers his subject," says Donald Murray. It is "discovery of meaning, discovery of form — and the writer works back and forth [. . .]" (7).

Conclusion

All of this would suggest that the best way to teach basic writers is through both process and a respect for the social discovery that ensues as one composes. To negate or trivialize the context in which they write is to alienate students and relegate them to a passive process of imitating others rather than learning to create and synthesize information from their own world. "Bartholomae's pedagogy," writes Richard Boyd, "sets up a kind of master/slave relationship where the student-as-mimic is relegated to a perpetually subordinate role" (341). Indeed, to reduce writing to a series of "skills" and prescriptions does not teach empowered, creative thought. Rather, it marginalizes writers, telling them their experiences are not important, that composition is not about social critique but rules and obedience. It is the antithesis of Freire's vision for a liberated, problem-posing community.

Back in the writing center, composition is too often about imposed power, about learning to write for one's teacher, about learning a prefabricated, immutable form. It is too often about following orders. For Polly and Marcus, two basic writers who show incredible insight, ideas and experiences become submerged as they are coerced into joining this "university of writers." It is a practice that needs to be changed if we are ever to be truly democratic and inclusive in the way we teach college composition.

Works Cited

Bartholomae, David. "Inventing the University." *Perspectives on Literacy*. Ed. Eugene Kintgen, Barry Kroll, and Mike Rose. Carbondale: Southern Illinois UP, 1988. 273–85.

Boyd, Richard. "Imitate Me; Don't Imitate Me: Mimeticism in David Bartholo-
    mae's 'Inventing the University.'" *Journal of Advanced Composition* 11
    (1991): 335–45.
Elbow, Peter. *Writing without Teachers.* New York: Oxford UP, 1973.
Freire, Paulo. *Pedagogy of the Oppressed.* New York: Continuum, 1990.
hooks, bell. *Teaching to Transgress.* New York: Routledge, 1994.
Murray, Donald. *A Writer Teaches Writing.* Boston: Houghton, 1968.
Rosenblatt, Louise. *The Reader, the Text, the Poem.* Carbondale: Southern
    Illinois UP, 1978.
Shaughnessy, Mina. *Errors and Expectations.* New York: Oxford UP, 1977.

Classroom Activities

What happens when a student has a particular story to tell and needs
to tell it in his or her own voice, a voice that mirrors the streets or the
rural back roads, a voice with much to say, but in language often not
easy to hear? Shafer poses this important problem as he describes his
work as a tutor in the writing center and his discussions with teachers and students. One way to approach this issue is to discuss it
directly with students. Where do students find topics for "narrative"
writing assignments? What happens if their story doesn't fit the conventional five-paragraph essay format? How do students "negotiate"
the need to find their own voices and tell their own stories with the
need to write in "audience-appropriate" language that their instructors and tutors will accept as "correct"? This activity can be an opportunity to empower students, as Freire would have it, to begin to claim
their own education. Students can learn what kinds of questions to
ask of their teachers and of their writing center tutors in order to
learn and grow in their writing — and to not merely produce "what
the teacher wants." Moreover, teachers can see this discussion as an
opportunity to examine their own views about what "counts" as
acceptable prose in the basic writing course. Should the basic writing
course concern itself only with survival skills, such as writing five-
paragraph essays in academic discourse? Or should students new to
process-based writing (as many basic writing students often are) have
the opportunity to experiment with prose style and storytelling as a
way to learn the variety of rhetorical choices available to writers?

Thinking about Teaching

In your teaching journal, reflect on the questions presented above and
work out some of the difficult issues presented in Shafer's article.

Have you or a colleague ever received a paper similar to Marcus's "My Thug-Ass Cousin"? What was the response to this writing — and on what criteria was the response based? How were those criteria constructed in relation to the course requirements of basic writing and in relation to facilitating an opportunity for students to grow as writers? Shafer frames the question as follows: "Is it our job to assist students in becoming models of academic discourse, replete with properly placed commas and standard white English, or rather, is it our job to help them unleash the clamor and discord that rumbles inside their heads, a cacophony that can enliven their papers if it is allowed to become part of their discourse?" Perhaps this problem need not be posed as two diametrically opposing sides. Moreover, as Shafer suggests, "Writing is about more than either a monolithic model of the university essay or a personal vision of what the author has planned." There is, in fact, room for negotiation and for honoring process, which Shafer contends is often taken for granted more in composition courses than in the basic writing course. Consider other essays in this book that refer to the problematic nature of the basic writing course. Also take a look at Paulo Freire's germinal work, *Pedagogy of the Oppressed,* which provides an important perspective on student-centered learning. Consider facilitating an open discussion on this issue among teachers, students, and tutors. Perhaps such a discussion could be sponsored by the writing center and could involve a wide range of participants across the curriculum. Finally, consider writing an article on your own perspective on this issue, based on your ideas and experiences as a teacher in the basic writing classroom.

"Whispers of Coming and Going": Lessons from Fannie

Anne DiPardo

In the following article, first published in 1992 in The Writing Center Journal, *Anne DiPardo presents a case study of Fannie, a basic writing student who was the only Navajo at her predominantly white West Coast college. Fannie, DiPardo writes, "was still struggling to find her way both academically and socially, still working to overcome the scars of her troubled educational history." To document this struggle, DiPardo presents excerpts from transcripts of Fannie's tutoring sessions with Morgan, an African American student and writing center tutor. These young women from different economic and cultural backgrounds bring contrasting communication styles to their tutoring sessions, resulting in significant challenges for each. DiPardo chronicles these challenges and suggests implications for tutoring language minority students, as well as for training tutors.*

> *As a man with cut hair, he did not identify the rhythm of three strands, the whispers of coming and going, of twisting and tying and blending, of catching and of letting go, of braiding.*
>
> — Michael Dorris, *A Yellow Raft in Blue Water*

We all negotiate among multiple identities, moving between public and private selves, living in a present shadowed by the past, encountering periods in which time and circumstance converge to realign or even restructure our images of who we are. As increasing numbers of non-Anglo students pass through the doors of our writing centers, such knowledge of our own shape-shifting can help us begin — if *only* begin — to understand the social and linguistic challenges which inform their struggles with writing. When moved to talk about the complexities of their new situation, they so often describe a more radically chameleonic process, of living in non-contiguous worlds, of navigating between competing identities, competing loyalties. "It's like I have two cultures in me," one such student remarked to me recently, "but I can't choose." Choice becomes a moot point as boundaries blur, as formerly distinct selves become organically enmeshed, indistinguishable threads in a dynamic whole (Bakhtin 275; Cintron 24; Fischer 196).

Often placed on the front lines of efforts to provide respectful, insightful attention to these students' diverse struggles with academic discourse, writing tutors likewise occupy multiple roles, remaining learners even while emerging as teachers, perennially searching for a suitable social stance (Hawkins) — a stance existing somewhere along a continuum of detached toughness and warm empathy, and, which like all things ideal, can only be approximated, never definitively located. Even the strictly linguistic dimension of their task is rendered problematic by the continuing paucity of research on the writing of non-mainstream students (see Valdés; "Identifying Priorities"; "Language Issues") — a knowledge gap which likewise complicates our own efforts to provide effective tutor training and support. Over a decade has passed since Mina Shaughnessy eloquently advised basic writing teachers to become students, to consider what Glynda Hull and Mike Rose ("Rethinking," "Wooden Shack") have more recently called the "logic and history" of literacy events that seem at first glance inscrutable and strange. In this age of burgeoning diversity, we're still trying to meet that challenge, still struggling to encourage our tutors to appreciate its rich contours, to discover its hidden rigors, to wrestle with its endless vicissitudes.

This story is drawn from a semester-long study of a basic writing tutorial program at a west-coast university — a study which attempted to locate these tutor-led small groups within the larger contexts of a writing program and campus struggling to meet the instructional needs of non-Anglo students (see DiPardo, "Passport"). It is about one tutor and one student, both ethnic minorities at this overwhelmingly white, middle-class campus, both caught up in elusive dreams and uncertain beginnings. I tell their story not because it is either unusual or typical, but because it seems so richly revealing of the larger themes I noted again and again during my months of data collection — as unresolved tensions tugged continually at a fabric of institutional good intentions, and as tutors and students struggled, with ostensible good will and inexorable frustration, to make vital connection. I tell this story because I believe it has implications for all of us trying to be worthy students of our students, to make sense of our own responses to diversity, and to offer effective support to beginning educators entrusted to our mentorship.

"It, Like, Ruins Your Mind": Fannie's Educational History

Fannie was Navajo, and her dream was to one day teach in the reservation boarding schools she'd once so despised, to offer some of the intellectual, emotional, and linguistic support so sorely lacking in her own educational history. As a kindergartner, she had been sent to a school so far from her home that she could only visit family on weekends. Navajo was the only language spoken in her house, but at school all the teachers were Anglo, and only English was allowed. Fannie recalled that students had been punished for speaking their native language — adding with a wry smile that they'd spoken Navajo anyway, when the teachers weren't around. The elementary school curriculum had emphasized domestic skills — cooking, sewing, and especially, personal hygiene. "Boarding school taught me to be a housemaid," Fannie observed in one of her essays, "I was hardly taught how to read and write." All her literacy instruction had been in English, and she'd never become literate in Navajo. Raised in a culture that valued peer collaboration (cf. Philips 391–93), Fannie had long ago grasped that Anglo classrooms were places where teachers assume center stage, where the students are expected to perform individually: "No," her grade-school teachers had said when Fannie turned to classmates for help, "I want to hear *only* from *you*."

Estranged from her family and deeply unhappy, during fifth grade Fannie had stayed for a time with an aunt and attended a nearby public school. The experience there was much better, she recalled, but there soon followed a series of personal and educational disruptions as she moved among various relatives' homes and repeatedly switched schools. By the time she began high school, Fannie was wondering if the many friends and family members who'd dropped out had perhaps made the wiser choice. By her sophomore year, her grades had sunken "from A's and B's to D's and F's," and she was "hanging out with the wrong crowd." By mid-year, the school wrote her parents a letter indicating that she had stopped coming to class. When her family drove up to get her, it was generally assumed that Fannie's educational career was over.

Against all odds, Fannie finished high school after all. At her maternal grandmother's insistence, arrangements were made for Fannie to live with an aunt who had moved to a faraway west-coast town where the educational system was said to be much stronger. Her aunt's community was almost entirely Anglo, however, and Fannie was initially self-conscious about her English: "I had an accent really bad," she recalled, "I just couldn't communicate." But gradually, although homesick and sorely underprepared, she found that she was holding her own. Eventually, lured by the efforts of affirmative action recruiters, she took the unexpected step of enrolling in the nearby university. "I never thought I would ever graduate from high school," Fannie wrote in one of her essays, adding proudly that "I'm now on my second semester in college as a freshman." Her grandmother had died before witnessing either event, but Fannie spoke often of how pleased she would have been.[1]

Fannie was one of a handful of Native Americans on the campus, and the only Navajo. As a second-semester first-year student, she was still struggling to find her way both academically and socially, still working to overcome the scars of her troubled educational history. As she explained after listening to an audiotape of a tutorial session, chief among these was a lingering reluctance to speak up in English, particularly in group settings:

> *Fannie:* When, when, I'm talking . . . I'm shy. Because I always think I always say something not right, with my English, you know. (Pauses, then speaks very softly.) It's hard, though. Like with my friends, I do that too. Because I'll be quiet — they'll say, "Fannie, you're quiet." Or if I meet someone, I, I don't do it, let them do it, I let that person do the talking.
>
> *A.D.:* Do you wish you were more talkative?
>
> *Fannie:* I wish! Well I am, when I go home. But when I come here, you know I always think, English is my second language and I don't know that much, you know.

---

[1]"Fannie" was the actual name of this student's maternal grandmother. We decided to use it as her pseudonym to honor this lasting influence.

A.D.: So back home you're not a shy person?

Fannie: (laughing uproariously) No! (continues laughing).

I had a chance to glimpse Fannie's more audacious side later that semester, when she served as a campus tour guide to a group of students visiting from a distant Navajo high school. She was uncharacteristically feisty and vocal that week, a change strikingly evident on the tutorial audiotapes. Indeed, when I played back one of that week's sessions in a final interview, Fannie didn't recognize her own voice: "Who's that talking?" she asked at first. But even as she recalled her temporary elation, she described as well her gradual sense of loss:

> Sometimes I just feel so happy when someone's here, you know, I feel happy? I just get that way. And then (pauses, begins to speak very softly), and then it just wears off. And then they're leaving — I think, oh, they're leaving, you know.

While Fannie described their week together as "a great experience," she was disturbed to find that even among themselves, the Navajo students were speaking English: "That bothered me a lot," she admitted, surmising that "they're like embarrassed . . . to speak Navajo, because back home, speaking Navajo fluently all the time, that's like lower class." "If you don't know the language," Fannie wrote in one of her essays, "then you don't know who you are. . . . It's your identity . . . the language is very important." In striking contrast to these students who refused to learn the tribal language, Fannie's grandparents had never learned to speak English: "They were really into their culture, and tradition, and all of that," she explained, "but now we're not that way anymore, hardly, and it's like we're losing it, you know." Fannie hoped to attend a program at Navajo Community College where she could learn to read and write her native language, knowledge she could then pass on to her own students.

Fannie pointed to the high drop-out rate among young Navajos as the primary reason for her people's poverty, and spoke often of the need to encourage students to finish high school and go on to college. And yet, worried as she was about the growing loss of native language and tradition, Fannie also expressed concerns about the Anglicizing effects of schooling. Education is essential, she explained, but young Navajos must also understand its dangers:

> I mean like, sometimes if you get really educated, we don't really want that. Because then, it like ruins your mind, and you use it, to like betray your people, too. . . . That's what's happening a lot now.

By her own example, Fannie hoped to one day show her students that it is possible to be both bilingual and bicultural, that one can benefit from exposure to mainstream ways without surrendering one's own identity:

> If you know the white culture over here, and then you know your own culture, you can make a good living with that . . . when I go home, you know, I know Navajo, and I know English too. They say you can get a good job with that.

Back home, Fannie's extended family was watching her progress with warm pride, happily anticipating the day when she would return to the reservation to teach. When Fannie went back for a visit over spring break, she was surprised to find that they'd already built her a house: "They sure give me a lot of attention, that's for sure," she remarked with a smile. Many hadn't seen Fannie for some time, and they were struck by the change:

> Everybody still, kind of picture me, still, um, the girl from the past. The one who quit school — and they didn't think of me going to college at all. And they were surprised, they were really surprised. And they were like proud of me too . . . 'cause none of their family is going to college.

One delighted aunt, however, was the mother of a son who was also attending a west-coast college:

> She says, "I'm so happy! I can't wait to tell him, that you're going to college too! You stick in there, Fannie, now don't goof!" I'm like, "I'll try not to!"

"I Always Write Bad Essays": Fannie's Struggles with Writing

On the first day of class, Fannie's basic writing teacher handed out a questionnaire that probed students' perceptions of their strengths and weaknesses as writers. In response to the question, "What do you think is good about your writing?" Fannie wrote, "I still don't know what is good about my writing"; in response to "What do you think is bad about your writing?" she responded, "everything."

Fannie acknowledged that her early literacy education had been neither respectful of her heritage nor sensitive to the kinds of challenges she would face in the educational mainstream. She explained in an interview that her first instruction in essay writing had come at the eleventh hour, during her senior year of high school: "I never got the technique, I guess, of writing good essays," she explained, "I always write bad essays." While she named her "sentence structure, grammar, and punctuation" as significant weaknesses, she also adds that "I have a lot to say, but I can't put it on paper . . . it's like I can't find the vocabulary." Fannie described this enduring block in an in-class essay she wrote during the first week of class.

From my experience in writing essays were not the greatest. There were times my mind would be blank on thinking what I should write about.

In high school, I learned how to write an essay during my senior year. I learned a lot from my teacher but there was still something missing about my essays. I knew I was still having problems with my essay organization.

Now, I'm attending a university and having the same problems in writing essays. The university put me in basic writing, which is for students who did not pass the placement test. Of course, I did not pass it. Taking basic writing has helped me a lot on writing essays. There were times I had problems on what to write about.

There was one essay I had problems in writing because I could not express my feelings on a paper. My topic was on Mixed Emotions. I knew how I felt in my mind but I could not find the words for expressing my emotions.

Writing essays from my mind on to the paper is difficult for me. From this experience, I need to learn to write what I think on to a paper and expand my essays.

"Yes," her instructor wrote at the bottom of the page, "even within this essay — which is good — you need to provide specific detail, not just general statements." But what did Fannie's teacher find "good" about this essay — or was this opening praise only intended to soften the criticism that followed? Fannie had noted in an interview that she panicked when asked to produce something within forty-five minutes: "I just write anything," she'd observed, "but your mind goes blank, too." Still, while this assignment may not have been the most appropriate way to assess the ability of a student like Fannie, both she and her instructor felt it reflected her essential weakness — that is, an inability to develop her ideas in adequate detail.

At the end of the semester, her basic writing teacher confided that Fannie had just barely passed the course, and would no doubt face a considerable struggle in first-year composition. Although Fannie also worried about the next semester's challenge, she felt that her basic writing course had provided valuable opportunities. "I improved a lot," she said in a final interview, "I think I did — I know I did. 'Cause now I can know what I'm trying to say, and in an afternoon, get down to that topic." One of her later essays, entitled "Home," bears witness to Fannie's assertion:

The day is starting out a good day. The air smells fresh as if it just rained. The sky is full with clouds, forming to rain. From the triangle mountain, the land has such a great view. Below I see hills overlapping and I see six houses few feet from each other. One of them I live in. I can also see other houses miles apart.

It is so peaceful and beautiful. I can hear birds perching and dogs barking echos from long distance. I can not tell from which direction. Towards north I see eight horses grazing and towards east I hear sheep crying for their young ones. There are so many things going on at the same time.

It is beginning to get dark and breezy. It is about to rain. Small drops of rain are falling. It feels good, relieving the heat. The rain is increasing and thundering at the same time. Now I am soaked, I have the chills. The clouds is moving on and clearing the sky. It is close to late afternoon. The sun is shining and drying me off. The view of the land is more beautiful and looks greener. Like a refreshment.

Across from the mountain I am sitting is a mountain but then a plateau that stretches with no ending. From the side looks like a mountain but it is a long plateau. There are stores and more houses on top of the plateau.

My clothes are now dry and it is getting late. I hear my sister and my brother calling me that dinner is ready. It was beautiful day. I miss home.

"Good description," her instructor wrote on this essay, "I can really 'see' this scene." But meanwhile, she remained concerned about Fannie's lack of sophistication: "Try to use longer, more complex sentences," she added, "avoid short, choppy ones." Overwhelmed by the demands of composing and lacking strategies for working on this perceived weakness, Fannie took little away from such feedback aside from the impression that her writing remained inadequate.

Although Fannie was making important strides, she needed lots of patient, insightful support if she were to overcome her lack of experience with writing and formidable block. Only beginning to feel a bit more confident in writing about personal experience, she anticipated a struggle with the expository assignments that awaited her:

She's having us write from our experience. It'll be different if it's like in English 101, you know how the teacher tells you to write like this and that, and I find that one very hard, cause I see my other friends' papers and it's hard. I don't know if I can handle that class.

Fannie was trying to forge a sense of connection to class assignments — she wrote, for instance, about her Native American heritage, her dream of becoming a teacher, and about how her cultural background had shaped her concern for the environment. But meanwhile, as her instructor assessed Fannie's progress in an end-of-term evaluation, the focus returned to lingering weaknesses: "needs to expand ideas w/examples/description/explanation," the comments read, not specifying how or why or to whom. Somehow, Fannie had to fill in the gaps in her teacher's advice — and for the more individualized support she so sorely needed, she looked to the tutorials.

"Are You Learnin' Anything from Me?": The Tutorials

Morgan, Fannie's African American tutor, would soon be student teaching in a local high school, and she approached her work with basic writers as a trial run, a valuable opportunity to practice the various instructional strategies she'd heard about in workshops and seminars. Having grown up in the predominantly Anglo, middle-class community that surrounded the campus, Morgan met the criticisms of more politically involved ethnic students with dogged insistence: "I'm first and foremost a member of the *human* race," she often said, going on to describe her firm determination to work with students of all ethnicities, to help them see that success in the mainstream need not be regarded as cultural betrayal. During the term that I followed her — her second semester of tutoring and the first time she'd worked with non-Anglo students — this enthusiasm would be sorely tested, this ambition tempered by encounters with unforeseen obstacles.

Morgan's work with Fannie was a case in point. Although she had initially welcomed the challenge of drawing Fannie out, of helping this shy young woman overcome her apparent lack of self-confidence, by semester's end Morgan's initial compassion had been nearly overwhelmed by a sense of frustration. In an end-of-term interview, she confessed that one impression remained uppermost: "I just remember her sitting there," Morgan recalled, "and talking to her, and it's like, 'well I don't know, I don't know' . . . Fannie just has so many doubts, and she's such a hesitant person, she's so withdrawn, and mellow, and quiet. . . . A lot of times, she'd just say, 'well I don't know what I'm supposed to write. . . . Well I don't like this, I don't like my writing.'"

Although Fannie seldom had much to say, her words were often rich in untapped meaning. Early in the term, for instance, when Morgan asked why she was in college, Fannie searched unsuccessfully for words that would convey her strong but somewhat conflicted feelings:

Fannie: Well . . . (long pause) . . . it's hard . . .

Morgan: You wanna teach like, preschool? Well, as a person who wants to teach, what do you want outta your students?

Fannie: To get around in America you have to have education . . . (unclear).

Morgan: And what about if a student chose not to be educated — would that be ok?

Fannie: If that's what he wants . . .

At this point Morgan gave up and turned to the next student, missing the vital subtext — how Fannie's goal of becoming a teacher was enmeshed in her strong sense of connection to her people, how her belief that one needs an education "to get around" in the mainstream was tempered by insight into why some choose a different path. To understand Fannie's stance towards schooling, Morgan needed to grasp that she felt both this commitment *and* this ambivalence; but as was so often the case, Fannie's meager hints went unheeded.

A few weeks into the semester, Morgan labored one morning to move Fannie past her apparent block on a descriptive essay. Fannie said only that she was going to try to describe her grandmother, and Morgan began by asking a series of questions — about her grandmother's voice, her presence, her laugh, whatever came to Fannie's mind. Her questions greeted by long silences, Morgan admitted her gathering frustration: "Are you learnin' anything from me?" she asked. Morgan's voice sounded cordial and even a bit playful, but she was clearly concerned that Fannie didn't seem to be meeting her halfway. In the weeks that followed, Morgan would repeatedly adjust her approach, continually searching for a way to break through, "to spark something," as she often put it.

The first change — to a tougher, more demanding stance — was clearly signalled as the group brainstormed ideas for their next essays. Instead of waiting for Fannie to jump into the discussion, Morgan called upon her: "Ok, your turn in the hot seat," she announced. When Fannie noted that her essay would be about her home in Arizona, Morgan demanded to know "why it would be of possible interest to us." The ensuing exchange shed little light on the subject:

Fannie: Because it's my home!

Morgan: That's not good enough . . . that's telling me nothing.

Fannie: I was raised there.

Morgan: What's so special about it?

Fannie: (exasperated sigh) I don't know what's so special about

it . . .

Morgan: So why do you want to write about it, then?

Morgan's final question still unanswered, she eventually gave up and moved to another student. Again, a wealth of valuable information remained tacit; Morgan wouldn't learn for several weeks that Fannie had grown up on a reservation, and she'd understood nothing at all about her profound bond with this other world.

Two months into the semester, Morgan had an opportunity to attend the Conference on College Composition and Communication (CCCC), and it was there that some of her early training crystallized into a more definite plan of action, her early doubts subsumed by a new sense of authoritative expertise. Morgan thought a great deal about her work with Fannie as she attended numerous sessions on peer tutoring and a half-day workshop on collaborative learning. She returned to campus infused with a clear sense of direction: the solution, Morgan had concluded, was to assume an even more low-profile approach, speaking only to ask open-ended questions or to paraphrase Fannie's statements, steadfastly avoiding the temptation to fill silences with her own ideas and asides. As she anticipated her next encounter with Fannie, she couldn't wait to try out this more emphatic version of what had been called — in conference sessions and her earlier training — a "collaborative" or "non-directive" stance.

Still struggling to produce an already past-due essay on "values," Fannie arrived at this first post-CCCC tutorial hour with only preliminary ideas and nothing in writing. Remembering the advice of Conference participants, Morgan began by trying to nudge her towards a focus, repeatedly denying that she knew more than Fannie about how to approach the piece:

> *Morgan:* What would you say your basic theme is? And sometimes if you keep that in mind, then you can always, you know, keep that as a focus for what you're writing. And the reason I say that is 'cause when you say, "well living happily wasn't . . ."
>
> *Fannie:* (pause) . . . Well, America was a beautiful country, well, but it isn't beautiful anymore.
>
> *Morgan:* Um hm. Not as beautiful.
>
> *Fannie:* So I should just say, America was a beautiful country?
>
> *Morgan:* Yeah. But I dunno — what do you think your overall theme is, that you're saying?
>
> *Fannie:* (long pause) . . . I'm really, I'm just talking about America.
>
> *Morgan:* America? So America as . . . ?
>
> *Fannie:* (pause) . . . Um . . . (pause)
>
> *Morgan:* Land of free, uh, land of natural resources? As, um a place where there's a conflict, I mean, there, if you can narrow that, "America." What is it specifically, and think about what you've written, in the rest. Know what I mean?
>
> *Fannie:* (pause) . . . The riches of America, or the country? I don't know . . .
>
> *Morgan:* I think you do. I'm not saying there's any right answer, but I, I'm — for me, the reason I'm saying this, is I see this emerging as, you know, (pause) where you're really having a hard time with dealing with the exploitation that you see, of America, you know, you think that. And you're using two groups

to really illustrate, specifically, how two different attitudes toward, um the richness and beauty of America, two different, um, ways people have to approach this land. Does that, does this make any sense? Or am I just putting words in your mouth? I don't want to do that. I mean that's what I see emerge in your paper. But I could be way off base.

Fannie: I think I know what you're trying to say. And I can kind of relate it at times to what I'm trying to say.

Morgan: You know, I mean, this is like the theme I'm picking up . . . (pause) I think you know, you've got some real, you know, environmental issues here. I think you're a closet environmentalist here. Which are real true, know what I mean. (pause) And when you talk about pollution, and waste, and um, those types of things. So I mean, if you're looking at a theme of your paper, what could you pick out, of something of your underlying theme.

Fannie: (pause) . . . The resources, I guess?

Morgan: Well I mean, I don't want you to say, I want you to say, don't say "I guess," is that what you're talking about?

Fannie: Yeah.

Morgan: "Yeah?" I mean, it's your paper.

Fannie: I know, I want to talk about the land . . .

Morgan: Ok. So you want to talk about the land, and the beauty of the land . . .

Fannie: Um hm.

Morgan: . . . and then, um, and then also your topic for your, um, to spark your paper . . . what values, and morals, right? That's where you based off to write about America, and the land, you know. Maybe you can write some of these things down, as we're talking, as focusing things, you know. So you want to talk about the land, and then it's like, what do you want to say about the land?

What *did* Fannie "want to say about the land"? Whatever it was, one begins to wonder if it was perhaps lost in her tutor's inadvertent appropriation of these meanings — this despite Morgan's ostensible effort to simply elicit and reflect Fannie's thoughts. While Fannie may well have been struggling to articulate meanings which eluded clear expression in English, as Morgan worked to move her towards greater specificity, it became apparent that she was assuming the paper would express commonplace environmental concerns:

Fannie: I'll say, the country was, um, (pause), more like, I can't say perfect, I mean was, the tree was green, you know, I mean, um, it was clean. (long pause). I can't find the words for it.

Morgan: In a natural state? Um, un-, polluted, um, untouched, um, let me think, trying to get a . . .

Fannie: I mean everybody, I mean the Indians too, they didn't wear that (pointing to Morgan's clothes), they only wore buffalo clothing, you know for their clothing, they didn't wear like . . . these, you know, cotton and all that, they were so . . .

Morgan: Naturalistic.

Fannie: Yeah. "Naturalistic," I don't know if I'm gonna use that word . . . I wanna say, I wanna give a picture of the way the land was, before, you know what I'm, what I'm tryin' to say?

The Navajos' connection to the land is legendary — a spiritual nexus, many would maintain, that goes far beyond mainstream notions of what it means to be concerned about the environment. However, later in this session, Morgan observed that Fannie was writing about concerns that worry lots of people — citing recent publicity about the greenhouse effect, the hole in the ozone layer, and the growing interest in recycling. She then brought the session to a close by paraphrasing what she saw as the meat of the discussion and asking, "Is that something that you were tryin' to say, too?" Fannie replied, "Probably. I mean, I can't find the words for it, but you're finding the words for me." Morgan's rejoinder had been, "I'm just sparkin', I'm just sparkin' what you already have there, what you're sayin'. I mean I'm tryin' to tell you what I hear you sayin'."

Morgan laughed as, in an end-of-term interview, she listened again to Fannie's final comment: "I didn't *want* to find the words for her," she mused; "I wanted to show her how she could find 'em for herself." Still, she admitted, the directive impulse had been hard to resist: "I wanted to just give her ideas," Morgan observed, adding that although Fannie had some good things to say, "I wanted her to be able to articulate her ideas on a little higher level." Although it was obvious to Morgan that the ideas in Fannie's paper were of "deep-seated emotional concern," she also saw her as stuck in arid generalities: "'I don't know, it's just a beautiful country,'" Morgan echoed as she reviewed the audiotape. While Morgan emphasized that she "didn't wanna write the paper for her," she allowed that "it's difficult — it's really hard to want to take the bull by the horns and say, 'don't you see it this way?'" On the one hand, Morgan noted that she'd often asked Fannie what she was getting out of a session, "'cause sometimes I'll think I'm getting through and I'm explaining something really good, and then they won't catch it"; on the other hand, Morgan emphasized again and again that she didn't want to "give away" her own thoughts.

Although Morgan often did an almost heroic job of waiting out Fannie's lingering silences and deflecting appeals to her authority, she never really surrendered control; somehow, the message always came across that Morgan knew more than Fannie about the ideas at hand, and that if she would, she could simply turn over pre-packaged understandings. While her frustration was certainly understandable, I often had the sense that Morgan was insufficiently curious about Fannie's thoughts — insufficiently curious about how Fannie's understandings might have differed from her own, about how they had been shaped by Fannie's background and cultural orientation, or about what she stood to learn from them.

When asked about Fannie's block, a weary Morgan wrote it off to her cultural background:

> You know, I would have to say it's cultural; I'd have to say it's her you know, Native American background and growing up on a reservation . . . maybe . . . she's more sensitive to male-female roles, and the female role being quiet.

On a number of occasions Morgan had speculated that Navajo women are taught to be subservient, a perception that contrasted rather strikingly with Fannie's assertion that she wasn't at all shy or quiet back home.[2] Hoping to challenge Morgan's accustomed view of Fannie as bashful and retiring, in a final interview I played back one of their sessions from the week that a group of Navajo students were visiting the campus. Fannie was uncharacteristically vocal and even aggressive that morning, talking in a loud voice, repeatedly seizing and holding the floor:

> *Fannie:* You know what my essay's on? Different environments. Um, I'm talking, I'm not gonna talk about my relationship between my brothers, it's so boring, so I'm just gonna talked about both being raised, like my youngest brother being raised on the reservation, and the other being raised over here, and

---

[2]Morgan's assumption is also contradicted by published accounts of life among the Navajo, which from early on have emphasized the prestige and power of female members of the tribe. Gladys Reichard, an anthropologist who lived among the Navajos in the 1920s, reported that "the Navajo woman enjoys great economic and social prestige as the head of the house and clan and as the manager of economic affairs, and she is not excluded from religious ritual or from attaining political honors" (55). Navajo women often own substantial property, and children retain the surname of the matrilineal clan; the status accorded women is further reflected in the depictions of female deities in Navajo myths (Terrell 57; 255).

they both have very different, um, um, (Morgan starts to say something, but Fannie cuts her off and continues) characteristics or somethin' like that. You know, like their personalities, you know.

Morgan: Um. That's good. (Morgan starts to say something more, but Fannie keeps going.)

Fannie: It's funny, I'm cutting, I was totally mean to my brother here. (Morgan laughs.) Because, I called, I said that he's a wimp, you know, and my brother, my little brother's being raised on the reservation, is like, is like taught to be a man, he's brave and all that.

Luis: (a student in the group) That's being a man?!

Fannie: And . . .

Luis: That's not being a man, I don't find.

Fannie: (her voice raised) I'm sorry — but that's how I wrote, Ok?! That's your opinion, I mean, and it's . . .

Luis: I think a man is sensitive, caring, and lov —

Fannie: (cutting him off) No, no . . .

Luis: . . . and able to express his feelings. I don't think that if you can go kill someone, that makes you a man.

Fannie: I mean . . .

Luis: That's just my opinion (gets up and walks away for a moment).

Fannie: (watching Luis wander off) Dickhead.

Morgan listened with a widening smile to the rest of this session, obviously pleased with Fannie's sometimes combative manner and unflagging insistence that attention be directed back to her. "Ha! Fannie's so much more forceful," Morgan exclaimed, "And just more in control of what she wants, and what she needs." When asked what she thought might have accounted for this temporary change, Morgan sidestepped the influence of the visiting students:

> I would love to think that I made her feel safe that way. And that I really um, showed her that she had, you know, by my interactions with her, that she really had every right to be strong-willed and forceful and have her opinions and you know, say what she felt that she needed to say, and that she didn't have to be quiet, you know. People always tell me that I influence people that way. You know? (laughs). "You've been hangin' around with Morgan too much!"

Hungry for feedback that she'd influenced Fannie in a positive way, Morgan grasped this possible evidence with obvious pleasure. Fannie was not a student who offered many positive signals, and it was perhaps essential to Morgan's professional self-esteem that she find them wherever she could. In this credit-taking there was, however, a larger irony: if only she'd been encouraged to push a little farther in her own thinking, perhaps she would have found herself assisting more often in such moments of blossoming.

Conclusion: Students as Teachers, Teachers as Students

When Morgan returned from the CCCC with a vision of "collaboration" that cast it as a set of techniques rather than a new way to think about teaching and learning, the insights of panelists and workshop leaders devolved into a fossilized creed, a shield against more fundamental concerns. Morgan had somehow missed the importance of continually adjusting her approach in the light of the understandings students make available, of allowing their feedback to shape her reflections upon her own role. At semester's end, she still didn't know that Fannie was a non-native speaker of English; she didn't know the dimensions of Fannie's inexperience with academic writing, nor did she know the reasons behind Fannie's formidable block.

Even as Morgan labored to promote "collaborative" moments — making an ostensible effort to "talk less," to "sit back more," to enact an instructional mode that would seem more culturally appropriate — Fannie remembered a lifetime of classroom misadventure, and hung back, reluctant. Morgan needed to know something about this history, but she also needed to understand that much else was fluid and alive, that a revised sense of self was emerging from the dynamic interaction of Fannie's past and present. Emboldened by a few treasured days in the company of fellow Navajos, Fannie had momentarily stepped into a new stance, one that departed markedly from her accustomed behavior on reservation and campus alike; but if her confidence recalled an earlier self, her playful combativeness was, as Fannie observed in listening to the tape, a new and still-strange manifestation of something also oddly familiar, something left over from long ago.

Rather than frequent urgings to "talk less," perhaps what Morgan most needed was advice to *listen more* — for the clues students like Fannie would provide, for those moments when she might best shed her teacherly persona and become once again a learner. More than specific instructional strategies, Morgan needed the conceptual grounding that would allow her to understand that authentically collaborative learning is predicated upon fine-grained insight into individual students — of the nature of their Vygotskian "zones of proximal development," and, by association, of the sorts of instructional "scaffolding" most appropriate to their changing needs (Bruner; Applebee and Langer). So, too, did Morgan need to be encouraged toward the yet-elusive understanding that such learning is never unilateral, inevitably entailing a reciprocal influence, reciprocal advances in understanding (Dyson). As she struggled to come to terms with her own ethnic ambivalence, to defend herself against a vociferous chorus proclaiming her "not black enough," Morgan had reason to take heart in Fannie's dramatic and rather trying process of transition. Had she thought to ask, Morgan would no doubt have been fascinated by Fannie's descriptions of this other cultural and linguistic context, with its very different perspectives on education in particular and the world in general (John; Locust). Most of all, perhaps she would have been interested to know that Fannie was learning to inhabit both arenas, and in so doing enacting a negotiation of admirable complexity — a negotiation different in degree, perhaps, but certainly not in kind, from Morgan's own.

Having tutored only one semester previously, Morgan was understandably eager to abandon her lingering doubts about her effectiveness, eager for a surefooted sense that she was providing something worthwhile. Her idealism and good intentions were everywhere apparent — in her lengthy meditations on her work, in her eager enthusiasm at the CCCC, in her persistent efforts to try out new approaches, and in the reassurance she extended to me when I confessed that I'd be writing some fairly negative things about her vexed attempts to reach Fannie. Morgan had been offered relatively little by way of preparation and support: beyond a sprinkling of workshops and an occasional alliance with more experienced tutors, she was left largely on her own — alone with the substantial challenges and opportunities that students like Fannie presented, alone to deal with her frustration and occasional feelings of failure as best she could. Like all beginning educators, Morgan needed abundant support, instruction, and modeling if she were to learn to reflect critically upon her work, to question her assumptions about students like Fannie, to allow herself, even at this fledgling stage in her career, to become a reflective and therefore vulnerable practitioner. This is not to suggest that Morgan should have pried into hidden corners of Fannie's past, insisting that she reveal information about her background before she felt ready to do so; only that Morgan be respectfully curious, ever attentive to whatever clues Fannie might have been willing to offer, ever poised to revise old understandings in light of fresh evidence.

Those of us who work with linguistic minority students — and that's fast becoming all of us — must appreciate the evolving dimensions of our task, realizing that we have to reach further than ever if we're to do our jobs well. Regardless of our crowded schedules and shrinking budgets, we must also think realistically about the sorts of guidance new tutors and teachers need if they are to confront these rigors effectively, guiding them towards practical strategies informed by understandings from theory and research, and offering compelling reminders of the need to monitor one's ethnocentric biases and faulty assumptions. Most of all, we must serve as models of reflective practice — perennially inquisitive and self-critical, even as we find occasion both to bless and curse the discovery that becoming students of students means becoming students of ourselves as well.

Works Cited

Applebee, Arthur, and Judith Langer. "Reading and Writing Instruction: Toward a Theory of Teaching and Learning." *Review of Research in Education,* Vol. 13. Ed. E. Z. Rothkopf. Washington, DC: American Educational Research Association, 1986.

Bakhtin, Mikhail Mikhailovich. *The Dialogic Imagination: Four Essays by M. M. Bakhtin.* Ed. Michael Holquist, trans. Caryl Emerson and Michael Holquist. Austin: U of Texas P, 1981.

Bruner, Jerome. "The Role of Dialogue in Language Acquisition." *The Child's Conception of Language.* Ed. A. Sinclair. New York: Springer-Verlag, 1978.

Cintron, Ralph. "Reading and Writing Graffiti: A Reading." *The Quarterly Newsletter of the Laboratory of Comparative Human Cognition* 13 (1991): 21–24.

DiPardo, Anne. "Acquiring 'A Kind of Passport': The Teaching and Learning of Academic Discourse in Basic Writing Tutorials." Diss. UC Berkeley, 1991.

———. *"A Kind of Passport": A Basic Writing Adjunct Program and the Challenge of Student Diversity.* Urbana, IL: NCTE (1993).

Dorris, Michael. *A Yellow Raft in Blue Water.* New York: Holt, 1987.

Dyson, Anne. "Weaving Possibilities: Rethinking Metaphors for Early Literacy Development." *The Reading Teacher* 44 (1990): 202–13.

Fischer, Michael. "Ethnicity and the Postmodern Arts of Memory." *Writing Culture: The Poetics and Politics of Ethnography.* Eds. J. Clifford and G. E. Marcus. Berkeley: U of California P, 1986.

Hawkins, Thom. "Intimacy and Audience: The Relationship Between Revision and the Social Dimension of Peer Tutoring." *College English* 42 (1980): 64–68.

Hull, Glynda, and Mike Rose. "Rethinking Remediation: Toward a Social-Cognitive Understanding of Problematic Reading and Writing." *Written Communication* 6 (1989): 139–54.

———. "'This Wooden Shack Place': The Logic of an Unconventional Reading." *College Composition and Communication* 41 (1990): 287–98.

John, Vera P. "Styles of Learning — Styles of Teaching: Reflections on the Education of Navajo Children." *Functions of Language in the Classroom.* Ed. Courtney B. Cazden and Vera P. John. 1972. Prospect Heights, IL: Waveland, 1985.

Locust, Carol. "Wounding the Spirit: Discrimination and Traditional American Indian Belief Systems." *Harvard Educational Review* 58 (1988): 315–30.

Philips, Susan U. "Participant Structures and Communicative Competence: Warm Springs Children in Community and Classroom." *Functions of*

Language in the Classroom. Ed. Courtney B. Cazden and Vera P. John. 1972. Prospect Heights, IL: Waveland, 1985.

Reichard, Gladys. *Social Life of the Navajo Indians.* 1928. New York: AMS P, 1969.

Shaughnessy, Mina. "Diving In: An Introduction to Basic Writing." *College Composition and Communication* 27 (1976): 234–39.

Terrell, John Upton. *The Navajo: The Past and Present of a Great People.* 1970. New York: Perennial, 1972.

Valdés, Guadalupe. *Identifying Priorities in the Study of the Writing of Hispanic Background Students.* Grant No. OERI-G-008690004. Washington, DC: Office of Educational Research and Improvement, 1989.

———. "Language Issues in Writing: The Problem of Compartmentalization of Interest Areas Within CCCC." Paper presented at the Conference on College Composition and Communication. 21–23 March, 1991.

Vygotsky, Lev. *Mind in Society.* Cambridge: Harvard UP, 1978.

Classroom Activities

DiPardo's conclusion suggests that, despite the continuing challenges, there is much potential for developing writers and their tutors to benefit from participation in writing center activities. If your campus has a writing center, take your students on a tour or have a peer tutor or other personnel representative visit your class to talk about the writing center's services. Find out how your writing center recruits peer tutors, and be sure to recommend that interested students apply for those positions. If your campus does not have a writing center, have your students do research on other support systems that are available for developing writers and readers, both on and off campus. For instance, what kinds of tutoring services are available at public libraries or community centers? If you or your students are interested in finding more information about resources offered by writing centers at other campuses, visit the National Writing Centers Association home page at <http://iwca.syr.edu>. This site includes resources for writers, tutor stories, e-mail discussion groups, a writing center start-up kit, and more.

Thinking about Teaching

If your campus doesn't have a writing center, find out what is needed to create out-of-class support services for student writing. See, "Classroom Activities" above for appropriate Internet resources. If your campus has a learning center, rather than a writing center, ask what services are available specifically for students who need support with writing — whether there is "remedial" help or general feedback for more "advanced" students. If your campus does have a writing center, it may be possible for you to work there yourself. Some writing centers encourage faculty to hold office hours in the writing center or to work as tutors in the center. Meet with the director of your writing center to find out what his or her policy is on instructors working there. If either arrangement is viable given writing center policies and your own schedule, try spending time working there over the course of a semester. Be sure to keep a journal of your experiences. This opportunity will enable you to experience at first hand DiPardo's call for teachers to "serve as models of reflective practice — perennially inquisitive and self-critical, even as we find occasion both to bless and curse the discovery that becoming students of students means becoming students of ourselves as well."

About the Contributors

Gloria Anzaldúa was a prominent Chicana/tejana lesbian poet, essayist, and cultural theorist whose groundbreaking *Borderlands / La Frontera: The New Mestiza* (1987) combines bilingual poetry, memoir, and historical analysis to illuminate the transcultural Mexican American "borderland" experience. Her subsequent works include *Making Face, Making Soul / Haciendo Caras: Creative and Cultural Perspectives by Feminists of Color* (ed., 1990) and *Interviews / Entrevistas* (2000). She was the recipient of an NEA Fiction Award and the Sappho Award of Distinction. Before her death in 2004, Anzaldúa wrote and taught in northern California.

Susan Naomi Bernstein has published the third edition of *Teaching Developmental Writing: Background Readings,* as well as two previous editions (2004, 2001), two shorter ancillary versions (2000, 1998), and the textbook *A Brief Guide to the Novel* (2002). Her articles on teaching writing have appeared in the *Chronicle of Higher Education, Journal of Basic Writing, Modern Language Studies, English in Texas,* and elsewhere. Her poetry has appeared in *Teaching English in the Two-Year College,* the *Texas Observer,* and *Thirteenth Moon.* She is an assistant professor at the University of Cincinnati, where she works at the Center for Access and Transition. Bernstein has taught basic writing in Ohio, Pennsylvania, and Texas, and has worked as a writer-in-residence at a Houston public elementary school for the non-profit Writers in the Schools program. She currently is a cochair of the Conference on Basic Writing.

Irene Brosnahan is professor emerita of linguistics at Illinois State University, where she was the director of the ESL program. In her research with Janice Neuleib, she has promoted the integration of grammar instruction with general composition instruction and has written on the effects of personality on grammar pedagogy. Their article "Teaching Grammar Affectively: Learning to Like Grammar" appears in *The Place of Grammar in Writing Instruction* (1995), edited by Ray Wallace.

Patrick L. Bruch is associate professor of writing studies in the Department of Postsecondary Teaching and Learning at the University of Minnesota–Twin Cities. He is coeditor of *The Hope and the Legacy: The Past, Present, and Future of "Students' Right to Their Own Language"* (Hampton, 2005), and has published articles on the social dynamics of teaching writing in books and journals, including *College Composition and Communication, Symploké, Journal of Developmental Education, Journal of College Reading and Learning, Journal of Advanced Composition,* and *Rhetoric Review.* He is also coeditor of the writing textbooks *Cities, Cultures, Conversations* (Allyn and Bacon, 1998) and *Reading City Life* (Pearson Longman, 2005).

Sally I. Cannon teaches at Saginaw Valley State University in Saginaw, Michigan. She has written about the dynamics of basic writing assessment based on her experiences as writing coordinator of the SVSU English Department.

Martha Clark Cummings is a member of the Center for Language Research at the University of Aizu in Aizu-Wakamatsu, Japan. Currently, her research focuses on the differences between face-to-face and computer-mediated instruction.

Anne DiPardo, a professor of education at the University of Iowa, is a past recipient of the NCTE/CEE Meade Award for outstanding research in English education, the NCTE/CEL Best Article Award, and the NCTE Promising Researcher Award. DiPardo has published articles in such journals as *Reading Research Quarterly, Anthropology and Education Quarterly, Review of Educational Research,* and *Theory and Research in Social Education.* She has written two books: *A Kind of Passport: A Basic Writing Adjunct Program and the Challenge of Student Diversity* (1993) and *Teaching in Common: Challenges to Joint Work in Classrooms and Schools* (1999). She is currently coeditor of NCTE's empirical journal, *Research in the Teaching of English.*

Yu Ren Dong, an associate professor of English in the Department of Secondary Education and Youth Services at Queens College–the City University of New York, has devoted her research to the unique strengths that ESL students bring to writing classrooms and the role of teacher/student reflection in TESOL pedagogy. She has published articles in *TESOL Journal, International Journal of Bilingual Education and Bilingualism,* and *Journal of Teaching and Writing,* among others.

Peter Elbow is professor emeritus of English at the University of Massachusetts–Amherst. He directed the Writing Program there and at the State University of New York–Stony Brook — and taught at M.I.T., Franconia College, and Evergreen State College in Washington State. He is the author of *Writing Without Teachers* (1973) and *Writing With Power* (1981). His recent book, *Everyone Can Write: Essays Toward a Hopeful Theory of Writing and Teaching Writing* (2000), was given the James Britton Award by the Conference on English Education. With Pat Belanoff, he wrote a textbook, *Being a Writer* (2001). A short section, *Sharing and Responding,* is published separately as a guide to students for peer feedback. NCTE recently gave him the James Squire Award "for his transforming influence and lasting intellectual contribution."

Dana R. Ferris is a professor of English at California State University–Sacramento, where she teaches MA TESOL, linguistics, and writing courses and coordinates the writing program for multilingual (ESL) students. She has published four books and over twenty journal articles and book chapters on the topic of second language writing, particularly on topics related to teacher commentary and error correction. Her most recent book, coauthored with John Hedgcock, is *Teaching ESL Composition: Purpose, Process, & Practice* (2nd ed.), published by Erlbaum in 2005.

Michelle Gibson received her Ph.D. from Ohio University, where her areas of study were American literature, composition research and pedagogy, and creative writing. Her scholarship has continued in all three of these areas. Much of her work applies queer and postmodern identity theories to pedagogical practice. She also continues to write and publish poetry. With Jonathan Alexander, she edits *QP: Queer Poetry,* an online poetry journal, and she and Alexander also edited a strain of *JAC: Journal of Advanced Composition* entitled "Queer Composition(s)." She coedited (with Deborah Meem) *Femme / Butch: New Considerations of the Way We Want to Go* (2002) and *Lesbian Academic Couples* (2006). With Meem and Alexander she is writing *Context Queer,* an introductory textbook for use in introductory LGBT courses.

Barbara Gleason has been an associate professor of English since 1990 at the City College of New York, where she currently administers the master's program in language and literacy. She has also served as director of composition in the English Department and supervisor of writing consultants at the Center for Worker Education. Gleason's essays on writing curricula, program evaluation, basic writing, and returning adult students appear regularly in professional journals. She coedited *Composition in Four Keys: Inquiring into a Field* (1995) and *Cultural Tapestry* (1997). She currently serves as a member of the Conference on Basic Writing Executive Board.

Ann E. Green is an associate professor of English at Saint Joseph's University in Philadelphia. She is the founding director of the university writing center, which she ran from 1998 until 2004, and she has published in *College Composition and Communication* as well as several essay collections on race, class, gender, and writing. She regularly teaches service-learning courses as well as pedagogy courses in the master's program for writing studies.

Kay Harley, a professor of English at Saginaw Valley State University in Saginaw, Michigan, has written about the dynamics of basic writing assessment. She has also served as director of the Saginaw Valley National Writing Project.

Beth Hartman received her master's degree from the University of Minnesota and has published, with Elaine Tarone, in the anthology *Generation 1.5 Meets College Composition* (1999).

Jeanne Henry is an associate professor of literacy studies at Hofstra University in New York, where she teaches courses in adolescent literature, language variation, and teacher research. Henry also advises doctoral students, several of whom are conducting research on developmental reading or writing. Her on-going work in undergraduate reading education includes the development of a pleasure reading course for pre-med majors. Henry is currently researching language and literacy learning in Guatemala and other parts of Central America.

Glynda A. Hull is professor of language, literacy, and culture in the Graduate School of Education at the University of California–Berkeley. Her research examines digital technologies and new literacies; adult literacy and changing contexts and requirements for work; writing and students at-risk; and community/school/university partnerships. Her books include *Changing Work, Changing Workers: Critical Perspectives on Language, Literacy, and Skill* (1997, SUNY Press); *The New Work Order: Education and Literacy in the New Capitalism* (1996, Allen & Unwin; with James Gee and Colin Lankshear); and *School's Out! Bridging Out-of-School Literacies with Classroom Practice* (2001, Teachers College; with Katherine Schultz). She is cofounder of DUSTY (Digital Underground Storytelling for Youth), a community technology center in Oakland, California, where she designs and studies after-school programs on literacy and multimodal composing for children and adults.

June Jordan was a celebrated poet, novelist, essayist, and political activist. The author of twenty-six books, Jordan is the most published African American writer in history. Before her death in June 2002, she was a professor of African American studies at the University of California–Berkeley, where she founded and directed Poetry for the People. Local high schools, churches, and prisons participated in the popular outreach program. On the strength of her poetry and books such as *June Jordan's Poetry for the People: A Blueprint for the Revolution* (1995) and *Affirmative Acts: Political Essays* (1998), Jordan received numerous grants, fellowships, and awards. Her poems have appeared in more than thirty anthologies. Her memoir is *Soldier: A Poet's Childhood. Directed by Desire: The Collected Poems of June Jordan* (2005) and *Some of Us Did Not Die: New and Selected Essays of June Jordan* (2002) were published posthumously.

Valerie Kinloch is assistant professor of English education at Teachers College, Columbia University in New York. Her most recent work investigates democratic learning, literacy practices, and spatial affiliation in the education of diverse student populations. Her book on the life and literary contributions of poet June Jordan titled *June Jordan: Her Life and Letters,* was published in 2006. Kinloch's writings have appeared in *College Composition and Communication, English Education,* the *Journal of Advanced Composition, Developmental Education and Urban Literacy Monograph,* the *Encyclopedia of the Harlem*

Renaissance, and others. Her coedited book, *Still Seeking an Attitude: Critical Reflections on the Work of June Jordan,* was published in 2004. Currently, she is working on a grant-funded project on the writing processes and spatial narratives of African American and Latino high school students.

William B. Lalicker is an associate professor of English at West Chester University in West Chester, Pennsylvania, and serves on the board of directors of the Volunteer English Program in Chester County, Pennsylvania. He has published on composition theory and the role of imagination in multicultural writing, and maintains that bilingual education and interdisciplinary thinking draw power from an imagination-based epistemology that makes creative use of ambivalence and dialectic. Lalicker is an advisory editor for the journal *College Literature* and was cochair of the 2003 Conference on Basic Writing. He is codirector for Curriculum in the Composition Program at West Chester University.

Ilona Leki is professor of English and director of English as a Second Language at the University of Tennessee–Knoxville. She is the author of *Understanding ESL Writers: A Guide for Teachers* (1992), *Academic Writing: Exploring Processes and Strategies* (1998), *Academic Writing Programs: Case Studies in TESOL Practice* (2001) and coeditor of the *Journal of Second Language Writing.* She has shared her second-language writing research and pedagogy with other educators through training programs and conference presentations in Brazil, Colombia, Egypt, France, Turkey, the former Yugoslavia, Hong Kong, Taiwan, Morocco, and Canada.

Jane Maher is a professor in the Basic Education Program at Nassau Community College, where she has taught basic writing since 1987. In addition, for the past ten years, she has been the director of special programs in the college program at the Bedford Hills Correctional Facility for Women in Westchester, New York, sponsored by Marymount Manhattan College, where she developed and currently coordinates the Pre-College Program, in addition to teaching, tutoring, and mentoring. She is the author of five biographies, including two of extraordinary educators: *Mina Shaughnessy, Her Life and Work* (1997), published by NCTE, which shows the way Shaughnessy's work and vision made it possible for Open Admissions' students to find a place in the academy; and *Seeing Language in Sign* (1996), published by Gallaudet University Press, which describes the way that William C. Stokoe began the linguistic revolution in American Sign Language that lead to the Deaf President Now protest. She can be contacted at janemaher@aol.com.

Janice Neulieb is a professor of linguistics and the director of writing programs at Illinois State University. In her work with Irene Brosnahan, she calls for the integration of grammar instruction with general composition instruction. They have also written on the effects of personality on grammar pedagogy. Neuleib and Brosnahan's "Teaching Grammar Affectively: Learning to Like Grammar" appears in *The Place of Grammar in Writing Instruction* (1995), edited by Ray Wallace.

Sarah Nixon-Ponder is an associate professor at Missouri State University, where she teaches in the School of Teacher Education's Graduate Reading Program. She was formerly the assistant director of the Ohio Literacy Resource Center at Kent State University. Nixon-Ponder elucidates student-centered creative problem-solving as an effective classroom practice for teachers of adult literacy and composition.

Catherine Matthews Pavia is a Ph.D. student in rhetoric and composition at the University of Massachusetts–Amherst. She has published in the *Journal of Basic Writing.*

Richard Raymond teaches technical communication, composition theory, and persuasive writing at the University of Arkansas–Little Rock, where he also serves as chair of the Department of Rhetoric and Writing. In 1999, Raymond won *Teaching English in the Two-Year College*'s annual Best Article Award for the selection that is included in this book. Most recently, he has written for *Pedagogy and Writing Program Administration.*

Nancy Lawson Remler holds a Ph.D. in English education from the University of Georgia. Since 1992, she has taught freshman composition and upper-level writing courses at Armstrong Atlantic State University in Savannah, Georgia, where she is an associate professor of English.

Adrienne Rich is a prolific poet, theorist, and political activist whose influential writings have spanned more than half a century. Her commitment to social justice and the women's movement took shape during the mid-1960s, when she taught in a remedial English program for New York City's recent immigrants and other students who were underrepresented in college admissions. Her numerous volumes of poetry and collections of essays explore themes of linguistic privilege, sexual identity, and patriarchal systems of oppression. Rich has taught at Swarthmore College, Columbia University, Brandeis University, Rutgers University, Cornell University, San Jose State University, and Stanford University. She has been honored with the National Book Award, two Guggenheim Fellowships, the Book Critics Circle Award, and a MacArthur Fellowship, among other awards. She lives in northern California. Her recent book is *The School Among the Ruins: Poems 2000–2004* (2006).

Mike Rose identifies literacy — its definitions and its acquisition — among his principal teaching and research interests. As a professor of social research methodology at the University of California–Los Angeles, Rose explores the cognitive, linguistic, and cultural factors that affect engagement with written language. He recounts his experiences in his autobiographical work *Lives on the Boundary* (1989) and has also written *Possible Lives: The Promise of Public Education in America* (1995). Rose has recently published *The Mind at Work: Valuing the American Worker* (2004).

Gregory Shafer is a professor of English at Mott Community College in Flint, Michigan, and past president of the Michigan Council of Teachers of English. His publications include articles in *English Journal, Teaching English in the Two-Year College,* and the *Humanist;* and a book, *Process and Voice in the Writing Workshop* (2000). He is the former regional coordinator for the Michigan Council for the Arts and has received four Excellence in Education awards from the Kellogg Foundation. He is at work on a book, *Linguistics for Beginners,* which he hopes to use in his future classes.

Mina Shaughnessy began teaching composition at the City College of New York in 1967 and served as the director of the school's Basic Writing Program until her death in 1978. She founded the *Journal of Basic Writing,* and in her foundational work, *Errors and Expectations* (1977), examined the question of where it is "best to begin a course in basic writing." Many thinkers and teachers in the field of developmental writing trace their roots to Shaughnessy's early inquiries about writing pedagogy, which, above all, stressed respecting students and their strengths, rather than focusing exclusively on weaknesses or deficiencies.

Elaine E. Tarone is the director of the Center for Advanced Research on Language Acquisition (CARLA). She is also professor and head of the English as a Second Language Program in the Institute of Linguistics, English as a Second Language, and Slavic Languages and Literatures at the University of Minnesota. Professor Tarone's research publications focus on the impact of social context on learner language and second language acquisition. She has published work on interlanguage variation, learners' interactions in immersion classrooms, the communication strategies used by second language learners, language play, and genre analysis. She is a recipient of the College of Liberal Arts Distinguished Teaching Award, and the University of Minnesota Award for Outstanding Contributions to Postbaccalaureate, Graduate, and Professional Education.

Kay Thurston has taught at Pima Community College in Tucson, Arizona, and at Navajo Community College (renamed Diné College) in Tsaile, Arizona. In 1998, Thurston won *Teaching English in the Two-Year College's* Best Article Award for "Mitigating Barriers to Navajo Students' Success in English Courses." Thurston's consciousness of the educational obstacles faced by Native Americans informs her choices as an educator, as her classes explore Native American oral and written literature in the context of that culture.

Karen S. Uehling is an associate professor at Boise State University in Idaho, where she has taught since 1981. She specializes in basic writing and creative nonfiction, and teaches a range of writing courses as well as nonfiction literature. She has published two basic writing textbooks, *Starting Out or Starting Over* (1993) and *Vision and Revision* (1994), and articles on writing and teaching. She was the second chair of the Conference on Basic Writing (CBW) and helped keep the organization alive in its early years. She served on the executive board of CBW for many years and is on the editorial board of the *Journal of Basic Writing*. Her history of the first twenty-five years of CBW appeared in the *Bedford Bibliography for Teachers of Basic Writing,* 2nd ed. (2005).

Constance Weaver, professor emerita of English at Western Michigan University in Kalamazoo, taught courses in reading and writing and in language arts instruction. In addition to writing *Teaching Grammar in Context* (1996), Weaver has edited *Lessons to Share: On Teaching Grammar in Context* (1998), a collection of essays that offer a variety of perspectives and practical applications, including grammar instruction for ESL students. Weaver's other books include *Practicing What We Know: Informed Reading Instruction* (1998), *Reading Process and Practice: From Socio-Linguistics to Whole Language* (2nd ed., 2002), and *Success at Last: Helping AD(H)D Students Achieve Their Potential* (1994).

Linda Feldmeier White, a professor of English at Stephen F. Austin State University in Nacogdoches, Texas, has written and lectured on the learning disabled (LD) student experience in the college classroom and writing center. In her examination of LD pedagogy, White elucidates the educator's role in advocating for LD learners' access to higher education. Her articles have been published in *College Composition and Communication,* the *Writing Center Journal,* and *Children's Literature.*